D1251732

The Early Diary of Anaïs Nin

Volume Four

1927–1931

WORKS BY ANAÏS NIN

[Published by The Swallow Press]
D. H. Lawrence: An Unprofessional Study
House of Incest (a prose poem)
Winter of Artifice
Under a Glass Bell (stories)
Ladders to Fire
Children of the Albatross
The Four-Chambered Heart
A Spy in the House of Love
Solar Barque
Seduction of the Minotaur
Collages
Cities of the Interior
A Woman Speaks

[Published by Harcourt Brace Jovanovich]
The Diary of Anaïs Nin, 1931–1934
The Diary of Anaïs Nin, 1934–1939
The Diary of Anaïs Nin, 1939–1944
The Diary of Anaïs Nin, 1944–1947
The Diary of Anaïs Nin, 1947–1955
The Diary of Anaïs Nin, 1955–1966
The Diary of Anaïs Nin, 1966–1974
A Photographic Supplement to the Diary of Anaïs Nin
In Favor of the Sensitive Man and Other Essays
Delta of Venus: Erotica by Anaïs Nin
Linotte: The Early Diary of Anaïs Nin, 1914–1920
Little Birds: Erotica by Anaïs Nin
The Early Diary of Anaïs Nin, Volume II, 1920–1923
The Early Diary of Anaïs Nin, Volume III, 1923–1927
The Early Diary of Anaïs Nin, Volume IV, 1927–1931

[Published by Macmillan]
The Novel of the Future

With a Preface
by Joaquin Nin-Culmell

———

Harcourt Brace Jovanovich, Publishers
San Diego · New York · London

Nin, Anaïs

Linotte,

THE EARLY DIARY
OF ANAÏS NIN.
VOLUME FOUR 1927–1931

❧

MIDDLEBURY COLLEGE LIBRARY

7/1985
Am. Lit.

PS
3527
I865
Z522
1978
v. 4

Copyright © 1985, 1984 by Rupert Pole as Trustee
under the Last Will and Testament of Anaïs Nin
Preface copyright © 1985 by Joaquin Nin-Culmell

All rights reserved. No part of this publication may be reproduced
or transmitted in any form or by any means, electronic or mechanical,
including photocopy, recording, or any information storage and retrieval
system, without permission in writing from the publisher.

Requests for permission to make copies of any part of the work
should be mailed to: Permissions, Harcourt Brace Jovanovich, Publishers,
Orlando, FL 32887.

Portions of this book were previously published in
Anaïs: An International Journal, *Vol. 2, copyright © 1984*
by the Anaïs Nin Foundation and Gunther Stuhlmann.

LIBRARY OF CONGRESS CATALOGING IN PUBLICATION DATA

Nin, Anaïs, 1903–1977.
Linotte, the early diary of Anaïs Nin.

Vol. 1 translated from the French by Jean L. Sherman.
Vols. 2–4 have title: The early diary of Anaïs Nin.
Includes indexes.
Contents: [v. 1.] 1914–1920—v. 2. 1920–1923—[etc.]—v. 4. 1927–1931.
1. Nin, Anaïs, 1903–1977—Diaries.   2. Authors, American—20th century—
Biography.   I. Early diary of Anaïs Nin.   I. Title.
PS3527.I865Z522   1978   818'.5302 [B]   77–20314
ISBN 0–15–152488–2 (v. 1)
ISBN 0–15–127185–2 (v. 4)

Printed in the United States of America
First edition 1985

A B C D

❧ *Editor's Note* ❧

Like the previous volumes of *The Early Diary of Anaïs Nin*, Volume Four was prepared from Anaïs's own typescripts, which she produced almost simultaneously with the original handwritten versions. Unlike her transcriptions for Volumes Two and Three, however, this one was made faithfully and without self-censorship. Again the text is presented in a continuous chronology, edited only to eliminate repetitions and material of dubious interest to the reader.

The entries for the years 1927–1931 are drawn from journals number twenty-four through thirty-one. The first three books are bound in red leather and marbleized paper. As the Guiler fortunes ascended, together with the stock market, Anaïs indulged her love of luxury with three books bound in soft black Moroccan leather with vertical gilt borders and elegant gilt-edged paper. Journal thirty-one, reflecting the stock market crash, is once again bound in simple, inexpensive red leather.

These journals contain Anaïs's first extensive use of photographs on the title pages. Number twenty-five has cutouts of Miralles, her Spanish dancing teacher, performing and instructing; twenty-six, a photograph of the S. S. Pennland, on which the Guilers planned to return to Europe, until a collision sent them back to New York; twenty-seven, a cutout of Anaïs and John Erskine, taken from a group photograph; twenty-eight, photographs of Anaïs's Moorish interior design for the Boulevard Suchet apartment; thirty, a photograph of the Suchet furniture installed at

Louveciennes; and thirty-one, a photograph of Deyà Cove in Mallorca.

From the time of her marriage Anaïs signed her diaries "Anaïs Nin Guiler." But for volume twenty-nine she uses not one but two pseudonyms: "Anita Aguilera," the name she chose for public appearances as a Spanish dancer (her father told her she must never use the Nin name on the stage); and "Melisendra" (Spanish for "Melisande"), her new pen name, taken from Manuel de Falla's *Master Peter's Puppet Show*.

Volumes Two and Three of *The Early Diary* contained the titles "Diary of a Fiancée" and "Diary of a Wife." A number of titles were used for this volume: "John" (journal twenty-seven); "The House" (twenty-eight); and "Writing and Dancing" and "Eduardo" (twenty-nine). But journal thirty-one is dramatically titled "The Woman Who Died" and "Disintegration," beginning the pattern of prophetic titles that Anaïs was to maintain until 1947, when she ceased keeping a diary in bound notebooks (see *The Diary of Anaïs Nin, Volume Six*, pages 55–56).

In addition to providing titles and photographs for the opening of her journals, Anaïs also listed the places she lived during each period. Like the quality of the journal bindings, the various locations reflect the Guiler finances. The first three journals were written in the studio apartment at 11 Rue Schoelcher, but the next two proceed with increasing affluence from 13 Square du Port Royal to 47 Boulevard Suchet, a posh modern apartment where Anaïs finally had a chance to apply her unique imagination to interior design, uninhibited by financial limitations. The bubble burst in 1930, following the Crash—it came later in Europe—and in journals thirty and thirty-one the Guilers have retreated to an old run-down manor in the less expensive suburbs, Louveciennes, which Anaïs later made famous. It is here that *The Early Diary* ends, and here that Anaïs chose to begin when she decided to edit her Diary for publication.

Rupert Pole
Executor, The Anaïs Nin Trust

Los Angeles
July 1984

LIST OF ILLUSTRATIONS

⚜ *Preface* ⚜

The fourth and final volume of *The Early Diary of Anaïs Nin*
begins and ends after short visits to New York, both of which
were to give Anaïs a new perspective on her life in Paris and
encouragement to pursue the path she had chosen. It provides
the bridge to her diary of the early thirties, the first of the
journals to be published and the first of her work to bring her
literary fame.

In the years between 1927 and 1931, Anaïs and her husband,
Hugo Guiler, moved from the relatively modest studio apartment
on Rue Schoelcher in Paris to the well-appointed duplex on
Boulevard Suchet, facing the Bois de Boulogne. After the financial
crash of 1929, they finally moved to an old country house in
Louveciennes, just outside Paris. Louveciennes was the last place
where Anaïs, Hugo, my mother, and I lived under the same roof.
It was also the setting for Anaïs's first encounter with Henry
Miller, and it was there that she wrote her early stories, gathered
under the rather Proustian title *Waste of Timelessness*, and her
un-Proustian study of D. H. Lawrence.

After her initial resistance to Parisian life, Anaïs was finally
overcome by what Paris had to offer in the late 1920s. She literally
devoured contemporary French literature, as only Anaïs could
"chew" and assimilate books. Even before reading Proust, however, she had discovered the art of x-raying people in her own
way; before reading Colette she had discovered that she was no
longer the unbending puritan she had thought herself to be; be-

fore reading Jacques Rivière's *Rimbaud*, she had begun to explore the hidden depths of the unconscious.

Anaïs was now grateful to France for the intellectual development of what she intuitively already knew and for the cultural atmosphere that made this development possible. On the other hand, she never succumbed to the facile temptation of becoming a French writer. French was her first language, and there is no question that it had a lasting and evident influence on her use of English. English and American literature, however, was her model from the very beginning of her literary career. Further influenced by Hélène Boussinescq (Boussie), who taught English and American literature in a Parisian lycée, and by Eduardo Sánchez, her English-speaking Cuban cousin, as well as by her American husband, Anaïs turned to Sherwood Anderson, John Dos Passos, Waldo Frank, Theodore Dreiser, Sinclair Lewis, and finally D. H. Lawrence. There have been a number of distinguished foreigners who have written in French. Anaïs was a French-born "foreigner" who opted for writing in English.

The avant-garde review *transition*, which began in 1927, was another significant influence on Anaïs, even though she seemed to be more interested in the publication of Jung's comments on the artist and Jolas's theories about the hallucinatory than in the excerpts from James Joyce. She nevertheless stoutly defended Joyce at every opportunity. Books and ideas still "churned" her, and she read anything that might offer her the nutrition for her intellectual growth. One notable exception was Jacques Maritain, whose philosophical writings she barely glanced at before turning them over to me to read. Little did she realize the influence Maritain would have on my life.

Among the American writers whom Anaïs favored during this period was the novelist John Erskine. But her intellectual admiration for him gradually turned into a romantic obsession, clouding her honest opinion of him as a writer. Her "painful lucidity" (a favorite phrase) was partly restored when Erskine attacked the contemporary values she had begun to cherish. He also expressed some belated misgivings about the direction her life was taking. Both attitudes identified Erskine with the critical, dominating father-image so fervently abhorred by Anaïs. As she wrote, she would have liked to explain to a psychoanalyst "this horrible and endless intellectual and physical starvation and how much not having a father had to do with it."

Meanwhile, the diary continued to be her confessional, her sole but now somewhat restricted confidant, the source of her early literary flights, and the only tangible proof she had of the significance of her writing. She realized that it was her life line of communication with the world even when she felt alone, special, and different. She wrote: ". . . no woman ever looked down into herself with as much cold criticism, no woman ever analysed her ideas and actions more carefully, none was ever more doubtful of herself, more self-depreciating, more fearful of hypocrisy, more terrified of lies, more eager for truth, than I. You, my Journal, alone, know this."

Even Hugo felt that her early stories, though original in concept, could not be compared to the freedom of her Journal. "I really believe you have reached perfection in that form," he said, according to Anaïs, "and that you will never do anything else. [The Journal] will be your whole life's work." But the Journal, though splendidly articulate, was not enough. Anaïs was tired of writing just for herself. It was "like talking to a wall, like smoking in the dark." Why not incorporate the Journal into a book? Why not publish it as it was? For this she would have to wait until 1966.

While she posed herself such questions, Anaïs proceeded to gobble up life in large pieces, not in dainty morsels, recorded her multifaceted personality, and raided her beloved diary for a series of stories she now began to write. For one dangerous moment she entertained the possibility of a split personality by starting a diary within a diary and signing it "Imagy." The conflicts were real enough and so was her feeling of anguish at the idea of hurting those closest and dearest to her. She repeatedly quoted Mélisande's words to Golaud in *Pélleas et Mélisande*: "Je ne suis pas heureuse ici." The etherealness of the princess in the Maeterlinck-Debussy masterpiece was a far cry from Anaïs's "painful lucidity"—more painful to her, perhaps, than to others—but the difficulty of coming to terms with reality was common to both women. Besides, Anaïs could not do without her painful lucidity. Neither could she help writing what it dictated.

Although she was extraordinarily inventive in her ideas about homemaking, dressing, and entertaining, her favorite occupation was that of observing people and stimulating the good, bad, or indifferent artists who crossed her path and for whom she displayed a special weakness. She eventually saw through the self-centered music critic, the weak composer, the pedantic pianist, the temperamental painter, the erratic sculptor, and assorted social predators of Paris in the 1920s, but even then she was patient, loyal, and supportive.

In an effort to express her physical awakening and her ardent desire to shine in public, perhaps even to compete with her father or win his approval, Anaïs took up Spanish dancing, and Hugo became her most willing partner. In spite of her frailness, she danced with enormous vitality and made up for technical limitations with fiery intensity. Though much in demand at social and semiprofessional gatherings, she soon realized that to become a professional dancer she would need a stronger physique and a greater commitment. But after all, her love for writing was deeper than anything else, the major justification of her life. She soon outgrew dancing, as she had outgrown other enthusiasms in the past.

The arrival in Paris of her cousin Eduardo Sánchez gave her the intellectual companionship she so longed for and enabled her to discover new values that would change her life. Among them, and perhaps most important, were the writings of Freud and Jung, which obliged her, for one thing, to reconsider the absolute truthfulness of her diary. Her initial hostility to psychology, a field of study she had hitherto ignored, gave way to an instinctive acceptance of Freudian premises.

Another related interest that she shared with Eduardo was the work of D. H. Lawrence, which they discussed interminably. Eduardo detected signs of Lawrence's influence in her early stories, an observation that Anaïs, usually defensive, accepted with uncommon good grace. Lawrence had become her principal literary hero. And yet she could write the following about him in her diary: "He knows and he doesn't know. At least he doesn't know what to do with what he knows." Her fascination with Lawrence culminated in her book *D. H. Lawrence: An Unprofessional Study*, published in 1932.

If imagination was part of Anaïs's life, Eduardo made her aware that the unconscious was another part, but while he fussed about academic details, Anaïs began to soar beyond his orbit at the speed of light. It was to his credit that he never tried to hold her back, although he could not have known then what Hugo had already experienced: Anaïs was unholdable, ungraspable, or, to use a favorite French word of hers, "insaisissable."

After every crisis, every perilous adventure, she turned to Hugo as her sole friend. Only Hugo believed her capable of all things; and if she did accomplish what she set out to do, it was largely due to his unswerving faith and love. Anaïs could flirt with her middle-aged dancing teacher and long for a physical relationship with an already married American writer, but it was Hugo she adored, who held the key to her many abodes, and who could accurately interpret many if not all of her transformations.

In spite of Anaïs's misgivings about his all-absorbing dedication to the financial world, she was proud of his steady professional advancement. She observed that he applied to banking the imagination and vision of an artist; that he was "a poet of action, who works with forces obscure to me but of equal greatness to the creative ones." Years later, in a lecture Hugo (as Ian Hugo) delivered on his films, he stated: "It would be difficult for any man once planted in Anaïs Nin's magic garden not to produce some green leaves of his own."

This preface to *The Early Diary of Anaïs Nin* was written, like the earlier ones, in the intimacy of her apartment in New York, where I was surrounded by furniture and artworks chosen and arranged by her, and where dresses of hers were still hanging in the closet. No doubt I profited by these tangible though mute reminders of Anaïs, as I profited from the invaluable insights and comments of Hugo. And so I come to the end of my long journey through Anaïs's childhood, adolescence, young womanhood and marriage, reliving the many years I spent in her bright shadow. I have followed her astounding development, trying to understand every variation of those basic themes she established so early in life. I often felt that I was in the presence of a special camera that could record the germination, growth, and flowering of a plant in a matter of seconds. The more I discovered, however, the more I was left to discover. This volume completes the recorded cycle of Anaïs Nin's life. But does it complete her portrait? She once wrote about a woman who had a hundred faces, and having shown one face to each person, she required a hundred persons to write her biography. Anaïs, I believe, was that woman.

Joaquin Nin-Culmell
Berkeley, California
1984

The Early Diary of Anaïs Nin

Volume Four

1927–1931

≱ 1 9 2 7 ≱

July [?]. Paris.

Hugh[1] said rightly the other day: "There is enough bad in all of us; we must not try to develop it." Something or other has been developing the worst in me. I must have been a false ascetic before, because now spirituality is leaving me, I live with my body, I am led by many sensations I never felt before, and I am full of warmth and leapings and languors. To punish myself I devote myself to the house, my family, and my friends. I have dutifully attended to our mail, errands, shopping, reorganization of the household, the engagement of a new maid, cleaning and renting Mother's apartment.

Still I cannot forget that there is something wrong with me. It is as if in this complete and deep blossoming of myself which is taking place, the physical is trying to regain its place. I am harder emotionally. I am wide awake, strong, intensely alive, but less idealistic, and my moments of supreme spiritual goodness have gone.

The fear of hurting others, which was perhaps the key to my whole life, has left me too. As a result, I have become cruel because I am no longer submissive. The only cruelty I have not yet been guilty of is to write what might hurt others, and therefore I am beginning not to tell the whole truth to my Journal after fifteen years of faithful and absolute confidence. But then I

---

[1] *A.N.'s husband, Hugh Parker Guiler.*

hope to find a solution, to find that my badness is only temporary, that I shall find a way of living my life without pain to others. This sudden and absolute intellectual and physical freedom distresses me and yet intoxicates me.

July 19(?). I enjoyed the "economic" review of our two months' trip in my fat account book. Was glad to find we had a few francs left, so I am having Richard Maynard's painting [of A.N.] framed; Pussy [Hugh] bought me a book on costume and I tried to replace what he had in the lost valise. And then I will buy a new Journal.

Our trip to New York has given me confidence, courage, worship of life and a clear vision of what we have here. I don't know what has given me the strength I lacked before, this clarity and self-confidence. My imagination, which only teased me before, supports me now. I should be able to do the great things of which I have dreamed.

At the bottom of all this lies my eternal sorrow, my eternal regret for what has passed—for the old house in Richmond Hill, the lonely porch, the peace, the innocence, the sweetness, the purity of thoughts and delicacy of the senses. What is this brutal awakening beside that peace?

July 20(?). Sitting alone in dining room of Le Bon Marché. Couldn't have brought my big Journal here, but this notebook passes unnoticed and has its advantage. Came here to shop for a journal book, address book, alarm clock, clippers and hair brush. Have been happy and full of ideas even though the Devil in me is awakening noisily. But no one can say I didn't struggle two and a half years against European tolerance, humanity (which is another way of saying weakness), against its satanic flexibility, its lack of conscience, scruples and humility.

July 21(?). Irving Schwerke [the music critic] gave us two wonderful evenings: one for us alone when he revealed the beauty and resonance of the piano to our ears; and the seriousness, intensity and idealism of his own character, which is usually concealed by his bland smile.

The second evening he celebrated his birthday and introduced us to his friends.

He is kind, affectionate, demonstrative, and frankly egotistical. He threatens to write a book that will be called "Great Men Who Have Known Me." Meanwhile a book of his on music and musicians is coming out in a month. Manuel de Falla said to Joaquin[1] the evening they met: "Irving is your friend isn't he? Well, keep that friendship—you don't know what you have there."

He is a man who has a right to be egotistical, for all he has been and all he has accomplished, for his writing, his criticism, his influence over young people, his friendship with great musicians, his own wonderful knowledge of music and gift for the piano. Mother's jealousy makes his friendship for Joaquin a very unsatisfactory, uneven, and stormy relationship, which I must try to protect because I believe in him now.

August 3. The Bank[2] gives and takes, like some ancient God. Our offerings to it, our sacrifices are wasted hours spent on Bank people—teas, lunches, dinners, evenings of futility, mediocrity and boredom. But occasionally what compensations! This is an elaborate introduction for our car—a Citroën, for four people, picked without hesitation out of a whole exhibition, for its smartness and distinction. It is a rich, warm black and the leather "capote" [top] is a dark red. It will take us a year to pay for it. But it is worth it. For a week now, I haven't been able to think of anything else—and neither has the Cat [Hugh].

I am proud of our outwardly beautiful life because our mental life keeps perpetually ahead of it. It is no empty shell—it is the expression of all our ideas, devotions, taste, desires. I feel that each new power that has been put in our hands has been well used. And every power given us—marriage, house, salary, youth, unity—has been something to conquer, to understand, to control, to keep, to defend and to work with.

Our progress has been well balanced. Every visible addition has been preceded or accompanied by a spiritual one. I have no fear of wealth. Our hands are firm and strong. We both have capable, sensitive, intelligent hands. Dear Journal, you will certainly travel in that car—even though it is meant for four people. No more buses, trains, trolleys, taxis. I hope you are as grateful to the Humorous Banker [Hugh] as I am.

August 4. I sit in the deep armchair waiting for Hugh and Emilia Quintero. My old diaries must be full of Emilia when she lived with us at 158 West 75th Street [in New York]. She was part of

---

[1] *A.N.'s younger brother who was now seventeen.*
[2] *National City Bank, Hugh's employer.*

the family, kind, romantic, flattering, interesting, with her numerous mannerisms, her abundant conversation, her perpetual exclamations and superlatives, her long letters, her love and hankering for prettiness, her piano playing, her sentimentalism, her attachment to passing things. I think she taught me to take photographs on every important occasion; she gave me one of my diary books; she was one of our best, most loyal, and most troublesome friends.

She came for a moment the other day, admired everything, kissed Hugh like an old friend, reminded me, when I invited her to dinner, she could only eat fish, and allowed herself to be taken home. She leads a lonely life in Madrid—her only relatives live here—and I often wonder what became of her diary, which made a great impression on me when I was little. She was in love with the composer Pablo Sarasate, a hopeless love, and it was about this she let me read, but at that time, such feelings were strange to me, and I didn't understand.

Emilia hasn't arrived, and so I have time to describe the party last night. Mr. and Mrs. John Gunther have sublet Mother's apartment. John Gunther has written two novels and is a correspondent for the Chicago *Daily News*. His small, tousle-haired wife was once a press agent for the theatre. Finding them interesting, I helped them a great deal and we grew very friendly. Yesterday they invited us to their housewarming, and the guests included an American pianist, a painter, a designer, newspapermen, etc. The pianist, Richard Buhlig, interested me most.

He sought me out and we talked together most of the evening. He is a great reader, a linguist and an intellectual musician. Knew Father's[1] compositions and found them polished and cold. We compared languages, Paris and Vienna, criticized modern dancing, talked of the Menuhin boy and his parents, of Joaquin, of French civilization, etc. My contribution to such evenings is (or seems to be to most people) purely decorative. I am inevitably compared to the portrait of Mme. Récamier or to some other painting. Some men don't listen to what I say but just stare. I am touched to think I have been endowed with some resemblance to the old-fashioned faces, to faces chosen by painters. After days of self-criticism, self-depreciation, to find myself giving pleasure to the eyes consoles me and helps me.

[1] *Joaquin Nin, composer and concert pianist.*

August 5. We took Emilia to the Opéra, to hear *Thaïs.* I was touched by the music and disgusted with the acting and dancing. I am afraid I am going to hate opera. The African "tambour" excited me and reawakened my longing for Algeria, Egypt, India.

Thaïs's acting was unbelievable—mannequin, cocotte, society woman, all in one. John Brownlee's singing was marvelous, even though the voice has never yet moved me.

This morning is again offered up in sacrifice to the Bank, morning and afternoon. But tomorrow we get the car!

I think my self-criticism is becoming an illness, and I'll have to find a way of curing that. Last night I was worried by my vanity. I didn't want to walk through the foyer of the Opéra because I wasn't dressed up! After a struggle, I mortified myself by walking through leisurely.

How Erskine[1] would laugh at this. But then, I don't do this often, and apart from such moral struggles I don't waste a minute. I think too much—I think day and night. Music and love alone have stopped my thinking. And Enric.[2] My mind criticizes him, sees him as he is, inglorious, lazy, unintellectual, and yet when he is there I am drawn to him. I have no more mind—only feeling.

August 9. Keen enjoyment of the car, Saturday and Sunday. Yesterday I began my driving lessons and was overjoyed to find myself learning quickly. In the evening we drove leisurely to Irving's studio. Irving played again for us; I have never been so moved by any piano-playing and I told him so. And now I have begun to come up to the High Place[3] to write; began my letters— to Coqui, Joaquin, and Erskine. Coqui is in trouble and sorrow- ful—because his father has fled from his problems—and is arriving next Tuesday.[4] I shall do all to defend his young life and dreams and work. Joaquin writes thoughtfully and as if awakening to his lack of independence.

August 11. One of the Bank friends has only to suffer, and im- mediately my attitude changes. On ordinary days they bore me, they stifle me; I get almost hysterical fits of desperation and

[1] *John Erskine, the American writer and educator.*
[2] *Enric Madriguera, a young violinist who is in love with A.N.*
[3] *A servant's room with a balcony that A.N. used for a studio.*
[4] *A.N.'s cousin Gilbert Chase. His father was having marital problems.*

rebellion after spending a long evening with them. But when one of them gets in trouble everything disappears before my pity, and I begin doing things for them in all sincerity. Mrs. W. just came and cried a little because she is upset and is going to have a baby. Poor Mrs. W. Yesterday I hated her. Today everything is changed. Perhaps if I could feel useful to these people, if I could be a source of happiness and inspiration, my time would not be wasted; our relations would not be artificial and barren. On rare days when I am in the mood to see the usefulness of my existence I realize how much I have made even of that apparently empty part of my life. In that narrow little world, I have already set a standard of superficial beauty, at least, in decorating, dressing, etc. I am a decided influence and a help in small practical problems. A few sincere relationships have really developed. I look for the smallest traces of talents and draw them out; I respect the prosaic qualities and learn from them. I spread the love of drawing, music, traveling, and learn a lot about babies and cooking and marriage. Only most of the time I have to keep my foot on the brakes. I get no joy from this cautious driving, and when I get home, alone, I burst.

August 19. Too much to do. Another change of maids, the hatmaker, the seamstress, the cleaners, driving lessons, visits to Irving's studio, helping Mrs. Gunther with her own practical problems, writing letters, reading John Gunther's very promising two novels. No time for the High Place. We entertained the Gunthers at dinner, enjoyed listening to John Gunther's talk; then drove to visit their friends the Child-Munros, at a lovely, peaceful house with a garden near the Ecole Militaire. The mother sings, the daughter is a designer and married to a businessman, the two handsome sons are artists—one paints, the other carves wood and teaches. We met their friends. I had a headache and found conversation difficult, but discovered nobody missed it. I made a sensation without it. Without talk, without a single intelligent gesture. Hugh was told I was beautiful, that I looked like Dulac's paintings—Dulac, whom I love so much. A disconcerting success!

August 23. Three days of cheerfulness. Made Horace[1] laugh on Sunday afternoon while we visited Malmaison; made the Cat shake and roll himself with merriment last night when he felt

---

[1] *Horace Guicciardi, one of Hugh's Bank associates.*

most overwhelmingly sleepy, and made him laugh again this morning. What a record! Last night, as I said to him, I felt "brilliant." He was too sleepy to appreciate my sallies, so after a while my brilliancy died down.

All I remember of it is that I saw *through* Horace Sunday evening. He believes in Experience, in seeing all of life and studying all people indiscriminately when they come your way and also by going out to meet them. As I said to him, I have met many "dangerous" people—and a dangerous man, but so interesting— during expeditions directly inspired by his theory. And I was prepared to meet more of them. Horace feared for me, not for my intellect, but for my womanhood. He said I was so "feminine," and such relationships might bring men around me who would flirt with me, that in such worlds, as a woman—well, it wasn't right.

I thought it was the Spaniards who made laws for men only. It isn't safe, because I am so "feminine." Let the intellect starve. Oh, well, men like Horace are none the wiser for the many experiments and experiences they can safely pass through! I'll find a substitute.

Of course, at the time, the discussion did not seem as important to me as the place—a restaurant attached to the new Mosque. Soft multicolored lights; rugs on the ceilings, walls and floors; couches all along the walls, low copper trays for tables, low stools, hot food, ardent-eyed Algerians to serve us, and the most exciting, stirring music I have ever heard. Dulac's illustrations of the *Rubáiyát* without paleness and vagueness. Dulac's people, alive, with burning eyes.

The music, the rhythm of it, the chants and the tambour, the string instruments, were like old wine tingling through your flesh. I long to hear it again, to sit in that room of my dreams, or in the garden under low and frail-leaved trees—that exotic patio, that unbelievable place in the middle of a city like Paris.

The Orient attracts me as no other part of the world has ever done. I feel in it my deepest friend and my worst enemy. An enemy to that energy and clearness of mind I have achieved through long struggles, an enemy to my courage and my activity and my obstinacy. A friend to my hunger for beauty, for languor, for peace, for a life of the senses, for color, for self-abandonment. *August 24.* I am learning to drive. That is in keeping with my new sense of decision and control. I surprise Horace, and others. They think me incapable of excitement of the senses, of the love of sport, of anger, of domination, of independence—and now of driving! How deceptive is my quietness and thinness, my meekness and spirituality. What can I do to express fully what I really am? Frances[1] thought I couldn't dance Spanish dances because they are provocative, sensual and fiery. I also surprised my dance teacher. Hugh alone believes me capable of all things, and that is why I can do them. And I have utter faith in him, and that is why *he* is progressing.

Birthday Letter to Joaquin:

I can't let your birthday pass without writing you, even though just today I don't feel my imagination quite keyed up to the event, as I have been dabbling amidst petty occupations and living very choppy and uninteresting days. I have not even had time to read, much less to think or to invent a dazzling and novel way of greeting the anniversary of your birth, which I daily acknowledge as a blessing and a gift for which I am deeply grateful. Perhaps I might tell you why I am grateful for your birth. Well, first of all, just a plain, ordinary brother is a rather comforting thing to own. At first it gives a lot of trouble and ever afterwards too, but it has compensations. As for example when this brother comes on a rainy day to sit at the foot of my couch and ask me what I am making and when he offers to walk with me to the subway entrance. Occasionally, he musses up the books in the library, but then he knows what is inside those books. Of course, the best of it is that besides being an ordinary brother you are an extraordinary person. I mean you are capable of everything. You can be kind, you can be intellectual, creative, imaginative, literary. You are possessed of many gifts and many possibilities. I don't know yet what you have chosen to be or if you are going to try and be *all* of them. I have utter faith in you. You have intelligence, vision, will, and sincerity. I am glad you were born and glad you were born my brother. I apologize for thinking you red and ugly the first day I bent over your crib, but remember I was young and did not have much artistic appreciation at that time.

I am sorry if I ever spanked you. And as for the times you spanked me, well, it was worth it. However, all these phrases don't mean anything at all unless they take on some physical

---

[1] *Probably Frances Hyde, an American acquaintance.*

visibility. Even the old Wise Men who rushed to greet the Saviour gave us a tangible example of how spiritual admiration should be translated. Therefore, I offer you a check! And love from your brother and sister.

August 27. This High Place where I am writing is a blessing, a refuge, a tower from which I can look down on my life without disturbance, a place of meditation, concentration, where I can gather anew my scattered strength and splintered control. Downstairs, Clementine is scraping pots and pans; the iceman comes in with a few words to say on the topics of the day; the seamstress is bringing me some sewing; the cleaner is calling for Hugh's trousers. Here, peace, solitude. My writings are all parading on the shelf. My typewriter is on the green garden table with blank paper and carbon paper. I enjoy life. Especially on mornings when I begin to carry out a new and firm resolution. I have decided that I love Art too much or too many phases of it. I have been divided and attracted by every side of it: drawing, sculpturing, costume, acting, dancing, etc. etc., but I made a condensation of several items and decided to become a costume designer. Writing and dancing remain apart, and I won't drop them. But here is a work at last which combines artistry and usefulness. No more drifting and experiments. Here is a way to use my ideas on costume, my interest in its history, my love of it and facility for its creation. Here is a receptacle for color when it haunts me, for ideas when they keep me awake.

I began yesterday. When Hugh came home he thought my "teacher" had made drawings for me. He was elated to find I had made them myself—so was I. I shall attend the sketching class of "La Grande Poussière"[1] as before. Something is settled which makes me feel happier.

My mind is preoccupied with Politics, Anarchy, Anti-Americanism, Executions, Injustice, Demonstrations. We have seen violence in Paris these last days because two Anarchist assassins [Sacco and Vanzetti] were executed in Boston. The American Legion, on a visit, is feeling the full bitterness of the French and seeing examples of hatred they did not realize. The newspapers are disgusting. France, thanks to her tolerance, is no better than

---

[1] *The Great Dustiness, A.N.'s name for the Académie de la Grand Chaumière.*

ignorant Russia. Someone said rightly that France's tolerance for all ideas was due to her refusal to make choices. Being critical herself, she evades positions of such definite character that they can be criticized by others. While she speculates, thinks, tolerates, etc., the Anarchists eat her heart. We return to the idea that an open mind is a mind too weak to close itself to certain ideas, too cowardly to uphold those of its choice. That has been my suspicion in connection with men like Horace. We'll see.

My own tolerance has sprung from defeat, from weakness of the senses and the affections, and from fatigue from struggling as it did for two years. How many of my tolerant ideas have sprung from conviction? It wouldn't take long to mention them, but this is Saturday, a holiday, and I must keep faith in myself—faith in this poor infant Dress Designer just born yesterday.

August 29. A wonderful weekend has filled my head with pictures of hills, trees, heather, blue sky, white roads, sleepy villages. We drove through the valley of Chevreuse—la petite Suisse.

Yesterday morning we went to play tennis at the house of Mr. R. That is, Hugh played and I watched. I saw again the lady I had liked so much two years ago—but how changed! Submerged and embittered by housekeeping, the care of three children, servant problems. I have known three cases of "steady" home women going to pieces, for no apparent reason. It isn't moodiness, temperament, or anything like that. I can only explain it by a sudden sense of emptiness in their lives, or of suffocation. A regular life, such as they lead, housekeeping, canning fruit, sewing, gardening, nursing children, would drive me into an insane asylum. It makes these women irritable and restless. They have made such a frowning god of low occupations; they have let these duties rule them and dry them up, and then they expect sympathy from their husbands, gratitude from their children, love in return for the sacrifice of themselves, but how shocked they would be if they discovered that they don't deserve a bit of it. Canned fruit doesn't mean as much to a man as a living, joyful face. Some women manage to can fruit and keep their bodies beautiful and their minds awake, but as most of them can't, they ought to give up the canning. In all these cases the husband suffers. The household is a burden; he sees the strain, the fuss, the wrinkles, the drudgery. Offering him that is not giving him a home. A home should be a silent, smooth, unoppressive thing, a self-effacing, mysterious, comfort-giving machine.

If I am right, then the only remedy is to pull these women out of the rut, to awaken their imaginations, their interest in living, to force them to give the House its proper place, as a *background to life*. I am going to try it with Mrs. R. I'll call her my "Case" and do my best to help her.

Rebelliousness against social intercourse is one thing I have nearly conquered by bringing into it as much of my real life as is admitted into society. I seek to understand character, to develop it; but when that is done, I am bored. It takes me such a short time to discover everything and then I long to run away again, home, to my thoughts and occupations. While I am with younger people, (in a spiritual sense) I learn nothing. That makes me impatient and sad. When I am alone, or with "older" people, I try to make up for lost time, but it is difficult. Erskine says, "Cultivate your own garden." Why should I be taking care of the Bank's garden?

September 1. I admire Sherwood Anderson. I love the gentle way he probes people, this simple and yet deep understanding of suffering, of oddities, of fatalities, of dreams, of the torments of the imagination. I liked *Dark Laughter* but *The Triumph of the Egg* is even finer. Erskine does not admire him. He is preoccupied with intelligence and philosophy. Anderson is concerned with impulses, instincts, sensation, emotions, capacity for pain, sickness, spiritual entanglements. Anderson places understanding fingers on wounds. He has marvelously delicate and pitying fingers, and his tenderness for the things he discovers is like a double vision which reveals more than he realizes himself perhaps, reveals the very hazy unnamable things which are like that story "he cannot tell," that wonderful story he has no way to tell.

September 3. Richard Buhlig came last night. I expected an intellectual and scholarly man, but not an ardent mystic. He is an extraordinary man. Our talk began conventionally and turned to the appreciation of music. "It is greatest in Germany," he said, "and in Austria. And then in England. In America it is a transplanted appreciation. They have the desire to understand and to love it, but they can live without it, whereas in Vienna it is the very essence of their life."

And then to books. He exploded when we mentioned Erskine. "*Helen* [*The Private Life of Helen of Troy*] is terrible, terrible," he said, so earnestly that he startled us.

And then he made the same criticism I had made when trying to explain why Erskine could not mean very much to the French. "He is preoccupied with essentially Anglo-Saxon problems, problems of conduct, of morals, local struggles. So young, so futile, so unimportant to the European. Even though he seems so old, so essentially rational, even cynical, to Americans, to Europeans he seems to be applying his intelligence to the problems of childhood."

But even though Buhlig admitted Erskine was helping and guiding America to rid herself of cobwebs, he did not admit that conduct would be improved by witty discussions, paradoxes, sophisms, and studies of either antique or modern situations. No, there was something else. You began not by the lower plane of conduct, but by some high spiritual vision, some central worship or faith, something which settled all small, petty problems automatically.

It was at that moment I felt Buhlig held a key, not an intellectual, philosophical solution or explanation of life—but a mystic one.

"I am very near, very near to becoming a Roman Catholic," he said. "But it means so much to me, that I am terrified. Think of approaching and receiving Communion in an unworthy state. And then I am so full of intellectuality, so corroded by intellectuality, that there are intellectual questions which must be made to harmonize with my intuitions, with my spontaneous faith."

He had been reading Jacques Maritain's *Art et Scholastique*, the life and writings of Saint Theresa, all the Catholic theology and philosophy. He goes on Sundays to a small Dominican monastery to hear Mass accompanied by Gregorian chants.

At the end he said to us, *to us* who have been, up to yesterday, inflexible, intolerant, filled by our spiritual vision: "Do not temporize. All those books like Erskine's are temporizing."

I protested, "But Europe, old wise Europe has demanded temporizing, speculation, tolerance, as the first duty of the intelligence. It has demanded flexibility, open-mindedness. It says: Understand everything, see everything, be open to everything. Et à force de tout vouloir comprendre, ils ne comprennent rien" [And through wanting to understand everything, they understand nothing].

And there we stood, caught in the middle of our triumph for having at last reached Tolerance (we were celebrating only a month ago) through Buhlig's keen eyes, and grey-haired knowl-edge. There we stood, clasping hands firmly with a man who could have built Mont-St.-Michel and Chartres. A living man, when, for lack of him in our world, we haunted other centuries and chased shadows in damp castle halls and prisons.

September 7. A feeling of control, of comfort, of power. I go hum-ming through the streets. I feel that now I can work, because I have confidence, and because I have so much to say. Strange how I have called writing my "work" after spending a year effacing "writing" from my consciousness. Writing, after all, is more than dancing, more than drawing. Mais je ne dois me laisser distraire [But I should not let it distract me]—always talking about "work," oiling my typewriter, yes, and listening to the journals of others, which, I swear, interest me more than my own. I have an hour before Gilbert's visit with *his* journal.

"She possessed the true critical gift, that is, she had the power of steadily enlargening her mind, increasing her receptivity, and *destroying her prejudices* in the bud, thereby, holding herself in constant preparedness to understand." From *Immigrant Litera-ture,* by Georges Brandes, about Mme. de Staël. An ideal to live up to! But I am not a good critic, and even about literature, to which I apply all the intelligence I possess, I am emotional and personal—that is, I can't read without feeling: if it is sensual, I am disgusted; if it is vulgar, I won't read on; if it is fine, I am transported; if it is weak, I despise it; if it is strong, I am en-thusiastic and devoted—all *personal,* not literary, viewpoints.

I realize I *am* too personal—that all of my writing springs from my self. As soon as I write objectively, as soon as I talk in the third person, my work freezes. My "third person" is always ridiculous. It is a scarecrow which I endow with my thoughts and my emotions. It is never absolutely *somebody else,* because I don't know anybody else as deeply as I know myself. Besides, why should I dig into other minds while mine is full; why should I stand aside and help a shadow to walk when my own doings are so real and so vivid? In criticism, I don't know what a thing is in relation to a vast whole—I have a philosophy by which I measure, and emotions by which I judge. All wrong—I know.

September 8. The sun shines moderately, and I have dragged table and typewriter out on the terrace. But I can't begin, because I fall into Erskinian prose, pure imitation, or again into the clutches of my Journal, which has swallowed up every theme I have created during the years. To the imitation of Erskine I bring much verve and individuality but I feel his influences, and though I smile at what I write I cannot take it seriously. Remains the eternal problem—turn the Journal into a novel? Copy out the Journal as it is?

September 12. Gilbert is in a state of effervescence; he is discovering the world; he is applying a critical, analytical mind to literature and music. We have long and interesting discussions. He has a solid foundation of knowledge, a sound, rather formal way of expressing his ideas, principles of character, and a great love for Spain. He has the two eternal weaknesses of youth: supreme interest in himself and the inclination to talk about futile reforms. He demands only a listener, not an exchange of experience, and some of his guns are pointed at the moon.

He makes me realize how far I have traveled from a certain kind of talk because I am living and not just starting to live, and so many conclusions are reached by living not by reasoning. I don't know why, but I feel old, older than Eduardo[1] and Gilbert. My mind seeks more difficult ideas to follow; I seek the "denouement" of things; I can't follow roundabout talks; I feel that I am at the center already, and I am impatient to go forward from there. I seek old people, wise people. Youth has nothing to give me. I am full of energy, full of creation, full of enthusiasm already. It is not indifference to development, which has always interested me. It is a desire for deeper life. Or perhaps my old, painful, unexplainable restlessness. I could, if I let myself, be the most capricious, moody, unapproachable person. Instead I am mild and accessible and interested. And then, after an hour's effort, I rise and begin beating the walls of my prison. Yes, I am in a mood, that is all.

September 16. A wonderful evening—with Gustavo Morales, the young Cuban composer I met at Irving's home. He mimicked the "piano-playing systems" of New York with such humor that we laughed ourselves into tears. He has a knowledge and a love of Oriental philosophies: he is writing an opera on ancient Egyptian religion and history; he has already produced a "Royal Fandango" in New York. He is a brilliant talker, full of irony, enthusiasm,

[1] *A.N.'s cousin, Eduardo Sánchez.*

and frankness. He bolts from his chair, explodes when something is mentioned which he does not like, walks about to illustrate his descriptions, uses all his face with perfect art to punctuate his ideas. And he is rich in ideas, experience, opinions. He loves Albéniz; Granados is the Grieg of Spain—and he hates Grieg; he does not think Falla has genius. He went to listen to the opera *Louise* all ready to pounce on it, and found it charming. He has an English sweetheart with red-gold hair and green eyes. It was midnight when he went home. Morales had received, just as we had, a letter from Irving announcing his return on the twenty-second. Joaquin is not enthusiastic. He took fire too quickly, and is now tasting ashes.

September 19. We drove 250 kilometers, six and a half hours, to see a statuette from Tanagra, the Grecian city! We had really intended to see castles, but after driving three hours Saturday afternoon in angry rain and vicious wind, after finding all hotels in Orléans full, and finally landing in a boardinghouse, after spending the night awake with noises in the street, we surrendered and came home Sunday night, to our stove and books, and our own clean bed. But Orléans pleased me, even though I could hardly see it for the rain. We did not leave it before visiting its museums, its old houses and streets, and its cathedral. It was in the Musée Historique we saw a most interesting collection of carved coffers, Egyptian clothes and glass jars, and the statuette from Tanagra—exquisitely fine.

Today, by accident (we wanted to go to the movies), I saw the idiotic Legion parade. Clumsy, innocent, tactless, stupid, infantile Americans reveling in a parade which could only hurt the French, who are sick of military demonstrations, unnerved by ordinary and daily American invasions, and who, if anybody, should be the ones to do the parading. I stood there among a crowd that was trying to be civil; heard the swift, slangy remarks of workmen, the joking of the people, *felt like a Frenchwoman* before that pushy, boastful, indelicate, idiotic parade. "Please take me home," I begged. And we returned to our stove, and just as I hated Paris on some rainy nights when I first came and didn't understand it, today I hate Americans.

Hugh was reading some bank pamphlets on will trustees, inheritances, etc. I said to him: "If I died you would get my clothes allowance, and could live on it in perfect comfort ever after."

September 20. Joaquin objects rightly to my mixing pure and modern English—to my writing "tasting ashes" and, on the same page, "Lord, I'm hungry." Now I use flourished English humorously, affectionately; I can't forget that I once worshipped it, but direct and vivid English suits my thinking better.

Driving has been something to conquer, and I have suffered. It demands concentration that is painful to me. I have to stop thinking of anything but the road before me and its problems. What an effort for one who is used to dreaming in subways, thinking in buses, freely and at all times. And then I have had to learn certain scientific facts, which I hate, and to obey laws, to control and submerge my timidity, my nerves, my impatience, my detachment from earthly machinery. I have cried at night with anger and discouragement. I awake early to return to my torture; I obstinately face it over and over again. I force my hands, eyes, nerves and mind, enslave them. I have hated driving. And then when I drive well, I feel exultant and proud and as satisfied as if I had tamed a monster—not the car so much, as myself, this self who would choose only the easy tasks.

September 23. I had been sitting for an hour in a formal French salon with three old countesses. The maid had just taken away the tea tray. I had been very subdued, very conventional. I was dressed in a pastel blue dress and hat, and they wore black, brown, and navy blue. I had complimented one of the countesses on her tea; I had received a compliment on my hat; I had inquired about the painting of the other countess (she was doing peaches and bluebells). The third had mentioned a book, the life of a saint. We had talked about religion for half an hour. The countess at my right had an apostolic expression and a handbag full of relics.

Suddenly one of the countesses bent over toward me and said very slowly: "Have you made jam this year?"

I felt myself getting very small and my flowered hat growing very big and my medieval ring shining with unbearable brilliance. I wished my hands were less smooth and were stained with fruit juice. I looked up humbly at the three old countesses and said, "No, but I would like to—"

"Well, eleven pounds of prunes and five pounds of sugar, one hour's cooking—"

I listened gravely. I felt my hat forgiven and my ring. The talk turned to the parade. The three countesses had been there.

One of them said, "It will cement the beautiful friendship between the two countries."

"It was wonderful!" said another. "I wept when I saw it. One should seek such emotions! Of course you were there?" The three countesses looked at me.

"No, I don't believe—" And I told them what I really believed. There was a silence. Nobody understood.

"You weren't at the parade?"

Just then Hugh came in, kissed the hostess's hand gracefully, bowed before the other ladies, sat down and resumed a delicate conversation, repairing, by vague, general, meaningless statements, the effect of my frankness. Then we left the battlefield.

In the car I made rapid calculations. "I was there one hour and a half before you came, and I was good up to the last moment. Which means I can be tactful and idiotic for exactly one hour and a half but no longer, and you must not expect it."

Once home, I overflowed with humor. I even tripped about to warm up my mummified body, my jamified head. I gave fantastic descriptions of the afternoon. I went to say good night to Mother.

"Mother, Mother, have you made jam this year?"

Mother looked at me with round eyes. This morning I went into the kitchen where Eugénie was peeling potatoes.

"Eugénie, can you make jam?"

"Oui, madame."

"Buy eleven pounds of prunes and five pounds of sugar, and make jam."

"Oui, madame."

"And if anybody asks, I won't be home until twelve. I am going to my drawing lesson." I am not a countess.

Winter is coming. We have dinner by candlelight already. I have a blue velvet coat with squirrel trimming for the cold days. Disraeli, whose life touched me so much, also loved velvet and lace. He would have seen the true aspect of the parade, not its sentimental or naïve appearance. He would have spoken frankly about it. I feel mean afterward, overcritical, overcynical. Sitting in blue among the three harmless, conventional countesses, I see myself as a pleasantly disguised Devil who takes the bloom out of peaches, prunes, bluebells, jam, and parades.

What I dread always is to cripple myself fatally for friends; dread that the jam should clog my vivacity and spontaneity. I can't live in artificiality. In the eyes of people like the countesses, I see thoughts other than those they speak about, dimmed by a long habit of reserve, sometimes effaced completely. There remains nothing but a watchful guard set upon the thoughts of others, which they cannot tolerate. Hugh said rightly that the War was to them their sole real emotion, that in their dry, dead life, they cling to that emotion, are anxious to revive and maintain it.

P.S. The jam was very good.

September 24. How little there is that does not interest me. I make use of everything, of everybody, of every place and hour. Shopping with a domestic lady, I study other shoppers and salespeople. I gather expressions and small incidents. Formal calls of the most deadening nature have given rise to humorous pages in my Journal. Small trips downtown furnish me with ideas and innumerable fancies. A trolley ride provides me with more faces and guesses at people's characters. When I am trying on a dress, I am discovering my seamstress's life. A few Bank friends, bad movies, tennis matches have alone succeeded in boring me. Inaction, if I can't study anything, bores me. Everyday I am more interested in life and character, in living directly, vividly. In consequence, I read less poetry, which is about life and not life itself.

September 27. Just as I had written that line about poetry I was saved by the greatest poet alive today—Armand Godoy. We went to see him last night, Joaquin, Hugh, and I. He was dressed in black with a soft Baudelairean tie. After greeting his wife and children, we followed him to his library, an immense room, a sanctuary, "the most beautiful library in the world" (I quote from a dedication made to him). It was there he had shown us, two years ago, manuscripts of Baudelaire and Victor Hugo and others.

He read to us from his manuscript of poems with musical titles, inspired by music; read in a low, sober, stirring voice, simply, beautifully. The modulation and expression of his voice, human and divine in one, penetrated all my consciousness; his poetry has resounded in that inaccessible world of spiritual shadows where the sound of it can never be lost. I shall never read his printed words without hearing all those miraculous accents, those multiple and harmonious voices. I cried.

I wrote to him today: "You have received many tributes in words, but last night your poetry roused in me an ecstasy which could only be expressed by tears. So much beauty was never crowded in one hour . . ."

October 3. Saturday evening we had Irving Schwerke to dinner. After dinner we all sat in a circle, and each one of us read from his journal. Irving began with a description of his visit to a singer who had such a brilliant career and is now blind, old, and poor. He wrote with feeling about her; with sarcasm about some teas he attended; with spirit about famous people. He had some clever aphorisms and epigrams.

Joaquin read a description of the sea which was beautiful and poetic, and Byronic (though he has never read Byron); a comment on *Don Quixote*, which had insight and romanticism; and a description of a walk, which moved us like the best poetry. It was so profound that Hugh said, "I don't think you realize what you have written!" (He wrote in his journal later that he had read for Hugh and me; that he had felt *we* had understood him; Irving was too preoccupied in seeking the traces of *his* influence on Joaquin.)

Hugh read a page of pure poetry from his journal, which Irving appreciated. And then he made them laugh by reading what I had written in his journal, as if coming from him. I read my "Three Old Countesses," which also made everybody laugh.

Irving was rather surprised by everything. "We all write well!" he said. The lasting value of that evening was that it inspired everybody; gave each of us a sense of the journals' importance and charm.

Boussie[1] is home. Antonio[2] came today. Morales is going to Spain for a month. We have discovered an Indian book on love. I have bought castanets and found a teacher. Eduardo has written! I have tonsilitis, a good pretext for writing all day if I wish. Hugh, encouraged by an outsider's praise, is really turning to his writing again. What we all realized Saturday night was that Joaquin, less trained than any of us in the art of writing, had touched the source of communication directly and spontaneously. Hugh is, of course, a natural poet, but also an educated (and educated by Erskine!) poet. As for my "attitude toward writing," I write be-

[1] *Hélène Boussinescq, a teacher of English literature.*
[2] *Antonio Valencia, a young pianist.*

cause I feel, and only because I feel. But I don't think that at Joaquin's age I often wrote lines beneath which you feel the rumble of deep, interior life. For both of us, Godoy has been the true revealer of Poetry; by the miracle of his own *being*; by the realization that he is himself a pure Poet, and therefore the only dispenser of poetic understanding.

I owe my beloved [Henri Frédéric] Amiel a habit which is bringing a thousand scoldings upon my head from the Poetic Banker. Too often now he has said, looking crossly at me writing: "You use too many adjectives!" When I give him something I have written, he puts on a white apron like a butcher, picks up a bloody knife and slashes into my adjectives heartily. Still I insist each word I have used has a different "nuance" and it has a use in my phrase. But I can't fool the Poetic Banker like that. Amiel did not have such a watchdog. Poor Amiel!

Men like Horace, Eduardo, Enric, etc. have the power to make every woman feel as if she were the Only One. But I am never mystified now, and the other night (although Frances [Hyde] was in every snapshot taken by Horace during their vacation in Greece) Horace was soft-eyed, soft-spoken, and addressed both glances and words to me all evening. I wasn't caught! I understand now I am but a manifestation of Woman. Do they really make distinctions between women? Do they really see differences other than those of clothes, shapes of noses, or voices?

October 4. Formal dinner last night at Durand in a private room— all in gold and red brocade, stiff chairs and too many lights. Pheasant brought to us, wings and all, as if ready to fly off. Gastronomically an interesting dinner but conversationally boring. And my grippe growing worse every minute so that I could hardly talk, see, hear or smell. Relied entirely on my superficial qualities, which served me loyally. I think I achieved my highest mark in dressing: tight-fitting dark blue velvet dress with enormous medieval sleeves slit to show half of the arm, Mont-St.-Michel bracelet and rings, velvet turban softly and yet neatly framing the head, coat of the same sapphire-blue velvet, tight-waisted, wide at the bottom, trimmed with squirrel. I didn't need to talk.

Spending the day in bed writing letters to break all my "engagements" up to Thursday, when I hope to be well enough to attend Godoy's reception. I almost believe I am leading a conventional life. I can't be ill without upsetting the plans of several people. What slavery. I couldn't just disappear, leave for Italy or India, with my Journal, without causing comments and curiosity. That is all that social life means, the careful setting of a web. We feel that we are living because we feel the web *pulling* and feel we are *important* merely because our absence tears the web. This web, to most people, is a justification of their lives, and it is responsible for their illusions. To me it means nothing except when it communicates with the Exceptions. It is amusing to think that the telephone, pneumatique, and date book, all the web sustainers, can serve two widely different ideas; and tragic to realize that there is only one web—if you are in it, you are in with the Idiots and with the Exceptions—if you're out of it, you are alone and deprived of both. We chose to be in the web. Only the grippe or a trip saves me from its tentacles.

A sad day—head too heavy to absorb anything but biography. I don't mind being ill with a clear head, but this is terrible. Joaquin came to see me a little while. We talked about his work. The last year was in many ways disappointing. He is willing to admit it. Does he really lack the *force*, the will, the tenacity? He *looks* softer than I am, but both our faces may be deceptive—I know mine is. Before my awakening I was dreamy, drifty, indifferent to the exterior direction of my life. It may be the same with him. I await the full awakening because I have faith in him.

He interests many people—people who feel his intense musicality, his power to create, his sensitiveness and his intuition. Women are always his ally. They like his eyes, his manners, his romanticism. He is sincere, good, easily enthusiastic, and just as quickly disillusioned—which makes some people think he is fickle. He is not fickle—he is true to an ardent and uncritical nature, to spontaneous emotions, and a rich fund of affection. His only fault is that he argues badly. He makes proud and preposterous statements; he is guided by obscure and illogical attractions and dislikes; his reason vacillates. In arguments he either looks overbearing and overcertain of himself or like a tracked animal. Every idea is received by his heart, not his mind, and he is hurt at every attack or mere statement. Yet he shows in writing, and in calm tête-à-têtes, an inclination for philosophy, and a quick discernment of truth, which may in the end win out. But I fear to see him in the hands of enemies. I fear the decisions of his mind in moments of passion. So few people are going to understand my little "tracked animal," so few will find the gentle way into his head, so few will know the words he did not mean from the true ones, so many vain ones will take offense at his pride, which is such a pathetically thin shield for his sensitiveness.

Fortunately his journal now will be his favorite confidant. It makes him reflect and meditate—exemplifying all the miraculous properties of journal writing which I have described in pedantic essays, in speeches, and most effectively in my own Journal (didn't I convince myself?).

October 6. "Do things thoroughly or not at all!" I believe in this and carried it out faithfully by getting thoroughly and desperately ill with grippe, bronchitis, laryngitis, fever, etc. etc. Last night I could neither read nor breathe, nor hear, nor talk. What a punishment for a person like me. I think, in fact, that this was a Biblical revenge for my vanity, of which there are enough proofs in my Journal. All I regretted today was missing the Godoys' reception, where I was to meet the famous painter Beltran Massès.

Boussie came to see me for an hour. Talked of New York, Chartres, [Louis] Jouvet, new books, Godoy, [Waldo] Frank, [Sherwood] Anderson, Erskine, plays. She gave me life again! I offered her *Eglantine.* "Oh, I can live without Giraudoux!" she said. I can too; I am not fooled by him. I know quite well he has nothing to say, that he dissertates as any Frenchman can, before, during, or after dinner, that when you take the sum of any of his novels you hold nothing but air. Eglantine loved two old men; you could find a thousand women like her walking down the boulevards or through the Bois. The two old men were not exceptional. Everything in the book, in fact, is absolutely banal— people, places (and that gift of jewels made by Moise), restaurants, offices, houses. But that plain, stupid story is told with miraculous words, with the most exquisite finesse. It is eloquence wrapped about trivialities. I blame Giraudoux for two things: for not having discovered a few exceptional women who could talk well in addition to ornamenting beds, and for reducing his intelligent men to living for such small causes.

My days are cheered by the *History of Costume,* by the smell of Eucalyptol, by my book of clippings and my account book; yet I am bored because the sun is shining outside, and I am missing the Godoys' reception. I am no longer afraid of receptions. I seek the opportunity of meeting some interesting person. Timidity hardly ever bothers me now, though I have unexpected and irritating returns of that old illness. I have to learn much to keep up with my Humorous Banker, who, in the last year, has learned so much grace and tact. He has now, besides the deep qualities of the Anglo-Saxon, all the charms of a Latin.

The other night he was sitting on my bed speaking some affectionate words, his whole face alight, eyes and smile warm and expressive. I told him he had at that moment all that makes a Spaniard irresistible. He talks much more, very smoothly and richly. In fact, I sometimes wonder how much actually remains of the man I married four years ago—reticent, inexpressive, hesitant, vague in his desires. His work and responsibility have matured him in a virile, worldly way. I like to hear him talk with other men; he has command of language, vigor, reason, persuasiveness, judgment. He has all sorts of unexpected intuitions, which come from the poet. He has that quality which exists in few men in his profession: aristocracy. Everything he touches is made beautiful.

October 10. Slow return to life. Saturday I took my first walk. Sunday the Cat devoted himself to me, taking me out all day in the country among the heather. Our Scotch hill (Chevreuse) was beautiful. We sat there an hour. The sunshine healed me, the smells, the colors, the dry air.

This morning I sat cheerfully and organized my week with a method and care which suddenly reminded me of Father. Of course I realize that it is not only the bad qualities which are inherited. Like Father, I love a tidy house, filed papers, order in the library, etc. Bills are paid, letters answered, accounts revised, budget and expenses balanced, engagements made. No *confusion* in any detail. The same idea applies to dressing. The Frenchwoman excels in neatness, in *perfection of detail*, and there lies her secret.

I begin by a sermon—a good sign, as it shows my illness has not changed me in the least.

Am I in a worthy state to record an important conversation the Cat and I had this morning while we were having our usual breakfast in bed? The Cat said, speaking of that Indian book on love, "Do you think it is right that such books should be suppressed?"

"They might do a lot of harm to those who would use the knowledge badly."

"But what matter the harm done to the weak ones, compared to the good it can do."

"That is true."

"I believe such knowledge is necessary and beautiful."

"So far," I said, "it seems to have been mainly in the hands of vicious people—"

"In itself, it is a noble knowledge. Compare that lovely Indian idea of marriage to our own—ten days instead of a few hours before the physical expression of union; ten days of delicate attentions, of wooing, of preparation, of poetic coaxing—"

They have beautiful names for everything; a deep knowledge of feelings, instincts, physical emotions; profound wisdom in love, its spiritual and physical subtleties. Why is such absolute knowledge always distorted into something ugly? As Hugh says, it should be given to all. The most powerful charm in the world has been left to the devils by a few prudish old men! The most beautiful art—the art of love—even today has been abandoned in the hands of low men and women who can continue to make it seem their own. From today, the knowledge is ours.

Hugh is balancing my literary successes with his financial genius; edifying the Bank with his energy; pinning down cranky customers to huge promises; bluffing through difficulties; riding over his own native temperament, which is quiet, retiring, speculative, aristocratic, even snobbish; conquering timidity and hesitation; persuading "big men"; winning sympathy and cash; surprising his fellow workmen and his wife; electrifying the Manager, who had once thought him a pessimistic credit man who could pass judgment on but not *create* business. A triumph of character, of will and imagination. Even I did not expect so much. Without regret or sadness, I recognized that Johnnie and Thorvald[1] could do such things; but my Banker was a poet and a humorist, and I did not ask more. That he should be, in addition, a brilliant Banker is not only startling but admirable.

October 11. I will do my best writing, my truest writing, while it remains unknown, unappreciated, and unpublished. Afterward will come self-consciousness, vanity, adulation and, as in the cases of Anderson and Erskine, material comfort. And then? Anderson has ceased wandering and has settled in a stone house; he is less naïve. Erskine is also settled in a stone house, and writes

[1] *Hugh's brother, John Guiler, and A.N.'s older brother.*

Adam and Eve instead of poetry. No, I do not believe in writing for *anyone*. I never have and never will.

October 12. Joaquin's piano accentuates the blackness of my mood. It is not the grippe; it is Sherwood Anderson. His last book makes me feel like the days in New York when I was fourteen and cried desperately when I heard music. Boussie and I sat yesterday talking about him. The foolish things that are written about him make us angry. We love and understand his writing.

October 13. The emotions roused by Anderson's last book distilled into a letter to the *Literary Review*. I sit in a corner of the studio warmed by my "Middle West" stove (shown in American moving pictures as a footstool for the town Sheriff and the old gossips in the General Store). I write on the tea table, which gives that symbol of insipid friendships a new character. And then I boast a lot and do nothing! But, as usual, I am bursting with thoughts: useless thoughts, fantastic thoughts, illogical and incredible thoughts. As for example: Why not put my Journal into a book? I am tired of writing just for myself. It is like talking to a wall, like smoking in the dark. I know I could make others cry and make them infinitely, desperately, divinely alive. I know I say what they wish to say and cannot say. And some, if my writing reached them, this writing that I have done walking alone, would know that there are several of us walking alone, and that it is good to know it.

October 15. Erskine was the first to find the key to my writing and character: he said I was "reticent." For a year I have struggled with this reticence. Occasionally I have conquered it. Erskine's own writing liberated my intelligence from scruples and hesitations. Then Sherwood Anderson liberated my feelings and dreams from timidity and self-consciousness. I had so many fears, fear of hurting people, fear of ugliness, fear of being bad, impure, not aristocratic, not ideal. Now my freedom is complete. I write exactly what I think. Dancing has liberated my body. For the first time I am almost continuously myself. Last year such a freedom came only spasmodically. I still write reticent letters. There is no doubt that I am still afraid of Erskine.

At least I am no longer afraid of Boussie. We had a delightful evening together yesterday. We invited her and her little old mother for dinner. Warmth from the red stove, candlelight, exquisite food, water in blue glasses, a dessert of which Boussie took two helpings—all these things pleased them. Hugh was conversing freely in his soft French. Joaquin came in after dinner, and we sat in the library and lit the candles, which light up the books. A painter should have been there to see Boussie's little mother—so tiny, with a black bonnet and tight-waisted black dress and a red wool shawl. Her face is olive-colored, her nose large, aquiline, and a hundred wrinkles run evenly from her chin to her eyes. She has small bright eyes, which absorb everything.

October 17. Loneliness: because Hugh had to leave on business in Alsace for two nights and a day. We laughed at our own sentimentality last night when we kissed as for a long separation. I didn't sleep well.

The atmosphere of the art school depressed me. The model had a beautiful figure but such a bestial face; low forehead, big thick mouth, and flat, round nose. She walked about the room naked without reason, and the periods of rest caused me feelings of disgust. The men in the class could not help watching her. When I met their eyes their expression did not change, and I felt myself confused with the other woman, likened to her; felt myself made of the same flesh and attracting the same brutal curiosity.

I awakened without a kiss, had breakfast alone, dressed without talk; I had nobody to brush, to kiss good-bye; I am having lunch with Mother, and tonight I will sleep alone again. Am I glad to be alone? Was there anything I wanted to do while Hugh is away that I cannot do when he is here? No. I miss him deeply. I have no desires, no joy at my independence; and I feel as if I were half alive. This wonderful life I praise so often seems blank and stupid today. I could do without my mirror, without lovely clothes, without sunshine—none of these things are necessary when I am alone. I did a few things to take advantage of my solitude, sleeping on the left side of the bed, which I prefer to the right, and wearing gloves with cold cream. And then, of course, I was glad to have the bathroom to myself. Usually I have to scratch on the door and "miaow" desperately to be allowed in, and even then I often get a shoe or a clothes brush on the head. Also, I slept fifteen minutes longer than usual.

October 21. My dear Scotchman received the following letter from his Uncle George: "It may seem a long time since I received your letter of last year, but time passes quickly, especially when partly taken up by travel and its consequent results, and a mislaid letter does not help. Your letter was a sincere expression of your feelings and sorrow for past errors, and while without in any way wishing to enlarge upon or emphasize them, I wish to say that I appreciated your frank expression of regret. You know what regard I had for you, and so it is natural for me to wish that you may be led on to greater strength and courage along the right path of duty and conduct in life's long endeavor. With greetings from your affect. Uncle George."[1]

What can you say? Everybody can see that it was fitter to laugh—and so I said to my Scotchman: "Go and tack up that letter on the Lost Letter board of American Express. Dub it 'To an Erring Nephew,' and you will see all the Anglo-Saxon youths stand in a row. He is a real Parker," I said, too; "he has been parking for over a year."

My generous Cat deserved a better uncle. May that clumsy and noble man sleep in peace after writing his "dignified" letter (it came from London, of course). How could my Cat come from such a family? Secretly, on my "aristocratic" days, I despise them. Hugh explains reasonably that whenever men of his temperament appeared in the family, they were soon exterminated by the "public opinion" power of the family. He has been the only survivor; he has been strong, has escaped and rebelled against them. What a miracle of solitary growth is his open-mindedness, his humanness, his warmth, his largeness of mind and heart.

I have wanted to do his portrait. He has a marvelous profile, high forehead, moderately aquiline nose, a large but finely carved mouth, perfect teeth, and a determined chin. The firmness of his mouth hides its sensitiveness, just as the clear frankness of his eyes hides softness. The intonations of his voice, rich and varied, are also winning but firm. There are two things which appeal to me particularly: his hands, with their furry wrists and long, sensitive fingers, and the little valley on the back of his neck, just deep enough for a kiss, expressive of a nameless quality which is rare in men—a sort of carved fineness—the opposite of thick and bullish necks or the merely flabby ones. Enough for today— such a portrait always leads to sentimentality.

October 22. Fortunately, Hugh has the habit of being late, which is often the cause of my writing so much. If he came home early,

[1] *Hugh's family opposed his marriage to a Catholic.*

my Journal would be reduced by half. Yesterday was an important day; we received in the morning Godoy's new book, *Le Carnaval de Schumann*, with a beautiful inscription, and in the afternoon an affectionate letter from Erskine.

I write and I dance. When I get tired of typewriting, I take up my castanets and study the "arms" before the mirror, or I review my Sevillana entirely. It rests me from the drowsiness of sitting in a chair without moving; it rests me from thinking; and refreshed by the rhythm, I can return to my writing with more vigor.

October 24. My first dancing lesson with Señor Paco Miralles, teacher of professional Spanish dancers. I changed in a dark room like the dressing rooms of cheap theatres (see Colette's descriptions). The mirror has a bluish tone, the walls are lined with hooks on which are hung ballet dresses, tights, coats, fur neckpieces, stockings. I put on my wide cretonne skirt, whose volants are edged with black velvet, and my tight black velvet bodice and black velvet shoes. Then I went to the studio where Mr. Miralles was just finishing a lesson. He is a small, black-haired man, about forty, agile and graceful, with small hands and feet. He has the face of "un homme du peuple." I am sure he cannot write very well, but what a dancer he is!

Immediately he spied all my inexperience and faults: lack of flexibility, etc. I felt I would learn with him, and I admired his severity, his seriousness and earnestness.

The room is long and wide, and the end wall is all mirrors, with side lights as for a stage. At the other end of the room there is a piano, which a Frenchwoman plays indifferently, with her hat and coat on. The long bench on which she sits is piled high with music. Between each dance Miralles stirs up all the music and never finds the piece he wants. Next to the piano there are two straw chairs with holes in them. Miralles's coat is on one of them, because he teaches in his shirt sleeves and sweater. On the other there are castanets, usually. I sat there the first time I went to watch one of his lessons. It was hard to sit there while the others danced. After my lesson Monday, I watched that of a Spanish girl doing the Fandango and the Valenciana. I was excited beyond reason.

October 27. Two days ruined by grippe. Fits of choking gave me a real scare during the night. These are a mystery, because I have never been in better health. Sniffling and coughing, I went to my dancing lesson, and danced better than I have ever danced. Miralles is a magician. With a tap of his finger he curves my waist, with a sign of his head he makes me catch the lost rhythm; his neat, clean steps are easy to follow; he is patient but exact. I feel flexible and quick and full of spirit. I never get tired. Nothing hurt me that he made me do, and I was happy. At the end he looked pleased and said, "Ha adelantado mucho!" [You've made great progress!] It is a day of pure physical joy and work—a rest for the mind. I dress up for it: I paint my eyes heavily, rouge my lips more intensely than for ordinary days, curl my hair carefully. When I get home I feel really tired, pleasantly tired. I lie down with a book. Other days, in Colette's phrase, I have "le mouvement ralenti par la pensée" [action restrained by the mind]. On my dancing days, ma pensée est étouffé par le mouvement [my thoughts are smothered by action]. Without the two movements, life dies. I want both movements—quick and beautiful.

October 28. I have steered my life, as far as is humanly possible, but bad health conquers me every time. The more I defy it, the more it tortures me. Taking milk, Wonder Malt, naps, etc., are useless. In short, I'm discouraged, after four bad nights, four sad days. At last life can laugh at me; I'm pinned down by the most humiliating physical weaknesses. At the end of the second day of such tyranny I lose my sense of humor; the third day I get up and take a splendid dancing lesson; the fourth day I give up without humor and spirit, and I take up the conventional and Biblical lamentations, "Oh, Lord, look down upon Thy suffering servant."

No, it is not the suffering that bothers me. It is the fact that illness keeps me from living, that it affects my mind so I can't read, alters my writing, softens my legs so I can't dance, weakens my hands so I can't sculpture. All the power that makes my joy taken from me—eyes, hands, feet—all the senses dulled and crushed but the sense of pain, and a pain from which I have nothing to learn. If, at least, an earache revealed charity to me, if a body-rending cough revealed the meaning of life, if a feverish, sleepless night, a soreness from hair to toes taught me philosophy— at least, I wouldn't complain. No. A better prayer would be, "Lord, deliver me from useless suffering." The Cat has four days' holiday. At last I understand the use of a harem. A single woman cannot be depended on. Hugh could go off on his holiday with a grippe-less wife, and if this one should break her leg getting out of the car, a third wife could be mustered to entertain the waiting Bank friends next week. Mrs. G. would ask: "And where is your first wife?"

"She is being repaired just now. She had lost her voice and her coughing was dreadfully irritating."

"And your second wife?"

"She is having her leg changed at the hospital."

"Let's talk about cheerful things," the third will say. "Do you like my new fur coat?"

Now, when the two wives get well, they will also need fur coats. I suppose that is what has kept my dear Scotchman from getting a harem. One wife, even with the grippe, is more economical.

Joaquin has composed a wonderful dance of purely Spanish feeling. He played it for us last night. For two days he had not been studying very well, and yesterday he was overjoyed to be able to explain that it was due to "les douleurs de la maternité" [labor pains].

November 1. Four happy days: two afternoons spent in the country, two evenings seeing Jouvet in *Leopold le Bien Aimé* [Leopold the Beloved] and *Maya,* one rainy afternoon spent in the movies, the other resting and reading another book on Oriental love. The grippe, once or twice, claimed attention, but on the whole we conquered it by fresh air, the smell of heather, a tennis game and a generous dose of affection. Oh, the smell of heather! We are making plans for a house in the middle of the heather. A house of stone with a tower and a wild garden (pine, cypresses, and heather). Our ideal house, for which my plans have been ready for years.

Evening. Miralles's eyes shine humorously and kindly. He takes the trouble to show me how ridiculous a step looks badly done so that I may laugh. My, but I am hot, and my head spins from circling. No, I am not as flexible as I should be; there is so much to learn—this control of the legs, independently from the waist, and keeping my chest out and my feet pointed and my head high. "Bend! Bend! More, more—" I am looking at the floor, but upside down. My hair touches the floor and sweeps it. I tingle from head to foot with the music. The roll of the castanets gives me delightful shivers. How can I make mistakes! And yet I do, and when I make one I lose my head and make two, and three. And I even lose the rhythm, that rhythm which I feel so clearly in calm moments.

I know now why I admire particularly the style of La Argentina. She tells how vulgarity took possession of Spanish dancing through an overemphasis of sidelong glances and suggestive hip poses, how it became an entertainment for cabarets because it expressed sensuality and invitation and coquetry. She has purified it, freed it from the conventional, restricted, and vulgar forms. And now she leaves Paris for New York! No more Falla ballets, no more *Danza del Fuego*.

November 4. After my dancing lesson, Miralles came out of the studio with me and asked me to have a cup of coffee with him. We sat in a café and this is what he said: "I am making plans for you—I know what kind of things you will do—you will be a handsome Maja—a distinguished one. We are going to work well together because "me cae simpática" [we are compatible]. But there is a lot of work to be done. Look at my repertoire [in a notebook, four pages of names of dances taught and arranged by him]. Someday we'll take one of your father's compositions and I'll teach you what to do with it. But work, work a lot."

Then there is hope, I said to myself. Miralles dipped his sponge cake in his coffee and continued to talk about dancing and what he was going to do with me. Then he accompanied me to the bus stop. I made superhuman efforts to contain my excitement and my enthusiasm for my teacher, but my fist moved mysteriously during that bus trip, and I smiled so often that I was twice invited to another cup of coffee!

November 6. While Hugh and Joaquin played tennis together I went to Miralles's Sunday class to watch his pupils dancing together—ten girls and four boys. Three girls were interesting, but the atmosphere was frankly theatrical and cheap. The girls were on "show" for the boys. The air was bad. Miralles danced something with one of his pupils, and danced to perfection of course. But I decided not to join the ensemble. What I saw there encouraged me because nothing that was done by the three good pupils was inaccessible to me.

When I came home the fever had touched Hugh—he was practicing with my castanets! He is going to study and be my partner.

November 9. A dreary rain celebrates the opening of a new Diary. But I am not discouraged. I have written Godoy about his *Carnaval de Schumann*. Joaquin came in a little while and read some of my descriptions of life in New York, chuckled at what was intended to be chuckled at and said I had acquired my humor from my marriage with Hugh. Is that true? I am sure it is! Horace brought me incense from Greece. There is a statement few modern women could make. It amuses me to be able to record such a fact in 1927, a fact which has such a decided antique flavor.

November (?). Last night dinner for Horace and Frances, for the sake of making peace with Frances, whom Hugh never liked. I was startled to find her imitating my way of dressing. However, I still blamed myself for my doubts about her, assuring myself that if I had ceased liking her from that evening at Horace's apartment, it was merely because Horace liked her and she brought out the side in him which I dislike.

Just the same, the evening seemed long and painful. Horace was telling us about his trip to Greece. She repeated his phrases without adding to them. She talked a lot, made many gestures and expressions which seemed insincere to me, but then—I didn't trust my discernment. We'll see what the Humorous Banker thinks.

Later, as Hugh undressed for bed, he said, "Frances is nothing but a very good actress. She has set herself out to please Horace, and she is doing it by all sorts of unscrupulous ways: acting, pretending, imitating what she admires in you, quick to catch and to do what he wants."

How well she fooled me! Until the night at Horace's where I caught her making fun of Horace's father, and then hiding her expression when he looked at her, I had thought her simple, merry, and charmless. In a moment of impulsive liking I had introduced her to Horace. How naïve I was; how repentent for my doubts of her! I, who thought myself a good actress too (an emotional and sincere actress); who thought I possessed discernment of women. Well, I have learned a lot.

Hugh's shrewdness astounds me. He has had, in the worldly sense, so little experience with women. When he was in college, he dreamed about the princesses of the "Thousand and One Nights," but never talked to his college mates, or attended the dances. In Forest Hills he only knew a few tennis partners. Once he kissed a girl from Washington, and then immediately realized he did not love her and wrote her a letter to tell her so. He was always chasing after fancies, but never after the real thing. And then, as I said to him with a smile, he married me and has been kept at home ever since, sheltered and protected from any other experience! His knowledge comes not from practice, then, but from reflection and intuition.

Joaquin's dance composition made a strong impression on Antonio, who wants to play it at a concert he is giving. Irving was not so pleased and clumsily imposed some criticism with an authority and tactlessness which Joaquin rebelled against. In short, he tried to dominate him by breaking his spirit, and failed. He reminded him: "But of course you have always said I understood you better than anybody else."

"No," said Joaquin, "if I had said that I would have been disloyal to several people."

Irving's conceit is enormous, phenomenal. I think he is another who fooled me for a little while. Fortunately, nobody can deceive both Hugh and me at the same time. Together, we are unconquerable.

All that dark effervescence which worried me when I came back from New York, that sudden and violent expression of myself, has brought no bad results. It was a moment in my growth where everything was confused in a whirlpool, and I saw in the confusion and darkness of the water, signs of evil! It has all passed, like all the other crises, though it was really more severe than the others. I have kept only the faith, the poise, the courage, and some vanity, which I am now busily squelching.

Vanity! How did I pick *that* up in my wanderings? I, who was so well prepared against it by a childhood spent in self-depreciation. What turns my head? Hugh's love, Joaquin's faith, Mother's, Thorvald's—general compliments, particularly ones like Miralles's, who calls me "Guapa" [Good-looking]. It will pass. I am no longer afraid of such ghosts. I have spent my whole life at war with my character; I am well trained now, and I have much experience.

The dancing is going well—too well, because for the moment it absorbs my interest almost exclusively. The music stirs me. I learn steps quickly. I have a few difficulties, even when I am asked to "Camine, asi, despacio, como hacen las gitanas, y con mucho descaro" [walk thus, slowly, as the gypsies do, with much brazenness]. How to interpret "descaro" for a person who is combating vanity!

December (?). A new maid: Jeanne. A baby born to Mrs. G., which keeps me visiting the hospital and watching Mother sewing things for the poor lady, who has no mother. No desire to write. Feeling rather tired, as I usually do every year around Christmas. Yet the dancing goes well, and I admire my teacher enormously. When we finish at 4:30—that is, once a week—he always invites me to have coffee with him. Each time he tells me he takes more interest in me. I can see it is not for my dancing, which is not the best, by any means, among his pupils, nor for my looks, which fall about tenth in the series, but for something *personal* and inexplicable. I cannot justify it but I accept it, returning his compliments, his glances, his confidences with a sincere admiration of the man's talent, grace, and earnestness.

He told me today that when he was ten years old in Valencia he worked in a factory. He was very ambitious and worked well, and his hands were deft. At night he studied dancing. Pretty soon he showed a very special gift and began to teach his young comrades. His teacher was, as he said, the best in Spain. He died about six months ago. I read an article on Miralles saying he was the only one who was preserving the pure classical traditions of Spanish dancing.

We sat in a large, glaringly lighted café, talking. Then he walked with me to the bus stop and kissed my hand when he left me. No doubt, I thought, his gallantry is that of any dancing teacher for any of his pupils—because I am a woman—and he is a man not too old yet to have fancies . . .

December (?). Depression—fog outside and inside, in which dancing is the only light—a purely physical light which intoxicates me but does not heal me. Mother's perpetual contradictions irritate me. There are days when she will say "No" to anything you might say. But what a small thing compared to her power of sacrifice and work and devotion. I would like to be kinder and softer sometimes, but her combativeness hardens me. I know her to be good, but I try to argue with her, and it is here our tragedy begins. And this is the season of frosty joys and red ribbons and gifts; this is the time of year for jolliness and self-forgetfulness! I am not prepared for it.

Today was my first day at home for ten days or so. I tidied and wrote letters, studied my Granados dance, with Joaquin at the piano. Now I sit shivering and brooding. All these mysterious moods are easily explained by Science: "Get fatter," says the doctor, "and you will feel perfectly well." Therefore I eat a lot of butter and lie down when I can. And I keep calm even in the middle of parties, such as Saturday night's at the Egoist's [Irving's] studio, where we met Jan Hambourg, great patron of music and a musician himself. His violin-playing made me think of Enric and his pathetic life and of my softness with him. Music holds for me the very essence of life, the very mysteries which words never solve, the images which words never grasp. Music is above literature in that it says what can never be said, and it contains all the moods and aspects of life, sometimes in one note. But because I worship music, and yet I am a slave to words, I follow with words the meanings of music, I seek words to re-create the sensations which exalt and unhinge me. Godoy can accomplish this with poetry. I am no longer a poet. I will be content to worship—and to dance.

Miralles is usually patient, very industrious and very thorough with his pupils. Some days he is not in such good humor. I saw that he wasn't last Friday. But at the end of my lesson I had "unwrinkled" him, and he was smiling, with glowing eyes again. But I observed something else, which I suspected, and that is, I am not the only one who inspires his gallantry. Those many little gestures and glances of tribute, like [Charles Dana] Gibson's frequent "By golly but you're a handsome girl," when I was modeling, are distributed by way of friendly encouragement. Every day I find myself melting more and more into the Universal Woman, by my physical attributes, my coquetry, my desire to please, my dancing. I am no longer so naïve as to think myself a separate thing from the others, except at moments. These moments when I feel unique, special are: when I am thinking and seeing through myself and through other women; and when I am writing and reading philosophy or conversing intelligently— which are the product of Mind accidentally located in a feminine envelope.

December (?). More coffee with Miralles. He is a simple-hearted, generous, quixotic man, not clever at handling his material life, devoted to his work. As he says, he is not bold in moneymaking;

he is, in fact, shy in everything but on the boards. Again he wished I had seen him on the stage. "I look twenty years younger." He talked like a young boy about his successes. I would like to know his whole life. He is an uneducated man with delicacies which I can hardly grasp. For example, in money matters, I feel that I am the practical and forward one. I had to raise the price of my own lessons after we sat down together to figure out his expenses for studio and pianist. For a long time he felt he was not making enough, but he did not like to ask women for very much; he did ask a little more from men.

"But you are making ridiculously little," I said. "I am going to try to get you more pupils, and I'll tell them you want sixty francs."

"Sixty francs for a man—but for a woman, fifty francs."

I knew, however, that when he asked that price, he would not stick to it. He teaches through the whole hour without a pause; he hurries and usually gives five or ten minutes more than the hour. Last Wednesday I needed a hat for the Tango, and he insisted on going with me to the shop he recommended. So we walked from Place Clichy to Place Pigalle. I noticed he was careful to walk in step. Then he left me at the bus stop after kissing my hand more gracefully than many aristocrats I have known.

I always come home from my lesson exulted and enthusiastic. Last night I danced for the family: the Tango, España Cañi, the Sevillana, and half of Granados's dance. I ought to try to remember all that Miralles tells me about Spanish dancing, because very little is actually known about it, and almost nothing has been written about it. He is convinced that there is too much careless dancing in Spain, too much improvisation, while the true, ancient steps are disappearing. I asked him if it was true that the gypsies danced well. "No, no," he said. "They exaggerate, they invent, they have a lot of fire and energy, but they don't really know how to dance." Not even La Argentina, whose technique with the castanets is miraculous, not even La Argentina is entirely true to the old dances she sometimes promises to re-create.

I bought a Spanish dress used by a professional dancer. Some of its splendor has faded, but it has preserved an inimitable shape. It outlines the figure, and then swells into a thousand billows, which fascinate me. It is covered with paillettes and colored stones and painted flowers, and it catches the light with multicolored reflections. It is a stage dress, more showy than classical, but I have moods which it can express—my savage love of color and magnificence.

The Bank dance was far more agreeable than we expected it to be. The Paris Branch doesn't lack aristocracy, and almost every dance I danced was interesting. And then Hugh looked so proud of me that I was intensely happy. Horace asked for a dance, and I teased him and made him laugh, and did not give him a chance to hurt my feelings. I used to take too much interest in his fate, and now this preoccupation has been conquered.

December 8. Miralles is always interesting but a little too free with his hands, which I attribute to his stage life. There is the man, the little factory boy, the dancer, and the teacher. The man is like all men, the factory boy is simple-hearted and kind, the dancer is rightfully vain, the teacher is inspiring. I accept this mixture as well as all the others around me. I am beginning to understand that everybody is a mixture, that I am the worst one myself, that there is nothing to do about it.

My superficial life—dancing, dressing, flirting—seems to dominate everything. Yet because of this life I have attained my spiritual and intellectual independence. By a movement of the hips, by the wearing of an eccentric hat, I have gained mental assurance. In two months I have solved more problems of the intelligence, not by assiduous brooding over my typewriter, but by watching Miralles's expressive hands, studying the Sunday-morning classe d'ensemble, rushing back and forth in the bus, making swift and late appearances at teas, where my livingness creates a disturbance— I put my mosaics together without understanding what they mean, except at moments, rare moments of vision. But I know now that since I live more, I understand more.

December (?). For her fifty-seventh birthday, Mother gave a tea. Antonio played, the ladies talked. I came to it glowing from my dancing lesson. Mother looked exactly forty years old, with her hair neatly waved, her high color and perfect smile. Mrs. Varela thought I had taken on an Andalusian manner and walk, that I had changed considerably in a year. Yes, from a mouse to an Andalusian! I was proud of Mother, and she was pleased with me. Nobody likes a mouse, not even a Mother, who is supposed to like anything she has created.

I think often of Enric. Somebody who loves me without understanding me, who hates my Journal, who never reads, who lives only emotionally, and yet is animated by the only chaste love in his life—for what? The mouse, the thin, cold mouse of Richmond Hill? But she is dead. I want to know why he loves me, and he doesn't know. I accept mixtures, but I can't accept things without reason, without sense or meaning.

Years ago I analyzed ideas, and today I analyze sensations, because my puritanical soul revolts at this new life made of physical impulses. I feel bad because I live with my body, because now I touch life not only with my mind, but with my skin, my blood, my nerves. This physical contact with life exults and revolts me at the same time. It is full of shadows and abysses, full of degradations.

To understand Miralles, I must understand Miralles's hands, because I have felt them. Before I only had a mental revolt against the idea of those hands. My body felt nothing. It was always running away, running away, and carrying away all my understanding. Today I stay. I feel all life running through my body. It doesn't pass like a shooting star in the sky. It bites me, soils me, bleeds me. Because I don't run away now, I suspect myself of weakness. I am no longer afraid; then am I bad?

Saw one of the most extraordinary films in the world: *Metropolis*. A vast intellectual, imaginative, and symbolical conception of a city for which New York was but a seed—all that the scientific mind of man can possibly conceive, to the very limit of the imagination. Ideas of men against the Machine, of brain against hands, of power against pity. I understand now the horror, beauty, and power of Machinery. *Metropolis* does not pretend to propagandize; it denies any socialistic idea. But it works from the thesis that labor and brain depend on each other and do not understand each other, and that unjust laws govern both, and natural instincts make them brothers. The idea of "Evil" is masterfully incarnated in a Woman, as is the idea of Goodness. Religion appears as a consolation. The "hands" are oppressed by the "brain." The "brain" is a tyrannical, powerful man who rules the workmen. But the sense of social injustices, of the grinding oppression of Machinery over man, etc., is all comparatively unimportant. It is the enormous leaps of the imagination, the poetic, mystical, supernatural qualities of Science which impressed me. I felt last night that it is only in *film* that reality and unreality, poetry and science, can be fully achieved and communicated! It lacks only color and sound, and they will come later.

December 21. Midnight, after an opera. All evening, while I heard the music, I had dreams about myself, dreams of beauty, of intellectual achievements, of grace, expression in dancing, of passionate, desperate living. I felt myself burning with delirious fever; I saw myself at home, at teas, on the stage, in various countries, writing, dancing, moving, changing, changing. I was everywhere, I was everything, everybody. My life had no limitations, no boundaries, no end. The more I dreamed, the deeper grew my fever, until I suddenly realized I was dazzling myself with myself.

December 22. From what I wrote last night you might think me occupied in gracing a divan and fanning my fair face. Instead I have been shopping, sewing, cooking, dancing, wrapping packages, writing letters and cards, fighting off a cold and desperately ugly moods, swinging from extreme self-satisfaction to extreme self-depreciation; and thinking on the whole more about the Cat, the Lord and Master and Banker, than about anything else.

Yes, this week I realized I would be nothing without him; and he would be worth less also, if we had not found each other. It is the union of the two of us which has made this very brilliant career of ours, the envy of our friends. Alone, each one of us is hesitating, humble, too easily hurt, deceived, or won. Together, we each dispel the other's imaginary fears or self-doubts; our double judgment of people is infallible; deceit, disappointment do not touch us, because we have a fortress in our love.

December 23. There is, in the heart of it all, a perpetual ache. If it is a mood, it is a pretty persistent one. These busy days do not efface it. I go about taking the sorrows of others upon my shoulders. I feel the petty cruelties of people in the shops, the petty lies, the petty tyranny. I am no more philosophical about suffering than before, no more hardened, no more stoical. A terrible admission to make at the end of a wonderful year!

My life is rich, beautiful, creative, but I continue to suffer. Its sweetness does not dull my senses, my body; nor stop my questioning, restlessness, and brooding. It looks as if life could not spoil me. As far as I can see, the only thing that has turned my head is—my head. Hearing so much about my face, at last I have become overconscious of it. This next year's great war will be against Vanity!

December 26. The four of us spent Christmas Eve in Mother's apartment trimming a tree six feet high. Joaquin was lying in his small bed with the grippe. Hugh was busy at the top of the tree, I at the middle and Mother at the lowest branches.

When the candles were on and the tissue paper was spread at the foot of the tree, we all brought in our packages, with jokes and teasing. Mother's present, a dressing table, had to be brought up from the cellar. We first brought the stool, as if it were the only thing, and when Mother, rather dazed and puzzled, decided it might serve to support a plant, although she could not see why we bought such a thing, we brought in the table. (Hugh and I gave each other the big presents beforehand. We had shopped for them together; I bought him a black lacquer cigarette case, and he bought me a black mantilla and comb.) After the distribution of presents we went to bed too tired for midnight Mass. Hugh was so tired that he didn't write me my usual Christmas poem!

Christmas Day: Rain. Mother bustled all morning with the dinner. I helped. Hugh stood outside in the rain with a mechanic, giving the Car a thorough medical examination. At noon Antonio and the Danish cousins arrived. The tree was illumined—more presents given away. Mother's dinner was efficiently disposed of, without much grace or wit—the Danish spirit prevailing. Stupefied by the labor of digestion, all the family sat around in a circle: Manny, like a wilted flower; Liska, like a tired athlete; Emily, with her hands on her stomach and her knees wide apart; Betsy, with sagging shoulders. Joaquin and Antonio were whispering in a corner unconcerned and happy, but Hugh and I looked at each other with sadness.

As this "Dutch painting" grew more and more stolid and fixed, we decided to make one desperate effort to bring it back to life. Antonio was asked to play. I went out unnoticed, to put on my Spanish dress, the new one—orange silk and black lace flounces—with my high comb and black lace mantilla. Joaquin was warned to get ready to play "España Cañi." My first dance was cut short by my stage fright, which was so intense that my fingers were paralyzed and I was unable to play the castanets, and my mouth twitched as if I were about to sob. However, I conquered myself and went on. The last two dances were satisfactory and natural. Antonio was deeply surprised and pleased. Joaquin was particularly impressed with my appearance. Hugh's eyes shone with admiration. Mother was enthusiastic. The Danish cousins were impressed, scandalized perhaps.

I had a moment of very pure joy while dancing. For a moment Beauty entered that gray and sluggish day. Hugh gave us Laughter, by parodying my dances with the most subtle humor. Later we went off in the Car, through the Bois, speeding in the dark, breathing the damp air with pleasure, shaking off the oppression of that "Dutch Family."

December 27 (?). The lady I thought oppressed and irritated by the monotony of her life has deceived me. It is something more serious. The day we went to her home, and Hugh played tennis with her husband, there was a distant relative staying with them, a young man whom I observed to be stupid. Mrs. R. appeared only for lunch. Her husband had already asked me to see what I could do "because she was nervous and upset all the time." That day I tried to "awaken" her without success. At the table the relative was sitting next to her, and I next to him. She wore a summer dress with short sleeves. I don't know why that bare arm and the "relative" became associated in my mind with a feeling of something physical between them, an intuition which startled me. I put it out of my mind instantly, ashamed of myself and blaming myself for letting French novels influence me. Those books I am reading are upsetting me, I thought, and poisoning my imagination.

A few nights ago Hugh said, "Do you know that 'nervousness' of Mrs. R's we were worrying about?"

"I know exactly what you are going to say: There is something between Mrs. R. and this relative visiting them."

"How could you guess?"

"I felt it the day I was there, but I thought it was due to my reading. What have you discovered?"

"Mr. M. observed little things when he went to the house, but I was not convinced. Now, between his shrewd eyes and your feeling, I have no more doubts."

"It is terrible."

We could not go to sleep, thinking of the little children, of Mr. R.'s confidence, his ignorance, and we worried about their fate.

There *was* something lacking in her life, but not *that*! And yet whenever women find an emptiness in their lives they don't seek the cause of it within themselves, in their spiritual and intellectual life; no; they seek a man, they turn destructively upon the husband as if he were to blame, upon the children. They turn to mere physical sensation, to base deception—I can't understand.

December 29. I have had several dreams today—the desire to draw close to Eugene,[1] who is peculiarly in my thoughts all the time, even though we don't write to each other, and hardly talked in New York. Is it an illusion I have that he understands more than most people? Also, to draw close to Erskine. I dreamed how it would be if I could break my reticence and talk or write to Erskine as I do inwardly. Why does he frighten me so? I realize that I am now doing nothing but fulfilling dreams, nothing but materializing images, using my will to make all my desires tangible. Of course, I never dreamed all that I am doing. When I was younger, in Richmond Hill, I imagined my dancing, my writing, and marriage, though not quite like the real one, which surpasses the conceptions of a child. My imagination has been my lamp. I have only to desire wisely and intensely, and with my will, to fulfill.

Is this an illusion, a conceit of my will's power, so newly discovered that perhaps it has intoxicated me? It is so new for me to have an active will after years of merely imaginary activity. Even last year, walking down Boulevard Montparnasse, I asked myself what could happen if suddenly I said and did exactly what I wanted to say and do. I foresaw cataclysms. Yet I tried it. And the result? Nobody hurt—a few scandalized; more, pleased and proud; even more, influenced and enlivened by my activity. Every day I feel surer of myself, my desires soar higher, I feel power in myself, conviction. If it is conceit, a vast empty bubble of vanity, an illusion as false as my old modesty was false; if I am deceived, intellectually, by the fireworks of my life, if its *ascension* is the ascension of self-glory; if there is no spiritual value and philosophical significance to my life, then there is no truth and no sincerity in this world, because no woman ever looked down into herself with as much cold criticism, no woman ever analyzed her ideas and actions more carefully, none was ever more doubtful of herself, more self-depreciating, more fearful of hypocrisy, more terrified of lies, more eager for truth, than I. You, my Journal, alone, know that.

---

[1] *Eugene Graves, a close friend of Hugh's.*

December 31. "Saturday" always has a festive sound. This one ushers in a New Year. We have preserved it for ourselves, escaped cocktail parties, reveillon suppers, etc., and planned an evening to our taste. I don't feel in the mood to celebrate the occasion. Every year I make the same monotonous remarks: Calendric frontiers have never affected me, and my life has never followed any conventional design. I only mark Time with experience, and learning and suffering. I have aged deeply in these three years of European life. That is all I know.

❧ *1 9 2 8* ❧

January 3. I fear I am becoming enslaved by the movement of my life—that is, its routine and its chain of activities are beginning to push me when I should be pushing them. For example: today I wanted to write. I have been boiling thoughts in my head for many days; they were ready today. Tomorrow they will be spoiled. This morning, housekeeping, because I am saving money this month to steady our ever-tottering Budget. Essayage [trying on clothes], because I must dress—I cannot live in rags or in last month's design. Then lunch with Mother and Joaquin, which includes, of course, a little conversation. Then the inevitable and absolutely necessary nap. And now at three o'clock I am waiting for Boussie, and at four o'clock I must be next door to receive the Danish cousins, and at six o'clock back here for dinner and to dress up for one of the Egoist's musical evenings.

And I would like to be writing. How wise I have been to put my writing aside, to leave it alone, to pay no attention to it, to belittle it, to give the greatest importance to dancing. Now the rebellious, uncatchable, wretched, unconquerable gnome regrets his fantasies and whims. He sits abandoned and forlorn. And when at last I am ready for him, he comes, docile and repentent, and bows to all my desires. The real truth is that I love writing more deeply than anything else, that my living, my dancing, all activities, are like the voyage of the bee over the flowers. If I appear more devoted to the other things, it is because my writing can't thrive on adulation. I must leave it alone. That will be my plan for the year.

I have many plans. I seek tolerance for others and perfection for myself. I want to deepen and broaden my only virtue, which is pity. Pity is my most natural and instinctive quality. I want to conquer my faults, which are numerous: an irritable temper, vanity, facility for lying, procrastination, snobbishness, occasional insincerity, jealousy, restlessness, desire to shine, to outdo everybody! I want to continue to harden myself against pain, so that I can keep my intellect clear from passionate judgments, likings, and hates; from swift and illogical actions. I seek intelligence and wisdom.

I think my friends' New Year wishes have affected me. I am almost making resolutions.

Party at Irving's: two Poles, the Labunski brothers, out of a novel—tall, handsome, fair, romantic, but with something hard in their faces, a sort of restrained violence, and a false smile. Both of them have starchy manners, are aristocratic, and musically a little pretentious. I was at first attracted to Felix's impassible face, high forehead, inscrutable eyes, and fine manners, but as soon as we began to talk I felt myself on treacherous sand—this mixture of smoothness and hardness, romanticism and cynicism, pride and silence was full of dangers. I would like to read this enigma, even though my instincts warn me against it. The pianist brother played with great finesse, precision, perfection, and a little starchiness. Where emotion was required, he gave us sentiment. Felix himself, in his compositions, knew only two extremes: coldness and sentiment. He has composed a "languorous" tango, full of trailing notes.

At first sight they do not seem to have any sense of humor. But at the same time their seriousness and solemnity are not entirely born of sincerity. Poles, Slavs, these people have always suggested an enigma to me—I understand the Orient, and Europe, but not that midway race, made of both.

"Good-bye, Monsieur Labunski!"

He kissed my hand. "When will I see you again? When will you dance my tango?"

"Some evening you will come to our studio, and I'll dance your tango."

"Avec grand plaisir."

"Good-bye, Irving. It has been, as usual, a lovely evening."

"When will I see you again?"

"Come for dinner Friday night."

"Charmée." More hand-kissing.

"Write your names in the book as you go out," says Irving.

"May we take you home?" I say to a handsome Italian lady pianist who had come alone to the party because her husband, a businessman, had been too tired to come with her. I always feel sorry for businessmen's wives. Joaquin was pleased with the evening because he met a lady who gives musical teas once a week and pays the musicians who play. He had made himself agreeable to her. Is he developing a business flair?

January 5. Sacrée famille! [Damn family!] Illogical, passionate, emotional, combative, domineering—and until now I refused to see that Joaquin is part of it, enslaved, unconscious. Yesterday at last I had to realize it. He does not see how much I suffer with Mother ever since I have tried to build up my own life; he does not see that when I fight, I fight for my life, for my ideas, my home, my habits, my dreams, my friends, and that I fight alone, because Hugh, to preserve a precious appearance of understanding between himself and Mother, never contradicts her. And Joaquin *never*, even when his *friends* are in the balance, helps me. How terrible my struggle is. Hugh alone knows, because I am *still* under Mother's domination, and I am concerned about her opinion, and when she is most unreasonable, most cruel, I doubt myself. I act with the conviction that she does not *know what she is doing*, and I pity her deeply, desperately sometimes, and yet the danger is there, and it must be fought. She aims fatal blows at everything; she strikes at her children's *faith in themselves* first of all, so they will have to come back to her protection like babies. She is ready to kill the joys they find outside, away from her; her jealousy is greater than her love. Yet she would work night and day, kill herself to feed her children, to care for their illnesses; she is self-sacrificing; she would give everything but freedom!

There is only one thing which I can deduce from these useless complaints: I must stop suffering and getting angry. I must not let Mother develop in me, by constant bickering, the same vile temper. All parents are cannibals anyway, but eaters of souls instead of flesh. Let the Family crush out my pleasures, frown upon all I do—I don't care. Damn all the world—to hell with sentiment and filial loyalty. God made a law because He knew such slavery would not come naturally to man.

January 9. I write foolish things to encourage myself. At bottom, I am sadder than ever. All struggle is bearable and useful and creative except that within families. I am going to try my best to subdue this one.

And now, back to work! I am going to prepare writing for Erskine. Write to Eugene. Meet Boussie and Godoy at Vieux Colombier. Pose for Paquito [a sculptor]. Perfect the Valenciana. Housekeep and sew and cook.

Joaquin's music accompanies all my activities, colors my moods, accentuates my sadnesses, excites and soothes me. Now it is d'Indy's *Le Chant de la Montagne* he is studying—one of the most beautiful things I have ever heard. I forgive him for everything, but he must not know it. We are both keeping dignified attitudes: I am hurt, and will not show it; he knows he has hurt me, and he will not show it. In these cases I usually surrender first, meet him more than halfway, admit him to be in the right, and that is why he is spoiled.

And meanwhile his music pours harmony into both homes, silences quarrels and misunderstandings, lulls me, enchants me and saddens me. I forget the grayness of the sky, the discordant sounds in the street, the evil face I saw yesterday. Music melts the ugly, the bad, the discordant, and brings out only the gold.

Afternoon: Morales is very high strung; his thinking is like lightning, and he has, among several others, the gift of perfect expression. His whole face, body, and hands are expressive, like those of an actor always at the moment of a climax. He is full of ideas, bursting with independence, humor, and life. His black eyes are almost unbearably sharp and brilliant; his hands could make a woman envious, they are so fine and sensitive. He has a Latin physique, not athletic but well proportioned, medium height, curly black hair thinning at the top. His forehead is high and prominent, his nose acquiline, and the lower part of his face a little heavy, as in many Spaniards, but intelligence carves and animates it. He has composed three excellent things, of which he tried to give us an impression the other night. He has a strong dramatic sense, and his music is always for the stage, too.

What I liked best was his extreme sincerity and modesty, and his ardent enthusiasm. Here is another person "burning up." But his naturalness and vividness are enlivening for those around him, and I feel the charm of it. Nothing remains to describe but his voice, which is very rich. Until further changes! I am getting skeptical.

Irving fooled us so completely. We have discovered him to be an incurable egoist with unbelievable conceit. Morales saw through him in a month, but it took us a year!

January 16. I will never be able to write all that is happening. First I had coffee again with Miralles. He had given me a bunch of violets at the end of the lesson. In the café he talked about his teaching, about his desire to present two ballets he has in mind, of which he told me the stories, illustrating the dances with his fingers on the table. I grew enthusiastic about his ideas and told him I had so much faith in him. And he confided everything: how he first came to Paris to work at the Opéra, how rivalries finally forced him out; how he earned his living well by teaching but that he could not be happy off the stage. The only obstacle to the performance of his ballets was money and the fact that he had very few serious and dependable pupils.

"If only I had more pupils like you, with an intelligent understanding of what they are doing. In my ballet you will dance."

"No," I answered, "I am not good enough. The important thing is for *you* to dance. That is what I am waiting for. I will help you by talking, the way we are doing now."

I knew well we were achieving something by our talk. The man's hopes, faith in himself, and talent were burning again; while he watched my attentive face, his enthusiasm and energy were growing.

In between I have been busy posing for Paquito, who is doing some very fine work. I need more time to sketch him; his studio, his friends, and our talk.

We invited Gustavo to the Opéra-Comique. We like him better than ever. He has a curious whimsicality, and an unusually fertile imagination. Although he is not in the best of health, he is always producing ballets, songs, operas, novels, plays. He is both soft and strong, humorous and romantic. We want to do something for him too. The first thing we did was to speak of him to Godoy, and they are going to meet here Wednesday afternoon.

Godoy has just written his greatest and most powerful work, *Colloque de la Joie* [Dialogue of Joy]. He read it to us last night. A vast conception, embracing all of life, with many unforgettable phrases. It is dedicated to Antonio, who played the music which inspired it.

We went to a reception at his house Saturday afternoon. The

Cuban Minister was there. There were Cuban songs sung by a M. Bettancourt. We met Jean Royère, the pianist Ricardo Viñes, the poet Mariano Brull, the composer Manuel Ponce. Antonio played. Two mulâtresses danced the Rumba. There were, of course, many lovely ladies, some diplomats, a French woman writer, etc. But I wasn't happy. I was at war with myself. The good music destroyed my smiling mask and separated me from those who were laughing. In Royère, though excessively intelligent, friendly, talkative, I recognized the scientist, the analyst, the aesthetician. Royère, the laboratory of poetry! Royère, symbolical of France's genius, critical, analytical, creator of form, laws, aesthetics, theories, definitions (like "poésie pure," which is his). Godoy venerates him. And Royère admires Godoy above all poets. Here is a union stronger than the world and beyond my understanding. I would like to understand.

I am afraid of laboratories. Hugh says there is a little devil in me, a "creative" little devil, who needs sometimes to be tamed. This devil sees in science only dissection of dead bodies, not a living force.

"Science for me," I said, "has the face of Richard [Maynard] explaining the technique of writing. It kills my work. You see that since I have been in France."

"You have done your best writing," interrupted Hugh.

"Perhaps, but I suffer."

And at the same time Hugh compares me to Mélisande, whose character was as clear as water, who was surprised by evil, saddened by mysterious things, who was always far away.

"But all that is buried," I said. "I am no longer a delicate, weeping, unearthly being!"

"Those things never die."

Unfortunately. But why should they appear at Godoy's parties? What saved me from disgrace was my toilette—black velvet dress with black lace sleeves and a black hat with a veil over the eyes—and all my Florentine jewelry, which made people say I looked like a "dogaressa," etc. Meanwhile, Hugh made a very pleasant impression on Royère, who mentioned it to Godoy. Antonio's reaction to the honors conferred on him was a childlike mood, and a fit of pun-making. Why? Was he unnerved; is he incapable of a sustained intellectual and emotional effort? Joaquin has very generously effaced himself before the older pianist. Godoy still writes little poems for him. He told him all his ideas and plans for his next work, which is to be *Le poème de la Passion selon St. Mathieu*. He gave us his photograph.

January 19. Madame Culmell a donné un thé a ses amis dans son atelier de la Rue Schoelcher. Il y avait là des personalités artistiques, cosmopolites, et financières.[1] Yes, the place was crowded. But even I, who am not an expert social columnist, could recognize a few friends here and there. Gustavo came first, and then the Godoy family without its Head (alas!), and the Varela family (even the untamable and irascible Paquito) and Mrs. Mahl, and her shy husband (who uses a pen name for his writing but will not even divulge that to his friends) and Bettancourt, a singer of typical Cuban songs, and a rising young Cuban doctor, de la Torre. The Humorous Banker arrived last, and after him, unexpectedly, Boussie! (Whom I never guessed interested in Cuban-Spanish teas.)

While the Cuban songs were being softly chanted, I went out to dress in my orange-and-black Spanish dress. I started with the Tango, danced it with all the spirit and spunk I was capable of without altogether mastering my nervousness. The applause was spontaneous. Joaquin played beautifully after that, while I prepared myself for Cañi and Granados's Fifth. More nervousness, and yet joy. I counted a great deal on the experience to discourage or encourage my studies. It made me immensely happy to have the opinion of Mrs. Varela, a real malagueña who has danced a lot herself. She said my feet were lovely, as well as my expression, my spirit, my souplesse [suppleness]. She did not expect all she found, because she knows just how short a time I have been working, and she reminded me that she had promised me the absolute truth. She was really enthusiastic. Gustavo, who *knows*, was surprised and pleased. Joaquin was at last won over—provided I promise to do classical things. He is not so much impressed by the feet as by my face, which amuses me.

Today I posed for Paquito while he talked. Confidences: his ideas on love, marriage, women, life, art. Also confessions of his faults without any promise to change, and I actually resisted the temptation to preach!

All the same, he thinks my face naïve, showing "bonne foi"

---

[1] *Madame Culmell gave a tea for her friends at her studio on Rue Schoelcher. Present were artists, cosmopolites, and bankers.*

[sincerity], the desire to believe in the good, the desire to *believe*— I objected. Defended myself by mentioning that I did not look like I felt; that I did *know* life. I didn't convince him. Perhaps he is right. I am intelligent and yet I'm fooled by life and people, and will always continue to be fooled. Because I have faith. Voilà!

I even fool myself. Some days, when I see clearly into myself, I hate myself. But most of the time I live on my illusion of myself. For example, today I lived all day with the joyous conviction that *I can dance.*

Paquito, the first day I came to pose, lit the stove and pushed the furniture aside so that I could at least find my way to the model stand. As soon as he started to slash into the clay, a friend of his arrived to talk. The conversation, except when we are alone, is what is conventionally expected of studio talk—that is, rot.

Paquito is a disagreeable, willful, spoiled young man, with a good heart—as he says himself. That is exact. He is also sensual, fickle, and physically weak before women. He has a few good ideas in his head, talent, and temperament, and a good strong sense of independence, which I like. He works fitfully. He is not serious and he is not light (as he says again in his self-portrait); he means he finds it a strain to be any one thing too long. In other words, he is like a cork on a river.

I prefer him when we are alone, but that is rare. All his friends keep dropping in and, once there, they never go. I have to listen to all their ideas—mostly on women. Meanwhile I watch their faces. I notice the empty bottles of wine in a corner, the ties among the sketches, the sketches among the face towels, the coal behind a coal-colored curtain, the bust of a Frenchwoman begun a little before mine—and all over the walls, paintings by the studio owner's son. Paquito classifies my face as half Gothic, half Florentine. He is making my portrait while I make his, but he does not know it.

And now Boussie's cousin takes the small theatre on Place Denfert-Rochereau, and the Supreme Temptation has come to my very door, when Boussie says I should be given a decorative part in *Miguel de Mañara* [by Milosz]. If I keep a naïve face it is because my life is altogether too damn romantic and novelistic! *Everything I desire happens.*

January 20. My worst enemy is the "Grippe." Whenever I am busy, it comes to ruin my plans and my energy. To fight it I spend most of my courage and spirit. Twice this winter it has conquered me, but four times I have defeated it, have pursued my occupations, have treated it violently and angrily with port wine, pills, and hot water—remaining after the struggle as weak as if I had succumbed to it. I have been busy since Wednesday with my Grippe's last attack! I pose, run, write as usual, shivering, perspiring, but I won't surrender to it. This morning I helped Paquito look for a studio in the neighborhood. I ought to write letters, but I like to write lively ones, and the grippe "squashes" me. Instead, I hide myself in between engagements and bore my poor Journal with complaints.

But even with a grippe could I ever be as boring as Tolstoy? What a journal! "Today I took a bath. I borrowed some money. I visited some prostitutes. Oh, God help me to become a good man. Added a chapter to Adolescence. Saw Masha." "Today I didn't take a bath. I returned the money to B., but C. owes me some. Had dinner with Masha. Did not write. Played cards. O Lord, keep me from the sins of the flesh! Masha is a flirt. I like her. Tomorrow I will work."

I have found a better journal, Katherine Mansfield's—sensitive, penetrating, almost mystical—at least elfish and scarcely human, though full of human suffering. I love it. The only thing I do not like is its closeness to death. Even if a being is ill and detached from most of life, he can enter another life, between reality and death, which is even a deeper life. Katherine enters into it at times, then runs weakly into death, into destruction, into fear.

What terrible fancies I take to people. Now it is Gustavo. I fall from one enthusiasm into another. I take everything with too much fire. That is why Hugh has to be suspicious for both of us. He *pretends* to be more critical; at bottom, he is just as easily deceived (outside the Bank; inside he is quite shrewd and cautious). With Gustavo he is also enthusiastic. So what can I do about it, and where can I learn indifference?

January 22. Disregarding my grippe, I posed for Paquito Friday— and it conquered me. I came home and went to bed. But I was happy because the head is going to be worthwhile. I liked it from the very beginning, and Hugh's delight Friday finally settled the question. Paquito has a certain firmness and originality; and quite a shrewd perception of individuality.

Saturday Hugh took his dancing lesson alone. The pianist took the occasion to tell him a lot of agreeable things about me. I was lying on the couch in the studio when he came home with the news that Miralles liked him and had given him a fine lesson.

Every day I love Spain more—its music, its dancing, its writers, its language, and every picture I see of it arouses a deep longing in me. We shall see it on our next vacation. I don't know how we were able to wait so long.

Quiet Sunday, spent in reading Erskine's last book [*Adam and Eve*]. He has "illumined spots of life," but his choice of "spots" is disappointing. He goes into domestic troubles, into the "triangle," with a boring Adam, an imperfect mistress, and a rather human but depressing wife. All that, of course, with unsurpassed humor, philosophy, etc. It is an amusing and deep-cutting parody. But it is saddening. Such obvious problems of conduct. Adam is uniquely American, so is Eve. Lilith is inconsistent and nags as much as a wife.

Erskine is self-conscious about sex, obsessed by a desire for freedom, stunted by long habit of the opposite, and he compromises by a suggestion which is not satisfactory to either the puritan or the sensuous man. Feeling is suppressed, for the greater part; there is a dreadful and overpowering sense of truth; a profound and yet limited knowledge of woman. Erskine needs Europe, and should have had it before *Adam and Eve*. His education, surroundings, habits, have begun to limit his growth. His women are "hard"! They are instinctively wise, and yet tactless. They are loving and yet tyrannical. Such paradoxes are not always true. Lilith is pushy and pitiless, sometimes. The most extraordinary quality in it is its infinite sadness—"humor and tragedy meeting"—as Erskine told us that day we saw him.

January 23. "I am sure," said the Humorous Banker once, "that you would like nothing better than to be a confessor so that you could receive all the confidences of human beings."

"As a woman," I answered, "I hear more than a confessor. Men tell a woman not only all that they have done, but also what they dream of doing, and aspire to do, so as to show themselves at their best before her. I get a much more complete confession *that way*!"

Writing—to tell *everything* in little stories: the night we saved two girls; marrying artists, marrying a banker. Posings—

here and there. The maid's story. Concierge's change of character. Alarm in Paris. Adventures of a naïve person. The two sevillanas —smell of garlic. The two taxi men in New York—one threw change back; the other offered to take me where I wanted to go though I had no money. Story of taxi man's bad day (Marie's husband), to be done in detail, with inner meaning of everything, without seeking consequence and logic. Paradox, contradiction.

January 24. I am inordinately happy because Gustavo is coming tonight. (I need to be exiled to the North Pole for six months or so, or perhaps a Frigidaire might be sufficient.) It is strange that I disliked him when I first saw him at the Egoist's party. Because he was making fun of people. He is the kind of person who carries a circle of fire around him; if you are allowed within it, it is very enjoyable. If you stand outside, of course, it smarts. I noticed he did not use insincere phrases.

After that, he proved clever, amusing, enthusiastic. But I was not particularly struck again until the day we met him at the Opéra. He did not see me come, and was standing against a column, all in black, with a black hat larger than the average size. He looked essentially Spanish. Perhaps I like him because he needs friends. Or perhaps because he has a very expressive voice, colorful and changeable. I also like his work, his ideas. Patience. And get the Frigidaire.

January 25. Gustavo read us his plan for the Egyptian opera, a brilliant and philosophical work, very vivid and dramatic. Meanwhile, I was taking in other things, as usual. Detected signs of weakness of character, but cannot tell yet in what way it acts.

Hugh had one of his good evenings. He talked a lot and extremely well, and showed a deep sense of philosophy and a subtler knowledge of mysticism.

Yesterday was a special day for my writing. I conceived at last, a form for my ideas. I began to write immediately. I had a half hour before the poetry conference, and wrote the first story right off. I am going to be entirely free in this, writing for nobody but myself. Nobody is going to scare me into changing what I want to say, what I long to say, what I must say.

Later. Boussie and I took side balcony seats in the Vieux Colombier. The poetic session went well and quietly until Greta Prozor began to read some fragments from Apollinaire. A man in the audience with a very loud voice began to quote a different passage.

"Why don't you read that one?" he said.

Greta Prozor looked startled and displeased. "I don't see why I should change the program."

She read on. Someone hissed. Another interrupted with a "disgusting!" Private arguments were beginning. The actor Henry Verneuil began to read some lines. More objections. Hisses— applause. "Throw him out." But there was more than one agitator. They were forming into a group. A policeman walked down the aisle, making threatening speeches. Verneuil read on. A man ran down the aisle, up on the stage, up to Verneuil, and slapped his face. Verneuil looked scared and backed toward the wall. Four or five men came to his rescue. More objectors went on the stage. Many violent blows were given. The lonely policeman could not stop anything so he went out for help.

A man started to read a letter, which he said was written by Apollinaire, forbidding the reading of his poetry. By this time everybody was fighting either physically or verbally. Two policemen took away the most violent of the men. Several insulting speeches were made by one of the agitators, the possessor of the letter. As he spoke from the side balcony, we looked over his shoulder at the letter, which was printed.

Boussie said: "But what harm is being done reading poems which are published?"

"I'm his friend, and I forbid it," the man said furiously.

Boussie said nothing, but looked on with amusement. It was left to me to be sorry for Verneuil. Two more policemen, of higher rank, came to ask what the trouble was. Nobody knew. There was a hostile objection, but to what? And why? The policemen couldn't understand.

"Who is making the trouble?"

Two or three of the agitators hit their chests dramatically and said: "Moi." They were taken away. Boussie stayed until the end, which was peaceful. But I had invited a guest for dinner and was forced to rush away. I was struck by Verneuil's helplessness and femininity, by Boussie's nonchalance and indifference and amusement, by the incident of a white-haired, white-bearded, rotund little Frenchman who had rushed to Verneuil's help, into the thick of the fight and out again, after being shaken and jostled and squashed several times, without being able to do anything but receive blows, while keeping his dignity.

January 26. An afternoon wasted on a visit. But has anything been wasted for me? I have written about everything, and today when I am putting all my little stories together, I find I have obtained some of them from "wasted" afternoons! I am very happy and very sad, writing. It stirs up the depths, and problems, and doubts. It makes the rest of life, and people around me seem unreal and irritating, and useless. Eating seems an interruption. Conversation is burdensome. I am obsessed by my work. The day is too short.

January 28. At last I think I have the form. It has to be in the *first person,* the only way in which I can write. It has to be fragmentary—the coherent novel is too strict. Since I can tell my Journal little stories every day, I can tell them to others, in the first person. Reality, unreality mixed. Perfect freedom of utterance. People will talk as they *want* to talk, not as they actually *do* talk, which is meaningless. And I am going to tell everything. I know that nobody will like the book except Hugh and Eugene. I have written three stories already. Meanwhile, everything appears the same—the house, the maid, the errands, sewing, clothes, cleaner, hat-maker, visits—but I have changed.

Yesterday I was struck by Miralles's tenderness, that quality I miss deeply in France, and in Erskine. I was doing Granados's dance, which is slow and classical. He caught a mood in my face unknown to him before. He stood before me, put his hands on my arms, and leaned over to look at me.

"Está triste? [You are sad?]," he said, so delicately, so tenderly.

It struck me, that delicacy, compared to the terribly *hard* and *cruel* curiosity of the French, which makes me shrink. Even Boussie is never so compassionate, although, in her own way, she cares. But she cares so flippantly, so metallically, and you have to be constantly on your guard not to give away too much of your feelings.

February 3. Miralles is going to dance at Monte Carlo at a private reception. He is on his way now while I write. In preparation for his trip I had his silk evening scarf washed at home, and I bought him two good cigars, because I remembered seeing him smoke very poor ones, and I knew he had many hours of traveling to while away. He was touched by my thoughtfulness and kissed me unexpectedly and heartily on both cheeks and on the neck and then said hurriedly: "I take such an enormous interest in you —I wish, I wish sometimes I could pass all my knowledge of dancing to you."

We left the studio together and he asked me to accompany him at least part of the way to the station. I decided to get off at the Opéra, because he had his arm about my waist and I thought he would become overdemonstrative again. But I did not mind it the first time. Why not?

I was tempted today to keep a double journal, one for things which do happen, and one for imaginary incidents which pass through my head as a result of some insignificant happening on which I embroider. I live *doubly*. I'll write *doubly*.

I have been living through queer days, possessed by my book, writing in the Métro on my way to and from Paquito's studio, dancing every day, observing Miralles and his pupils, feeling myself split into two women—one, kind, loyal, pure, thoughtful; the other, restless and impure, acting strangely, loosened, wandering, seeking life and tasting all of it without fear, without convictions, without restraint, without principle, a demon whom I will call "Imagy," after the origin of its curse, imagination. For this demon I am not responsible. I don't love it. It is free, and uncontrollable. Imagy lives mostly in images and unrealities. I want to follow her doings because they are the ones which *haunt my writing*.

Meanwhile, "me," the real me, has been keeping house, sewing, doing errands, looking up studios for Paquito, lunching alone, helping my Beloved to write a letter to the New Family [the Guilers], again harassing us on the religious question.

Today, after seeing Miralles off, Miralles excited and happy about his engagement, I went to buy tickets for a Shaw play, which Hugh and I will see tomorrow night. I had a need of *realities*—I was glad to feel rain on my face, to be obliged to run for my bus, to argue with the Russian woman at the desk for good seats. Imagy was leading me, confusing me, and I felt dizzy, hot-headed, and lost. I wanted to re-enter my world. I banged the door of Miralles's taxi hard to wake myself. I crossed the street swiftly and went into the Bank. I wanted to see Hugh, but he was not there. A touch of his hand has always dispelled all my ghosts. I went out again into the rain and felt the water going through my satin shoes. And I said to myself: Nothing like this is happening to Miralles. He is probably enjoying his cigar and thinking what a cute woman I am, and wondering why I dropped my handbag when he—but it was Imagy he kissed, not me, not me!

I am lying in bed. I have turned the electric heater on myself. I have changed my stockings. Mother just came in from a tea. She was telling me about it and I could not listen to her. I said, "Oh, yes," three times. I feel sad, and I feel like writing a story. I prefer writing my own to listening to anybody else's; more things happen to me than to a thousand women put together.

February 4. The Farruca is animated and full of undulations of the hips. It is done with a tambourine. Now I have finished the Sevillana, Valenciana, España Cañi, Granados's Fifth, and the Tango. Miralles says my arms are getting lovely.

February 5. A curious happening; met Count Guicciardi, Horace, and Frances in the lobby of the theatre last night. Count G. was very demonstrative: "How pretty you are looking, what a becoming hat!" etc. Horace assented eagerly and seemed immensely pleased to see us, but Frances was not. For the first time she forgot to act and showed plainly an intense displeasure. She could hardly talk, and her ever-shining smile failed her. I felt sorry for her, although I suddenly realized that this was probably what had kept Horace away from us this winter.

Frances realizes I am not a child any more, that I am outgrowing her, and I worry her. To worry an experienced ex-actress, a good sport, and a woman of her assurance gives me a proof of my development. I enjoy the disapproval of other women.

Evening: My love for the stage is increasing every day. Sometimes it is even painful. Today at the Théâtre des Champs-Elysées (watching fine dancing done without intelligent meaning) I felt this desire and this aching fever. I have the capacity to live several lives—one does not satisfy me. How can I get to the stage? What have I? A face, a bad memory, a small voice, an *intense understanding* of acting.

To the Cat, reading a Financial Statement: "Pussy, are you still violently opposed to my going on the stage?"

"What is this new problem? Isn't your dancing enough?"

"No, it is not enough."

"No, I don't like the idea of your going on the stage"—this, after a while.

"It will have to be sooner or later."

"Let it be later."

February 6. I felt sorry for Frances the other night because I realized perfectly well that Horace is always enthusiastic about the Other Woman. When we were on board ship, his eyes were on a little French actress; when we went out with him and one of the Frost girls, his eyes were on some little dancer, etc., etc. Enfin, he is always restless, always fickle, always wandering off. At one time, I had all his attention, and I noticed it had to be won every time. Now he has had Frances almost a year, and even if this should become a permanent habit, he is already turning his head around, noticing other women, raving about me to her, paying more attention to any and all Other Women than to the one next to him. It amuses me, and makes me sad at the same time. As far as I am concerned, I am determined to remain the Other Woman; it is much more pleasant.

Dancing almost every day. I want to reach perfection in that. The stage career can wait. Dancing and writing *are enough*, and I must remember, there is a limit to my physical endurance. Posing for Paquito is mostly a hardship: his studio is freezing cold. He drinks far too much, doesn't sleep enough, works unevenly and without concentration. And I don't like his friends. There is one who talks too much, and so stupidly. Flappers' conversations in Forest Hills were no worse than this attempt at Parisian "blague" [joking] and cynicism.

I lie in bed, in the glow of the electric heater, waiting for Hugh. I love this hour, the end of day, when I can brood on things. My book doesn't grow, but I do. I am like an overflowing *sponge*. Have discovered several things. That we get the wanderlust every six months. That our budget will never be satisfactory. That we are naturally generous. That I never see the end of my desires.

February 16. Dinner chez un ménage Français [Dinner in a French couple's home]. Small apartment, wood paneling, waxed floors, Louis XV chairs, prints on the walls, bric-a-brac, hard ceiling lights in the dining room. Two ladies conventionally dressed in *Vogue* winter number, conservative models, dark colors. Talk full of "ma chère," "ravissant," "charmant," "delicieux," "tordant," "amusant" . . . for everything: books, paintings, the latest murder, newest car, Russians, etc. As bad as the Forest Hills "How nice!"—but with a higher degree of culture and a cover-deep knowledge of literature. In France, Art is a fad, a sport. Everybody talks about it and knows everything but feels nothing.

Cocktails have finally been introduced in France. They take the place of the apéritif. I couldn't bring myself to taste one.

Last night, for the first time, I was struck with the fear of death, with a horrible fear of leaving life, which I worship so desperately, fear of annihilation, of the tomb, of the end of everything, of the dissolution of my body, *of my face*, so radiant in the mirrors, of my feelings, so sharp, so burning, so exquisite. I know I will never want to die, will never resign myself to becoming old.

February 17. A profound play, *Dibbouk,* seen with Gustavo and his sister. Discovered new qualities and new faults in Gustavo. He possesses the gift of drollery, of utter indifference to the crowd. But he is overcritical and overcurious; and overfrank. I decided his acute observation would intimidate me and that in self-defense I would flirt with him!

And then a poetry conference, given by a lady I am too charitable to mention, including a reading of Godoy's poem "Havana." We all went to it, Mother, Joaquin, Mme. Varela, Nena de la Torre. A terrible conference, with a painfully correct list of all the banalities and bromides in the world, monotonous, endless, ridiculous. Every poem (except "Havana") read in breaking and sobbing voices. And what poems! We consoled ourselves with mockery. Nena said it was like the Grand Guignol. Joaquin said other things, at which I laughed as one can only laugh in church and other forbidding places.

We consoled ourselves with tea at a fashionable place on the Champs-Elysées. I was excited by the whole afternoon, with my observations. I delighted in that tearoom, and thought that I well understood the love of frivolity in people, the love of luxury, idleness and sweet emptiness which has the appearance of an *intoxicating fullness.* I felt I was being fooled myself, and that I really believed that moment in the tearoom was very important and beautiful and worth living.

"I understand the *pleasure* you take in these things," I said secretly to the Varelas. And all of a sudden I realized they were *not* taking much pleasure in it, not half as much as I was, and that even tearooms have an aspect for me that they have for no other human being.

February 20. We rarely miss anything good. With the *Semaine à Paris*, the *Guide des Concerts*, and Boussie, we see and hear everything! Beautiful Hindoo songs, Hindoo dancing, Jewish drama, La Argentina. Joaquin gives the alarm on pianists, etc. We do a lot of seeking and watching ourselves. Between the things we seek out and those which are forced on us by blind destiny and blind friends, our days are full.

I try to follow the black lines of orderly facts because my head is so unsteady and dizzy and light, and my imagination is leaping like a baby goat. I think so disconnectedly. That Miralles spends a lot on coffee, for his pupils. That the Seine is swollen and has covered the banks and surrounded the trees, so that there is very little space beneath the bridges for the boats. That Hugh looks strikingly handsome in his black velvet Spanish suit with orange silk band and orange kerchief for his head. His profile and his smile are Latin, not Scotch. I never understood how such a man could come from the Guiler alliance. No wonder they do not recognize him and call him a Black Sheep. He is thirty, and we have been married five years. Sans regrets.

February 26. Wednesday after the lesson Miralles said to me: "I have to dance Friday night at the Académie Deauville; will you dance with me?"

"I am not good enough yet," I said. "I'm not *ready*."

"You are. It is a very fashionable place, where it would be good for me to dance to advertise myself. We'll do the Cañi and the Valenciana together, and you'll do the Tango, and I, Alegrías, and if they like it, España."

Of course, I must explain that it was out of the question for him to engage any of his "best" professional pupils, who would expect to be paid. I was chosen only among the amateurs! I was happy, and yet frightened. Four months of study only. Miralles was being unwise and sentimental. He was taking fearful chances in choosing me. However, I accepted the dare to please and help him, although I spent three days with a sinking feeling in the pit of my stomach. We rehearsed with costumes. He was impressed by my "sparkly" dress, the one that belonged to a dancer, and by my orange Maja costume. I insisted he should watch my feet instead of my face, but he found everything satisfactory and showed his satisfaction in varied ways.

Friday afternoon I took one last lesson, and then I went home to rest. At nine o'clock I began to dress as a Maja, pinning three red carnations to my hair, securing the high comb. (Blessed be long hair!) I got into the car with difficulty on account of the comb, and then had to sit bent slightly forward. Hugh carried an immense hatbox with my other costume. We called for Miralles, who was also powdered and painted and wore a red velvet vest, black trousers, black hat, and a magnificently embroidered cape. He looked younger. The pianist came with us, carrying music.

We arrived at a rather fine-looking apartment and landed in the middle of a party, having to cross the salon to get to the bedroom, our "dressing room." My stomach sank again, but it picked up when I noticed the men "whizzing" at my appearance and smiling at me. In the dressing room the four of us waited, occupied with details. We were offered champagne.

The "patron," as Miralles called him, was handsome, tall, white-haired. The salon, Hugh reported after inspection, was half full of that crowd we knew so well and hoped never to see duplicated again. The other half was French.

I was announced as Nina Guilera! We danced our program. I saw stolid faces staring at me unresponsively. I had them on every side. I felt they did not understand. And then I was afraid. Miralles was completely different, terribly swift in his movements, full of improvisations, curlicues, and disconcerting novelties. I made a tremendous effort, smiled continuously, unmoved and undaunted by several technical mistakes, which I quickly covered. I gave all I had to those unresponsive faces.

And then I rushed away as soon as we were finished, with hatbox, Hugh, and the pianist, because Hugh did not want me to stay. So although my ears were filled with the sound of applause, I left without knowing what Miralles thought.

I slept heavily that night. Hugh had said it was lovely and successful, but I did not believe him. I was thinking of all my mistakes, and my fear. The next day I rushed to my lesson a half hour earlier, anxious and worried. Miralles came in with a happy face. The evening had been a success: he had won two pupils. He had received many compliments for me: I had so much "chic," so much gracefulness, I was so pretty and carried my arms so beautifully, etc. etc.

"Poor little thing, you were afraid, and I felt sorry for you, but it is good for you to have an experience like that. You'll dance with me at other soirées—we'll share the benefit."

I was happy, and so surprised. But as far as other engagements are concerned, Hugh has set his Scotch mind against them!

February 27. Living, to me at least, is like a fever, consuming and devastating. But before, I only felt this fever in my head, and now every bit of my body is on fire. I am experiencing all the sensations that it is possible for a woman to know. Miralles's admiration and gallantry, which I fan with persistent coquetry, give a disturbing keenness to my lessons. Perhaps I do not live enough now with my head. I have lost it—and I feel happy without it!

I am through with Gustavo. He is uncharitable and not terribly intelligent, full of enthusiasm for his own doings and critical of others. And I, who spend so much enthusiasm for others, get tired of giving him encouragement, interest, and sympathy—heavy portions of it, which he drinks placidly and contentedly.

Another mistake! So many of them, in so little time. I am beginning to fear my *inflammable* nature. I must invest in that Frigidaire.

March 1. I smoke a lot, work on my dances untiringly, housekeep, sew, dream, laugh, flirt with Miralles. His phrases are not new to me, his way of saying them. He has gestures which are painfully familiar. And I like succeeding Lolita, Joselita, Rita, etc. in his affection. Just now I am the favorite. He talks about me, exhibits me, makes me work doubly hard, gives me red carnations, and is altogether most illogically and unreasonably charming. How long will it last?

So many types have crowded his life. I see them come and go, I know when he likes or dislikes them. I study them mercilessly and with keen interest. Their faces, bodies, voices, talk, expressions, characters. Miralles thinks I am watching their dancing only.

I live on exultation and illusions most of the time. Now and then they fail me. At such moments I reach the bottom of self-doubt and self-depreciation. I see myself as lucidly as I see others. I would like to be as lucid every moment, but then I would kill myself.

In that rough world, among theatre people, artificial, full of inflated personalities, unintelligence, where I find essential *truths*, I feel sometimes like a Lost Lady. In my disguise I draw close to them, fool them, and am sometimes caught myself by their good-heartedness, warmth, vitality, and expressiveness.

In stage life, everything is *personal*. You don't sell your judgment, your business ability, your training, your efficiency, but something closer: your eyes, your feet, your voice, your whole body, yourself, your charm. Stage men and women stake their careers, success, achievement, on physical possessions and personal talent. They tend these precious selves, pamper them, feed them, develop them; it is their business. So you see the stage man and woman as a definite and gigantic Personality with overdeveloped self-consciousness, with human frailties and qualities twice the normal size: vanity, jealousy, etc. Add to that an abnormal quantity of insincerity and flexibility, born of the habit of transformation, and you behold the actor, the dancer.

March 2. I don't sleep well, I cry when I am alone and hear Joaquin playing, I feel an almost physical pain in my body, an ache, a hunger, an emptiness and burning which nothing soothes. Music, men's admiring eyes keep me stirred like the earth in the fields. It is spring, the new sap, the awakening of a once-cold virgin.

Evening. I see Miralles so clearly: his middle age, his black and oily hair, his kindly eyes of undetermined color, his worn eyelashes, his heavy features, his nervous and fine hands, his short but graceful figure. He looks younger when he dances, and old and tired when he walks home with his music holder under his arm. He is too good, easily deceived, modest, hard-working, ignorant, generous. His coat is worn at the sleeves but his collar and cuffs are always clean. If I had money I would let him present his ballets. Meanwhile, I am his most devoted pupil.

"The more I like you, the better you seem to dance," he said.

And the more I like *him*, the more I understand and learn, the closer I feel to Spanish dancing.

March 4. Yesterday afternoon, just as the sun was setting behind the ivied wall in front of our window, our Party began in my Studio. Shining silverware, smell of carnations and roses, soft lights, cigarette smoke, tinkling of teacups, blood-colored Porto, talk, laughter; Paquito's sculpture was examined and commented on. Boussie was there, the Guicciardis, Mr. Rey of the Philharmonic Society, the Varelas, the Godoys, others. At six o'clock we moved to Mother's studio. Joaquin played while Hugh and I dressed. Then we danced España Cañi with a great deal of expression in spite of my nervousness. People grew excited. When we were finished the applause was not only highly enthusiastic but they began to scream "Bis, bis" [Again, again]. Hugh and I were completely overwhelmed. We danced it over again. Hugh's face and smile were dazzling.

Joaquin played Falla excellently. I did the Farruca in the paillette dress with less success. I was frightened and the dance appealed less, being subtler. Besides, I did not have my very appealing partner! The Valenciana brought down another storm of applause, and "bis"; we had to dance it over again. People's faces were alight with pleasure and excitement. What compliments we received. Everybody was marveling at Hugh's transformation and miraculous achievement in two months' study. Mrs. Varela had tears in her eyes and said we had reminded her of her own country. Count Guicciardi was loudly enthusiastic: "You are a perfect artist," he said to me. "Your gestures are beautiful, you have an innate gift for dancing. It was beautiful, beautiful. And Mr. Guiler! Why, I was never so surprised in my life!"

Horace said: "It was *wonderful*! I always knew you were graceful, but I never imagined so much fire and energy and expression in you."

Mrs. Godoy was won over by Hugh's smile. For a moment I had a circle of men around me kissing my hand, and all exclaiming at the same time.

Joaquin played d'Indy's *Chant de la Montagne* in such a marvelous way that Hugh and I nearly broke down and cried—after so much tenseness, so much emotion. The whole afternoon was an unexpected and unbelievable success. Rey was impressed with Joaquin. Hugh and I were engaged for two appearances—at the Godoys' and the National City Club. Hugh was definitely convinced of his power. The surprise his dancing gave to the bankers was a source of joy and humor to him, which kept him laughing through half the night.

March 6. My first quiet day at home for a year, it seems to me. Sorely needed calm and rest. I mended stockings, made out my accounts, looked over my wardrobe, and observed I needed spring clothes; read the fashion magazines, wrote letters, tidied my papers; noticed I have stopped writing my little stories and decided I would keep them for my old age. I also drank my Jemalt (a chocolaty medicine), took a nap, and realized that for a long time I have been going over my "energy allowance"—as well as my clothes allowance and the entertainment and amusement allowance! This last, because we had to see La Argentina dance.

She is a beautiful woman, not in the Grecian style, but with power, expression, and intelligence. Enormous fiery eyes, and a too dazzling smile, gypsy features, heavy and large, brown hair; arms and legs not beautiful but living and expressive; neither are her shoulders beautiful, but her bust and waist are mature and satisfying. She has vital charm and power. Her dancing gives an emotional and sensuous pleasure of the deepest kind. In detail I find that the carriage of her head, the expressions of her face ("the face of a thorough and admirable actress") were among her principal charms. And her arms, her castanets, her poses, her swirls are incomparable. But her feet were inexpressive, vague, and uninteresting.

In all the dances that expressed passion and intenseness, languor and coquetry, naïveté and simplicity, she was perfect. But she missed two things: sadness (as in the Córdoba, which she danced lightly and joyously), and the sensuous movements of the hips. The repetition of steps, of which she knows few, in the end grew monotonous. Her Granados's Fifth dance, in a black velvet dress, was full of grace; the Tango Andaluz, languid, violent, and sensuous. But the others were too alike, always joyous, always animated, always wild. She is however, I am certain, the greatest dancer alive and has shown me the most complete and profound beauty of Spanish dancing.

Miralles was there, but she was beyond his understanding. He was worrying too much about the *roots*, the feet, and though I agreed with him, I felt that her genius was too fine for him, too independent and too free. I prefer him as a teacher. Let me begin with the roots and expression will come afterward.

The real story about Miralles is that I feel sorry for him, for his goodness and modesty and simplicity and lack of talent for earning money and fame. I would like to help him. But we don't always speak the same language, and to evade misunderstanding, to fill the gaps, I choose the easiest and simplest way, which is by affection. I heal his hurt feelings when he hears Escudero is going to dance at the Grande Salle Pleyel. I console him when one of his pupils plays a mean trick on him (so many of them do: go away without paying, announce themselves pupils of another, deceive him, make use of him for their own ends). Poor Miralles, who is so sensitive and kind that he cries when a peanut vendor at the café turns out to be a Spaniard too long away from Spain, his wife and children. He always receives me demonstratively, tells me his troubles, and that he doesn't like "chiquillas" [young girls] and that he wants to pass all his knowledge of dancing to me because he likes me; and "here is a carnation."

"Have you found a studio yet, Miralles?" I want him to have his own studio, so that he can advertise himself. Now his pupils must go here and there at odd hours. Meanwhile, he tells the editor Garzon how I am progressing, and that I have already danced with him, which Garzon, who is a friend of Father's, will tell him immediately, and I like to imagine Father's face!

I spoil people with my ever-fresh interest in their lives and feeling for their troubles, and they spoil me. So in the end, the balance is even, and I am pleased with life.

Pleased with life, and never with myself. Hugh says he is sure I spank myself every time I entertain a conceited thought. In that case my body must be very sore. How I like compliments! Irving tells me over the telephone that I looked beautiful the other night at La Argentina's concert (he was seated in a box with four rich old ladies) and that I looked more Spanish than anybody there.

I see Boussie less often. I have emptied her out. I love her but she is limited by the boundaries of socialism; and having guided me to the Atelier, the Comédie des Champs-Elysées, Chartres, Anderson, Frank, actors, poets, she leaves me there and refuses to go further.

Hugh warns me that my writing is getting "cheap" and careless. At the same time he says I have written some things far superior to anything else I have ever done; both facts are due to my new life. I am usually in a hurry, tired, and seldom in a meditative mood.

March 7. I sleep well again. I am calm and happy. We may have to move into a larger apartment on account of my Spanish dresses! Last night we talked about babies. We don't feel any desire for children yet. We feel young and free and more like lovers than responsible parents. Our life is full enough.

A sad day, full of sighs, of futile dreaming, of languor, of apathy. Miralles was in bad humor, the pianist had the grippe, and I didn't feel like dancing. Then I saw pretty spring hats and dresses which I can't buy because my allowance is all gone on

Spanish costumes. And Joaquin played d'Indy more touchingly than ever just as I came into the studio and dropped my valise wearily.

I smoke. I close my eyes. My body and my mind are tired. I am tired of "willing" so intensely and exclusively to become good and an artist. That in itself is a contradiction. An artist is ever restless and curious. I not only see everything, absorb everything, but sometimes I use my own self as an instrument of discovery; I exploit my charm in return for knowledge.

March 8. I go to Music Halls now for the sake of Spanish dancing, trying to see as much of it as possible. I endure the rest of the program, although I feel so much sympathy for the poor performers' efforts. Went in to buy a pair of ballet slippers for the Granados.

"Are you from the Casino?" said the patron of the shop.

With the little I do see of dancers, and the much I imagine, I am almost from the Casino. That life is clear to me now, as it was for Colette. But I don't see it the same way. I am too often *outside*. Colette was *inside*.

I danced, wrote, and sculptured. And I ate my dinner with virtuous bourgeois satisfaction. My little statuettes are intensely alive, if not technically plausible. I ought to have a secretary with Richard's talent to finish the many things I blow life into. All I do is suggestive, alluring, expressive, but perishable because there is no science in it, no roots, no logic. I am not a human and inspired artist. I am an elf, a disturbance in the world, haunting all the arts, haunted by them.

March 10. Miralles tells me: "He soñado contigo" [I dreamed of you], and overwhelms me with his tenderness. We had a wonderful lesson. I danced well and he was patient and happy. We invited him for dinner tomorrow night. I went to the Spanish shop and bought rice, stuffed olives, bacalao [cod] a la Vizcaina, buñatos [sweet potatoes], turrón [nougat], everything Spanish I could find. We want to show him a dance for which Joaquin has composed the music and see what the three of us can do with it.

March 12. Miralles appeared in a new role yesterday, beautifully and carefully dressed, carrying a gold-headed cane. He enjoyed his Spanish dinner, took an interest in Joaquin and liked his dance. He told many stories about his life, his dancing partners, his sisters in Valencia. Then he made me dance with him for the family. Joaquin took a liking to him, observed as I did that he is simple, good, and that he knows *all about Spanish dancing* in a thorough and absolute way, that he has a talent for teaching. We want to see him dance in public next year.

A new enemy, or, rather, my oldest enemy attacking me in a different way. Reticence. First of all it was reticence in writing, which Erskine discovered and lamented. Now it is reticence of physical expression. My real feelings do not come out. In dancing I am gaining a little headway, but I *still* give an impression of sweetness, of delicacy, not of intensity. I am not free yet. When will I be? I am twenty-five, and not yet a fully matured woman, still "insaissisable" [elusive] and elfin. Savagery, intensity, sorrow are deeply buried behind gentle and timorous manners. What a tiresome struggle! But I have won in *writing* and will win out in other ways too. I tell everything and let the mask of delicacy, sweetness, and softness drop from my face and from my body.

March 13. Last night we saw Falla's *La Vida Breve* and *Amor Brujo*. The last, a perfect thing, musically, visually, dramatically. La Argentina was unforgettable in it, as an actress and as a dancer, as a creator and interpreter. She was obliged to repeat the "Danse du Feu." I discovered that night the beauty of her walk and her intense individuality. She danced with twelve or fifteen other gypsies, and surpassed them all in expression, in the keen arching of her body, in the violence of her contrasts and the *wholeness* and sincerity of her dancing. Her dancing comes from the inner woman, permeates and takes absolute hold of her like an ecstasy. The music haunts me yet. It haunts Joaquin, who has been playing it all day.

March 16. I am so inordinately happy and danced wildly for Miralles, who is so terribly kind to me. He does not know how to express his liking. He tries to do it with his eyes, and they are eloquent enough, but they remind me of Enric's eyes, and so I am not pleased and I look away.

Joaquin came to play his dance for us, and Miralles planned steps for it. Then he watched me go through my repertoire. Joaquin and I came home together, both elated by the air and light, regretting having to come home, Joaquin for his piano and I because my supply of energy is finished for the day. Such a meager supply for a being like me! I have more spirit than energy, fortunately, and I can sometimes laugh at my muscles' weakness.

What I need more than energy are friends. I bother too much with Miralles because he is someone to bother about, to take care of, to love, to help, to encourage. In spite of the dancing and writing I still have this terrible hunger for a friend, the desire to love and be loved. Hugh is never there. Joaquin is always at his piano. Boussie is too intellectual. Mother is too emotional. I had counted on Gustavo, but he is in Spain. I am lonely, yet not *everybody* will do. I don't know why some people fill the gaps and others emphasize my loneliness. In reality those who satisfy me are those who simply allow me to live with my "idea" of them.

Joaquin is playing Debussy, which upsets and churns me. Small things at such moments (at the end of the day when the house is quiet and soft and empty) become very large and important.

Hugh's thoughts are on Egyptian Civilization. He thinks the little Pussy is very lovable, but a little mad sometimes (and if he knew, I am mad most of the time) and goes on reading his book without trying to heal me. He is home now, with a smile and greeting. Why isn't it enough? Je ne suis pas heureuse ici.[1]

March 20. Banquet in honor of Prince Cantacuzène. Restaurant Gougeon. A very literary and very smart affair. We were all seated at the same table, Mother, Joaquin, Hugh and I, with Mr. and Mrs. Godoy, Mr. Brull, a famous architect and sculptor, a Spanish writer, a famous surgeon, Camille Mauclair and his wife, a beautiful Cuban lady, Marquesa de Casa Mauri, Beltran Massès, a handsome Spanish diplomat, a handsome French writer, M. Dumesnil, the daughter of the Princess, etc., etc. I was across from Massès. I did not know him and was surprised to see this quiet man staring at me. I had the idea that night of wearing a gold lamé turban around my head, to go with my draped lamé dress. Joaquin was the first to be struck by the effect and said that if he met a woman like me at a party, "il ferait des bêtises" [he would do something foolish]. This turban was a great success! I was neither witty nor interesting, just *scared* and "sauvage" [unsociable], but my face saved the evening. All night I was

[1] *"I am not happy here." A quote from Mélisande in* Pelléas and Mélisande.

flattered by Massès, the handsome Spanish diplomat, the French writer, and M. Dumesnil. Men asked Joaquin who I was. Men asked Mother if she knew me. An old Spaniard asked me if I would dance for a Spanish charitable organization. I worried the lovely Cuban lady. Thus the dinner passed, and then we turned to the enjoyment of very witty speeches. I didn't like the Poet Prince but admired his fair sweet wife, who was a delicate and aristocratic beauty.

We rushed away to hear the end of Falla's concert at the Salle Pleyel. Arrived in time to hear *Nuits dans les Jardins d'Espagne* and then went to the Salon des Artistes to greet him and Viñes. Father was there with his wife and mother-in-law. He fortunately remained in the opposite corner. We spoke to Falla—a keen-eyed and ascetic-looking man—and then left, with mixed feelings: I, pitying Father; Joaquin, indifferent; Mother, triumphant; Hugh, disturbed. What an evening!

March 21. We took our dancing lesson yesterday evening, and I gave Miralles my opinion of Escudero from what we saw Saturday night: a pretentious monkey, giving a parody of Spanish dancing, vulgar, unmusical, burlesque. We hissed him and were furious with the idiocy of the crowd, who saw little difference between him and La Argentina. A third of the people were intelligent enough to leave with us before the end.

I am working on my little stories again. In my own life, I live dramatically. I am, in reality, equally impulsive and thoughtful. In writing, only thoughtful. My stories won't be complete until they contain both elements of life.

Coming out of the studio, Miralles said: "Other men play cards, play billiards, or drink. I have never done any of these things because I have always been devoted to dancing only. Dancing has been my fiancée—has been everything to me."

And then he told me: "Years ago in Spain it was the custom to have dancing after every play. Dancers at that time could earn their living. But later, actors began to think the dancers were an extra expense, that it would be cheaper if they could replace the dancing with a short comedy. Slowly dancers were edged out of the theatre; they could not support themselves. Many of them dropped dancing altogether. Others worked in café-concerts. And that is how things were spoiled."

"But there is a great interest in Spanish dancing in Paris," I said. "Spain will take the place of Russia in Paris. For years it has been only Russian dancing and Russian music, but today it is all Spain."

"Yes, but Russia was well organized to produce its dancing and music. Russia had schools, and Russians worked in unison at their arts. In Spain there is no school, there is no interest and no unity. Just now Falla has won the interest of Paris. Spain has more to give than any other country, but who will present it, who is capable of organizing it, of putting it all together?"

"You could found a school in Paris," I said. "All those who care for music and dancing come to Paris."

"That is true."

I am still thinking of my beloved and marvelous Spain, of its unknown treasures of color, rhythms, and expressions, of its unvisited and uncatalogued beauties, of its dances.

From the Diary of Imagy. I take pleasure in my "transformations." I look quiet and consistent, but few know how many women there are in me. I smile to think of myself at the banquet, where I struck men as "reserved and mysterious," and then, in my dancing, animated and coquettish and wild. I change, inwardly and outwardly. I don't need the stage. I deceive others, and I deceive myself, because I enter every phase wholeheartedly and completely, slipping in and out blithely, untouched. No, that is a lie. I *am* touched, altered, changed.

And at the same time the real me makes the Cat happy, takes care of his buttons and socks, cuddles him, entertains him, watches out for his pleasures, does all to make him proud of me, and, above all, loves him. He is happy, busy, fond of his work and his dancing, trying hard to gain weight, enjoying dance festivals and the theatre and music and Merejskowski's book on Egypt, and reading about his stocks in the paper.

I feel that I will never write anything but my Journal and the Journal of Imagy. And yet—perhaps something else, when I am older and the fever for living has abated and my hunger is satisfied. Just now, I cannot retire within myself for more than a moment. In Richmond Hill I was always meditating, eating my own thoughts. Am I destined to a dramatic life or to storytelling? I shall have nothing to show Erskine when he comes but a new woman.

March 23. I have become interested in dancing with a wholeness I have never given to anything else. I have refused to study the technique of writing, I have eluded the science of all the other arts I have practiced—drawing, sculpture, decoration, costume design. But dancing I have approached scientifically, elementally. I have been perseverant, thorough, patient, and devoted. I *work hard.* I love not only the practice, but also the theory, the history, the entire aspect of the subject. I would like to understand and express Spanish dancing with perfection. Miralles has inspired me not only with enthusiasm for it, but also with respect for it, and a desire to serve it, and preserve it.

Mother looks so well these days, so young and so active. We go shopping together, we sew together. She is almost always in good humor and takes an interest in dressing well for her concerts, teas, etc. She is now quite proud of our dancing. My family is so close to me, but I hardly see them, although I watch Joaquin's development, and although we have good talks together, little quarrels, great pleasures. I would like to keep some of those sweet moments of companionship with Mother, which remind me of my girlish adoration of her, and those with Joaquin and the curious, almost ludicrous admiration we have for each other. I do not want to forget anything: Joaquin at the piano, filling the two apartments with disturbing music; Mother sewing, or rushing off to market, or reminding me to take my Jemalt.

Now and then Joaquin and I travel downtown together, and I find out all he has been doing. Some evenings we go to concerts, share the delights of Falla and La Argentina. Sunday night he brings back news of the Godoys, with whom he usually spends the day. He often walks in to look over my Journal (although it is hidden now when I am not writing in it), and to ask me if he should break noisily with Irving. I advise hypocrisy.

"You have become *too* nice to everybody," he says.

"So you preferred me in my savage state?"

"Perhaps."

He resents my being friendly to people he *knows* I dislike, and who bore me. He is amused by my new-found liveliness, pleased with my dancing. I am amused by his aggressive love of Debussy and of d'Indy, and pleased with his musical progress. I peep into his Journal, find that he too is preoccupied with unreasonable sorrows.

March 25. "Classe d'ensemble" with Hugh. Miralles pleased because we were six in all. He became enthusiastic and showed off two superb dances with his best pupil—Irene, of the Opéra, a big, brown-skinned girl full of energy, steady-legged, and temperamental. Their dances excited us. It was the finest Hugh and I have seen this winter. What a success they would have on the stage!

In the dressing room, afterward, I told Irene I admired her dancing. She answered that she was always afraid of not being Spanish enough, having had so much classical training.

"For instance you," she said, "you have gestures that are so characteristic."

We went on complimenting each other. She has been studying two years, and I hope someday my dancing may resemble hers.

We had an "audience" of five persons or so, and Hugh and I danced the Sevillana for them. While we dressed afterward, the girls were frankly careless of what they showed, leaving the dressing-room door open, so that Miralles saw me in my chemise— perfect theatrical atmosphere! I was a bit startled, and yet amused. What struck me today (and last night at Bonifacio's performance) was the deep seriousness of Spanish dancing. Some gestures move me and send electric shivers through my body. Today Irene's steps and movements were so provocative; and Miralles's, so suggestive of pursuit. It is a sensuousness which pleases me and satisfies me. I would like to be able to express what I truly feel when I dance— that inward delirium, restlessness, worship, desire, fear, *everything*. It will come.

March 26. More dancing: Nyota-Inyoka—a beautiful brown body, so soft and supple, so much harmony and sensuousness and snakiness. A very expressive face, brilliant smile and roguish eyes. Her first dances were too African, too savage and too acrobatic, but the second part (of a later period in India) as beautiful as I had dreamed them. One Egyptian dance was done with classical restraint, and was supremely evocative of sculptures and reliefs of Egypt. Hugh and I were delighted. Between acts we talked about dancing, and wondered why all human beings should not have been taught at least to walk beautifully, like animals.

We are becoming thoroughly Parisian. We gaze around us in theatres and concert halls, comment on the people we see, study faces, criticize, pick to pieces, and discourse at length on the spectacle. Everywhere we go now we see people we know. Paris seems small and intimate; we have penetrated its musical, literary, and theatrical life. We recognize its coteries, its types, fake and real, its truly great people, its notorious and its popular children of the moment, its elite.

We don't follow its whims and judgments. I have not cut my hair, I have never worn pearls, we don't drink cocktails, we don't like the radio, we have not ridden in an aeroplane, we have no ultramodern furniture in our home.

March 27. Mornings spent in housekeeping and dress fittings, sewing, and tidying. Most of the time I think of dancing; I read very little and write only in my Journal. I am becoming superficial!

Yesterday I said to Miralles: "Please be hard on me, and scold me, and let nothing slip by. I want to dance well. I love dancing."

It is the thing he loves best, more than flirting, so that he responded immediately and we worked hard. He is happy because the "audience" Sunday complimented him on my dancing, my "charm and gracefulness." They too are encouraging him to give a concert in June with Irene, at which he would also present his pupils.

A letter from Tia Antolina[1] announcing their coming in June, but Thorvald[2] can't come, alas, and I will miss him seriously. The New Family [the Guilers] is coming too, but I am not happy. In New York I discovered that Hugh's mother does not love me; his father, yes, and his sisters, but they are still unwilling to meet my family, and I have made all the imaginable sacrifices and now I am *through*. So is Hugh. I wish they would not come.

Godoy calls up to inquire after Joaquin's health (he was slightly unwell yesterday), because he was deeply struck by the discovery that Joaquin writes poetry (not very good poetry, to my mind, but Godoy likes it). I told Joaquin that one is rarely appreciated by one's own family—we laughed, because in our family that is so untrue. Secretly we think ourselves a very favored and interesting family!

March 29. I said to Miralles: "In June, for your concert, I think you should only dance with Irene, and alone, so as to make a perfect and purely professional impression, and then *later* you will introduce your pupils."

---

[1] Antolina Culmell de Cárdenas, a sister of A.N.'s mother, who lived in Cuba.
[2] A.N.'s older brother lived with the Cárdenas family.

"I wouldn't think of it," he answered quickly. "I'm doing this thing for *you* anyway, because you have encouraged me, and because I want to please you, and I am even thinking of doing a dance with you, and of having you do your brother's dance as a solo, and the Farruca."

And he became more sentimental than ever and worked with the greatest tenderness, keeping me overtime, and begging me to stay through the other pupil's lesson, just to keep him company. He acts like Enric in Richmond Hill, and I respond with enthusiastic affection. He likes me because I am like him, he says, serious about my work and docile.

"When I was studying in Spain I was so obedient and so well behaved. I don't like willful and silly people, 'gente loca' [crazy people] like that little girl who comes and doesn't listen to me." He doesn't like vulgarity and *obvious* coquetry, and doesn't respond to roughness and nerve. All the opposite of what I expected. Meanwhile I am happy, and wondering just how sincere he is, and how long it is going to last.

Tonight he offered to come and work over Joaquin's dance, and I invited him for dinner. Paquito is coming too, later, because he has begun to work on a head of Hugh. Hugh sits and smokes in his favorite armchair while Paquito works. And I sew, and we have pleasant talks together.

The more I misbehave, the more I love Hugh. But the more I flirt, the lovelier I am in the evenings for Hugh. When I lived waiting for him, I was restless and miserable. Now that I live independently during the day, in the evenings I am exactly tuned to Hugh's mood. While he talks about the Bank, stocks, trust funds, I think about Miralles. If he is tired I don't mind because I have had my day, and I am contented. He leaves me alone too much. I tried for four years to live only for him and nearly went mad. To wait *all day* and then to hear about the Bank, to find him preoccupied and tired! He works for our home, our marriage, and me, but also because he *likes* it.

I am grateful but not blindly so. I made the sacrifice of marrying a banker, and few people know what a misfortune that is! Of course, I try to take an interest in his work, and sometimes I do it naturally and easily, but he always overdoses me. So few things bore me, but the Stock Exchange is the first one on the list. For four years I gave him all my thoughts, time, and attention. He was happy. Now for a year I have only given him these things occasionally, and he is still happy. He has not *missed what I give to others*, and this discovery has made me desperate; four years wasted on foolish loyalty! A paradox: by being less good I become a better wife.

I am beginning to feel again that snapping of once-sacred beliefs. I feel the abysm of logical, intelligent living opening to me, and the laws of the sentimental becoming empty of meaning. Just today, just this moment, I am confused by values and results. My instincts lead me on—I could not give up the sweetness of my freedom—and old habits pull me back. I can't reason any more. I give myself away, and yet have more to give Hugh. I am no longer wholly his, integrally, uniquely, supremely his, and yet he has missed nothing. I don't know if this can last. If he finds it out, or if he should feel the need of this freedom too?

It all seems far removed from the outwardly peaceful regularity of our marriage. Hugh is confident and untroubled. Everybody is convinced we are exceptionally happy and beautifully mated. We keep assuring each other that we love each other. We prove it by devotion, not by sparks and flames and inward leapings. As usual, I alone see problems and imagine storms. I think too much. But I have done my best not to think, not to analyze that fearful thirst which makes me live several lives while Hugh lives one. From the beginning I feared that he could occupy only part of me, that he is the Master of one life and no more. I am, against my will, a vagabond, a wanderer, a complex troublemaker. I must at least live without hurting him.

March 30. From the Diary of Imagy. Everybody sees him [Miralles] as an old man, a man of the people, a man who is not handsome. I see only the grace of his carriage and the ardor of his eyes. There is no conversation possible between us; we have few interests in common, but a handclasp is sufficient to make us happy, a small act of thoughtfulness. I find in him a deep racial beauty and kinship of character which I have never found in France. We are both *Believers*, ardent, naïve, sincere, full of an affection few people want or understand. He carries pictures of me in his pocket. Today as I stepped out of the bus I saw him walking down the street with a very preoccupied air, his head bent down. When he saw me his whole face was illumined. The concierge had told him I had called up to say I was ill and could not come (a mistake in names), and he was so unhappy. Sentimentality? I don't know. It soothes the perpetual sadness and pain

I feel when I am left alone. I make someone happy, I *give* something, I am useful. Et j'ai tant besoin de tendresse, et j'ai tant de tendresse a donner! [And I so need tenderness, and I have so much tenderness to give!]

As to my own life, I coax the Humorous Banker for a little extra money.

"You always come home and say you have made so much on stocks. Why do I never see the money? I want a little money to fix up the house for the New Family, and to make a Valenciana dress."

I tease him, cuddle him, mix entreaties with witticism and kisses. The Cat laughs. He believes in saving. I believe in it but I can't do it. I see so many things I like! He holds some Dunhill stocks. I asked him if he wouldn't sell one little pipe for me. He laughs, but he doesn't give in. I ask for three thousand francs. He may give me half of it.

Meanwhile, we are going off on a ten-day vacation in the mountains. I am glad. I need nature, purity, to find myself. I would like to recapture my old intellectual life again, my love of theories and philosophy, which seem to have been destroyed by my dancing.

April 1. From the Diary of Imagy. Gypsy mine, I would like to give you little kisses everywhere. I dream of you every night. How happy I would be if I had a little woman as affectionate as you are. I have seen so many women, have traveled so much, have known many, so many women but none like you. I don't know what it is you have or what you have given me to drink for me to think thus, I who have never thought of anything else but my work. My gypsy, gypsy mine! How smooth your skin, as smooth as silk.[1]

April 5. Parted yesterday from Miralles, who is also going on an Easter vacation. I made all our preparations in a wretched state of mind and body. An inexplicable sadness, a terrible emptiness, a burning of the blood. A feeling that I am being penetrated by new perception, a new sensitiveness to life. I suffer most of all from a breaking up of myself, from a lack of wholeness. I feel weak, soft, multiple. Je suis femme, avec les faiblesses de la femme [I am woman, with the weaknesses of woman].

[1] *Translated from the Spanish.*

April 7. On the train. Gide says [in *Strait Is the Gate*] abandonment is not living but restraint, and that it is by passing through the Porte Etroite [Narrow Gate] that one can reach the keenest life. La Porte Etroite! Self-control, sacrifice, restraint—I have always practiced them, and all I gained was an insensible body and a painfully awake intellect.

And now I have found warmth and physical sensitiveness, and with them *understanding*, the power to act, to forget myself. And has the intellect been harmed? I confess, yes. I have lost my balance. I feel only my body, its burnings, its languors, its desires, and its defects. I cannot think. But I will find measure.

Montana-Vermala, Switzerland.
Mother dear:

I am writing to you from my sun-drenched chaise longue. The sun melts the snow, Hugo's business thoughts, and my choreographic preoccupations. We think of nothing else but eating and sleeping the most we can. The Swiss meals are made for mountaineers and so we climb two or three small mountains every day in order to help our digestion. All very healthy and filling. Everything shines with cleanliness. We will hug you probably Sunday night. A kiss without Colombine's make-up and with the taste of Swiss chocolate.[1]

April 9. The beauties of nature touch me far less than they did in Richmond Hill, where I could be passionately attached to a tree, upset by the death of a flower, transported by the call of a bird. But I love these mountains, the sharpness and purity of the air, the violence of the sunshine, the smell of pines. We take long walks, lie in chaises longues in a pavilion next to the hotel, read and talk, and we sometimes practice our dancing outdoors, where the pine needles make a soft but dangerous carpet. The castanets echo, and the sound brings curious workmen peeping from behind the trees.

I love the calm, the solitude, and I spend long hours with an open book on my knees, unwilling to read, occupied with dreams and incoherent thoughts. The fever has died down. My body is numb and responds only to the joys of healthy living. I am poised again, though unchanged, and denying nothing of the past.

[1] *Translated from the French.*

Hugh looks younger—reminds me of the Hugh I first met. He fits in perfectly with the surroundings. He reads serious books seriously. He laughs at my sallies, but quickly returns to philosophy.

Will he ever lose his assurance, his confidence, his frankness? Will he, too, go through a crisis? I will help him, then. He is not *simple* (none of us is) but his complex side is calm now, because he is satisfied with his work, his home, his wife, and his books. He is kind to me, thoughtful, confiding. He says there are no secrets between us; Paquito was wrong in saying that no man ever knew the thoughts of women. Men who say that are those who never stay long enough with one woman.

"Do you know my thoughts?"

"Yes."

I looked at the pine needles on the ground, at the crocuses. Hugh was looking at the snow-capped mountains. The phrase passed, and I let it pass. I never, never want to hurt him. We are so beautifully mated, physically, mentally, temperamentally. But I cannot stay at home. I have a desperate desire to know life, and to live in order to reach maturity. Our marriage has given me but one kind of knowledge. Unless I am mistaken, Hugh, whose mind it always open to new ideas, whose mind tolerates mistakes when they are made in a sincere struggle for truths, Hugh will forgive me.

April 10. In Godoy's salon I guess at many things which I do not altogether understand; social differences which I have never, by education or by instinct, learned to untangle, since for me there are only three classes: aristocrats by birth, intellectual aristocrats, and mediocre people. In Godoy's salon there are more classes than that. I can't make them out: there are rich and important people whom it would never occur to me to speak to if Mother did not make me. There are celebrities like Massès, the painter, and [Francis de] Miomandre, the writer, whom I would never have noticed if Godoy had not made me. There are diplomats, who seem to have nothing to do but flirt. There are decorative ladies of nonprofessional appearance and status, who, nevertheless, are expert amateurs. There are a few really aristocratic ladies, also highly decorative, but who never read Godoy's poetry. A little of everything. Godoy does not choose.

The only thing which is clearly indicated is that you must be well dressed. As to manners, a Marquise nearly sat on me and effectively crushed my dress one day while talking to Viñes. The rest is all a matter of luck. You may have a talk with Royère, or with a young woman who can dance the Rumba. The Frenchman who sat next to me at the banquet is universally known as a flirt, but a very pernicious and assiduous one. I began to dislike him intensely—I always hate a professional lover, and, above all, a French one. That cocky and cynical pursuit antagonizes me. Flippancy, that is what repels me.

How often will I be persuaded to appear in Godoy's salon? It will always be an artificial effort, made, perhaps, for the sake of a glimpse of Godoy himself.

What do I think about during these long, sweet days? That if Hugh were always so absorbingly companionable I would never stray from home. That his new-found religion, or, perhaps, non-religion, in Merejskowski's book, *Mystères de l'Orient*, is satisfactory but impractical, and could not be explained to our children in time to evade their natural questions! That I have ceased to believe in the improvement of character, although I don't give up the struggle and only hope for a deep *understanding*. It is too late to continue dreaming of a perfect woman, since I am twenty-five. I will always be too soft, and too impulsive, and too thoughtful, and too analytical. Like Proust, I don't look at people; "Je les radiographie" [I X-ray them]. But at the same time, their troubles upset me. I have so much sympathy for Proust and so much admiration. What intellectual energy, patience, and lucidity—the literature of half tones and quarter tones, as in Oriental music, which the Occidental ear can scarcely perceive. I see these quarter tones, these almost intransmissible nuances, and marvel at his rendition of them.

The Wind—I hate the Wind, the gusty, noisy, violent destroyer of Peace. It was furiously sweeping the mountains, shaking our pine trees, filling our eyes with dust. So we came up to our room (Hotel Alpina, modest, far removed from the village, hearty dinners, spotless and dainty place). Our white furniture and woodwork reflect the last rays of the sun. I shouldn't be writing, because my eyes are tired, but sometimes I could not stop writing even if I were mortally ill. I love my writing above *everything*— I know it now. The feelings I have when I slip my hand into my pocket and caress my polished castanets are keen and overwhelming, but I feel even more when I am alone, or sad, or overjoyed, or overfull of thoughts and I open my Journal. My *truest* half resides here.

My *mind* will never perish, and therefore neither will my writing. My dancing will perish because it is ephemeral, a mood, an emotion, which contains only one aspect of beauty. I oscillate perpetually between the two lives. I will never find a center, and I will never find a harmony between the two, because each holds me completely and jealously. And I will never be able to stop writing my Journal until I find peace. Ce que je ne trouverais jamais [Which I will never find].

April 11. Proust has revealed to me how I too live intensely in the Past and outside the usual boundaries of time; and how a smell, a sound, a color, some small thing, will easily re-create in me an entire portion of my life—very lucidly, and with the additional tang of complete understanding. What Proust does not have is an intuition of the future, the power to imagine places never seen, the patience to build up preconceptions. This additional activity of the imagination helps to fuse the three "Times" [past, present, future] so harmoniously that you can grasp the links that bind them, you can follow their moments of unity. Proust finds little unity, besides his central idea of Time and Timelessness, found and fixed by memory, and by observation only. I think I shall find more unity in life.

Today, besides thinking of Proust, I brood on a strange evening, which has brought a great change in me. The wind was hissing through the valley with furious vigor last night. All the pine trees were bowing and lamenting. Our windows shook.

We sat quietly in our room, smoking and arguing philosophically about literature and life. At some point in the conversation Hugh began to glorify our marriage with a graver voice than usual, as if more fully conscious than ever of its importance. He spoke of how deeply it had changed him, how he did not begin to live until five years ago, how it was a force which could accomplish unbelievable things, how together we had reached a balance and an élan which no man alone, however great, could ever reach. He said many more things, talking about our marriage as an eternal and mysterious power, an unearthly ideal, all in a steady, calm voice. Looking at his confident face, I suddenly realized the enormous strength of our union; and Hugh, talking so steadily on that stormy night, seemed for a moment a symbol of the most

indestructible ideal. My fever died down, and all my small tear-
ings at that almost inhuman ideal seemed futile; I sat very quiet,
listening and staring while, without knowing it, Hugh was winning me back, with his voice, his faith, his dream.

Yet, the old dream, for me, has lost its living warmth because
it demands chastity, sacrifice, restraint, and those things cannot
hold me. I can return for a moment to purity, to thought, to a detached existence, concentrate on one love (a love which does not
belong to me alone; Hugh, for the sake of love, gives his energy
to seeking power). I can return, as I have returned to nature, to
peace, to solitude, but now my desire to *understand* is greater, to
understand for the sake of our Ideal, too, because I want to bring
to it the devotion of a woman not of a child.

I thought of these things last night; I was caught, and held
again, yes. But from that high mountain where we dominate petty
obstacles and face our true desires Hugh descends to earn power,
and I shall descend to earn understanding. I can no longer be the
spotless, detached, inhuman self of old—that mummy who inspired
men with dreams. What I want now is a proof that this mummy is
dead. I have had it lately in Paris, moments when I felt sure it
was dead. But not the ultimate proof.

A long time after our talk, as I sat silently, Hugh asked me
what I was thinking of.

"I will never forget tonight," I said.

April 12. The idea in Proust on which I have brooded persistently
is this: "Une heure n'est pas qu'une heure, c'est un vase rempli de
parfums, du sons, de projets, et de climats" [An hour is not merely
an hour, it is a vase full of perfumes, sounds, projects and atmo-
spheres]. This is his simplest expression of a mystical idea which
obsesses him and pervades all his books—*A la Recherche du Temps
Perdu* and, particularly, *Le Temps Retrouvé*. It is an idea that has
come to me very often, at strange moments, when I did not know
where I was and felt all demarcations of time and space destroyed—a terrifying and ecstatic emotion which I treasure and
have rarely attempted to describe. (It is true that the most important ideas and feelings are often left out of this book, as they
are from all books and all the human forms of expression.) When
I mentioned this to Hugh, he said: "Oh, I am glad you have
understood it. It is an idea I have liked for a long time, and from
which you can pass into innumerable perceptions. Now that you

are ready for it, read this (from Merejskowski's *Mystères de l'Orient*): "Even the man who ignores the Trinity lives in the Trinity like a fish in the water and like a bird in the air. He may have broken the logic but he cannot escape it unless he is completely mad. As long as he thinks, he will think according to the Trinity, for all of the fundamental categories of human thought— space and time—are ternary. Three dimensions in space: line, plane and volume; three dimensions in time: present, past and future."[1]

The sense of these three dimensions *in one*, without boundary lines, and with unity is what I understand.

This has been a sufficiently nutritive idea for this vacation. Each vacation of ours has been stamped with the discovery of an idea—Ferrero in Fiesole, Unamuno that quiet summer month in Paris, Rolland in Luchon, Proust and Merejskowski here.

We fly from people, we evade the entire hotel, seek isolated walks and places. We seek only each other, we draw close to each other, we open our hearts to each other. We discover anew what complete companions we are, and lovers.

The idea I have been pursuing these last months by experiments and analysis, the one which has occupied me most persistently, is the *decentralization* of personality, which I find in Proust, who has arrived at it by different means, mainly by way of meditation and microscopic analysis.

When I told Hugh about this, he said: "I don't like that idea." Because he fears its influence on action. Proust had no fear of that because he was not a man of action. Besides, true to the French philosophy, he was not preoccupied with conduct or any ultimate result—merely with the statement of mental discoveries. These last months I have felt the same way, and I reached the idea of lack of unity in character through a simple acceptance of the facts before my eyes—that is, that *I* did not act with any unity whatever, in spite of my desire for and admiration of consistency.

Which brings me to an important difference between French and English literature and mentality. Hugh was describing Conrad's heroes in *Nostromo*. I said, "These taciturn and firm men do not interest me any more. Their only actions are based on noble principles—admirable, yes, but I am no longer interested in mere conduct, in character. I am sure this man you tell me about knew

[1] *Translated from the French.*

very little about life, and thought very little. That is why I am abandoning English literature, although I was under its exclusive influence all the years of my girlhood. It is too elementary and too simple. Today I prefer French literature, where *understanding* life is the main object—ideas, intelligence, curiosity. Erskine, you remember, seeks that exclusively."

"What influence have those ideas had on you?"

"They have made me seek mental activity rather than adhesion to principles. I understand life better. Erskine believes in curiosity, in unlimited research, and has reached the most open-minded theories without letting them change his private life—so far."

I did not say that this new influence had destroyed many of my old "principles." Hugh is not ready for that yet. He can admire Conrad's men, whereas their silences do not impress me any more and I even suspect them of stupidity; their lifelong and absolute devotion to an ideal seems to me like the unnecessary and unadmirable (according to Erskine) death of the Light Brigade.

"And yet," says Hugh, "there is something mysterious about life which the French do not grasp."

And I agree with him.

I have been writing in the bedroom all morning, because it is snowing. We took a small walk for health's sake and for art's sake—the place is so beautiful! But now comes the sunshine, timidly, and all the beauty is melting and we will have to wear rubbers. We wait for the dinner bell. Hugh reads Conrad. In our room, white and clean like a sanatorium, we lead a simple and rustic life. Paris seems unbelievable, chaotic, compared to this. I get sleepy when I think of the things which await us.

Whenever I go away, and find myself alone, je me retrouve, et avec plaisir [I find myself again, and with pleasure]. It reminds me of Woodstock, where I wrote so much and talked so little; of the days in Richmond Hill when I believed that was all I was born for—to write, write, write. *I regret nothing.* I write less, talk more, and in spite of my Proust-like mentality, je marche [I go on], oh, with tremendous energy. Experiments and analysis don't paralyze me. I use everything for fuel—indiscriminately, and on I go, on and on, back to Paris!

Later: Hugh says over the newspaper: "My stocks have gone up!"

"I don't care, I will never see the money, so why should I rejoice?"

"For the wife of a banker you are too practical. I have made ten thousand francs."

"Yet I am sure if I asked you for two thousand you could not give it to me."

"No, because I can't sell the stocks now. I expect them to go up still more. If I had listened to you, you little hard-headed Catalonian peasant, we would not have bought any stocks or made any money."

"I grant, you were clever—but still, I would rather have that money in a stocking, where I might get at it more conveniently. And all that fictitious gain, after all, what good does it do us? Today you rejoice because the stock is up, tomorrow you are gloomy because it goes down—don't you know yet that that is its natural way to act? Ever since I have observed it, that is all it does, mechanically, up and down like sand in an hourglass. Then why the excitement?"

"You are too literal," said Hugh helplessly, laughing. "And you are too occult, too mystical, for me."

We both laugh, but I don't get a cent to fix up the studio for the New Family and Tia Antolina.

April 13. Yesterday evening I explained everything to Hugh, told him how my attitude toward things had changed, how my ideal of goodness conflicted with my desire for maturity, how my sense of principles had snapped, how I sought to feel as a woman does and exposed myself to the conventional experience of woman and how these experiences gave me what he appreciated in me today far more than the old book learning. "How far can one go in that direction?"

"Nothing that you do," said Hugh, "can be wrong. I trust you."

"But you must not," I said. "I need to know—you must tell me."

"Well, we have nothing to hold us from acting as we please: we have no religion, we have no sense of the conventional ties of marriage. Our religion is love, our love; as long as you believe in that."

"As long as I respect our love, then."

"When people believe in nothing, their lives go to pieces, and that happens to everybody around us. You do not want that to happen to us. You have seen in literature and in France what your ideas, carried to extreme, lead to: mediocre unfaithfulness."

"You have used the only argument which could move me: if I believe in our love. I do. I don't think I can make mistakes now. Our idea of freedom can never resemble that cowardly and superficial drifting of people who do not have the strength to devote themselves to anything."

Put into plain words, it all sounds simple, and it is all easily solved. Hugh's summary is as exact as I could make it, but it does not contain everything. I am not assailed by black-and-white problems. I feel there are a thousand inexpressible subtleties that I will have to meet, and work out alone.

"I trust you. We live for our love, we believe in our love," Hugh says. Here, everything is balanced, clear, pure. But when we return to misty and chaotic Paris . . .

"You understand, dear, that now I have come into the center of living—for wisdom and for human warmth. For a woman, knowledge of human nature is knowledge of man—Erskine said the opposite; for man, it is woman—so I must *listen*, and will you tolerate that? The days of introspection and reading are over, and you remember you found me too unearthly then?"

"No," says Hugh, regretfully, but when I insist, "You *do* remember," he merely looks away. Oh, he does not like my new feelings, as a husband, but he must admit them intellectually and he does, as bravely and as broadly as possible. Meanwhile, he holds my hand, and his eyes say: "You won't go too far—I love you. I need you. Ideas have been the bread of our life, but our love is more."

He trusts me, and I am so soft, I lean over to listen, lean over too much; and what I seek in other eyes troubles me. And I don't always find wisdom.

When he goes away in the mornings, I, too, call him back. "I need you. Power is a great thing in your hands, but our love is more." Still, he goes away, with a hurried kiss, he goes away for days and days, and he finds joys in testing his power (as I test mine), in judging, helping, advancing, and handling men (as I do in inspiring, pleasing men), in gaining praise, in triumphing (as I do), in exercising his mind, his character, his theories (like me), in making discoveries, in learning, in *living* (as I do).

"Don't exaggerate," says the poor Banker, growing worried. "You have your art, your writing!"

"They never helped me to become a woman," I answered.

Curious days, as we rediscover each other. Hugh finds with

surprise that I fit in among the mountains—he had forgotten Luchon! He observes that my skin looks transparent and dazzling in the sunshine. He reminds me of a walk we took in Forest Hills one evening after a tennis match, long before we married, when we talked about our love for children.

Today we took a long walk up the mountain; we felt carefree and loving and young. He did not even remember his stocks, and I suddenly realized that for five months I have been in the best of tempers and no longer need to worry about the irritability which Paris seems to accentuate.

Hugh asks me to put a very clear Post Scriptum to my Problem: P.S. Remember, principally, that I have a jealous husband.

April 17. Home again. Everything *seemed* changed up in the mountains, and yet everything has remained the *same*, except that I live with more lucidity and more anxiety. I am, even to myself, a bag of surprises, "Pochette à surprise," such as they sell in the movies. What attracts me, tempts me perpetually, is the opportunity to live out a new self—such as I do with Miralles. Women see themselves as in a mirror, in the eyes of the men who love them. I have seen in each man a different woman—and a different life.

April 18. Horace and Frances are to be married. Hugh says: "Horace has chosen a mediocre life." Poor Horace confesses that he has *thought* about it a long time, and is *still thinking*; the irresistible impulse is lacking! I am disappointed, theoretically, but cannot help hoping for their happiness. He is a lost friend, because Frances will keep him away from us, and from me.

Evening. Home from my dancing lesson. Depressed, troubled, up in dense clouds, suspended. The Journal of Imagy is growing in my mind. It is going to be a separate and special Journal. I can't live within reality—I must live *within stories*. Then I will *fuse both* and surrender the real me and Imagy to the world as One.

I begin today. I want to clarify: Frances and Horace together; Gustavo, whose friendship I crave; Labunski, who intrigues me. I would like to see Enric again, and Eduardo. A need for friends—never felt before!

Antonio has dropped out of our life because of physical inertia, and a sense of Latin discomfort because he owes us money. Boussie is in Chartres, and remains brittle. I do not find with her the old glamour of inexhaustible talks; she has limited her intellectual life too closely. Perhaps I am mistaken. Godoy lives in another world and does not understand me. Oh, Erskine —I expect him impatiently.

Miralles said, while we took coffee together, "How wonderful it would be if we could dance together at soirées, and on the stage. You make me do so much, and I am absolutely certain we would be successful."

I did not have the heart to mention the contrast which makes us physically incongruous. Each day, however, I become more earthy, like him, and give more volume to my dancing, more substance. But my face will never change. I am not *physically* Spanish; I lack the thickness and strength of their features. Then why . . .

Journal of Imagy. Then why does he love me? That man loves me. I must believe it now. He proves it in a thousand ways, and I don't need proofs. I feel it.

April 20. Horace and Frances for dinner. A new Frances, sweet, domestic (already), eager to please him, full of the preoccupations of homemaking, and very soft and happy. If this was a new piece of acting, I was caught, felt affection and concern for her, and completely softened. Horace is unchanged. Together, they make the most curious effect of being a perfectly nice, ordinary couple, not overinteresting, just *banal*. They talk about children and electric toasters. Horace has given himself up to simplicity and to a girl who loves a "clear, sweet, fresh home," with cretonnes and rustic furniture.

But Hugh has the last word. "The trouble with Frances is that everything is *acquired*—nothing comes from the *inside*. I have always seen through that and been displeased with it. And Horace will never see it. He is really very dense." Horace is going to be "simplified" by Frances. What does that mean exactly? I must see.

April 21. Huge success at the Godoys. (Hugh and I danced España Cañi and the Valenciana; and I, the Farruca.) Compliments from Jean Royère, the pernicious Frenchman; from the Cuban Minister (who asked us to dance at his next reception); from a writer for [the Spanish magazine] *Blanco y Negro*; and from other miscellaneous friends. The Godoys very proud and pleased. It was not a succès d'amis, because the public was, in general, blasé, indifferent, and very few people knew us. A dreamy-faced Italian, to whom I have not been introduced but who always stares at me a great deal, courageously complimented me with his eyes alone.

Suddenly Godoy's salon ceased to frighten me; I had broken its shell, won a place for myself as a dancer. I couldn't have done it any other way, because I realize now that I can't talk well except in intimacy, and that my intellectual life has clamish habits. I am happy, however, to deceive them. In that body they admired lives a spirit they shall never know.

April 23. Mrs. Godoy sends us a "cachet" [fee]—three hundred francs and more compliments. Joaquin, who played for us, receives seven hundred and is overjoyed. It seems that the wife of the Cuban Minister was moved by the fact that I resembled her mother, who was a Roman. Several people were struck by the distinctive style of my dancing, which they said resembled La Argentina's.

To Imagy, Miralles says: "Now that you are given so many compliments, you won't forget me? I am your prisoner—I don't know what you have done to me. And God knows I am tired of seeing women—but with you, the third lesson, your eyes drew me, hypnotized me. I felt something *different*."

We were sitting at our usual table, at the usual café, Place de Clichy.

"Do whatever you like with me, ask whatever you wish, but don't forbid me to kiss you—I couldn't live without that now. I am not usually like this—for years nobody has tempted me. I don't like the kind of love most men do. Women who invite me in the street repulse me. I have loved very seldom."

Imagy listens; and tries hard to destroy a little smile which persists, because Miralles looks so serious . . . but she listens.

Hugh said just now, leaning over me while I worked on my accounts, "I am glad that people are allowed to see, now and then, what an extraordinary person you are."

"Nobody but you thinks me extraordinary."

"Saturday at the Godoys', they had a glimpse of it. But it is true, I know you best. You have expressions and confidences for me that you never show to the others. If you showed only half of your transformations on the stage, I don't know what the crowd would do—go mad, probably."

And then later, because I had been smiling to myself.

"You little devil, you've been flirting. I can tell now."

But soon he plunges again into banking, and I am left alone to look over my mosaics, to put them together, to try to find a design, a unity, a meaning to all those little pieces.

April 25. First day of softness, sunshine, and warmth. My body relaxes. I am deeply happy. I feel beautiful, soft, and womanly. I feel, at moments, *wise*. My senses are more keenly awake than ever. I see everything with a painful lucidity. My body is like an instrument, vibrant and sensitive. My reason alone is wavering and overwhelmed by impulses. I fear my imagination and my emotions. Je brûle et je souffre et je suis heureuse, heureuse, heureuse . . . [I burn and I suffer and I am happy . . .].

I am filled with Proust, with his slowness, the development of his phrases, the long rhythm of his thoughts, the "sondages" [soundings] he makes of the smallest details of existence, his ascension into spheres never before visited by words. He gives to life the exact measure of time life needs to unfold, and to thought all the care it requires to develop.

I who work, live, think by explosions, and I who (even though I pass through slow growth) bring to writing only a résumé of my struggles, am baffled by such precision and marvel at his superiority.

May 1. On board the S.S. *Aquitania.* A sorrow for which there are no words: Hugh's father has died. Hugh's suffering was terrible to see. The first night we cried all through the night; I remembered his father's eyes, his kindness, his tired shoulders, and his hands. Every moment Hugh discovered new despairs: he had not loved him enough, he had not expressed his love, he had not done enough for him. Ten more days and we were to have seen him. He died two days before they sailed. Thank God we were kind to him in New York, and gave in to all his demands on the religious question.[1]

The terrible rush and work of those two days before we sailed saved us from utter despair. Only the nights were unendurable.

The trip has soothed Hugh a little. We have talked quietly about his father, and he has written a poem to him. I stifled my

[1] *He had asked Hugh to leave the Catholic Church.*

own regrets to care for Hugh, but at night I was haunted by memories too and struggled to understand death. Did Hugh's father understand that I loved him? He never knew that it was my softness which brought about the reconciliation and surrender.

On the surface there is nothing changed; we eat, sleep, work, talk, but something terrible has happened to us inwardly. There is a new emptiness in our hearts, a new fear, and much of our confidence and our eagerness has crumbled. So much fever, so much struggle, so much labor, for that sudden end? I cannot believe that Hugh's father has disappeared.

May 10. New York—Forest Hills. Hugh sits in *his* chair at the table, wears *his* kimono. I have seen his pipe, his glasses, his golf sticks. And he is now a handful of ashes in an urn. For two days I felt him in the house, felt he might come in among us, as before, and sink in his armchair and tell me one of his stories, because they were all new to me. But when I realized that he would never again be among us, then I understood death, and knew Hugh and I would never be the same again. He died looking at his wife, and his face, they tell me, was wonderfully peaceful. If he is safe from pain, we should not regret his death.

The keenest pain was given to us in church Sunday, the church he loved. Hugh missed him so deeply that he broke down and cried, and I had to leave him alone because I had no strength to give him. That day in church I could see him burning (he was cremated), and the vision was so horrible that I nearly went mad. We could not understand how the others could bear to stay in the house, touch his clothes, see the book he read last, smoke cigarettes from a pack he had begun, talk about him.

All the while, the house ran normally; Hugh's sister Edith drove the car; his brother, Johnnie, fixed a blown fuse, saying, "Daddy used to do all that; we feel so helpless without him."

Hugh's mother did not know where the money would come from when the bank account was closed. Edith had trouble learning to run the hot-water furnace; they could not find the keys for things. In the evenings, before we arrived, they used to jump at every noise in the house (Johnnie was not there).

May 19. On board the S.S. *Pennland*. We came on board last night at eleven o'clock, according to the new fashion. We let only Eugene [Graves] come to see us off, and sat with him in the library for a last talk. This morning at nine, just as we were about to get up, our ship collided with a cargo ship, which made a large gash in our hull, just above water level, and a small hole below water level. When I first felt the shock I realized immediately that something had happened. Hugh grasped the fact a half a minute later but showed great presence of mind and immediately took down the life preservers and tied one around me and said: "You stay here until I find out what happened. I will come back for you." I stayed in the cabin with the life preserver around me and nothing on but my pajamas and slippers and boudoir cap. I had three thoughts: would I be able to take my Journal along with me; did I have time to dress; and how long would the ship take to sink? After a minute I took off the life preserver, because it looked rather ridiculous, and I stuck my head out the door. Several persons were walking quickly up and down with their life preservers on. I asked the stewardess if she knew what happened.

"I don't know, but you'd better dress," she said.

So I put my coat on, and stuck my head out the door again. I was so happy when I saw Hugh coming.

"There is a hole in the ship but no danger. However, let's get dressed and go up on deck."

We went up and looked at the hole, a rent which had given a great shock to the couple whose cabin wall was dented. From the smaller hole our ship was losing oil. But seeing that it was not sinking, we went down to breakfast, and Hugh enjoyed his kippered herring.

It is seven o'clock. We haven't moved. We are surrounded by a thick fog, which was the cause of the accident. Also on account of the fog, it seems we had not sailed until six A.M., so that we are only three hours away from New York. Two or three ships are around us, also caught in the fog. They blow their fog-horns continuously, and we cannot see them. We have spent a peaceful day talking, smoking, and writing. We don't know yet if the ship can be repaired here and we can go on or if we must return to New York. A small ship came with engineers, etc., who examined the holes. But no news is given to the passengers (as in time of war, soldiers receive only commands and little information).

I am thinking of our arrival in New York. It was six o'clock. Edith was waiting for us, all in black. I made Hugh go alone with her to Forest Hills, and I stayed in a hotel. I wanted Hugh's family to have him all to themselves and did not want to intrude on their sorrow. I wrote Hugh's mother to explain this and to tell her she occupied, always, the first place in his heart, which is true, if you consider that the heart seems to be made particularly for the family, and peculiarly for mothers, whereas lovers seek other things. Staying in that hotel that night helped me to understand real loneliness such as I never experienced in my whole life.

But Hugh called me up at nine the next morning. "Mother wants you to come down."

"Are you sure she really wants me to?"

"Absolutely. Everything is all right. The girls [Edith and Ethel] need you."

He telephoned Eugene and we met for lunch before going down to Forest Hills. I found him as understanding as ever; sad-eyed, thoughtful, human; susceptible to my ways and ideas and presence; wise and well informed. He desires this freedom from principles which I have found. He was keenly interested in some parts of my Journal, which I read to him so that he could understand our life in Paris. Can I communicate such a freedom or is it only to be found by suffering and living and dancing? He finds a relief and a joy in modern freedom of utterance; he likes modern literature for the very reasons that I like it. We tried to make him promise to come to Paris, and he assured us he would be with us in a year.

I left Forest Hills every day for a few hours and saw the Erskines, the Maynards [Richard and Lorraine], Eduardo, Tia Coco,[1] Uncle Gilbert and Gilbert. Stuck to my promise not to see Enric, although I nearly telephoned him twice. Richard let me read his novel, and I let him and Lorraine read what I had type-written out of my Journal. Their most definite gift to me this year was the enthusiasm they showed for my Journal, which surprised and encouraged me beyond reason.

Did I give them as much as they gave me? Richard is affected by my mere entrance into his studio, which makes him feel like doing great things. Lorraine exclaimed (according to Richard) that she was glad I came as such a great relief from their ordinary friends. But I couldn't give them sincere approval of their writing, and Richard's novel oppressed me, like a stronger echo of

---

[1] *Edelmira Culmell de Chase, a sister of A.N.'s mother, married to Gilbert Chase.*

my *Aline* and all the ideas, style, life that I am desperately running away from. There is in friendship a tragic inequality, as in love sometimes. I do not like to love less than I am loved, to be given more than I give.

May 21. On board the S.S. *Pennland.* Yesterday after lunch the fog lifted and we discovered that thirteen ships were waiting with us for relief from the blinding vapors. We all started together toward New York and the sight was very dramatic. At the pier we were met by cameramen, reporters, insurance men, etc. The reporters questioned Mr. Clark, who was in the damaged cabin. The cameramen photographed the gash. Other men interviewed the captain, and a diver was sent to investigate the hole below the water level. Hugh and I watched him from the deck, a little tense for the man's life. While waiting for the results of the examination we went to the pier to telephone the family and the Maynards. Everybody had been anxious. The newspaper headlines read: "Six ships collide in the fog," and gave many dramatic details. Another ship was far more seriously damaged than ours and the passengers were taken off in lifeboats. At seven o'clock we were told that repairs would take a week and that we were free to change over to another ship. At last the accident began to tell on our nerves, and the romantic element in it began to fade. We slept badly, ate our breakfast and packed grouchily, and now Hugh is gone to make new arrangements. I was so anxious to get to Paris and had no desire to see New York again. I long for Mother, for my brother, for our home, for my dancing, for all our life there. Two days' delay seems a great trial to me.

May 23. On board the S.S. *Mauretania.* We spent two days in New York at the Pennsylvania Hotel. I was physically comfortable (lovely room, telephone, radio, private bathroom, prompt and pleasant service, breakfast in the room, etc.) but mentally distressed. I go *forward* in life with so much impetus that an accident which takes me back to the place I have left, and makes me go through the same events twice (going to Forest Hills, inviting Eduardo for a second lunch, talking with Eugene, having lunch with the Maynards) upsets me, and destroys the harmony of my life (not of my thinking, no, because in that I am perpetually elastic and ever ready for surprises). I felt I needed repairing as much as our ship, and that this stopping of wheels, which I do *willfully* in my own mind every day by analysis, is perfectly futile when it happens physically. I learned nothing.

On second thought, perhaps I did. Perhaps such a retracing of steps would save me from mistakes. I just realized that it helped me to clear up Eduardo.

However, I am glad now to be on my way home, to feel the ship speeding away from New York. I am thinking of Paris. I am relieved to escape the hellish days I have lived in New York, although I must write about them, and I don't regret having passed through them.

The *Mauretania* (second class) vibrates so much that it is difficult to write, even more difficult to sleep and even distressing to eat, so most of the time I lie on my deck chair dreaming and dozing. Although I write very little, I have just discovered a new justification of my Journal, a definite use for it. I have discovered that I owe to it much that I am and much of the success of my life. I owe to it what some people owe to psychology: knowledge of myself, extreme consciousness of what in others is vague and unconscious, a knowledge of my desires, of my weaknesses, of my dreams, of my talents. There is more than that to psychology, but in writing about it I am entering an unfamiliar world.

The science was utterly unknown to me until the day I met Eduardo in New York. He told me almost immediately that he was being psychoanalyzed and that at last he knew what was wrong with him.

"I never knew that there was anything wrong with you," I said. And then, after thinking a while, I had to add: "Not seriously wrong. You were always dreaming a little too much and you were vague about yourself but I assumed these were the natural weaknesses of an extremely artistic nature."

"I was not only vague, but always unhappy, and I could never concentrate my energies, or draw close to reality. There was something seriously wrong; something that partly explains my unhappy and far too ethereal love for you."

"Please tell me as much as you can about it, what this knowledge has done to you, what it means."

"I can't tell you very much, because the analysis is not finished yet. I go to see this woman every day for an hour. She makes me lie down on a couch and sits where I can't see her, and then makes me talk. I tell her everything I remember from my earliest childhood. There are days when I rebel against this knowledge. It makes me very unhappy but I know in the end it will help me. Until the end of it, I can make no plans. The doctor does nothing to influence me in any of my actions."

"When you have all the knowledge of yourself, will you still remain your own master?"

"Yes, I will be able to concentrate my energies and to understand reality."

He talked all through our lunch, and I asked a few questions and listened. The whole thing was at first a great shock to me. I know life, and I know facts, and I know reality, and therefore I know homosexuality but not from so near. My own romantic and lovable cousin, become a reality instead of a poetic and beloved ghost. I knew he lacked character and he lacked a warm connection with life such as I found in marriage, but I never imagined that science instead of human love was required to cure him, to gather up his energies, to fortify his will. My first reaction was a feeling of strangeness. I tried to understand. If I had seen Eduardo just once, I might have remained distressed, as one might feel at suddenly seeing a very sick man whom one believed until yesterday to be in perfect health. I am glad now that I saw him again. In four days I had become accustomed to the fact, and could act. First I realized I must read and learn something about it. Then I had to think of ways of helping him.

We both, for different reasons, hate the ethereal love we felt in the past. Perhaps we realize the incompleteness, the futility and weakness of it. Perhaps we blame each other for it. He could have made me a woman as Hugh did a few years later. Perhaps I could have made him a man if I had been a woman then.

Eduardo wants to get rid of that past, as I want to get rid of it. He wants to write about it. I have already done that and it did not bother me very much. Before I help him I must gather up all my strength and all my reason to understand this new thing. I have been, until yesterday, my own analyst. I am proud of never having had to turn to another for any explanations of myself. I have felt, and particularly this last year, that I was fulfilling all my dreams, that my will was growing stronger, that I am extremely conscious and lucid, strong, and successful. Does psychology hold any surprises for me? Have I evaded any truths, have I been timid, have I been repressed, or fearful, or unconscious of anything?

"Don't be afraid," said Eduardo to me the first time.

The second time I asked him why he had said that, because it annoyed me. "You looked afraid," he answered.

"Well, from now on, never mind my face," I said crisply.

As usual, the one who knows more about it is Hugh. He loves life, he loves facts. He is at once poetic and scientific. He is sensitive and yet fearless. He took up the psychology book with more determination than I did. It was not new to him, except in detail and in wording. He is less clear-minded about his life than I am, but he has more character. I know what I am about and he sees that I carry it through. I often tell him what he is about. We have been truly each other's analysts (with the help of my Journal) and more, because when scientific clarity was lacking we supplied a physical lesson, a human example.

That second time I saw Eduardo I was impressed with the improvement in him: at least here he was facing truths, pulling himself together, using his mind; at all other times he had been so vague and so pointless. Of course he brings to psychology all his habitual weakness: his moods, his despairs, his lack of unity; but toward the end of the analysis, he may do something. Here I find myself believing and relying on the analysis!

May 28. Oh, such an endless trip. My intense desire to get home, one day of rough sea and seasickness, and several sleepless nights have made this the longest trip I have ever known. In second class there is little to observe but mediocrity, and mediocrity is monotonous. One lonely man from Montana spoke to us last evening while we were reading in the lounge. But otherwise we have jealously preserved our solitude. That is all we have to make us happy, and except for seasickness it is an infallible cure.

New York this time was a great trial to me, and it is a wonder I have kept my faith in myself. Added to the sadness I felt at the death of Hugh's father was the bitter realization that he never understood or appreciated his son, our life, and our marriage. And this attitude still exists in the mother. They made me come to Forest Hills, but they wanted to treat me as a guest. Of course I understand that formality is a natural habit with Anglo-Saxons (or shall I say vice). It does not mean unfriendliness, but in the case of formality expressed by a mother-in-law for me (at a moment when she should have been forgetful of her usual restraint) it was a delicate problem to deal with. I struggled to free them by taking an interest in the house, by sharing the work, by sewing, helping, by giving them some of that abundant thoughtfulness I give to my own family. I gave them so much! I swallowed my pride; I was gentle and patient. They began to treat me differently. The mother became confidential, talked to me about Hugh's father, about the love affairs of the girls, and the girls began to tease me. But as soon as one battle was won, I was faced with a new one. Visitors came. It was a renewal of the judgment to be passed on me, from which my sensitiveness shrank. However, they all liked me. Even their lovable old minister, a warm-hearted and liberal man, called me a "lovely French girl" and was deeply impressed by my "beautiful eyes." And then what happened? Too much praise of me was not wanted either and was received without pleasure. A lady painter who happened to come for a visit at Uncle Parker's house one afternoon also praised my "beauty" but received no response. And Aunt Lisa said (I learned later) that she had a sister with an expression of the eyes like mine who died of heart trouble, and should I not be examined?

Of course, the aunts and uncles were each separate and enormous problems. Uncle George never talked to me, and merely shook hands with me dutifully. A fat, loud, humorous, overfriendly aunt, fond of protecting young men, spread her rather vulgar ways before us and at least the New Family were truthful enough to find her "tiring." But of course, my opinion was not asked, heureusement [happily].

Hugh's mother is really a pathetic and helpless person, with very limited feeling and no understanding whatsoever. I make tremendous efforts to love her but find it utterly impossible. Why? Because when they all became resigned to my existence, I discovered it was Hugh himself they *did not understand*. I had to defend his ideas (oh, mildly), his ways, explain him to his own mother! That is why I can't love her.

Toward the end of the visit they became so natural that they began to criticize and to meddle: Hugh must not give up sports for dancing; he smokes too much and too quickly; I must put on weight. We were both good-natured about it. We had come to help Hugh's mother, to make her happy. I often cried at night. I suffered in my pride.

There is hope for the girls and I want to help them. I also try to make up to Hugh for his sadness at not being able to be really proud of his family. I try to remember all the lovable traits in them, and remind him it is his father he resembles, not his mother; his father, who was really a man of great strength of character, feeling, and of fineness beneath the rough exterior. And why, anyway, should our family weigh on us? Each one of us carries an independent seed of greatness. Families give us life and nourishment and a beginning. We can do the rest. And yet we like to have them great, understanding if possible. What a lot we ask.

The Maynards did me a lot of good that last time I saw them (another thing I owe to the collision). They pinned me down to certain facts about my writing which I evade conscientiously. My Journal was wonderful, but why were there pages missing? Things too personal to be copied out. And I told them, as an example, about my father and mother's quarrels. They sat and gasped at this story, which I told with all the ease I get from thinking so often at concerts of how it might be written.

"Wonderful things happen to me all the time," I ended, "but I can't tell them all."

"That is wrong," they said. "You are a cheat in your writing. You might use all that in fiction, give yourself more elbow room."

"Yes, I suppose you are right. It must have been that feeling which prompted me to begin the journal of another person, in which I would not only be free to tell everything but to invent if I pleased."

"There you are—you yourself have recognized the limitations of your journal. Now if you would read [Thomas] Uzzell on the technique of . . ."

Lorraine interrupted Richard. "Anaïs does all those things *instinctively*; she doesn't need to be taught." For which I gave her a grateful look.

"But she can't know everything instinctively," said Richard. "That's impossible."

"I will read Uzzell when I get home," I said, but I already regret that promise. Of course I know I have often come up against terrible technical difficulties, but they never stop me. I invent what I miss, and leave out the problematic parts, and what is left makes people laugh and cry all the same. Richard's theories do me good theoretically, but actually my writing cannot be changed by them. It will remain unconscious and unscientific and ungovernable. Perhaps I am proud of this, as of being my own analyst, and if someday Erskine says so, I'll try to find another way.

Strong visual talent in the violinist on board. If the trip were longer he would certainly strain his eyes. I happened by mistake to smile with him at something, and the consequences are serious, as serious as if I had smiled directly for him. The man from Montana wants to know what takes the place in Paris of the American burlesque show. "You know, the rough kind, with girls with nothing on." I taught him to pronounce Folies-Bergère. He was very willing and very absorbed. He had taken over Hugh's chair while Hugh had gone for a haircut. When Hugh came back and the man was gone he said: "More charity affairs?"

"I only gave him suggestions."

"Good, Freckles. Come down to lunch." And because I made a little joke, which I enjoyed more than he did, he said: "You are, at bottom, just a little girl."

I had sworn that this time Erskine would not scare me, but he did. Our evening with him was calculated to intimidate me. First of all, we were served a young lobster, which required a ridiculous amount of attention. And then, Erskine had just returned from a lecture tour and was talking about the West and the Middle West of which I knew nothing. And then, Mrs. Erskine was intent on questioning me on material life in Paris, since they are coming in September, and I can never make this subject attractive or even bearable. She remembered the curdled cream I had been sold and which spoiled my dessert the day they came to have lunch with us.

"Have you found a place to buy fresh cream?" she asked me, smiling.

"No. We have just become used to sour cream, that's all."

Erskine was subtly more "American" than before and a little too self-satisfied. He read us two perfectly delightful stories in his old manner, and one that was more modern, which I disliked because it was a sort of exhaustive repetition of himself and a little obvious. I didn't hesitate to tell him that Eve [in *Adam and Eve*] was essentially American, whereas he intended her to be universal. That is when I became scared. My criticism was instinctive (damn it) and stood on no legs at all. I'll have to make up in writing for that momentous impulse. The rest of the evening was comparatively smooth. We laughed at his stories but couldn't laugh as heartily as he did himself. He read them with a strong colloquial accent, which accentuated the rougher aspects of his face, and for no sound reason I was a little disappointed. I have such faith in Erskine's mind. But his thundering, ogrelike laugh rolls over everything and makes me feel small and sad.

An evening Hugh and I spent in the Sevilla restaurant (Alice Foot McDougall's Spanish restaurant), also due to the collision, is one of my sweetest memories of New York. We had not really been alone for dinner for a long time, it seemed to us (only two weeks), and we felt and acted like lovers. The setting was appropriate (that woman has such a genius for creating atmosphere), but it made me realize with immense regrets that we could not see Spain this year. This trip has upset our budget quite seriously, even threatened Hugh's precious Dunhill pipes and international telephone stock unless Mother Guiler helps us.

Which brings us to a financial question which will have great importance in our life. Hugh's retirement from business is now definitely uncertain because Father Guiler, to frighten Johnnie, who was in love with an ordinary Catholic working girl, showed him a will in which all those marrying into a non-Protestant family were cut off! He intended to rearrange this later. Mother Guiler said she would do the right thing, but Uncle Parker is there to see and to tell her what is the right thing, this little, uncompromising, inflexible, un-Christian uncle who is now, according to Scotch standards, the head of the family when it should be Hugh. But evidently Scotch fathers never abdicate— they die and another Scotch father, lawyer, and banker takes care of everything. Up to the time of his great rebellion, Hugh was treated like a child. It took a tragic break, marriage, to make him self-reliant, to teach him to run a furnace, a car, and a house, and a woman.

June 8. At home, as usual, writing on my dressing table. Exciting homecoming that Tuesday, with Mother, Joaquin, and Thorvald at the station to meet us. Dinner all together at a restaurant. Thorvald and Mother left us after dinner to see the doctor, who examined Thorvald and planned a regime and ordained a month's stay. Thorvald is entirely *new*. I have had to get used to him and get to understand him as if he were a newly acquired friend. Will have to make his portrait soon, when I know him well enough. But will I have time? Tia Anaïs[1] is here with her daughters, Graziella and Ana Maria. Tia Antolina and Baby[2] are arriving Sunday and later Tio Enrique and Tia Julia.[3]

[1] *Anaïs Culmell de Sanchez, a sister of A.N.'s mother.*
[2] *Antolinita (Antolina) de Cárdenas, A.N.'s cousin.*
[3] *Enrique Culmell and his wife, Julia.*

Thorvald has to be entertained; he does not relish solitude, nor books nor quiet domestic talks. We have already danced for Tia Anaïs and my cousins, had dinner out with them, visits from them. The apartment was painted by Mother, cleaned, polished, etc., and I had to add the last touches to an entirely new decorative scheme. I float through the days at the will of the family.

Hugh is made Trust Officer and is leaving credit work. The only realities, definite realities, are my dancing and my account book. I can't float over them, although I have deprived Miralles of Imagy by the mere presence of Ana Maria, who is learning the Farruca. And the Budget, as usual, groans loudly and demands a raise.

Gustavo was instantly reinstated to his old place of honor in our friendship on our receiving a delightful, spontaneous, affectionate letter from him in Valencia. Since he admits he is self-centered, it is no use holding it against him. He is witty and alive and that is all I ask now. Other things can be had from aunts, uncles, cousins, second cousins, as a compensation for their intellectual apathy.

Gustavo awakens the Imp. He is really a rare and precious friend. Why must he live in Spain? And Ana Maria is here instead of Eduardo, and Erskine is not coming until September.

June 11. Hugh and I took a day off yesterday and fled to Fontainebleau, all alone. We talked, rested, walked, and prepared mentally and physically for a strenuous month. No more solitude, no more peace for a while. The whole month will be offered to his family, mine, relatives of all denominations.

Tia Antolina and Baby arrived at midnight yesterday, eager for a good and lively time. The mere mention of their intentions and ambitions tired me. We began by taking them to the Café de la Paix for coffee and brioche by way of a first chapter to the Parisian life. Baby wanted to walk all through Paris, but we finally persuaded her to leave that for today.

Through it all I cling to my dancing and, visibly, to my writing. But I get sad when I waste time, and when I feel myself throwing away precious days. Fortunately the new maid, Alphonsine, frees me from many tasks, and I may be able to make up in the mornings for other things that should be punished and are punished with immediate evils. Every tea, show, exhibit, visit creates a void where there was wealth before, and I feel my head getting emptier and lighter.

June 20. Wasted days. Shopping and eating and guiding the family through Paris. But I don't stop dancing. Last night La Argentina filled me with enthusiasm again with her Ballet Español at the Femina. I danced once for the Sánchez family, once for an America party we gave Thorvald (when for the first time we introduced bridge tables and cards in our home) and again, impromptu, at a tea to celebrate Joaquin's diploma.[1] (He has passed brilliantly, with all honors, and only two pupils passed out of the whole class.) Mrs. Varela is my most faithful admirer and the one who best realizes my progress. Joaquin wants to write a ballet for me. Even Thorvald is interested. Poor Thorvald is in bad health, physically and morally. He has at last decided to stay, after many pleadings.

I believe in permanent waves, in express traveling, in local chastity. Hell is on earth, and heaven is in extermination. We sleep at night because if we were awake all the time and could follow out a thought to ultimate clarity we would lose our reason. Our reason was made fragile so we would not notice the imperfections of the world.

June 27. I keep my eyes and ears open as usual but find nothing to satisfy my ever-hungry mind. I am tired of the family, even though I love them. None of our tastes are alike, nor our ideas. The one word that does not exist for me is the most important in their lives: boredom. Baby is always bored, all of them are bored. Thorvald has caught the malady and is bored, so easily that while he was here I lived on charcoal pills.

On Monday Mother and Thorvald left for Hendaye, Tia Antolina and Baby for Plombières. But Tio Enrique and Julia arrived today. Tia Anaïs, Graziella, and Ana Maria are leaving next Tuesday, but the Guilers are arriving the same day.

When I am home I lie in bed. I am tired, empty, and sad. Miralles has lost Imagy. I work hard at my dancing when it comes. I can't write and I can't think. What I see in tearooms and shops and revues is not worth painting. Occasionally I get visual pleasure from Spanish shawls, silk dresses, colorful scarves, a smart handbag, or a dashing hat, but a pleasure tinged with desire. I love luxury too well, far too well. I want too many things, things which I could endure seeing others buy if they loved them

[1] *Diplôme Supérieur de Piano from the Schola Cantorum.*

as keenly as I do. But their unenthusiastic possession rouses my envy. I am perpetually upset about beauty I can't own, about money, about my desire to shine, to live showily and brilliantly and exceptionally. The apathy, the dullness, the boredom of rich people make me desperate.

June 29. Today while Hugh was playing tennis I pretended to have an engagement, locked myself in our apartment and slept and dreamed and then wrote letters. Horace and Frances rang the doorbell—I saw their car from the window—and I didn't answer.

Miralles still loves me. I am dancing well; that is a consolation. Yesterday I felt very light and very poised, and the angular lines of my dancing are melting into harmony. Miralles is pleased, and keeps composing new themes for me. His scoldings, his devotion, his intensive teaching, I appreciate deeply.

July 1. Sunday morning. A beautiful moment, all alone in the studio, listening to a Hebrew melody on the phonograph. I am happiest alone, with music and thoughts. I like my own company, the sound of my own ideas, and the sealike movements of my feelings, more intense than all the rest of my life, more than other people's lives, more than books, more than plays. I used to fear emptying myself, but it has never happened. I get empty only when I am with other people, feeling their emptiness, bruising myself against their walled-in intelligence, against their stony apathy. Alone, I overflow, I am rich, I am alive, I shall never dry up until I die.

July 14. Hugh is playing tennis, and everybody else believes I am with him. The studio is deliciously hot and I am scantily dressed. I have listened to the Hebrew melody, I have conquered my desire to set forth all alone to some play, since it would worry the Cat, and I have dreamed heavy dreams of an unquenchable restlessness. I sin by the imagination. I go everywhere and explore everything.

These days of purely social life (entertaining the Guilers, Gilbert Chase and a friend of his) contain nothing in themselves, but my imagination runs wild. The hot breath of untried experiences burns my face. I feel again those mystical withdrawals from life, but this time I withdraw heavily charged with sensuous richness, upon which I feed for days—remembrance of a stranger's glance, new names invented for me by Miralles, the profound delight of physically expressing Albéniz's "Sevilla," the words of a Spanish song, the Ballet Español again, the intensely blue eyes of Gilbert's friend, which remind me of Ramiro Collazo in Havana. I withdraw because life is too strong, too powerfully sweet, too exquisitely painful, too crowded with small miracles.

"You must feel this step as I do," says Miralles, with a caress of his eyes. And immediately I feel it, as he does himself, and it is not strange that he says I dance better since he loves me.

The rest is simple. I try to make myself love the Guilers. I wish a miracle would happen here. But it doesn't. I do it by deft, clever, thoughtful shopping for them, by helping them. I will really love Edie when she grows up. Ethel and I are more alike, but she knows how to make people give to her, how to hold them without paying them, and at this sort of game I always lose heavily. Edie pays me with affection, that's all I ask.

Saw Horace and Frances married. She lives against a yellow paper background, a shade off the artistic track. But she has eliminated the museum atmosphere of the Guicciardi apartment. Horace and Frances together look "thick." I don't know what has gone out of breezy and floating Horace. A certain curiosity. Does he find marriage an end? Is he satisfied with life, with Frances and yellow wallpaper and his secondhand car? I look at him with cool eyes; whereas he clings to our friendship. When I cease to feel, as a woman does, I analyze cruelly, like a doctor. Did I expect too much from him? I probably did. I usually expect too much even from myself.

July 16. Mixed impressions, without unity. Tennis matches seen in tropical heat, much flirtation, July Fourteenth celebrations in the streets, problem of evading Guilers, and Tia Antolina arrives tonight. I once boasted of directing my life as I pleased, but I did not foresee the invasion of the family nor my helplessness before their demands. I remember old favors so well; I am grateful. I owe to Tia Antolina my five months in Havana, I owe her *Aline*, my first and bad novel, and so many unwithered memories. In exchange for all that here are my precious days, my treasured hours, a portion of this life I worship and find too short, the greatest gift I can make anyone.

Said how do you do and good-bye to Boussie one morning

last week. She also thinks Erskine's *Eve* is uniquely American. What will Paris do to Erskine?

"Well," says Boussie, "you have a wonderful brother." I agree with her; I can't help it. I am so proud of him. The two of them are good friends. Joaquin deafens her with praise and explanations of Spain. She loaned him Waldo Frank's *Virgin Spain*. When I didn't go to see her, Joaquin did and explained: "Poor Anaïs, she won't come because she feels 'empty' and she is ashamed. She has been leading a stupid life."

I don't even read, but I dance, dance so well. After vivacity, technical maturity, broadening of repertoire, general facility comes harmony, the melting of all knowledge, suavity, poise, and Miralles scolds, works, and gives himself pain to perfect me. And now and then his eyes shine, and he tells me: "Me entusiasmas!" And kisses my hand, and makes me work harder.

"Flirt" is a mild word for my behavior. I like to arouse feelings, and I like to pretend. I like to create confidence between the man I am interested in and me, so that I may know him well, deeply, and so that he may know me, and enjoy me, without ever owning me. I give a great deal, too, so that I have no remorse. I have been, in a theoretical way, Miralles's companion and helpmate. I have penetrated his life. I am useful to him, consoling. I have his thoughts and his devotion. I hear of every detail of his existence. He offers up to me as a gift the confession that the other night at the café he sat alone and realized his loneliness, that he also realized he was old and could not make a success on the stage, that most people were selfish and their word could not be believed. Another time he showed me an atomizer he bought for his sister in Valencia (wholesale price, but they would never know). The choice of atomizer in a distasteful green with gold stripes and a silver handle brought back painful memories of Spanish interiors and Cuban wedding gifts. I could imagine his house in Valencia. At the fair he buys two gold vases at two francs apiece for his mother's grave, to be filled with artificial flowers. Another day he has trouble with pupils who have not paid their lessons. He is invited to stay at a wonderful house full of empty rooms for friends, and he can't sleep, thinking of people who have empty rooms when he lives permanently in one small airless one.

July 21. Orders from the Omnipotent Bank to visit Le Havre. Pretended regrets, but really glad to leave shopping, teas, evenings out. Put my Journal in the valise first of all. And then permitted myself the unusual luxury of a breakdown, from excessive weariness. One day and a half of depression, shivering, heavy head, blurred eyes, nervousness, crossness, but as soon as I found myself alone with Hugh on a hill, looking down on the sea, five hours away from Paris (by Citroën), I recovered. The sun shines on what I write and on my newly shorn locks. It is unbelievable, but my hair was cut a week ago and permanently curled, yet left long enough so that I can still put it up and it can flutter in the breeze. It makes me feel like Shelley. It is in harmony with my new breezy spirit. Whatever I wear, cut, or curl is symbolic of an idea, a mood, an aspiration. It is not due to the influence of some crafty saleslady or to a drawing in *Vogue*.

Gustavo is a problem. I miss him when he is away and like him less when he is here. He is more malicious than I remembered him, more flashy, more of a fire cracker. He stayed in Valencia all this time and wrote half a book, a modern book, without plot, vivacious, like his own conversation, odd, interesting, whimsical, neurotic, coarse, incoherent, immature. Two chapters in it are arresting, gems of impressionism and imagination. It sounds at times like a good parody of the ultramodern style and sometimes like an echo of better books. He wants to make money. What to do with him? Encourage him—he needs it. He is stimulated by our company, worried that we think him corrupt, defends himself warmly, was puzzled because we told him conduct did not worry us. Of course he is a mixture but he wants to be thought good. I can safely look at him through my cigarette smoke. He does not understand me.

He is not sure that he likes me. I am not sure I like him. Something in us clashes mysteriously. His maliciousness and my lucid faith, his Spanish disregard of intelligent women and my mental fever. He lacks a little poetry and imagination in treating me. He is a true imp, not quite human, not good, not a woman's friend, like Joaquin, Eduardo, or Enric; a problem, a diverting problem, a likable problem, seen like this from the top of a hill with the sea below and the sun shining on my writing. On darker days I know Gustavo, in some way or other, is going to hurt me.

July 22. Sunday morning on the hilltop. The air is fresh, intoxicating, and the sun is soothing. A three-funnel ship is coming into the bay. Little ones move about, bows pointed in many directions.

And Hugh is fittingly reading Conrad. Moi, je divague [As for me, I ramble]. I should be writing letters but I cling affectionately and unreasonably to my poor Journal. Just now I remembered an idea of Gustavo's which I meant to clear up. According to him the greatest sin is coldness, and the greatest saint was Mary Magdalen, who was capable of passion. He does not admire those who reach perfection by renunciation, indifference to the flesh, or mere insensibility. That is exactly my idea. Asceticism did appeal to me at one time, as an ideal, but now I seek its opposite: I seek living. I was overjoyed the day I discovered I had a sensitive body, although at one time nothing seemed important but a sensitive brain. I am today fully capable of passion in the most complete and absolute sense of the word. I have thrown off asceticism, separation from life, aloofness. Girlish sentimentality caused harm. My head developed first, and out of proportion. I regret my mistake deeply, but at least it has helped me to realize the full preciousness of what I once despised. Gustavo never sinned by coldness, I am certain. Neither did Enric, nor Hugh. Hugh humanized me. Is this a story that would help anyone, or is it stupidly banal?

July 30. Two strange days spent in Dinard [Brittany] with Hugh's family. Strange because we found Johnnie engaged and the family upset. I looked the girl over. Phyllis is English, and has narrow, inexpressive eyes, a frank smile, a strong handshake. She plays tennis. Johnnie is in love. What can one say?

However, we enjoyed our visit. Hugh played tennis with his mother, and then they played doubles with Phyllis and Ethel, and then Hugh played with Johnnie, and then Johnnie played with his mother, and then they played with the two girls, and then Phyllis's mother with her daughter, and the daughter with Hugh, and Hugh with Johnnie again . . . I got nearly hysterical.

Fortunately, the next day we went to St.-Malo. I do love Edie and Ethel. I gave them a facial treatment, and Edie fixed my hair. They dressed me in real sports clothes and raved about me. We talked together intimately and naturally. They are the only girls who can make me change my eyelash dye, or my hair, or the tone of my face powder. I like to give up my fierce individuality and let them fuss over me. It is such a sweet novelty to have sisters. I try to open up their minds, tell them stories of traveling, all I know about men (how that subject fascinates them). I call Ethel "Diablito" [little Devil] (she is pretty, ardent, flirtatious) and tease her. Edie's soulfulness and thoughtfulness exceed my own, and for the first time in my life I find someone who gives more in little ways than I do and who can spoil me and make me feel selfish. Ethel said, I was told, the more she knew me, the more she liked me, that I grew on one. I stimulate them, tear down their conventionalities, prejudices. I shocked Johnnie, who did not know my sprightly moods. I used to be so passive and pensive.

Now I run about the ramparts of St.-Malo, hair flying, threatening everybody with my artistic photography, placing them in the right doorways, etc., and in the little boat I had a moment of uncontrollable laughter at myself because I felt again like a soap bubble, and I used to think of myself as solemn.

We arrived in Paris this morning at seven, had breakfast in a café. We are sunburned, we feel strong, our lungs are full of fresh, marvelous air. I have lost forever, forever, a certain weakness in living. My body now must follow my mind.

August 3. I miss Miralles. Dancing alone is different. I am helpless. I realize now what a domineering maestro he is and how thoroughly he teaches me, leads me. I consequently answered his letter with a very affectionate and comforting one, which may ultimately make it harder for me to take Imagy away from him. And it is about time Imagy attends to other things; she is taking too large a place in my life.

August 8. Journal of Imagy: Does one come to France to learn the power, the inevitable power of the body? I have leapings of sensuousness entirely separate from myself, from my dreams, my soul, my feelings. There are moments when I do not belong to myself. This mystery, this frightful division exists, then? Sudden desires for an unknown love, sudden curiosity about an unknown man, a sudden melting of the body into a dream, a surrender. And this does not happen in moments of idleness, but unexpectedly, in the middle of my life, during a drive through the country, while I dance, while I walk through a shop. The real world goes to pieces and I am another woman, dissolved by passion, conquered by a love that belongs to no one, and to anyone, outside of myself, and yet possessing all of me.

I adore, I worship Hugh with my body and soul. But I have a surplus of affection, of enthusiasm, which is pent up because he does not need it all. My devilish, demoniac imagination takes advantage of it, and the little seed that might have been thrown away because it was left over, is nursed, and becomes a tree, another life, another love, another journal.

A lady in Le Havre made a strong impression on me, and I surprised her. We both thought we were going to meet plain boring women, as bankers' wives usually are, and were not looking forward to the encounter. I found a lovely house, a studio, sculptures, exquisite taste and comfort, Merejskowski's book on the parlor table. And then the lady came in, handsome in a southern way, dressed in white sports clothes, with brown, muscular arms and wearing a wide, flat silver bracelet. She was, however, conventionally witty. There is a conventional wit in France as easily recognized as the Kew Gardens jargon. No, she didn't talk very well. She was impressive more through her work, her house, her appearance. Her husband, a coffee merchant, and an Egyptologist, was given to caustic remarks. The lady and I found more to study in each other. I was dressed in sapphire blue, with my hair bound in a blue turban. At a certain moment, when asked what dessert she wanted (we were having lunch at a restaurant overlooking the sea), she expressed a desire for "des fruits très mures" [some very ripe fruit], and the way she said it, the suavity, the controlled modulation and studied charm of her phrase, immediately made me feel the symbolic relationship between her dark, rich beauty and the ripe fruit, and I felt very, very young. However, while she ate the ripe peaches and prunes, I was making more discoveries than she was. I perplexed her. I wasn't dull, and yet I wasn't caustic, and my toilette was neither bad nor strictly good. I detected a grain of social snobbishness; which I disappointed by not mentioning my friends by name as she did, knowing I must have seen those names in the social columns. Against that, she loves music, and she receives all the musicians who pass through Le Havre.

What disdain she has for Le Havre, Le Havre which seems romantic to me. Ah, Paris. She couldn't live away from it and comes to it often. Will I see her again? No. Our lives are too much alike: she reigns alone over hers, as I do over mine. We both realized it. My friends would like her and her friends would like me. "I wouldn't mind," my eyes said frankly. "You interest me enormously." But hers did not respond, dark eyes of a ripe woman who knows better than I that it is not good to give friendship to a woman.

Gustavo invites me to take coffee with him; even more agreeable than with Miralles! He looks so Spanish with his black hat. His hands are immaculate and his nails polished. He is obsessed with sex and sensationalism, but these things, once he is published, may not worry him any more. I like his talk. He gave me his first compliment: "You are growing prettier every day," so I immediately invited him to dinner Saturday night. It is funny to observe that because Hugh is absent, he showed his liking for me, which I doubted. Spanish respect for husbands.

August 9. We were invited to a second banquet, for the celebration of Hugh's victory at tennis. I felt unsociable and unhappy at the idea of a wasted evening. I watched the tennis reluctantly. We sat out in the garden of the tennis club. One of the tennis players was a very witty and mischievous Frenchman who kept the whole table merry from beginning to end. At one end of the table sat Alice (I had seen her often at the Bank, but we had talked little), staring at me, a friendly stare which I did not mind. After dinner she came and sat next to me. "I love the way you wear your hair," she said. "It is lovely, it is unusual, it's artistic, and it suits you. You remind me of an angel in the Cathedral of Rheims."

I was intimidated. "Vous êtes bien gentille," I said, conventionally.

"Oh," she said, "I am not being polite. I never say things to be polite. I love your hair, really."

"But I am glad you do," I said, feeling stirred by her exaggerated seriousness.

"For a long time I have wanted to talk to you; I always felt you would understand."

Gently, I made her talk, questioned her, and found her highly sensitive, hopelessly and admirably idealistic, fond of reading, lonely, rebellious, bitter, and intense. While she talked I felt an immense sympathy for her. Her eyes, so eager, so restless, so consuming, held me. Her face was moist from the effort to surmount her timidity and her nervousness. I told her I would ask her to come and see me, and show her my books. I knew our life would help her in her wild, desperate search for beauty, in her loneliness, and I wanted to pour a balm over her rebellion. Her parting handshake was like the grasp of someone in distress. Her eyes had not left my face once.

I was tired that night. I felt old, because for the first time I had met someone more eager, more dreamful, than myself. She is now as I was. She is at the age when I cried over *Jean Christophe* and fought the whole world, and worked, and went through hell discovering ugliness.

August 11. Had dinner in the country with Horace and Frances. She has settled down; she is very domestic, thoughtful, fresh, and nice. Horace is happy. She is, above all, adaptable, which is a beautiful quality. You can no longer separate the real from the acted: marriage has fused everything. I feel friendly toward them. Horace's contentment has somehow taken the sharpness and brilliancy out of his character. Frances makes a noble virtue out of being uncritical and easygoing, and Horace sinks in his deep armchair, puts his slippers on, and enjoys a bourgeois happiness. Why do I resent their comfortableness and plainness? It is none of my business. Little joys, little sorrows, little desires, little lives. They are afraid of analysis, afraid of thought, afraid of restlessness; they have chosen placidity and stagnation.

Meanwhile, Hugh and I are getting our wits sharpened by our uncomfortable lives. Last night at the dinner I was witty enough to please and tickle him. He was more profoundly happy than Horace. He knew it. And he knows, too, that it is because he does not seek peace but me. I have my peaceful days, when I'm tired, when the rain depresses me, but as a rule I have all the defects of Guinivere without her looks, and I am certainly one of the troublesome women of the world. How do I get away with it? Mild manners that betray in no way my nature, nice dresses that divert attention from my restless intelligence, and the habit of writing more than I talk, which makes me altogether harmless.

August 30. Hugh was obliged to go to Geneva on business, and so I went down to be with Mother for two days in Hendaye. Then I rushed back to help Hugh's family with their shopping. A week wasted, frittered away, and I nearly broke down under the strain of a terrible depression. I am alone in bed, trying to rest. I can't throw off my worries. All the families are away, but their whims, weaknesses, restlessness, ignorance, pettiness, selfishness weigh me down, as well as their indelicate generosities, their ever-mentioned gifts. What a sad summer. Hugh is like me, devoted to his family. They tire and depress and irritate him. We are both too stupid and too unselfish. We come back to each other for comfort, for peace, to heal each other's wounds.

September 1. At last I have been lifted out of my muddy life. Gustavo came to dinner last night. With an eager face and sinuous movements of his hands, he told us about theosophy. I kept staring at the four lighted black candles and felt a heavy burden lifting from me, and wondered where I had been for three months, three unhappy, lifeless months. On a fast, certainly, without food or light. How we talked last night. Hugh proposed giving a high place to love, with no distinction between the spiritual and the physical. Gustavo talked of planes, density, progress, and of the perfect men who achieved wisdom. We went to his apartment to get the little book he has been reading. He read us another chapter of his own book, a futile one; but we encouraged him to finish it so that we could judge the whole.

We had promised to read him a little out of our journals. He expressed a doubt of the *truthfulness* of journals.

"Nobody tells everything," he said, "none of the bad thoughts of which they are not proud."

I was piqued, especially when I have been so painfully truthful lately. So I showed him three intimate and unflattering descriptions of myself. He was a little startled and silent. Silence in Gustavo is ominous, dangerous, inexplicable, because it is so rare. I was elated at my recklessness. I am so tired of selecting beauty for the others. I don't care what Gustavo thinks.

The three of us smoked, pondered, argued. At midnight we parted.

And today is a holy and blessed Saturday, and we can enjoy it alone, but I'm sick. I have been too unhappy and too tired. One evening of theosophy is not enough to heal me, because the summer is over and I cannot be consoled.

Keats worried about his brother and his sister. Poor Keats. I am not the only fool. My mother is like my child; her sorrows are mine. All the sorrows and all the deceptions of the world are mine, every vibration pulls at my strings, and I am never silent, never indifferent. All those who do not believe in souls can come and feel how I twist and quiver at every pain.

And in the same way, I respond to joy, with all of myself. I have earned the right to die earlier than others. But first I must write my book, create a second Hugh, because the first one is so unutterably perfect, and the pattern must not be lost.

September 2. I played tennis to please Hugh, which, incidentally, cured me mentally and physically. Humor returned to me as I ran across the red sand courts, chasing a ball, which rarely escaped me. I am going to play tennis with accuracy, swiftness, and spirit, said Hugh proudly, while I wonder why I wouldn't give him this pleasure before.

Sweet, restful days, in the exhilarating fall sunshine. We drive together, we eat out, we take naps, we go to bed early, we talk. We build up again, higher than before, so that no visiting relatives can tear down life and strength.

Theosophy, Gustavo, tennis.

I wrote Mother a comforting letter just now. My Journal has suffered from the fact that I write to her every day.

September 3. After a restful weekend it is easier to make wise plans. First obstacle: Gustavo has my typewriter. Second obstacle: I have no quiet place to work. Studio is at the mercy of the butcher, iceman, cleaner, etc. No daylight in the bedroom but plenty of noise. Bathroom is an unconventional place, often needed by others, but I'll have to have it and dedicate it to a new use. Noise can be excluded by a closed window. First of all I must get a pair of glasses. I need them. Now that this is settled I can write about Gustavo.

Gustavo is abnormally self-conscious, self-critical, and sensitive. He wants so much to be liked. It is already an accepted fact that we do like him. But his imagination will soon create another doubt. Does his talk tire us? Do we think him corrupt on account of his novel? His book on theosophy proved a very childish set of conventional laws of goodness and conduct. What could be simpler and more banal than this: discrimination, desirelessness, good conduct, love. Yet this appeals to his complicated mind, and he naïvely tries to live it out. What can one do with such a mixture of imp, devil, child, and man? Money slips through his fine hands. Women protect him but he doesn't make love to them. He is overanalytical and yet dangerously impulsive. Is he wise? He doesn't give that impression, but then, most wise men never show their wisdom.

September 7. Miralles is back in Paris. We begin our lessons again, twice a week. He is unchanged, but I am no longer the same. Imagy tires me and does not bring me much knowledge. Hugh is right after all about essential experiences and ideas. Have I been trifling with little feelings? Perhaps. But I'm wiser and must accept this wisdom unquestioningly. Perhaps I am tired of everything, just now. Today I could only sleep and wish for somebody else to worry about instead of Miralles. I am afraid of winter, the rain, short, dark days. It has not come yet. Today was soft and sunny, but at 7:30 a mist came over the city with the darkness, and I imagined that winter was watching, waiting, crouching not far away.

September 11. One Saturday we visited Louis Kromberg, a friend of Luis Mora, for whom I posed when I was a model in New York. He showed us some of his beautiful paintings of Spanish dancers. The man who introduced us to him was what I call a Seller of Personalities. He is a middle-aged American dentist, kind-hearted, boisterous, sociable, settled for twenty-five years in Paris, devoted to queens, kings, princesses, marshals, maharajahs, poor but famous artists, rising young men. Only well-known names appear in his conversation: Ruth Elder, Lindbergh, Marshal Foch, Monsieur Meunier. How enthusiastically he sells one to the other: "You love music? Oh, well, you should meet So-and-so. She is really wonderful." "Not interested in music? I'll have to introduce you to Loie Fuller." "The day I received Lindbergh, Meunier was there, and he said to me . . ."

He has stories for everything about everything. Talking thus, he invited us to dinner at his sumptuously conventional apartment, together with Sidney Veit, one of the three oldest members of the American colony, a delightful, bright-eyed, neat, and refined old man to whom I took a great liking.

Mr. Veit's apartment is a real museum of valuable and lovely etchings, paintings, bric-a-brac, etc. He showed us through it and invited us for dinner next week with the old dentist and the painter, Kromberg, who really interests me. The dentist's mania has so far proved a blessing.

More talk, confidences, discussions with Gustavo—personal, philosophical, sentimental, religious, pagan. Sympathy growing stronger. Gustavo understands me. He likes my faith, my faith in him, in life, in art, in myself. He has none, but I have enough for two. And on we talk, until we feel sleepy, and he goes home to think over us while Hugh and I talk him over.

Sunday was sweet. Tennis, sunshine, rest. A new job given me by the Humorous Banker, who hates personal accounts: two hundred pages or so of stock correspondence to straighten out. I did it. And I could never pass in Arithmetic or Algebra. Interest, dividends, complications of Mother Guiler's stocks mixed with ours, personal loans, a car loan, monthly installments buying National City Bank stock—all that to be made clear, logical, and to be balanced in the Fat Book. This little triumph elated me.

Also invented a little trick by which Richard can reconstruct our studio out of snapshots pasted together on paper and made to stand up like the walls themselves.

The music we heard with our dinner one evening at the Rotonde was so bad that I said to Hugh: "It must have been composed by someone who could not pay for his dinner."

September 15. Saturday. A day like any other, since Hugh is away playing golf with Tio Enrique and I am invited to the theatre with Tia Julia. I'm in a bad mood merely because I am writing badly, meagerly, anemically. Living itself takes too much energy, too much thought, too much of one's preciously gathered wisdom. There is nothing left but a bad taste in one's mouth and the strong desire to forget. Forgetting is not my job: I choose eternal remembrance; I choose to suffer twice, in actuality and in the telling of it; I choose double living. And at the same time I am fully convinced I love life so much that I find its physical duration too short. Those who believe in reincarnation believe they return again and again until they have found knowledge. But I don't think I shall ever be given another chance, because I am making so much use of this life, and I am so intense, so alive and so restless, that surely at sixty I shall have known and felt everything, and I will die in exactly the way I have lived.

Gustavo is Hugh's friend, not mine. Yesterday I came to a curious realization of this fact. We have several effeminate friends, and they naturally are more attracted by Hugh. As I said to Hugh: "I feel very jealous." In a play we saw, an elderly man advised a pretty lady to let a certain man flirt with her.

"But he's not sincere," said the lady. "He makes love to all the women he sees."

"Why that proves him to be a wonderful man. There are so few men nowadays who love women."

What am I going to do? The big manly Cat doesn't need friends. He's too busy. Besides, he doesn't like effeminate men; he likes women. Whereas I get lonely sometimes. Gustavo is not exactly effeminate, although he uses powder and lipstick. He likes perfume and is worried about his few wrinkles. But I know he appreciates woman; he is in love with an American beauty. However, he lacks hardness, and he finds it in Hugh. I won't worry about Gustavo. He likes both of us, and we both like him. I am at bottom very pleased with anyone who realizes Hugh's value. But just the same, it is a rather comical situation.

How much jealousy enters into my thoughts and actions? I resented Horace's happiness because I had not created it. I am not a monster and yet there is no doubt that I lost interest in Horace the minute I could no longer help him. I never do harm. I write it! And then I always discover it, atone, confess in silence, without bother to anyone, even to Hugh. Dear Journal, who keeps me out of mischief. There is no doubt that I am jealous. I love to be loved, alone, uniquely. But I swear that this feeling shall never harm anyone. Thank God I know myself, and I have the will power to rule myself.

September 19. Hugh comes home from Lille and laughs at my confession of jealousy. "You have never been jealous of superior people. And you *never* do harm."

The one night we were separated and which I spent with the Sánchezes makes reunion sweeter.

I am free, strong. But there are moments when I must begin from the beginning in order to gain a foothold. I get lost now and then. I got lost yesterday when Hugh was in Lille. I was alone in the Sánchezes' hotel apartment. I could have been unmarried, visiting them in Havana. I could have dreamed everything that has happened in the last six years. The nightmare wrapped me. I felt small, fragile. I imagined I was just beginning, and had nothing but a pretty face and very little knowledge of life, and my body was numb and mousy, and my mind was timorous and lost in vague desires.

Oh, the horror of that thought! I jumped from my armchair to answer the doorbell. It was a telegram from Hugh to say he was arriving at nine.

September 21. The lady from Le Havre appears in the social columns, attends the races, but does not call on me. Someday, if she ever finds her portrait in my book, she will be sorry not to have noticed I appreciated her.

Mother and Joaquin arrived yesterday. I was so happy to

have them near again. Mother became sprightly when invitations poured on her.

Just now I am alone. Gustavo has my typewriter, so I write letters, to Frances Schiff, now Mrs. Whitney Bolton, to others. Pretexts for not working. Tonight we are invited to dinner with Veit, the dentist, and Kromberg. Facts. Empty facts. Ne serais-je qu'une danseuse? [Will I be nothing but a dancer?] How restful. No more digging, digging, digging into life. Yet there is sunshine, the studio is golden, harmonious, beautiful. Hugh is coming home soon, and he loves me.

September 24. I know that Gustavo is unreliable, scattered, impulsive, sensual, yet he interests me. I have read his novel and found it attractive, *alive.* He is complex, and I should never have tried to condense him into a phrase. At times he appeals to me as a pathetically eager and sensitive person; at other times he appears weak, curious about too many futile things, too unpoetic. But he lives so *absolutely*, and for the moment this seems to me the most important thing. Therefore likes and dislikes are to be hushed. He is to be watched. He is interesting. I want to help him.

Yesterday we went with him to a boring play, Giraudoux's *Siegfried*. He criticized it heartily with us, and at the end acted and talked like the conventionally grateful guest and thanked us for an enjoyable afternoon. But he admired Hugh's tie and shoes as much as my peach dress, and didn't he say the other day over the telephone: "Give my love to Hugh—I hope you don't mind"?

Mother's violent dislike of him makes matters difficult. Because he is interested in Joaquin. What would she do if she had read his novel, "Sexicology and Otherwise"?

I write Imagy's Journal in another book. She was getting troublesome and occupying too much space, considering her unreality. She and Gustavo must make friends; what a pair they are together. Resemblances: the same restlessness, lucidity, the same mixture of boldness and timidity, impulsiveness and reticence, the same desire for admiration and the need of faith, the same inaccurate, unartful writing. They watch each other; both love acting.

Are you acting now? Are you sincere? They never know. He has lived enormously, through everything; his face and language and his novel show it. Imagy's living is still a little theoretical, deduced from reflection and observation. She watches him. But he is sometimes impressed with her intuitive knowledge and wonders how much, just how much, she knows.

Yesterday, in the theatre, between acts, while we smoked and walked, I glanced swiftly at a man whose extremely intense but idealistic eyes were worth noticing. Gustavo caught my glance immediately, lost interest in the conversation, and studied the man. He was mad not to understand the simplicity of my observation. In a moment he had built up stories. Why did you look at this man? He is taller than I am. Do you like tall men? You don't like me? He gave me credit for an interest, a fickleness, a complexity I did not feel. And I could have cleared up his vain, jealous malaise in a moment but I kept quiet, mysteriously suggestive, and let his imagination fly. He can't conceive of simplicity, and I sometimes enjoy seeing him blunder. I am *acting* wisdom, to intrigue him, to tease him, because I don't want him to know the real me, yet. What good would it do him? He has a talent for distorting things, just as I have. His imagination butts into everything. He has sand in his eyes, sea shells in his ears, and foam under his feet. He ought to write a journal and have no friends, like me.

September 25. Kromberg made an uninteresting dinner partner the other night, even though he talked about his idea of painting all the dancers of the world. But when he invited us to his studio today to meet a Spanish painter, I hurriedly accepted. His work has fascinated me, and his interest in dancing. Blessed be the old dentist who introduced us, and who wore a purple bow tie at dinner. I dressed for Kromberg—hair up and slick (with water), earrings, black velvet dress, and my shawl from Granada, Joaquin's present, for which he starved himself. Today I am also dressing for Kromberg, not for Gustavo, who is invited but who may find the Spanish painter more interesting than me and his tie more attractive than my dress.

September 27. Gustavo burst in Tuesday with my First Book [drawn from the Journal] under his arm, full of interest in me, my life, my writing. I was so startled, so pleased, that I nearly said aloud: "Have I found a friend?" Neither one of us wanted to go to Kromberg's studio—that first moment of complete understanding was so valuable—but we had to go. The Spanish painter del Pinto—friend of my father, Segovia, Iturbi, La Argentina—

thought I looked Russian. (I wore a black silk coat, coral silk dress, very tight-fitting, with a row of black buttons, and a three-cornered black hat with a veil. Are these the things which misled him?) Gustavo protested: I looked like a Botticelli woman, absolutely. Kromberg just winked at me in a friendly way. I like him. Gustavo watched me all the time, and made a scene afterward because I was too self-possessed. Such a hearty quarrel we had, such a delicious bursting out. Hugh was not home yet. Gustavo accused me of reticence, secrecy, conventionality. He was so eager to find me out all at once. He begged me for my raw journal, not typewritten or recopied. And although I confessed to a great desire to throw off my reticence, I refused him. "Why, why?" he asked.

"I suppose I like to be secretive."

He did not have the time to pull my hair and get the key of my safety box. Hugh came in, and things quieted down. Gustavo was asked to leave because we had to dress up for a dinner at the Café de Paris with two bank vice-presidents, the manager of the Paris Branch, and a sub-manager.

Caviar and chicken and ice cream. American jazz. One of the vice-presidents was a big, fat Dutchman who was fond of dancing. He gave me an enormous amount of attention. I danced all night, collected compliments. Three Americans seated next to our table never once took their eyes off me. The sub-manager said to Hugh: "Look out for Mrs. Guiler. That man who is watching her is a prominent actor. He is terribly interested in her."

The next day I remembered nothing except Gustavo's eagerness to tear down the barriers which separate and isolate us all.

Winter is here. It surprised everyone but me. I had felt it hovering over us, sensed its nearness, when everybody else was enjoying the sunshine and the mildness. My old enemy and tormentor is here. The days end at seven, the studio is cold, the sun is powerless, the leaves are dying.

Yet I love winter clothes. I wear heavy, rich, warm things with sensuous pleasure. I hide like a jewel in a velvet jewel box. You can see only my nose and chin. I will always have that terrible frailty before the winter and that great longing for a perpetual summer. Ridiculous. Like ladies who died of love, or of desire for their native land. I must find a way of falling in love with winter, permanently, that nasty fellow. What does he give me? The right to wear velvet and fur, the intimacy of closed doors and windows, and a fire, and an abundance of concerts and plays.

October 2. The Erskines arrived unexpectedly Friday at four and called us at six. I was startled out of my wits but so happy. The next day they all came to lunch, John Erskine, Pauline, Graham, and Anna. We talked all afternoon. He still frightens me. I lose my wit, my poise, my age. No progress made in that direction. But my eyes and ears are open, and I watch him and I see him so clearly.

No time for literature or character analysis. Mrs. Erskine requires a home. Agencies, taxi drives, walks upstairs and down-stairs, through old-fashioned French apartments declared un-inhabitable (at three thousand francs a month); modern ones an improvement but not perfection yet. John stays at the hotel, writing. Graham plays tennis with me. Anna has already sized me up as the kind of person you can get most anything out of. Exactly. That's why I'm running after apartments while John writes, and the very sound of his typewriter gave me an incisive ache which lasted all day. There is genius—and here is a possibility.

We haven't seen our dear genius since Sunday. Hugh is thinking of how rich we are going to be someday because his Trust work is flourishing. Joaquin is here, my darling, beautiful, alive, affectionate and thoughtful, and so rich inwardly. Mother cooks and sews. Gustavo calls me up: "When are we going to meet?" And I dance. I want a studio for myself, where I can hide and work. My head is full, and I bother too much about other people's lives, and I am wasting time.

October 9. Next Tuesday the Erskines will be in their own home. Three high points: the evening we took Erskine to see Godoy; Saturday afternoon, when Erskine took us to lunch and the Folies-Bergère; and the moment I discovered how to lose my shyness with him—by being thoroughly and outrageously French, which intimidates him, or at least puzzles him and gives me time to catch my breath.

The evening with Godoy was unbelievably literary and un-believably perfect. They talked directly to each other, each wittier than the other, both lucid, critical, amusing, finding interests in common. Erskine was forced to realize that he is not known in France, but how tactfully, how suavely Godoy let him know it. Today all Erskine's books are in Godoy's hands, and all Godoy's poetry is in Erskine's hotel room. Together they executed the critics, disagreed on the greatness of Racine, admired Poe (whom Godoy is translating), belittled Proust and Gide, lauded Baudelaire and Verlaine.

Julia Godoy's profile made an impression on Erskine. But it was at the Folies-Bergère I realized that he is very susceptible to women's beauty. He is also difficult to live with, willful, a little overcritical. He has the admirable power of concentration, works anywhere, leaves an unfinished page in the typewriter at night and can go right on with it when he returns to it in the morning. I like his big voice, his manner of speaking, the swiftness and subtlety of his mind, his wit.

In order to help him to know France I have become French. I show him the extreme incarnation of his French ideas—I exaggerate them a little. Thus I find out he is *slightly hypocritical* about woman, slightly proper Anglo-Saxon malgré lui [in spite of himself]. When I get rational, intelligent, reasonable, then *he* comes up with the old hackneyed "conduct affecting the life of others," "kindness," and other sentimentalities. I don't know any more what to think of the human mind if Erskine contradicts himself. Ah, Proust. Proust may be right; there is no unity, there is no fixed personality. Sand, broken necklaces, dead leaves, scattered mosaics, a kaleidoscope.

October 13. Erskine came back yesterday to something I had said about tragedy not existing in France. I also told him I had found out that the Parisian point of view on love is entirely physical. His ideas on love include companionship. But I am wiser and did not condemn the French philosophy. I insinuated there was something necessary in it and suggested that even his own formula of love and companionship is not enough. There is also the love of life, which leads one on and on (into experience). He said I was cynical. I said I was a woman, and had had occasion to test my ideas. He was half convinced. Not only was my language frank, but I admitted the physical so entirely that he knew I was not theorizing.

Then in the evening, I was inwardly upset by the discovery that above everything else, Erskine is sincerely seeking the truth.

The sure failure of his search (hasn't it maddened me, this search?) gave me an unbearable sting of pity and sympathy.

The secret worry about Erskine's mind was effaced this morning by a conversation with Gustavo over the telephone. A new voice, deep and slow: he is hurt because I postponed his visit twice. So he did his best to hurt me, and I promised atonement. For the second time we were entirely sincere with each other. He, sad and moody, and I, confessing my liking for him, and worried over the discovery of another sensitive nature, as brittle, as raw, as weak, as deep, as impossible as mine.

The conversation with Erskine on love, on the French, etc. was interrupted each time Mrs. Erskine came into the room. Yet one day, shopping, we talked, and she showed that she understood him, knew his failings (susceptibility to flattery); knew he sought romance and could no longer connect it with her; saw clearly his problems, a desire for all knowledge and experience, a pagan thirst for living, so incompatible with loyalty; his restlessness ("the torment of my life").

Joaquin is so busy, too, that we can't talk. He teases me about my "worldliness," my poise. I know he wants to shake me and find me breaking up into little wild untamable bits. No, I'm getting invulnerable, at least outwardly. Nothing now can drown my eyelash paste, rub off my face powder, disturb the red design of my mouth, wrinkle my dress.

Our first quarrel: Gustavo's eyes are narrow, and his smile twisted. His precious vanity is sore, and his inferiority complex is aroused, just as we were beginning to understand each other. We had a boring session of explanation, and I finally realized I would have to be insincere and artificial—queer how people love hypocrisy. I can never say again: "Gustavo, I can't see you, I'm busy, I'm tired." No. He wants to be a duty, an obligation, and heaven help me if there is another broken engagement. But he was not happy, not confiding, and he was tactless enough to mention some friends who "spoiled" him, which immediately had the effect of killing my enthusiasm, because I dislike competition.

I met Madame Rachilde at that famous literary banquet for the Prince Cantacuzène. She wore dark red and black lace, and a sort of skullcap, red, like that of a pope. She was fat and impressive, so I bought one of her books. Alas. Echoes of some poor man's writer, sentimentality, three or four good phrases. I may have been deceived in English by the Victorians, but I cannot be taken in in French. Rachilde: mush.

October 15. Erskine's mind fascinates me. I have spent a sleepless night thinking of him. We went, the four of us, to a "boîte" [night club]. In between acts we talked. He told me that a few years ago he came to the realization that he had to be sincere about something, so he started a notebook in which he writes exactly what he thinks about everything. He talks "les yeux dans les yeux" [looking into one's eyes], and his eyes are really sad, while he smiles. I was so upset by that sadness, that smile, his talk that I decided to talk to him openly about his problem, and mine, when the opportunity came.

October 16. Gustavo again, with all his vanity and brilliancy. But suddenly I realize that only a great intellect, a fervent intellect can completely win me. Gustavo is fervent, but not great, not mature. Not a man. Yet I have promised atonement, so I am going out with him Thursday evening while Hugh and Erskine attend the Columbia University dinner. Last night Hugh and I discussed Gustavo's novel. Hugh said I could write a better one, which hurt me, because it is so, and yet I lack Gustavo's assurance and boldness. I am still smoking in the dark and talking to a wall, shopping with Mrs. Erskine and running errands. But at least I have refused to call on Mrs. S., who is expecting a baby, and on Mrs. G., who is bringing up hers, where I must hear about hospitals, regimes, a milk shortage, nurses, new teeth, etc. That, I can't stand.

October 17. My vanity is satisfied these days by the discovery that the sapphire-blue fur coat I designed last year is offered this year as the creation of the great couturiers. "It doesn't come from Lanvin," I said this morning to all the Cuban relatives, who wanted to know. "I designed it last year and wore it to death." And I feel swollen with pride, while new ideas continue to come, faster than my allowance, into my well-hatted head, which looks fragile and useless.

We said good-bye to the Sánchez family at the Gare St. Lazare. They are going back with eight trunks and less knowledge and fewer ideas than ever. They don't understand, they never will. That Hugh is in banking and progressing is the only fact they can gleefully record. What is Eduardo going to hear from them?

I think so much during the long bus rides to my dancing lesson, think of Erskine, Gustavo, Joaquin, of what I read in the

Mercure de France and the latest book, of truth, people, faces, ideas, art, design, dressing, the house, the maid, myself. When I think about myself I get sad. I see this buoyant self so clearly and wonder how I seem to others. I am alive, good, weak, complex, frank with myself in my Journal, an actress the rest of the time.

All this thinking in the bus while men brush my knee, even speak to me, touch my sleeve, all this thinking, futile and unending—not futile when I can offer it up to a man like Erskine; or through it, understand his thinking. But it brings me nothing outside of a profound ache. And Erskine would be satisfied with Nina Aguilera, ballerina española.

While Hugh and Erskine were at their Columbia University dinner, I went out with Gustavo. I knew he would imagine I was thinking: Surely he'll make love to me. I made certain I would disappoint his theory. So we started off gaily, guarded against our own mischievous imaginations. He took me to the Foire [fair] on the Place de Clichy.

"You expected me to take you to the movies and hold your hand."

"I didn't," said my eyes, faces, gestures, but so mockingly, so sure of themselves, he became angry.

"You think me incapable of falling in love with you?"

"Yes. You love somebody in New York; you told me."

"She is too far away. You are more subtle, you are an infiltration. One can't realize you suddenly, entirely. I am beginning to fall in love with you."

I laughed. As we walked, our talk was half drowned by the music of the merry-go-round. I would not become a child to please him, especially when I felt that his very black eyes and caressing voice would make me laugh. When we had seen everything, we had our fortunes told by a toothless woman. We wanted to see her blunder, so we asked to have them told together. She announced trips, no babies, good fortune, no separation, and someone who wished us bad luck. It was frightfully banal.

"Let's go to a café and talk, but not to a glary place," said Gustavo.

I suggested the Mosquée.

I teased Gustavo almost to the end, but we were, on the whole, serious. My inaccessibility tempted him. He tried to break through it. Were we truthful? He had doubts about my "coldness." His knee touched mine. My blood leaped to my face.

"I did that to shock you."

He realized he had not shocked me, but that I was sensitive. He asked: "Why do you think I did not kiss you in the taxi on the way?"

"Because you did not feel like it."

"No."

"Because it would embarrass you."

"You are wrong again. What would you do if I did it now?"

I didn't answer. So he took my hand and held it. He felt me quivering from head to foot, looked once at my face, and let my hand slip away. No puritan there, just sensitiveness, danger.

"I have broken through, I have shaken you, Anaïs."

"What have you found out?"

"We are playing with dangerous things. You are alive, Anaïs. I'm in love with you."

"Tonight, because you have nothing better to do." I surrendered once, now I escape again. I give him mocking glances. He is angry. But he remembers the quivering. So he talks about his sadness, his loneliness, his dreams. I tell him about my sadness, my loneliness, my dreams. They resemble each other; we ought to be friends.

"A cold word. For me, everything or nothing. I'll keep away. I don't want to disturb your life."

The usual banal adventure, apparently. We are acting like everybody else, half seriously, half laughing at ourselves. Underneath, a persistent current of understanding, pathetic earnestness.

October 20. Gustavo, over the telephone: "You are not alone?"

"No."

"As usual. You are too well watched, your husband, your mother, your brother. Have they found out yet what I am? Spanish, therefore a seducer of virgins. Have you been scolded?"

"No. I do as I please. Don't let your imagination go wild. Nobody is watching me, and nobody thinks that. What are you doing? That lady who wants to take you to Italy for a week, is she taking good care of you?"

"As well as she can, with limitations, since I am not crazy about her."

I felt like saying: nor about me, because I am not sensual enough. I said, "Call me up again."

I am letting Gustavo tell *me* what I think. Yesterday he

said: "You are glad because you have found something to play with, a thrill, an excitement."

"That isn't it," I said.

"You are glad then, because you have found a friend."

"Who loves me a little and won't go beyond that."

"If you wish it."

Sophistry, of course.

October 22. A successful party for the Erskines. Hugh and I danced well. Erskine and Joaquin played the piano for us. Boussie made sharp remarks, and her dear little old mother enjoyed everything. Moi j'avais le diable au corps [As for me, I was possessed]. For La Jota I made faces, naïveté and coquetry mixed. No more nervousness, a deep thrill, a feeling of plenitude. But it was impossible to know what Erskine thought and felt. Sometimes I hate Anglo-Saxons for that lack of expressiveness.

I missed Gustavo and told him so. The night at the Mosquée remains the most beautiful of the week. But I don't know yet how serious he is. I have moments of infinite sorrow in the very middle of the most brilliant hours of my life. He says he has, too. Could two sorrows of such mysterious origin make a moment of beauty?

He has lived so much more than I. I laugh so he won't find out what a child I am. I am afraid of his jaded appetite, his sensual mouth, and I can't let him find out how little I know, how much I guess at.

Last night at the theatre Erskine told me his secret, and I told him mine. He has noticed that I am going through a phase. He thinks I am under the influence of his books. He tells me the result of his philosophy to warn me. He himself has found tragedy.

"Don't you do anything foolish," he said. We talked a lot about his friend Lilith. She is like the Lilith of his book. They love each other. She writes beautifully, and she loves music. We talk always "les yeux dans les yeux," but this time he was tormenting his lower lip and looking worried and human. Whenever there was anything clever in the play we looked at each other. His mind is so intensely interesting that I envy Lilith his companionship.

"Temptation," he said, "never worried me before because it always came in such vulgar forms. But when I found my ideal . . ." He sacrifices his life to his children and remains fond of Pauline because she is so fine. He has remorse. "There is always the ghost of the wronged one between you and your love." Erskine's sadness weighs on me today. His profound idealism torments and maddens me as much as that inaccessible truth I forever seek.

October 24. I'm sick, hooray. I can write all day today. I got out of bed for dinner last night to receive Gustavo. I have read the libretto of his Egyptian opera, and I like it. "Human beings are serious, and the gods are humorous," says Gustavo. If so, they have taken the best for themselves, and it is only fair if a few great men laugh at them now and then. While Gustavo read the prologue I watched his face. It has a sort of burned-out expression, which I like. His hands are very fine. While I lie here I miss only shopping with Mrs. Erskine and two dancing lessons. I am happier brooding and writing. Yesterday I began the Second Book drawn from my Journal; it will be full of inventions, exaggerations, Imagy's life, unreality. I am beginning to feel the need of fiction, of a disguise.

Gustavo says my actions toward him are partly devilish, partly romantic, partly serious, partly playful. How well he sees through me.

I said: "Are you sure you can distinguish between deviltry and tenderness? I'll be afraid to call you up lest you think I am passionately interested in you."

"No, I know that is just friendliness."

My shawl became caught in the embroidery of my dress. "That is deviltry," he said, "because in helping you to fix it [and he helped me] you knew I would come near you and that this would upset my resolution to be circumspect." And he kissed my hand.

His sudden gesture upset me, and so does his utter frankness about himself, his occasional crudeness in speaking, his lucidity, his knowing so well I was influenced by the atmosphere of the Mosquée, his knowing the end of our adventure before it even began.

"Now I leave you to think over what I said and what you said!"

"What makes you so sure I will think about it?"

"Because I will, as soon as I get home."

He is always right. He foresees my thoughts, my impulses; he knows my childishness, my fear of certain words. "It was *pleasure* which made you blush at the Mosquée," he said, when I had written "sensitiveness."

October 27. The whole thing lies in my not getting serious, and not needing him too much. While Erskine is here I am deeply satisfied, because his mind is a perpetual miracle. The other night we were invited to hear him speak at the American Women's Club. Mellowness and wit, a capacity for expressing what he reads, and a profound sense of comedy. I have never seen eyes or mouth so rich in meaning. He read us two chapters from his *Uncle Sam.*

I said to him: "I would like to hear more about Lilith and to see some of her writing." He loves so to talk about her.

"I have nothing with me here, but I will bring you some. When I return I'll come to see you alone and we'll have a great talk about everything."

"Please," I said. He is trying to understand me. Why does he watch me? As a "case"? His books may have influenced me, but he himself does so much more.

The Embassy yesterday, hot, languid, crowded. Argentine tangos, sad singing, handsome women in black furs, jewelry, lamés and velvets. The afternoon-tea men possess the same languid, caressing manner and ardent eyes of women who are professional love-makers—a beauty sought by some, like opium, a dissolution of mind and scruples. I feel it wrapping me like a perfumed, insidious smoke. The desires of these men caress me, cling to me. Their eyes draw me. And as I am bending over the abyss of life, just to see, I feel violently called back. I pick up my gloves, my bag, my coat. I walk swiftly between the tables, seeing nothing. Fortunately, the night is cold. The perfume and the languor are brushed away. Hugh says: "Those teas bore me."

Invitations, too many invitations. We are a nice couple. Everybody likes us. We weaken. Tonight we dance for Ferrara, the Cuban Ambassador to Washington.

October 28. Yesterday's party a great success. Ferrara's eyes twinkle. Mrs. Ferrara is peaceful and a Christian Scientist. Tio Enrique is glad to be my uncle. I am asked how I make myself up to look so Spanish. My petticoat hangs now in the closet with a tear in it; we have finished talking about the party, we have slept on it, eaten the leftover cakes.

I have told Hugh the plan of my novel, which shocks him because there is no plan.

"When you think too deeply there is no end to anything," I said. "I only believe in the present moment, in the detail, in the momentary glimpse of truth."

October 31. Gustavo takes me to the Louvre. Arm in arm we stare at da Vinci's faces, talk about them, dream about them. He has a wonderful way of explaining paintings. He goes further than I do by intuition. He brings music and philosophy and poetry to bear on everything. Then we sat in a little café on the quay and talked. He walked home, to think about it all, and wrote a story about a wonderful husband, a lovely wife, who loves a certain Robert in spite of herself, and she has a child, whom the husband brings up thinking it is his own, etc., down to a tragic end.

"That might happen to us," he said.

I laughed at him: "You go too quickly. I'm only at the first chapter, about that lovely afternoon at the Louvre." His imagination certainly beats mine.

We took a walk through the Luxembourg. He began to ask me the conventional questions: "How often have you loved? Are you happy?" Which I didn't answer. And then he said: "You understand me better than anybody else, Anaïs."

Of course that touched me, and I suppose it was this which pushed us deeper into our story, deeper than the first chapter anyway. We opened up completely to each other. He said at first I seemed sweet, reticent, and puritanical. I told him at first he seemed superficial and bold. He ends with the threat that someday he is going to kiss me, to add piquancy to the situation.

I no longer live only with my mind, but with all of myself, that richly sensitive self so long ignored, sensitive to the very fingertips, vibrant, expansive, uncontrollable. Feelings, warm and immense, overwhelm me. I burn at last completely, and living is revealed to me in a thousand ways: by that moment of drowsy enchantment in the taxi after the Louvre; by that moment at home lying on my bed, when a wave of sensuousness melted my whole body. . . . Before, I gave only the cold radiation of my thoughts; I give now my burning flesh and leaping blood. I am woman.

Together, Hugh and I came to this: all writing is an *extension* of one's self. He worries about some of my writing lately, which he says is looking "wild." He offered to listen to my Journal and I put him off.

I remain confronted with this new problem just as I was peacefully undressing for bed, the problem of influence—the influence of others and of one's own self, the development of seeds which otherwise remain harmless. Et, alors, that sexy book of Gustavo's? I'll have to write a nicer journal, and I don't want to. Let the Journal be the extension, and I will go on writing more harmfully than I live. Reticence in writing induces reticence in living. Freedom in writing induces free living. Overfree living will force my writing into reticence again.

Meanwhile, Hugh gets sad. "I want to be your only friend. My work means nothing to me. You alone mean anything to me."

I have been a perfect wife for five years. What am I now?

November 3. "Leave innocence to children, who do it better than we do," I said to Gustavo. Why does he persist in liking me for my passionate flowings toward one idea when I seek the cleverness, the triviality, the playfulness, the complexities, the indecisions of the byroads. He belittles the wit and the cleverness of Erskine's vagabondage. I have had enough of unity. A man with one idea is like a horse with blinkers, which oblige him to look in front of him. I have looked in front of me with a deadening faithfulness, stumbled over many things. Now that I drop the blinkers to pry into everything, now that I have learned to talk for no purpose at all, to mask my eagerness in humorous phrases, to be interested in everything and in everybody, to appear nonchalant, to display only civilized enthusiasm, to accommodate myself to the refined cynicism of the salons, now Gustavo stirs up the old fire.

When he talks about unity I am moved. I regret having abandoned Unamuno for Erskine. I look at Gustavo's intensely brilliant eyes, his eagerness and his terrible seriousness, and I don't laugh. Comedy is not native to me; I tried to acquire it. Blind, window-breaking enthusiasms, ridiculous and futile suffering, those are my natural ways. But what is the use of struggling to be consistent?

Pauline tells me she wishes John had sown his wild oats in his youth. She sees and says things plainly. But both of them are thick-skinned at times, and jokes pass in their home which would destroy ours. The evening before he left they invited us for dinner. We drank champagne to his trip.

"May you not stay away ten years," I said, thinking of Ulysses.

"And if I do," he answered, "may it be for the same reason."

We were invited, as they said frankly, to relieve the strain of the last evening. Pauline knew about Lilith. She knew John was returning to New York to see her. She suffers and I feel sorry for her. She has a certain control which sometimes fails her.

John dotes on the children and listens with great pleasure to Graham, who has a real talent for drawing. He loves to eat, to sleep, to play the piano, and to be compared to French writers. I think his writing fertile, and superior to the French writers he admires. But I also find in it now a lack of *feeling*, which leads to sterility. Unless he gets a strong emotional shock very soon this bitterness and dryness in his writing will predominate. I have thought a lot about him. I live with his ideas.

November 5. Joaquin looks at me with reproachful eyes. "I don't like you these days. You are too flippant, too clever, too worldly, too frivolous."

I can't endure his not understanding. I try to explain: "It is a phase. I am conscious of what I am going through. I am conscious of the *end*. I haven't lost my ideals. Be patient."

He is younger than I am. I was like him at his age. I can't go back just to be with him. I must go forward all alone; I must have confidence in myself, in the life which pushes me, in the openness of my mind, in the impulses of my imagination.

I knew what I was doing when I went out in Havana society, though Charles[1] thought I was being blinded. I have never been blind. I must go in and through everything. I like to feel myself not on the shore, watching the boats sailing away, but in the sea, fighting the waves. Gilbert thinks I am dazzled by the superficial world, because I can't conceive now of desert islands with books, ink, and the prospect of a withered yellow face. I have already been a savage on a desert island (Richmond Hill). I have lived with books, bathed in ink, worshipped the inward life blindly; I have renounced half the beauty of the world (when I slapped the faces of the men who desired me). I have been the most chaste

[1] *Carlos de Cárdenas, her cousin.*

woman, the most desperate dreamer, the most innocent child, the most self-effacing sister, the most obedient daughter, the most virtuous of housewives. I feared to hurt, to disturb, to take up too much room; I left defiance, rebellion to noisier, bigger people. I had enough with being loved.

Today I am a woman. I defy the hate, the criticism, the envy, the scandalized faces around me. Even Joaquin's eyes can't stop me, though they hurt. I have my dream. I'll follow it alone, always, against the world. I haven't much self-confidence. It is the same with my dancing. Miralles thinks I am a star. I have been offered a job in the Café de Paris. Yet I was thinking of starting as a chorus girl. At last Hugh gives me permission to try the stage. Joaquin does not. Mother looks worried.

November 10. I am getting to need Gustavo, his ideas, his outbursts, his fantasies. For three afternoons we worked together on the correction of his novel. Intimacy and understanding grew from the shared work. He said at least one thing was certain: He could not live without me.

We find that we can analyze *all* that springs from our companionship without killing it. To both of us, analysis is not the destructive, deadening conclusion but the beginning of living.

He is a realist, as only a Spaniard can be sometimes. There is no word in the world he is shy of mentioning. He is amused by my innocence, by the fact that I can be made to blush against the very will of my intelligence. He likes my quickness, my understanding, my liveliness, my habit of thought.

I feel with him, too, a new perception of truth, not because he is sometimes violently truthful, but because he foresees my evasions, destroys my ways of escape, tears the veil off my phrases so I can see my ideas.[1] He needs an ear (a pretty ear it must be) and while I listen, I see a fine thread of resemblance between him and Eduardo and Enric—in the hands, in the musicality, in the sensitiveness, in the *femininity*, in the need of me, in a slight, almost mystical lack of balance. They are not steady, rooted, fixed, immutable men. They are not protectors of women. That is all they have in common.

Eduardo was sweet, helpless, poetic, weak. Enric was stronger temperamentally, emotionally, but limited intellectually. Gustavo

[1] *See similar passage on p. 144.*

looks weak but has a capacity for work; he requires tenderness and petting. He can't control life, money, events, except with his mind, but he *acts*, finishes things. He has his share of deviltry and cruelty. He has many of women's faults. But I know how to take him—as a child, sometimes, as a woman, as a writer; and how glad he is when I don't take his words literally but pursue with that playing with phrases, of which we are both fond. Yes, I understand him. I see through his cynicism to his naïveté. I am not impressed with the boldness of his writing. I don't try to fit him into a design. I just follow his pranks and tricks, the changes and motions of his mind, his elastic mind. He is not a sword swallower, not red blooded, and yet not empty of all that stuffs a man: love, egoism, desire for admiration, for greatness. He breathes deeply when he talks of greatness. He has a great man's capacity for great feelings and thoughts. His responsiveness to life is absolute. Will he make art of it?

Here is my pretty ear, my help, my companionship. But no man, either weak or strong, dreamer or realist, can endure a woman who belongs to herself.

November 11. We met last night a Mrs. Velasco, really beautiful *and* intelligent. I was charmed with her in so many ways. And sad. Because I am only beautiful at moments, here and there, by a trick of clothes, or expression, or emotion. She was really absolutely beautiful, immutably so. While I have my days, my face changes perpetually, with an idea, with a hat which invokes the East, with the expression of my dancing. Looked at coldly, I have a small face suggestive of old paintings but not strictly classical, fine features and big eyes but teeth like a mouse's, just a hint of sauciness in the nose, and hair that is neither black nor blond. How often I have described myself but never with such cynicism. I have met many handsome women I never think of again because they were not interesting, but when I meet someone who is both intelligent and lovely, then I feel Hugh did not get much out of life.

November 12. Consolation. I am loved. I am, to Gustavo, a Botticelli. I have, according to him, a beautiful body. I can make him miserable or happy. After those three days of work, which sealed our understanding, we can't stop teasing and talking and flirting.

He takes a slightly superior tone to tell me, the child, stories meant to instruct me in the knowledge of men—that is, of himself.

The only story he will not make up for me is that of a separation. He doesn't see anything amusing about that.

"And yet, and yet," I said, "I want to give you something *new*. You have been loved already, you have lived with married women, you have been a lover and a seducer of virgins. . . . I'll be *different*."

"Do anything you please except drop me. Not that."

Alas, his face was really serious. Does he take stories seriously?

November 14. At Antonio's concert, d'Indy sitting four rows ahead of us; all Antonio's friends; Joaquin clapping his hands to pieces. Gustavo sits at my right, critical, analytical, while the music pours over me like a balm. The flute, plaintive, solitary, with the sweetness of singing pain, almost made me weep.

I met Bonifacio, the dancer, after the concert, a small, slender, serious young man. Extremely likable. Gustavo sulks because Mother is icy toward him, and my sweetness doesn't calm his ruffled feathers. I try to help him by introducing him here and there. He is on the whole an unhappy man, oversensitive and vain. The only story which is really true is that he is going to make me suffer.

Today in a café, near the Odéon, we met secretly. He said that he loved me because I had the kind of physical beauty he admired, because I had intelligence and wisdom, because, in spite of that, I was *intensely feminine*, very seductive, and a little wicked. And when I had told him what I liked in him, he said, "How do you feel about my faults?"

"I understand them, don't mind them, accept them. Mine you don't know yet, but they will show up."

Driven out of the café by a bunch of noisy students, we walked about in the rain. I said: "You have been romantic today, walking in the rain, oblivious to surroundings."

"Women do these things naturally for the person they like. That is what I love in them. They dare everything, defy everything, forget everything. When a man does the same thing he is termed romantic." He had his novel under his arm, and was going later to visit his publisher. I talked to him as I do to only a few people. In return he showed me what he shows to only a few people: tenderness and sincerity. His black hat, black hair, black eyes, and very white face make most other faces look empty.

November 21. Took a walk through the Bois with Gustavo. He said, "Explain to me why Joaquin and your mother dislike me so much."

"Because your vehemence and strongly accentuated personality demand equally strong and accentuated feelings. People either hate you or love you. You are terribly frank, terribly critical, you *see* everything and say so. . . ."

"But I am good at heart, really."

"Of course. I know that, but not everybody does."

A squeeze of the arm. Understanding. Satisfaction. The autumn leaves smell poignantly. Twilight. "The hour loved best by all women," says Gustavo. So I make again the discovery that I am feminine.

The café. More talk. I couldn't add up now the number of cafés crèmes I have absorbed this year at corner tables, feeling tossed up like driftwood, homeless, husbandless, after riding for hours on the waves of adventure. No, the real shipwrecky feeling comes when I get home, to my account book, to the thirty pages of my novel, to Mother's consulation on the next dress, to Thorvald's definition of intelligence, "capacity to make money," and to Hugh's calculations for a peaceful and comfortable retirement.

November 22. What I want sounds very simple, and yet I can't get it: to have friends; to go out, to cafés or plays or in taxis, or to the Bois; to live, to be intimate with men without falling immediately into complications.

"My dear, don't flirt, and don't let them make love to you."

But then I cannot be close to them. A little love helps a lot, but then it gets bigger, and, alas, I find myself floating in the usual story.

"Be cynical, be indifferent."

I am. I cheat. I elude the ultimate surrender, the direct questions, the dangerous places and hours. I give only the little promises, the hand, the glance, which can fill at least an hour and postpone the climax. If I didn't, I wouldn't have any friends. That word in my vocabulary makes every man laugh. I contradict the anodynic effect of it by my softness, my perfume, my femininity.

Evening: My shopping is not real shopping. Ideas buzz into my head like insects, and I go about digging. I choose quickly, always know what I want, never have regrets, buy what makes others say: "Where on earth did you find this?" I am really watching faces, listening to conversations, evolving theories, building stories.

And yet my novel is terrible. Thirty-five pages of rot. Darling Journal, I am punished for wanting to divorce you. I am really a damn sentimentalist, trying to be clever. I know only myself well. I should mind my own business.

November 26. From the New York *Herald*, Paris, November 25: "Brilliant reception yesterday at the home of M. and Madame Armand Godoy. . . . M. and Madame Guiler danced with great success and the pianist Nin-Culmell was strongly applauded."

This was the greatest success of our dancing career, judging by the quality of the compliments we received.

Then last night we danced for Bonifacio. Surprise! He is delighted, enthusiastic, shouts encore for the Jota, says this is no amateur work, dwells on my natural ability, expressiveness, animation. "Comme une couleuvre" [Like a serpent], says Leyritz, the sculptor. Antonio remarks, "Great progress made in seductiveness." Joaquin kisses me.

Bonifacio's admiration is a great triumph, because we disagree on methods of dancing: he is a modernist. For that reason he will not give me a job until he modernizes me, my dances, and I won't do it, not until I myself understand and feel this new concept sincerely.

Hugh is immensely proud of me. Today all my dresses and petticoats are squeezed back into my closet. We are preparing to leave for Nice and Monte Carlo "on business."

I write my book everywhere, in the bus, on my dressing table, in bed. Learning to discard and to develop. My defects are: impatience with details, reticence in development. I see and think far more than I write, due to a habit of writing for myself, when I know what I mean. It has all been written mentally in French, then translated.

November 30. Sadness, excitement, and tension yesterday when Gustavo and I spent our last afternoon together reading over my Journal and novel.

"Our two enthusiasms would explode the world," we said.

"What I could do with your faith," he said. Our minds are terribly alike. We both have that self-possession which made Enric say I couldn't love, but which is merely the livingness of the intellect. I always leave him in time to cool myself off. But I feel a terrible heart-rending at giving up a mystery, half solved.

Tomorrow morning I will regret Gustavo less. His pent-up, half-expressed, or suddenly flaring love will not upset the balance of my life. And this perpetual "I need you" is such an old and such an irresistible trap.

December 1. Monte Carlo, Hôtel de Paris. Evening: A day spent alone. Like a spider I have woven my web all about me, thoughts chained one to another, delicately, beginning with my lunch alone, my drowsy rest in the room, my walk between the sea and the cactus and pines, and my reading of [Francis] Carco. I love his writing because of his power to convince me of places, faces, and feelings I do not know.

I feel all Carco's moods more keenly in this hotel room, alone, in a strange city, his multiple living, his despair, his way of *doping himself with experiences.* How else to describe these half dreams? I drug myself with images, words, sensations. Everything thickens this veil between me and facts.

"Carco is simply a rotter," I have heard. There is always a diabolical light around favored heads, these people who come from nowhere, to me; because no one told me about Carco. I went blindly to his books, understood them, sought more of them, alone; the same with Colette, whose five senses are more miraculously sensitive than anybody else's in the world. Thus, too, I follow my own ghosts, my own precious mysteries.

"Me" in a red-and-black Grecian dress, having dinner in the Hôtel de Paris. Too many waiters—one to light my cigarette; one to pour water; one to present the meat, another the desserts, and another the bill. I try pathetically to find a real meal in this dangerously deceptive luxury. Why does my potato salad taste of mint, why do my chops look like a flower, why are the beets sliced paper thin, and why does the bread vanish with a sound of crisp paper? Millions of things are brought on rolling tables, and I find nothing real. Sauces, sauces, herbs, everything finely chopped, unseemingly red, unnaturally pink, impossibly yellow. To tease the appetite of rich people, everything must taste like something else. I sit with dignity, listening to anemic music; I smoke stoically. Impeccable nails, idle hands, jewels. Very high ceilings arch over my head, sculptured, carved, gilded. A waiter has just poured plain water with such an absorbed air that I am sure it is going to taste like champagne.

December 4. Conscientiously, religiously, I worship the Sun, my God, the God of my moods, the only God. I open the shutters in the morning with a keen joy. It shines straight into my eyes, over the sea, falls at once over the brown rug, the blue chairs, and the yellow quilt. The breakfast tray is transformed; the butter shines, the milk radiates. We lie in a bed of snow and gold.

I have seen the gamblers at the Casino, crowding around enormous green tables, men and women of all ages and classes. I do not like their faces. And as for the game, I prefer the hazards, excitements, fears, doubts, intoxications, joys, despairs of love. But here they are, swayed by a great power, fascinated, drugged.

I was tempted. Hugh would have let me throw away all the money he has so carefully earned—that is his way—to see pleasure and life on my face. I had a pang of disgust, pulled myself together, and asked him to take me home.

All around me I hear talk about the game—in the room next to ours, at the table in the dining room, on the streets, on the benches along the promenade. If in Montparnasse we see the whims and fantasies of poverty, here are those of riches. There is an old woman in the dining room who looks like a witch. She is always cold, employs six waiters constantly during her lunch, sends for scarves, veils, pillows, scolds and tyrannizes. I see many ill-assorted groups, no sense of class. The luxury stands: overornamented and gilded hotels, the rich, natural beauty of the sea, trees, hills. At least I am getting the conventional education of a novelist. I feel I have seen the world, more or less, which means nothing to me and to the books I will write, since in everything and in everybody I always see something else.

Those who take a walk at four o'clock, at twilight, see Imagy sitting alone, all in white, and looking down at the ground when men pass. But she is not alone. She talks to Gustavo.

I hate the word "God" applied to the mystery I love. I don't mind so much applying it to the elements, to the sun, because it defines beauty and power in the sun, in love, in us. I see the unity and I have no name for it. We are gods; only through us are these forces manifested. But don't say God to me, God the bearded old man.

"You are so literal," says Hugh reproachfully when I talked about this with him. We were having lunch in a small place on the quay, under an orange awning. Orange, blue sky, white pavement. Two yachts tied to the pier. That vivid coloring gives me shivers of pleasure. It was there before my eyes all day, even at twilight when I was walking back slowly to the hotel.

Gustavo, I would have liked to have you here, walking with me, seeing the orange and blue and gold fade into a dark blue and purple darkness, seeing the red, yellow, and purple lights of the city burst and crown the bay, seeing the black cactus spread against cream walls, dwarf trees projected heavy and still over the sea, cars purring up the hilly road to the peak of gilded luxury, the Casino and the Hôtel de Paris. My walk is slow and languid. When I am alone I take myself back, gather myself up; I could sleep in a circle, like a cat, self-possessed, selfish, calm. I stand now before the mirror and say: "I don't love anybody just now." I have become unreal with so much weaving of my own dreams, being so much with myself, and yet away from myself, because I don't feel my body. If Gustavo were here he would remind me of it. His hands would impulsively touch me, his shoulders would press mine, even his mouth would come so near, so near, and his desire would surround me with heat and fever.

"Dear pussycat," scolds the Humorous Banker, "we are here for business. Get dressed tonight. We dine with the Stewarts."

"No, no, no. Didn't you love our lunch alone, there on the quay, and our talk about God, and my nice white ensemble, and the very little table where there was no room for my bag?"

"Yes, of course. But you know this has been a great day."

"For the Bank?"

"Yes. Listen."

Imagy, don't lie in a circle like a well-fed and indifferent cat. Don the Grecian dress, brush your curls, shine your nails against your husband's woollen underwear, put on your cheap jewelry. I still have that orange awning, the sky, the sea, the sun, the pavement before my eyes; my walk with a Gustavo who does not love me, who is interested in the cactus spread like a tense, giant animal hand with sharp nails.

December 5. Last night Hugh said: "You have never looked more beautiful. Your face looks waxen."

This is *my* place, my climate, the place where I *feel* beautiful. My blood flows evenly, not in cold and fitful patches as in Paris. My thoughts flow evenly too. I feel clothed in a brilliant lamé like the sea, intoxicated with light.

Colette and I have points of resemblance: Colette has a pointed chin. I have one. Colette loves cats. I love cats. Colette is like a cat. I am like a cat.

But she says mon derrière and I never mention it. She loves women. I love men.

Colette smells, touches, sees everything. As I do. Colette is individual. So am I. Colette is independent. Ditto. Colette is saucy. Ditto.

Only, she grew up differently, in the country, familiar with animals, with a physical, more natural connection with everything. I grew up as I could, Mother naïve. Colette read everything; alas, I read English. Colette calls a spade a spade, and worse. I am shy. She was human every moment. I passed through a phase of asceticism. No intellectual pose in Colette; in me, yes, even a tendency to moralize. She has the gift of mockery. I am sentimental. She lived. I thought too much.

But I'm catching up now. (I was franker, sharper in my earlier Journal in French, until I fell into Victorianism. Can I ever make up for that blunder?) Colette writes in French, thank God! English is such an evasive language. Colette, you are miraculous. I am not. But I know how to appreciate you.

We are both at our best writing about ourselves. Half humorously, half tenderly, she reiterates her traits and physical attributes: animal grace, pointed chin, long eyes, supple figure, charm. As for my favorite possessions (did I say I was jealous of a really static beauty? I didn't mean it), I think the only things I really dislike are my mouse-teeth and my overfine hair, and I always wished my nose pointed down like the Spaniards' and that I had smaller hands and ample breasts.

Oh, well, everything you live with for a long time you get to love, even inanimate furniture, and everything has memories. . . . Enric pulled my hair, painters loved my hands, Boris [Hoppe] would lose his head when I smiled. Speak, Colette, your frankness has shaken me like a powerful wind. I haven't really got *it*.

Colette, you are more real than I, more human. Both your feet are on the earth. I have one leg halfway out, always ready to run off. You know how to brush off the foam from your enthusiasms and drink only the real thing. I swallow foam and all.

As a result I am a little crazier than you are, and I am not always entirely where I seem to be. You don't leave Paris, for example. And you never have to get your feet wet in order to find yourself again.

I would like to draw close to you. I want to be a woman, *altogether* woman.

December 8. A day of exultation about my book. After a week of thinking fitfully about it, I have reached a new concept. In my real Journal I am sentimental about myself. In the book I will laugh at myself. Because there is nothing funnier than a naturally *believing* person trying to be skeptical. There is nothing funnier than my restlessness. Nobody worthier of being tricked. *So* the Humorous Banker will play the trick and give me the freedom I pine for!

I write and tear up, write and tear up. Discovered I can only work with interest and enthusiasm. What I do in other moods is useless. Yesterday after working three hours I suddenly grew cold and disgusted. Whatever I do at such a moment is destructive and flat. I will achieve fresh, living writing but never the other kind. I really don't *work*—I create. And that's all. I am very weak in rewriting, polishing. And then I am always watched by the Critic in me. I think I had better stick to dancing.

December 11. Our last day. No sunshine, so my regrets are subdued. Hugh says we will come back. I love this place. I have lived here with myself and my thoughts, and I do know how to entertain myself successfully. Everything amuses me: my fervent desire for skepticism, my occasional deviltry, my ridiculous sentimentality, my abnormal susceptibility to color, sounds, smells, cheap music. . . Suddenly the idea of painting the ridiculous side of myself and making the Humorous Banker the great character of my novel fascinates and hurts me. I think it is the first time I have laughed at myself. I see so well the foolishness of my actions. But I can't stop them. Feeling is stronger in me than thought.

December 13. Paris. Arrived Wednesday. I ran to the telephone, sought out Gustavo, walked into the lion's mouth. Although desperately busy with Christmas shopping, letter writing, and addressing Xmas cards I found time to see him, talk to him, to begin again the same old round of fencing and parrying with words while our feelings belie us, and go further than our intentions. Neither one of us could sleep that night, wondering what had become of our joyous flirtation of the first days. But Hugh and I are going back to Monte Carlo, and this second trip may cure me.

Erskine is here. Joaquin works with Bonifacio. Hugh talks about the Bank, but cuddles and spoils me. I have lost my sense of humor and gained two kilos.

December 25. Hôtel Eden, Cap d'Ail. An important thing happened in Paris. John came to see me alone, and I became his confidante and he my friend. *A day I have long desired.* I read to him from my Journal about himself. He questioned me for more details. I told him what I thought of his face, character, and ideas. When I lost my shyness, I talked about my problems. He said: "If you will forgive me for saying so, these things you worry about seem unessential to me. Hugh is a great man. You are his ideal. He loves you. Meanwhile, remember, you are extremely pretty, and you have an extraordinary amount of charm—all men will take pleasure in hunting you down. To be loved is a great temptation, and very flattering but . . ."

I understand him so well he did not need to finish his phrase. I want him to like me. We started with the utmost frankness from the very beginning. But when I read him from my Journal, merely to nourish our conversation, his attention was more taken with style, and he said: "beautiful, beautiful."

Though I read him only eight pages or so he commented on my "clarity" and told Hugh afterward: "She is a genius. All she needs is to find herself now and her writing will *coagulate* into something absolutely her own."

I was so upset by his judgment that I couldn't sleep.

Hugh said the next morning: "What will you work on during our vacation?" I answered: "I will try to coagulate." But I was not laughing. John has always been my most discerning critic. I will never forget how he put his finger on my "reticence" and cured me. I told him so.

Since that afternoon I have felt my enthusiasm for him reach its highest point and also a permanent, immutable place in my life. Because now I know the man, I know his life, I know his contradictions, his character, his feelings. When I read him about himself he was struck with the truth of what I said. (I feel with him a new perception of truth, because he foresees evasions, destroys all ways of escape.)

"I wish," he said, "you would keep these things for my biography after I die. You seem to know so well not so much what I *have* done, because I don't think I have done it yet, but what I most want to do."

He was shocked and startled that I should have discovered bitterness in his writing. He did not think it had shown through. He said, half regretfully, half admiringly: "My, but you're a sensitive reader. I am not by nature a bitter man."

"Of course not," I said impulsively, thinking of his natural kindness, generosity, and interest in other people, his patience with his students and disciples.

I told him that if Lilith did not write his biography I would. "Oh, she is a woman of action," he said. "She is more preoccupied with *living* my biography."

He said about the first time we met, five years ago in New York at lunch, that I looked extremely fine but when he heard of the various experiences I had already had the thought: But why doesn't it show more?

Finally I told him about my little problems. "I have no sentimental blindness about myself. I am not posing as a misunderstood or neglected wife. Nobody understands or loves me as well as Hugh, but still *I get into trouble*. I am attracted to so many things, to musicality, to ideas, to creativeness. You *know* I really seek intellectual companionship." My face was aflame with sincerity, and John had to believe me. He said: "I know."

John loves to talk about Lilith. She is over forty. Not strictly beautiful in features but she is tall and splendid. I see a generous mouth in her photograph and clear eyes. John seemed shocked that I should express a spontaneous desire to meet her someday.

"You are Pauline's friend," he said, with a return of his New England scruples, which annoyed me.

"Will you think me too French if I serve as an alibi when you want to see her?" (Lilith is in Paris now.) I feel French, and yet absolutely sincere. John realized this, and accepted, with his logic this time, a situation his character cannot endure. Each of us can see the other person's problems so clearly, and we are so blind about our own!

❧ 1 9 2 9 ❧

January 9. Paris. The year began with a triumph for my "great man," who was made sub-manager of the Branch, and who received a new raise in salary—the whole thing due to his vision and initiative. I feel as proud of him as if he had written a book, because I have seen him apply to banking the imaginative and creative forces of an artist. The confirmation of the news came to us while we were in Cap d'Ail, where we attempted a vacation and failed. I was ill for a week. Hugh had lumbago. The weather was cold and gray. My only joys were ravenous reading and three parties at which I displayed a coquetry which brought on complications. A bad beginning, but I am not superstitious and hope to improve in conduct the rest of the year.

As a final misfortune I finished my Journal no. 26, and since I can't write my Journal in anything but the consecrated pages, I languished, brooded, wrote nothing and longed for home. At last we came back. And then I had regrets—I missed the lack of domestic responsibilities, the luxurious hotel, the five musicians, the dancing in the evening, the walks downhill to the sea, the odd plants, the occasional sunshine, and my solitude.

I have already seen John and Gustavo. I am in a social mood, hungry for talk and excitement, very unhappy and very happy. Unhappy to admit that life subjugates my emotions in spite of my lucidity; I am not as strong as John or as good as Hugh. Happy to discover my power to please increasing and my courage to face criticism. Now that I am no longer reticent I receive plenty of hard criticism. Before, when I was sweet and unobtrusive, everybody liked me. I knew it, and felt I couldn't live without approbation. Today I live without it, though it hurts. Mother thinks I am "hors de mon assiette" [out of sorts]. Joaquin condemns my liveliness, Hugh confesses my expression is changing, Gustavo accuses me of being unfaithful, because I received John alone.

There was one day in the hotel when I could have written a book. The day had been long and I had spent my time magnifying realistic details while my cold prevented me from embroidering anything with imagination. I stared persistently at the bottle of eucalyptus and at the glass of Vichy, listened to my neighbors: the man was ransacking the drawers of his trunk and the lady was humming "Ol' Man River" (this immediately fixes the epoch of my story as 1928).

But however ill I am, I can never reach abject misery and helplessness. I love sadness, but not weakness. An overdose of negative, passive, fatalistic, realistic living is repulsive to me. I love action. Jumping into the river is not action; it is madness. Particularly when there is so much to do and see and smell and hear. The illness of timidity is especially irritating to me because I went through it and I have relapses.

The morning after *three nights before* is something to write about. The proverbial headache, I observed, was not so painful and I did not require towels and ice. I was sorry, because white is becoming to me, and it was in a long white dress I conquered my Lawyer. I did drink all of a bottle of champagne—I became drunk by premeditation, at the idea of having to pass the evening with bankers and bankers' wives; I was afraid of being bored. Besides, I had been ill and felt the need of artificial strength. So we entertained nine bankers and wives at our hotel. The next evening they entertained us at the Hôtel de Paris, and then the Lawyer entertained us at the Negresco in Nice. With the champagne, twelve hours of dancing, good music, a white evening dress, a red carnation, Molyneux "Fête" perfume, pink and yellow balloons, I turned the head of a rich forty-eight-year-old lawyer from New York, Mr. F. We started to flirt merely to liven up the dinner. He seemed a fit and able partner to the game, and a man who would never bother too much about one woman on account of a general interest in all of them. I must add that he was bald, but a good dancer, fond of actresses, of Personality, a good critic of ladies, and I never could resist tempting a connoisseur, just as a matter of statistics: I always want to know how I rate.

By the third evening he was out of my control. I couldn't keep him outside the half-yard distance I usually insist on, his eyes were overbold, his hands restless, his brain unsteady and his remarks insidious. And I was stupidly surprised at the effects of such harmless beginnings. After all, I talked to amuse him. He was planning a trip to Egypt and Spain and offered to give them up to *see* me in Paris. Here, I was really firm and showed him I was not serious. I probably won't see him again, but he has the honor of having scared me off flirting—for a few days.

Why a page to such nonsense? Because it is new to me. Frailness of conduct interests me more than immortality. There must be an attraction to the frailness, since we sometimes give up immortality for it.

Deflation—after the first exhilarating contact with Paris, my friends, my dancing. Experienced a physical pain in myself yesterday accompanying a sudden and unreasonable desire to see Gustavo, whom I had seen the day before. I am curious about his love of me, as if it were a strange, impersonal thing. To divert my thoughts from it, I turn to other occupations.

Discovered Gilbert writing a truly fine book on Spain, poetic form, touched by mysticism, irony, appreciation of surface and of depths. The minute he showed me three pages I judged it to be something good and showed an enthusiasm which led him to finish the book in less than a month. He came two or three mornings to read me from it. I forgave him then for having failed to charm me, and for always presenting *with creation* a full list of his laboratory accessories.

I am becoming tolerant of the mechanics of writing. But I am glad to notice John is equally independent of aesthetics and forms. No one could be more critical, more scholastic, and yet give a true place to the means. He seems so utterly free of it. He never gives the impression of a second thought about composition. I have three chapters of his *Uncle Sam,* and the growing conviction that I could write his life by gleanings from his own writings!

Did I write deflation? I felt it only for a second. Cold and fog are torture for me and they sometimes flatten out my spirits, but my more normal state is: a keen elation at the discovery that I now possess the power of irony, that I can upset the hold of tragedy on my imagination by self-mockery, that I can see through the poses of others, that I can understand the doubts of others and yet *believe,* believe in life, people, myself, beauty, the ideal. The most mystical thing of all is the effect of my belief on Gilbert, who writes his book by the heat of it; on Gustavo, who rushes home to work after he talks with me; on Miralles, who takes up his teaching with new vigor; on Richard, who embarks courageously on my religion of self-development; and this force I give frightens me because I feel that if I should "fail" in my own eyes by a crime against the ideal, I will lose it, lose my miraculous power, and the justification of my existence. The power to work miracles was denied to the unbelievers and the impure. Is my abnormal capacity for passion an impurity?

The criticism which hurts me most is that of superficiality, because I *shine* superficially and keep the rest for my Journal. Also because I empty out the heavy sadnesses into phrases and go on living and looking for other sadnesses. Gilbert thinks me a lightweight intellect. He thinks I *only* see the joy of color and dancing in Spain—my Spain. I remember now Gustavo gave me the same impression, and I made that mistake about him. I thought I could brave criticism, but I find myself unhappy and sore, because I make such tremendous, such intense efforts to understand the true inner self of others.

When I draw Gustavo I feel like pressing down heavily on my pen to make dark lines. His versatile nature is like mine, only more highly colored, more powerfully accentuated—the swift, the critical, the impulsive in him is more unfettered. When his mind leaps to some idea, something unexpected, unreal, or so piercingly lucid and cynical, or poetic and fantastic, I follow him, though some details of his private life worry me: his incapacity to bow to discipline, to labor, as Hugh does, to sacrifice his liberty so as not to have to depend on others for his material existence. But can you be intellectually free and fertile and sensitive while entirely disciplined? I admire so much those who are, who control the terrestrial and the divine together.

The day Gustavo accepted Hugh's help, while loving me, something happened to me. Hugh in giving, while knowing, was so divinely generous. I was humiliated by Gustavo's weakness, although it seems inevitably to be a part of such men. All I feel, at the moment of their distress, is a strong desire to help. Once or twice I have compared myself to them, thinking that, after all, I was one of the helpless ones, cared for by Hugh on account of my sex—but no, I know I am not. In New York I worked harder than any other girl posing or modeling. Though I wrote in lunch hours, dreamed, I was never late, I was never indifferent. I gave all my strength, I sympathized with the artists. Conscientious—like a little bourgeoise, industrious. Why talk about these things? I am deeply unhappy to be analyzing a person I am fond of, as if it were an act of disloyalty. One could believe I am trying to reason myself out of an emotional attitude. I can't. When Gustavo says, "May I come today—estoy loco por verte" [I'm crazy to see you], I say: "Come." And break all my other engagements.

We always begin intellectually and ceremoniously. He kisses my hand and returns the two or three books he has borrowed, with comments. While we argue I take his coat and hat, arrange the pillows on the couch, light a cigarette. He reads me from his writings. He asks for my Journal. I refuse. We quarrel. I bring it down, pick out personal and impersonal things. He likes my thoughts, but he does not think me a genius—I don't mind. We have coffee and brioche. He tells me "stories." We have little scenes of jealousy, of teasing. He threatens to marry a small, fat, faithful Spanish woman who will stay home, never think, and believe him a god.

"But you will get tired of her in a year."

"Oh, no, I'll go off and visit women like you."

By that he insinuates that I can be a mistress but not a wife, which amuses me. At the same time the first thing he intends to do when he has money is to carry me off. Yet I tell him plainly I have no intention of moving and of having an ordinary love affair. I am safe, since he has barely enough to live on and owns but a small room in a hotel, where he freezes. I sent him an electric heater. He brings me the first mimosa.

Last night Godoy read us his poem on the "Elements," a superb, cosmic, touching piece of work. Burns's poems were on his desk and Hugh asked him why. He then told us the story of his fortune. "I owe it to a phrase of Burns in which he said money was necessary to an artist because he needed independence more than any man. I was fourteen and had been writing poetry from the age of ten. I decided to begin to work. Spoke to my father. This was in Lima. He sent me to a small bank branch, three days' trip from the capital. I couldn't even multiply. I learned banking at night. In three weeks I knew it. The bookkeeper was bad, and I was given his place. Later I became the master. I saved money. Went back to Lima to improve my situation. Followed a man who was going to open a bank in Havana. The affair fell through. My father ordered me to come home, but I disobeyed. He cut off my allowance. The money my mother sent me secretly I proudly returned, and I ate only once a day. I got a job in a tobacco factory. Then in a bank. Meanwhile, I married. Suddenly I made a good investment. I left Havana and gave myself up to poetry again." He quoted the poem in Spanish in which he sings his return to poetry.

He called us a sensitive audience, enjoyed our emotion, and advised us to read *Les Termites* by Maeterlinck, and Silva, the poet whom he loves to translate. Gilbert talked all the way home of Whitman, Poe, and Moody, and disregarded my desire for silence. Joaquin made spiritually beautiful remarks which lacked reason and logic. Fortunately, he is another I understand in spite of himself.

I suppose that although I spend so much time explaining myself, others will interpret me in their own way. I say that sadly, because the only man who understands me is working in a bank.

And yet, with all the best will in the world I can't help getting *bored* with his work because he overdoses me. To please him I have trained myself to understand all that goes on inside the Bank. I am well informed, I know all the men, the routine, the problems, the departments, the clients; I know so much that Hugh has sometimes asked my advice, and he always asks my opinion of the men he has to handle and work with. Why won't he understand how much *dryness* there is to banking for a person like me? He spares me nothing.

We are in bed. He thinks himself wronged because after an hour I asked him to talk of something else. He admitted the other day that the big effort had been made for his promotion, the strain was over, and he would begin to enjoy life. But nothing has changed. I have a desire to receive friends, and he is tired, indifferent. I am not complaining but giving the only justification I know for some of my actions. May I be forgiven for my *vagabondage*.

A corner of the world I love is near the Place de Clichy, Rue de Liège and Rue de Clichy, where I go for dance lessons. There is a little bakery where I have coffee and brioche, a bookstore where I borrow modern books, a jewelry shop where I have my earrings and bracelets repaired, a shop of modern artwork which evocates Egypt for me. The bus that takes me there is full of special people. Many of them get off at the Apollo and the Casino. While we stop there, I sit in the glare of signpost lights and feel a desire for the stage. I like the shoe dealers and hat makers who ask me, "Are you from the Casino?" I live, in that section, some of my dreams—cheap dreams of heavy make-up, brilliant lights, a dark audience applauding, and, backstage, disappointments and people whose hardness still has the power to surprise me.

I would chose black velvet among all the other stuffs in the world. I embroider too many paillettes, these days. My eyes are tired of their glare. In star shapes, sunbursts, serpents, I see the symbols of a fantastic destiny. When I walk alone, quickly, because it is cold, in these sad streets of Paris with their fog-colored houses, my eyes seek the lights, crude artificial lights, illuminating drugstores, hot-water bags, toothbrushes dancing on soaps; endlessly circling Michelin tires; burning in red darts down the dark stairs of the Métro; jumping and skipping for the Revue de Paris; shining white on imitation jewelry. All in black, I follow the lights. I glance critically at the shop windows. A young man stops me; a burned-up face, burned-up with cheap living, a handsome face, lined before its time, with eyes that have seen everything. He smiles a smile that whips you with its humiliating lucidity, certain of its charm. "Tu es trop jolie pour te promener seule" [You are too pretty to walk alone]. I decide to cross the street. I look to the right and to the left, swiftly. I step forward. But a taxi, which has been parked, suddenly backs out. It touches me, barely. The young man pulls me back in time, without a smile, without a word. I dart across the street again, walk without looking at the shops.

I was a little late for my lesson. When I came out, the evening mist had dimmed the lights, a mist that does not come down from the skies but rises like the breath of the earth, through the hard pavements.

January 12. I read with passionate interest Herriot's life of Madame Récamier, taking a greater interest in what it reveals of Madame de Staël. I am filled with the realization that in some ways I resemble these two women and that their lives are what I need to encourage me. The *purity* of biographies is going to turn me away definitely from novels. I have read few things as impressive and lasting as the life of *Zélide*, Benjamin Constant's *Adolphe*, this history of Mme. Récamier, and of Keats, the journal of Marie Bashkirtsev and Katherine Mansfield, and others of the same kind.

The life of the salon does not appeal to me as a life occupation. Mme. Récamier stayed at home most of the time, had things read to her, wrote letters, intrigued to protect her friends, but led, as a whole, a passive life, a life of influence on others, in which I could not find a sufficient intellectual satisfaction. Political movements were given too large a place. I admire her beauty, her charm, her genius as a confidante, as a "trait d'union" [link] between great men, her genius for friendship. I would prefer to see her friends "en mouvement" [in motion] for something other than political intrigue. France, who has been more preoccupied with small intrigues than any other nation, does not govern herself any more wisely for it. It must be that France loves intrigue for its own sake, like talking.

Persecutions by the family because of my unwise and bohemian choice of friends. For Gustavo's sake I think I have suffered everything. The hardest attack today from Mother, in tears. I discover violent opposition from Gilbert; Joaquin also is against him. And I have guessed John to be theoretically opposed. Hugh wants above all to please me, but he can no longer disguise his disapproval. As none of them know Récamier's life, I can't tell them that she had a "tendresse passionnée" [passionate fondness] for Chateaubriand, who was, as far as I can see, an impossible and detestable character. I haven't a "tendresse passionnée" and Gustavo does not have a detestable character. But so the situation appears to others. I do lack wisdom to make no secret of my impulses, and the more meanly Gustavo is persecuted, the more naturally and warmly I defend him. Our "séances" [sessions] of reading, coffee drinking, and badinage seem no less than a tragedy to Mother. She puts the whole world on my shoulder to crush me down: Hugh's reputation and dignity, criticism of all my other friends, bad example for Joaquin, bad risks for my morality.

Now I feel the issue is not between Gustavo and Mother or Hugh, but between Gustavo and John. Must there be a choice? I don't feel that any of this talk changes my opinion of Gustavo, but I suffer just the same, because I cannot bear to hurt Mother or Hugh, nor to lose John's respect. If Gustavo were rich, independent, and happy, I could more easily give him up, but the only thing he has now is my interest.

Willing at least to compromise, I decided to see him fewer than three times a week. We met yesterday at four at the Lutetia café. I felt cheerless and discouraged. But he was sizzling and had a new chapter of his second book to read me. We forgot our coffee. I read with him over his shoulder. Each time I have decided to like him less, he has charmed me.

But I worship Hugh, Hugh's energy and Hugh's greatness of heart. I suffer to see him tired, although he *would work just the same if I were not there.*

I suffer to see him silent—happy but inexpressive, content that all the ideas should come from me, and it is his tranquillity which sometimes makes me sad and lonely, his great interest is his work. Fundamentally, he is sounder and richer in thought than anybody—he understands music, philosophy, religion, poetry, mysticism, literature, psychology. But on a million things he has no opinion.

The effect of life on him is not a brilliant response, not a colored enthusiasm, but a misty appreciation, a passive and calm rumination.

If I turn elsewhere for the kind of stirring creativeness such as John has to the highest degree, may I be forgiven. I am cursed by a perpetually starved mind. I would like to love Hugh better, absolutely, uniquely. The danger with me is that my intellectual enthusiasms are colored with tenderness, with pity, with the desire to help. I have already discovered that what I give to others does not impoverish Hugh—up to a certain point. A dangerous discovery. I must understand him better—there are so many kinds of greatness; his is almost mystical, self-effacing, obscured to ordinary eyes, not brilliant, not startling, but deep and so unbelievably *fine*.

January 16. Nobody understands that if Gustavo is not satisfying, I am the one who suffers from his shortcomings; and that what he does give me is precious, that the fact that he understands me *pretty well* is already a miracle, that I need *special* friends, that I can't like everybody. When he gets tired of the hostility, I shall be alone again. This week I have seen him only once.

Salutary, all this, for it throws me back on my writing. Today I worked with a tragic furor, just as a man takes to drink.

There is a struggle between my feelings and my intelligence. Truth hurts. I receive it with pain and therefore more deeply than those who make it a pastime of the intellect. Grasping truth is not to me an acrobatic feat but plain living.

Antonio passed through a somewhat similar phase. He was criticized last year for "moping," for nursing his melancholy, for seeking solitude and sorrowful thoughts; this year, for superficiality. We laughed about it together. He came to lunch.

"Oh, Hugh isn't coming!" he observed.

"No."

"So we are going to have a lovely tête-à-tête."

"Yes, it's a long time since you have wanted to take the risk!"

He introduced us to a Frenchwoman of great charm, Madame Peignot [Marie André], exhilarating, hospitable, a handsome woman of forty who wears her red-gold hair short in a chignon of curls on her neck; lovely shoulders, a great deal of animation, interest in art, and always up-to-date. I thanked him for the gift.

Her salon is, furthermore, franco-espagnole—the Bonifacios and the Viñeses were there last time, her daughter Alyette danced Spanish dances. It was one of the soirées I enjoyed most.

January 18. My mornings are spent looking for a new Home, an occupation I delight in because I like the exercise of imagining how each one could be decorated and furnished. Tonight at five my darling is signing up for a studio apartment at 47 Boulevard Suchet. I am restless, pleased, and unhappy. A new separation, a new loss. I can't go through the change of background without a lot of sentimentality and evocations! It hurts me to have this place so highly praised, always. But I want to turn away from the regrets and think only of the future home, so much more splendid and healthy and luxurious. We are near the Godoys, near the Bois; we have room for our dancing, a fireplace, a big bedroom, a beautiful studio; quiet at night, more intimacy.

January 19. We see the Erskines only en famille. Anna occupies my attention with demonstrations of affection. Graham shows me his drawings. Pauline and I talk about dressmakers, the price of gloves, etc. John talks superficially about his work.

I am very busy and yet lonely. Yesterday we met accidentally in the bus, Gustavo and I. He looked miserable because the evening before we had tried a "soirée" of five persons, which he did not enjoy because he could not talk with me. I was miserable because I had been living with myself for ten days, with books, my Journal, my work, and my dancing. Gustavo's admiration was fanned by the praise of a friend he brought to meet me, a lovely Swedish woman, who said "she could not take her eyes off me—I was so exquisite, so fine, so dainty, so Italian-looking, so charming, so interesting."

I will cultivate passivity, self-sufficiency, and a lower temperature so as to moderate my desires for affection and companionship. The worst of it is that I don't care for women, as a rule. I admire unreservedly great living women writers, dancers, beauties; but women in everyday life don't inspire me. I don't like to talk about maids, babies, housekeeping, dressmakers, illness, deaths, marriages, the cost of living. When they criticize the conduct of other women, my tolerance always makes a bad impression and reflects on my own moral status. Besides, they never like me. I am "stagy," painted, and always in the mood to please. They reproach me for *always* being dressed up—nobody has ever seen me in a stained dress, worn-out slippers, with uncombed hair, or unpowdered face or unpolished nails, at any hour. I dress out of love of dressing—I would dress on a desert island.

Conchita was astonished I should take the trouble to put on a cretonne dress, earrings, and a shawl to work at my dancing, for Miralles! No, not for anybody. For that illusion, that reflection I am going to see in the mirror, which is going to delight my eyes, give me my daily dose of beauty, affect my mood and my inward vision, and without which I would feel like someone who had not eaten a dinner. It is my food, my natural sustenance.

January 21. I really believe I am cowardly enough to suffer from Joaquin's utter misunderstanding of me. We had such a foolish argument last night over this statement he made: A woman who practices the art of dressing is superficial. In with this he threw decoration and other visual expressions. He makes an exception for me, but what illogical and emotional arguments he gave me, so much like Mother's. Did I talk in this way when I was twenty? I was then getting married, emancipating myself.

John calls up—to ask for a piano tuner. Gustavo will come this afternoon with a wounded vanity for me to heal. I write every day and wonder when I will coagulate. I scold the maid for cheating in her accounts, and because she cries, I nearly do too. That is what you might call natural socialism. I fondle my darling. At least on weekends he turns into a real lover. Monday, I always have rings under my eyes.

Evening. Poor Gustavo came, hurt and upset by his former sweetheart's letter about his book, "Sexicology and Otherwise": "You have been influenced by the *decay* of Paris . . . the lower side of your nature, which I never knew . . . disgusting, shocking, nauseating . . . remain among your own people, Americans won't understand your book; they love clean books and clean plays . . . what awful people you must have been going around with to write a book like that . . . only spiritual things count . . . where are the days when you used to speak so much about beauty," etc.

"Poor little Lyndall," I said, "she won't mean that in a few years—she is just young. Don't be angry with her."

But it was too late. He had written her a severe letter asking her not to be so personal, but objective, if she could. He took hold of my little finger while he read and interrupted himself to say, "You understand everything though you are almost Lyndall's age. You are the most broad-minded person I have ever met."

"Oh, no. I used to say personal things like that."

I wanted to protect Lyndall and hated to take advantage of my triumph in understanding, but it was too late. Gustavo was definitely estranged from his American Beauty.

He said: "I had hoped to make something of her as nearly like you as possible, although she would never have had your special kind of beauty or your special kind of mind—she is conventional in her face and thinking, and now her provincialism seems hopeless. From the very beginning you understood me better than Lyndall did after four years. I love you more every day."

So often I have wished he had the money to return to New York and marry Lyndall, who is twenty-two, free, and not unwilling. How often I have pointed out to him that he could be happier with a younger person he could mold, whereas I, besides being fettered and unwilling, already have too many ideas of my own. Of course, I don't take this "break" seriously. Lyndall's red-gold hair, emerald eyes, little nose, laughter, and youthfulness, *when present*, will make up for all the provincialism in the world.

January 23. I have only one proof that my writing is good. Every time I read one of my old Journals I experience the same things all over, as keenly as if I were living through them again; and not in a personal way, but detached. Nothing seems to be peculiarly mine, but pain, sorrow, triumph, struggle, vision, all flowing from some common, eternal source. I write for other people, *even* when I say "I am alone, I am special, I am different."

I am so preoccupied with telling all I am going through that I don't have time to realize what I am doing. Now and then someone like John praises me. I am intensely happy for a day, then I forget about it and go to work. Hugh and others have observed that I very rarely talk about my writing, that most of the time, I sadly assume I am not doing anything. Now and then when I read over old things and get a little light-headed, poor Hugh really thinks I am at last going to get self-confident. He is disgusted with my steady evasion of publicity. I seem to be made to encourage others to write. This morning I have faith. I would like to read to somebody. I am sizzling.

Visited Princess Troubetskoi, who is a painter and decorator. I had heard of her furniture and wanted to see it for my future home. While I admired the furniture she admired me: "You have a dream-face. I must paint you, like that, in your sapphire-blue coat against the background of this chair (her own work, copper designed with figures of a Pushkin legend and inlaid with colored stones). You like this furniture? Pure Russian. No—all Russian wouldn't do as a setting for you, too heavy. Russian-Oriental. Yes, a delicate Oriental. When will you come? I am going out to get a 'toile' [canvas] right now."

Appointment at 10:30, to give her time to do her housework. A lovely, enthusiastic woman, lovely smile, intelligent blue eyes, Slavic head. Detests modern woman of the wholesale type. Her studio is *my* dream. The copperwork with the stones shining and the designs of the legend growing slowly into your imagination, the thronelike chairs, sapphire-blue woodwork, and silver and gold hangings all please me. The Orient has finally won me, subtly, insidiously, through my imagination and passion for color and richness.

January 24. Suddenly, I am surrounded by friends, and many things begin to happen. The Princess has made a deep impression on me—her enthusiasm, frankness, her genius for color and decoration, the quality of her mind, her *love of legends*, her understanding of sadness. We talked about Merejskowski, compared the Spanish and the Russians, agreed on our opinion of the French. Every moment she would say something I liked and expressed a broad-mindedness, an ideal of art, of beauty very similar to my own. Her seeing me as a romantic, legendary person, now Oriental, now a Spanish Infanta, now a child and again as a person who "has known sorrow in some previous existence," all drew me back into the unreal world I first sprang from. I feel that my dreams of a fantastic destiny will inevitably prove stronger than my quiet plans for a wise life! What I feel in her studio has a stronger hold upon my imagination than any other emotion. One of these days the passion roused in me by splendor, jewels, gold, color, richness will push me into some new creation of background and living, so far but faintly suggested.

There is no expression in the world as entrancing as the one in the eyes of an artist at work, in a good creative mood and "after something," as the Princess is now.

January 25. After meeting the Princess in the afternoon, I went to a soirée chez Mme. Demange-Barrès, sister of Maurice Barrès, where Godoy's poems were read. Replica of Guicciardi's salon, but three of them and overcrowded, all French people except Godoy and ourselves. First I met the Lady of the House, homely but friendly. Talked with a man who knows "tout Paris," and admires my dancing; but immediately an old General, who smelled of horse, with big white whiskers and black eyes almost drowned in surplus flesh, began to circle around me and to make his plans for a campaign. He opened the conversation with the usual boulevard phrase: "Didn't I meet you at Madame Aurel's?"

Never thinking salon tactics were the same everywhere, I answered in all sincerity. Afterward I couldn't get rid of him. His jokes passed over my head. I was wishing the poetry would begin. Instead I noticed a lady who seemed terribly struck by me the minute she came in. I was beginning to think I knew her when she got herself introduced by the General.

"I am a painter and I must paint you," she said without warning. She introduced her husband, a writer. Other men were talking to me, but she guided me off into a corner of the second salon, sat me there and stared at me the rest of the evening. Men came and went. I still couldn't understand their jokes, but the tone of the woman's laughter helped me to guess.

I was thankful that night for my face, which made repartee unnecessary. After a while, however, my face became a liability. The Old General came close and started some knee conversation, which I promptly interrupted by trying to sit into the wall. The Lady Painter was inwardly laughing at my unfriendliness. She caressed my naked shoulder with overardent eyes. When would the poetry begin?

More men, more eyes, more accidental bumps against me, *even* a pinch. The poetry did not help. Nobody understood or cared. The reader thundered. Godoy looked pensive. Everybody was waiting for the end. I couldn't believe my eyes and ears and knees and continued to look for intellectual faces and literary or artistic people. They must have been talking to the Lady of the House.

I was anxious to go. The Lady Painter clung to me. A man

with a very refined face said to me: "You shouldn't go so early. You will deprive me of the immense privilege of looking at your face."

The Lady Painter pushed me: "A dozen in one evening—pretty good, but you must learn how to get rid of them. Give them the rendezvous they ask, name the place, and then go and stand half a block away and laugh at them."

The man had heard her. He had very sad eyes. At last I found Hugh and Mother. When I spoke to the Lady of the House, the same man was standing next to her and was formally introduced to me: another painter, begging me to come to his studio. The Lady Painter was boiling. "I thought he was only a flirt and he's a painter—some nerve, trying to do me out of a priceless model."

The man and I were talking. She suddenly pushed Hugh between us like a bomb and said, "Presentez lui votre mari, presentez lui donc!" [Introduce your husband to him!] I murmured an introduction. The painter invited Hugh to come to his studio with me. The Lady Painter pulled me away. Her husband said: "Quand vous êtes la Madame, tout le monde veux se faire peintre" [When you are la Madame, the whole world wants to paint you]. The two painters' cards are still untouched in my handbag.

January 26. I am too occupied with the Princess and almost too happy to find out she has very few friends and that she wants me to "come upstairs as often as possible," because I fit into her background.

With Pauline yesterday. We don't talk about John but I know what she is going through, and his poor escape of a few hours a day seems dearly paid for. Do parents really think such a tense and unhappy atmosphere is a "home" for children? Do they think they can fool the children? How well I remember when I was eight years old, sensing hostility in the air and getting hysterical when I heard Father and Mother quarrel. May I have the strength to give up Hugh nobly when the day comes.

February 14. I was still upset by my experiences at the Demange-Barrès salon, when Hugh came home to tell me to dress up, because we were taking Queen Siddika Begum, Her Majesty's brother, the Sheik Abdul Khalig of Mangrol, her son, Prince Gutam, Moinuddin Khan, and her daughter, the Princess Mumtaz

Jehan, to the Folies-Bergère! The whole court was staying at the Continental for a few days and wanted to be entertained. What the Queen liked best, she said, was music and dancing.

From the very first moment, she made a profound impression on me. She is a small, thin woman with a very calm and graceful manner; sweet, lovely, low-voiced; queenly every moment in such a delicate, poetic way. She had a small face, enormous sad and dreamy eyes, delicate features, and a brilliant smile. I was so moved by her face I could hardly speak. I thought of the *Rubáiyát* and Dulac's illustrations. In a box at the theatre I enjoyed her pleasure at the show, her childlike questions, her gestures. Her embroidered Hindu costume of pastel shades delighted me.

Her walk was halting and difficult because she was recently operated on in America. She suffered from the cold, and I was overcome with pity. Hugh and I took such care of her. The rest of the court, even the handsome, ardent-eyed Sheik and a very charming Prince, hardly existed for me while the dream Queen was there.

I made plans for a party at home Sunday night. They all came, including the Prime Minister. The Queen came dressed in purple with silver embroidery; the Princess, in white. The Queen sat near my divan and said, pointing to it, "It reminds me of home." But when I inquired further about her home, I discovered that all the rest of her furniture was European. We danced for them: Sevilla de Sentis, Sevilla de Albéniz, the Farruca and the Jota. My little Queen had moist eyes and said, "I would like to see you dance all the rest of my life. How wonderful you are! Your gypsy dress looks just like the dresses we wore in India some time ago. Let me see your castanets."

The Sheik wanted to learn the Tango. I gave him a lesson. The little Princess was restless in her chair, wishing her religion did not forbid her to dance. In talking about it, the Queen said, "I get such joy from your dancing because I feel almost as if I were doing it myself. I never feel this in India, because the dancers are all paid, common women." They enjoyed Joaquin's playing. The Sheik sang a few Hindu songs and talked music with Joaquin.

The next day I went to say good-bye to the Queen and to get the photograph of her she had promised me. She seemed sorry to say good-bye and asked if we could not all come to dinner the next evening, before their trip. Big table at the Continental; I wore my purple evening dress and the turban. Joaquin sat at the Queen's right. I had to endure the diplomatic talk of the Prime Minister. Hugh was away in Monte Carlo, and the Sheik was showing the proverbial sheik interest in ladies. He was really astonishingly handsome, cultured, and charming—about Joaquin's height, with very noble features and ardent eyes. Upstairs in their salon we danced the Tango, the Sheik and I, and then watched "movies" of their trip to America. The Queen had bought herself a pair of castanets and all the Spanish records she could find. I gave them several they did not have. I went to see them off. In the train she made room for me next to her with such a sweet manner, and in that dark station and crowded train she was as lovely, as regal, as unique as everywhere.

Those few days left me dazed and dreaming, as when I used to read three books in four hours. I hardly realized that in between I had given Anna a birthday party at the Blue Tea Room and danced a lot with John and talked in spite of the jazz band; that Joaquin's two compositions had been played by Antonio at the Salle Erard with moderate success; that I had met Gustavo for tea and began to feel the first signs of disillusion. He can only *envy* the experiences of others, neither share them nor work for them himself, as Hugh and I have worked for ours.

Every morning I posed for the Princess. John came to see me for two hours, and we talked about Lilith. I finally went to see Mme. Jeanne D., the painter, liked her work, and consented to pose for her. I was really tired out, but I couldn't stop living. Hugh's absence of a few days did not weigh on me because I was so terrifically busy, but when he arrived Saturday morning, impetuous, adoring, tyrannical, I realized that his great understanding love was the mainspring of my life.

A whirlwind: visit to our new apartment, consultations with the architect, letter writing, theatre and dinner with the Erskines, three hours at the Cour de Cassation, where Erskine spoke wonderfully in French, posing for the Princess in the mornings, for Mme. D. in the afternoons, seeing Gustavo at the Rotonde, dancing, attending the Fête Espagnole at the Godoy's, where Julia [Godoy] pursued me meanly with implaccable jealousy and pushed me into the background—all due to my former success in her salon with my dancing. No use giving the details of what a woman can do when she hates you. Women have a genius for petty cruelty.

Tuesday we gave a party, mainly to show Mme. D. our dances, so she can make plans for her big painting. A great success.

Mme. D. was startled by the contrast between my "sad-eyed, dreamy face" and the extreme vigor, character, and vividness of my dancing. The Munros thought I surpassed La Argentina!

With Gustavo it was another thing. He liked me at moments, but remained on the whole his usual detached, unemotional, critical self; he, the man who needs such tremendous doses of faith and enthusiasm from others! He felt jealous seeing other men kissing my hand and raving. I sensed a desire in him to *dominate* me by being, of all my friends, the least flattering, the least subjugated.

I met him for coffee today. He waited fifteen minutes in the bitter cold for me. He was sorry to have been so "technical" over the telephone. He ended by begging me not to misunderstand him, because "if you did there is nothing left for me but to shoot myself. You must try to understand my need of fundamental faith. On top of that you can pile up all the criticism you like."

Then he started to tell me what he did love, but I laughed at him, which made him angry. However, toward the end we were reconciled.

I am thinking of my firm and complete friendship with John and Lilith. I called on her for an hour the day before they left for New York and found her just as he had described her. Only, more woman, even, softness mixed with firmness, which I love. Her eyes are of a rich blue and very steady and powerful. A slight shadow of embarrassment before me, with a very feminine rush for a little powder on her nose before sitting down, appealed to me more than the absolute self-assurance I expected. She was surprised at my babyishness, evidently expecting a real woman. We clasped hands like two real, honest friends, elated by a moment of understanding, and John was happy when we each termed the other "wonderful."

February 27. I am now twenty-six and have done nothing. No book, no stage career, a lot of unsatisfied desires, and a realization that I am but half of what I hope to be. But I am terribly, profoundly happy, and terribly, profoundly unhappy—I am alive, thank God!

Everything fascinates me, teaches me: the discovery of Mme. D.'s vulgarity, her bad, superficial painting of me (thank God, out of the house); discovery of a talented Russian painter, Liphart. He comes in the mornings, distressingly handsome, with enormous blue eyes, dreamy and sad, woman's hands, an appearance of aristocracy, fineness and seriousness. His painting of me gives me, for the first time, the signs of intelligence. He is the first to see my sad eyes and constantly smiling mouth—"Léonardesque," he said.

This year spring will kill me. The sap rising in the trees does not rise each year with greater strength, but life rises in me each year with greater strength, and can I endure it? The symphonic concerts of the birds do not get louder, but my cries of exultation, yes, and can others endure it? My Journal? I felt spring long before anybody else, ten days ago, lying in bed—a stillness, a softness, through the frost. My eyes are open to color as they never were before. I have always loved color; my first wish was to be a painter.

Today all this has come to a climax, when, dreaming of our next home, I bought paints, glue, cardboard, scissors, brushes, to prepare a tiny cardboard stage. I have started to mix, study, and handle color. The new perception gave me a new joy. I make great efforts to design, working without experience or teaching. At night I almost have a fever from visions of gold, Persian blue, pomegranate, violet, emerald green, lacquer white, burnt sienna, cobalt blue, vermillion—Byzantium! I am obsessed with Byzantium!

And very slowly my cardboard apartment grows, small, crude, pitiful in comparison to the dream. M. Liphart looks kindly upon my Persian designs made with a pen dipped in gold. Gustavo sniffs, walks about like a caged animal because Mme. D. is there on his afternoon.

I have nothing but a desire to be left alone with my work. Friends have never lasted me more than a few months. None of them have been worth as much as my solitude. Why do I sometimes feel I can't live without them? It is true they enrich my life, fill my mind, so that afterward my solitude is an active, thoughtful, ruminating kind, that keeps me from having to feed always on myself. Now, I suppose I am in a mood for rumination. I want everybody to leave me alone—with my Journal and cardboard home and my paints and my overcrowded ideas.

Mme. D. called me "petite cocotte, mon amour, ma fille, ma beauté" and other concierge's pet names. She raved about "my veiled, mysterious eyes, my heavy eyelids, my adorable mouth, the purity of my features, the innocence of my expression, the delicacy of my coloring, my charm." She painted me like a magazine-cover woman, with enormous empty eyes, a luminous nose, a carnal mouth. Her husband thought I looked like the incarnation of the Dance itself, that the painting exposed my "delicately violent soul," and meanwhile he sized me up as a desirable morsel and began calling on me when his wife was not there. While we talked about his poetry one evening, he covered the distance of a yard and put his hand on my knee. I got up and took a little walk around the room, wondering if it had been an accident and what I should say. The second time, I felt he was breathing me in. I gave him a cold look and took another walk. When it was clear that he was hunting me down, I played him the trick of continuing with an impersonal conversation, which annoyed him more than if I had become angry (to the French, a source of amusement and ridicule), so in the end he must have thought I was not inaccessible but inaccessible to him, which is the worst punishment you can inflict on a man of his miraculous vanity. Miraculous because he is small and ugly, with pig eyes and a twisted smile.

"Alphonsine, when this man comes again you will say I am not at home."

Mme. D.'s utter lack of intelligence struck me the first day of my posing. The second day I knew her intimate story—a deceived wife in quest of some physical nourishment. She made a dash for all the young men I had at my party, at the same time being overdemonstrative with me. Liphart frankly snubbed her. Gustavo called on her once. He is less quick to sense coarseness. Monsieur et Mme. Chien, good-bye!

The Family agrees that I need a warning, so en masse they fall on me with "You are wasting time posing for all these people." To their surprise, I answer, "I posing for them? Ha! Ha! You think they are making my portrait? You are wrong. They are posing for me, and I am making *their* portraits, and I am not wasting a minute."

March 2. Danced at the opening of a Grande Maison de Couture, Avenue de l'Opéra, a paid engagement. Arrived at nine o'clock with my Maja dress and gypsy dress in a hatbox. Ushered into the dressing rooms with the mannequins, a blonde and a brunette. Ushered into the Past. I was poor again. I had to earn my living. Here I was. The mannequins were friendly because I was of their class. Not so very long ago, I was a mannequin. I knew what it was to rush in and out of dresses, to have one's hair pulled, to walk out attractively, displaying clothes one never could hope to own.

I danced well, alone. Miralles was kind and flattering. Hugh was waiting for me, but I felt far away. I could see myself walking before the buyers in New York. "You're a darn good-looking girl, but you don't smile enough." It was shyness. I was too sweet with the other girls. I always offered to wear the heaviest dresses (we showed winter suits in the summer) because I felt the heat less, in reality because I loved to help. I read *Jean Christophe* when I had time. I went without lunch to write in my Journal. The money I made sank into an abysmal blankness. There would never be enough. The buyers asked me out. When I was on duty at twelve o'clock, left alone, in my black slip, the brother of the owner tormented me. One time while I was answering the telephone he came up behind me and tried to feel my breasts. I kicked him. The designer would call me upstairs to measure something, and his hands were insidious and sneaky, and I always left him in a temper, to be scolded afterward if the clothes did not fit me.

The evening was over. I was very hot and very tired. I put my big shawl over my head in the Hindu fashion, picked up my hatbox, said good-bye to everybody, collected compliments. Hugh helped to get my big dress into our little red-and-black car. He covered me with the fur rug. Home. Comfort. Security. Compliments from the Humorous Banker. Love. All the rest was the Past.

March 5. Joaquin and I are not alike anymore, although we understand each other always. His exultation takes a religious form. His feelings soar to the heavens. His thinking is vague, pious, illogical. There is no religion in me but for individuality, and human understanding and artistic inspiration. I love life fervently. I love the body. I never think of heaven. My mysticism is not religious. I don't believe in renunciation. I am not resigned. I never pray. Out of habit, I sometimes exclaim angrily against a blundering God. I fear death, which is passing into the Universe, into some other body.

Organ music, nature sometimes give me what might be called a religious feeling. The face of the Madonna in Florentine paintings, too. No bearded old man, no priests, no sermons; Christ, yes, who is suffering. I reject the human manifestations of religion. I don't believe in spending this life in contemplation of the next, which is theoretical. How literal I am! Yet I believe in *every human, interior manifestation of God in us, like genius, charity, pity, love.*

March 6. This has been the Winter of the Painters. Carl Bohnen came last night to see our apartment. Offered to pay part of the expenses by making my portrait, but I have never yet had to *pay* to be painted, so we refused. Liphart's portrait is finished—hard, intelligent, sad-eyed face, not pretty at all, but it pleases me. Today comes M. [Georges] Wakhevitch, whom I met at the Godoys' yesterday.

Pauline's comments on my vanity sadden me a little; I wear too many bracelets, make-up, very personal and special clothes, interesting hats, I love color and never wear neutral tones, I don't have babies. Tia Antolina writes that she prefers me as a sub-manager's wife rather than as a dancer. Elvira Viñes is astonished to discover I can read, write occasionally, and think clearly. I am now convinced that you arrive at a greater understanding of human character by idealization, such as I practice, than by skepticism.

I seek signs of intelligence, understanding, pity with such fervor that no flicker of it on *any* face escapes me. I begin with faith; I cling to all the illusions held out to me. Everybody else begins the other way round: I. Faith in themselves. II. Expecting the worst—of others. III. Preconceptions. For example: A handsome woman must be stupid; a dancer can't be a mystic.

Made friends in the last month with the Viñeses—Ricardo, the famous pianist, his brother, José, his brother's wife, and their children, Hernando and Elvira, who are our age, more or less. Hernando is a painter and a subtle guitarist. Elvira reads—and dances like a true gypsy. We danced, both of us, Saturday evening, here at home. She has long, strong black hair, green eyes, an aquiline profile, a plump, earthy figure—intelligence, character all through. She dances from the waist up, with her arms, and her face, and expressions, real flamenco, to Hernando's playing. It was wonderful to see and hear them. By contrast my own dancing seemed purely classical—with less pantomime and fewer static moments. I am more Oriental in the hip movements and very light in the Jota. I want to be a complete dancer and will try now to perfect my arms and to show all I feel in my face. Everything that Miralles has told me about Spanish dancing is now said in a dance magazine by an expert.

March 8. Soirée, Chez Mme. Aurel, in honor of Jean Royère. A house in a quiet street. Stained-glass windows. Four salons opening into one another—the main one with a canary-colored rug and walls. A lot of people, mostly old and not very pleasing aesthetically.

The Lady of the House was fascinating—a woman of forty-five, perhaps, with red-gold hair worn à la Récamier, with a silver net instead of the ribbon; an eighteenth-century face, very serious, very determined, and very domineering. Her husband was tall, bearded, with close-set eyes, an aquiline nose, and a witty tongue. She is a writer, and he seems to be interested in the theatre and has just adapted an Italian play for the Parisian stage.

Royère was feted with admiring speeches and the reading of his mysterious and senseless poems—"hermetique" is the right word, air-tight. A great man for the philosophy and development of poetry, but certainly obscure and involved himself. Mme. Aurel informally introduced everyone who spoke. She defended a play she admired which had been hooted by the critics. She introduced a little-known and little-appreciated author. Then she asked a question which was supposed to bring on a heated discussion. It concerned a book in which a sensualist asserted that what he reached by his senses remained a permanent perception, whereas what he perceived with his intellect was mutable and unreliable. Nobody picked up the argument. The whole thing was too artificial. There was a little more private talk and people began to leave.

Met the Old General, who asked forgiveness for the letter he wrote me offering me many dancing engagements if I came to see him. M. Mortier, Aurel's husband (Aurel is her pen name), had been, throughout, perhaps the wittiest and most unaffected of all the people there. His little eyes shone sharply and pleasantly. Both of them asked me very specially to come back. I promised.

But now I know what literary salons are: literature dressed up, unreal, starched, overdecorated, lifeless, bloodless, and dusty. Just the same, I love to penetrate into that old, overcarved, overfine, wordy French civilization, where Style and Form were born. I admire their intellectual exercises, the looseness of their tongues; I feel carried back to Madame Récamier's salon.

Evening. Two delightful hours spent with Gustavo, walking in the Luxembourg and sitting at the Viking. He gave me his best self, all his charm and livingness. I forgot to drink my tea and he lost his sense of direction. We talked about music, dancing, his new friends, Mme. Récamier's life, French salons, Isadora Duncan, Hindu philosophy, Arabian fairy tales, his book, La Argentina, Plato, Marcus Aurelius, and the Erskines.

He said, "Apart from my love, I *admire* you, Anaïs. If I did not love you as a woman, I would still love to be with you. You are very extraordinary. I am proud of you, of being liked by you. It is because I admire you so much that I can never make the definite manly gesture that would spoil our relationship and bring everything to a human and everyday climax. I don't feel that I want to swallow you up in an ordinary love, but that I want to give you everything I can. *You* have given me so much."

I am grateful to him for this feeling. This amitié passionée [passionate friendship] has meant a great deal to both of us. If his deep susceptibility to environment and people makes him a little caméléonesque [chameleon-like] and difficult for most people to understand, at least for me he has been consistently a living personage among many dead ones.

March 19. Dancing for a charity affair—for old ladies. Success and encores, and I collected seventy francs in my tambourine for the poor! Elvira, very sweet. Two men, only, in the audience. Many mousy little women in dark clothes absorbed by the tremendous task of selling miscellaneous objects to other mousy ladies. One of the mousy ladies was the wife of an admiral. She made me repeat Sevilla so her husband could see it when he came to take her home. I spent on that affair the amount I made at the dressmaking house. Hugh said I was at least self-supporting!

Quiet studio: Carl Bohnen, Chicago painter of celebrities, is working and waiting for us to move out. I make a lot of notes of what I must do.

Unexpected business trip, which I hailed as an escape from half-invaded apartment and a thousand other troubles. Cimiez reminds me of Fiesole, with its cypresses, height, church and cloister. Left alone in the hotel I sit down to write and to rest. Resting was easy; writing, impossible. It is appalling to discover how much I think and wriggle and how little I produce, aside from my Journal. I am deeply dissatisfied with myself—I am really a fake.

March 22. Street musicians: first there were two of them, an old man bent permanently by rheumatism over an asthmatic guitar and a younger man who sang with an operatic aggressiveness. But it was early in the morning, the sunlight dissolved all critical faculties, I was overloaded with pennies, and there was a spare envelope in the scrap basket. I did not feel very much like working, so I leaned out the window and smiled at the serenaders.

How sweet life was! I was swimming in warmth and in light, floating in cotton. At the same time I felt the old familiar pain all music gives me, which is like the strumming and pulling of a multitude of chords in myself. The man in the next room threw money from the window in a cigarette box, and he was laughing. I threw my envelope, but I was sad. Perhaps if I did not move from the sunlight for a long time and let it soothe me for many years, as I listened to those cheap songs, it would make a shell around me. The two musicians finished. A woman came up the hill with a hand organ and a little boy. She began to play, but the handle came off now and then. The man next door shut his window. I had no more pennies, but I had an idea for my work.

Mr. Rey took us to St.-Paul, the artists' colony, to meet two friends of his, two American old maids. One was middle-aged, but energetic, practical, wide awake, frank, talkative; the other was old, wasted, emaciated, ill, with hardly any voice, but with beautiful, sad, dreamy eyes. I couldn't endure their gaze. The first talked about stocks with Hugh. I was silent, watching, listening.

We had in common the love of good books and of artists. I could have echoed all they said but I didn't talk—I watched them. We parted. I will probably never see them again. They must have thought me sweet and quiet. Yet I understood them, perhaps like no one else, too well, too well to tell them, too well to tell even myself.

I saw ghosts and strange horrors as I sat quietly at lunch on the terrace of the auberge, with the sunshine glittering on the checkered tablecloth, on the yellow pottery, and on Miss Lemer's blue earrings, and Miss Martin's parched skin.

Even Hugh felt something. He said to me in the evening, "Darling, I don't want you to miss anything—life is too short. I don't want you to get old without having had all you desire. I have had more than I deserve in getting you. I don't want you to have regrets."

March 23. I said to the Humorous Banker last night, "I'm sorry, dear, but I can't work in this place. This morning I listened to the musicians, copied a few things, made a few improvements. The sunshine affects me. I want to be out of doors. Don't scold me. I won't have anything to show John—I'm sorry."

"Don't worry," said the Cat, generously.

We started to dress for dinner. I, being ready first, picked up my Journal idly and finding I had written something, read it to him. The Humorous Banker grunted (he was shaving) and stopped to say, "You haven't wasted your day."

March 24. Sunday evening. The Cat and I are sitting before the fire, after a day of love, reading, tennis, a carriage ride, and sun-worship. At last we are both calm, nerveless, philosophical, well fed and well rested—ready for Paris.

We came up to our room immediately after dinner, finding no interest in the marches and movie music they play for us, and tired of making bad guesses at the nationality of our neighbors. Every day outward signs grow less and less visible; there are fewer differences in clothes, and even if you listen, the French can talk English English, and the Russians can talk good French, etc.

The light is bad, I feel lazy and dull, but I can't keep away from my Journal. Hugh is at last enjoying Proust, and I am wondering if a book could be written combining Proust's mysticism with a little more clarity. I lived for an hour today with Hugh the Poet. He was wishing that instead of all that successful banking he could have achieved a single poem. Reading Proust has upset him, made him restless and regretful. Is it a phase, a crisis, or a real renunciation of what he has already done in favor of literature? I watched his face while he talked, questioning the extent of his regrets. He was telling me about his feelings, his brooding observation of life, his desire to fashion poetry, lines that would haunt one like certain pieces of music, that would intensify, realize the essence of life. Is it possible he should have such a desire and not write a line for six years? If it is true, I am not the one to hold him back. I have always, always pulled him away from banking. To-day, any day, this very minute, any minute, I would give up everything and live with him in a hole, anywhere, and write. He is the first to say, "I need luxury. I need power. I love comfort, privacy, independence, expensive things." He wants me in a car, not in trolleys and buses. We love play-going. We love costume and dancing. We love beauty, in the home, in our surroundings. Would he, today, choose poetry?

Or are these little regrets suggested by Proust, by a romantic hour in the garden, by my own writing? How is one ever to know the secrets of another, in spite of love, which fuses, in spite of understanding, in spite of everlasting conversations?

Just a day before leaving, writing comes to me in an irrepressible torrent. I feel myself wholly possessed by words—too late! Time to go. Paris and a million occupations will swallow me. But I will see John, I will see John!!!

I heard serenaders again. They came to play under our window. I said to Hugh, "How much more touching they are than the very great musicians, who give us perfection, but so far removed from our own lives, so inaccessible. Look at these two— guitarist and violinist. Their playing resembles our lives, which are really pathetically out of tune sometimes; how many of us play ridiculous melodies with rheumatic fingers on such cheap instruments. The great musicians transport me, but these men make me cry.

"Hear that funny little note, that screech, that long-drawn note absolutely off key—doesn't it make you think of the time you were seasick on our honeymoon voyage; of the day in Luchon you cried when I told you about my first dish-washing; of me walking in our bedroom in my fur-edged slippers, which make me look like a half-skinned chicken; of you in your B.V.D.s making a scene because I wasn't writing enough; of the time we stayed in an expensive hotel, and, wanting to economize, told the manager we had had dinner, then went out to a modest neighboring restaurant, which turned out to be run by the hotel and where the manager greeted us amicably. Give the musicians a franc!"

Paris. Rain, cold. John's return still uncertain. Lilith keeps him. So I threw my new book into a corner, in a fit of disappointment. Alphonsine leaves me because she is ill. Bohnen works in my studio. For once, I am conquered by Disorder, which I hate. But my mind is orderly, and I have mastered the situation. I saw Gustavo today.

"If I were not tied," he said, "I would write a Spanish Chauve-Souris [The Bat—*Die Fledermaus*], mostly for you, and we would tour the world!"

Such ideas help him to work. I smile. I pay for the coffee. Went to my dancing lesson, with renewed fervor.

Discovered in Madame Aurel (*Le Couple*) a philosopher on love. Good plain rational thinking, which endangers the life of the average French novel. A special, intelligent study of adultery. "Real genius consists in making the man for you out of the man you have." She has a justified disdain for the "love" which can thrive on an hour's meeting somewhere for physical union. What a modest lover, who can thus be satisfied, and what an avaricious woman, who can be content with such a gift!

She is trying to make "honesty" fashionable. For centuries the devoted or chaste wife has been an object of ridicule in France. She was either "cold" or a "hick," but certainly neither womanly nor smart. How many women, influenced by this ridicule, turned to adultery! I like her ideas because they are not based on moral grounds, but on intelligence and wisdom, and a realization of life's extreme brevity.

Aurel has clarified the philosophy my feelings were ready to obey. I have known the fever, the restlessness, the weakness, the disorder, the impulses, the regrets, the futility, the error, and recognized, in less than a year, the absolute falseness of my voyage. I return from cafés, secret meetings, and talk (*nothing* but talk— but talk and imagination are sufficient for some people), cured, apaisée [calmed], lucid, wiser, and profoundly, irrevocably in love with Hugh. It is only my imagination which travels and stumbles, the eternal, diabolical deceiver. But I'm home now, to stay, and Hugh senses his full return to absolute favor and gives me more love.

Prescription against dangerous exultation: let the Subject talk himself out; write your journal instead of the letters he demands; take several short trips; make a study of your husband's Personality, as if about to lose him; *wait.* "He" will become an Ordinary Friend. And your husband will appear greater than before.

April 9. A colored girl with the poetic name of Gracieuse is taking care of our home. Mr. Bohnen is taking care of occupying my studio. Hugh is taking care of our future, of our stocks, and the safety of our salary. Mother is taking care of Joaquin, Joaquin of Mother. So I can sit down and write.

An afternoon spent in Sceaux, visiting Liphart's cousin, in an old house with an old garden, reminded me of Richmond Hill and depressed me so thoroughly that I wonder what the Past has done to me. It would seem as if I were not sure enough yet of the Present and of my strength. A forsythia bush in Florence can throw me back into a feeling of timidity, pale idealism, and child-like innocence; a day with Tia Anaïs, away from my home and without Hugh, can suffocate me with a fear of not having lived all these creative years of our marriage; a branch of dogwood tree in Nice can rouse again in me the feebly romantic love of love, symbolized by Eduardo's fair face and green eyes; an old house in the country, chilly, paintless, ready to tumble down can re-awaken the distress of poverty and of physical powerlessness. It would seem as if all my brilliant efforts and my self were issued out of a pale dream and could instantaneously vanish the minute I ceased to believe or lost my Lamp, my vision—in the midst of physical security, of home, marriage, and love, while Mother cooks my lunch, while Joaquin works at his piano. To feel this frailness and transitoriness—surely that is the hell reserved to poets and to mystics, and I am evidently condemned to it.

April 15. A keen, particular joy at meeting John at the station, and he in exactly the same mood. Lilith sends him back happy and buoyant and natural. He took my arm with an impulsive and youthful gesture. He insists on our going to Beaune with him and the family, and we leave Friday by train to meet them at Dijon.

A keen, particular pain at leaving our little apartment. We move Wednesday temporarily to 13 Square de Port-Royal, Rue de la Santé. The books (450) are all packed and the bookcase looks miserable. The walls are bare of John's photograph and paintings of me. Richard's statuette is on Joaquin's piano. Mother is storing my Oriental bed, lamps, coffee set, armchairs. I pack with method and order according to an ideal of mine.

Meanwhile, we see a beautiful play, *La Prisonnière,* and resolve that the best inheritance parents can leave their children is having been great and wonderful themselves, rather than the usual collection of "sacrifices" and "renunciations," to be eternally mentioned afterward as a reproach.

April 23. The trip to Beaune with the Erskines gave me what I had long expected and been hungry for—a few moments of perfect communion with John, a few moments of unique exultation and that fever, that kind of wasting fever, from which I come out always wiser and saner. I wanted to understand John. From the first moment he met us at the station at Dijon and I read on his face that he was glad to see us, I let myself be penetrated by all his moods, expressions, thoughts, and words. I felt him entirely, with all my being, in the same way the mystics perceived truths never seen by ordinary men: John greeting us at the station, spirited, in spite of a severe cold; John talking to Hugh while we drove to Beaune; John introducing us to the old patron of the hotel, introducing us to his Past, to a moment in his life which changed his whole life. John, at the dinner table, choosing the best of Burgundy's wine. We talked while I tasted those exquisite, extraordinary, almost intangible wines, all essence, all finesse. I looked at him over my enormous glass. His talk and the wine were inexpressibly alike. The subtle fermentation in my head, at least, was just the same. He drank to the "personal" parts of my Journal, we drank to his new novel, *Sincerity*. He mixed his talk of the present with allusions to the trip ten years ago which brought him to Beaune, in a uniform, to the Camp, to his first freedom, and to the Legion of Honor and the title Citizen of Beaune.

"Here we used to come for dinners, occasionally. That same girl, standing over there by the door, waited on us. In the next room, we had the banquet, with the Mayor, and other government officials. And now we'll visit Beaune."

Beaune in full moonlight. Hugh and Pauline walked together. I have seen many medieval towns. Beaune, too, had a church, little old streets, old trees, but all transformed by John's memories and enthusiasm. France was his intellectual Mother, the most civilized of all countries.

He told me the story of the new novel. We were in the hotel, by then. Good night! Good night!

Not good night. Ideas, the bells tolling the hours, the fever, John's rich eyes blazing, John's ideas blazing. No peace. I had been hungry, and here was fullness, which could not be contained in a day, consuming half the night. I had to wait ten hours for all the things we had not talked about. Twelve hours, because John was asleep, in the room below ours, when Hugh and I came out in the full morning sun, to get him medicine for his cold and some flowers for Pauline. I was reading *Uncle Sam* in the garden. Anna came down first. Then John. We talked until Pauline came down with Graham. In a group, we visited the museum and the famous Hospice.

In the afternoon we were driven to the place where the Camp used to be. John showed us the house in the fields where he had his room. Most of the other houses had been pulled down, but we saw the floor of the "theatre" and dance hall built by the soldiers. John's little stories about these things were simple and not unusual, but all of them had a special meaning for him and had contributed in some subtle way to his discovery of himself.

Meanwhile, the banquet was being prepared; answers to his invitations were coming in. The Mayor was too old and too ill to come, but all the other officials and their wives were there, and it was the artist of the town who took charge, stimulating the sentiment and memories on which the evening was built. John, at the middle of the long table, talked French in his rich voice. Photographs of the American invaders were passed around. Each little old man had a story to tell. Two of them made speeches. My neighbors sang old Burgundian songs to wine. The artist, small, swift, wiry, with serious eyes and pointed beard, never missed a chance to click glasses and to make neat, sonorous phrases. John spoke, as always, humorously, but over the level of the audience. I could only see faces such as I had seen all over France—wine merchants, petit bourgeois, cozy government employees—but John's pleasure gave to the whole evening the color of a quaint and memorable experience.

We had enough to talk about the next day in the car, on our way to Orléans, though no intimate talk was possible, and I had to bite my tongue several times and restrain from all spontaneous remarks. At Orléans, where we spent the night, we went for a walk after dinner, Graham, Hugh, John, and I. John and I had wished it, plotted for it; we walked together talking at last about Lilith, about our problems of living, about Wordsworth's love affair with a Frenchwoman.

En route earlier, a little incident led to John's carrying me in his arms! We were arguing about the seating in the car. Pauline and I wanted the men to sit in the back seat, because they were all uncomfortable and too big for the front ones. So, being the first one in, I sat in the front seat. John asked me to move, politely at first, then more domineeringly, then half angry, and observing my stubbornness, he threatened to carry me to the back seat by force. Hoping he would, I said, laughing: "I prefer to be carried!" And this he did. Afterward he did not talk at all, or look at me. I regretted my impulse, desiring for a minute to have him transport me physically as he does intellectually. At Orléans I asked him, when I had a chance, whether he was angry with me. He said, "Heavens, no. Who could be angry with you?" And I saw he had not guessed at the feminine cause of my "stubbornness" and would never guess.

At the door of our house, while Pauline was in the car with the children, the chauffeur lifting down the valises, Hugh counting them, John said: "May I come to hear the new parts of the Journal?"

"When can you come?"

"Tomorrow morning."

The next day I couldn't realize he was sitting there on the couch and that we could talk. I was not at all calm, but did not show it. We went directly to our most intimate problem: pagan living—when to restrain ourselves and why.

"I am so *hungry*," I said.

"That is the word, the exact word," said John, who was not calm either. "We are hungrier than other people."

I didn't say: Is Lilith *enough*? If she were, John would not have been sitting there this morning after three days of traveling together.

"Read me from your Journal."

So I read all I had copied out in Nice. He was so wonderfully responsive, to the humorous parts, to the poetic, to everything. He seemed struck by the style, said the "fog" pages were "pure poetry," the descriptions "vivid." He thought I had a great deal of philosophy, a wide understanding, that there was a unity in the work due to the consistency of the personality and attitude. He was surprised that it was not at all an egotistical journal, that the background was rich and varied and the stories spoke for themselves.

"I can see you are a writer, Anaïs, because things come out in your writing which do not show in your talk, or in you, generally. It is your true means of expression."

Of course, he had to say something. I was happy, but far more so when he spoke to Hugh two days later of his own accord and said, "I have been thinking of Anaïs's writing objectively and cannot change my feeling that it is great—I am really very much impressed!"

This was a turning point in my life. A great confidence came to me, and for the second time a deep conviction of my strength and power. John is essentially a very *lucid critic*, of writing, life, and people. He could have made a mistake while I was reading to him, but he had time afterward to revise his judgment.

I was happy. I sang all day. My life was full, full, to overflowing. Singing was not enough, even dancing was not enough, and one couldn't write while ideas burst. I needed to throw something overboard. An intense sadness quieted me. Wednesday night we heard Joaquin's Trio, played by him, a young cellist and a young violinist. The first time I had heard it, played by Joaquin on the piano alone, I cried desperately. Wednesday, I controlled myself, but I was completely broken up and in a desperate mood. His music is terribly moving. There are in it moments of deep struggle, of triumph, of clarity, of exultation, rising to the purest harmony, the purest melody.

Elvira and I had to dance afterward. I was so upset, so detached from all visual pleasures, that technique alone carried me through, along with an almost savage desire to conquer my pain.

The next day a physical numbness overwhelmed me. An emotional crisis from which I came out strong, calm, wise, deeply self-possessed, *whole*—as if the struggle were only an effort toward unity, a gathering up of small, vague, fragmentary, lost parts. Suddenly I felt I would never again be as pliant, as soft, as timid. I have the courage to be entirely myself.

Hugh says: "You seem to have finished just *suffering* life and are beginning to dominate it."

Just suffering life is not enough. I know.

End to Eduardo's Story—quoted from a letter from Baby. "I see Eddie often. I think he got over all his troubles. He smokes big cigars, drinks, and goes to all the dances, so I don't think you need worry about him. He works in the National City Bank for twenty-five dollars a week."

Out with John and Pauline. Upset by an idea of his which is to go into the new novel—sincerity of the woman who returns to her husband, but an intellectual sincerity, because her *feelings* are not satisfied. Struggle between the ideal and the senses. How the devil does he find these things out? Also, this woman reaches a certain stage in her "experiences" away from her husband where she cannot any longer write of them and becomes insincere as an author by the process of reticence! Damnable little twists and turns and borings of the intelligence by which John reaches the most uncomfortable naked truths. And always women, women, turned inside out.

I have an annoyingly persistent idea that John and I together could grasp the most elusive truths of character. I feel it when we talk. We reach the same hilltop by different ways. We get the same inordinate pleasure from such mental elucidations and analysis as most people are too sleepy to undertake. But what is the use? He has a family, Lilith, and lives in New York. The little moments have been small explosions. But that is all I will have! His elbow on the arm of my theatre seat, fitful confidences, ordained by circumstances, and a few rare, premeditated visits. And after that I'll have to light my own bombs.

As I finished writing, Max Wald came in. In my quest for friends I chose him because he seemed quiet and wise and understanding. Discovered an ardent, eager, passionate man, who has lived thoroughly and fearlessly, coming through gloriously and ingloriously, with an intact love of truth and ultimate sincerity. What he told me of his life, I liked and told him so. He said it "sounded right" to me because I loved color and intensity but that he had seen some very inglorious moments and had not always come out untouched.

Inglorious moments—when things happen in spite of yourself, when the senses betray you, when you find your philosophy is based on a paradox, when truth is a paradox. Also when you understand and can't *talk*. *I can't talk*. I am convinced now. I sit and suffer, like the dumb, and am driven to the pencil.

Gustavo tells me, "The first day I met you it was impossible to say what you were; you did not talk." John tells me, "Things come out in your writing which don't show in your talk." It is always the same from everybody: "I never *knew* you—never guessed." Hugh laughs himself sick when I tell him this; to him, to those I know well, I talk. His laugh consoles me. At least in intimacy, after six years of marriage, I make a little progress.

Hugh lives so much through me and would get such a joy from seeing my work published, yet I don't care. I am too preoccupied with the perfection of it, I see too well what remains undone. Furthermore, I feel that what I do requires a secrecy, which I have deliberately maintained. But all the things I have been told these days are fermenting in my head, and I can't help being pleased.

May 8. Volcanic session of five hours with John. Talk—interminable, upsetting; confidences, literary and personal. Admissions of mistakes and defeats. Encouragements: I to him. "John, you have not *missed* anything. You know and you possess as much as do men who have actually tasted everything. You carry richness in yourself, your imagination" (telling him what I have not proved to myself yet). And he answers me, "Anaïs, you have not missed anything. You carry creative power within yourself. You will live in that, and by that more profoundly than the others." (But we did not say what I thought of afterward: imaginative experience is very fine philosophically, but it makes you so helpless before real experience—so awkward!)

His stories, his renunciations, are loaded with an excitement which communicates itself to me. Didn't I guess Lilith was not enough? He escapes by a miracle from other seductions—physical, experimental, impulsive—only because he always considers the consequences and the aftermath and he fears disaster and disintegration. I am surprised by his stoicism, and I am not admiring. I tell him, "But you have *done* these things with your mind— then why not altogether?" He has wished, he has sometimes given way to kisses and caresses. At last I understand from his talk that he is moved by passion, today, now, as he never was, and that he is passing through a profound sexual upheaval. I feel the overflow. There are tense moments in our conversation. He knows that because our ideas, curiosities, imaginings are alike, our feelings are alike too.

He reads me from his intimate notebook. "A lot can be done with the imagination," says John, fearing that I would personally test some of his plain statements.

"How much?"

He doesn't know. So he tells me the story of the woman who offered herself to him. I commented that he seemed to have got a lot out of saying "no"; the whole incident was such a source of knowledge to him.

Sincerity, as a sketch, was read to me. It is very real comedy, unexpected, intricate, and psychologically sound, humanly so. John is saturated with French novels. In them he has expanded physically. But because he is not French, he takes his expansion intensely and thoroughly, and not objectively. To take French ideas seriously is disastrous. Technically, he has not surrendered yet. But in reality he has. He was afraid that because he feels so restless and feverish, it would be plainly visible to everybody. I said: "You tell me you feel 'safe' in your own writing because most of the people don't understand. Well, you are equally safe in society. It is all *visible* to me because I know you."

I certainly do, today. If I was convinced long ago of his

intellectual livingness, yesterday I learned just how susceptible he can be emotionally and physically. I still feel, while I write, the immense excitement that possessed him, I can feel his struggles to emancipate himself from all scruples—but, like me, he has days of triumph and days of defeat. He triumphed yesterday, spurred by my receptivity; and next time—I may find him cooled off. How much time wasted on deliberation! Curse thought and wisdom which arrest impulse.

Quietly retired today after too emotional an afternoon spent with John. Complications, because I want to live and learn with the least possible sacrifice—not of myself, for which I fear nothing —but of the one I love best, of Hugh. Besides, living thus with the fevers of others, following all John's feelings, entering so thoroughly into them, I feel as tired, as beaten as if I had done it all myself. And I have moments of disgust with myself for wriggling so much and so ridiculously at the least little whim of the Winds.

I have a curious conviction about my writing, and it is that I say enough, I say the essential thing. John urges me to develop my themes into a novel. It is his first mistake about me. I see things that way, swiftly, condensed, brief, all the opposite of Proust; I can't develop. I haven't the temperament, the mood, the obstinacy to do so. It is not my way. And yet I don't want to be superficial.

Hugh and John are perhaps the only men who remain the same when they are *among men*. John reminds me of a story of a girl who disguised herself in order to see men among men, and who, as a result, never loved. (John is against all men, except Hugh, of course—warning me paternally?) I know Gustavo tells filthy stories when ladies are not there—Gustavo, Enric, and many others—and they speak of their lady loves in very unpoetic terms. My father was one of those. It is no wonder I told John what I think of Hugh's character, which is "incredible." John's prediction is that Hugh will be a great man in a quiet way, that although I have by far a wider range, he has unity, which may help me.

"Of the two of us," I said, "he is the superior."

"Both of you are remarkable people. But it is clear you have all the genius in the family."

May 10. Unable to bear the burden of my talk with John. Why be so emotional about intellectual debates? *Why was he emotional?* So I plunged into another person's life—a dead one, to whom my enthusiasm can go freely, my dear Proust, Proust illumined by Léon-Pierre Quint[1] in a marvelous book. Then we went to see Ibsen's *Canard Sauvage* [*Wild Duck*]. So last night I collapsed! I went to sleep in Hugh's arms worn out, exhausted, weak, and woke up with a temporary desire to eliminate all *thought* from my life.

Went to see the carpenter who is making my furniture. But on the way back noticed an incredible street, Rue Jean Dolent, alongside the wall of the Prison de la Santé. A black wall as high as a house, windowless, stretching as far as I could see. I imagined a story about the little houses on the Rue Jean Dolent. And I felt very happy because I realized I possess a power of magic— I can see through walls. I can by an idea change the placid face of the world. I can also ruin my life, make upsetting relations out of an ordinary friendship, destroy the balance of a well-designed destiny—all with my diabolical mind.

Peace. Gracieuse is setting the table. I can smell the filet de soles and the asparagus. John is in Bordeaux. But Gustavo is coming at three. No use burning my own poor little mind. I will always have those of my friends to worry about.

Adding a new knowledge to my dancing: Elvira Viñes's way of handling her arms, the gypsy sensuousness and subtlety. We work together every Thursday. She is a fervent Catholic, with a Spanish prejudice against the theatre.

May 11. The theatre! Gustavo literally burst in yesterday just as I wrote that word and said without a stop, "My ballet is almost accepted by the American theatre; you will star in it, I love you; lend me five hundred francs until Monday; I have to go to Berlin with the German orchestra director who wants to present *The Scorpion*; I made an engagement for you at five o'clock. Put on your loveliest clothes—to see the Director; I want to buy a monkey now—that is all I need to be happy. I have to move from the hotel; they won't stand for my late payments any more. I'm a wreck."

He slumped down on the divan. "Feel my hands." They were frozen. So were mine. He started telling me what my role would be, and to play my dances, and to show me photographs of the production as it was done by the Playhouse in New York. I went

[1] *Proust's first important critic.*

to get dressed up. Accentuated my make-up and donned my turquoise Grecian cape and dress and my black hat. Gustavo pinned my veil, ordered an accroche coeur[1] on my forehead, supervised my make-up and thanked heaven for my docility!

We rushed to the Vieux Colombier. Met the expected hardboiled Director, who looked me over, studied my photograph in Spanish costume, said I had "it" and that if they didn't produce the ballet would I take the role of Salomé—Oscar Wilde's—and "hang around as often as possible." Gustavo was selling me. He counted on his interest in me for final acceptance, but there is an *if*: the expense, musicians, two other dancers, three men actors and a troupe, etc. On this hangs the whole thing now, and I'll know on the fourteenth. Even if I don't do it, I have had the joy of standing on the stage of the Vieux Colombier (to try out the floor) and of having Gustavo sit in the front row and gasp. Of course, Gustavo at this moment is no judge of me or of my stage presence!

Hugh, having eliminated music-hall and all "cheap" theatres, could only be pleased with the Vieux Colombier—though at first he paced the room, played a sad Scotch song, and smoked a cigarette without enthusiasm, because, he admitted, he "hated to share" me. And I had a curious feeling of being pulled two ways, with a fear of losing him, and of loving him *more than before*. What is John going to say?

May 15. Concert of Yehudi Menuhin, the most religious and profound experience I have ever known. A sense of the *miracle*. Moved to heights never known, by his deep, clear, classical, pure expression of the best feelings known to man—a child of twelve, who has not yet lived! No sentimentality, no overemphasis; the true, the exact, the wise, with an astonishing perfection.

I have been watching Hugh for some time, as if he were new to me, seeing him with my new eyes, as a woman, in the middle of my fever and struggles. I called him passive. He is passive because he is not creative, but he has a genius for receptivity and for comprehension. No one has such an absolute lack of egotism, which can be mistaken for lack of individuality. Because he lacks outward brilliance he is difficult to understand.

In my struggle for sincerity—as I see sincerity, not as John

[1] *A spit curl—literally, a hearthooker.*

does—I always catch myself. It occurred to me I was giving a lot of understanding to others and that I had not given it actively to Hugh (of course, fundamentally, he thinks I understand him all the time). As a result I have fallen more deeply in love with him. It is true he is maturing and changing. That I have learned to draw him out. But whatever it is, I know things about him now that I can never unlearn. The beauty of his character grows. While other men wriggle, lie, evade, fall in and out of moods and illusions and appetites, he remains incredibly wise, loyal, whole, balanced. I, who feel the sands moving under my feet so often, look up now to his magnificent trueness and force. Why, say the philosophers, stake all your faith in human nature, which is defective and unreliable? So we turn to art and to creation, to philosophy and to science. In every respect I have found this true—except about Hugh.

I want to write him down without lyricism, and I can't. I have loved him so absolutely and so desperately and so humbly these last days. I find a new taste to our quiet evenings at home, when we both lie on the same couch reading; when he plays his guitar and sings while I write in my Journal; when we talk and smoke; when I show him my cardboard Home and he laughs at the little paper chairs, at the red logs I painted inside the paper fireplace; a new taste to our early-morning breakfast together because the next thing he said after saying he hated to share me was "And now you'll have to sleep in, in the mornings, and I'll have to have my breakfast alone."

With what desolation he said this; as if the breaking of this little habit implied a fantastic change in our life! And with what desolation I responded, petting, consoling him, without succeeding in consoling myself.

Meanwhile, Gustavo exults in the success of his work, in the prospect of our "business and art partnership," which I insist primly is to take the place of nonsense. He calls me fourteen times a day: "Can you get me a girl for the group? Have you a wig maker? Do you know a music copyist? Can Miralles get the 'Prince'?" (Poor old Miralles balked *here* and refused all help, feeling he should have been asked.) Under pouring rain we rush about on little errands.

The two producers and the Director still want me for Salomé, because they have the idea that she was like me—young, innocent-looking, dreamy, and yet devilish! But I can't do both things.

"Come and help me choose a new suit," says Gustavito in a pleading voice. But here I quit.

In two weeks we move to our new Home, and I must buy face towels, teacups, pans, sheets, rugs, etc. So I went off to Printemps alone, humming, talking to myself, acting Salomé discreetly before the mirrors while waiting for my change.

"Do you really want to do this?" asks the Humorous Banker wistfully.

"Well, I want to go on having breakfast with you, having our quiet evenings—and I want to do this too."

"In itself it is not a very big thing—"

"Nothing has ever been a *really big thing*—posing, Havana, society, dancing—but I have always got so much out of it!" So I hum in the streets, drink a lot of Jemalt to get fatter, dream, wonder what my fundamental, native, incurable timidity will do in all this.

May 17. When John and I sat all afternoon on a divan discovering each other's character, intimate thoughts, desires, defeats, we felt that all-disturbing Impulse, resisted it, and faced it all again yesterday. We refused to admit we had flirted. No. He couldn't flirt with Hugh's wife, and I couldn't flirt with Lilith's lover. And yet—he has been wanting for some time to kiss me. And I had been wanting to see him forget himself. And when it happened all the rest of the world ceased to exist, for a minute at least.

And then, when he was gone, everything turned black. I lay on the bed, limp and miserable. I said to myself, Now I must not take this kiss too seriously. This is only "une amitié passionée." But my ice-cold hands, leaping heart, thumping temples, blurred eyes, and the fever which took hold of me were not so simple to dispel. So this was the overflow, in him and in me. One moment of great happiness, hours and hours of distress, of bouleversement [confusion]. Because that is the way I am. And he?

He called up the next day to see if we could all play tennis together on Sunday morning. I found myself saying, in an altered voice, a far deeper voice than I usually have: "Would you like us to take you to the Foire tonight?" He agreed with eagerness. But in the end, we went to the theatre, Hugh, he, and I. We were gay—talked a lot. I tried to read his inward feelings and couldn't. He was very gentle and thoughtful but self-possessed. So was I, outwardly.

We played tennis this morning. I didn't play so well; couldn't understand how things could go on running so normally when I was so broken up inside. Easy to explain. Nobody could feel all I feel. Well, I would be a "good sport" (how unnatural for me, when I am so raw, so sensitive, so incapable of throwing off whatever touches me!), but I didn't want John to think I was sentimental.

Meanwhile, I think *this* has been my worst crisis, because I expected help from John and stumbled on the greatest of all my complications, because I can't understand him as easily as the others, because I can't rid myself of him as easily. Enric and Gustavo never dominated me. John does. Through his maturity, has age, his force, his greatness.

I must not take his kiss seriously. I must not. I must keep my mind clear, my senses clear. I have wanted this, sought it, provoked it—it is enough. It came from a man who is very self-possessed, does not often lose his head, and has the best possible reasons for not doing so. I was happy—as a woman who loves to be loved; as an artist, because he repeated I was "extraordinary"; happy in a wicked way, a great way, a divine way.

May 20. I had three feelings about you. The first day I was terribly happy because you kissed me, and terribly unhappy because I knew that kiss was an overflow of enthusiasm like the one you gave that lady after your concert. The second day I wanted desperately to know what it meant to you so that I could guide my life by it; if it meant more than the one you gave the night of your concert, then I will never flirt with another person; if it meant the same, then I will do *all* to forget it. That day was the saddest of all. I felt more restlessness, more unappeased hunger, more despair than ever. The third day I tried to conquer myself to please you, because I know you don't like a magnifying of sentiment. So the third day I decided to take it all as an ephemeral joy, for which I am thankful. Which feeling do you like best?

You have sad days, flippant days, days of humor—which one is it today, John?

I don't want to deceive you; I'm not really a good sport—no more than the Elaine [in Arthurian legend] who drowned herself. I mean that I can't forget that kiss. Can you? And do you want me to?

There is not much room in your life for me, but I have found a beautiful name for the feeling which binds us—une amitié passionnée. That can include all you can give without in the least impoverishing Lilith.

Only the climax was perfect. Before and after, there were in him and in me, hesitations, analysis, thought, thought, thought. He himself said, "I, being such a cerebral . . ." And I, such an "imaginative . . ." that my conception of what the moment *should* be, what it would seem to him afterward, in retrospect, and to me, crushes me.

Little by little, I came out of all these states: physical ecstasy, mental turmoil, sadness, and joy. John being away for two days, I talked to him only here, and dreamed. The senses grew calm, and my head clear.

I have only a painful, profound, absolute need of seeing him again once before he goes to New York. I know now the whole thing will mean more to me than to him, because I am made that way, because I am a bottomless well, full of echoes and re-echoes, unsoundable.

It was Thursday evening at Mother's, for the playing of Joaquin's Trio, that he finally felt attracted. The week before, we had had a long talk. He knew then what I didn't know, that he wanted to kiss me. Thursday night I apparently looked better than usual. I was aglow with the excitement of my "theatre engagement." Our eyes met during the music with an alarmingly personal brilliance; we didn't know what the other was thinking, but, whatever it was, it was for no one else in the room.

I felt his excitement Friday. We had only talked an hour. I had an engagement. I put on my jade-green cape and gave him his copy of *Uncle Sam*; he was standing up and watching me. I went to the desk to get my key, feeling nervous and upset. When he walked toward me I knew instantly what was going to happen. His grip on my shoulders was very strong. I had my back turned to him at the moment; he turned me toward him and bent over me. All I had was a blind surging up of all my being to him, a desire to drink, to absorb him. His tongue in my mouth seemed like his very own flesh penetrating me. It was a long kiss—strong, possessive, absolute. And that was all that counted—the rest, his words, mine, his reluctance to go away, my calling up to break my engagement, the other hour and a half we spent together, were misty and unsatisfactory. I couldn't tell whether he was talking about indifferent things to cover a feeling or because the feeling was gone. I was surprised because when I called up about my engagement, he said, "I'm glad to see you have trouble with the telephone too—I was always afraid it was due to my bad French." A plain little sentence. But wasn't I saying them too, to cover the turmoil. Silly things. Things I didn't mean. And I was annoyed because my hands were ice-cold; he had never seen this happen to anyone and he teased me about it, and I showed him how they grew warm again when we talked about philosophy!

He should not have stayed so long. I wanted to be alone, to gather myself up and all my poor scattered feelings. And what depression afterward—always, after small excitements, after music, dinners, evenings out, talk, and doubly so after that afternoon—a terrible depression. A bad night—fitful, dreamful, and a sudden realization that Thursday night I had *dreamed* that John kissed me, dreamed all that did happen. Visible signs of a strange destiny overpowering me. Yet I want to be wise, rational, and John would be the first to laugh at all this, if I told him.

The next morning, Saturday, I was restless, moving endlessly about the house, making desperate efforts to write a coherent letter to Lorraine [Maynard]. When the telephone rang my heart gave such a jump that I couldn't answer it at first. When I did, in a deep voice, John asked if we could play tennis with him Sunday morning.

Today on the tennis court, though, I couldn't rest from thoughts of John for a second. But with my racket in hand, hitting hard balls, smelling the flowers, and being burned by the blessed sun, I felt very courageous and very strong and very woman and shouted defiantly to my great man: "Oh, I'll get over your kiss."

I know how insincere I am, because if he came in this minute and said again what I *didn't believe* the other day, "I love Lilith and *you*, too," in a tone that would convince me, I wouldn't try any more to cure myself, but would make a permanent place in my life for it.

May 21. I am so conscious of the wonder of life that when Lorraine writes me a letter in which regret and inertia show clearly, I take an hour off to write her a long comforting letter, trying not only to inject my own enthusiasm into her but to communicate to her my own life, so as to carry her up in it—though I can't tell her what is really happening, because it would break up her ideal world. And in the end I tell her, so she won't be sad, that she carries the most precious of all worlds within herself in her writing, because now I know *this is true*. All the madness and turmoil of these last days disappeared last night after I had written. I kept only the most supernatural ecstasy and sense of enrichment. In John, the kiss might be dissolved by other incidents, but I possess it now until I die, buried deep within me, fixed, imprisoned; and I can live it over again as often as I desire.

May 23. He came while I was out this afternoon, and I went out because I couldn't face the possible disappointment of his not coming; we had made no appointment. But it was his first day back from Bordeaux.

In the taxi, driving home at a furious pace, nearly met annihilation, and for a second I *desired* it. Because I am always afraid when I have reached a peak of life, of its being the highest and the last.

May 25. Formal dinner given by John for some of his friends at Lapérouse. When he offered his arm to me, he pressed mine hard and I responded. I who had come all in white, in a quiet mood outwardly, felt my restraint broken and madness again holding me. At the table he drank to me directly. After dinner, which seemed interminable, he insisted on being taken home by us though there was no room in the car. I realized suddenly he was burning up, as I was. I would have liked to feel his forehead, his heart.

In his apartment, we talked; he read to us from *The Sleeping Beauty*. Pauline and Graham were falling asleep. Hugh and I prepared to leave. "I'll go with you," said John. Pauline left the room angrily. It was half past twelve. In the car, on the way over, John pressed my knee in his hand. I sat close to him. I could feel his excitement and he, mine. We came up to the apartment. I opened the door to the balcony and suggested we sit there. There was a full moon. We put the lights out.

Hugh went to the kitchen to get something to drink. John and I stood there, facing each other, tendue par un désir affolant [taut with mad desire]. Yet we had to sit there, talking, only looking at each other, and twice I thought that in front of Hugh he would kiss me as he did the other night, and that all my life would explode. Looking at me, into me, he said he had not slept for several nights. I had a desperate desire to be tender to him, to soothe him, to be his. His fever and mine were melting into one another in spite of all barriers.

At half past two, as he stood by the door, ready to go, his eyes devoured me again, and I almost screamed: "I'll come with you." The pain of seeing him going away alone was intolerable. He wanted me. So did Hugh want me. I almost went crazy when we started to undress and he said softly: "I loved you tonight, little Pussy."

For the first time, I didn't babble, as I always do, about all my thoughts, which amuses Hugh, who smiles, assents, shakes his head, while he undresses. He was surprised and said, "Did you catch cold on the balcony?" John! John!

Evening. After the kiss, John teased me about Lilith.

"Do you still like her?" he asked.

"Of course," I answered truthfully enough. It does not hurt me that we talk about her; that she is his great love. She is the woman for him, so much older, wiser, braver, and more *humorous*. She has more to give him. I am only his little love—just more than a flirt, and for a few days. He will return entirely to Lilith now, and to flirtations with the many women who propose to him after reading his novels. His life is really overcrowded with love.

May 27. This morning when the doorbell rang, I knew it was he. I knew, too, that he wanted to say an ordinary good-bye and that he thought we could escape the feeling of the other night. He walked from the door through the hallway into the parlor; I closed the door. The maid was out. We stood for a minute facing each other. I wore a red-and-white sheer chiffon dress without sleeves. It was very hot but my body was as always cool. I had been doing my accounts—had put away the fever of thought. He had been terribly busy with the details of his trip. We were facing each other in the brilliant morning, clearheaded, self-possessed, for only a second. Even now I can't understand the all-sweeping force of that impulse which again drew us together, in spite of terrible obstacles, in spite of Lilith and of Hugh, and of all our ideas and dreams. He drew me to the divan, and we kissed, kissed, kissed, profoundly, desperately, hungrily.

"This isn't fair," murmured John, "but so lovely, so lovely." His hands caressed all of my body, sought my breasts, and my most secret, most sensitive part. "I want to kiss your breasts—go and put something else on. I want to see them—I don't want to tear this dress."

I stood up. Something he had written came to my mind, about

our right to see the body we love. I took my Spanish shawl to my room and came back to him wrapped in it alone. He carried me to the divan and stretched himself next to me. He kissed me, caressed me, penetrated my legs, was bathed in the moisture of my desire, but could not penetrate me entirely. He was powerless. He murmured plaintively, "I love you too much—I have thought too much about this, and now I think of Hugh. I love *you, you,* all of you, your mind, your unique self."

"I understand," I said. "It really all happened the other night. This is not the moment, not the mood. Don't be sad, don't be sad."

"Forgive me." All our strength had gone into dreams! "Lovely one—how beautiful your body is. Stand up; let me look at you."

I stood up and opened my shawl.

"The body of a dancer, Anaïs—what a precious gift you've made me, letting me see you."

When I came back, dressed, he was standing by the window.

"You are not sad?" I asked.

"It was our destiny, Anaïs—perhaps it was better so. At first I hated myself for being unable to pay tribute to a beautiful lady, but you are not only *that,* to me, today. But now I am a little bit glad because of Hugh—though I want you. Oh, I want you, and someday I'm going to possess you entirely."

We sat on the couch—he held me close. He fondled my breasts, which he found incredibly sensitive to his touch, hard-tipped, quivering.

"Lovely breasts. You are like a little faun—so sensitive, so little, so fine, darling little pagan." And, because I looked disappointed, "This is a compliment, you know."

"A faun is not a woman," I said.

"You are both" (kissing the *woman*). "You know I came this morning just to see you, not to make love to you, which is in a way, a higher compliment. But I couldn't help myself."

After a while: "You won't hate Lilith, because she thinks so much of you."

"No, I can't dislike her. She makes you happy. She is really the woman for you."

"It is absolutely true that I love her and you."

And a little later, "You won't experiment with love any more?"

"I couldn't play now, or endure anything mediocre after you."

"That is a wonderful thing for you to say, Anaïs."

I asked him, "What did you think after that first kiss?"

"I didn't think at all—it was lovely. I just wanted another."

It is strange. I wasn't hurt at his powerlessness. I felt his love surging up, surrounding me, in spite of the fact that it was not consummated. We were both happy for the *others*, though frank enough to laugh at our *technical* faithfulness, and John said it was unbelievable we could be happy merely because we didn't surrender entirely physically and yet so entirely in every other way.

"Neither one of us was cut out for the life of a Don Juan. We *feel*, we *think*, our passions."

After many more kisses we said good-bye.

Last night, *the* last night, he took us out to dinner and to dance. He was alternately sad and flippant. I was dazed. When we danced he showed me again the most intense desire and a love of my body. He spoke beautifully to me while Hugh and Pauline danced. "I really paid you the highest compliment the other day, Anaïs. You didn't rouse the rake to a forgetfulness of your wonder —yet ever since, I have been haunted by your beauty, your lovely, unbelievable, sensitive body, so much your *own*, like your mind and your face. I didn't realize until now what a miracle individuality is—such as yours—little faun, little faun with the sensitive breasts—how I have thought of them—I must be careful not to describe them. Oh, Anaïs, you are going to make many men bad. You have the power."

After a while we couldn't stand dancing together any more. One more desperate embrace of all our selves, and we parted really. This morning at the station it was only a pale, sad, domestic scene, far removed from the true separation. He surprised everybody, however, by showing his sadness. His sister Rhoda said, "Extraordinary to see John have regrets. He is always looking *forward*, enthusiastic about what he leaves but also about what he is going to meet."

I didn't lose my courage until afterward—alone. I realized then how much I had given, how much I had received, and I felt a déchirement [rending] which his absence of a few months would not explain, but my secret feeling is that we are separated for good and that Lilith will keep him now, and that I must remember I belong to Hugh.

I began even the day John came so near to possessing me to make up to Hugh by an increase of devotion, of energy in the creation of our life together. I built up a new conception of his own value and of what I must do for him. I couldn't understand John worrying about *me*. I don't care about myself. I *love* all the pain and all the struggle that comes to me. But Hugh is now my Religion, my God, the end of my life. I must give him more than I have taken away from him. John has genius and power; Hugh has a mystical quality which appears only in the greatest poets. I am going to inspire him and then free him of me, whenever he wants. All this could be destroyed in a minute if I broke his faith in me, since I am his *religion*, his all. I won't break this faith; I'll even bring *lies* upon myself, into my life. They won't do me any harm. My lies are here—this book will be sealed. I have sifted everything; only beauty remains. Everything human, weak that happens to me will not remain so. I take, even from John, only what is finest. The white heat. In such a white heat, you can mold anything. And on myself, above all, I work with merciless fingers. These fingers are soft and tender only for others.

If Hugh knew today what I am, he would crumble. If I learned today that Hugh is what I am, has done what I have, I would *understand*. My happiness would crumble but not my understanding or my pity; and not my love of life.

I discovered the qualities that are missing from John's writing: tenderness, pity, a tragic sense of life—the knowledge of the poets. He told me Monday how his heartaches were always covered by facetiousness—that he was never wittier than when he was suffering. He always *shakes* off sorrow by humor, like the French, refuses to let it penetrate him, to let it make too long an impress. Partly "pudeur" [reserve], partly stoicism, partly an intellectual fear of sentiment. He, so eager to possess all precious experiences, actually rejects the most profound of them all.

With me he must have suffered; I made him doubt himself, his philosophy, his love. Lilith is a triumphant, liberated, happy woman. I am the faun, little and wistful, mystical, and sensuous. He loved me despite all his wisdom. What will happen? I haven't made him happy—I have made him restless. He was sometimes afraid of looking into me, so he teased me, made me suffer, made hard remarks about little things. I smiled—I always smile. He was moved.

If he can go on being merely witty, clever, brilliant after this, if he does not reach a profounder feeling of life and of woman, then he lacks the ultimate concept. I have faith in him. Today he does not understand me altogether, but he will later. I am so much older than he knows. Through an intensity of the imagination and of the body, millions of things have happened to me, and I know a great deal; I am old.

May 30. I have had few days as sad as yesterday, known few times when I could control myself as little. I cried in the street, walking home, and today it is worse. I miss him more than I ever imagined. I think of him every second. What surprised me most is that he inspired me to write about him, though it hurt me so much. A sorrowful desire for *preservation.* After I had done it I felt happier and had no more fears of *losing* it all.

In a way he knew best when he said the separation would have been unbearable if we had been more closely united. But I can't rejoice, because I know now it will never take place. And if I am glad of anything, it is that by the fact of his absence I may liberate myself from the need of him.

I don't do Hugh any harm. Ultimately what he wants is my love and me. He still has them. I have the power to multiply myself. I am not one woman. He has the greater part of me. I have never been so prodigal with anyone as I have with him. I have only one secret from him. Everything else he knows, he holds, is his. The strange paradox is that these last days he has loved me more—I don't know why. He finds me lovelier, he is astonished by new expressions, by my ideas, by the rayonnement physique et intellectuel [physical and intellectual radiance] which emanates from me. A discovery to madden me and make me doubt all truth.

John had said before the first kiss: "You look adventuresome, but your journal discloses another character. It is really a sad journal, because you are preoccupied with real values."

May 31. I am going to write a novel someday about a woman who loved men while they were in trouble, defeated, unhappy, unsuccessful, and loved them until they triumphed over life, achieved their destiny, satisfied their ambitions, and after that, lost interest in them altogether. Because she was not a woman so much as an artist—a creator of lives, occupied with struggle, construction, not with climaxes.

It is a curious thing how I sustained Gustavo with an unblinking faith when he was penniless, unknown, alone, friendless, dejected, abandoned, unlucky. I never loved him, heavens no, but I found plenty of affection, encouragement, patience, tenderness, tolerance for him—enough to warm him up when he was freezing literally and symbolically. And out of all this issued his vigor, and he went out to see people, and he began to make friends. Today all kinds of offers and hopes are held out to him. He is about to meet La Argentina, to have his songs put on records, to have his music played in London and in Berlin. And he wants me to star in everything because he thinks we can work miracles together. I'm satisfied, though, to disappear now. He is rising up. My work is done. What kind of a monster am I? Do I love people or ideas and work—my creation?

He says I have changed incredibly in a year. I was, he believed, a sweet Spanish woman, malleable, attentive; a real doormat, such as the Spaniard loves. Today he finds me independent and ready to fly off—the Winged Doormat! I tease him, laugh at him, stir up his ideas. He is half angry, half tantalized. I thank him, for I am really grateful for all he has taught me. The "Mensonge Vital" I have let him have, his illusion about my true feelings, is justified by the miraculous power it has had on his life.

Truth, I know now, is not always *creative*. There is something else—the "Mensonge Vital," the illusion, when used at the right moment. Truth in *itself* is not worth more or is not more right than untruth, loyalty than disloyalty, sincerity than insincerity; but wisdom lies in knowing how and when to justly use them all. Ibsen, who was not such an old-fashioned writer as we like to think, blames the man, "the Wild Duck," who comes to destroy his friend's life, which was beautifully built on a lie that had long ago ceased to be harmful and had been transformed into good. He has nothing to offer in place of the desolation he spreads but a sort of moral satisfaction, which is in itself not very substantial nourishment.

June 1. When I tell Hugh the idea of my novel he seems delighted: "The first bit of cheerful news I have had in the last few months."

"Cheerful news?"

"Well, doesn't that idea explain *you* and all your friends? And even John, who, though successful, was lonely here without Lilith, so that now, when he no longer needs you, you will lose interest in him?" He is half serious, half flippant.

I laugh. "Well, if it makes you happy."

"It does. It is the sort of explanation I need lately. As you know, I've been jealous and sad."

"Yes, I know."

"Go ahead, write it—it's a great idea!" He was laughing like a boy.

Sometime before, I "confessed" to Hugh that I had had an overfull week, with visits from John, Gustavo, Mr. Wald and M. Liphart, and that I was ready to take my "sermon" from him; if he was really displeased—to go ahead and scold me. I knew I deserved it. And I waited. Hugh looked at my face, softened, and said quietly, "I only wish they would not smoke all my cigarettes!"

And afterwards, he humorously observed the supply of cigarettes. Monday the package on the table remained untouched, though John had spent an hour and a half with me. Hugh noticed that and said gaily: "This is a worse sign than all the others." I didn't laugh. He suddenly grew silent and then said, "Darling, I have tried to be nice and patient, but I'm glad John is going away. I am beginning to feel jealous of him."

Today, I am glad, too, that John has gone away. I am not entirely like the woman in my novel, because I really love, but today I realize that Hugh needs me more than John does—that he has staked all his happiness on me.

For two days now I have lost the taste for living. How flat all people seem to me! Before, courtesy, pity, sympathy saved me from discarding and disdaining mediocre people. And the other day, in spite of the interest of the work we are doing together, I discovered all Gustavo's faults, realized I didn't like the expression of his face, or his smallness, or his Spanishness, which charmed me before. John has worked strange influences on me. He has destroyed my taste for ordinary things.

Evening. It is serious—my illness. I refuse to dance for a charity affair. Nobody knows what is wrong with me. It is worse not being able to talk about John, about the *real* John. Everybody attributes our enthusiasm to his work alone. At Mother's I get restless and nearly explode. Nothing helps me—neither the sunshine nor the warmth, nor the nuns' party in the garden that I watched from my window, nor books, nor my work.

I walk down Boulevard Montparnasse facing the sun, blinded by it, my black cape floating behind me. My sadness is so strong that my body aches.

June 3. Gustavo is studying scales on my piano in preparation for his interview with La Argentina. I came away to my bedroom with my typewriter. I opened my Journal. Am I just making scales, too, studying for a real work? And when will I do this real work? Already, the praises I received are wearing off and I look at my Journal uncharitably.

Three or four times now I have hurt Hugh when the Bank has nearly drowned him. He would let the best of life pass him by. When I know he is wrong, I struggle, I pull him my way. I know that for a few hours he will resent it, be miserable. But I persist. We quarrel, we talk, we cry, we fall asleep in each other's arms. He confesses he was angry because he knew I was right. My only reward is, now and then, his recognition of the wonder of the life *I* have planned for and built and fought for. But I get tired of obstacles. I desire, secretly, independence, not having to plead for beauty and life, being able to direct it all myself. I feel in me a dangerous power which every day becomes more impossible to keep enslaved by a Bank, by the meagre authority of people who are worth a quarter of what Hugh and I are worth.

I could earn money, I could help Hugh. But he won't give me up, nor our breakfasts together in the morning. And I see a million things pass me by which I can't reach for. Prisonnière. I love Hugh, adore him—I also love life. I have the gift of *desiring*, of inventing more and more desires, of never knowing satiation and dullness. And I am cursed with the lack of genius for *renunciation*.

June 4. Hugh, sensing, perhaps, a danger for his happiness, woos me with infinite delicacy. We are incredibly united, in spite of my secret and my treachery. His love and his faith grow day by day. And I feel the other love to be entirely outside of our life, as if I were a separate woman for John and yet another for Hugh. The other love cannot diminish or alter this one. And deep within me I have the conviction that this one, Hugh's, is the enduring one, the eternal one, out of reach of all human and terrestrial destruction. When I think of it, I almost go mad. How can I explain that I should be richer in tenderness than ever before, more absolute in moments of passion, that I should dazzle him with new expressions of beauty, that I should be more lovable, and feel and look *noble* . . . while yet a liar?

My secret does not poison me! I feel glorious and strong and right. I bow today before the facts of my strange self—a woman who was not contented with one life but embraced several—as others do within a longer space of time. But I have no sense of time. There are no barriers for me. I am going through several incarnations *now*, all in one.

I want to copy here things Hugh has written about me in his journal which please me. While traveling through Italy: "And that is another reason for me to worship Anaïs—above all the other women I have ever seen or known she is exquisitely feminine. Such beauty, reflected from within, is hers; her lovely, liquid sad eyes, her soft, delicately molded mouth, her fine nose and chin, her downy skin, so white that it actually illumines, her fine, wispy hair bound high over her head, her goddesslike grace . . . Traveling with her is like a continuous Fourth of July parade, so much does everyone stare at her. Women and men, whether they are English or French, Italian or German or Russian, are intensely attracted to her and I have been told a hundred times by people of every nationality that there is something special about her beauty which they have never seen before. None seems to be able quite to make out what she is made up of and each nationality seems to see in her a little of the best of their own race."

Irritated by my overtipping on trips, Hugh said: "You're not a traveler—you're a philanthropist."

After a very full day, I asked Hugh what he thought, what he had liked, disliked, criticized, or praised, etc. But he was sleepy and unresponsive. He said he had thought nothing, and then teasingly: "What are you performing—a dissection?"

"No," I said, "an autopsy."

At a railroad station I tried to weigh myself on the baggage scale and the hands did not move. Hugh said that was the only thing I didn't make an impression on during the trip.

June 28. Five days spent in London to attend Johnnie's wedding, five days spent entirely on pleasing Hugh's family, on making a friend of his Aunt Annie and his cousin Betty, etc., etc., as an ending to a lonely, terrible month nearly drove me mad. I am ill. Mother and Joaquin have gone to Hendaye.

John sends me a book instead of a letter. Where shall I turn? To my work, to myself. I have paid dearly for that moment on the Peak! I cannot find rest and coolness anywhere, though I work on writing and on the new Home. For the first time in my life *everybody bores me.* After those talks with John, the tension of our curiosity, the fever of our ideas, the whole world looks dull.

My habit of observation keeps working, mechanically unfortunately, so does my outward cheerfulness, responsiveness; and my *body* dances! How long will this last? I long for the continuous "white heat" and lack the strength to endure a milder temperature and solitude.

There is at the bottom of my sadness, the eternal question of the value of human experience, a doubt, a disappointment. All my living—creative, intellectual, emotional—culminated in a minute of human worship—but how short that minute, how ephemeral, and how dissatisfied it has left me!

In art, I can achieve alone. What I give or fail to give is all my own affair. At moments, when I feel furiously individual, shrinking back from human love because its *fullness*, as I visualize it, is denied to me, I imagine that I want to remain alone, that I despise the partnership forced on us by human love.

Yet I can't maintain such a renunciation. I love. I prefer a moment, a single moment of white heat, and, after it, destruction.

Gilbert is translating; Gustavo is trying to sell his mediocre music; Horace is having his car painted over; Boussie is vegetating in a congealed socialism and still attending Jouvet's mediocre plays; Joaquin has bought a breviary and a life of St. Teresa; Godoy writes unconventional invocations to Foch; the Princess is in Aix-les-Bains with her lover; Mr. Wald is followed everywhere by a naïve English girl and talks about her "reactions" to Paris, which I don't want to know.

I'm hellishly lonely.

June 29. After writing in my Journal yesterday, I dressed up to keep a formal engagement—lunch with one of Hugh's millionaire clients. But after the lunch I drooped again, surrendered to my physical weakness, came home, secretly happy, to my writing, to solitude, to the same old keen disappointment before the empty letter box. I worked on copying and arranging my old Journals, from 1919 to 1929. Then I wrote a strange, mystical story, which John won't like because he admires sanity and normal thinking, but which pleased Hugh. And then I read. [Hermann Alexander] Keyserling, a wonderful thinker—marking his "Figure Symboliques" with exclamations of satisfaction.

I am dominating life and pain again. I slept soundly for the first time since John went away. I felt my head full of images, of ideas, of inventions, a world in itself; and I felt an occult power, with which, it seemed to me, nothing that I *desired* in all the world could be denied to me since I myself could create it with my mind, and live with it. Wasn't it John's mind I loved? Since he could give me only a little of himself, I would fill the void with other thoughts—with Proust, Léon-Pierre Quint, with Keyserling, with self-made stories.

Evening. Hugh says: "Your story is good, but nothing compared to your Journal. I really believe you have reached perfection in that form and that you will never do anything else. That will be your whole life's work."

June 30. Thought of John all day, and though I cannot quite understand what keeps him from writing me, I am going to be a "good sport" and attend to all those things which made him love me for a few days.

Sitting alone at the tennis club (the fashionable Circle du Bois), drowsy after a game of tennis with Hugh, I watched the children playing around and saw a little girl I wanted to have—an eery child, with a secret smile at thoughts of her own, running lightly to dry her hands, which she had dipped in the lake.

I must be beaten, I thought sadly, for I am beginning to want to pass my life on to another. Until now I never wanted children. I called them "interruptions," "renunciations," knowing too well that they might be like neither Hugh nor myself, not even perhaps an extension or a development of our ideals, but a mere repetition of ordinary patterns. Yet this child fascinated me. She drew me out of myself—perhaps that was the blessing. I chased after her fragile self, in yellow, red; left all my weariness far away. She was happy to have wet hands, she was happy because the sun was drying them, she was happy to be running. All of a sudden she stood before me, wide-eyed, startled, her arms wide open, her little yellow dress fluttering. I felt a second of struggle, as if the child were demanding a kind of surrender. And though my body was sore with passion, with hunger, with pain, I smiled, and she liked my smile and ran away, and ran back, and around my chair, until her mother called her.

I will never give myself entirely to anything. I will never escape from myself, neither by love, by maternity, by art. My "I" is like the God of the weak faithful who see Him everywhere, always, and can never escape the vision that haunts them.[1]

---

[1] *Translated from the French.*

I have desired self-perfection and greatness, a very immense conceit, and now I am crushed by the weight of my ambition. I would like to pass the burden to a child.

Evidently my story is universal. I read that the illness of our century is dissatisfaction. We struggled against fetters—there are no more fetters—yet we are still dissatisfied. Exactly. But why worry? Keyserling seems to think we can't accomplish anything worthwhile without that fever. So walking down Montparnasse on petty errands, I looked up at the gray sky and swore to rejoice over my discontent. And so the rain began to fall. I looked down again and thought: "Will John come in the autumn?"

7:30. "Pussy, get ready to go to the theatre. Mr. Silver invited us."

"I'm sorry, dear, my cold is worse after my dancing lesson. Please, put it off until tomorrow."

I can't stand the sight of *any* man. I turn my face away from men who admire me in the street, almost angrily. I don't want to see any theatre, any dancing. I hated my dancing today. Have I ever been bad for such a long time?

July 1. I asked Mr. Wald if he had read Virginia Woolf's *Orlando.*

"No. There is a group I know who spoiled it for me. They take such an attitude to anyone who has not read *Orlando*, as they did before to anyone who had not read Proust, and they are such terrible snobs about literature that I felt antagonized and read neither Proust nor *Orlando.*"

"I never knew about such coteries," I said. "I thought they existed only for the sake of rank, money, and name. I read so much according to my own fancy. I would hate them. They spoiled one good book for you, at least."

"There is such a group, too, devoted to Erskine and another who hates him. I must say, my friends belong to the last."

"And you?"

"I have no opinion," he said. But after I talked very "literarily" about John, he confessed he really didn't know Erskine but that he could see he would be a person to inspire either great devotion or hate—which is the case with all great personalities.

This book, mine, I mean, I had not intended to be about John. But I need material for his biography.

I send him Ségur's *Mariage Charnel [Carnal Union]* with a

little card, a monument of reticence: "I don't believe you have received this from Galland as until now Ségur had written nothing interesting. *The Enchanted Garden* was *exquisite*—there are so many sides to you. Don't forget I would like to read *Hearts Enduring* and to know how Uncle Sam affects people. Anaïs." And meanwhile I break my head trying to understand why he doesn't write.

July 3. What do I discover, alas? That I have been traveling in a circle, that I have come back to *poetry*. I have been asking rather anxiously to those who would hear: What is the matter with my writing? It doesn't coagulate into a novel or a story. "Hear this," I said to Gilbert. "What would you call it?" and I read him what I wrote on the child. "It's poetry," said Gilbert. "Pure poetry."

John used that word, so did Max Wald, so does Hugh!

"There are two kinds of poetry—strict poetry, which is like a flashlight on a crystallized mood or idea, and the less formal kind, which is extensive, developed. Yours is the second kind. You should put it into free verse."

That's the trouble, then. I am still lyrical in attitude, and that is why my novels are ridiculous. I am not mature yet. I was lyrical about John, about the fog, about my discovery of the joys of the senses, about a child, a few days ago. A unity, with a central theme that flowers into details, is required by the novel rather than a surprised excitement held together merely by personality. It does not appear to me that I have advanced, except that my poetic attitude is built on a very fleshy basis now.

I don't understand what has happened. I can't lose the *child* in me, and I can't lose the *poet*, though I am woman. The Princess tells me: "What I like about you is that at the bottom of the woman, the woman's seductiveness, there is always the child— direct and natural and *true*. I want to make a work of art out of this. In the first painting I only caught the poetry. Now I see the woman. You see this other woman (prostitute in vivid red velvet, dazzling blond hair, heavy eyes and mouth, caught in a gigantic spider web), she is dramatic, impressive, but one tires of her. She shows only one side. I want to make you dramatic and haunting too, in a different way."

My body has matured, not slowly and gradually but in a sudden miracle. My breasts are so full, so firm and pointed that they hurt. All the curves are softening and filling. In less than a month it has happened.

July 5. Entertained John's sister Rhoda at tea. Was nervous, excited, tense, because it was *his* sister, and she would see him in a few days, and I wanted her so much to like me—and afterward I was worn out and terribly sad again. I came home and put on the chiffon flowered dress. I am working very hard, on the decoration of our new Home, on my story, in making Hugh happy.

It seems that Anna told Rhoda that I was not like other women, that I was not interested in recipes, servants, shopping, but that I liked things her father liked—that I was like a man! She herself is showing such strong domestic attitudes.

The Home is growing in my mind. I stay awake thinking of new ideas, of corners, niches, arrangements of color.

"You have an adorable husband," says Rhoda Erskine. "And you look so happy together. Anna thinks you are a perfect couple."

If she tells John that we look happy, busy, contented, he will realize how little truth appears on the surface of life.

July 6. Last night, since I could not sleep, I finished my creation of our new Home. That is, I *visualized* it. Rugs, curtains, furniture, books, lamps, everything was *placed*. I was stuck with the problem of the doors, which are absolutely necessary and yet ugly. I tossed and turned in my bed and thought and thought until the image grew in me, formed out of an intense desire for color and richness—an image of stained glass heavily painted and studded with imitation stones, and shaped like my chairs in the essence of the Oriental outline; and the woodwork would be painted a slightly lighter bleu d'orient than the rug; against the gold walls it would be marvelous. I see it now as a mystic place—as something rising out of the labor of a dream. I build my prison out of velvet, gold paint, silk, colored glass, soft cushions, a royal bed. I transform my desires for the whole world into one lovely place. And all the time I cannot sleep and I feel my imprisoned anger gnawing me.

When I woke up this morning after a few hours of sleep, I faced the eternal anticlimax to all my fantastic imaginings: a tennis match, and a banquet offered to the players by a Vice-President: "And please don't let Mrs. Guiler fail to come."

I'll wear an indescribable green dress made by the Russian woman according to my design, a subtle, insidious dress, revealing and concealing the figure at the same time, Oriental in essence, complex in its embroidery, entirely unintelligible to all the people who will be there.

Hugh reads *Harper's Magazine*, to which Richard has enslaved me, and I go out on little errands to oblige Gilbert, to whom my attitude has changed. His book *Cities and Souls* conquered me.

We disagree however on reading the popular philosophers, such as [Will] Durant and Keyserling.

"They are quacks," says Gilbert. "Just serving up odd dishes in facile style. I prefer to go back to the original sources."

"Not I—provided I am convinced of the intelligence of my secondhand dealer, provided I believe he knows how to collect, select, sift, and choose the essentials, I am willing to entrust myself to his secondhand philosophies. I have a flair for the essential. I know when I get it. I know Keyserling has a good collection. I know and admit frankly I will never find time to read Kant, Spengler, Schopenhauer, Nietzsche. I like to make use of the indirect knowledge I get from critical studies. Durant was fine, you know."

Hugh and I: resemblance is based on the poetic attitude, and on our infernal gloominess. For that I love him. All women like him for his smile, his frankness, his trueness, his manners, his manliness, but he knows that they see only half of him and that the rest would surprise and baffle them. He is outwardly a nice, lovely man, direct and simple. Not really. When he looks into me, he sees his restlessness, his possibilities for passion, for will, for creation, for destruction . . . that is why he understands me, everlastingly, untiringly, and lives *through* me the greater part of his life. That is why, though I sometimes make him suffer so much more than these other peaceful women would, he loves me as one loves his own life.

Meanwhile, I crystallize my idea of Proust, whose writing is so *true*, so real that I am bored by his soirées and visits! Quint has achieved a work of art, independent of the interest of the subject. He has written an intellectual biography so illuminating and universal and profound that it is, to my mind, at least as great as Proust's own work.

Proust's subject matter discourages me, though I admit his treatment is unique. Through him, I feel I have lived in society and know it, and hate it.

Sometimes, when I draw near other women, I realize my resemblance to them (which I deny at other moments) and also to my father. He was a verbal lover of the "ideal," captivated by its appearance, by its charm, by its eternal prestige, but incapable of enacting it, guided by selfish motives always and his physical appetites; a sophist of the most pernicious kind, a sophist entirely deceived by himself.

Such a resemblance to him is my only *human fear*. The outlines of our two lives do not resemble each other, but some of the outlines of our deceptions do. Nobody has sought sincerity more passionately than I have, because I *doubt myself*! Is there any connection between my father's infatuations and my exultations? None, none, none. The whole basis is different—the *soul* (poor worn word!), the *meaning*.

Since I showed Gustavo an inkling of my true opinion of him, he is showing me an inkling of his other sides. We more or less quarrel by telephone. The bonfires of his brilliancy don't warm me up any more, all the crackling and spitting and illuminations. His musical promise was so untrue! Seeing that I missed manliness in him, seeing I had observed his helplessness before life, which is pardonable in a genius, but which in him came from his "cocotte" nature—in other words, that he likes to be supported not only by women but by those women's husbands and lovers—he thought he could destroy my discovery by a systematic boasting, assertiveness, and strutting. Manliness is one quality I never make mistakes about. I watched him strut—as I watched everything else—and let him, for the last time, buy me flowers with money he borrowed from me ten minutes before, in the café, where I also paid the bill.

Slowly, however, I balanced my gratitude against the miracle I performed in his life—lifting him up from absolutely hopeless situations to a promising one—against electric radiators and warm encouragements, against coffee and a constant softening of his many ruffled feathers.

Unfortunately, these experiments do not end as neatly as the final phrases one can use on them. For me, it ends here. For him, there will be a few more calls, and perhaps accusations of my having turned away from him through the influence of John, which is partly true.

July 8. This idea of liberation, which in each century takes merely a different form, now appears to me directed against ourselves, against self-constructed institutions of marriage, against the tyranny of self-invented conscience. We suddenly discover that our fetters are ideas and attitudes within ourselves, like our ideal of loyalty or morality. Logically, we have deduced that our mental attitude should change.

Eugene, who suffered from a morbid hate of ugliness, found in the modern novel an attitude of callousness, and having bathed his sore mind in that healing anesthetic, feels liberated. John, whose senses are now unfettered, delights in the feeling of painlessness, remorselessness.

Liberation from pain, scruples—yes, I myself have stood on such hilltops, self-possessed, reasonable, when I knew all things existed only in the imagination and that we could rid ourselves of all that bothered us by closing our minds.

Dangerous pleasures . . . because they exclude sensibility. The minute we cease to feel jealousies, dislikes, fears, hesitations, we lose with them our guidance to subterranean worlds. With loss of pain, we lose also keener joys.

Lilith has slipped cleverly between the dragons, shrewd and agile, but I will be devoured, and will find out all the things which exist inside the dragons' bellies.

J'ai l'impression qu'elle se soucie moins que moi de creuser le sens des choses [I have the impression that she cares less than I do about digging into the meaning of things]. John is fond of digging too. He asks what the purpose of our lives can be. Evidently Lilith laughs at such questions and casts them off by a fullness of action and movement.

Hugh doesn't resent my rebellion against three days wasted on tennis matches and banquets. He understands I seek "real things" more and more intensely, more and more exclusively, now that he has less need of my submission to create his position in the Bank. If it still helps him, to have me admired by the Vice-Presidents and liked by everybody in the Bank, from the clerks to the stenographers, at least he needs it less, and I begin to see a way of escape.

Hugh said he doesn't feel as sorry for me as he should because I *always get something out of it*, to which I retorted: "But you don't know how much more I would get out of life left to my own fancy." And as there was no answer to that, he went to sleep after swearing never to enter another championship, because they make him lose weight.

July 9. I wrote about the "dragons" yesterday in a taxi while doing errands for the house and preparing to receive the New Family. We met them at the station, had them to dinner, and took them for a drive in the moonlight. And all this time my head felt separate from my body, as if it were a balloon floating independently over the earth, connected to it by a trailing cord. The only thing which held my attention for a while was the beauty of the sweet peas I had on the table and the empty letter box. The sweet peas are still there, bathed in a cool, fake sunshine (I was warm only one day this summer), and I am about to plunge into "real" existence again—a dress fitting, shopping with the New Family, dinner with them.

Hugh teased me when I asked him what he thought of what I wrote. "I like dragon stories," he said.

July 28. That first week of July the New Family found me in a daze and left me quite wide awake and hurt. I worked my head off for them, but they made me suffer again with their undervaluation of me and utter misunderstanding of Hugh and our life. What a long martyrdom it has been, this relationship. I have truly offered the other cheek so that Hugh would not lose them. I have shown the greatest generosity in my life—my one act of absolute goodness. And Hugh's father died wronging us, misjudging us, but Hugh, through me, had been reconciled to him, had forgiven him and had nothing to regret. It will be the same with his mother. The psychology of it all is complicated and not worth unraveling.

We spent a weekend together at Le Fouquet, where our differences of ideas almost caused an explosion. And then we came back to our new Home, and I to my most tremendous task in homemaking. Blessed be work!

We moved Wednesday, July 17. House not finished and full of workmen. Until Sunday I never sat down except for my meals, which we ate at a pension almost next door.

I had the concierge to tame and bribe; the moving men to direct; two servants, electricians, plumbers, a window cleaner, and a hundred other persons to handle; fourteen baskets of books to unpack, seven trunks; Mother's apartment to arrange at the same time. Sweltering heat, which made me happy but which upset the others.

First night—just the bed made. No hot water, or telephone, or gas, or light. I was worn out but cheerful and hungry, and I felt a great sense of power because the whole thing was done with order and a thousand obstacles were quickly overcome.

In a few days I knew all the electrical terms and all the details of plumbing, the qualities and kinds of woods. I had all my closets made. I bought some paint and started some experiments with color. Even the first night, the house was tidy. Hugh never lacked a button. I kept a notebook, my keys in a bunch with tags on them. I interviewed the architect, had conferences with the concierge, spotted the defects, had them repaired, followed up the workmen, tipped, smiled, offered beer, craftily evaded deceit and cheating, didn't once lose my temper, and learned in a week to handle these perspiring, smelly brutes.

July 30. Physical exhaustion but mental elation at the feeling that I am using my force, fully at last, on tangible work. My poor Journal is such an obscure achievement. Dancing was a bright-enough one, but less subtle. On this homemaking I am using imagination, sense of color, of form, of comfort, of beautiful living. The only ungrateful, dismal part of the work is combating the laziness and stupidity of others and repairing their mistakes.

Now I'm in bed, alone. Hugh had to go to London for two days. I have a bad cold I don't pay any attention to. I feel queer, lonely. One side of me *does*, the other asks unanswerable questions. At night I compose long letters to John, which he shall never read.

Today I am happy because I find everything out alone. Nobody ever *studied* less. I never had a real education, never learned to draw, to mix colors, to decorate, to build, to calculate, but I arrive at everything alone, with my own mind. I have learned to mix colors and create some which surprise the painters. I have designed furniture, have quickly caught on to the proportions, etc. I can figure out how much wood it takes to make a closet (and I could never pass an arithmetic test!). The men who have to work for me are surprised that I understand all their trades, that I never change my mind, and always know exactly what I want.

So I console myself with little talents for my big faults!

I was also happy today because Gilbert answers my note on his last poems with a deeply grateful letter and says I am the only one who understands. I want to understand as well as create. I am so pleased that my judgment of his poems should have been un-usually accurate, as pleased as if I had written something myself.

Tonight, before coming to bed (a very, very large, wide bed with a Moorish headboard, a beautiful thing I bought in an antique shop and for which I have already been offered twice the price), I looked at the edge of the Bois, which fringes the lower part of our window (all the rest of it is pure sky) and thought: I have lost my desire to write because it hurts.

But so much hammering, sawing of wood, scraping of floors, turmoil, and hard physical labor has somewhat drowned all thought and I hesitate to seek it out again.

August 1. I console myself by observing that at twenty Proust wrote a book, *Plaisirs et les Jours,* which is as sentimental and as poor as *Aline.* If I don't write a fairly decent novel at thirty, then I will give myself up and remain just a dancer and the wife of a sub-manager.

I have just had my breakfast on a four-legged tray. I can see twelve inches of treetops and a yard and a half of clouded sky. My spacious, royal bedroom pleases me. The dressing table, of my design, with three mirrors, symbolizes the importance I give to appearance, but there will also be a desk. This part of the apartment will be my refuge. I can close two doors against the world and lock them.

August 9. While sewing gold thread on a sapphire-blue pillow I thought about the spiritual value of Decoration. Through it, I realize, I have gained in assurance, audacity, authority. I, who could still cry a month ago because I had to scold my maid, have learned firmness in this business with workmen.

Besides all the keen, profound delight I get from an assembling of color, stuffs, wood, and stone, I feel the joy of a visibly beautiful work. The immense studio is already painted, turquoise blue with more Veronese green than usual so it will harmonize with the blue-and-gold fireplace. The large Hindu lamp is hung. While the sawing of wood, hammering, and painting are going on, I make pillows or I paint room designs on the paper I should be using for that famous Novel.

Last Sunday, on my breakfast tray, I found John's letter. It gave me a queer feeling, like stage fright. I couldn't open it for a little while. I shouldn't have been so startled. It was a quiet, conventional letter, only handwritten instead of dictated to a secretary, as all his letters usually are. News of his activities, of Lilith's trip to her parents' home, and "Faithfully—John." Nothing between the lines, even for my wild imaginative power, except for that very quietness, reticence, whose meaning I cannot quite grasp.

It is here in my Journal.

Suddenly I felt that that was his way of being wise—not taking risks, with life, with complicated relationships. I am neither sentimental nor reckless and I wouldn't have written anything disturbing, but still—something more expressive. As it is, my answer is more *natural*, more real, more unafraid. Oh, well. Scotchmen are afraid not so much of their own volcanoes, which they can manage, but of other people's, and particularly of special persons like me.

My desire was for a letter without emotion or feeling, but with the same warm intellectual and human nourishment John gave me before the kiss.

August 11. Hugh was obliged to go to Nice for three days, and he was unhappy because I couldn't go. I sent him away just loaded down with tenderness and love and thoughtfulness. My love for him is my religion. I love him with words; as I look at him I say to myself: Look how fine his head is, how tall he is, how sensitive his furry hands, how high his forehead. I love him with my senses. I love him with re-creations of our life together, of past love. I love him with my mind, admire him. I love him gratefully for his wide understanding, his love of me. I *want* to love him, because he *ought* to be loved. I hate myself for whatever I make him suffer for. I have moments when I know that no multiple lives or loves can be worth his love, when I desire desperately to be able to control the overflow of my excessive nature and imagination. I love, *really*, only him.

As long as he wants me, I shall be his. His own trueness must not be meagerly, meanly repaid. May I have the courage, when the time comes, to give up other joys, other ecstasies, as he does for me, for doesn't he miss all the sweetness other women could give him?

August 12. Folded over and into myself. For a month now I have not seen anybody outside of the men working for me. I become unsociable again, shrink from renewing old contacts, marvel at my old desire for companionship, and find in utter solitude a bittersweet feeling, a sadness and a joy I never know with people.

Why couldn't John have written a letter like a talk, a nice talk. Poor John—he must have felt uncomfortable, writing me. Because he thought I expected either a work of art or a demonstration of affection, and what the devil does he expect from me?

I started mine, so naturally. Now I can't finish it. I always want to give people what they desire—and it is impossible for me to know what John desires.

Can it possibly be that John's literacy, clairvoyance, imagination, do not extend into his own life, that they are not spread all through his acts, that he can have understood Helen of Troy better than he will ever understand me?

Because the sun was shining I went out and bought myself an 11 frs. 25 necklace. Hugh says we are going to be rich. I feel rich already, with my wild enjoyment of little things, and my deep appreciation of the big ones, like this house. In my love for Hugh there is gratefulness for his courage in marrying me—and for the way he gives me things poetically, invested not only with material but also with mystical value.

Gilbert writes: " . . . very anxious to see you, discouraged about my literary career . . ." I answer: "Why should you be? You must have tried to bully it, or have asked indiscreet questions, or pressed it for security, or assurance of help for your marriage; that's one thing literary careers won't stand for. They are so mystically outside and beyond our human will."

August 13. I have moments, sitting in a taxi, in my best costume, gloved, while passing along the Avenue des Champs-Elysée, when I feel poised, worldly, triumphant, powerful—and that delectable feeling lasts until I reach my destination: a visit where I shall be sweeter and smaller than my real thoughts; an interview with the furrier, where I shall believe his flattering remarks and be more credulous than most women with a good critical sense.

Today I tried on an astrakhan fur coat which was beyond my means. It suited me beautifully, seemed made for me. It cost twenty-eight thousand francs, and I just want to know if someday that will seem a small sum. The furrier's remarks were artificial: Model created, shown, applauded, but no woman dared buy it and wear it, but how well I carried it off!

However, I did hear the whispered remarks of the mannequins, not made for my ears: that I wore it like a mannequin.

Yes, of course. Plenty of experience at Jaeckel's Fifth Avenue! Cheap little story of a sensational climb: Coat Model Becomes Wife of Sub-Manager.

August 15. Hugh comes back a day earlier because he couldn't endure being away. Making himself small, so his head can rest on my breast, he sighs and whispers his love and woos me. I put away my unfinished letter to John and listened to the story of the expansion of the Trust Work, source of all our comforts and pleasures.

I also received Gilbert and heard all about Kathleen, an English-Danish girl he is going to marry in November, who has a sincere love of literature and is utterly devoted to his own writing, but, says Gilbert, "she lacks certain external things which I hope you will teach her. I don't know quite how to describe it. And she didn't understand my poetry."

"But she is young, only twenty-one, and she has the most important thing," I said, "sincerity."

"I know now," said Gilbert, "what your reserve meant when I talked foolish nonsense about a spiritual monk's life containing all—you knew all the time about the *human*. How I feel it now!"

He did look more human, reservedly happy, secretly figuring how he could add to Kathleen what he likes in me, so as to have everything. But I have an intuition I'm going to like her. She is the fourth woman brought to me by her husband to learn "externals."

John's letter:

I'm sending with this the little play *Hearts Enduring* of which I spoke. And my thanks for the book, which came a few days ago. How good of you to keep me in touch with ideas which seemed natural in Paris, but which to most of the residents of Wilton will always be foreign. I enjoyed the novel immensely, but I wondered why you wanted me to read it. I confess I wondered. It seemed to me ingenious, but less subtle than the things you usually like. There's a lot of truth in it, of course, but expounded with an almost professional dogmatism, I thought. We must talk it over when next we meet, which I hope will be before long.

I see by the address that you and Hugh are in your new home, in that lovely part of town. Congratulations! I'm glad I saw the spot, so that I can visualize you as you are.

We settled quickly into our routine here. The farm never seemed so beautiful, Pauline quickly found a good outfit of servants and we started in for the summer. Graham is at the Summer Session of Columbia for six weeks in July and August. He has been painting, and both he and Anna speak constantly of Paris and yearn to be back.

Since our return, I've been frightfully busy, but happily so. I've almost completed that new novel, *Sincerity*, of which I told you the plot. It's to come out in October or November. As soon as it's done I've promised to write a libretto for an opera George Antheil is to compose and produce in Germany. If it really comes off I may want to go to Germany next Spring as soon as I can get away. I'd like to go to Bordeaux to collect a degree. But my plans are chiefly wishes at present.

Until about ten days ago I spent five days a week in N.Y. Then Lilith went to Colorado to see her parents and I've been here since. Tonight I go off to Chautauqua for a fortnight to play. I'll take my typewriter along, however.

Pauline is very well—begins to look even a little stout. Her winter in Paris did her good, and she still says she'd like to go back and stay. We all got something from the trip.

I wrote Hugh that I can't thank you both, not in any adequate way, for your kindness to me all year. The next time I come I'll be a sensational Parisian and get along without calling so often on your patience. Meanwhile I'll be on the watch for a chance really to show how much I value what you both did for us all.

Will you write me news of the dancing and the acting, and all the news? My letters come best to the School, 49 East 52, N.Y.

And will you give my love to Hugh and your Mother and Joaquin. We think and speak of you all constantly.

Dear John:

I appreciated your handwritten letter, and *Hearts Enduring*. In the play you certainly achieved the effect you desired. I don't know if you had a chance to discover how strong is the visual impression it makes, even read (precisely because each gesture does mean something), and how the phrases endure in one's mind. It is really deeply moving—I hope someday I may act in it. But just now I couldn't even show it to the producers, as I have broken completely with their theatre by my refusal to act in *Salomé*. I also gave up the ballet dancing temporarily. Whenever we talked about it, Hugh said yes but sang Scotch songs, with undue emphasis on their wistfulness, and I know what that means. He also thought that if I danced every evening I wouldn't be able to get up early in the morning to keep him company at breakfast.

So I turned Decorator! When your letter came I was up on a ladder, painting, and the paper bought for the novel is being used for drawing. I do write, too, at the Club in the Bois, while Hugh plays tennis. I have added a great deal to your biography.

Tell Pauline her fears for Hugh's happiness were fully justified: Hugh had to go one day without shaving while I lacquered his shaving-brush handle.

You are right, John, I do prefer more subtle things than the *Mariage Charnel* but very often I take ideas where I can find them, and sometimes in books that have no other value. I believe you do, too, and that is why I have passed on to you books which in themselves were not of great value but which had a little truth or the seed of an idea. So few books are rich all through. But occasionally I don't mind the stripped, artless, scientific analysis which the French use to gain clearness—do you?

Of course, to all ways I prefer yours, which is a kind of lyrical lucidity. I did think, didn't you, that the description of the woman entering the room to meet her lover was lovely. Ségur, however, doesn't deserve any more of your attention—he usually imitates d'Annunzio and Anatole France together. He might have found a better mixture.

I had hoped for a few lines from the notebook, so as to have news of your thoughts, but you write that you are "frightfully busy." Does that mean you have less time to write in it?

I hope I've given you all the news you wanted. I didn't tell you that I'm trying to make up for the limitation of Spanish dancing by developing its more Oriental sides; that Joaquin and I discovered that musicians do think, but in notes, and that is why they don't appear very intellectual in conversation, that I wrote a story about a woman who takes a long bus ride on a sad, rainy, foggy evening. Affected by the temperature, people let their streets pass without getting off. Also affected by the temperature, the woman begins to tell everybody the absolute truth about themselves. Immediately there is a scramble for the stop signal.

Will Lilith's clever play be produced?

I suppose you have missed your *Mercure*. It has been going to the bank by mistake. I'm going down today to give them your address.

Votre amie

Since I was a child I always had a gift for attitudes, poses, a way of walking, sitting, which satisfied the artists and suggested pictures. Now, since I dance, I realize this is even more accentuated. It makes me happy. Nobody believes it's natural, but I don't mind.

I am beginning to love unreality, artificiality, which Modern Art expresses so perfectly. Some of the ultramodern rooms look symbolical, inhuman, impossible . . . and I like it. I read future ages in it, far off, impossible almost to imagine today, just as today was unimaginable six hundred years ago.

I love the coral glass trees as much as the real ones, the unreal turquoise of my studio as well as the real colors of sky and sea, my exotic but not strictly Oriental furniture as much as the authentic bazaar stuff. What reality lacks, a lie will give—a beautiful lie.

Complexity. I am beginning to seek it, or at least not to fight it, as all sane people do.

In *real* things, I seek only spiritual values, intellectual values. There, I can't stand artificiality or any substitute. I hate Godoy's salon and Godoy's literary friends, and all other literary salons. I know now I only liked them because I was admired in them.

August 18. Je vous presente [I introduce] Madame Melnikoff— Russian-Japanese woman, thirty-nine or forty, dressmaker, artist, a genius in her profession, erratic, undisciplined, always late, missing three-quarters of our rendezvous, addicted to drugs, poor, rescued when on the verge of suicide, ungrateful, rapacious, inventive, inspired, the one woman who knows how to dress me and whom I am now supporting and whom I am recommending to all my friends.

Together our minds create costumes which are really works of art.

Now I find that her father, Malioutine, a rough uncultured man, was a great artist in decoration and furniture making, for whom the Princess Ténicheff created a workship and founded a school. He is dead. The furniture is in museums, and I have been given access to the unique book of his designs. A revelation. Rustic foundation, intricate decoration, stylization carried to a high degree, suggestive of Fairyland, of the Orient, of Byzantium, and yet just Russian.

Again Russia gives me more than all other countries in color, form, temperament, rough inspiration. I can't use this art just as I find it. The rusticity of it doesn't suit me, but its beauty moves me and pushes me onward to seek a coagulation all my own between the refined and the unreal, the modern and the traditional. Out of all this, my mystic, fairy home will grow.

Time is overprecious for me, and yet I don't regret the many hours I have spent tracing out those designs so as to accustom myself to their rhythm and character, the many hours I intend spending on decoration of every object in the house.

Princess Troubetskoi spent two years on her furniture. I won't do that. I have other work at hand, but I do want with my own hands to create an outward reflection of my visions, a chair or a door that will be a symbol, holding in itself the meaning, the emotion, the beauty, the evocation of an entire land, like a voyage to Egypt, a night in India; though I may never see either place, or live that emotion, the key to the dream will be there.

All unlived emotions turn to inanity, as is plainly visible in the eery writings of so many Anglo-Saxons—James Barrie, Stella Benson, Walter de la Mare, who are so beautifully mad, fantastic, strange. Only in an inexpressive race was the most inexpressible madness so highly cultivated. We, the Latins, constantly verbally free, impulsive, natural, fantastic, have remained quite sane, and lesser poets.

What happens when you don't live out physically and humanly an idea in your head, a dream, a desire?

Psychologists are tired of detecting the ravages caused by frustration. Barrie, Benson, etc. were not frustrated, but I know their imaginations went wild within them because they didn't turn to vapor in the fresh air of light conversations (no, since the Anglo-Saxons either say the opposite of what they feel, or grunt) or into actions, which would have dissolved the purely literary outburst.

We talk. Our dreams evaporate.

Will I thus see the world and all that I am hungry for, through fantasy, with a bandage over my eyes (because Hugh feels they attract trouble) and a little chain around my neck (I must be home at six o'clock), and what will happen?

I will know the Anglo-Saxon madness—ecstasies of a vast imaginative world while sitting still, by Hugh's side, while he smokes.

I am only afraid of my body.

I have exhausted French literature, absorbed all its neuroticism, and all else it could teach me. I turn with gladness to English again, and have the luck to grasp Ford Madox Ford at the library, finding in it a far more substantial food for the mind. The others were for the body entirely. Ford satisfies both.

I like Ford's style—complicated and plain, invented when the occasion requires it, undisciplined, excessive. I like the undercurrents. There are no undercurrents in French books, except electrical, devastating physical ones, with scintillating vocabulary to adorn the hunting scenes.

Hugh, who wears his little chain, too (his bank work, the need of money, for me too, alas!) is longing for home and literature exclusively. But that happens every weekend. Monday he'll devour the stock market column more hungrily than his roll and be thrilled by the day's quotations.

September 5. The New Family came. They were overpowered by the apartment, frankly swept off their feet; the Mother, for ten minutes, really admired me. The Cat was bursting with pride. We even danced for them Thursday night in the Chinese-red room, with its stage-light effect.

Now I realize I have made a work of art—a very personal and very special thing. Ethel voiced the fears of my friends when she said: "When you spoke of Oriental essence I imagined something oldish and stuffyish. I never expected this perfect mixture of modernism and livableness, plus atmosphere."

It is a fact that the apartment is a perplexing mixture of comfort, airiness, freshness, practicability and strangeness. I'm happy, terribly happy. Through creating, I fought off the depression weighing on me after John's departure. I surmounted my own character and made something beautiful. Hugh wonders how I can externalize such subtle ideas, how the apartment can so express us, our feelings and dreams.

Thought begins again. I am back to my hole and keep on writing storyless things, and wondering what's wrong with my poetic but ineffective, unsuccessful, unprintable stuff.

Still, it is all so consistent, so beautifully bound—my home, my costume, my life, Hugh in the center of it all, my dancing, and my unpublished writing! I work for working's sake and without proof of the value of what I do.

September 7. Courage—it sometimes fails me, in the middle of my feverish shopping for the house, because of the intense heat and because John likes formal letters! I go to Sherry's, drink a frosted chocolate, smoke a cigarette, stare at all the American women who remind me of Lilith, and come home tired out but restless. It isn't work I need—I've been overworking. But I'm going to *pull through,* by all the pagan gods, and be a strong, triumphant *creator* and less woman, which is too painful and too dangerous.

I sit at my own desk, of my own design, facing the window, the trees. The seamstress interrupts me to decide on the length of the curtains. All around me things come up, come out, grow, and they are all beautiful, while every day I have less strength and more hunger. Here's a house, here's Hugh's happiness, here is my writing, here is my dancing. I feel like giving them away as I give my ideas, with an indifference which infuriates Hugh—because, as I tell him, "I've got plenty of other ideas in my head."

Edith has gone back with a blue replica of my turquoise costume with my black hat. Ethel has my antique bracelet-watch and other things. John took away my contentment. I never get anything back in exchange!

Nonsense. I got a formal letter, which included the thanks for my kindness. Kindness, hell. Enthusiasm, devotion, overflow of all kinds of things which men get rarely from intelligent or wise women. I'm too damn generous. People like a feeling like mine, but it's rather cumbersome. You can't file it, you can't leave it around when you have a wife and a mistress and a curious public; and when you're at bottom just an honest Scotchman, you are uncomfortable. So you write a formal letter to your dear little faun, and she turns into a sedate decorator of a nest for a perfect married couple—and writes bitter things and stares at the hundred Liliths who are walking through Paris with her eyes, her hair, her walk, her——conquering air.

September 8. I am not very proud of what I wrote yesterday. It was a moment of weakness. My "illness" (missing John) comes back unexpectedly when I think I'm cured. It rather baffles me. I don't find anything to replace our talks—those long talks about his problems and Lilith—and I wonder rather wickedly why John liked to talk to *me* about these things instead of to his other women friends, and why I much preferred hearing all about Lilith from him rather than about my own miraculous charm from Gustavo. All the time I realized none of these things—we were both dreadfully sincere. If he gave me a compliment, it was accidentally. If I gave him one, it was on literary grounds. Now, when I think about all these things, my eyes slant, and my mouth curls upward to the left, and I am at once terribly amused and terribly sad. I think if I get another formal letter I will be entirely cured. I'll set another test for him: if John doesn't come to Paris this Fall, then I'm cured—sworn to on a fresh Saturday morning, with very wide-open eyes.

September 9. Hugh and I went off to the country to heal our frayed nerves. We lay on the heather. We smoked. We read Huxley, we made love, we talked. To cap it all we had a dinner with cheap music at a Moorish restaurant—and I love cheap music. It acts on me like champagne, makes me tipsy and happy and even witty. I asked Hugh silly questions. Why couldn't I talk just as I wrote, as well as I wrote? Why did all Huxley's little sarcasms about my pet ideas bother me? Why was I so anxious for perfection that I constantly put myself on trial? Am I sincere? Am I whole? Do I know what is worthwhile? It is just a shade of difference which separates me from the sophists, the sentimentalists, the poseurs, the egoists. It is so easy to slip into these things; I watch myself and take Huxley's people (in *Barren Leaves*) as a warning.

"Have a lamb chop," said Hugh, "and don't worry. You're all right."

"But I'm not," I said, my head buzzing with the cheap music. "The fact that you say so doesn't convince me." My attention was caught by a very sophisticated woman who sat near us. "There's an exotic-looking woman."

Hugh studied her a second. "From the Jungles of Montparnasse." Can cheap music possibly affect him too?

A cool morning. The books are in the new bookcases; it was that ceremony I enjoyed most of all and I didn't let anybody help me. John's books are in the best part. I'm strong again. Ready, if necessary, to build another house. How can you believe in the mind when a breath of pine and heather, a long-stepped walk, and a day of sunshine can cure you of almost anything?

September 11. For the first time I get up and find only three little things to do on my list, which can wait until this afternoon. The apartment begins to look livable, although two weeks ago it already looked interesting. I can begin to brood a little. I have made up my mind about one thing: that John's kiss was a whim; that if he comes this fall it will be with Lilith, and that I will be remarkably self-possessed and platonic!

It's all over. It was wonderful. So is my getting over it. It's curious how I now have a feeling that holding John's love for a few minutes is the only experience I couldn't endure missing. Nothing else can come up to that, or to my love for Hugh.

Everything else would be a mediocre echo of these two experiences. All other feelings resemble these, fundamentally. All the living imaginable is contained in these two aspects of love. And I couldn't bear a repetition: there is only one Hugh and only one John. For me, there are no other men worth knowing. It seems to me that I should be contented. Let me build on that from now on, without backward glances, and without *mediocrity*.

The morning is fresh and good smells come from the Bois. My desk is ready. My home is built. Hugh loves me and is happy. I have beautiful dresses in my closet, a pair of Perugia sandals, Eustion perfumes on my dressing table. I'm going to *work*.

Now that I have no rendezvous with anybody, I evade the cafés when I'm alone and go to the little bakeries, where nothing happens. The waitress stops mending her stockings by the side of the cash counter to bring me a cup of coffee, which doesn't sit very steadily on the bread crumbs left by other people. The flowers in the little jar are faded. Children come in for their goûter [snack] of bread and chocolate. The whiteness of the bakery ·walls is like the whiteness of a sanatorium—and here indeed I am recuperating from the fever of smoky cafés, where apparently all men are lonely and I was the only woman who could make them happy.

I have said before that I don't like "intellectual infancy"— the first tooth, the first time it walked, cried, talked, etc.

[Francis de] Miomandre makes a watercolor novel, that novel most writers just can't help writing about their youth, in which I can see clearly he is obsessed by visions of a certain sentimental, tender-hearted young man, who appears now and then in his grown-up world endowed with the inevitable anemic ideals, and with the audacity to write poetry.

Those men who have a genius for creating moments of white-heat living are the very men who don't know how to make them last. Their own enthusiasm flares and dies, and you can't expect anything from them outside of that intense moment. And how blank the moments in between! They are dull, they are sleepy, they are in a period of "warming," like the silkworm, in preparation for the dazzling minute. Who wants to be caught like that in such a mirage of fitful, spasmodic beauty?

Joaquin played his Trio, which I love so much, in the little apartment on Port-Royal one morning. I sang the words each note meant to me. He was startled.

"Didn't you imagine such a meaning?" I asked.

"Yes, but in *notes*. All that happens to me, all that I know are *notes*, not words."

"Like a direct language that doesn't become conscious *words*. A direct transfusion, different from mine, from feeling into sound instead of from feeling into words. Yours could be compared to water in an alchemist's bottle, mine to sand. You work in fluid matter. I, in solid. I must transmute water or sound into sand or words to understand completely."

Those who don't know this accuse musicians of not thinking, of not being intellectual; they are, in another language, which remains for them on that plane until we, the word makers, translate (they hate translations!).

In London, Hugh's mother and I had this conversation. She was worrying about Johnnie's wife—and giving me a respite.

"They say her father is Welsh. I have heard the Welsh are such unreliable people! Do you know anything about them, Anaïs?"

"I'm sorry—not a thing. All I remember reading is that the Welsh were once part of England and are now separated."

"I wonder *why* they separated," said Hugh's little mother in a tone in which women say: "I wonder why he divorced her."

I shouldn't have written that nothing happens in bakeries. The other day in the one in Place Blanche a little four-year-old boy came in for a chocolate roll. The lady waited on him with very ostensible fondness. Then she talked about him when he was gone: "He is not like the other kids. His mother dances at the Moulin Rouge. The little one sings, he acts in the cinema—the other day he played the son of a king—he did everything they told him to. He comes every morning to fetch his roll. He doesn't make a fuss when we ask him to sing. He is not an ordinary kid."[1]

The least little thing upsets my balance again. The other night music set me off dreaming feverishly of lives I will never

[1] *Translated from the French.*

know. At the same time I am lucid enough to know that ten lives such as I imagine would not be worth one with Hugh—and yet I long. I long, and all I want conflicts with Hugh's precious happiness; all but writing quietly at home, owl-like, mouse-like, unseen, as in a harem. I cannot live on that alone. But I'll try. I have yet a lot of resources: myself, small illuminations, which give me for a moment the illusion of white heat, and spirit to go through, cheerfully and generously, experiences which I only criticize in my Journal. Only last night Hugh was surprised at the wholehearted way I entertained some absolutely colorless Bank people.

Together with all these divagations or, rather, in the middle of them, I took out my small box of tools and rescrewed the toilet top, which had come off, and filed off a superfluous rosette from an iron lamp. I am not always occupied in futile things!

September 15. Palace Hôtel de Caux, Caux/Montreux, Switzerland. Let's not get lyrical. I am sitting on a large balcony, suspended high over Lake Geneva in company with the misty clouds, facing a semicircle of extremely majestic mountains. We have had our breakfast. Hugh is already looking rested and ruddy and Scotch. I have discovered a book I wish I had written. I have written a spontaneous letter to John. Hugh has figured that he will be able to retire at forty, and I planned that we would give up our apartment in Paris to lessen expenses—live in it only perhaps one month a year to see the plays and hear the concerts; then we would take a little chalet up here and write; and move perhaps to India and write; and visit Egypt and write; find a balcony overhanging the Mediterranean and write. We would seek out just the people we want to know to make up for all those we don't want to know. We might meet on the way John and Lilith traveling too. John and I might have a talk.

I might get my Journal published. I would dance only for my friends. Might act Salomé for a charity affair, with plenty of clothes on.

A marvelous life.

But let's not get lyrical. The mist is floating away. The lake steamer makes a white snaky trail along the absolutely placid water. We are in our tennis clothes, ready to play later on. I have passed the exceptional book to Hugh (*Le Dieu des Corps*— Jules Romain). My letter to John is safe under the blotting paper.

Hugh was worrying yesterday about the time he was wasting

on reading Huxley's *Barren Leaves*. "I suppose it's the Scotch in me. I feel I ought to make better use of my time. I ought to read some heavy, stodgy philosophy."

"There is time for everything," I said. "Well-diluted philosophy such as you get in *Barren Leaves*, concentrated philosophy, and Huxley's refined disenchantment—they're all useful."

We know several social snobs. Hugh said they were hateful. I confessed I thought myself an intellectual snob. Hugh protested. He tried to remember all the unintelligent and good-hearted people I had been kind to. He had to admit that although I visited them at the hospital and knitted booties for their babies, I dropped them as soon as decently possible. And even the intelligent ones who didn't develop—Eduardo, Enric, Gustavo—I dropped.

"The difference is," said Hugh with his usual vacation brightness, "is that a social snob is not concerned with real values but with unreal ones, whereas your snobbery—since you insist on the word—is motivated by a sincere desire for progress. You discard only worthless things."

"That's a consolation. It makes me feel better to believe it."

Hugh, on our vacations, becomes really talkative. He turns to literature. He reads a lot . . . but just as he begins to get interesting, it's time to go.

There is a Lady Godiva in the hotel—at least, half of one, the hair half. I doubt whether the other half would be effective, except at a distance. It's a little massive, and on horseback it would wallow. Still, the man who eats with her seems satisfied with the ensemble, although it doesn't keep him from analyzing my own slender possessions, and from exclaiming in Italian when I pass and while the Lady is buying postcards at the desk.

September 19. What ecstasy, what sweet, excruciatingly sweet moments I have known through my writing. The day before yesterday I sat on the balcony with Hugh, looking over my Copied Journal, and came across something rather fantastic I once wrote in Paris. Suddenly I said: "Darling, I have an idea of how to use the Journal."

That's happened before, so Hugh didn't get worried. But I started then and there. Separate stories, united by resemblance in personality, an enigmatic resemblance. And tricks! I never had so many ideas. When we took a walk I was sizzling, fermenting.

I told Hugh this story and that. All of a sudden, like a miracle, I was coagulating!

I wrote today. The first drafts, and speedily done, were all good. Not cheap, not unlike the Journal.

I wrote John—about other things, *Le Dieu des Corps*, Mann, and that I was far from quitting, as he feared I might. Two lines about the fever which fills me.

Hugh has gone to Milan for two days. I finished the first and longest story. The second is three-quarters done, the third half done. Now I know I'm on the right road. My face is aflame, my eyes are worn out.

And I have to go down to dinner like a real lady!

I know I have one quality which I owe my Journal. I discard the conventional and futile details and go straight to the center, to draw the *essence*, and only the essence, of my experience.

How I Came to Sit Inside a Coffee Cup.

The other morning the milkman brought in a big package containing my fur coat while we were finishing breakfast. I laid the breakfast tray at the foot of my bed. I jumped out of bed, slipped off my nightgown and reached for my chemise, wanting to dress quickly so I could try on the coat. Hugh pretended to be overtaken by a violent desire for me and also jumped out of his bed. "Don't dress yet, little Pussy. I want to play with you."

"No, no, no," I said, hurrying into my chemise. But before I had it half on, Hugh walked toward me, laughing. I started to run back and forth, laughing, too, so I couldn't put my chemise on but held fast to it so it covered my front. Finally, in desperation, to escape Hugh, I leaped backward and sat on my bed, on the tray, in the coffee cup, and Hugh had to lift me up.

A big love can be held together by little phrases. Hugh calls me: Pussy Willow, White Rabbit, Foxy, Pussy, Little Dog (when I spill something on the table). He says my eyes are too big for my face—and my mouth too small to eat with. "How do you feed yourself?"

I call his manhood "Toby"—"Down, Toby," I say, when it points upward. I call him "Cootie" because he sticks to me so; "Tomcat"; "Little Boy," when he makes irresistible eyes at me. I said: "Don't use the same dirty tricks on me that I use on you." To imitate the lowering of my eyelids he pretends to pull down a long shade. When he wants me to love him he comes miaowing, licking my neck, purring, scratching. I chew up his soft ears. His forehead has a peculiar, fruity, woody, milky smell. He has a trick of kissing in the air, very fast. It sounds like drops of water falling. I say: "There's a leak." And stop it with my own mouth. We call love "playing," my longing "a trickling."

Hugh's idea is that the test of a great love is endurance. There is no other way of telling.

Then what I have for him *is* a great love. It surpasses, outlasts, everything else. I haven't doubted, one second, the ultimate strength of it. Other feelings have passed through it without affecting it. It is almost *religious*, mystical.

I would have liked one life, just one life, however, with John.

September 20. Hugh came back this morning early from his business trip. While he slept after breakfast, I sat out on the balcony and wrote my "mystical" story. I read it to him after lunch, and he cried over it. Then he exclaimed: "That's perfect, absolutely perfect. It's the most beautiful thing you've ever done."

I feel a joy which I can only rank second to that of love.

The seed of it was in my Journal. I had written a cheap version of it once at Port-Royal. This new version tormented me for two days; the idea wouldn't become clear enough, and yet wouldn't leave me. Finally this morning it came all in one dash, and I wrote to the very last word without one change.

September 21. I have been so happy here, and I don't want to go home! Hugh, sunburned, dour-looking, but feeling well; my books, my writing, the "coagulation"; the marvelous static mountains, the peace rising from the lake; our walks through the mountains, tennis (I play well now and so hard and firm a game); above all, the inward clarity and force, the flow of ideas; the sense of my gift—of my blessed solitude in the world, of my own possession of the world, of my domination of love, of loneliness, and all the things which want to beat me down.

September 23. We arrived home at night. It was soft and luxurious and beautiful, but I was still far away, walking through the mountain roads.

I began early this morning: inspection of Mother's apartment, new, painted; watching new rugs arrive, making the menu. But I didn't care about all this. I wanted the mountains, my ideas and my writing. But I'll come down again.

The maid is neat and pretty, and brings me mail on a tray.
Lovely dresses wait in the closet.

And my fur coat defies the sinister winters.

But I want to go back to the mountains, to my ideas and my writing.

Evening. The house bewitches me. The lamps are lighted. A dreamy beauty hangs over it, an exotic, far-awayness, a strangeness. It gives me a desire to live again, as a woman, to seduce and to enchant, to love, and to love unwisely. The fantastic shadows cast by the colored lights on the red lacquer walls, the watery effects of the ceilings, the soft shimmering of the lamé, the languid depths of the pillows, the radiance of the Hindu lamp, the mellowness of the rugs—all affects me, softens me, envelops me.

I couldn't go back tonight to the mountains.

September 24. I didn't go back to the mountains but I went back to work. I rewrote my mystical story and the other called (ironically) "Faithfulness." Wrote until my back ached. Then Hugh walked in, surprised I was not on the watch for him. Lunch, a smoke, a little talk, a little nap. Writing again, until my eyes sting. Coffee. Work on the house.

Mme. Melnikoff says my life is exceptional but that I must not become conscious of it or it will bring me bad luck. Just Russian philosophy. How in hell does she think my life became exceptional? Just by a miracle? Was it not deliberately, consciously planned to be exceptional? I laughed. The dresses she makes me now are inspired by the setting. I didn't tell her that my setting, consciously and painstakingly worked out, is influencing me.

I do not have a triumphant face, however (I've been ailing a little since I came home). Yet the lawyer I flirted with at New Year's does not forget me and tried to see me. Hugh told him I had stayed in Switzerland. I didn't mind.

I'm trying to be funny—found a deep source of humor in my hand: myself. I'm laughing in all my stories at certain familiar little foibles and tricks and thoughts. Seen like that, I'm rather a comical character: ludicrous overflow of energy, enthusiasm, avidity for the inaccessible, moon-gazing (but not the silent kind), worship of genius, impulsive, emotional ascents and descents, like the chute-the-chute of Coney Island; and with all that, the neat little habits and common abilities of middle-class women, and tenderness winning over my temporary fits of madness.

I am playing a trick on myself, using the first person at first so as not to antagonize my very capricious Self, who refuses to tell other people's stories.

Here, Puss, Puss, I say every day. Now listen. I'm going to tell a story to myself in the first person.

And someday I'll be able to say, Here, Puss, Puss, I'm going to tell a story to myself in the third person.

And by that time Puss, Puss will be tamed and like other writers who prefer not to take too intimate a responsibility for their ideas.

Beloved Journal, Je t'épluche! [I am sifting you!]

But you'll be glad, someday. I'm giving you a chance to reach airier quarters—in your new form. How clear it all is for me now. A book of verses from your lyrical pages, and a book of stories. To be finished by Christmas.

And Life, with inevitable capital "L," begins again. I mean the Social Life, the worst of my problems, because I hate it, in general, and can't live or write without it. Every day I get a shock of this kind now from Hugh: "There's a Vice-President we must entertain, dear." I don't hate people individually—but it's like a plunge in ice-cold water again, after work and comparative solitude. It's something for which I am eminently unfitted. I'm not clever at small talk. I get fits of shyness unexpectedly, at the worst moments. Beforehand, my first instinct is always: escape—like a hunted animal. Then I think either of Hugh's future or of the happiness of finding someone like John; or, the last and basest: I am going to be liked, admired. In the end I dress carefully and get a great deal out of everybody—especially stories. Real companionship, no.

I have become an upholsterer, too. Covered a chair seat with bluish lamé; my toolbox is very complete and very impressive. I have sixteen kinds of nails and know how to use them.

Hugh has a genius for appreciation, continuous, inspiring, warm. I thrive on it. It is a rare talent, and should be ranked among the creative ones. I realize now how constantly he supports my writing, my decoration, my dressing, my dancing. Why always aspire to make over people in one's own image? Why must I wish Hugh expressive, artistically creative, brilliant, arresting? His comprehension is infinite, unfailing; he is calm in his genius. There is nothing aggressive or flamboyant in him, but he is even, steady, and profound.

It is in clearness and quickness that we do not meet. I am amazed sometimes at the mistiness which covers his memories of childhood and adolescence. Almost no awareness of himself, no desires—a vagueness and a drifting. A miracle of effort along with stubbornness, wisdom, cautiousness, personal charm, and the confidence he inspires, gives him such a strong grasp of financial achievement. He is distinguished-looking, talks well, has a fine voice, is cultured. Our marriage, responsibilities, suddenly bring out in him all kinds of steel qualities. Beautiful strength of will, although physically he is weaker than most men.

He showed tremendous courage marrying me—losing his family for me, his father's support. That, too, was a slow decision, though, and it nearly did not come in time. He would have missed what he most wanted by simply not knowing, ever, what he wanted.

Even now, I have never seen such waverings, about meals, ties, all kinds of futile things. And time means nothing to his calm, vague ways. Only in his work is he direct, sure, decisive.

September 29. A letter from John, newsy, chatty, trying to please me, but conventional. Caution? Lack of imagination. I passed it to Hugh. Hugh said: "I am glad to see John doesn't understand you."

This hit me in a blaze of acute truth, which I, very cowardly, had tried to evade. I knew it from the first moment of intimacy—that John doesn't understand me. Four times I found we spoke a different language. Correspondence has made this plain.

I suffered as much in facing this fact as I did from his departure. My consolation is to see Hugh so happy to be the only one who understands me!

We play the phonograph after dinner, hear Segovia on his miraculous guitar—"The Hebrew Melody," Falla's "Jota"—Hugh reads. We have talked about his silent meditations and habit of brooding. "Eighty percent of that is Bank thought, but the rest, darling, isn't even thinking. It's a sort of vague state, and I want you to help me get out of it. It makes me lonely sometimes."

He was amazed to find this out. He leaned over tenderly, anxiously, humbly, to excuse himself.

"Of course," I said, "I talk perhaps too much—I babble—that may annoy you!"

"Oh, no, I love it—I couldn't live without it. It's what makes you interesting, little Puss."

In five years he may be able to retire. He wants to study, to read, to write poetry. This prospect of a scholarly life enchants me. Seclusion. Life in the country. Traveling in between. Our life is too sweet, too sweet.

We want to go to Oxford together. I'm going to work to be a Doctor of Philosophy. (I who only had half a year of high school and nothing else.)

September 30. Gilbert comes back with a rather fine philosophic survey of the world. He gets from Waldo Frank these words about America, which can be applied to everything and might serve as a subtitle to my whole life: "Accept, with the spirit. Understand, with the mind. Transfigure, with art." He informs me that all Europe is dead, as a philosophic creator, except Spain, which has a strong and vital spiritual value (as, for example, its power to discard comfort, its power to understand mysticism).

"You don't mean a religious spirituality," I said suspiciously.

"No," said Gilbert. "If it weren't Catholicism it would be something else. Spain just had the capacity, the temperament for the fervor of the soul. That's why it's still vital."

"We can't discard France."

"It still has an intellectual value, but it is all more or less static. . . . We begin," he says, "by a consciousness of ourselves, then of humanity, then of the whole. It's the only way we can work. We will always be accused of egotism."

"Yes—because some of us forget to transfer the understanding from ourselves to others. Or we don't do it quickly enough." I had him in mind. Well, of course, it is only a phase. I went through it. I thought the limits of my self-knowledge were the limits of the universe. Dangerous thing, consciousness of self. You forget you are dissecting a human being to see how human beings are made. You begin to take a kind of personal interest in the heart pulsations, a feeling of sympathy for the pain—dangerous! dangerous! I catch myself doing it.

Anyhow, Gilbert is thinking hard—he is trying to see the whole. Pretty soon he will be where I am: that is, when understanding is beginning to become less important than the transfiguration, once mastered, and work begins. You talk less, you are less eager to listen; you want to work.

Is passion superior to creation? Their joys resemble each other. They are both peaks, climaxes. They are interwoven, fatally so. They cannot be ranked. But why does passion have the power to annihilate creation, while creation cannot annihilate passion? We can live without creation. We cannot live without passion. At moments of passion I have forgotten my ideas, my philosophy, the existence of my mind.

I can't give up either element, and yet I don't think both can be lived fully without detriment to each other. I don't believe a creator should be a hermit. But I doubt if he can be a great lover, a whole lover. The mind is a damn independent monster—exacting, too. Passion requires a certain blindness.

My passionate friendships—look how I spoil them with an exacting mind. And John probably does the same thing. I may be even now disappointing him.

I hadn't thought of this last point. I was walking down the boulevards. I saw myself in a shop mirror, unexpectedly. Exultant face, blazing eyes, a winged walk, with the wind swelling my cape, and I flung out, across the Atlantic: Oh, John, you don't know what you're missing!

He isn't missing anything—he's talking with Lilith. He has the heart to write me that she is surprised at his book, his writing so truly of things he is really ignorant of, "and when I tell her I am not ignorant, she goes off with that laugh of hers, and kisses me."

These are the things we used to talk about, so pleasurably. I have lost interest in them.

Today when Gilbert was speaking out many minor ideas, I realized he was doing his thinking aloud. And I also realized how I *sifted* my talk, how I burdened only my Journal with lamentations, overanalysis, doubts, hesitations, so that I come to others chastened, brief, and clear. I scour my mind before I go out. I would hate to be judged by my Journal. So many bad moods and complaints are dumped in here which I never carry about with me. Poor Journal! Faithful sifter.

October 1. Two hours of writing in the morning (wrote a story this morning), which include fifteen minutes of struggle with myself to take up rewriting, which I hate.

Invitations are coming in, from Godoy, the salons, friends back from summer trips. There is on the horizon a threatening possibility of a dinner with the President of the Bank.

My darling doesn't sleep well—his health is not so good, so I try to love him more, to stay awake with him. We talk. Yesterday I advised him on a Bank problem; he, uses my knowledge of the character of the men he works with.

I realized that through him I have learned to understand the poetry of Power, the vision of great men in business, to be admired whatever the use it is put to. I reacted against a book, *So Big* (Edna Ferber), in which a man is looked down on merely because he "sells bonds" instead of being an architect, for instance. The supremacy of every artist is now a joke for me. I wish Hugh could write about this. He is fitted for it. He has applied even fine spiritual values to his work; he has used all the qualities usually confined to art.

October 2. I am at my desk, all dressed, ready for business. It is a gray day and the winter is crouching near, but I don't mind. I am still sated by Hugh's enthusiasm for the house last night when all the lamps were lighted. "It looks unreal; it looks like Dulac's pictures for the *Rubáiyát*; like a set for a play; it looks marvelous!" He sat in different corners to savor the various effects.

"You made it with your daily hard work," I said, caressing his strained forehead.

"You made it with your genius," he answered.

At night I was awakened by a windstorm. I lay awake thinking about tenderness and how it could surpass passion. In days of passion I have felt selfish, stormy, almost destructive. I sought infinite climaxes, appeasement of a ravenous hunger, of exacting, fantastic desires. Tenderness is not domineering and demanding. It's a gift. I surround Hugh with it, with sweet words, with thoughts of his health, of his comfort, of his pleasure, with appreciation of his efforts, of his work; sympathy for his tiredness, pity for his silences and his apathy, with caresses, cuddling, petting, crooning over him as if he were a child; smiling, watching at the window for his coming home; sifting books for him; following his talk of the Bank . . . an immense, overwhelming tenderness, infiltrating his life so much more subtly than passion.

And this morning when I woke up I thought, I am only twenty-six!

I read in *Harper's*: "By exposing himself to the radiation of the older culture [the American] may absorb some of the qualities in which the younger is deficient: an understanding of the complexities of organic growth, sympathy with the process of slow ripening; distrust of simple explanations, short cuts and purely mechanistic remedies; impatience with mere action for action's sake regardless of its end; respect for abstract, unapplied thought."

Funny—yesterday I was trying to unlearn that, by appreciating the genius of the President of the Bank and of my own husband.

October 3. Wrote another story, just like that, yesterday before dinner! That makes eight stories in two weeks or so. Of course, parts of them were already written. This one is called, temporarily, "Fear of Nice." And last night I couldn't go to sleep because I had thought of another. The rest of the things I keep on doing, efficiently but indifferently, seem Lilliputian.

I'm also rejoicing over Mother's and Joaquin's arrival tonight. Have been putting the finishing touches to their apartment.

My ambition, and I know I will reach it, is to write clearly of impenetrable, nameless, and usually undescribable things; to give form to evanescent, subtle and fluid thoughts; and to give force to spiritual values that are usually mentioned in a vague, general way, a light most people follow but can't really *understand*.

I'm going to look into that world with clear eyes and transparent words. No dramatic searchlights, incantations to Mysterious Omnipotence, hazy language, witchcraft. No. Clarity, supreme clarity.

October 4. Superb and thrilling family reunion. We kiss over and over again and enrage the porters and taxi drivers who are waiting in the rain. Joaquin's love gives me a profound joy. But what a surprise, his journal—in Spanish, religious, lyrical, very beautiful. And what a surprise the house is to them! A mousy Spanish maid has come with them, and two canaries. Mother makes fun of my very large bed and objects to walking a mile around it to kiss Hugh good morning. They invaded our place, touched and commented on everything again this morning.

I have a suspicion Joaquin deals as freely with the Spanish language in his journal as I do with English, and always shapes his own molds. He has found in Spanish the language for his thoughts, as I have found in English the language for mine. There had to be a difference between us. We move now in different spheres. But we are still intimately, oddly, united.

October 6. Hugh and I had a lovely day. Saw a sizzling comedy which I enjoyed to the point of tears—and afterward realized that French plays leave an impression of civilized mellowness, a lovely feeling.

We were driving home, at twilight, up the Champs-Elysées. The Salon de l'Automobile has just opened. It was lighted up with gold and red lights. The fountains were all playing and illuminated. There was a great bustling of cars, people were walking and parading or sitting at Le Berry and Fouquet, and smart women brightened the crowds in their white furs. The excitement and theatricalness of the setting was communicative. I caught the fever. I wanted to go to a Russian tearoom. I glanced hungrily at the faces. I suddenly desired the social life I had discarded.

Hugh preferred to come home. I fixed our Sunday supper. Then I turned on the phonograph and happened to play a Tango. I began to dance to it alone, and an overwhelming pain pierced me, a leaping, unsatisfied desire, just as raw as ever, the memory of that other Tango and the farewell embrace—so long ago; but why so keen, when my mind has put the experience aside, and been disappointed in it?

I wrote John yesterday, at least without timidity, with even a virile boldness, frankness, and directness, having sworn he shall know me whether he likes it or not, because I can't stand his misunderstanding and prefer hate. Don't know what he will think of me. I raved on, naturally, casually, incisively for four type-written pages. Flung all my moods at him: intellectuality, mysticism, humor, a little malice, a little sweetness . . . terrible recklessness, because there is no fundamental understanding, and my words may have a different sense for him. I wrote to the genius, to his clairvoyance, to his mind, and may stumble on his Americanism, on some preconception he may have about my Frenchness. I don't know what.

It's terrible that my instinct clamors so distinctly for his love.

What I endure very badly are comparisons. I am proud enough to believe that I am a strong entity and should be blamed or praised as such. It isn't a cult of myself, because on the whole I know both my gifts and my defects too well, but, rather, a cult of my individuality, which I have painfully nursed and fostered, risking ignorance by giving up an education which happened to conflict with my ideals, respecting no opinion my mind would not absorb, preferring to rediscover all theories and facts myself, preferring loneliness to inferior friends, being throughout bravely myself with a true thirst for progress.

Why should I be more difficult to understand than Helen of Troy? Or Guinevere?[1]

October 7. Gray days, and, by contrast, the house just *glows.* Joaquin is studying in my studio. I realize that if I lived alone I would not have any social life at all—would live like an owl. It is either Joaquin who gets me into it (since he came back he has, by telephone, drawn all his friends to the house) or Mother or Hugh. Joaquin calls up Godoy. Godoy asks us all to come and hear his new poem to the Virgin. I sit back. Everybody is seeking to renew the thread—the gigantic spider web. I should be calling up the Princess and Boussie. And in the middle of our visit to Godoy, I go off into a solitary mood, so far off that I pinch myself physically to bring myself back.

Hugh made me laugh the other night after the visit to Godoy. We were undressing, and Hugh was saying half humorously that he had found the forty-nine-page poem a little long, that he was a little tired of those people who always had something to read to you. One minute after, I had forgotten his remark and jumped up and said: "Oh, I forgot to read you something I wrote in my Journal today!"

"Oh, dear," he wailed, slumping down on the bed. "I brought one of them home with me!"

October 9. Now I know why the Parisian winter evenings have always made a strong impression on me, which I tried many times to analyze and couldn't. They give me a mixed feeling of anxiety and excitement, of depression and restlessness, because the short days that end at five o'clock are like a summons to live faster and more intensely.

So different from the feelings of long summer days, of daylight dreams, of sunlit walks and thoughts. A breath of sensuousness rises from these early winter evenings. The dark pushes you into tearooms, into taxis, into home, and artificial heat overcomes you suddenly, melting your cool body with a shock of pleasure.

And I sit in the corner of a taxi, with my cheek on my fur

[1] *Both, characters in books by John Erskine.*

collar, smoking, and I feel my heart getting tight and shivery, because it's dark and I haven't written a good story today.

October 11. In my mystical story a woman who has made a wish for a real world finds herself in a bus going to other worlds, and then wants very much to be taken back to the Opéra. My fear of going away has always been a very real one, of "going away" from human affections, from home life, from pleasures, and superficial occupations. Today I was taken away, and it frightened me. I wrote all morning (novel of Lyndall and Vivien) and all afternoon until Miralles came to rehearse my program, and I didn't *care about the dancing.*

In the evenings we always have a little music. Joaquin plays. I'm learning his songs. We laugh. And then in the middle of it, I go and write my Journal in some corner or on the piano, because they have taken the best lamp. I laugh at their jokes and teasings, and go on writing, and I cry because Joaquin plays a bar of *Pelléas,* and go on writing. Hugh says I could be hung on a tree and I would write on the leaves.

October 14. Mr. _____ is here from Barcelona. We have invited him out for Sunday-night supper and the theatre. Mr. _____ is always very nice to me, always giving me compliments, but he doesn't understand the house or anything but the Bank. He and Hugh had a great deal to talk over. I listened, thinking of my business novel, but oh! dear, at eleven o'clock I could have blown up the whole world so as to end the evening! At midnight I smoked myself to the point of suicide by choking; at one o'clock I nudged Hugh's arm firmly; I had finished studying all the people who sat around us at Le Berry. At 1:30 I undressed spiritlessly and wished Hugh were an artist, even of the lowest degree, but an artist. And this morning I woke up chastened and secretly grateful to the monstrous old Bank to whom I will soon owe a trip to Spain!

Evening. This living with myself as closely as others live with husband, wife, mother or brother is a strange thing. I get from it a continuous exhilaration. From solitude I get the fermentation others get from active happenings. It is then my "fire" really gets going, and I pray to an inclement and deaf God to spare me interruptions.

Anyhow, with or without interruptions I'm working. I copied

all morning, and planned to write a novel about a writer, thoroughly and frankly. After lunch I gave myself indigestion writing the first chapter. Why call it a chapter? I'm really writing, like Proust, a formidable ensemble which will not be one book or novel but several things connected, as all life is.

What I call "the Spanish Opening," Vivien and Lyndall's life, and the business story are all one, because they all come from the same head.

October 16. Had to stop so my eyes could be repaired. Was so unhappy that I sat before my typewriter, smoking and thinking, hating to do anything else. Was aghast to discover that my gift for social intercourse is not natural, and that I need to keep in practice. Found myself reticent, shy, absent-minded, and small-voiced before all the friends we are again beginning to see. So the struggle is to be repeated. Oh, well, it's fun to master one's self.

Wald came last night, in splendid form, telling the funniest and most colorful stories about people I'd like to know. He doesn't intimidate me. I told him it was better to have open enemies than to have friends who like you for what you are not and misunderstand you in all ways. He won me by his admiration of the house. But he stayed late, Mother and Hugh were tired, and I could see he classified our life as more or less dull, or at least conventional, because we were bright at seven A.M. and sleepy at ten P.M. In his world, one gets bright with the night.

Of course what keeps me from a full enjoyment of people is that I have become detached from them by these months of utter preoccupation with my work. Max Wald said last night he had come to prefer the "worldly" people, the human, to the ascetic— unless the ascetic is a *born* ascetic, like some of the saintly hermits.

No one could have been more human and worldly than myself last winter. I loved the physical expression of my dancing; I loved to be moved by others' desire; I loved triumphing in salons, loved to be painted, loved to have friends. I was vain, seductive, hungry, and alive to an amazing degree. Where did it all lead me? To passion, and to the destruction of all the more delicate values; worst of all, to the destruction of Hugh.

Then what happens? I come to. I find the ecstasy has a bitter aftertaste. I come back to my introspective life, to my writing. That week in Switzerland took me back to my first attitude toward life—tender and idealistic, not self-seeking.

Am I a natural ascetic? Is this only a phase? Which is the true me? Primarily the writer, to the extent of realizing that the passionate being is only food for the writer.

I rejoice, after my blundering and stumbling and inglorious worldliness, because it has helped me to understand. This, I can write, on a calm day, when illness makes my body silent and unprotesting, and only the mind is watchful.

Mon Dieu, what am I destined for? I am afraid of only one thing: of not being a great-enough writer; and I could have given all my time to being a great woman, or a courtesan. What would I be if my worship of Hugh did not hold me? Is it merely for love of Hugh that I escape into creation? I observe with a deep irony that Hugh is happiest when I am hidden to human eyes, by my existence within thought. There, I am secure, secure from love, from the intoxication of adulation, from social contact. And I myself wake up in the middle of my fevered dream and say: At least now I'm not harming anybody.

For most people, no such choice is necessary. For me, yes, because I do things so wholly: if I live for passion, everything else can explode and disappear. I won't notice it. If I live for my writing the real world can go to hell! A paradox, since my writing springs from reality, but a reality I am now finished handling. And yet, God knows, it fascinates me.

Evening: Hugh so childishly pleased because I tell him I observed his mental qualities in business to be precisely of that brilliant, incisive, swift temper I miss in him when he is home. He is so humble! So pleased when I appreciate him.

October 17. Up from bed for a business lunch at Café de Paris. Don my fur coat (the unattainable fur coat at twenty-eight thousand francs, stripped of a few foxes and reduced to eighteen thousand). A Ford Company Manager and his wife. And what is happening to me? I take a great liking to both of them, and what a winning and attractive personality the Manager has, a mixture of pure Anglo-Saxon with Spanish polish, acquired in traveling, a singing way of speaking English.

He talks about his work. I listen. Know a lot about Fords now, sales, rigorous discipline; Spain consumes only thirty thousand cars a year and could not, under the circumstances, produce either a Ford or a Citroën.

I'm bored, but the man is worth meeting. What tickles me

is that he thinks I'm pretty but not particularly brainy. I just can't exhibit my brains in society. Of course, this is an improvement on the reforms I attempted at Columbia on the harmless and idiotic boys who courted me. And Mother had to say to me with a dolorous voice: "You're going to ruin all your chances for marriage if you go on insisting on talking only to 'literary' men."

Nothing forbiddingly scholarly about me now—the very last word in fatuous femininity, not the clinging vine, but the *agreeing* one.

October 19. What I owe to dancing I never calculated before, but it struck me forcibly yesterday. I have lived a month now on writing. It makes me inhuman, intellectual and melancholic. I turn *away* from life, literally.

Yesterday I was again feeling solitary, egotistical, ascetic, and sad. Then I had to dress up and go to my dancing lesson. I became instantly woman. The beating of the blood silenced the beating of ideas. What I saw in the mirror startled me. A lively body transfigured by the music and the dancing, emerging from its coolness and deadness of the past weeks as vibrant and vivid as ever. It is a real resuscitation.

I must never forget that I am not balanced without it, that I lose my womanhood outside of it. Why must I be so excessive, always leaning one way or another, never quite poised between gulfs, but always tumbling?

October 21. "Come to my charity sale," writes a lady. "When will you call on me?" asks another, who is a social flower. I can't tell them I'm upholstering a chair with lamé, beginning to encrust it with colored stones, hammering flat my fingers, counting on my calendar the days it may take to bring a letter from John, working on two balky novels, and reading *Elmer Gantry* with breathless interest, half fear, half awe, mostly thunderstruck by the power of its satire and formidable veracity and ferocity; and I can't tell them that it is the Princess I want to see, whose temperament and individuality are so uncomfortable and so inspiring. Every day I hate common women and flabby ones more acutely.

Horace and Frances called on us Saturday, sweet and refreshing and uninteresting; and pleased with the house, but rendered speechless by my sandaled feet and suspending judgment in the way well-united couples have, until bedtime. Curious opinions come out at such a moment, a meeting of two minds, for better or for worse.

I'm not charitable. I forgot to say Frances looks soft and pleasing and very comforting, and that I almost wished she could like me a little, but she doesn't. I no longer have that apostolic severity toward those different from ourselves, but a quick impulse to defend them against Hugh's ideal measuring tape. Because, as I said to Hugh last night, mastery of ourselves is only a fitful and temporary thing—any day, our real character can betray us. We only have *moments* of high living, of ideal living; we have mostly aspirations, and the best we ever do is struggle for them. Perfection, we know, alas, is a sterile thing, a lifeless, static, condition. Hugh believes in it. I don't know what I believe. I do love perfection, beauty, the ideal, but I don't love *only* them. I love rare sensations. I love knowing everything real, ugly, ferocious. I eat up life *whole*, don't pick the choice and dainty morsels. Curiosity of the mind? Perhaps. My idea of perfection begins to look like this: instead of a choice of the lovely things of the world, it is a containing of the whole world, mastered, understood, and used for creation. I speak as a writer, then, not as a woman. Because, again, I want the woman to serve the creator, body and soul.

My saintliness consists in my worship of creation and in the struggle I make not to destroy either human happiness or truths which are life-giving even if not quite true. I don't tell the truth any more to those who can't make use of it. I tell it mostly to myself, because it always changes me, does something to me.

Afternoon: Amusing situation with the young decorator, whom I had to convoke for the design of the couch. He is twenty-five, very handsome, with lovely manners and stylish clothes. He stays much longer than necessary, comes every day on some futile excuse, struggles to reduce the price for me, and we talk about decoration by the hour.

Finally today he made a humorous remark about my pile of cushions on the two flat valises near the window . . . said he particularly admired my elegant divan. I answered that it was, above all, as soft as the thing he proposed to me.

I was amused, and annoyed at myself, because I had dressed up for our business talk! Are these literary experiments?

Listen here, make literature out of something else.

October 23. Passion, of course, doesn't unite. What unites is Hugh asking me this morning, with a little boy's voice, to come with him this evening to the Doctor to hold his hand while he is radiographed. What unites is Hugh and I solving together the problem of an insurgent white-haired man in his department. What unites is the tender solicitude I have for his happiness, and the overflow of sweet words to heal his sleeplessness or his tummy aches.

October 24. I work now on one novel, now on the other, and wrote a little story in between. And then I got defeated because it occurs to me that I can't live without John's approval. I have moments of such lack of self-confidence that when I see certain words I used in my letters to him, I feel the blood rush to my head, and I would give anything to have remained misunderstood and liked. I have renounced religion or I would pray fervently, desperately, for a favorable answer; another formal letter will end all my hopes. But I *must* be prepared for a disappointment. Or I will never, never be cured.

Evening. The decorator comes to say—almost nothing. And stays. And we laugh because the couch is shrinking in size each time he comes so as to stay within my income.

October 27. My "great man" has written a book [*Sincerity*] which has disappointed me. If he had described mediocre, poverty-stricken temperaments with a satirical intention I could have understood, but no such lucidity shows through. It could have been a great comedy—if the actions of the three characters had permitted—and the failure to achieve sincerity could have been tragic, but for the deadness of the characters, who are mere mouthpieces for slightly superficial ideas. Isabel learns nothing in Europe except how to wear sheer negligees and that certain rituals precede ecstasy in love—but the "fadeur" [insipidity] of her character is distressing. Winthrop does wake up (and that is at last like John) at the end of the book. The polemics involving morals, the need of doing something out of the ordinary so as not to stagnate in peace (so he gives a swimming pool to the town's children) frankly tired me.

I had to make a tremendous effort to judge the book. I felt John sitting next to me, excited as a boy, saying he very much wanted my approval, reading me the sketch of the book, which sounded, at first, very shrewd, like the idea of *Uncle Sam*. I had to tear myself apart, forget his eyes and his mouth as he read, his enthusiasm for his words. I had to see. I couldn't blur my mind with his presence.

It is precisely what those pages lack, his presence, his greatness. I don't recognize him in the poverty of Isabel's experience, in the stark simplicity of her theories, in the emptiness of those ten years abroad. Ten years of personal liberty, and she only finds a Carl and a nobleman to learn from, and gathers a flimsy knowledge of physical love, and comes back to a Winthrop. And there exists a Winthrop who can live ten years with a Mary, who is neither hunchback, nor bow-legged, nor dumb, and they are not lovers; he isn't a man anyway, not a real live one. How little warmth and impulse, and how much dry talk. How could John live with them, as he did, for 350 pages without irony, without stifling? No. He takes them seriously. He places in their hands the subtle, diabolical problem of sincerity.

And I almost cry with despair and shame because I am too woman, too hellishly woman to stand up and tell John what I think!

I also tried to look at it from a philosophic standpoint. Sincerity, as an inflexible doctrine, is like all formulas, destructive. Whatever the intelligence does not mold, make supple, apply, is a failure. Sincerity is not a logical event. So far John is—just John. That is the best I can say. But I come back to why he talks through limited figures. Comedy is made out of the ridiculous mess people make of ideas, formulas, and philosophies when they don't understand them. So is tragedy. But these three characters make a mess that somehow does not seem funny to me or tragic. It just fails to strike me as *great*. John was inspired at first, then he wrote the story with scholastic precision; he loves his themes, his symbols, *making his point*. The poor characters move bloodlessly, like so many of those created by ideologues—Shaw and Ibsen, for instance; but he is not carried away, his characters are not carried away, and I'm not carried away.

And I strike my chest contritely, three times, three times penitently and sorrowfully, saying each time: Je suis femme, je ne lui dirais rien, je suis femme, je ne lui dirais rien. Pardonnez moi, Siegneur! [I am woman, I will say nothing to him. Forgive me, Lord!]

Saw a play today, by Elmer Rice, perfect, complete, absolute, hair-raising realism but ineffective, meaningless. It lacked a great supporting idea or a single theme to raise it above accurate reporting. It was called *Dans la Rue* [Street Scene], and was characteristically enough translated by Carco. There was nothing lacking: the house, the front "stoop," as we called it in New York, a woman screaming because she expects a baby, cats fighting, policemen on patrol, the grue [prostitute], the voyou [urchin], the taxi driver, the unfaithful wife, the virtuous young lady, etc.— but it was dead.

And to finish my Literary Sifting for the week, I must damn my story-novelette of Lyndall and Vivien, which ends so abruptly and is so badly developed that I am the only one who understands what it means.

October 28. Hugh is going to Milan. We kiss tenderly, as if it were a long voyage, and laugh because nobody knows it's only a separation of two days. He says it is painful to go away from me. He finally compliments me on my eyes, after six years of stubborn refusal, because he said everybody talked about my eyes, so he wouldn't, and he preferred my mouth anyway.

I fall asleep reading Armen Ohanian's memoirs. There must be some Asiatic blood in me, because I enter that life as naturally as if I had always known it. Thursday, thank the pagan gods, I'm seeing Vanah Yami about lessons in Oriental dancing.

I sew yards and yards of turquoise-green velvet for the studio window.

I put off writing John.

I tell Jeanne to cook what she damn pleases—food doesn't interest me. If I were an old maid I would thrive on bananas and purple figs.

Evening: My scrapbooks are characteristic: one for decoration; one for dancers and dancing costumes; one for costumes and dress designs; one for literary articles; one for pictures of babies, Oriental fantasies, madonnas, and all the portraits artists did of me in New York; and one for traveling and trips already taken and to be taken. I work on them on some forlorn afternoon when I have no dancing lesson, no visitors, no desire to write and nothing to sew. I work until my tube of glue gives out.

I want to free myself from all faith, from faith in John, as in others, from these moments of blindness which prevent my intelligence from expanding and growing. How naïve I am! I pass from one idolatry to another, I give myself, I idealize, I illuminate, I transform, I adore. And when I open my eyes one day, I feel stronger for having freed myself from this bondage.

I have dared to criticize John, his book, his work, his life, his lack of understanding—and I feel free of him. He only dominated me for five months.[1]

I don't know what this cry means, except that I have wanted to be liberated. Queer how liberation always comes through the intellect, how, by a judgment of the mind, I quiet the tumult of my senses.

If John, by a stroke of genius could show an understanding of Europe and of me, I would be glad to bow my head again. Is there anything I can do? He is merely stifled by his surroundings. And yet, no. Lewis, in *Elmer Gantry* bursts out with magnificent irony, using precisely the same ground and people, and makes an epic of American hypocrisy. What can one do when a genius fails, as he has in his last two books? Criticism is hopeless; he would not take it from me. When I ventured comment on *Uncle Sam*, he said I couldn't understand because it was American and I was European. He can also say that about *Sincerity*.

And even if I were listened to, what could I give him? He needs suffering, to become humanized, he needs to get rid of the poisons of puritanism, of America as he sees it (the new America— Waldo Frank's, Sinclair Lewis's, Sherwood Anderson's—he does not know). He needs Europe *deeply*—and not the Moulin Rouge. How unfair he is to Europe in his survey of it, even through a mediocre woman's eyes! How unsubtle!

I see, as I write, his big, heavy-lidded eyes, twinkling—I thought he understood everything. But not me. He didn't get me at all. I'm French, Spanish, Christian, Jew, and Oriental. If he had understood me, he would have learned enough.

John, John—I think it would have hurt me less if you had disappointed me as a man, but your greatness of mind must not fail me. I have loved you so much for it.

November 1. I had a moment of pure, simple happiness tonight. Hugh and I were sitting by the fire. Joaquin sat at my feet, poking at the fire, talking to me. Mother was there too, warming her slippered feet. Something of that sacred family peace came over

[1] *Translated from the French.*

me, a reverence for the precious home that holds all one loves under its roof. And for those moments, I ceased to be a discontented wanderer, and I felt almost religiously grateful.

My adoration of Joaquin is a special thing. He has been my child, almost, my constant preoccupation. He has repaid my concern by an equal devotion. I hear from Elvira what he thinks of me. Now I almost wish there were not five years' difference between us, so I could confide in him completely. But apart from that, and from religion, how wonderfully we understand each other. Since we moved here, we are together more often, because I take him for walks in the Bois, and we can talk. Sometimes after the strain of his composing and of my writing, we get talking quite foolishly and merrily—even making puns.

Now while I write, Mother is going to bed, Joaquin is studying his harmony, Hugh reads a book I enjoyed keenly, and I meditate on the possibilities of my becoming, someday, domesticated and quiet.

My Spanish Story is an underground, introspective affair . . . autobiographical with fifty percent fantasy. I finished "Appearances" as a novelette. It's good, with an unexpected ending. Now I have (temporary titles):

The Idealist*
Pity
Three Old Countesses
The Russian Who Didn't Believe in Miracles [and Why]*
Mystical Story [Tishnar]*
Apartment for Rent
Fear of Nice*
Faithfulness*
Dancer
Essay on the Journal

If I were really French I would not be sad at the clever way I have written John about his book—veiling criticism in irony, granting him intentions and reserves that he did not have, giving him the benefit of the doubt, saying, as if it were unconscious, what he intended to do, which I know he did not do.

If he is sincere as an artist he will say: "No, that was not what I intended." If he is insincere he will accept my praise. Or he may simply not get the irony and accept the compliments. I'm

* Published in *Waste of Timelessness and Other Early Stories.*

afraid he just won't get it; he is at heart so naïve—and not terribly acute. And I'll be left friendless with mere intellectual satisfaction, which is a poor substitute. Mon Dieu, I prefer my friend. The letter will remain here.

Have thrashed out my ideas on God; Hugh thinks I do my weakest thinking on that subject. That, too, will remain here.

While Hugh sits reading by the fire, I go into the red room, turn on the phonograph and begin my Sentimental Journey around the world: the Tangos, so sensual, evoke the atmosphere of tearooms and the searching glance of strange men; the Spanish dances carry me on the stage, in an Egyptian town, on my way to other engagements in India; the Cuban song reawakens my life in Havana; and Segovia's guitar raises all kinds of delicate emotions. And meanwhile, through the transparent lamé curtain, as through a mist, I see Hugh reading peacefully, the fire sparkling, the lamps shedding short circles of light and shadows, and the smoke of Hugh's cigarette rising—all so tranquil, so unreal, almost unattainable, so far removed from the demoniac fever agitating me, making me dance Tangos to recall other Tangos.

I open the curtains, come in quietly. Hugh's kiss is so cool and his hand so friendly and so warm. And I go back, after a while, to the other room, now in the dark, and sit down by the mirror and cover my eyes, to recall other lives and other moments.

Something in me curses away all peace.

November 5. Tea. Chocolate cake. Friends. The house has become a curiosity and a museum. I used to talk about the mystical meaning of it and how I would judge people by their understanding of it. What does it mean, then, that *everybody* likes it, that I find myself a popular decorator, that anybody would confide his home to me to do? Popularity! Unexpected and startling.

A formal philosopher opens my eyes to the weakness of lone studies—and to the impossibility of understanding philosophy without initiation. I listen to her doctoral voice. Although quite peaceful and balanced, she enchants me. She is half Dutch, half Mexican.

So now I have found something to worry about. I can't endure the idea of missing philosophy by my random reading.

She knows that writers often can't talk. Good for her. I agree, pretending to be objective, though I've learned the fact from cruel personal discoveries. She ranks music superior to all arts, as I do. But she has learned Latin. Languages? Oh, but I love ideas, no matter the language. But as you learn a language you get special ideas. Yes, that's true. Some Spanish ideas are so Spanish, no language but Spanish can convey them. What are the Latin ideas? I don't know. I ought to learn Latin. No. I prefer to learn the modern language of the super-over-realists.

November 6. I took a liking to Vanah Yami, Oriental dancer, and she came today to see me dance and to decide if I am an interesting subject. I danced badly, was nervous with stage-fright, but she managed to see the possibilities. We begin Friday. We talked longer than necessary. She seemed to like me, while I cursed myself inwardly for my lack of poise and my childishness.

I was angry because I didn't write today. I had intended to discipline myself so thoroughly that I would be able to write without inspiration. What a task! Nobody was ever more uneven. Yet now I sit like a business woman, and *write* whether I like it or not. And today I nearly spoiled my novel with a stupid chapter.

November 7. I arrived yesterday morning at a clear plan for my Spanish Story, now definitely the Novelist's Own Novel. And I am writing a story that is to be mystical and at the same time as clear as water.

At teatime I let Boussie read two stories. She didn't understand the mystical one, but she found "Faithfulness" vivid and alive; she agreed with Hugh that I should strive for more artistic *objectivity.* Alas! So I went to bed full of confidence in the originality of what I am doing, since criticism just can't kill me. At the same time I felt sad. Technique. Am I going to stumble on *that*? Not me. You wait and see.

This morning I worked with furor on that hellish *rewriting.* It's not my fault that each time I work on old things I get ideas for new ones.

November 12. A day to record. Hugh comes home for the third time, frenzied because of the Wall Street Crash. Each time, I encouraged him. He is inordinately worried about losing our capital. Instead of worrying with him I found in myself the most profound courage, and tried to pass it over to him. What if the worst happens? It is only an outside misfortune. It will be good for us. I'll work. Our life will grow more chastened, more severe, stripped of social artificialities, of compromises. But what matters is our other life, I said. What are you, anyway, poet or business-man?

Not so good, the logic, but what mattered is that I was strong and unmoved, full of detachment, able to measure values, capable of combating a despair fostered merely by the influence of the men around him, whose fears I understand because they have *nothing else* to live for.

For the first time I understood the full power of philosophy. Hugh is weak because he judges and lives outside of it. Today, he came near collapse, because of someone else's losses on the Ex-change. He observes we have lost nothing yet, but he cannot endure even the mere idea of it. Nothing else counts. Not me, not our love, not the riches of our life. For a moment I see no trace of his mind's possessions. He is only counting money. Where is the past? He is submerged by the values of another world. Mon Dieu, can this other world have such an influence over him? For the first time I realize it has. It overwhelms me. I feel I alone carry the other treasures. I'll come someday to speak a language he may not understand. Already, today, my talk, fervent and power-ful, does not touch him. We walk together, looking at two ruins—he, the ruin of his speculations; I, the ruin of his philosophic armor.

He has had his days of courage. Now it is my turn. We help each other, but I am sad to see him so dominated by something I am free of.

My poor darling—

Evening: I was so happy last night because Gilbert gasped at my essay on the Journal and said the rest of my writing was a revelation to him, etc., etc. Yes, yes—surprised, by funny things coming unexpectedly from *me*. What a small voice I read them with, and at each page I looked up to see if he looked bored.

We called it, ironically, the Festival Anaïs—precisely be-cause it doesn't happen so very much, and I have so few chances of making myself heard. When he jumped up and exclaimed, really startled, I made efforts to hold back an infantile smile of glee—tried to look natural.

This morning I worked on the "Writer's Own Novel," as a result of the encouragement . . . damn hard and ticklish. When *that's* done, I'll come back to something human and light again, for a rest.

Elvira Velasco thinks I am as fond of her as she is getting of me. It is a terrible misunderstanding. She is sincere, I am not. She is drawn to me by the purity of my face, the sweetness of my acts. I listen to her, admire her dancing. When I discover her mind to be active, warm, but limited, I draw away. It's too late. She is used to me. She may be slightly disturbed by what she discovers in my mind, but it doesn't change her affectionate interest, which feeds on simpler things. And I feel devoid of humanity, because I can't love simply.

With tremendous efforts, I have now conquered natural and lively jealousy, by logic, by a desire to be just, by a desire to be fair. It was deep set in my temperament. It is in Hugh, too. But I tried to get rid of mine.

I felt it first because of Elvira's beauty. Women in my situation try to depreciate, to belittle. I did the opposite. I tried to discover all that formed this beauty, found her intelligent, sweet, tried to love her. I kept my head clear, refused to dislike her and her husband or deprive Hugh of their society. I went so far that I feel I could *understand* Hugh loving someone prettier than I am.

I hate jealousy, the forms it takes. I have suffered from it in other women. Now I pity those who can't master it. Yet mine was so keen, because I aspire so much to beauty and to talent and can recognize them more quickly than anybody and appreciate them. I have been jealous often, and profoundly, painfully so. If I can't prevent jealousy coming to me at moments, at least I prevent it from being venomous, harmful, from blinding my appreciation or altering my actions.

Elvira believes I am wonderfully free of jealousy—for example, about dancing, because I was generous in the appreciation of her talent. I'm glad, I'm glad.

November 13. Sad days for everybody. Many ruined lives, and suicides. At last I made my darling strong. But when he said the true mettle had showed in me, I reminded him that *he*, by his work, had given me the leisure with which I built an inner world. We pity those who have nothing else.

The Velascos come to be consoled, though their situation is ten times better than our own. It has been a chastening blow, just the same. Sometimes after talking showily to Hugh I have wobbled inside. All expenses to be cut short. Mother and Joaquin now entirely in our charge. No savings for accidents, illness, or traveling. Just the salary, which has never been quite enough.

Quite consciously, I use the anxiety to test myself. I drive myself to corrections of old writings; I economize; I pull myself together. I want to teach dancing, to fight, to help. For myself, I'm glad to be deprived *again*—all my childhood was spent in that state—but I worry for Hugh, for Mother and Joaquin. I myself have had too many pleasures, I have had everything I ever dreamed of. I have been too spoiled.

Of course, I foresaw this. We were too happy.

November 15. A purely "social" concert gives me a fit of neurasthenia. I shrink at the sight of people, friends, acquaintances, and am irritated by praise.

It's the writing. I shut myself up with it. I become another woman. Each day I add only one page or two to the Writer's Own Novel, but each one is packed tight with condensed and unrelenting thinking. Hugh says my style is punk. I don't watch it. I write on—never stopping, in my effort to name the unnamable, to elucidate the most subterranean ideas. I follow my ideas so intently that I push language aside, twist the meanings, shake up the phrases so as to dig up my own new meaning—not a *new* meaning, but a meaning congealed in phrases people repeat like a Catechism, phrases they are used to.

I get lonely writing, lonely for a supermind to talk with. And I dig into myself, saying things which must be said and which are not *attractive*, which won't please anybody—a real work after my own heart—dry, charmless, avid in exactitude, veracity, and depth.

When my eyes are worn out I clean up the closet, inspect Hugh's underclothes, call up the electrician, interview the decorator (he makes me sick). I go out on errands. Take the subway. We are going back to the simple life. I had forgotten what it was like to be shoved. In the middle of my errands I begin thinking again of the man in my novel, a writer—the portent of his words reaches only some of those they were written for.

I come straight home and without taking off my hat or coat, write a page.

I *know* my style is degenerating. I'm so eager to say difficult things that the English language doesn't stand a chance. Besides, in moments of strain, the genuine foreigner reappears. I use

French words—Spanish composition. And the English word I like best is "damn" because I feel so depressed.

Meanwhile, our "capital," our poor savings, are almost annihilated, and Mother Guiler must come to the rescue with a guarantee for our loan. But until the stocks are sold and our loss is irreparable, I won't cry. Not even then. I'll be too busy. We'll have to sell the Oriental Palace and move to the country.

Perhaps it will all straighten out; the stocks will go up again. It is queer, this little taste of poverty, fear, and anxiety after the feeling of ease and security.

Fortunately, Hugh is brave now. I made him some fine speeches. He said the crisis was worthwhile, because it showed what I was made of, that he loved me more. And as usual, after putting on a nice front to the world, I come here and show my real lack of mettle.

November 19. I kept calm and lucid. Comforted Hugh. We went through some terrible days. Then it all improved. The stocks are recovering. We are saved.

Just the same, I'm going to teach dancing. We are going to live more strictly, according to Hugh's salary, and the whole experience was salutary. But how pitiful the others, who are not young, or who have children.

A strange experience. A huge banquet offered Godoy by Farrère and Les Amis des Lettres Françaises. Chic. Everybody there.

Suddenly, instead of being impressed or moved, I felt myself judging the hollow speeches, the political flatteries, the tactful diplomatic moves, the bromides of so-called great men, the insincerity of these lovers of literature. I found myself seeing through Claude Farrère, Paul Fort, and others, men who don't take words seriously, who make a business of literature.

I sat between two oldish men, and thought.

Nobody else there was *thinking*. They were acting under a kind of collective friction. They were talking with a kind of contagious fever, called thought but which is caused by public opinion. I thought less of Godoy for seeking such homage and accepting it. One requires encouragement and criticism from a few real minds, not from a crowd.

Those who know the pernicious effect of it, like Falla, smile at it and go away to continue their work. It is an *obstacle* to work.

I sat there alone and observed that none of these men dared to think alone. Suddenly, I had a sense of danger, a belated fear that I might have been in this vast impulse, part of the herd. With effort, I had stood off, and I had a distinct feeling that I would continue to stand off, would nurse my instinct against the crowd. I had the feeling that my individuality was my salvation, that what I ran away from was the world, so I could raise my own thoughts without contamination.

The temptations are so appealing. It is so sweet to have friends, to have many people admire you, to be famous.

Thank heavens, I have had praise only for my face and my dancing—very little for my writing. My audience is composed of exactly five persons. Today I swear to continue in my seclusion, never to desire to be known, to go on with my work, as I have always done, without any popular encouragement.

What would I do if I had been given a banquet such as Godoy was offered last night? God, I'd be so sickened, so sad, I could never write again.

Godoy, Sherwood Anderson, and John have let the world judge their works and been satisfied. And immediately, like a punishment from Genius, they have ceased thinking with the power and independence of a mind liberated from the desire to please.

After the banquet, the family pitied me because I had been seated between two old men, whereas Hugh had a young and attractive partner, but I was miles away and felt old, indifferent, and invulnerable.

Hugh was surprised at my attitude last night. I said to him when he spoke of feeling tired and unnerved by the events of last week: "Rest on me, darling. I feel so terribly strong."

I have rid myself of the need of John. Secretly, I still plead inwardly for one or two friends. I do need them—but if I can't get the best, I'll stay alone. What will knock me down, now? I wonder. Is my strength real or based on a dream, and will it vanish like all other moments of temporary wisdom?

And then, in strength there is always a lack of charity and pity. As soon as I get strong, I am less woman. I am all mind.

I think my supply of pity is ample enough. I better concentrate on my critical faculties, too often tempered by the woman: I must proclaim, at least to myself, that the books of Miomandre, l'enfant charmant [the charming child], the delight of salons, should be read at infancy; that the novels of André David, the handsome poet, should be auctioned for eight cents at the Dime Novel Book Store; that Royère cannot be very sure of what he means and that it would be useless to ask him; that Paul Fort (who scared me stiff the first time I met him because of his prestige) writes poetry that has been done before.

To *see*! What a blessing after being dazzled blind so many years by a naïve hero worship. To see! After ten years, when the mere sight of a writer turned my blood cold, made me stutter, rendered me speechless, and kept me awake for two nights. To see, face to face, eye to eye, these men whom I thought lovers of literature, and closer to it than I was.

There was a time when I could hardly hear John when he talked. I trembled physically before him; when I went into his house it was as if I entered a church.

I was like a savage, superstitiously dominated by lightning, fooled by the witches' incantations, terrified by masks. What a capacity for faith! I laugh now. And I stop laughing. I regret a little the end of all that exciting unreality I lived in.

Hugh comments that I have been late in finding all this out but because I have tried to mature without becoming cynical— that is, by a recognition of the impossibility of attaining the ideal while believing that the ideal does exist.

I observed sadly, though, that a preoccupation with self-perfection is dangerous. In this crisis I was so intent on not weakening, not crumbling, that I forgot to sympathize with the troubles and ruins of others.

November 21. A pathetic effort to write John without hurting him, a return of my old loneliness, and I call out to him to *please* be great so as to preserve the really wonderful feeling I had for him.

And I plead with Hugh not to talk about finances any more.

The struggle to make something great out of myself without being egotistical is almost impossible to endure.

I have always wanted to be with people superior to me; it has been my everlasting hunger. I couldn't learn from teachers who could not dominate me. I could not talk with people of my age who did not know more than I did. I aspired constantly to ascension, to growth. I have needed more desperately than anyone, a *big* mind, older than mine. At such moments, I, who am so undisciplined, become the most docile and attentive of disciples. When

I respect, I learn. While I thought Miralles was learned in his art, I was docile. When I learned more than he knows, I went away. Mentally, I am *always* unsatisfied. John's mind dazed me, but he lacks the talent for friendship. His genius does not animate all of his life; he missed knowing me intimately because he can't write letters.

I'm going to concentrate on the art of *understanding*; I'm going to make a science and a religion of it. I have already inaugurated the first expressions of it: to be able to tell people what you do understand, which is so hard.

When John first came to me, to talk about Pauline and Lilith, I understood. He liked what I had written about him. He came back. Why couldn't he at least encourage this very rare preoccupation of mine to elucidate him? It was all I asked—for him to stay there. He does not even have the magical power to transport himself, to be with me, in letters. I have ceased to expect that he should have understood me. What I mean by understood is *appreciated*—he has not appreciated me! Be frank, child. He's too busy.

I think myself strong, invulnerable, intellectually independent, and today I *cried* in the bus because a man who looked a little like John sat next to me. And then I grew proud again, and I confessed to myself that John did not know what he was getting, that later he may realize it, and that by that time it will be of no difference to me because I will be cured. I can accomplish what I want, with time. I have wanted to be free of John, but I hope he stays away all winter!

November 25. My greatest pleasure now, what I most enjoy, are the Symphonic Concerts to which we go every Sunday afternoon. Hugh, Joaquin, Mother, and I. Joaquin has made me share his love of Debussy. I was overwhelmed yesterday by the beauty of "Fêtes" and "Dialogue du Vent et de la Mer." I fill myself with music, and it echoes all through me for a long time after.

I told Hugh last night that I had the intuition I should cultivate my faults—disregard details—because I feel I am going to accomplish something special with this part-blindness . . . an invulnerability such as masculine minds can embrace but a woman rarely, and that this peculiar outlook (like Merejskowski's), coming from a woman, might influence other women.

Woman is bound to the earth by blood. Blood clogs her vision. She must always remain bound because it is her destiny, but she must be lucid, too. I feel that I am turning now from the intensely personal analysis, which is feminine, to a perception of the world which is man's; but I want to bring to this perception of the world, woman's finesse and acuteness, sensibilities and flair.

November 27. Vanah Yami thinks I have des dispositions particulières pour la dance [a special aptitude for dance]. We study in our bathing suits before her mirror. We lie on the floor looking at her rare books on Cambodian dances. She shows me her roof garden, her bunnies, her cat, and her idol facing the sun. Her surroundings and her dress are plain and unimaginative. She does not live out her dance. She was rather startled yesterday when I appeared in my black turban: "But—it suits you extraordinarily well!" She has independent means and takes on only pupils who interest her, so I can have faith in what she says. But what a perpetual temptation, to have facility and enthusiasm for so many things. I feel that I am penetrating the East through its dancing. I also feel I should stay home and stick to one thing. Just the same I await her visits and lessons with impatience. She explains Oriental dancing to me, tells me that the "dance du ventre" is the most formidable animal thing she has ever seen, that ignoble-looking women do it to the point of frenzy, and drive all the men wild. Also, what is less known, that it has its masculine counterpart: a man wearing a belt with a rubber phallus attached, which dances and moves as he moves and dances, and drives the women wild. As a contrast to this, the human, Orientals have innumerable temple dances, mystical salutations and invocations.

This dancing suits me better than the Spanish in one way, that it is softer. My Spanish dancing has always been the least bit oversoft. I want to fuse and acquire both, since both are in me.

But sometimes I wish I were without any gift but one. I fear this spreading out, unless one has da Vinci's energy and genius to follow all things to an end. If I can be a great writer *and* a great dancer, tant mieux [so much the better]. I'll try.

At thirty I'll settle down.

Dear Elvira, fussing around my irreligion with an anxious air, passing me books by good Christians who are rotten artists, and

so I shall never be converted. Meager philosophy, the Christian—
you always feel the *wall*, the limitation.

So I ate the Russian cakes, and talked little, and felt bad. And
gave Elvira my yellow Spanish dress, because she had nothing to
study in—the one I liked best, and I regret it terribly, and find it
so damn hard to be good.

Every day I become more irrevocably, more hopelessly myself, a sour mixture nobody really sees through—thanks to a
childishness and impenetrability of face, which must be an Oriental
inheritance. Only the eyes, like those of harem women, watching
and speaking, and waiting, and longing . . .

And Elvira knits for a charity bazaar, reads holy books, and
thinks me lovable. She can talk and laugh and be the proud and
gushy godmother of someone else's baby; and be the wise one
when one speaks of life's troubles. She reads Lamartine to her
maid (but why Lamartine?) and upsets me by announcing in the
middle of my foolish withdrawal from the noise of the tea that
she is learning English to read my works!

November 28. At least once a year we have these "crises" in our
marriage, always over Hugh's absorption in his work. When I
make him realize now and then that he is losing himself, he has
terrible regrets, but does nothing. Last night he confessed himself
incapable, utterly incapable of doing more than one thing at a
time. I said I realized that our sharing of the work was a failure,
since all I did was of no use to him. For months now we have sat
together in the evening and he has thought of *nothing* but *stocks*
and his difficulties with Mr. B. and his talk with F. and his report
to a visiting Vice-President. I have gone nearly mad with loneliness. Last night I could not control myself when he spoke of a
talk with Velasco, who writes a journal and reads voraciously. He
said that sometimes he wished Eugene were here to talk with. I
answered: "If Eugene were here you would talk to him about the
Bank."

This, we have often gone over, ending with tears and kisses
and promises. Last night the climax was different. As he stood
there with a sorrowful face, admitting his powerlessness, and
wishing he could prove to me how, if he had the time, he could
give himself to literature, I suddenly saw as clearly as I saw him
before me that he was meant to be a banker because he could be
nothing else. I saw that the day he would give up this tangible

proof of his talent, this fine work of his, it would be a tragedy. Because he would realize what I see now. I made a mistake to encourage him to fight for his intellectual life. No one who has it in him *needs* encouragement and urging. I could not tell him what I had discovered because the whole structure of our marriage is based on faith. To deprive him of my faith would be like depriving him of my love, or of life. He has gone as far as he can go—achieved a magnificent work in which he has used up all his imagination and vision. He will remain now a sweetly appreciative, passive man, superb in qualities of character, but quiet in mind, sad-faced, pathetic, infinitely lovable. I yearned over him, at the same time that I realized starkly, mercilessly, his insufficiency. The sudden realization that inevitably, even if he gave all his life to literature, I would outstrip him mentally gave me such despair that after talking very quietly and tenderly with him, holding myself in, I slipped into the bed and began to shiver violently, overtaken by a deathly feeling of cold, and then I felt I couldn't breathe any more; I gasped for a few minutes while my poor darling called to me, and I couldn't answer.

For six years I have tormented him, *to keep him by my side.* He has been wonderfully willing and has made efforts. Last night he asked me again for another chance. But last night was the last time I shall ever mention the subject. Now I am going to be a woman like the others: I'm going to concern myself with his health and his happiness, rather than with his greatness.

His poor, tired face, overwhelmed by an effort beyond his strength, will become smooth again, like Horace's.

Mon Dieu, mon Dieu, this is the one separation I couldn't endure, and it is the one I must bear quietly. I would rather be a thousand times deceived physically, abandoned, beaten, starved, than disappointed intellectually. And now the hardest thing of all will be to grow at his side, without noise and without appearing to be moving, to grow gently without molesting or bothering him, to grow without his encouragement, to keep *him* from making comparisons that will make him unhappy. To write, to create, to achieve quietly—not to seem to do any more than what he has done in his own work; not to seek companionship anywhere else, since that hurts him. To sacrifice all human pleasures to that mind which has even taken away from me the possibility of a perfect marriage.

This has been the most unhappy day of my life.

The realization, too, of my own monstrosity, this insatiable hunger of the mind, of which I am ashamed, drives me mad. I'll have to give something very great to justify it. As great as Hugh's human accomplishment. Let me admire him for what he has done with other instruments and on another plane. Let me be fair. After all, he is a man superior to all other men. Thank heavens, perhaps, that he is not an artist; instead of one cannibal, there would be two.

Hugh is in reality so far superior to me. He works, he suffers, he lives without the hope of outliving the span of his life with his thoughts. I, at least, at some moments, feel a bond with all the thought in the world, a sense of fusion with the minds of the world, which is my heaven.

November 29. Peace and tenderness cover up the pain. Hugh even makes jokes. Revolution in the Art Department, he says. And goes off to play tennis while Gilbert and I have a fine talk, from which, I gather, Kathleen is now what I was five years ago. To say what I can teach her, Gilbert is forced to give me compliments, but that comes easier to him because he now frankly admires my writing, especially the essay on the Journal and "Anita." He is becoming more human, and I understand him better. Queer, how we began with clashes of two egos.

I read William James attentively and a book on Amiel, in which a certain habit of reading is compared to a drug. But whose fault is it if books act like a drug instead of a powerful dynamite? Books set me off! I explode. I jump. I change my life. I clean up the flabby ideas. I disinfect the rotten traditions. I shake up the congealed or inherited attitudes.

Books convert me and de-convert me, make me restless and active. No, they don't fall on me like an avalanche and bury me, in my armchair, by the fireside. They simmer under my chair, perpetually, like half-active volcanoes, and keep me awake and watching, and every week or so they erupt violently and carry me off to a new place, sometimes the other side of the earth.

Books made Amiel ruminate, reflect, criticize, analyze, ponder, weigh—and stay home. It was not the books' fault. No. Poor Amiel—I'm less gentle with him, since I have grown up.

December 1. Glory be to modern plays and to the age I live in! We lived intensely and fantastically this weekend through *Crimi-*

nals [by Ferdinand Bruckner] at the Théâtre des Arts, with Ludmilla Pitoeff. New technique results in a fuller expression of life. The set, a house seen all at once from the attic rooms down to the kitchen. Several lives developing simultaneously. Intricate and arresting—almost too strong a dose for normal minds and eyes, but how satisfyingly rich. From a boîte [night club], which occupies one part of the house, comes the sound of jazz from a phonograph all during the last act, while in other parts of the house come death, moments of sorrow, tenderness, at the same time as vice and debauchery. Suddenly all the action stops. Titine (Mme. Pitoeff) lies dead. A voice says: "Tout passe, tout continue" [Everything passes, everything continues] and the noise, laughter, dancing, love-making begin again.

Evening: I write sweetly to Pauline because I feel sorry for her. I write affectionately to Tia Anaïs because I feel sorry for her. Twenty-five Christmas cards. Xmas shopping. I certainly live down to earth, like Titine [in *Criminals*], who, a half hour before poisoning herself, offers the product of her act with heartfelt interest: "Goutez-moi cette mayonnaise!" [Taste that mayonnaise!]

To Anna I write: "You would be surprised. I finally bought myself a real sport suit, sweater and skirt and real walking shoes, and everything, and I looked and felt American. The trouble is I can't stay that way. The next moment I wear again all the trinkets which made you ask me if I were afraid to leave them home on account of burglars."

A typical example of how I "discover" things. Found twice while writing a need of the word "nacre." Asked Hugh for the English equivalent. Hugh said he didn't think it existed. In the dictionary I could only find a translation of "nacre" as "mother-of-pearl"—but not the adjective. Like a hunter, I continued to sniff the air, and I spotted the word "nacreous" in Huxley's novel!

December 5. The realization that there is something the matter with our friends kept me from sleeping soundly last night. In the first place I have never chosen them; they came as accidents. Mother's old friends; friends of these friends; admirers of Joaquín; Cubans, who are in themselves a vast social prison, with their passion for society; Bank friends; business compromises; and among them all a few rare cases of selection, like Irving, Gustavo —but even then selection by relative values. I mean that if I had been asked to choose between Gustavo and, say, Merejskowski, I would not have chosen Gustavo. Each year the handful, those accidentally thrust on me, have made me unhappy. Basically, all *safe*, rather conventional, even Catholics, sometimes artistic, but in such a pale way. No wonder John appeared like a giant among them and overwhelmed me.

A very social week! We danced at Mme. Peignot's house—Elvira, Bonifacio, Alyette, Hugh and I. Hugh came out, definitely out, of his shell and danced marvelously, with insolence and vividness. He collected the biggest load of compliments. Our Jota made people scream. I did a Cuadro Flamenco with a long-tail purple dress. But I never felt as vainglorious and exultant as I did last year. When I sat on the floor to watch the others dance, I saw myself in a mirror, among the purple billows of my dress, pale-faced, with colored combs and flowers and earrings and many bracelets, and I appeared sad and a little remote.

Every morning, before writing, I get into a one-piece bathing suit, turn on the phonograph and do the Oriental gymnastics. My body is getting more and more supple, and I am growing fatter. I like dancing against the black curtains and the red walls, to the rhythm of Tangos. I give myself a little show.

What my book needs now is "Mayonnaise" . . . so Anita won't be what Huxley called Shelley—a mere "flying slug."

December 10. It was no surprise to find that Aldous Huxley was the son of a man of science. He takes literature as a science. He dissects and he classifies.

In *Point Counter Point* he describes himself in Philip, "loyal only to the cool indifferent flux of intellectual curiosity" and inhuman—all theory. Also condemns his own novel through Philip's notes: "The great defect of a novel of ideas is that it's a made-up affair. Necessarily; for people who can reel off neatly formulated notions are not quite real. They're slightly monstrous. Living with monsters becomes rather tiresome in the long run."

As a matter of fact, I have lived with Huxley's monsters and did not get tired, although I missed two things: warmth and pity, and the execution of theories, which is passion. These two are dried up in an atmosphere of intensive polemics and cool analysis. For once I was given some of my own medicine: People ever ready for ideology. Did I like them? Did I prefer Philip and Spandrell to my actual friends? Yes. Now and then I felt the lack of air and movement. The laboratory experiments were a bit inexorable and terse. Character is more than a chemist's mixture. There is, outside of the laboratory, mystery and mysticism, defying the best set notions. And when I feel too near death—dissection is a study of dead things—then I must come out of Huxley's books into, say, de la Mare.

Could not have picked a better contrast to Huxley than Sinclair Lewis, particularly in the matter of style. Huxley is long-winded, scholarly, profuse, florid, though always in the best of English taste, but often guided by the pleasant flow of words, of which he knows more, I think, than any other living author. Lewis is terse, precise, incredibly vivid, American in his naturalness and unscholarly roughness, a master of his language but injecting into it the living qualities of men of action and men who have no time to waste.

I prefer Lewis. He may be sensational and is certainly not classic, but he is a force, and he has precisely what Huxley lacks —exuberant, irresistible, formidable life. Ideas, in Lewis, push men and women into fantastic, tragic, horrible, sublime actions. Ideas, in Huxley, stultify human beings. Compare a laboratory with Niagara Falls. I would rather be at the Falls. Literature for me is not static. It is wind, lightning, cyclones, volcanoes, eclipses, astral phenomena, conflagrations.

December 12. "Sit down," says Elvira, "and write a nice little note to this lady who let you know about the advent of her baby."

"But I only met her once! I hardly remember. What can I say?" I write: "Chère Madame, I am very touched [hypocrisy] about your darling little girl . . . I hope," etc. "With fondness," etc.

Satisfied, Elvira pockets my card and goes off to visit the baby in question.

I guess I'm a barbarian. Such formalities weigh me down. Ouf! Elvira breathes and swims about in a profusion of such things so comfortably; in fact, such things take the place of her own living: self-effacement, devotion to obscure duties, charity of a visible kind—booties for poor children, scarves to be sold at charity affairs, teaching children for first communion. Meanwhile I sit and try to understand infinity—and instead of knitting, I look at people with a dreamwise penetration, and see all their lives in their eyes.

So Elvira knits, and I know now that she is hungry for a husband, a baby, and a day at home, and all the curious reverence of the world for a woman legally stationed by society.

Evening: After all, I am composed of such chemicals as will surely prevent me from growing either inhuman or peaceful. I give every day the same barometrical zigzags as the weather reports. I begin the day cheerfully and get sadder in the evening. I have never yet come to the end of a day without sentimentality —mush; I can be ironical only a few hours, clownish less, humorous in writing only. To be safe from a lopsided Journal I have written it at different hours.

December 13. It's when I read the old biographies (*P. B. Shelley* by Edward Dowden) that I realize the moderns have progressed in depth. In the romantic biography there is a kind of superficiality. I'm beginning to think that it wasn't Shelley who was a "flying slug" but the man who wrote about him and deformed reality with this false conception of beauty; beauty is not absence of ugliness, but form, creation, and strength. Shelley had all of these.

What is discouraging, however, is that there is so little progress and so much time wasted on readjusting extreme swings. Today Shelley would be no more justly interpreted than he was years ago. Today they would find some vice in him to assure his humanness and reality—equally wrong. A mere reaction against the slugs and fairies.

Met among the Cubans a woman of thirty or so who seems to understand. Overcome with surprise, I talk to her, questioningly, desperately, awkwardly, surprising others with my sudden talkativeness when they had all been warned that I was timid and reticent. She is Maria Teresa Freyre de Andrade, a great reader, who confessed to me that she kept "terse and pedantic" notes of her thoughts and had a keen desire to write. All the time we talked (philosophy, the Spanish Renaissance, South American legends, Bernard Shaw, Valéry, Claudel, languages, life in Havana, etc.), her eyes understood, and I could see in her what I often do to others, with that expression of comprehension which drives others to talk to me, endlessly.

But I am punished severely for my "sauvagerie." In the spring she had written to me asking if we could meet because she was Thorvald's friend. I evaded the meeting with many excuses, let the summer pass. Only an accident brought us together, and now she is returning to Havana for at least two years and I have only seen her three times.

She is delicate in health, pretty, bright-faced—we have promised to correspond. She said to me, pressing her forehead with two fingers: "It is quite evident that you live in here, a world apart. When you're silent in ordinary talk, you go there, among your ideas. You live there, too. But I live there more coolly than you do. You are imaginative about it, you embellish philosophy. I think I'm more analytical."

Not with her sensibility—I wondered what she meant. I will find out.

I think things out, rather amateurishly and blunderingly and then come upon them, neat and professional, in some book or other. But I'm glad to have got there alone, like a man without a map—who, upon getting it, finds himself where he wanted to be and rejoices over his flair.

Having read in one day Barrès's *Greco*, Waldo Frank, and part of James's psychology, I feel top-heavy and utterly unfit for social intercourse. Mr. and Mrs. B. are coming to dinner. How much more tiring it will be to focus on their child's bright sayings, on the lady's newspaper work, on the gentleman's long-winded Southern stories, on general news, and I'm always so ignorant of even the newspaper headlines.

When Hugh comes home at last I even find it hard to talk to him. I'm so afraid that the most delicate attention will bring forth (and uncover) the whole story of the business conference. He picks up the irresistible *Mantrap* [by Sinclair Lewis], and I sigh with relief.

Mrs. B., though the most sentimental of newspaper writers, whose stories are full of mush and bromides, showed the most generous appreciation of my work yesterday, which touched me. I only let her read two of the shortest stories, but she found them exciting, subtle, and full of surprises and thought and humor. I was so pleased I had to hide a broad, uncontrollable grin. My influence on her is useful—she is going straight home to write to please herself and not the "public."

Mother and Joaquin are astonished at my "feverishness" and "inquietude." I made them laugh by saying I had an intellectual tapeworm. Joaquin pities me a little. He is, in comparison to me, serene.

I saw it all more simply today. It's just this: I write. When I write I feel exulted. When I feel exulted and excited mentally I want to *act*. My friends are irritatingly "insuffisant" [insufficient]. Dancing is all right, but I can't do it often enough. Having such a temperament is like having a shameful illness.

Am I beginning to lose my balance again? My disquietude is apparent even to a family who is used to my ways. Joaquin understands but does not share my feelings—all the while, I know he wants to say: Try religion.

And all the while, I know that all this is necessary to my work, that if I were contented I would not write "Anita" with such intensity—page by page—warm, fleshly ideology, mind and blood running together.

Composition done coolly and indifferently must be a curious thing. It isn't in me. When I work, my head grows hot and my hands and feet cold. Today I burned some incense and smoked too. All sensation was concentrated in the head and in the nose. I felt bodiless.

Evening: A strange thing happened to me which will change my life. I discovered today the infinite power of the imagination, its occult power.

I had been writing all morning; from three to four I read and studied. At four I dressed slowly and meticulously for a banal visit. I put on black underwear, my black velvet dress, coral earrings and bracelet, Egyptian perfume, my black hat and fur coat. And then I thought to myself: What a shame that I'm doing all this just to call on Mrs. D. If I were going to meet John, how differently I would feel. As I went out in the very sharp-aired darkness, I began to imagine I was going to see John, that I was walking toward the place where we would meet. I walked fast. My fur collar deadened the sounds of the street. Because I couldn't hear very distinctly, and it was dark, I felt more acutely the tumult of my senses, the joy and keenness of anticipation. All my body was quivering with pleasure. John was waiting for me. Already I felt his bigness, his warmth, his livingness, his own overflowing emotion. I walked quickly, entranced, to the climax of my dream.

Mrs. D.'s butler opened the door. Mrs. D. was not in yet. I was led to her boudoir. I sat by the fire. I had been very happy, almost as happy as that night on the balcony, as the morning he came to say good-bye.

Slowly I began to look at the room, so as to return. It was

not painful. I had my dream, as I had the kisses. When Mrs. D. came in I was able to say: "Waiting in this room was no hardship; how I like your salmon-pink curtains and the Japanese lamps." And we talked and drank tea. I was still sustained by my illusion, and the day was less sad than if I had just the writing and the visit to Mrs. D.

It was only when I came home that the exultant feelings died down—because I could not greet Hugh with them. And so I put them willfully, as a thing apart, into the dream.

I had read with such skepticism and mockery *Quand le Navire*, where Lucianne "appears" to her husband and he to her because they think of each other so intently. I said it was cheap. Now it has happened to me, and I don't know what to think. I'm beginning to "see things." Through the imagination I am living out those things which are forbidden me. It frightens me. How much I can do with my own mind; what will become of me? Just now, nothing to fear. I feel as if I had lived through a precious moment, relived all the sweetness I have missed, the sensuous plenitude.

December 15. Something in the human repulses the dream, alas, fights it. After the ecstasy yesterday I crumbled today into the most horrible depression. Could hardly endure the tea party here today—any moment I feared I would break down. "How beautiful your house! How beautiful your dress! How well you dance!" they say. And I cry inwardly while they talk. They bore me. "And is your sister's sore throat better? Is your new cook satisfactory? Yes, things do cost ten percent more out here. Oh, dear, is that so? Children *are* troublesome. I'm sorry you hate long dresses. I rather like them. Yes, my hair is permanently waved. You want the address? Go to M. Pierre, he'll take good care of you. Isn't it awful, the traffic! Don't take your children to see the toys on a Thursday. I was almost stifled myself. Did they tell you that? La Argentina is intelligent, just the same, even if there are better dancers. What has intelligence got to do with dancing, you say? Oh, I couldn't tell you. I just imagine it's necessary. Yes, English is a good thing for your children to learn. It's good for business? Indispensable. Yes, there *is* rather a fine English literature." (I see their faces look tired.) "I did read a translation of some English detective stories," says a lady cheerfully.

Mon Dieu, these people are going to make me egotistical and

neurasthenic. I must not let them. Let's see what I can find in them. The strain tires me so. I collapse when they are only half-way out of the house.

This is the way I am being slowly starved. And John has no pity.

December 20. To understand is to forgive? Yes. I read a startling explanation of the American woman by Waldo Frank—I, who had often misjudged her from a European point of view. A beautiful and tragic justification, which overwhelmed me with pity and sympathy.

Understanding is the most beautiful miracle of the intelligence. If all we learn only served for that, it would be enough. That is what I want to strive for, with all my strength.

Met another intelligent Cuban woman, a decorator, painter, and writer, Lydia Cabrera, but one embittered by criticism, indifferent now to people, unsociable, who never tries to please—and who is lonely. Her reserve broke down yesterday, in the atmosphere of Joaquin's music, my talk—how I talk when people give a hint of philosophic or literary interests! She knows Waldo Frank and Havelock Ellis, reached Spain through them. From Spain to the Orient, I said. She looked at me with a significant smile. She studies Hindu art and thought. She and her sister (a shadow) stayed longer than they had intended. And we may meet again. Yet the first time we invited her, she wouldn't come. I know what she feared. This finally convinces me we must take chances.

This *universal* loneliness begins to show to me its ironic sides; its universality is a comic paradox. In Havana I know two women groping and starving, yet they are not friends. Probably unconsciously they do not want it. Solitude has its strength. Yet so has love, as Frank says, and to possess strength, will power, is not enough. Love is the transfigurer. I know that. That is why, though I fold myself up into myself, grow inwardly instead of outwardly, cultivate my independence and self-sufficiency, I do not cease to love, to love unwisely and fervently.

What the American woman has gained, spiritually, from pioneering and becoming like a man is the "sense of sportsmanship" I so admire and miss in Continental women.

I told Hugh sadly that for that alone I would have wished myself American. Hugh said: "You had your pioneering in the bungalow, tending the furnace, cleaning the cellar, washing the laundry, etc. You have masculine qualities plus femininity." I looked doubtful. I thought of Lilith. Lilith's breezy simplicity and directness, Lilith's man-to-man talk. All at once I felt I could do all that a Lilith could do—that I understood Lilith, but that the Liliths would always misjudge me by *appearance*. I remember Frances (another's Lilith) laughing at the mere thought of *me* trying to climb the Greek mountains as she had done with Horace! "Can you just *imagine* Anaïs doing that?" Such hilarity!

It is only Hugh who believes, and it is only for Hugh that I can be at once a Lilith and a European.

December 23. Among our Christmas cards, which we were opening cheerfully, we got a telegram telling us of Uncle George's death—poor dear man, so noble and so upright, whose strict ideals made me suffer, but at the last how well we understood each other, and how reconciled we all were at Johnnie's wedding. This helped to make Hugh less miserable, less regretful, but what sadness for my poor darling. He is off to London to attend the funeral and to see Aunt Susie. Last night we wrote difficult and heart-rending letters to Mother Guiler and Lisa, his wife, the more terrible because they were not sincere: we *know* how horrible death is, that there is no consolation, and that life in the spirit is *not* sufficient—and while we offered our affection and sweet words, we felt desperately unreal because we wanted to express rebellion and bitterness.

We meet death with the affirmation that only the human presence is taken away from us, but what would we not give to find again the lost one, partaking of food with us, laughing and talking. Too well we love the human, with our blood, and it is only because we are beaten by it that we recognize the eternity of the image of the mind, which we love *less*, really less, and it is human life we are desperate to share with those we love.

The worst, the most unbearable, paradox: the words with which we lull our human pain.

I have two memories carved cruelly in me forever: Mother Guiler playfully chewing the hair on the back of Father Guiler's hands when we were in a taxi coming from a merry evening together, and now he is dead; Uncle George eating very fast and hungrily one evening at Aunt Annie's house, his cheeks grown pink with health, and now he is dead. These intensely physical moments of their lives come back to me. And the other day I was watching Mother having her lunch, enjoying her food, her cheeks a little flushed, too, and I remember watching her with an overwhelming joy and gratitude for her physical presence—which I was observing like some precious, precious fact.

December 24. I hardly slept last night, listening to the wind, which made me anxious for Hugh's safety on the Channel, yearning for him, overwhelmed with pity, with tenderness, swearing over and over again to be steady, absolutely true, for he deserves it so.

Before going to bed I wrote him a real love letter, repeating all I have written about him, adding to it, making wild promises, feeling hot with shame, icy with fears of myself, and desiring death because I live with a saint whom I can't love enough, nor wholly, nor divinely enough.

I could only prove how precious he is to me, how profound and infinite is my imperfect and human love for him, if he should die, because I know that I would not live without him one moment. And I know now that my love will be whole and complete and that I shall struggle to make it so—that his image, his being in me is irrevocable, eternal, that we have mingled beyond dissolution, that in my fitful way there *is* a consistency and a loyalty, because I always *worship* him even when I do not desire him.

I feel such pity for him, for all of him, for his delicate health, his sleeplessness, his nervousness, for his sadness, for the deaths which have hurt him, for his pathetic eyes, his thinness, his sensitiveness, his devotion to his family, his tenderness, his own pity of others.

Sometimes I feel that, with differences, we balance each other, that my feeling of singleness is only due to my work's being different from his, that I would feel single even if he were writing now by my side.

Strange how death pushes one into life, how death urges one to live. I know that at this moment Hugh craves the comfort of my love—my poor darling—and that is why I wrote him a love letter.

Evening: I read a strange and wonderful book (*Women in Love* by D. H. Lawrence), concerned only with the description of feelings, sensations, conscious and unconscious, with ideas, and with the physical only as a transcription of spirit—though recognized as having a life in itself, as in Gerald. To do it, Lawrence had to torment and transform ordinary language; words are twisted and mishandled, sometimes beyond recognition. And he is also given to loathing and loathsomeness, which is an individual feeling that is rarely mixed with love in such an absurd way, except in people who are emotionally dissolved so it all flows together. Apart from that, he has an occult power over human life and sees deeper than almost anyone I know. He never comes off the plane—lives permanently, naturally, and thoroughly *within*, and if it is sometimes airless, again it is, as with Huxley, a matter of being overtruthful, as sick people are who don't care so very much for life.

But I care for life, in spite of a tragic sense of its meaning and its futility, in spite of death, of my perpetual singleness, of all the curses around us. And so I live two hours with Huxley, two hours with Lawrence, and escape again, feeling they don't know everything.

How much they do know impresses me, formidably. They know more than John. They are fearless; they have almost disintegrated themselves to know; they have risked their personal lives; the lives of their characters; and their grammar (Huxley, too, because he has extended language, though correctly, like a tightly drawn elastic until it wears thin).

Lawrence is dangerous to the mind, though, because he flounders. He knows and he doesn't know. At least, he doesn't know what to do with what he knows.

December 25. Sad Xmas Eve, spent, to please Mother and Joaquin, at the house of their friends the Couteaus. Midnight Mass, eating and dancing, and my only pleasure the playing of Joaquin's Trio. We went to bed at five o'clock.

My thoughts are constantly on Hugh, with sadness, humility, remorse, and a painful, intense reiteration of promises, a great desire to love him as he deserves.

A bleak, windy day. Last night I was more than ever out of my element, and the gaiety of the young hurt me. I felt so remote that I could even watch with detached, almost literary, curiosity, my peculiar effect on the young men there, though I sat among the elders and was self-effacing and quiet. There were boys and girls of twenty or so, half developed; the young men looked at me over their champagne, drew near, and talked for my sake and were drawn and held and a bit puzzled. Their awkward talk and gestures to interest me seemed strange and made me feel old. It touched me that as a married woman of twenty-six, among five fresh and attractive "jeunes filles," I could still be singled out and courted, and asked to dance.

The people in general, fifteen of them or so, were plain, simple, good-hearted, musical—but certainly neither smart nor modern, quaint and obsolete like the garlands of flowers on the mirror and like the piano covered with brocade.

St.-Paul, Auberge Colombe d'Or. Up on a hill—medieval Provençal town. Doves eating corn before the door of the auberge. Hall of the auberge filled with artists, writers, journalists, actors. Hugh wailed: "I'm afraid to go in. If they find out I'm a banker they will throw me out." (He found out afterward that two bankers had made the place by having a blowout in front and discovering the exquisite cooking of Mère Roux.) I pushed Hugh in. We have lived here ever since. There are two immense fireplaces—the French sit around one, the Anglo-Saxons around the other. I feel literally between two fires. The walls are covered with paintings and drawings. Roux is a painter himself. The d'Or's livre [guest-book] is filled with signatures of celebrities. Roux tears out the rest. Artists often go away without paying their bills. All these are newspaper legends. But the place is good just the same. The old maids paint the doves fooling around Virgil's olive trees. In reality they spend most of their time eating corn and gurgling on the roof. The artists flaunt their unshaved faces and play bridge like ordinary men.

We overeat, admire the historic and eminently paintable town, take long walks, praise Waldo Frank and wonder what the devil he means by "compassionate ferocity." I guess that's what I practice.

During the first days I hankered after Caux. Then I realized it was not so much Caux I loved as the mountain roads, freedom to roam, and time to work.

By the most amusing coincidence I have seen Gerald Leake here, the painter who took me to Woodstock and then wanted me to be "nice," besides being a model. I enjoyed seeing his weak chin and furtive eyes, in which a spark of recognition was soon snuffed out when he remembered.

S. Wilenski

*Anaïs in Spanish
costume and wearing
her "accroche coeur"
(spit curl)*

Anaïs's husband, Hugh (Hugo) Parker Guiler

Anaïs's father, Joaquin Nin, the composer and concert pianist

*The apartment at 47
Boulevard Suchet, de-
scribed by Anaïs as "a
modernization of the
Oriental style"*

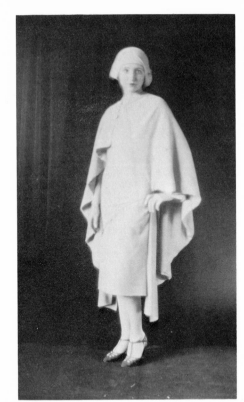

Anaïs in a dress of her own design

Joaquin Nin-Culmell, Anaïs's younger brother, in 1928

A portrait of Anaïs, possibly by Brassai, in one of her dance costumes

Anaïs posing in several of her dance costumes. As Joaquin writes, ". . . she danced with enormous vitality and made up for technical limitations with fiery intensity."

S. Wilenski

*Anaïs and Hugh as
dancing partners*

Hugh with his guitar

A concert program that featured piano pieces by Joaquin and Spanish dances performed by Anaïs, as "Mme. Anita Aguilera"

SALLE D'IÉNA
ANCIEN HOTEL DU PRINCE ROLAND BONAPARTE
10, AVENUE D'IÉNA, 10

LE VENDREDI 7 MARS A 16 H. 30
9° CONCERT
DONNÉ PAR
La REVUE INTERNATIONALE
DE MUSIQUE ET DE DANSE
DIRECTEUR : CAROL-BÉRARD

PROGRAMME
1re PARTIE

I. Novelettes .... GLAZOUNOW
    a) Alla Spagnola
    b) Interludium in modo antiquo
    c) Valse
    Quatuor SCHWARTZ (L. Schwartz, Blareau, L. Chalaton, A. Cruque)

II. Trois Impressions .... Joaquin N. CULMELL
    a) Habanera
    b) Un Jardin de Tolède (dédié à Marie André)
    c) Les Marchandes d'eau (Goya)
    Mme Marie ANDRÉ

III. Tres Canciones misticas (Trois Chansons mystiques) . Joaquin N. CULMELL
    a) Sin duda Senor que amais pues florais (Ledesma)
    b) Cuando no pude quejar... (Cardona)
    c) Pastor que con tus silbos amorosos... (Lope de Véga)
    Mme Suzanne PEIGNOT — Au piano : M. Maurice Béché

IV. Sevilla .... ALBENIZ
    Alegrias .... MONREAL
    Mme Anita AGUILERA

ENTR'ACTE DE 10 MINUTES
2e PARTIE

I. Quatuor : Sostenuto - Allegro - Largo - Allegro molto....... Ellen COLEMAN
    Quatuor SCHWARTZ (L. Schwartz, Blareau, L. Chalaton, A. Cruque)

II. Cinq Préludes (destinés à l'orchestre)................. Jacques BERNARD-NAUDIN
    a) Enjoué   d) Evocation, grave
    b) Lamento, in memoriam   e) Burlesque
    c) Scherzo
    Mme Marie ANDRÉ

III. Le Gloxinia .... AURIC
    Berceuse .... MILHAUD
    Les trois Présents .... G. TAILLEFERRE
    Air romantique .... POULENC
    Air champêtre ....
    Mme Suzanne PEIGNOT — Au Piano : M. Maurice Béché

IV. Jota.. V. ROMERO
    Farruca Meruna .... P. EXPERT
    Mme Anita AGUILERA
    PIANO PLEYEL

Photographs of Anaïs's dancing teacher, Paco Miralles, that she cut out and pasted in her journal

John Erskine, Anaïs, and the Erskine children, Anna and Graham

Hugh and Anaïs with Erskine and the children on a trip to Beaune (Burgundy) in 1928. Graham Erskine recalls that the chauffeur kept the car polished with rancid butter.

Courtesy of
Anna Crouse Murch

Anaïs took this excerpt from the group photograph (opposite, bottom) to decorate the opening page of her journal titled "John."

A pencil drawing by Princess Natasha Troubetskoi, described by Anaïs as "Natasha's idea of what will happen to me if I continue dancing and become more and more frail. I will be so light I will fly up to the ceiling of the studio and remain uncatchable."

Hugh in the Bois de
Boulogne

Anaïs and the portrait by Natasha Troubetskoi

Hugh, probably at the Auberge Colombe d'Or in St.-Paul

*Eduardo Sánchez,
Anaïs's beloved cousin,
in 1935*

Hugh in the late 1920s

OPPOSITE: *An entry
from Anaïs's Journal
for June 28, 1929, with
a photograph of the
Boulevard Suchet
apartment*

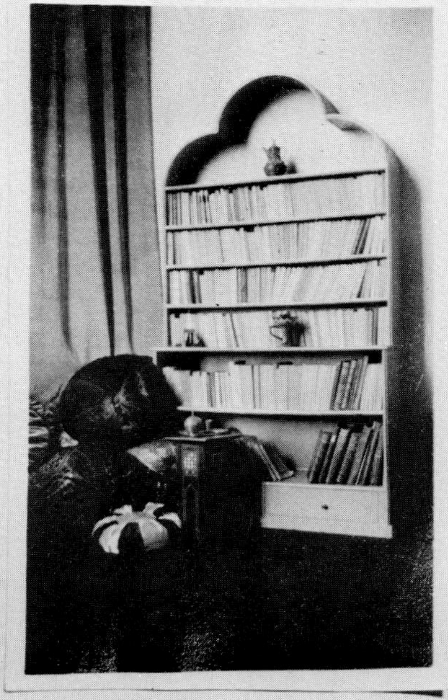

Hugh, Eduardo, and Anaïs in the garden at Louveciennes, early 1930s

Hugh and Anaïs in the 1930s; the photographer may have been Man Ray.

❦ *1 9 3 0* ❦

January 1. The New Year found us asleep after Hugh tore me away from the festivities. "I hate parties," he said. I do too, in general, but this time I had on my best green dress and gold slippers, and the artists were interested in me, so I was not so keen on leaving. But afterward Hugh elaborated. "Besides, the real reason is that I hate to have you dancing around with everybody—especially artists—and don't you think I didn't see them staring at you. And then there is another thing. You know those three or four healthy boisterous young college boys—well, they are just the type who always looked down on me a bit in college and who didn't understand me, and thought me "slow" with the girls—well, it gave me pleasure to walk off with the best-looking woman there and to keep them from dancing with you."

"My, my," I said, "a case for Freud [whom I haven't read yet], a real complex. Well, if you're satisfied, I am. I enjoy your being jealous." And we went to bed and read ourselves to sleep. At four o'clock I heard the others come into their rooms. This morning they looked frowsy, and also puzzled. We felt rested and fit enough to enjoy a two-hour walk in the sunshine. But our talk was on a higher plane than Hugh's jealousy complex. I was urging him, in spite of all my promises, not to constantly postpone his writing. He has come, all by himself, to the conclusion that his work will not ultimately satisfy him unless he extracts from it the essence and makes art of it. I said dispiritedly that all my work seemed useless except to give him an indirect satisfaction; he is the indirect cause of all I do and am, since he has made it materially possible. Hugh said no, that his own realization now was due to my constant pressure, for which, I said bitterly, I "even risked his hating me." Anyway, he is filled with aspirations, but hasn't written a line. And so it goes on, even though he himself says he is perhaps today the only poet in the business world. But a mute poet. "I'm tired," he said. But I reminded him how after working eight hours a day on the house I was still able to write lyrical pages about it—automatically, almost mechanically.

Even though our vacations are always physical convalescences, I can write. He has a single-track mind and a great power of concentration. I have more flexibility, but the trouble with flexibility is that it leads to excessive expansion and superficiality. And then people look for perfection, where the two faces of every virtue and vice are apparent to the most infantile intellect. They look for perfection with incurable naïveté in each New Year—just as I am doing now. And Hugh says, hopefully, "You wait and see, when I drop business, how I shall give literature the same concentration and absolute devotion I gave banking." "Why wait?" I ask with wifely, irritating stubbornness. "Write as you think. You do think, don't you? In fact, you cook and boil and parboil and recook and warm up your ideas over and over again and *never* get *rid* of them."

Hugh, on vacations, gets so bright and talkative and shows an innate wisdom which it takes me days and days to acquire. His remarks have the finality of a man who has controlled both the world and himself—and his wife. I like very often to submit to his will (like last night) so as to measure the force of this will, which he has fashioned in a chaotic world out of the hesitancy, the vague speculations, the imaginative marshes, the flowing sands and changing climates of the *pack*. I do admire him for all that, and for his sincerity, his true passion for real values, for which he is willing to suffer; and for his profound desire to reach invisible heights when he could be satisfied with his sub-managership!

This place has been fertile in walks, morning sunshine, drowsy sweetness by the fireside, an atmosphere of ease and artiness, exceptional meals; but our studio room, sunless, damp, rugless, chairless, with curtains half torn from their rods, no closet, no hangers, no shoes cleaned, no servant to answer the bell, no reading light, is my inferno. At four o'clock the sun is down. I can't write or read. If we go to the main room to enjoy the fire, the talking of people keeps me from working, too. Even now I write with my coat on because I have the fire before me but the door is opened constantly and I feel the wind on my neck. I find it hard not to hear the loud conversations. Above us, around the top of the room, we have a fine, stylized frieze by Buckley MacGurrin—three snaky and inhumanly proportioned but interesting ladies reclining among tropical vegetation, a swan, a monkey, and birds of paradise. In the gray room, with its smell of dampness, it glows. But it doesn't warm me. I have been racked by neuralgic pains for six days now, and I look at bohemianism with an unfriendly eye. MacGurrin himself sits behind us at lunch. He has a reddish-blond beard and a lady companion I don't like, and he has studied my anatomy, color, class, quite thoroughly. At mail time (9:30 at the old Provençal buffet by the door) we bump into each other. I smile with my eyes. "You *are* a good painter," I would say, if it could interest him, but I doubt it. His stylized women have scarcely any brows. They are part of the jungle. Reddish-haired MacGurrin, I know, uses them for the orgies of his fresco in the garden wall—Bacchus, with the grapes and a dilated stomach (he should wear a special corset like Hugh's), grabs the fruit and women's breasts at the same time—and for the decoration and enlivenment of his studio in Paris. (His card hangs on the door of the room below ours.)

Hugh is writing! He picked up my notebook. I can hardly stick to my chair. It is six o'clock and Mme. Roux is covering the tables with red-checkered tablecloths. At seven the artists will begin to walk in. Leake will evade my eyes. MacGurrin will take off his beret and his hair will stand up. His lady will rejoice that I am in my woolen suit with tennis sneakers and a faded blue hat. We will only be ten or so at dinner. All the visitors, tourists, admirers of the town came to lunch. At dinner we are en famille. But Hugh keeps intimacy away. He has read the Waldo Frank and ruminated over it, which means that he makes me feel as if I had not read it. All would be perfect but for the cavernous room where my pain will begin again, and where I shall long for my soft, carpeted warm bedroom at home.

Le Père Roux, described by a newspaper as having the face of a "toréador désaffecté"—I would say "retired," except that toreadors never live to retire—will have to charge me for extra ink. He watches me with curiosity. What did Stella Benson do when she came here? And Marie Bashkirtsev? They ate roasted chickens. And so with Michael Arlen, Bernard Shaw, Pierre Louÿs, etc.

January 2. Hugh having to go to Nice on business, I worked all afternoon. But I had to ask for a spare room with a *fireplace*. I have such a pile of imperfect, unpublished work and instead of rewriting I go on composing. Alas! How I loathe rewriting. When I was a child I loathed soup. I used to say: "The first thing I'll do when I'm grown up and free is not to eat soup." The first thing I'll do when I have published and have enough nerve is not to rewrite.

Hôtel Regina, Cimiez. To be nearer Hugh's work we came here. Finding myself in a sunny room and warm, I began to work well.

All my *ascension* of the past months to an understanding of Hugh has culminated in a formidable set of pages in "Anita," in which he is a thousand times vindicated and proved superior. It is the end of the book, the climax to her story and mine, and it is the most heated, the most inspired writing I have ever done. It appears to me now that I have truly transfigured our life and his character.

If I write nothing else about him, I am satisfied. It seems to me this is the least I can do, to thus consecrate all my work to an expression of him—the rarest of men.

Meanwhile, he writes in his journal a kind of examination of conscience, although he is suffering from a toothache. I see him with new eyes and my new love, and I feel that I have placed this love now in a secure place, binding myself so closely to it that he shall never be hurt again.

I don't know quite what is happening. I am, in some ways, congealing. By concentration on writing, I become impervious to music, to admiration, to people, to my own body, to all the mellow pleasures of existence. I look at the sea, sky, and palm trees as settings to the writing. I am quite stoical in the face of such disappointments as Hugh's not getting a raise in salary when we most need it, and the only things which continue to mean something to me are Hugh's health, Mother's happiness, Joaquin's progress, Thorvald's advancement. John doesn't answer my letters though he sends a cable for Xmas. But that doesn't hurt now, and it is even a help to me in my struggle for absolute love of Hugh.

January 9. At seven o'clock Tuesday when the mail arrived I noticed Hugh opening it brusquely and anxiously, and I realized with immense pity that he still had hopes of a raise. But there was no raise. He went off on a business call, and I went straight up to my room, sat before my typewriter and said: Now. I'm going to write something to help Hugh earn money. And right off I began a novelette temporarily called "A Russian Salad in Paris," which is an entirely humorous parody of the Russians. It is now five pages long and makes Hugh laugh, although he has a cold and had his tooth extracted.

January 11. In spite of rain, Hugh's ailments, and mine, I have worked wonderfully, having rewritten everything, often recomposing and altering, having added to my Journal essay, and finishing "Anita."

I visit a delightful lady of sixty, a Bank acquaintance, with whom I spend a delicious moment and who unexpectedly springs at me:

"But what do you do with yourself all day, a pretty young thing like you? You must get awfully lonely. And I'm sure you *could* have a lot of companionship. I'm sure many men would be only too glad to spend the day with you. How do you solve that problem? When I was your age, I was in a terrible fix. My first husband was in the diplomatic service. I had such a good time. Men made love to me, and you can't be very hard on a man who *adores* you, can you? And afterward, when I married a banker, and was left alone all day, I didn't know what to do. And I never liked lots of women friends—always preferred men. They're *interesting.*"

"I had a hard time for a few years," I said, "but now I have just ended the problem by work. I just work, work, work. No men friends, because it means love and flirtation. Just work."

"But you *can't* work all the time, my dear."

"I'm trying to—till I become dried up and inhuman, and intellectual."

"I'm sixty, and should be able to give you advice, yet I can't. There is no solution. There's a husband who works and is sleepy when he gets home and grunts when you talk. And there is the whole wonderful day and other men who want you, and your youth flowing away. And yet the husband wants *you* and *no one else*—won't give you up and won't forgive unfaithfulness. My poor child, I feel sorry for you. I'm sixty and I've never found a solution."

"*Work,*" I said stubbornly.

Portrait: This American woman had lived twenty years in Paris, and through her husband's diplomatic position knew the most aristocratic of Frenchwomen. Among them, she didn't find one faithful wife—all of them had had lovers. The "wise" philosophy of the French, said Mrs. B., was originally created by the Church, which forbade divorce. All these old French families were Catholics. They did not divorce, for the sake of religion, home, and children. Mrs. B. says that she *knows* these women confessed their adulteries and were exonerated, that the Church privately accepted such a situation, just as society did, for the sake of law and order. The happiness, or at least fulfillment of these women's lives, *plus* the extensive reading of French literature, had made a profound impression on Mrs. B. She had come to doubt the strict ideals—even the American experiments with divorce every time either husband or wife desired a change.

Whether she had had any love affair, I don't know. But I could see she was still aware of the problem, and I wondered why she was so powerfully sympathetic toward my half-lived life. When I said that I loved my husband, she answered: "Of course, why not? But one *can* love two men, I believe. I really do."

She practically urged me to take a lover, secretly. I was, inwardly, much upset by her frankness and human simplicity. I theoretically accepted her advice. And then I said: "Suppose my husband finds out? You know, as well as I do, that he won't forgive, that our marriage would never again be the same."

"I know," she floundered helplessly—a very vivacious, pretty old lady with the latest French novel within reach of her hand. Her curiosity, interest, and restlessness hurt me. I had hoped for one thing: that at sixty, at least, I would be quiet. But here I saw what I would have: a great pity for young and lovable young women, a great desire to see *them* live and do what I didn't do, a very active and disturbing feeling of participating in their troubles and of sharing their problems. So there would never be *quiet*, and the problem I wouldn't face now would simply live on within me.

Within myself, I have come to certain conclusions: that Hugh is worth *waiting* for, that if he wants me whole, he has the first choice, that loving another man is deceiving and cheating him, and that since I am creative, I can transmit the energy for other loves to writing, and since I have enough will, I shall see that I keep my desire for full living squelched and play fair. The worst of it is that I know that if Hugh were free of work, he too would want another love, so that just now he gives himself *wholly* to me because that is all he has time and energy for. What a thing to know! Which I can't prove until he retires, and then it will be too late.

When I read this last paragraph to Hugh in a moment of

courage, he said I was deeply mistaken about him, a fool even to suggest such a thing and wicked to say so when he couldn't disprove anything. And gave me a good Scotch sermon and afterward made love to me.

January 14. I love to come home after a trip, to see with fresh eyes my really beautiful kingdom. I like to unpack because I know there is a place for everything. I even enjoy sitting down to the business of my kingdom, sending checks, calling up about the broken vacuum cleaner, nailing up new photographs in the "art gallery" in the foyer. I like it all, the petty and the lovely. It is even slowly curing me of the hunger for traveling, although what I get from going away is priceless, too. In one week, cooped up in my hotel room, I did more work than I do at home in a month. Up there in Cimiez, too, I saw with a more severe eye what I have to do to help Hugh. As he *counts* on my creative work, I can't leave it to take an ordinary job, which would hurt his position in the Bank anyway. But I could do newspaper work, which is a neighbor to literature, and which would give me time for literature—that and teaching dancing.

As for pleasures, I have stopped the Oriental dancing lessons, keeping the exercises simply for body development and health. I take the subway, I buy no more dresses, I rent books instead of buying them, I cut down all social activities not strictly needed for business. (Each friend I have had has cost Hugh money!) In that way I will help to build up not only our almost vanished capital, but also my love and Hugh's happiness.

And so I began today, with the same élan which made me an artist's model and dress model—with a feeling of settling down again to austerity and self-denial, and I feel scornful of my past softness.

January 16. Amy Lowell says of Keats that although his life was painful and full of sorrows he was not an unhappy man all the time because he had the unequaled joy of feeling in himself the creative force. How right she is!

This feeling may be the reason why I am always, fundamentally, attached to life and why these last months, though unhappy in my friendships and worried by Hugh's health and financial difficulties, I have been strong and happy in one sense. I am filled with strength, with self-sustaining force; I work like the very devil—write, rewrite, doing book reviews in the hopes of getting a job.

Perhaps my last human experiment, being a disappointment, was intended to throw me back into myself so I wouldn't waste time on friendships and entanglements. In human relationships I am as luxuriant as in writing, as prolific—I remember how much time, energy, thought, I gave my friends. Most of it, I can see now, is futile, and falls short. It empties you and brings you nothing but regrets.

Yet I can't say I have tamed the desire for companionship and affection. The hunger is always there, very painful, very persistent. In friendship I have been a humble beggar, though never contented and never pleased but with the best. Those I thought the best, I refused nothing. I will never understand John's indifference.

January 17. Hugh discovers this: that I'm a brilliant writer, that I'm rich in ideas, but weak on details. My essay, which I wrote seven times over, remained defective because I am blind to the detail of composition. I see, seven times, the ideas, always the ideas, repeating the mistakes in phraseology. There is a remedy: Hugh's corrections. But his correction of a few words will change my paragraph so much that I feel the very impulse of it is endangered. He tames, sometimes obliterates the very brilliancy, because his writing is different, and he can't put himself in my place, of course. On the other hand, I myself don't see the error, and can't correct it in my own way. It's just as if I were far-sighted, *blind* to detail, aware of the whole. Hugh admires the breadth of my vision but wants to prevent me from overlooking language. He believes that my mastery of English is not equal to my thinking. When I saw my essay all mangled again I cried. I felt I had really tripped over the details I despise. It was a terrible blow to me. I had been so confident, I felt so free and so eloquent. It is strange that my defects do not appear when I *read* my things aloud, making Gilbert gasp, Hugh cry, Joaquin laugh. But on close inspection—oh, the bitterness of it.

January 18. I set out yesterday morning to master my terrible imperfections of technique, since I love writing beyond myself, my pride. There is no doubt that Hugh's mangling of my work cut me to the quick, and when I see a whole paragraph of mine crumble because he takes out a word "that can't be said in English," I'm helpless. What can't be said in English is now my permanent problem. This may be a result of the way I read English—skipping and jumping, gathering effects impressionistically. To cure myself of that I'm reading slowly, taking notes, studying the phrases thoroughly.

Last night, reading Amy Lowell, I said to Hugh rather cattily: "She uses slang: 'there was the rub.' "

"That's not slang," said Hugh, "that's Shakespeare."

"Well, did Shakespeare also say, 'It was raining cats and dogs'?" I asked, refusing to be downed.

"Don't seek justifications of your mistakes in other writers," he said. As a literary critic, he's just as inexorable as I have been as a critic of his life, thank heavens.

January 20. For three days I let Hugh rewrite my essay. He killed it. All the vivacity and surprise and jolts in it were gone. I wept all afternoon over it. Then I told Hugh to leave me alone. If I had done all Richard and Hugh advised me to do, I would never have written my "improbable" stories, now recognized by Hugh as resembling D. H. Lawrence's and accepted by him.

I am full of *confidence* in myself. I feel that I must believe in myself because nobody else does, that only by stubbornness will I survive against other influences and pressure. But inside, I feel horribly quaky and small—because of the *foreignness*, and my beautiful assurance is only a challenge to a weakness I recognize. Alas, Hugh downed me after a week of courage and constant work. He has broken *something* in my mechanism. I sit before my typewriter panic-stricken, deprived of my élan. He has corrected fussily and with a magnifying glass, not just bad English, but trying to make me over into a scholarly, staid, Anglo-Saxon, which I can never be.

He *understands* the power in me, talks about my brilliancy, but *sits on it* just the same by the mere evocation of my foreignness, against which I am helpless.

This afternoon, for once, the springs were broken. I cried as I worked, irritated beyond description by his alterations, so fatal to the phrase and the idea that no rewriting could recapture it. My essay is lost—it is stilted, boiled down to a boring thing, still clear, if you wish, but oh, so dead. I don't know what is going to become of me now. I'm going to write, believing in myself, but irrevocably weakened by this *doubt* about my English, instilled by the best intentioned of critics.

January 21. Hugh is convinced that this individuality can't be changed, that it may not be perfect now but that it is headed for *something* as yet obscure. I *sense* the ultimate discovery. I feel a blind faith. I have literally fought for my freedom. Hugh has agreed to correct the English only, and to make general criticisms, but not to *make me over.* He has an idea about writing, his own personal ideal, which he thought I would fulfill; instead he has to realize I am doing something else. He has to readjust himself to the difference. At the same time I submit to his knowledge and look at my work closely, but I have submitted as far as I think fit and no further.

I felt yesterday, for the first time, the occultism in my work— that is, the lack of *conscious, mechanical* work, done by formula. All I do is improvised, from an inner conviction and drive. Laws do not exist. Richard never did convince me how a short story or novel *should* be done. That is why I have matured slowly.

January 25. Hugh gives one morning to the correction of my work. Reluctantly, I go to a tea, and I'm glad afterward, for my mind is full of faces, and I recollect many samples of stupid conversation, including my own—to be used later. Alas, I'm not hard-boiled—I feel a warm sympathy for these people, but at the same time a desire to *kill myself.*

Last night I realized finally that there is the possibility in me of a *mad* action—that the more subjugated I am by my love of Hugh and my intellectual life, the worse will be the explosion. Will it really happen? I *fear* myself profoundly; I don't know what more I can do. I cultivate a passion for Hugh, a passion for my work and writing, and in spite of them I feel the unsteadiness, the demoniac force unhinging me.

No outward signs, thank goodness—a keen, rather brilliant face; people call it animation. I saw the same "overflowing" look on John's face, but, God knows, I do not desire his sexual upheaval. What, then?

I feel no control over my blood, my mind or heart. About me I don't care, but Hugh . . . What *is* it in me that boils up, steams, pushes me?

Hugh has gone to sleep, tired after his tennis, poor boy.

From Joaquin's room comes music—violin and piano—I cry as I write, from solitude, excessive responsiveness and unfulfilled desires—desires for an absolutism in passion and in ideas which I cannot find—not in serenity and quietism, not in religion, not in Paganism, not in art or creation, not in human love. And the most haunting call of all is in music—restless, ceaseless, unfinal music. I shall be just sea, with tides and never-ending movement, even after death, since I have so carefully perpetuated the movement here—in a book.

January 28. Have been utterly absorbed by Keats's life, living within it—moved both to much feeling and to much thought, by admiration of Amy Lowell's discernment, by a strong attachment to Keats. As I go along I make notes on what relates to Keats and what relates to creative work in general. Amy Lowell has a great deal to say about this.

About work—since I'm not ready yet to write about Keats—found this: "This, of course, is carpentry [filling in lines] but carpentry necessitated by inspiration. Faultless inspiration in his conception—carpentry, unfortunately, of not too high a grade. All poetry consists of flashes of subconscious mind and herculean efforts on the part of the conscious mind to equal them. This is where training comes in. The more expert the poet, the better will he fill in the gaps in his inspiration. Revising is the act of consciously improving what has been unconsciously done."

Healthy and true. I bow my head. There is no doubt in my mind now that I write prose as poetry is written—there is the point of all my tearful struggle against Maynard's consciousness, which I could not work with. But here also are my old torturers, revision and training. Poor dear Keats had to use them. Where he found two good lines sprung in his head, he had to find twelve more to make a poem—to hold them up. These twelve lines I'm always looking for. I write them badly. Hugh pounces on them. The poem falls down. I get neurasthenic, carrying my two precious lines about like a talisman—useless two lines. Alas, there's the book "Anita," full of gaps and holes, written in a delicious frenzy, also to be revised. Where are the connections? asks the Family. In gentler moods, they call me abrupt, careless, shifting, strange.

Anyway, I'm *revising*. I'm in the state that always brings on *something*. When I wanted to dance, I asked questions, bothered everybody, looked up old friends, wrote letters, until I reached my end. The Family looked on with a martyred look. Now, I want a job—and I'm so insistent, so obsessed, so annoying, that I'm going to get it. I caught the newborn *Revue Exchange*, just out, and just what I want to get into. *Burrowed* until I got the telephone number.

Godoy was well impressed with the mystical story—though I'm not so awfully impressed with his impressionability.

February 3. First appearance of a physical weakness, which may seriously alter my life—a real heart crisis after several days of dance training for a party. A weakness against which the will is helpless. Unable to read, write, or move. Just that gasping inner feeling—dissolution, tumult, faintness. Had to lie down all day. Doctors had observed first signs long ago, advised me against childbearing and anxiety—but I 'didn't take them seriously. I hate the unsteadiness of my hand as I write. I'm writing to see if I *can* write.

Evening. "Nothing but a strong nervous depression," says the doctor, and gives me a sedative. And pernicious anemia. So that's that.

I have been deeply upset by the reading of Keats's life—have lived all through it and couldn't face the manner of his death. Made a superhuman effort to read it through—couldn't understand that all of Fanny's passionate tenderness and self-forgetfulness shouldn't have gone to him and stayed by him until the last. Feminine impression, of course, to think he was not well loved—ungenerously so—and his longing, distress, hunger, and despair are terrible to read of. I'm too near to it to write, even, and certainly cannot think coherently.

Mother's party was eminently successful and brilliant. Thirty persons. Beautiful musical program, our dances. Showers of compliments on the house, on the dances, on my medieval rose dress. Pujol, Viñes and Brocqua, the composer, gave us a zarzuela—*Las Tres Ratas* [The Three Rats]—which was one of the funniest sights I have ever seen in my life; they were inspired by the spirit of the party. Mlle. Couteau looked the prettiest. Hugh's Corrida was "bissed" [encored], and he carried off the success of the dancing program. Not a dull moment. The Princess was beaming because her portrait of me was hung in the [Salon des] Independents, and engaged me to pose in my purple train dress. Liphart reappeared after months away—an enigma to me. Enthusiastic and intimate with us, suddenly indifferent, yesterday gushingly appreciative of the house, and yet, as I felt, partly insincere—perhaps entirely so. Just at present I dislike him intensely because I might have liked him more than he deserves, and I'm sick of my lack of discernment. Pujol, the guitarist, is a real warm-hearted, artistic, and delectable Spaniard—very appreciative of Joaquin. Hernando Viñes is a consummate flirt, who wonders what I am doing among my churchgoing friends, who talk of morbidness as if it were appendicitis. He gives me compliments that he is always half ready to retract—if I should get scared.

Mother was praised for her cakes and sweets. Joaquin's compositions attracted much attention and enthusiasm. There were fourteen nationalities. It was a grand party. Nobody would go home. The house looked truly magical and exotic. I lay awake four hours, crying.

February 4. I shouldn't write—I'm too depressed, physically and mentally. But I may succeed in winding myself up by repeating over and over again that I have nothing to be depressed about. My only problem is not being able to find a pen name among the family 57 varieties: Christensen, Vaurigaud, Farona, Castellanos, Nin, Guiler, Parker. The real ones are out of the question because of Hugh's work. Chantal is too romantic, so is Anita; Annette is a diminutive.

February 6. It is quite evident that I cannot measure my physical strength and stop straining myself in time. I overdose myself with the sedative medicine to sleep. I add up my year's worries—loss of John's affection and loss of our capital—both things not easily remedied, though the hurt about John will never heal, and what I most hate about it is that I can't understand it.

I have a sense of futility and emptiness. These days, what I see is death, a horribly flat, futile end to our great suffering and exalted creation. While I write, visualize, paint, carve, draw, sew, mold, I see the skeleton—I see my own enthusiasm, detachedly, as a pathetic, useless, and ephemeral log fire. I see myself burning more brilliantly and hotly than others with my mind and my body, but for exactly the same purposes—ashes. Keats is ashes. People say he lives on in images, in people who remember. He lives in Hugh, for instance, who is moved by his presence. But, God, it isn't Keats any more, it's Hugh's understanding and idea of Keats, it's Hugh's image, made out of Hugh's own feelings, and own imagination.

With what anguish we create Individuality. And it's that Individuality, precisely, which dies. Am I weeping over the death of Self? Indeed, I can't accept melting into the Whole, because the Whole is imperfect; it's only a magnified Individual, that's all.

To discover, in plain fact, that there is no end, that the world was made to perpetuate struggle, imperfection, sheer movement, is to know the first moment of profound madness; to know that each one is only a particle in a simple boiling and reboiling process, as ceaseless as the sea; to know the first moment of eternal fatigue.

To all was added the cruelty of a desire for an end that would appeal to our reason; and the cruelty of death coming just when we begin to get used to movement for its own sake, to be lulled by it. And even in death, when we submit to it—"submit," they say, to put it mildly for the relatives—we are not promised peace— merely destruction of a carefully created self. Who was the fool who misplaced Hell both on the map and in the timetable (they say it comes at the end of life) when it's in us—in our knowledge that there is no fulfillment of Desire, which was made to perpetuate movement, as a spectacle—and for whom?

February 15. Go to it! *Drive* the body! I take medicines, but I go on posing for the Princess in the mornings, rehearsing in the afternoons for charity affairs. I write stories in the Métro, strain my eyes and get a sty.

Emilio Pujol, the gentle, the sensitive, the musical Spaniard, gives a successful concert. Joaquin's composition for the guitar is warmly received. Everybody there that we know.

The Princess turns out to be the only woman who has ever appreciated me fully, because she realizes the artist in me, the everlasting artist, dressing, moving, house making, dancing, writing, for creation and beauty's own sake. No artifice, no exhibitionism, no man hunting, though after the work is done I love appreciation. I posed for the same reason. Pauline once said I did it because I liked to hear the comments on my face. Of course, but it is a secondary thought. There is first a love of painting, a passion for creation, for fine work (the proof is I don't pose for bad painters). No woman would endure the physical martyrdom of two hours' posing in a dancing attitude for the sake of a few compliments that I can get without a painting. Anyway, the Princess understands, and the result is that she says we paint *together*, that she can only work well with me because of my enthusiasm and my participation in the painting.

February 17. Due perhaps to the fervent admiration of the Princess, or to Pujol's compliments on my "extraordinary" eyes ("deep seeing, and full of meaning"), I'm reviving. Rehearsals for the charity affair have begun, with Bonifacio, who talks, breathes, eats and drinks dancing, so that my own enthusiasm is rekindled.

Health coming back slowly, a late arrival, treated rather high handedly, as of secondary importance, out of a pure boasting spirit, since I know I can't do without it—yet I won't let it think for a minute that it can run me. I take the liver concentrate, but I also take the Métro and don't pamper myself. Lovely feeling to be coming out on top again. How I plumbed the depths, not only of sorrow and death and illness, but also of understanding—for now I understand debauchery, a violent desire for strong sensations, which is one way of gripping an ever-fleeting life, a wild grasping of physical animal roots. I have the desire—theoretically. I would never indulge it because I know the results, but I understand those who do.

Coming soon to my human birthday, twenty-seven years. I refuse to make a balance sheet. I've done great things this year, artistically speaking, that's all. I've also made mistakes. Have learned to do without friends. I believe in will power. I believe in myself. Amen.

February 19. "Come in," says the Princess. "Look, just look at that painting!" Overnight, she had worked on the eyes, from memory. What eyes she made! I stared at them, transfixed. They were not only enormous but absolutely dazzling, unearthly, haunting. Like Pygmalion's statue, they came alive, and she says they haunt her, that she feels there is something *miraculous* about the painting, and I could see the miracle of her creation. For that moment I am willing to get tired. She praises me, my face, my influence on her, and I look at her and marvel at her genius. We both live in dreams, live *within*, sure of our individuality. She, in her broken language, I in my fluent literary one, reach the moments of creation together. I feel myself painting—she feels me urging her, loving what she does.

February 24. Joaquin's compositions played by Marie André are attracting attention. Spend my birthday evening at her house. The Pujols give us a supremely beautiful evening with their guitars. Pujol is a man I have great admiration for—a profound and sincere musician, with a mystical and poetic nature, sensitive, modest, humorous, kindly, intelligent. His writings on the guitar are erudite, discerning, and imaginative. He and Joaquin have much in common, musically and temperamentally. He has, perhaps, what I feel to be the truest and best Spanish qualities. To the idiots who see only the flamboyance, the dagger and the heel-clicking of Spain, Pujol is not understandable. Anyway, that evening we had a memorable talk on mysticism, interrupted by the jokes and laughter of the others. Pujol treats me like his guitar, with infinite delicacy and subtlety. He idealizes me—sees me like a dream—something fragile and unearthly. Curious how that image of me will not die in spite of my blunders and limitations.

Everywhere we go now, concerts, teas, soirées, we meet more or less the same group—the Pujols, the Viñeses, Marie André, Liphart, the Bonifacios, the Zoubaloffs, Couteau, Wald, etc. Brocqua is a fine composer, generously appreciative of Joaquin. I've taken a liking to him; he is fifty, sincere, enthusiastic, an admirer of my dancing. At moments, like Marie André's soirée, when the music was so exceptional and these people so expressive and attractive, I warm up to them and draw close to them. It was that night Carol Berard, director of the Revue International de Musique et de Danse, definitely engaged me to dance at a concert at the Salle d'Iéna, for which I'm working hard. That night I also met Fabian de Castro, the celebrated gypsy guitarist and painter.

John, I hear, is lecturing in Canada. My health is picking up. My life is full enough, and I feel the writing slowly ripening as I live. I have no time for restlessness—that is the best way. Carlyle's old way.

March 3. On the day of the rehearsal, I realized my passion for the stage and my stage personality. I took to it with astonishing assurance and rapidity; I loved it. No tripping, no timorousness, no blunders. I felt at home in the dressing room, backstage. The Princess gave me an intricate box of make-up and taught me how to handle it. I realized I had at last the tools, the place, the material for perpetual climaxes, fullness of artistic work. The rehearsal, to other eyes, was a poor affair. It drew me out of myself, made me steady, vivid, amply expressive, sure-footed.

We raised the dust in the old theatre. The piano was a frying pan; the lights were dead white; the background untidy and atrocious. No matter. Here was my world—planks, defective or not, strong lights, and the opportunity to play up to five minutes of concentrated intensity. How I did dance! Elvira tore her petticoat, tripped over a folded rug, walked out the wrong door.

The day of the "representation" I arrive first, of course, with my two maids. Hairpins, safety pins, combs, rouge sticks, all tidy and methodically prepared two days before. Eyelashes already waxed like a movie star's, done with infinite pains. I dress as a Maja, while the others trail in. The dressing room is a yard square. It's dirty, dingy. I love it all.

"En scène pour le premier acte!" They begin with a playlet. We have time to make up Elvira's face. Joaquin comes and pretends to kiss me; Liphart suddenly turns into a faithful, devoted, hard-working, utterly enthusiastic and thoughtful person, lugging my coat around, covering me (it's cold and drafty here, and there are no chairs to sit on). Upstairs, when we get to it, there is a big, invigorating bustle. Electricians are perched up on the left. The applause sounds distant. There are delays, counterorders, scenes— the singer immediately hates us, violently. She's fuming because the good piano has not arrived.

Now—Bonifacio and Elvira—success, encore. Bonifacio alone. Success. I alone. Sevilla. I'm blinded by the spotlight. I dance just a bit shyly on account of it. Success, anyway. Bonifacio—success. Elvira alone—warm applause. Success. I change into the train dress. Hot stuff. I dance with the devil in me. Have to take three bows. People cry out but the curtain comes down. The singer ordered it. She and Bonifacio start a scrap. She says there are too many Spanish dances, that we tire the public. She decides to interrupt and sing before we do the Jota. She wins.

I go down to change. My maid hands me a card while I'm dressing. I read it—"Hugh Guiler." He comes and kisses Madame Aguilera's hand. What fun! After the Jota lots of people come while the last play is going on. Compliments. Inwardly I know I should have done much better. I'm worn out.

And Sunday night D. H. Lawrence died—the deeply appreciated, the well-loved mind. I am stunned and intolerably hurt. He is dead, and my letter to him, with a review of his books, lies in my drawer. Aldous Huxley was there when he died. I went to bed early, worn out from dancing, and did not *feel* him die. His books are there, but *he* is dead, and I cannot understand this immortality they speak of. I feel the world emptier, and I know I can shout in vain my appreciation of him. He will never know.

March 8. Life takes hold of me again and, for a while, wholly. The posing has stopped, but I had to send invitations to the concert. Wednesday afternoon I rehearsed at the Salle d'Iéna and felt a kinship with it, an earthly love of all its trappings, new and lovely this time—fine lights and a kindly electrician. Despair at my physical weakness. Constant fainting at the merest provocation, not enough strength to do my four dances uninterrupted. No inkling whatever of what was to come, no forebodings. Realization that I was far from perfection and that my opportunity had come too early. Made changes in the dances and tried to feel my way out of the steps so as to leave a loophole for the imagination.

Bad night before the concert, weakened by sedatives. Glad to see the morning and glad for the hot coffee. Rest. Lunch in bed. Dressing, oh so carefully. My panties, so as not to shock anyone, are camouflaged with ruffles. Make-up as prescribed by the Princess.

Salle d'Iéna. Berard lets me in with my two maids, dresses and valise. The dressing room, almost next to the stage, is large and full of mirrors. But I share it with the singer and the pianist, Marie André. M. Senet ("Tout Paris") comes to see me. Being a painter, he inspects my make-up and approves it. The hall is filling up, they tell me. The quartet is late. The singer studies her music; Marie André massages her arm. I paint and repaint, adjust comb, flowers, mantilla, wet the soles of my shoes. A man comes from *Paris-Presse* to ask when I can be photographed for the paper. Bonifacio comes, sweetly and generously, to see about the lights, to straighten a ruffle, and help me in and out.

Program begins. I love the sound of the clapping. I hear Joaquin's beautiful things, and they move me for the hundredth time. They are enthusiastically received.

When my turn comes I'm nervous but not frightened. I have an enormous, fantastic desire to dance beautifully—to that vast, still expectancy. The stage personality, feeling, and atmosphere grip me. A new woman, free, daring, and assured, is released.

Into the Alegrías I poured both nobility and sinuousness. (Was troubled one minute because I thought I recognized Father in the front row. Shall never know if he was there.) The applause was vigorous. I had to take five bows. I thought I had done moderately well. Bonifacio said it was wonderful.

I dress for the Farruca. Eastern feeling. Last-minute inventions run loose in the gypsy dress.

Jota. Here I plunge into creation. Knowing myself not a Jota type, I became an imp, faun, whimsical and mischievous. What applause and shouts, and the feelings of the crowd are wafted up. I dance it again.

It's done. Fifty or sixty persons come to speak to me. I didn't know I had done so well. I can distinguish easily between the sincere and insincere compliments. There are all my friends plus new ones who want to know me. It is evident that my dancing was alive, in no way automatic, full of freshness, impulse, and improvisation, and personal things. All this helps to point out to me the direction in which I should develop: expansion, subtilization of Spanish character into universal feelings; purification and development of Eastern sources; wider separation between Andalusian and gypsy; more room for mimicry and individuality. I feel strong, encouraged, triumphant. I'm surprised by it all, never expecting such a success—such assurance and grit in myself, the power to create just as well on the stage before six hundred people as alone; in fact, moved to a climax of effort by the stage itself. But at night I thought of Lawrence again, wistfully—"Tout passe, tout continue."

March 11. My health, which I mocked, decided to play a trick on me. Saturday night as I was writing, a formidable neuralgic pain gripped my arm, shoulder, and back. What made me furious was not so much the pain as the fact that I couldn't reach out for the ink bottle. After a while I stopped and cried. All night, the smallest movement was torture and so was lying still. Here I am today, still in bed, worn down, half paralyzed, and as cross as the devil. Engagements broken. Can't typewrite. Can't even read for very long.

Two typical reactions to my creative work: Mme. Melnikoff, with moist eyes, telling me she never, since she first heard Chaliapin sing when she was sixteen, had such a thrill from anything as she got from my dancing, how she arrived cross, harassed, depressed, and went away elated and full of energy, how she could scarcely recognize the timorous, sweet, soft person she knew. And Miralles, growling, talking badly about me, furious because of the changes I made in the dances, refusing to acknowledge me as a pupil any more!!! He writes that the thirty-two steps he gave me I replaced by thirty-two vulgar and inadequate changes.

Then Vanah Yami says, "Trop enfant, pas assez charnelle, animale, provocante. Jota, good" [Too childlike, not sensual, animal, provocative enough]. Pujols: "You must make a career of it. You have *everything* for it!" Mrs. Pujol asks me to watch my turns and foot stamping, my stage control and entrées, and gets me the precious address of the gypsy Joselita, whom I have warmly admired in La Argentina Ballets.

If the general impression was enthusiastic, the way the details are mentioned is taking it for granted that I am headed for something big. It's done. Hugh bets on me. My career is begun. Isn't this what I wanted? And yet, I am doomed to conflict. When I am given a full physical life, I long for retirement, for mystical withdrawals. In the middle of praise, criticism, and all the stir I get intolerably sad and want to give it all up; I despise it, depreciate it, judge it devoid of value.

Engagement to dance at a big social affair, at the Edmundsons', before the Infanta of Spain. Health very bad. Mood terrible. Thinking of Lawrence's irreparable death. I copy my essay [on journal writing] to mail to an agent. I cut out flattering newspaper clippings about my dancing. I write Miralles a letter, full of cold logic, which he won't understand, and reasoning superior to his ignorant, blind jealousy, which is not what he needs.

March 23. It's all over, thank heavens. It seemed to me something in the nature of a flood, fire, or war. The morning after, I awoke with a sweet feeling of release, and as if I were beginning a convalescence. I love it and I hate it. I love the art in it, the excitement, the plenitude of dramatic living; I hate the personal conflict afterward. I can act and dance on the stage, but let me go home after the performance and not go near the crowd. *That* contact is intolerable. At that Grand Party—five hundred people, with numerous duchesses, marquises, countesses, princesses—I went through hell.

The first night of rehearsal all the young society boys and girls took to me, until I danced. Then some of the young ladies held me at a distance. One of them, who was to do one Spanish dance, suddenly decided to do two. There was instantly a sort of division of feeling. I came, as far as they were concerned, from nowhere. My friend Brocqua, who took me there, then retired from the theatrical field and talked with the old ladies. A few knew me as the daughter of Nin. Many young men liked me for myself.

Second evening of rehearsal. Mixed atmosphere. Suddenly asked to do two dances instead of three.

Day of performance, matinée. The other girl appears in the Alegrías I had been asked not to do and dances well. But I dance the Sevilla even better, and these people, who have no artistic standards, who only want to know who does what, are pleased in spite of themselves. Society girl does gypsy dance well. But I do the Jota and carry off the excitement. All the worse for me. Young man of the house, Georges Edmundson, gets panicky because of social problem involved and suddenly strives to star Mlle. Virginia Klappenback. So Virginia, a good dancer, and with many qualities of assurance I do not possess, is announced as the "grande vedette" [big star] at the Evening Show. Crowd amused. She dances boldly and well. I dance better. Again, all the worse for me. When she does the gypsy dance and the clapping is over, Georges says to the announcer, "Announce an encore." The announcer, who is one of my admirers, laughs at this. Without announcement and in silence Virginia reappears. But the dance, to this audience, looks just like the other. There is polite clapping. I rouse enthusiasm again with my Jota. It was hard, doing it merrily in the face of the plotting and lack of sympathy. I steeled myself to it. Beforehand, I sat there quietly, in control of my sinking feeling, able to admire the good in Miss Klappenback outside of my feeling. I had won, technically, but what a joyless fight. It all disgusted me so much that in the middle of compliments and talk and that empty smartness my eyes love so well, in the middle of a shower of lights, gorgeous wilting flowers, beautiful women parading in long dresses, young men kissing my hand, I left. And if my eyes had not been waxed and highly painted, there would have been a moment of liquid weakness. But there wasn't. Hugh had seen the petty play and felt hot about it. I felt revulsion and was very wilted, and very sad, but already withdrawing.

The trouble is, I come to dancing with the raw sensitiveness of solitary living, with a kind of humorless concentration on fine and perfect work, without the preparation and experience of all the worldly tactics involved, with an ignorance of the personal feelings that obsess women. Though I am so infinitely *woman*, jealous, vain, egotistic, fond of adulation, all that dies in me instantly before creative work: fine writing, fine dancing, fine painting. This submission, in a Society affair full of Who's Whos, was out of place. I should have been equally arrogant, assertive, self-confident, aristocratic in a noisy way. I wasn't. I should have realized there was a competition of prestige going on, not of art. I should not have said Virginia was gifted (because she was), but: "My grandfather was the Danish Consul in Havana. My father is decorated with the Legion of Honor. I am the wife of a Trust Officer and Sub-Manager. I live on Boulevard Suchet. My dress was made by Maison Melnikoff. Bon soir!"

Meanwhile, little currents of compliments travel around and come back to me unexpectedly, and a giant basket of red flowers is wilting in my house also, with a card from Georges, who was such a rotten impresario that he let me hear and see all kinds of things which made a bad impression on me, but then the theatre, large or small, does strain people's characters, like war, and all the weak spots give way.

I'm resting, deeply, thoroughly—for a day. Tomorrow it begins again. I wished for it all. When I didn't have it, I was restless. Now I'm squelched. I would give a great deal for the old empty days with the typewriter and nothing else.

April 4. Old lady Juarez comes to call—sweet, kindly, thoughtful, with her saphead grandson, Mr. Georges Edmundson, who innocently believes I will do "something artistic" with him sometime in May. Anita Aguilera in bed (a beautiful bed with turquoise-green bedspread), and because the curtains were half drawn and I had time to powder and rouge, I couldn't have looked so bad. I chuckled inwardly, first at myself, for being so sensitive to atmosphere and little tricks, and second at dear saphead Georges for not knowing anything about sensitiveness and coming to call cheerfully on a lovely spring day—after *that* evening.

Oh, well, I'm up and doing and not looking so pretty in the morning light. Regiments of medicines march behind and before me. Hugh and I plan a life-saving trip to beloved Caux. I've lost two kilos. But I'm cured of many things. In spite of spring (I thought it would betray me because it brings out sentimentality), I'm cured of John!

After all, it is better to do without friends. Having them is too lovely, too soft, too sweet a thing. Not having them makes me grow cold, hard, and braver, and I certainly create more. And I concentrate otherwise dispersed feelings on Hugh, who seems to like it.

April 5. The Princess is now difficult, wayward, moody, self-centered. How well I understand her! She is fond of me and yet she resented my illness—just as I did—on account of the painting. Hugh was scandalized at her lack of humanity. I wasn't. When I finally went to her yesterday, weak and wan, I instantly realized she had been very cross and miserable for three days. She was all bristly when I arrived. Her blue eyes were hard. She led me straight to the model stand. She asked for no news. Oh, how I understood! I saw her selfishness, and yet I felt distressed about the painting, drying, hardening, stiffening. So I stood and posed, though my body quivered.

I posed two hours. She grew softer and happier. She made me rest, and put some Russian songs on the phonograph. At the end she wished me luck and health on my trip and made cheerful plans of how she would work on the background while I was away. I think if I had been another woman, Natasha would have scraped the painting and that would have ended our friendship and perhaps the possibility of a good piece of work.

In most relationships, I first ply myself, waver, meet, seem to surrender, until I have absorbed, so to speak, the other person, until I have *understood*. But a part of me, the center of me, remains "infranchissable" [impassable], and this part, after a while, calls back to itself all the wandering extensions, the explorers, the selfless portions—and I'm whole again. Just now I am whole.

Yesterday, an outsider, suddenly walking into Natasha's studio, would have said: "Anaïs is in Natasha's hands—such selflessness she showed, such concern over Natasha's state of mind, her painting." But it was not so. It was I who was self-possessed. I dominated Natasha. I kept her from being angry, from scraping the painting, from hating me.

I'm planning a study of Lawrence's writing—reading all his books. Crudely entitled, for the moment, "When D. H. Lawrence Found Himself."

April 8. But my health affects my temper and strains me to a breaking point. I long for our departure. I shop wearily. I hide from people and flee social life. I write, revise; among my papers I'm happy. So many ideas, so many plans. I must finish "Anita," which is written in a remarkably modern tempo, and publish the Journal tel que [as it is], because the woman that was, yesterday, no longer exists today. She is an old coat. Today's woman is my own. And tomorrow's. I must work at that appreciation of Lawrence, which is sadly lacking. Write tales—all the tales in my head. Bury John, with the finality of the written word. Offer everything to the Man who made it all possible—the writing, the dancing, the house, my own life and fulfillment—my darling Cat.

April 15. Caux, to receive me, planned a very decorative snow-storm. Simply because I couldn't help it, I went to bed immediately with a gorgeous cold. This I really owe to two Englishwomen who kept all the windows open on the train—two ruddy-cheeked and generally cheeky Englishwomen, rendered antagonistic, as usual, by my pale, wan attractiveness, to whom, as they could see, my Anglo-Saxon husband (oh, the traitor) was utterly devoted. With D. H. Lawrence in hand, the greatest of all Englishmen, the tenderest and most passionate of poets, misjudged, belittled, I heartily hated these women, with their bland eyes, polite conversation (imagine polite conversation going on between a mother and daughter instead of plain talk) and utter incomprehension of the effects of drafts on delicate persons. Or maybe they *knew.* They guessed that I love Lawrence and hated them.

The days are long, though white and cheerful; I give all my time to absorbing Lawrence. I live in his world. His idea of love is ours. He moves us both to incalculable depths.

April 17. Snow falling continuously. Trees heavy and still—the hotel still. We are the only guests. Both of us have been ailing a little but quietly and without rebellion—with a true Christian resignation.

In the midst of the whiteness and quietness, came a letter from John to Hugh, in immediate answer to Hugh's, telling about the success of *Sincerity*, about his new book on Diane de Poitiers—friendly and conventional, disregarding the humor in Hugh's own letter. Was it his plain homely little old American conscience which pricked him into silence—"I couldn't flirt with Hugh's wife," he said once, the dear, noble Anglo-Saxon, who, at other times has proved he *could* be intelligent. I am not so disappointed that he should have a conscience—I have none, in that way—because, of course, geographically speaking, he belongs to Lilith, and should not cross the green or purple borders—but simply distressed that he should do it all, the crossing, the recrossing, and the flight back to security away from dangerous friendships with so little imagination and so little understanding of the fact that I can be more than any woman, a friend without danger!

So it goes—a story lamely finished, rather colorless and made homely only by his view of it, for in my mind it was something else. When will I bury John *definitely*?

April 18. The snow-mantled place is so soothing. Our nerves are embalmed. It is only our ideas which flit back and forth, sharp and clear. Hugh talks a lot, about Keats's life and mind, love and philosophy, about the finite and the infinite. So far we are distressed, like poor Keats, who believed in the infinite but not in immortality or a second world. Yet if we were convinced that there is no survival, as Hugh says, why not lie back and live like animals, or take to opium to still our consciousness forever, instead of doing everything to render it more acute by thought, creation, passion. If we believe it all futile and perishable, why not surrender? Both of us strain our eyes, our senses, our minds to know and perceive more each day.

We came to the conclusion that the center of our universe is our love, both as a finite, physical, human climax, and also as an infinite thing, for, said Hugh, "I certainly see and love in you not only your body, your breasts, your legs, your love-moisture, but the you beyond yourself, the you that sparks the 'little flame between us,' as Lawrence says."

That is all we believe in. How often, in my most miserable moments, have I not seen the "little flame" burning outside of the *present* moment, imperishable even when I was not tending it, even when I ran far off from it—I saw it, and wrote of that love outside myself, surpassing me, and transcending all human contacts.

Hugh says that when he writes about me, he will stress the things nobody knows: my good sportsmanship and courage, my intellectuality and my character when roused. That is, my character is not the Anglo-Saxon state of perpetual stiffness and inflexibility based on principles, but an experiment guided by the mind. I'm soft-hearted and flexible—beginning with the servants and dealers up to my highest friends. But if I am betrayed or cheated, I harden and inflict punishment; I throw out my maid, I force the carpenter to reduce his dishonest bill, I throw out my friend! A funny character. It frightens people. My servants, who thought me quite stupid and easy to impose on, have had the frights of their lives when I woke up.

Hugh is more inclined to be suspicious, reserved, and to seem hard from the very first—the softness is discovered afterward, if you have proved yourself worthy of it. I so much prefer his way.

I have written twenty postcards and twenty letters. It makes me wish I were born a foundling. And, oh, dear, how grand events dwindle when you describe them to Aunt So-and-So, who only cares about babies or Christian Science or sewing or visiting. I get colder and colder as I write. And sometimes I forget who I am writing to and write a really lovely and fantastic letter and then I'm sorry it is all going to be wasted.

Lawrence has loosened my own tongue so much, broken down my reticence, given me a world to live in, a world where I fit. Over and over again, in his descriptions of women I find myself. In his treatment of language, in the poetic intensity of his prose, I find courage for my own writing. I find, at last, a kind of home, or nook. He would have understood my writing and me. In a way, too, by his own fervor and naturalness, he has uncovered, crystallized, my love for Hugh. I marvel that I should have been so long reticent about it, shy of it—though there was no shyness or reticence about my feelings.

It was in writing about passion that I mistrusted my usual directness and clarity of language. Perhaps I felt as Hugh did until now, that such things required poetry. Hugh is as convinced now, as I am, that prose of Lawrence's quality has nothing to fear. Even then, Hugh would take refuge in poetry and gasps a little at the things I write down, so firmly and so clearly, as I wrote down this morning's talk. He is all for poetry, for suggestion, indirectness and mistiness and symbolism. Not I. And it is amusing to observe that he, who has the direct character, loves misty expression and I, who am indirect in nature and in my ways, am direct and clear in writing. Both of us, Hugh said, do conceal a lot of ourselves, behind appearances. Oh, we do. Women think him simple, and me naïve. His complexities are not apparent, nor is my lucidity. Men have come to me so unwary, and talked to my soft eyes, while I read deep down into their minds. Women offer to Hugh's simple, clear, frank ways the gift of their simple, clear, frank tastes and lives, which he really dislikes. To each other alone we are no mystery, except for the fascinating mystery of our constant growth; and each in his own way, Hugh's firm, mine tottering, we go on, awaiting an ultimate splendor.

April 19. The mist and grayness weigh on me, grip me, hurt me. All my body hurts. And suddenly I can see how one could accept death, like sleep, and a solution.

Yet there is always something left undone—I haven't written enough about Lawrence. Besides, Hugh awaits life from me. And he has written John! So—what a pathetic farce—Hugh explaining my wonder to John. Crusading for me. While I suddenly realized that the explanation was simple: John is fonder of Hugh than of me. Surely I can understand that. I can understand that Hugh should be loved above all else. I feel it myself. I would rather have it that way than to think it was some petty reason.

Later. When I work on my old stories ("The Idealist," for instance) I cannot believe I wrote them before I read Lawrence. They are so much in Lawrence's spirit; I see things as he does. Finding him has only given me the courage of my own writing; it has made me feel less blind.

April 22. On Easter Sunday, the sun came out, and I came to life again. I dropped my coat, grew chirpy, walked with Hugh, basked on the terrace, and while he took a nap before dinner I added a few pages to "Anita," now called "She," a nameless woman. I have kept my notebook in my pocket for two days now, and write in it a little at odd moments, planting seeds for work when Hugh reads or sleeps. Sunday night I thought of a story, "The Man Who Could Not Sin"—wrote half before going to sleep and the other half yesterday. It is ironic and whimsical. Have also outlined "Tango." Also keep adding to notes on Lawrence. I'm very happy when I write. And I worship this place, where my mind fairly blazes, where I feel my strength, my individuality, my solitude.

April 23. The funniest thing in the world: Hugh gives me his nerve-soothing medicine to keep me from writing, so I will really rest. And he wins. I'm quiet now—my poor buzzing ideas, like the ants under the snow, are just waiting for a chance to stick their noses out again. But I needed the rest. So I keep very still. In spite of it, last night, I did have another idea—saw a connection between my last stories, which I can gather under one title, something like *A Rogue's Gallery of Women*—for they are all certainly intent on mischief.

May 7. Paris. The fire is burning in the blue-and-gold fireplace. Joaquin is writing in his journal. John's *Uncle Sam*, inscribed, lies on the floor, with the ink bottle, a notebook, a blotter. Joaquin and I are on the floor, too. I asked Lola to take a picture of us. And I am thinking of Caux, where I went in quest of physical health and found something else.

Hugh and I were walking slowly uphill and nearing our hotel. I was very weak and sad to be so weak—when I looked for the tenth time at a little sign on the road, "Casutza receives Guests," and I felt irritated by the reserve and aristocracy of the phrasing and powerfully curious. I said to Hugh, "I am going down this road to find out what this Casutza is who receives guests."

Hugh said, "You are too tired. Come on home."

"No, I want to go!" (Exactly like a spoiled female.)

"Some other day," said the Cat with patience and sweetness.

"No, today." And I began to walk down the little side road straight to Casutza, with Hugh following me saying, "You are crazy, darling."

We came upon a quaint house, rambling and fanciful, with a little arched door with glass "eyes" in it. Inside, the chairs and tables were small, and so were the doors. Out of one of them came an old lady in a purple kimono and purple cap with very white hair showing on her temples. Her face was questioning, unfriendly.

"We would like some information about this place."

"It is not a hotel," said the old lady emphatically. "But we receive guests now and then. I will show you through."

As she did so, our enthusiasm for the Casutza grew, and she gradually became friendly. We learned she was an artist, now ruined, now in terrible need of money, now obliged to charge for hospitality she used to give away. Her eyes were intensely brilliant. She spoke of how wonderful I would be to draw. In the end (we stayed an hour) she had shown us her own studio and her drawings, and we promised to come in July. And at the very end, she invited us to tea. That was Eugénie Kazimir.

Four days later she "received" me in Casutza—coming up the road to meet me in a black dress, with her black dog, while Hugh traveled down on his way to Paris.

Her talk flowed; what words did not say, her face expressed completely. Her eyes, brittle, dark, intense, fixed, bothered me. This was not only an artist looking at lines, watching my gestures, analyzing my face bit by bit, but something else. It was a Mad

Fairy guessing at my mind and soul, reading into them, and making strange signs of elation at what she found. My eyes were searching her. I found the crevices in her armorlike will. I never got lost in her flowing talk, in which she sometimes wandered. I saw the madness, the wise madness, in her. She saw the wise madness in me. We were discovered. I knew her life, her struggles, her Idea, her strength—she, mine. The fourth evening, I kissed her goodnight.

I was to know that others had observed the Kazimir eyes and feared them. They were her force and her weakness. With them she divined, she subjugated, she magnetized. But with them, she was made helpless before beauty of form. But the "blindness" did not last very long. The beauty she found in me she quickly related to my inner self. If there had been no relationship, she would not have loved me long.

She herself had a plastically irregular face, beautiful with her inner beauty. Hugh and I were surprised to hear she had been considered an ugly duckling. She had been rich—had studied drawing, singing, and the piano. She has known the "grand monde" and the bohemian. At twenty-six she devoted herself to a woman—Helley —who was Russian, educated in Germany, a gifted writer, a fantastic creature. Eugénie is modern, frank, naturalistic, as well as idealistic. She knows good and evil. She has force, so she is both. She saw fit to consecrate this force and passion to a woman—not to man. Man, in her time, forty years ago, expected an abdication she would not make. She would have hated the being she also loved.

She lives in Casutza—though it is financially a folly—to keep in contact with people, with a faith in the invisible threads that will draw certain people together. A thread drew me there. That is what she lives for, and leaving Casutza to those who deserve it, through creation. It seemed to me, at first, a mad idea. Then I saw she lived within it, with all her imagination, energy, and will, sacrificing to it a cozy old age in a little place she could have somewhere if she sold Casutza. But Casutza is symbolical, Casutza has a spirit in it, it is a force, an influence. She wants not only to die in it, but also to find those who will carry on her idea.

Meanwhile, she goes through hell, enduring cold, debts, hunger sometimes, when she has no guests. And even the most ordinary guests are affected by her mad idealism, unsettled by her disdain for money, her all-seeing eyes.

But I have no dread of her. She saw through me as a transparent thing. She saw my two most obstinate dreams: beauty and growth. She saw in me the aesthetic sense abnormally developed, the lack of animalism and femaleness, *but oh*, the danger of *perversity*—because of my imagination, the overflow of temperament. She wrote that I was both woman and virgin—that I lived half in the mystic world—that, like her, I clung to my Idea and was true first of all to my élan. She came to my room once to tell me how I had liberated her by my power to write, to analyze and clarify her own mad revolving thoughts, that I had made her expand, and feel her strength again. On the other hand, I saw in her this miracle: a woman who without man's love reached understanding of all things, fulfillment, and intellectual and physical "rayonnement" [radiance].

In Caux, I have always found my own strength. I live there in intense clarity. The true size and relation of things appear exact. There, experiments appeared futile and unworthy in the face of such divination as was possible to a woman like the Mad Fairy. Like her, I shall be able to sense all things by the sharpness of my senses, imagination, and passionate feelings. She is an example to me of how concentrated strength (experiments are scattered strength) can achieve heights without bitterness, without narrowness. I shall know by listening, by having the power to listen to others. So many are anxious to pour out their anxiety. Eugénie herself talked out her soul to me because I listened. Oh, the marvel of this liberation, which enables me to love Hugh exclusively, wholly, eternally, as I desire to love him, while yet growing to be what he himself would have me be.

It was a painful shock to me to return to the world. The second night after my arrival we all went to hear Falla play his concerto. He is a genius, and his music is the most beautiful of our epoch; I was entranced by him. But afterward, in the reception room, plunged into the group of our winter friends, how I hated it. Something had happened to me. They were strangers to me. I had gone off alone on my own travelings—I had gone too far to return. All the elements in me are reduced to one mad desire: to grow higher, higher, ever higher, with creation. Solitude gives me such a consciousness of my elevation, such a fierce devotion to it, that when I come back into the world I find a new courage to break with my old friends because I know that I cannot grow by their side. They stifle me. In spite of my affection, I break away. No human tie can hold me when once I have found a friend small. I must go on.

When I feel a head over them, then I must struggle to reach what is a head over me—an inhuman, fierce reaching for whatever is higher. I have no feeling of being monstrous, but simply a feeling of power, as of flying in one's dreams. It is the mere impetus of my flight that carries me off from one place to another—that everlasting torment and ecstasy of growth.

In spite of the flights—or, rather, within the flights, because we fly *together* now—Hugh and I are better lovers. After the trip, we rediscovered each other—began, in a sense, a new life. He has understood everything. He said: "Drop me, too, if I am not worthwhile!" But he is the most worthwhile man I know.

At Caux I had the idea for my second book, *Three Lies*—wrote the first page during a concert I didn't like. I am inflated both with creative energy and with "hot air" and egoism. Somehow, when you blow oxygen into yourself, some hot air gets in too.

May 11. I just realized that I have not told you about my big, big failure. While I was away, the agent, Francis Jones, sent me back "Journal Writing Revalued," "Fear of Nice," "Talkies," "Three Old Countesses," saying they were "too slight for the magazines."

May 13. As soon as I was settled at home, I began to write again. In two days I have rewritten twenty-six pages of my book *She*, with courageous slashings and additions. I owe a great deal of my energy to Kay B., who read the book in Caux and was so excited and moved by it that it was a revelation to me. She has remained my friend. I shall say more about her later.

I am terribly happy in my work—just writing. There is no question of my dancing, because my heart gives me trouble. I faint often and cannot climb stairs, but I would not dance anyway, not until I empty my head out, and that will take a long time.

In a few days I shall have finished the Book—then notes on Lawrence. In July I'll write the *Three Lies*. I am moralless, fearless of conventions and of opinion and very stubborn in my ideas. I have been rewarded. Hugh, glancing over a page of my book, one of the best ones, was moved and said, "Thank heavens I didn't insist on your writing like me. You have found your own way, and the faults you made were of no importance—I see now."

The steel is coming out. I owe some of it to love, some to being badly loved!

May 14. I am transported by a morning of writing, of splendid writing. The book is emerging out of chaos, sharp and weird. I am worn out and pleased with myself. I am twenty-seven and I have written an old book.

May 16. Yesterday was a great day in my life. In the morning I finished the Book, writing its tenderest pages just before the end, transposing three pages of ordinary prose fiction into one of almost pure poetry, leading to the last phrase—"a woman who would never go away again." I was in a great fever, having done the whole in four mornings; the best of the new writing, all in one breath, so to speak. I felt I had gone far and high—but it might have been mere inflation.

I gave it to Joaquin to read at six o'clock. My feelings grew more and more feverish. Hugh and I went out for our usual walk. When I came back Joaquin kissed me and said, "I am proud of you; it's wonderful."

I had to wait till after dinner for Hugh to settle down to it. He read a while, then went to bed with it. My feet and hands were ice, and my head fire. Then I saw feeling rising in him; once, he said, "This is the high-water mark of the book"; then he found a second and a third high-water mark. At the end he cried. I don't remember just what he said, but something like: "It's a masterpiece, the greatest thing you've ever done. It moved me like great poetry— Keats and Lawrence. There is mysticism and tenderness—and humanity. I was moved physically by the Pagan pages. The end is beautiful. And how wonderful, the way you have left out details— as in Japanese painting. Each person is known only by one physical thing—one, by the voice; the other, by a wrist [the furry wrist of the Scotchman]." He loved the Scotchman, as I love him.

I have been so free in the book, and it has given me such deep joys. What I felt at the concert when I danced was nothing compared to this. Hugh says I can sit back now and write nothing else, but I know I can do something better.

May 19. My mind is fermenting constantly, and I want to write but haven't the physical strength for it. What a defeat! I must rest, quiet myself, or I shall go crazy and lose my strength altogether. In desperation, I began a painting yesterday. And this week shall be devoted to Clothes and the House, but in these things, too, I pour out imagination, a feverish energy and thought. In vain I appeal to Sedobrol [a sedative]. When I put my hand on my forehead, because it feels as if it would burst, I feel the ticking, the currents, the vibrations. At night, instead of sleeping, I write the first page of the Second Book.

May 20. Had to refuse to dance with Bonifacio at the Salle Pleyel —also in a ballet by [Tristan] Klingsor. The springs are broken this time. The machinery will not work—more so because it is cold —in May!—and to be cheated of warmth is the greatest calamity I know of.

I owe so much to Kay B. From the very first she encouraged me in my writing, urging me to finish up those fragments I had in September, turning my mind to the idea of a climax, to the idea of publication, and finally introducing me to her agent. She herself has had a great deal published, has done a lot of back work, and I have turned her mind to her own superior possibilities, have warned her against banalities and sentimentality. In Caux she stayed a day and night with me, and then I really discovered her life. From the way she read the formless rough draft of the book and responded to it, I also discovered her mind, so superior to what she writes. She was incredibly generous with me, sincere, and helpful. We reached a firm plane of almost man-to-man friendship. I want to give her as much as she has given me. There is no femininity in our relationship. We are both working—we have precisely opposite methods of working—we want to help each other. We have in many ways the same temperament and tastes. I try to point out how she can develop her writing; she, how I can make mine practicable.

She is pretty, has charm; we are the same age. She considers my writing highbrow, I consider hers vivid and attractive. She can tell a story, I can't. She can write with virility and persuasiveness. I make detours and imply most things. She is concrete, and I am abstract and symbolical.

May 23. I lie on the divans, sit on the rug before the fire, like a cat seeking comfort, but the truth is I am terribly weak. And I crave the balm of beautiful and soft things. Joaquin has tea with me. The sun makes occasional timorous appearances but is immediately swept off by a cloud. In my head the second book stirs, like a baby. I long for Caux again, and only writing, just writing—no people, no dancing, no visible shining. It's dangerous to love living with one's self. At moments I am frightened and think I am almost loving myself.

At the same time I dress Kay up in my clothes for an important wedding, trying to make her look as pretty as possible, and Hugh is flabbergasted. "You certainly are generous! Why, I hate your doing that. I'm jealous for you."

That made me happy. Then he suddenly remembered I had done the same for his sisters, given them all my ideas and discoveries. "And you are never loved the better for it," he said. "You have never found anyone as big as you."

With that I went to bed—with that, and the fear of loving myself and solitude too much.

May 24. I came away from the studio where Hugh is studying his Spanish dancing because it made me sad not to be able to do it too. I don't feel equal to it at all. I feel very strange, weak physically and strong mentally, concentrated and curiously entire. I feel as if I were carrying a baby—this new strength of mine—jealously guarding it, nurturing it, cultivating it, obsessed by it, enslaved by it.

I feel so many things growing—my individuality, my confidence; I feel lines of my character growing stronger. I'm really sprouting, springing up, with mixed feelings of tenderness and bitterness, faith and disillusion, hardness and softness. I have never felt so clearly what my Self is—obscurely and stubbornly self-made.

Was overjoyed last night to receive this note from my agent, Mr. Jones (after the first refusal). "Thanks for three manuscripts ["Faithfulness," "The Idealist," "A Dangerous Perfume"]. I like these very much indeed. They are very well written. I don't know that they will sell but I will do my best. They are unusual and magazines here don't seem to like the unusual! Send me some more stories."

May 26. Invitations! Invitations! No way of getting away. God! Hugh doesn't realize how ill I am. If I had the money I would go away alone this minute. For the first time we disagree and quarrel —all due to physical causes. Because he is nervous he dominates and nags; because I'm nervous I rebel and break down. Always on the question of entertaining. His Bank runs him. In matters of banking he is an automaton and a sheep. Even I do not count. I get desperately sad and act exactly like a tracked animal. I go to my writing with a wild hope of finding my balance and strength there. Poor Hugh; discipline, habit keep him up and going. He is only himself when he is on vacations. Be a good sport! That idiotic American slave-driving phrase, which means doing the stupid things before the others.

Evening. After that little fit of temper, I pulled myself together and went to work. Also entertained Kay and her friends, but felt worn out afterward. Now I sit by the fire. Hugh plays his guitar. Had a dream last night of a John grown cold and sarcastic, and as most of my dreams turn out to be true afterward, I considered this a fair warning of what to expect. But John may have the same dream about me, and it will also be accurate!

June 7. Thursday I worked my head off—rewrote my book, which is really only a long story (8,500 words), and is finally called "The Woman No Man Could Hold." Mailed it this morning to Jones with faint hopes— it is too lyrical. But Hugh loves it, Gilbert wishes he had written it, and Boussie said, "Très bien, très bien," and Kay was moved. Gilbert said I had done something that had never been done, that it is almost impossible to do that kind of abstract writing, that I had done it as well as it could be done. But I know I can do better. When I am less afraid of filling in, between intense and poetical writing, with human, consciously written pages, the work will be more complete and have more blood. Already I have mastered that mingling of the fantastic and the concrete.

I live constantly now on that plane—giving my imagination utter freedom and no longer afraid of my feelings, which I can express without sentimentality. But how difficult to keep up the other life. We entertained a man from the Bank, and I forgot to telephone for the dessert, and forgot the guest towel in the bathroom. Hugh said, "Those little things annoy me." The poor darling; afterward he forgot about it, because I looked pretty in my turquoise chiffon dress and turquoise cape.

That evening I was sad. I had dressed so carefully. But what for? A blue-eyed, young, slow-thinking, slow-speaking, slow-moving, half-developed man—on whom I just couldn't keep my attention. And talk of the Bank, of tennis, of Le Touquet—I won't say what. All the time, I spent imagining another kind of evening.

Today was the birth of "Melisendra," my pen name, the Spanish of Mélisande, used by Falla.

I have made myself a nook by the window, on a long divan— my favorite corner. I write here now. It is warm. I'm resting, with Hugh, for three days.

June 9. Resting! To me that means going for walks, theatre, etc. while thinking of Lawrence's study and *Three Lies*. And every now and then I jot down some notes.

Hugh was quite startled by something I said the other night apropos of Boussie's surprise at the happy ending of "T.W.N.M.C.H." I will write happy endings, not because of optimism or false idealism, but simply because I am balanced and always see the other side of the case. Mine is a creative philosophy, in spite of my deep sense of sorrow and of futility.

I am even beginning to see that the reason and end of our existence are contained within the span of this life, in the multiple climaxes of sensual and intellectual joys. The idea of the ultimate climax is only a kind of urge, which causes growth, only the gathering of many smaller climaxes by which we may arrive at a superior place in Thought—therefore, returning to the abstract we came from. In other words, satisfaction is *here*.

June 11. It is a positive fact that I must rely on myself entirely now—that I must build up a strong world within myself, so rich and so full that it will be enough. I must find all things in myself, create them. I must reach my own climaxes of strength and creation with my work. I have had too great a need of people; it is a sign of lack in one's self. My last need was the most foolish one of all—need of John. It was a fine thing for me that John had no need of me. It hurt me. It taught me a great deal.

John looks so powerful and so certain. I know he is not. I should feel sorry for him, but I don't. Because he disappointed me. I would like the hurt not to hurt any more. That is why I talk so much about being strong. I am not. As soon as I stop writing I am woman again. Nothing in the world will turn me into a pen, as was said of Ibsen: he was a pen, not a man. I am both pen and woman —hopelessly. While I shop and finger pastel-colored little dresses (189 francs is the highest I can go this month), I talk to myself about my self-sufficiency and my vast intellectual plenitude—and all the while I look aloof when young men bother me, and softer when men of forty-nine or fifty (John used to insist he was forty-nine) do the same. I hate cheapness. Why was there cheapness in me today? I did not buy the little 189-franc dress, was too conscious of its not being suited to my taste and style. If I can know my physical value (over 189 francs), can I not judge my mind's worth and say quite bravely, "John is not worth my concern"?

Found an excellent book on Lawrence by Potter—which makes my notes useless. But I developed one side of the question Potter had left out, took from my ideas only those that did not resemble his—and the Study is going to be mailed to my agent on Saturday.

June 16. Hugh and I scrapped over my Lawrence Study, and he said my essays were the worst side of my writing. He corrected it to shreds, I spent a wakeful night over it, then I rewrote it my own way, accepting only the essential changes, and sent it.

After that we saw a perfect and admirable play, *Etienne*, by Jacques Deval, one of the best I have ever seen. And also an odious one today—dirty and melodramatic—called *L'Acheteuse* [The Buyer—by Steve Passeur].

Joaquin gave us the deep joy of winning his pianist's diploma brilliantly. En famille we took a walk in the Bois and saw Pershing taking a walk, too.

Sweet weekend—not so sweet a self. Terrific fear of growing egotistical. Wonderful talk with Boussie Friday on a philosophic plane. At my age, she said, she would have felt and written such a story as "The Woman No Man Could Hold," but now she believes in letting growth come to you and not making too many efforts or thinking too much about it. She thought the woman in the story was overintellectual. Otherwise she admires the story and its modernism. Her admission that she had once felt such feelings gave me pleasure, and I was worried only by the fact that the story is young rather than old. I exacted and received truth from her, and let me always be as sincerely ready for truth.

June 17. Hugh has made me very unhappy by going into the Stock Market again after the first loss, and absolutely against my advice, my pleading and coaxing. We have lost again—our capital is not $1,000. All stocks sold. But older men have made the same mistake —so there is nothing to say, but a great deal to *do*. I am making plans to readjust our life: the most painful of all is to give up the house, my creation; I must also save so as to build up a reserve for emergencies, write like the devil, dance like the devil, or at least teach.

Meanwhile, we make joyful preparations for our vacation. Mother and I spent a sweet afternoon together shopping—100-franc dresses and 40-franc hats. She has bound my first diaries in three volumes, beautifully and carefully. Joaquin shows off a photograph taken of Falla in which he appears. The trunks are in the foyer. I clean up closets, prepare the house and sew. My typewriter is being overhauled, so I don't write. The mail brings us news of Edie's wedding, of Baby as a married woman, of Graziella's wedding, of Eduardo's possible engagement to a Cuban girl; and a letter from Eugene filled with a beautiful understanding of "The Woman No Man Could Hold." Kay says that *Aline*, my truly first novel, has fine possibilities, that she will whip it up so we can sell it together as a potboiler to a newspaper syndicate, it being sentimental enough for any or all the shopgirls in the world.

In the "other world," peace. *Three Lies* is slumbering. I am planning "practical" articles with photographs—to *sell*—ha-ha! Reading a once-scorned book given me by Uncle Gilbert called *88 Ways of Making Money by Writing*. I will try one way.

Soft weather, which has a tremendous, incredible effect on me. Good appetite. Good-bye visits to everyone. I look very well in Melnikoff's Grande Maison models, subtly cut and embroidered, theatrical and languid, and suggestive of imaginative living; but *also* in 100-franc dresses, small, dainty, pastel-colored, washable and *sweet*—ugh! The essential writer, friend of the Magic Lady in Casutza, has become the simple, clean-faced one.

Only last night I went out in full sail—vaporous turquoise dress and cape and hat, hair made black with water, eyelashes heavy with paint, eyelids painted green (as per suggestion of Natasha) and, oh, very crimson lips and tinkling bracelets, and all the cheap seductions (except for the perfume, because it is not cheap enough). In all this, there is no room for John, who has now dwindled to the position of "a famous writer in New York whose *Private Life of Helen of Troy* was once a best seller, you know, and with whom we were intimate when he was in Paris" (this, for the edification of friends who like celebrities). "Yes, he has just written *Uncle Sam* and is planning a book on Diane de Poitiers." And, as Boussie said naïvely, "Why?"

June 18. My Journal is my true source of balance, my great stabilizer. I found it so in my relations with Mother. Yesterday and today, I found my old tenderness and demonstrativeness for her, which has been partly withheld because of the constant struggle between our two strong characters. Often I have wanted to be very loving, but finding Mother in a combative mood has stopped me, just as Mother, finding me so self-reliant and willful, has felt the loss of her "Little Girl." I found this little girl in my first Journal, my cult of Mother for her courage, Motherliness, and a thousand proofs that she understood the child and was an extraordinary Mother to it. The vision of Mother *then* took the little wall down—there was no wall, really, just a slight, slight feeling of reserve and watchfulness for our independence. I never thought we could be the same, because Mother wanted the impossible, wanted the little girl, but I am so much myself now, so grown, that I can afford not to assert myself any more and to be soft. A new feeling has come to me, at least, one I want to keep. I am sorry it did not come before, though it was always there when Mother needed it, when she was unhappy or ill. The evocation of my childhood . . . There is so much one must not forget. We do forget. That is the cause of half our crimes.

June 27. Corner couch of the bedroom. Corner of the world. I, here; everything else, *there*, only while I write. As soon as I stop writing I shall be deeply *there* and *into* everything. Yesterday I was *in* the departure of Mother and Joaquin, always sad—my dear, constant responsibilities, of whom I think so much, and for whom, if it were necessary, I would instantly give up all writing, dancing, and pleasures. I am decidedly a family person for my immediate family. Well, anyway, Joaquin and Mother are gone for a happy summer, both contented and in good health. That's that. Part of my heart is at ease. Now I must see about Hugh's tummy ache.

The house, details, packing . . . Money is terribly scarce. We ourselves wait until July 1 to go, hoping someone will rent the house. I devote myself to minute orderliness, which I love. Everything is in its place, filed, sorted, glued, in folders, boxes, mothballs. I could sit in the corner with a housewifely smile, basking in the peace of orderliness. No, it's not housewifery; it must be aestheticism. Everything for me must bear a prettier name. Even tidiness can be an art, a beautiful thing, a mental quality. That is it. A house is a mental quality. There must be logic in it, and at the same time it must take the breath away and show only the poetry. So, this house. It takes my own breath away while I show it to strangers. I must say, some of them are not impressed at all, but I don't mind; I delight in my own effects, revel in arched lines and the fold of a curtain and the plenitude of coloring.

In the middle of it all comes a cable announcing Eduardo's

arrival. Now the Eduardo who left the stage and drowses in Havana is not the one it thrills me to see. Besides, there is Hugh's tummy ache, which prevents us from delaying our trip, there is our terribly, terribly worn-out pocketbook, there is my own lack of enthusiasm, and so Eduardo shall wait a while—the charming person, with whom, as Hugh said, "one cannot get angry."

Gilbert said yesterday with great enthusiasm, "I have a marvelous idea about Lawrence—will write about it. Will judge his book from the point of view of what is passion and what obscurity, and why *Lady Chatterley's Lover* should not be banned."

"I am sorry," I said sweetly, "but that is what I have done in my essay 'Sex or Mysticism?' But of course you must go ahead . . . it is a difficult thing to say, and you had better try it. I may not have done it well." I gave him all I have of Lawrence's books, plus notes and clippings and information. But I could see that it wasn't Lawrence whom Gilbert loved, and certainly not my essay, about which no more was said.

"What will you give me," said Joaquin, "if I finish my diary book this summer?"

"Another diary book," I said.

My head aches from a new permanent wave; I have filed John's letters to Hugh; I have said good-bye to all our winter friends. Alida [van der Henst] was revulsed by the "conduct" of my heroine in "The Woman No Man Could Hold." She was so upset by four pages of sensuality that she missed twenty-six pages of philosophy and intellectual quests. She was so busy being scandalized that she overlooked the mysticism. Virtuous, clear-eyed, honest Alida! Such a clean soul, she; if I were a man and had to live with that white cement wall, it would make me a thorough débauché.

June 28. Opinion expressed by an American real estate agent for our house: "Quite a place you have there. It doesn't appeal to me *personally*, but I suppose you have spent a fortune on it. I myself don't care for that sort of thing. It makes me feel as if I had to have my dress suit on all the time." A fortune! $3,000 for seven rooms! Ha! Ha! Fake effects, tricks, wisdom, hard work— and there's the miracle.

I'm doing copy work at 1.50 francs a page. It takes me three hours to do thirty pages! Two-finger system. Just "pin money," you know, but I didn't buy pins. I paid a cleaner's bill. So pleased

I can be useful. Intend to go on doing little odd jobs, because my "creative" work doesn't sell. Jones writes me sweetly that "The Woman No Man Could Hold" is a well-told story, indeed, but will not suit the need of American magazines, and he suggests I write "straight young romantic love stories that can be read in a family circle"—these are his words, incredible as they may seem. I am born to upset family circles! But he didn't return it, which is something.

What I am copying is a rollickingly bad play in verse called *Violanda* by Constant. I laugh as I do it. Constant must be very young, younger than I am, anyway, and if he had written in prose I would have suggested him as a candidate for Mr. Jones. The word "honor" comes up seventeen times in twenty-eight pages. "Amadeo, dear hero," has black hair and a pale face, as if made of ebony and ivory. He reminds me of David Sterling, my first hero, who also had "sensitive hands." Jones would have liked me at twenty. But I'm not a clock you can turn backward.

July 3. Caux at last. My wonderful Caux. We sit in a field in the sun. Down the hill a man is cutting the grass and the smells are rich and gorgeous. I wear a sky-blue little dress and blue linen hat, very fresh and dainty. Lawrence's *Assorted Articles* lies next to me with my cretonne bag and cretonne umbrella. I am so happy, so contented, so smoothed out, I cannot think.

July 5. Long, peaceful days, sunshine, meals out of doors, Eugénie's flowing talk of the past and against the modern spirit. I meet a lovely Scotch lady, Miss Hamilton, who teaches in Toronto and who introduces me to the *Canadian Forum*, urging me to send my essays there. She likes my work. I like her clear blue eyes and earnestness and clear-cut mind. Beautiful breakfasts on the balcony, naps, walks, writing, mending stockings.

I received Kay. I am directly responsible for her having a lover—the only full happiness she has had in her life. So her whole visit was a pouring out of confidences. "Thank you for Lawrence," said my dear little friend, who has that American love of evading sexual issues. At the same time I say "You are welcome," I quake a bit, wondering if she will have the courage, the beauty and power to live it all through, the adultery and the playacting and the emotional splitting. There must be no *feeling* of wrongdoing, or cobwebby remorse, or the slightest timorousness, or the untrue interpretation of lying—if you *think* you lie, you lie. If you know what you are doing, you know the real meaning of lie; a lie is not something you tell others, but yourself.

Kay is a gallant woman, who has been very unselfish, very selfless, and who is now listening to the urges of her own nature, which is alive and rich.

I was upset by her happiness, her tumult—"He has such a beautiful body—it was the first time I felt any joy"—seeing in the sensitiveness and feeling which pushed her into this the same power that might push her into destruction. Such a thin line of demarcation! I have roused and directed the flow. Have I power to preserve her from disintegration? Doesn't it lie entirely in herself? She is joyous today. She says very lightly, "Thank you for Lawrence," and I am thinking far ahead, far ahead, wishing she would not thank me; poor Lawrence and I . . . our philosophy is a sharp cry which we almost wish at times nobody would hear.

July 6. My agent Jones writes: "Received your study of Lawrence, which I like. Have already sent it out." But nothing sold yet! There is a peculiar distinction in my work between the solid constructions and the lightly sketched things. The sketched ones stand well together because they form an atmosphere. I shall not be satisfied and satisfactory to others until all the stories are published together.

A friend of Kay, whom she brought to my apartment, after seeing the place and hearing from Kay about my writing and dancing, said she felt like crawling into a hole and staying there— so much creation made her feel that way. Why? It is as natural to me as breathing.

Copied from notes: R. L. Stevenson urged Barrie not to be too funny, as I would urge John. But Stevenson was older than Barrie. It is no wonder, after all, that John has no use for me as a critic. There are twenty years between us.

I have written an article: "Original Foreign Homes: A Modernization of the Oriental Style. With photographs." How is that for trying one of the *88 Ways of Making Money by Writing*?

Glenway Wescott said I wrote "exotic English." Is that so?

To Hugh, who had confessed to speaking with an American lady on the train (reproachfully): "I'm sure you didn't tell her you were married!"

He answered, "Do you wish that we had reached such a

degree of intimacy in the conversation that I should *have* to tell her I was married?"

From notes: My evocations of other centuries in dressing are particularly frowned on by other women. There have been so many natures like mine who have delved into the past, worshipped the present, re-created and invented and renewed outwardly and inwardly. But when they weren't damned as "theatrical" (Isadora Duncan) or "affected, eccentrics, or fond of publicity," they were dubbed simply mad by those who were satisfied with a single century of thinking and dressing.

Pure philosophic truths do not interest me as much as the testing and execution of them, and I do not use them until I have lived them and accepted them, just as Proust did with Bergson's formulas and theories, dramatizing and humanizing them. And for this experiment I give *myself*.

Hugh says sometimes when I am writing: "Little Pussy, I'm sleepy. . . ." It reminds me of Mother's eternal, "Fifille, va te coucher—il est tard" [Little girl, go to bed—it is late]. All the household was asleep when I wrote my Journal. It was easy for them to give up the day, but for me the real tasting of things was just beginning.

One taste destroys another. If you believe in individuality you can't help seeing that multiple love destroys itself. The touch of flesh is the same, only the feeling transforms it. If you exhaust the feeling, you exhaust the difference. The taste of lips is strangely the same, and the physical union can remind you of the person who fills your mind, not the one who is stretched next to you.

Hugh, in the theatre, leaned over unexpectedly to say: "You are so *pure*, I know all the time that your thoughts run on a high plane. You are never disappointing." *Is* there a difference? I feel sometimes I can do the same thing that other women do but with a different mind. It is an astonishment to me that when I think myself most pagan or skeptical, what I discover in other minds is vulgar and far off the mark of my own thoughts. Is it just a difference of form and language or one of attitude? The poetic attitude, I would like to believe. I said once to John, "I have an abnormal capacity for passion." John said casually: "Many artists are oversexed." Which is not it at all. Oversexed implies a purely physical overflow, while my "passion" includes all feelings. Perhaps the whole difference lies in the poetry.

If it is that, Hugh has been consistently the truest poet. He has not written anything, but in every moment of his life, in every word, he has been a poet. In our love, in the language for our love, in not only intellectual and literary moments but also in everyday life, Hugh has never once been vulgar, though we have the sharpest and most intimate jokes about our coming together, and though we often laugh at everything. With poetry one does not evade facts; we face facts, scientifically, facts of sex, birth, death, relations, illness, vices. We know all; but just as there are two ways of saying a thing, there are two ways of thinking about it. It is by that subtle expression that I judge mind and character. I find truth in the very opposite of what people say, just as Proust did.

July 9. Today, I finished and padded the funny story "A Russian Salad in Paris." I'm afraid I enjoyed writing it more than people will enjoy reading it.

Nobody will understand the mystifying gravity and humor of the "miracle" in "The Woman No Man Could Hold." The more I read it myself, the more I realize its complexity, its power to stretch according to the imagination of the reader. *Within* the story, I am all the time explaining it, giving the key to its symbolism, pointing to its double meaning, indicating the varied angles from which it can be seen and thought about. It is a mystifying, mischievous, and at once a dreadfully serious story. When I copied it out for the fourth time, I was still impressed and felt that most people did not get how much there is in it; it was full of surprises even for me.

We call a "Scotch celebration" the one celebration that does not cost anything—at least between husband and wife. How marvelous the Scotch. Hear this from R. L. Stevenson about the wind: "snell, blae, nirly and scowthering." What could be more like the winds' own talk?

July 10. Eugénie's "flowing" talk has turned out to be an inundation, and all of us are calling for an Ark. When you hear for the *seventh* time that when she saw the moors of Scotland she was struck speechless for several days, you wish she had talked then and not now. (Hugh says, "Or you wish there were moors here.")

It is more serious than that. Her personality is heavy, oppressive, domineering, intense. I have seen her be mean and foolish. Her love for me has become a burden to me, and I don't know how long I can conceal my revulsion. I am strangely obliged to come back to my *first* impulsive judgment, which Hugh remembers well. When we were talking about my staying ten days with her at Easter I said, "She is interesting, but I wonder if she is not almost *too much* of a personality to live with." But curiosity and a certain attraction made me forget this. The ten days were interesting. These last nine days were the "too much" in the prophecy. The meals are lectures. If she is talking in German with the German girl, and I try to talk to Miss Hamilton, she pounces on our talk to force away my attention, appropriates it, squashes it, and then goes on. Logical conversation is impossible. I see in her now the worst of the Slavic faults: disorder, hysteria, moodiness, unreasonableness, cruelty, overintensity.

An Italian came in yesterday while we were having lunch in the garden, a well-mannered man who excused himself quietly for disturbing us and asked if there were rooms to rent (there are three of them). Eugénie's face took on an ugly look; she tightened her mouth and said with childish disdain: "Non, monsieur," in such a tone that all of us were frozen stiff. I cannot forget that look. Then, when he had gone, she said, "He is a Bolshevik! No one but a Bolshevik would interrupt a meal."

"But he seemed just a polite Italian," protested Miss Hamilton (she has studied logic) feebly. I was so disgusted I didn't say a word. Such little things, for me, destroy all possible affection. Of all the things I hate, unreasonableness is the greatest. I'm a visionary too, but I like my visions, my intuitions to be tempered by the intellect.

Mists, rain, thunder, a lonely breakfast while Hugh visits the doctor at Lausanne. Miss H. and I sit working together; she, on her dissertation for her doctorate, I on this.

July 12. Sending the nonsense story and "Slippery Floor" to Jones. Preparing article on Casutza. Evening—Hugh plays his guitar. He's happy and tender because I went to meet him at the station last night under pouring rain and he knows how I hate rain. Eugénie begins a portrait of me. She made the very shrewd remark that expression and character are neither in the eyes nor mouth but in the play of the facial muscles.

July 13. We talk now against the tide, snap up opportunities when Eugénie has something to say in German to the German girl.

Hugh began writing his journal, very dolefully, calculating his misfortunes and loss of capital. I happened to be taking a sunbath on the chaise longue. He happened to look at me—and the course of his ideas changed. A little later he told me I had performed a true miracle: from that minute he ceased to think he was a ruined man!

July 16. I've been working on little things, with *Three Lies* in the back of my head all the time—not quite ready. This morning we went out at ten to sit in the sun on a hill, and I straightaway wrote five good pages, succeeded almost immediately in the tone, the rhythm, and the manner of the telling.

I read one of my 1925 Journals—a painful reading. Naïveté, puritanism, romanticism, and a style not my own at all. Oh, God, what shall I think five years from now of what I am writing today? How much I owe France for the development of my intelligence! Am I still young, underdeveloped? I can't endure the thought. Does romanticism keep me from developing? How can it? I've never thought so much, read so much, worked so much—but I did all that in 1925 and it didn't help. If ever I have a baby I shall give him Boccaccio at four years, Anatole France, d'Annunzio, Erskine, Mencken, Lawrence; and then see what happens. I myself was certainly not an "enfant prodige" [child prodigy], but a kind of Peter Pan, keeping a journal. Unthinkable! Incredible!

I read the old Journal, curse it, and at the same time I think to myself, Well there was something pathetic about her, even appealing—poor thing—she was so sincere. So after all, I'm not grown yet, with all my unscrupulousness, paganism, etc. Not while I pat Peter Pan's sister on the back, even discreetly. It is no wonder Hugh says I should be covered by a tea cozy when I am cold. Exactly. Just about my measure, and someday if I write great books, people will simply say, "Her books are bigger than she is."

July 17. Sometimes I have the feeling that Hugh is a real baby and easily influenced. He has acted most foolishly today with a stupid doctor, fallen for everything. Then when he came home with the whole illogical story and I pointed out the flaws in it, he was angry, of course. I dread that trait in him, not having a mind of his own that can react quickly. It is mainly the cause of his failure in the market; he listens to everybody, gets in a muddle, and then acts emotionally and suddenly.

He has gone for a walk. I sit alone on the balcony. It will take him at least four hours to see my point—to see the whole story. 1. Doctor from Lausanne listens to reports of other visits to doctors, reads the summary of the radiographs made in Paris. 2. Orders visit to hospital for a radiograph (Hugh understood it would be a very different kind). This was already superfluous and illogical, since exactly the same kind of thing was already taken. 3. Doctor examines radiograph, taps Hugh's stomach, repeats what two other doctors have said, vaguely, has nothing to add, has no particular theory or plan. But casually orders us to go some place other than Caux. Hugh immediately runs to some casual English acquaintances to let himself be talked to about a new place.

When he came home, I said, "A man who doesn't know what is the matter with you has no right to dictate about a change of place." Also, "Why did you let the same kind of radiograph be taken when the doctor had the verbal reports and the radiograph taken in Paris?"

So Hugh went out for a walk, with a book, and a sense of deep injury, and I remain with my logic, satisfied with the logic, but upset by his childishness. When he came back we didn't talk to each other. After dinner he talked very loudly about it all, and I said, "Don't talk so loudly." And he went on defiantly, louder. I asker him three times to talk less loudly. Then as he went on I flew into a rage and struck him three times with closed fists without seemingly or actually hurting him the least bit. He was really *amused*, deeply amused by my act. I cried—and afterward we made up, and he agreed with all I had said, and I took back some of the criticism, laying all the blame on the doctor, and we have been very harmonious since. He is still laughing about my striking him. He said he thought I looked handsome when I was angry.

When two more boarders arrived we went on strike; the dinners had become a real ordeal. I played a little comedy, inspired by Hugh's nervous indigestion, and obtained the grace of eating in our room. Miss Hamilton, whose character seems more wonderful to us every day, helped me—in fact, suggested the plan to me. We only miss *her*.

I am ashamed of my poor judgment, though Eugénie alone

with me was quite another person. All this has upset me, and I haven't been working. What a flimsy excuse. A better one is that my eyes are very sore in spite of the glasses. Incidentally, I might mention that Miss H. has made communists of us—not very aggressive or active ones, but theoretical. We have been reading books on Russia—Dreiser's for one!

July 20. A really peaceful day. Only a glimpse of Eugénie. I get back to work, beginning a sort of *Book of Dreams and Nightmares,* full of fantasies, of which three stories are already written. Planning a serial story for shopgirls, inspired by our desperate budget. As I see Hugh's health going, I think now he will be *forced* to retire early. Get a kind letter from Gilbert sweetly denying me the only gift I do have: that of originality. He tells me I read too much, meaning I have been influenced by Lawrence. I have—influenced to write a startlingly different thing from Lawrence, urged on, spurred on by similarities of feeling and thought, which gave me the courage to be myself. Because I was able to explain the form of my "Woman No Man Could Hold," Gilbert thinks now I wrote it according to formula.

Had another dream of a John most sarcastic—and of myself equally so. Gosh, there will be a thunderbolt when we meet! But no rain, I mean, no explanations. No relief!

I hand Colette a gold cup full of Beaune wine for *Sido,* a masterpiece of description. Savory phrases, vivid, natural, rich in reality, rich in suggestion. She has the most powerful descriptive style of all the women in Literature.

Financial Fever Chart of Guilers. So that Hugh might retire from the Bank at forty, we must get $100,000. In order to have this we must save, and can only save with difficulty, 5,000 francs a month. 5,000 frs. × 12 = 60,000 a year—in 9 years, 540,000 francs or $21,600. We can reach $25,000 in savings when Hugh gets a raise in salary. The rest I have to make: by decoration, dancing, writing. Gosh! $75,000! Plans: I give up 47 Boulevard Suchet and take a cheap house in the country. I take a job on a newspaper, and I teach dancing.

July 26. Meanwhile, I have ideas, ideas, ideas. I continue "Woman No Man Could Hold"; the same character of woman, having passed through experiments, is now wise. I write an introduction to the book of dreams, now called: *Life on the Moon,* which Hugh describes as brilliant and profound. Jones writes he is pleased with article on Decoration. I amalgamate "Slippery Floor" and "Appearances" (remember two women, Vivien and Lyndall?) to form a longer story. I keep the post office busy.

After two weeks the rain is off. Others are suffering from earthquakes. Hugh says he would prefer earthquakes, because they last only a day. But here is the sun. Last night, thinking about my Life on the Moon ideas, I couldn't go to sleep. We had been invited to dance at the Palace by clients of the Bank. I *ought* to like that life; I am always so flattered and spoiled by it— yet I don't. Double merit, says Hugh, who is getting more and more complimentary as I gain weight. I don't want to exaggerate, but I think I have gained two kilos.

Eduardo is sulking. I write him that the Bible (which I have never read) says to follow your husband wherever he goes, and gives no indications as to chers cousins.

I write Gilbert that I have no "acquired tendencies," only "potent" artistic impulses. Ever see me acquire anything, except Anglo-Saxon self-control, which doesn't come naturally to me but through marriage?

July 28. Wrote article on "Casutza," and now, ouf, I'm tired, and for the rest of the week I will take a lot of Sedabrol, the sedative, and keep quiet.

The Rothenstein family who are staying in the house (the father is a painter, the son a writer) are quiet and interesting. The son asked to see my writing and I gave him the book of stories. He was quite put out by "Woman No Man Could Hold"—so put out he could not pronounce judgment until he read it a second time. Then he came up to our room and said, "It is quite re-markable." He had never read anything like it, so at first he did not know what to think, but he had copied down some of the phrases which had struck him particularly, and all his choices were after my own heart. I was terribly pleased and excited. He seemed to be particularly impressed by the portentousness of the phrases, the summaries of experience between the dia-logue. He found the essay on Lawrence "most illuminating," enjoyed the nonsense story, and thought "Russian Who Didn't Believe in Miracles" could be presented as a short play in two scenes. He advised sending them to Curtis Brown, agents in London. His own novel is appearing in the fall.

August 3. On the train to Paris. It's all over. I'm rather depressed, because I have enjoyed my husband's companionship so deeply—and I can say we love each other more. A marvelous life, being together, reading, talking; his helping me with my writing and, toward the last, getting an idea for a play himself. And the sun baths, the quiet meals alone—and at last four kilos gained, one for Hugh. We face each other on the train and observe the improvements. I make plans in my notebook, for house hunting, articles to write, books to read.

August 5. Paris. Eduardo. We meet after years of separation, after traveling by different roads. We look at each other. Who are you? Where are you? Suddenly we find ourselves in the same world, in Lawrence's world! Extraordinary. And there we are. Instead of being strangers, we are so *close* that we get tense, excited, exhilarated, sizzling (as we always did when we were younger), so much so we are almost ill over it. What a joy! What a discovery! He comes to me handsomer, more mature, rich with ideas, escaping again from his family—rich with experiences, terrible experiences, aspiring again, but more firmly, more knowingly. I bring my new self also—my costuming, ease, experience—a wakened woman—and my writing. Immediately all those things I grudge giving others or that I have given sadly, I pour out with zest and pleasure. He breathes the atmosphere of the house, rejoices in the spectacle of my costumes, in the changes of my face, and I spread my mind before him. I rejoice over his splendid body and noble, diverting, unique face, and his slowly revealed mysteries, and his language—Lawrence's language, mine, through which understanding flows like a force, rushing us into intimacies, silent communications, electric currents of livingness.

Wonderful ideas—on the tablecloth of the restaurant table; he drew a circle and circles within the circle, calling it a bowl. The inmost circle begins more or less with the idea of what we *should* do and feel. Then it widens, pushed out by personality. We enlarge and enlarge the horizon of our acts. Some of us go to the very end, the very edge of the circle, even fall out: Gide, Proust, da Vinci, Lawrence. Eduardo pursued one of the roads to the end, fell out of the bowl. He lived, he says, as a Cuban, exhausted his physical impulses, drank, ate, copulated, played tricks, wandered—then he returned. He did not want *that* climax. Now he hesitates between da Vinci's way, absolute and fearful *intellectual* control, or Lawrence's, which is to seek an intensity of both mind and body—melted into one another—impulses not *controlled* by mind but intellectualized, emotion—such as I found. Isadora Duncan, he says, lived her physical life to the limit of intensity. Good for her. But it destroyed her mind; she was not strong enough. Eduardo's emotions and impulses are destroyed by his mind: they are not strong enough. Mine are equal, which is just as bad. I fall out of the bowl because I cannot love merely intellectually.

"You are not in Lawrence's world," says Eduardo, "if you have moments of detachment—your mind from your body."

"Yes, I am. But those moments of detachment are those by which I return from outside the bowl—you can only return through the mind, to get your balance again." Oh, God, the struggle again, his and mine—thirst, hunger, the capacity to reach the bottom of all emotions, to fall out of the bowl (how sweet, how sweet the moment of the fall!), the capacity to return with the mind, as I have returned many times, only to go away again.

In two days I got used to him—so used to him that I hated to see him go to Hendaye. I went to see him at the station. He left me two of his notebooks, written while he was being psycho-analyzed in New York.

I was sad after the reading. Inchoate, tragic struggles—they weigh heavily on me, all those words; I, who always tried to clarify and lighten him. But my clarity is useless. I cannot work on him with thought. He must also find his own impulses. I do not have enough power.

We did feel in those two days that there was a tremendous livingness between us. We almost could not stand it—too many memories, too many surprises. The idea: We *should* have been lovers—it *might* have changed the course of his life—was always between us.

But when I read the notes I feared that the livingness would continue to be, as in the past, spasmodic. In between there would be recurrences of his wanderings. Now he is in Hendaye. I realize with a pang he will probably love Joaquin. It doesn't matter, since Joaquin, Eduardo, and I are united mentally. But it matters to Eduardo's own life—another frustrated passion. And it does matter to me. I see a great deal of suffering in store for me. I must have understanding; I must be natural, warm, and yet never cling; I must know when he wants me and when he does not want me. I think I have always known such things, yet can I always resist my own impulses? Symbolically—I took his arm at the station, and he was pleased.

The role of a woman a man always comes back to is a sad one. But I prefer it. He gives others momentary impulses, *seemingly* whole, followed by revulsion or total indifference. I'm not afraid of pain. I'm only afraid of being woman, of clinging. There is only one way of curing yourself of one man, and that is by another man. I see already that Eduardo will cure me of John, but that I must find someone to cure me of Eduardo.

He doesn't like irony, though he is amused by mine. He says, "Life is too serious for that—too serious for that amused detachment." "But irony is a form of lucidity. It is a cooling off of the mind." What fun to disagree. His eyes blaze, but I blaze back, and a little blood comes to his cheeks. We try to convince each other with the eyes, but no, our ideas clash. Wonderful!

"Lawrence," he says, "was not an artist in the strictest sense of the word. His prose should have been poetry."

"No. He made new prose, enriched prose, with the intensity of poetry."

"But it is not artistic, all in all."

"In parts it is perfect poetic prose, just as perfect as poetry."

"I don't believe in poetic prose. I believe in poetry."

"Well, I believe in poetic prose. I'm doing it."

"You've put Anglo-Saxon poetical ideas in a French mold, concentration and brevity and sharpness. That doesn't work."

"It *will* work. I'm just not perfect yet."

Eduardo seeks in poetry what Lawrence has said in prose. He read me Blake. (In that, he is like Hugh.) I dig pearl-lacquered nails into the tablecloth, with the fever of delectable discord. In the taxi, on the way to the station, I tell him why he is going away: to digest these two days, two strange days. He admits it. We admit we need a rest. But my digestion is better than his. In two days I have absorbed the miracles—with ink and paper. In him the ideas will simply beat, chaotically, hopelessly.

At the train, he kisses my hand. His eyes are very pleasingly alight. I know they could be equally so for many other people. Wholesale charm. I like exclusivity. But there I stand, battling my exacting self—smiling at the face so many women have seen with the same expression, smiling indulgently, affectionately, responsive but not dangerously. God, how the little girl of eighteen would have been caught!

Hugh sensed last night that I was off on another journey. I was doing what Eduardo had asked me to do, reading over my youthful letters to him, reading his journal, writing in mine. When we turned off the light he lay very close to me and said in a low voice, "I *know* I can never hope to satisfy you entirely, that I cannot be everything to you. I don't want to limit you. In a way you are like John—you need many persons."

"But *I* cannot be everything to *you*."

"Oh, yes, you can. You are like a harem, to me. You are so varied, even your body changes and gives me new pleasures."

"But *you* change," I said hesitatingly. His voice was so beautiful and generous. Then I added, "Let us try to include in our marriage *all* possible experiences, *all* kinds of emotions."

"Do you think it can be done?"

"No," I said sadly. "There are some feelings we can no longer give to each other."

"Don't say that. We cannot let it be so. What can we do? I can't give you up; yet I don't want to limit you—you are made for multiple living."

"Don't think of it. Perhaps—perhaps—mental changes can create a change in our physical feelings, a constant renewal."

"Do you believe that?" How his voice pleaded! I didn't answer him until this morning. It came to me while I was walking, the beauty of his generosity, the incredible depth of his understanding, the rare unselfishness. When I got home I said, "For example, for what you said last night I love you more today. It was wonderful, what you said."

And then against that, there is Eduardo's stumbling, chaotic life, his driftings, his self-seeking, the face turned adoringly to men, to whores, to insipid, marriageable girls, and to me, with the self-same power of attraction.

August 9. Post card—Joaquin and Eduardo off to Granada. Days cold and windy whip me into solitariness and self-suffering again. Hugh and I enjoy long quiet evenings in bed and go to sleep reading literary reviews. Swamped by mechanics of my "profession" (!), taking photos, etc., to get my potboiler work done for the month. My good work waits. In August we have autumn. I feel seasonless, now. Nothing comes from the outside, no causes.

All this is circumventing the fact that I am miserable because we are seeing new houses, mostly ugly houses, and I feel too tired to begin again; and all of them need to be rebuilt, nothing less.

I would prefer to be writing. Hugh, who doesn't know all this, says I'm a good sport, but I know I am not. I will miss this place terribly—the energy and imagination I poured into it, the finality of it, the dreams I had of spending the rest of my life making it more beautiful, the personal character of it—an image of us, to be sold. Oh, well, what is the use of brooding? So I begin other designs, other ideas—with less freedom this time, less money, less of a foundation. I must simply remedy what is already there—use ready-made fireplaces, wood carvings, papered walls—horrors, some of them, to be concealed by tricks. I won't let the whole thing put my writing in the background for four months, as it did before. In fact, I will begin to write tomorrow morning.

Not that I dislike seeing houses. Wonderful thing, to enter other people's frames, smell their atmosphere, observe their taste, catch them living—cooking, gardening, reading—beds unmade, books scattered, photographs on the walls, the radio turned on, the hairbrush full of hair, the bathtub full of water, newly made jam on the dining-room table being labeled, the automobile being washed, the laundry being hung to dry—titters from the children, barking from the dogs, the cat slinking away. At a glance, I feel the people's lives. It gives me an uneasy feeling, *sensing* so many other lives of which I am so utterly unaware while I am engrossed in work. Uneasily aware of so many who might have something to say about what I write. That old man in the garden, that young girl who is annoyed by our intrusion, a more adventurous one who likes being looked over, that man in his shirt sleeves, growling because we see his room, his bed, his clothes, his magazines, his bad paintings, and himself filing his nails a second before . . . people, like animals, so mindless, some of them. You catch them at living and there is nothing: a kind of burrowing, scurrying, seeming activity, no imprint of a *person*, no one striking, unique person clamoring through.

August 11. Hugh laughs because I have a very neat file for my literary work where I mark on little cards, " 'Faithfulness' mailed to Jones May 1930—returned." Now I am kept busy writing "returned," which I write very conscientiously and quietly. And Hugh laughs.

Enthusiasm might be a substitute for willpower. Eduardo has no willpower. Could enthusiasm ignite him? He has nearly retraced his steps, retrogressed, by entering Cambridge, to be with people who are *preparing* to live and talking about living. So I write him fervently about enthusiasm. He wanted to find discipline in Cambridge, give himself into others' hands; whereas work itself and solitude are discipline, and the only important discipline is *self-discipline*! What is the use of learning obedience?

On willpower, Eduardo said justly that Hugh had too much of it. He needed it to make a great banker out of a poet. Now he cannot stop. He is tense and watchful always, except on vacations. His banker's gestures are stiff, awkward. He has never relaxed for *ten years*! Poor darling. I hope that by the time I free him, he will not have forgotten. He has never known what he wanted until too late. He talks wistfully of wanting to be an actor. Yet long before he met me he chose the safe bank. And our whole life might have been different if he had been an actor. Marvelous. But he didn't know. It was a real struggle to make him see he dreamed of retiring, that it wasn't banking he loved; and so until now we never made a definite attempt to bring it about. He would have thought of it at sixty, too late, my misty-minded, chaotic darling. God, I'm like a trolley conductor, a lighthouse keeper, a signalman!

August 18. Yesterday we signed the lease for our House in the Country! I came home, and as we sat talking about it, my eyes wandered off to the turquoise walls, so high and spacious, and I began to cry . . . intolerable pangs of regret for my beautiful, beautiful place. Yet the other house is lovely, in a different way. It is old, rambly, quaint, with thick walls and a huge garden and an attic over the garage for me alone and a magnificent study for Joaquin.

After combing St.-Cloud, Vaucresson, etc., we drove out yesterday rather casually to Marly. In Marly our agent took us to Louveciennes. Quaint village, lovely old church, beautiful old castle a few steps away— a big, big strong gate. We went twice through the house and took it. Hugh, the quiet Scotchman, was enthusiastic. I was, too, but so broken-hearted about the other home. Though from now on I won't mention the subject again. I have less spirit to do the new place, less energy. I must make an effort. This is my background—not the other. I had dreamed of being *near* everything. I am still so curious, so hungry, so restless, and I love the City. The big gate will close on me now— the kind of life I wanted later, much later.

Hugh had his moment of weakness the other night—here, in the studio. The beauty of it struck him. He said woefully: "Can you make anything else as beautiful as this?"

"I can, I can!" I said to please him. But I thought of Natasha trying to repeat the miracle of her first painting of me.

Such a saving of money for my Beloved's retirement. Look back on the Financial Fever Chart. We are saving 25,000 francs a year on rent alone. In Richmond Hill I was stuck in a hole and wondered how I would get out of it. I dreamed of better things. Yet Hugh found me there. I have a childhood fear of "holes." Will Louveciennes be one? Our financial debacle—is it a hole I am crawling into again? Is it? Is it? I ask myself during my last nuits blanches.

A good thing. I was beginning to be proud of *myself* for having crawled out—whereas I see now it was money and Hugh who helped me prodigiously. Now that the money is gone, let us see what I can do, whether I can climb out alone and help *him*. How I wish for strength! If I had the physical endurance some people have, I really think I could be a most remarkable person. I could build not one but five houses, I could make a dancer's career, I could—no—I couldn't write more than I do.

Just now I'm *fat* from our vacation. Hugh is so pleased, he says, because there is more of me. If it could last! I see in the mirror I am not only rounding but *maturing*, growing really shapely. And let's think only about that retirement—in nine years—when Hugh will be able to rest, to get well. He is not strong. He is really weaker than I am. Funny, he never worries about holes. His head is stuck in the Bank, like a blind man. On vacations he discovers the world, he is hungry, he has regrets. But from now on I'm watching. It was I who decided that money could only be made by economizing, not by stock dealings. Hugh didn't believe me, until lately. Now he relies on that, rests his head on the plan, with a new feeling of security. We had squabbles over it. He said, "Buy stocks." I said, "Save." Finally we agreed he would go on buying stocks and I would save—save on the salary, save all the money I make. Yes, sir, if we get money for this place it is *mine*—to save! So here goes. Stick your head down, Lady, you were getting stuck up about your magnificent destiny—always charitable, oh, yes, but inwardly stuck up, with a feeling of having *climbed* into fur coats, lovely settings, a brilliant life—whereas it was the money that paid it all. Oh, I agree it was *well-used* money, artistically used money, but still, it was money—and the proof is that now that it is gone you're in a hole: less theatre, fewer friends, less *giving* to others, less pleasure, less brilliance. And slowly my "charm" is getting pulled out like a chicken molting (do they molt?), and I'm losing my setting, my Melnikoff gowns, my perfumes. Let us see, all stripped, what you can do, old lady of twenty-seven. I know I can make a marvelous life, yet—but not so visibly marvelous, not quite so smooth (run for the train! run through the grimy station, run, run, old lady—). How many ladies you know would love to see you *squashed*! No longer dangerous. A half hour by train from Gare St. Lazare. Country life. Chickens in the background—you know— simpler gowns—none of that artificial allure, that laid-on sex appeal. Oh, but I'm vulgar today—but it's *their* feelings not mine. We'll see. O Magic, turn a pumpkin into a royal carriage. That is what I will do. You will see. I will crawl out again, don't worry.

Evening. I'm in bed. Hugh plays his guitar. Chekhov's plays are open at page seventeen. A letter with heather in it made me think of Berta Hamilton, who spent two days here with us. She has the Scotch charms—kindliness, a warm heart, a cool intelligence, well poised. I like her. Think she will be a great influence as a teacher because she has the remarkable gift of not pressing the point, of not letting you feel any influence. Outwardly a person of half tones in her dress and manners, rich in appreciation and generous. Scotch tweed, walking in the rain, sense of solitude and hospitality, charity but with clouded judgment (of Eugénie, for instance), logic, a certain power to live for general causes, denoting unselfishness. Voilà Berta.

August 20. Submitting manuscripts to Edward Titus and to a London agent; making drawings for the new house; receiving very exultant post cards from Eduardo; dreaming that John is firmly convinced I am a wicked person it is safer to keep away from. Meanwhile, I realize my health will never be right again and the stage is forever closed to me. The least things affect my heart, keep me awake at night, and my hands tremble when I write. Thinking, merely thinking over a few ideas, in the bus makes me hot and cold and quaky. I hand my MS to Titus's secretary with honest trembling. Nerves so raw that when people come in, strangers, I am like a *photographic plate* and feel physically the "impression" they make on my visual sense, on my mind, on my nerves, all through my body. Extremely useful for writing. This is not mere observation; it is eating people. From that point of view the instrument is in good order. Love functioning perfectly. Hugh is deeply happy, wrapped up, swathed in tenderness; he says the way we live together is an art. I think there are only two or three things with which we annoy each other. He is untidy, always late and slow. I am impatient, too early, and I leave the toothpaste tube open. He gladly discovers that my other defects are Hindu: gentleness of manner (against the fierce dynamic strength of the Liliths), childish appearance (against an air of intelligence and of being all there), disarmingly sweet and nonintellectual smile. Oriental. Yes, sir. Enigmatic.

August 23. Hugh says we are living in a Chekhov play. The precious apartment is being sold, he dances, and in the middle of it all I write four perfect pages—terse, poetical, final, of my second story, a kind of sequel to "Woman No Man Could Hold," on the subject of imagination, creation, sensuality. Eduardo arrives early this morning. Then I receive the news that my article on Lawrence is to be published in *Canadian Forum.* How fitting a beginning—praising my Lawrence. Could anything be more perfect? I don't get paid; that will come.

Didn't sleep most of the night, thinking of my story. My body ached, my chest felt oppressed, and my heart seemed to be beating in my feet and gone from its normal abode. The morning coffee, blessed coffee, revived me. Eduardo talks. Joaquin, I hear, is jealous. I smile. I am so jealous too, deeply so, but I never admit it. I want Joaquin's independence before everything else— before his love. So I do nothing to absorb and hold all his love. Then he thinks I don't love him enough. It hurts him. So it goes. And it must stay that way: not to cling, not to dominate. And all the while, really, I am jealous and possessive and domineering and tyrannical—in my Journal.

Hugh gets cross and domineering because Eduardo is here. He doesn't like it. So I muster a double supply of thoughtfulness— must be everywhere at once.

I have another idea about multiple lives of which I am going to make a story. But this hellish lyrical writing makes itself rare and capricious. It comes slowly, really, though I am a quiet writer, and there is no conscious work to equal it. So I wait, writing all the while, which keeps the pen smooth, symbolically speaking.

The day is cold. I shiver. I have pains all over. Let me think only of praise of "my" Lawrence coming out in print, under a remote name, not my own yet—Melisendra. Who is Melisendra? Looking in from the outside, only at the writing, as people will, what image will they see? What new me will they create, and I, like a dutiful actress, live out?

August 24. The three of us, Hugh, Eduardo, and I, visit our country house and talk—wonderfully, about multiple living, memory, the past, Lawrence, men and animals, Blake. They tease me because I talk less and, an hour after, ask me if I have already written it down, which of course makes it impossible for me to do so. But it all sinks into me—and talk after my own dreams, after my own heart, affects me that way, as if it were too sweet to realize.

Eduardo says the creator is never satisfied with experience—never can be. The moderns, he has read somewhere, do shoddy and swift art work because they believe in living more. And just the day before he arrived, I wrote of how creative intensity leads to intense living. Eduardo calls genius an illness—creation. I call it a poison. I am sometimes startled to hear him talk. There is a difference in our way of thinking and a powerful resemblance in our feelings, so we are constantly meeting in fact, bumping into each other. Suddenly, I remember a letter from a woman he did not succeed in loving: "When you do love me one hundred percent, let me know." Why one hundred percent? An ordinary request, an unimaginative request. Eduardo can't do it. Lawrence couldn't do it. It is not emotional poverty or impotence; it is the insufficiency of everything for the artist. A curse. Is intensity—white-heat living—only to be found in creation? Yes. But creation calls for it. So I am doomed to overflowing, both in living and in imagination. Those who can regulate their temperature, who can be passive, neutral, appreciative, who "have cured themselves of the illness," understanding all—those healthy ones—what do I think of them? It is good they exist. But I prefer my illness, and, thank heavens, Eduardo does too, and Hugh is about to choose to be ill deliberately, when he might have remained a banker.

My writing, the writing that counts, as in "Woman No Man Could Hold," requires an explanation and preparation. Eduardo was put out and did not understand it either. It must be something new—a new attitude must be created for it. I will have a very difficult time over it if that is the case. Yet I am so sure I am right, and I'm going right on, trying only to do it better.

August 25. Eduardo says: homosexuality is an *immaturity* of nature. His only morality is a desire not to live against nature. He wants to find maturity in creation—intensity—then normal love. I told him I had tried it and that creation led again to unwise experience. I put it more strongly. I said, "Suppose Lawrence comes to you and says, 'Eduardo, leave your painting and come and live with me.' What would you do?"

"Leave my painting, because that would be the ideal of intense living."

Then I said, "Lawrences *have* come to me, and intense living was offered to me. And I went."

"But you knew you couldn't stay—that the little kernel of creation in you would make you return."

"Of course. Not wanting to destroy."

"But the ideal would be to live with Lawrence and work. And that is what I want to do. Live, and find my Lawrence woman. And you should work and live intensely when you have your Lawrence man. But Lawrence men are so rare, so rare. Have you really met one?"

"*Pieces* of Lawrence," I confessed frankly, "just pieces." He laughed. We talked about our slow, sincere development, step by step, complete and solid. In that we have been alike—seeking *integrity*, but not the mob meaning of integrity, which is to obey laws. We obey nature and fulfillment and the urge to create. We have the same problems, the same desires, except that he is more sick than I am.

We had such a swift, direct, concise, almost final talk on that subject that we refused to talk about anything else. Eduardo hit his forehead, as if it hurt, to have it all over so quickly, I banged my Journal closed (I had also read from the sequel to "W.N.M.C.H."), and he went to his room.

The apartment is rented, at a profit to me, for my work, of 25,000 francs.

August 26. Hugh had a dinner with Vice-Presidents. Eduardo and I went to the theatre and to the Mosquée. He said I was a Lawrence woman and I said he was a Lawrence man. We thought aloud together, we didn't talk. Yet coming home in the jolting taxi he said: "I have a presentiment that we will never be anything but brother and sister—that I will lose you again, through my own fault."

"To the right or left?" shouted the taxi driver.

"To the left," cried Eduardo, and then, "It's terrible."

And that is the end of it all. We can communicate, we are tied by dreams—only.

I said I didn't mind, let us enjoy the present. I didn't mean what I said. For a moment we were so curiously, so strangely tuned to the same measure—so wonderful, that intensity and sameness of mind, always the right answer, the continuation of one's own dream. We see that we walk the same way, feel the same way, plod, seek—and it is simply the fact of not being alone which gives joy. Yet he is saying I want to be alone and work, and I am saying I want to be alone. Yet we linger at a bar table, although our talk, face to face, only brings disorder, pain, and restlessness. We talked about intensity of living, a physical communication with life; the stage and the delusion of the stage; art and the possibility of perfection in solitary art. Yet, of course, we are overlooking one kind of intensity—that of our companionship, which cannot be complete or satisfying or anything but a disappointment, a delusion, even a danger, since he cannot love woman.

Sometimes I doubt whether I am really an artist, for I love living to the point of madness, and I would, I could, destroy the creative kernel for the sake of an hour of living.

I took the bus and went on all kinds of petty errands. I often get back my philosophy that way. Today it was hot, and the bus jogged my ideas, shook them up so that it is a wonder I could cling to them, and all the while I felt limp and defeated. When I came home and dropped my little packages, I said to myself, This freedom that is forced on me (yes, I couldn't say this freedom I obtained for myself) I am thankful for, after all. And I began making a great show of work among my papers—and all the while I knew that if I were not an artist I would be a woman not worth loving, not worth anything at all.

Evening. After I wrote here, I began a story I have had in mind: about a woman who, made to be an actress, cannot be one and tries multiple living in three parts in real life. At the crucial moment she recovers a stage voice and is able to return to the stage. Moral: acting multiple characters is for actors and cannot be carried out in real life. I played with my idea and wrote flowingly until Hugh came home. And when Eduardo came for dinner I was not woman any more. I talked from my "artist's promontory," so poised and self-possessed.

August 28. Warm, brilliant morning. Eduardo and I set out to look for a studio for him. I wear a light-green dress and picture hat. I am gay and light and free and clear-minded. We sit in the bus. Eduardo feels the lightness. He is suddenly delivered of his own heaviness. He says, "I love your insouciance!" (Always, man's fear of having a woman around his neck like a stone.) The atmosphere is suddenly cleared up. There is no more discomfort. I ask nothing; he gives me all he can give. I look fearlessly and quietly into his face, and he is glad for the fearlessness and the quietness. His confidence comes back. He takes my arm. And how we talk. There is to be an artistic fulfillment: he will illustrate my mystical stories. We dream of that. I am delighted. Art, art, is a fulfillment, is a fulfillment. The day is bright and warm; the bus shakes us. I am so light, so light—a stone, no more. Where is that brooding intensity, the brewing storm that was going to break our relationship? I have dissolved it. It is crystal clearness now. Clearness and lightness—man to man, almost. And what of my pale-green dress and ivory arms and coral bracelet and his hand on my arm and his green eyes and the sensuousness of his face and walk? Delight, delight, and nothing more. His freedom, my freedom.

There is no doubt that I am an artist, which makes a fine woman out of me; not a stone, not a housekeeper, not a nurse—a free, pliable, busy being, who weighs on nobody—carrying a world, not demanding one.

Go, my dear, go, I say. I can stay then, says Eduardo. He sees the strength in me; and I see it too, and I smile. Because nobody saw me yesterday.

It works this way: I may be in the car with Hugh, driving to the library. And I say unexpectedly, "I have an idea." And I tell him the story of my actress and her multiple lives. Or I may talk of another story to Berta Hamilton while she is trying on a hat. Or one comes to me while Eduardo is looking up Rue des Volontaires on the Métro map. Or I sometimes say to Hugh when he is half asleep, "I have the end of my story."

Last night Hugh was asleep. And the end of my actress story

came to me, and it was really wonderful. Then a mosquito woke him up and I was able to tell him. With great difficulty, I finally get to sleep. I hear myself saying, "I have an idea." It is the beginning of everything. It is my favorite phrase. When I can say that, the day is rich. I have found my view, my style, my form. The "actress" story runs quickly. A lyrical treatment and the terseness of a play. The sequel to "W.N.M.C.H.," more slowly.

The old things are kept in the mail, traveling. My file box is up to date. I think that "I have an idea" makes me happier than "I have a friend." It is *my* idea. A friend—a friend is an accident. Lawrence should have been my friend. Then I would not be so sure which was more precious.

August 29. Eduardo gives me some interesting criticisms: First, my Journal is more perfect than my "W.N.M.C.H." story, so far, because the psychology is more true—true to me. What I invented in the story is more or less false, to me.

"But that is not a *literary* criticism," I said.

"No. It is only because I know you, and I dare say you, as you are, are more interesting than the woman in the story." Oh, well. "Second," Eduardo said, "your love pages are directly influenced by Lawrence—too much so." Agreed. "Third, the new stories show more invention; you are coming out of yourself, and they have their own psychology."

"True," I said, "they are becoming more artistic. Would you have enjoyed reading the story if I had not written it?"

"Yes," said Eduardo. "I like it. It is intellectual acrobatics . . . like Gide." He gives me [Gide's] *Paludes* to read, and I enjoy it vastly. "To explain your book is to restrict the meaning of it. Let others explain the sense of it to you. There is a vast portion of unconscious meaning which you may not know about." Thus speaks Gide, so wisely, at a youthful age.

Eduardo scolds me because I don't know the names of trees. Why should I? "Because you make a friend of it. This tree, for instance, is a plane tree. You come and say, 'Hello, plane tree.'"

"But perhaps, although it is a plane tree, it may have the feeling of some other kind of tree. Why pigeonhole it like that?"

"That's true. This tree has the character of an oak. It is like me—I don't want you to judge me by my face."

Eduardo said yesterday my face really didn't suit my character—that it was deceptively sweet, when there was really so much strength in me. Monday he moves into his studio. As Gide says, "I can think better about a person when he is not there." So I shall wait.

Later. Eduardo reads me Lawrence's poetry while I sew a button on his shirt. He tells me he feels very self-conscious going out with me because people stare at me so much, turn around to look at me twice, turn somersaults to look at me; which, of course, I enjoy hearing! Offered to try to look mousy again but he won't have it.

Observations: my writing is getting poor. My grammar worse. So I am everyday more and more modern.

August 30. Heat—distracting to everybody but which I relish. Peace. Physical languor and relaxation. Less thinking. Eduardo has a byway mode of thinking. He stops at every word and thought to explore. My method of leaping directness helps him. At the same time there is that comforting feeling that we are both seeking truth. So we arrive at the same conclusions, with the same feeling about things. An astonishing thing: he suggested ending "W.N.M.C.H." with the same words I have carried within me for ten years and used in *Aline*: "Then she sat down and began a book."

While I was typewriting for him and helping him with a difficult letter having to do with his new decisions, I noticed that he has very, very long blond eyelashes. It is a strange thing that these men who cannot love women hold a sensuous appeal for them, quite a definite one, and one which must cause a great deal of pain to both the woman and the man.

He said yesterday I answered Lawrence's description of the modern woman—the woman who is cocksure—who has the power of the man; but such cocksure women are *impossible*—unless they are at once cocksure *and* demure. I am demure and therefore can "get away" with a great deal of modernism, and with all I want to get away with.

He showed me a letter he received from the man he loved. They have agreed to separate, each fighting off his tendency. The letter was very beautiful—intelligent, restrained, noble, almost classical in tone, and I told Eduardo so.

What struck me immediately was, why does Eduardo love men of fine mettle and mediocre or inane women? I asked him. I told him I didn't see how he would ever outgrow the other love if he matched inferior women against superior men. He answered:

"Because superior men inspire harmonious love in me. That is, I can love a superior man physically and mentally. But with women there is no harmony; I cannot love women who appeal to my intellect. And sometimes when I have a *feeling* of love for a woman, whatever woman, to save myself, I devote myself to this feeling, and try to increase it, and hope that the neutral companionship I crave, I may be able to teach her. Immediately I think, How wonderful if I could love her, marry her. The rest I can teach her."

Meanwhile, I thought how terrible such a disharmony must be—how tragic his friend and their love.

September 1. Eduardo finished reading all my stories yesterday and said: "It is *uncanny*, absolutely uncanny how you have put yourself into *all* your stories. I suppose it is due to your journal writing."

"Anything wrong with that?" I asked anxiously.

"I don't know," said Eduardo. "You are creating your own world like Lawrence, with you at the center of it. It is a problem to know whether it should be done thus. You rarely invent another character entirely. You did in 'Slippery Floor.' I like that story. The mother is very well done. Of course," he added thoughtfully, "why shouldn't you do it? I have rarely seen such an interesting woman as you. I think you are the most interesting woman I have ever known. So your stories are interesting—everything that relates to you. But I should think you would do well to keep all that *you* for your journal, your *best* work, and invent in your stories, because it seems a pity to waste yourself on little stories. . . ." He talked very quietly, coolly analyzing. I was struck by his acuteness.

"I feel I know Hugh now, too," Eduardo said, "and I know he was seasick on his honeymoon."

When we got over that, we got serious again. I was worried to have been so transparent. I asked if I had merely *copied*. Had I not transformed? Yes. I know that I *am* in the process of working away from the Journal, of working without the Journal. Already my last two stories swim in their own water. I used to dive from the Journal—often came back to it when I felt unsure of my strength. But it was so strange to have Eduardo understand my work so completely, and understand me and the exact separation between me and my work. It is so sweet to be really known—not to be confused with your own talk and writing. I stayed awake for an hour last night in the dark, purposely to savor the deep keen pleasure I felt.

Yesterday he came very near loving me. We were leaning

over Blake's book of poems, in the car. I felt that he was moved. And then we went on with the party, which was a picnic in the Marly woods. We were very foolish and playful. Eduardo climbed trees and went on with his botany lessons for my exclusive benefit, "This is an oak, Anaïs; this is a locust tree, this is a birch, and here are some honeysuckle flowers." He had lost two buttons off his shirt and his chest was bare. But I did not respond to him as a *man* with a bare chest. I felt nothing. His face shone with extraordinary intensity; his eyes were brilliant and soft, deeply green. He was like Blake's book of poems open on my knees.

The night covered us with such delicate stillness that Eduardo felt almost sentimental. As we walked, each wrapped more or less in his own world, we sometimes brushed each other, sometimes walked a few steps behind the other. And I had a clear vision of our two heads facing each other, two brilliant faces looking at each other, separate from our bodies. Intensity was gathered in our faces. The two worlds of ideas sought unity—two separate bodies fled from each other. Perpetually attracted, perpetually separate . . .

September 2. Yesterday he moved to his own studio. I went with him, made his bed, hung up his clothes while he unpacked, and then we went shopping, played at a bohemian life and had coffee at the Dôme. He suddenly grew serious and said: "Have men ever told you they wanted to destroy you? Well, I feel like that. You obsess me. The mental connection between us obsesses me. I cannot stop thinking about it. I know I shall never find anything like it in the world. I know that would be the ideal. I *want* to love you. I wish we had never begun by that mental connection, wish we had not begun by *dreaming* together, for now I cannot *touch* you— there is a veil before you. I want to touch you, to grasp you in another way than the mental, and it must be by a physical grasping—and I long for that, and yet I cannot do it—and I fear to lose you, and I won't be satisfied with that fulfillment in art you talk about. I don't want any half measures; either *everything* or nothing. It is all my fault of course. How well I know you! I know every word you have written in your Journal. Wasn't the picnic perfect? I didn't *think* then, I just let myself be. It was the most perfect day of all. . . ."

Either everything or nothing! I knew it would be nothing. As we sat there, the physical current was so slight, more like a tremor . . . I knew he could never touch me, and that even if he touched me he could never *hold* me. So I savored the sound of his voice, dropping so low: "I want to love you"; I savored the moment, the way we sat, shoulder to shoulder, touching; I, quite aware of the contact, quite aware of the caress of his eyes on the outline of my body—while he was only aware of that slight, unreal tremor in himself, a tremor of the mind, a passion of the mind only, while the passion of the man lay so profoundly still—dead perhaps—in spite of that "I want," in spite of his tragic struggle against the sterile love of man and the sterile love of intellect.

So we decided—or he decided, for I said almost nothing yesterday—to wait a while for his maturity, and then, if it did not come, we would give each other up altogether so he will no longer be obsessed. I knew that if he reaches his maturity, that is all he will have and that is all I want to help him find, because *me* he won't reach or have—not the integral me. My vagabondage is over. As in the sequel of "Woman No Man Could Hold," I know and have guessed all I want to know of living. I lived yesterday a whole long life with Eduardo in those few moments at a café table. There would be tenderness and sharpness; a bare chest which would not seem like a bare chest; satanic, deceitful beauty, unreachable, untouchable; feelings that would not be feeling; there would be an insufficiency, something always falling short, evanescent, teasing, incomplete—the *illusion of passion*. And always the face and mind shining resplendently, not the body . . . Curse my too clear eyes, which have recognized poverty. I want—to believe!

Eduardo moved yesterday, and he was here this morning. He said, "Will you have tea with me this afternoon?" I refused, saying I couldn't see him until Thursday. Then I went to work. But I couldn't work. I guess I am obsessed, too!

It is like an illness: the desire to see someone, the strong, deep yearning. Yet you have just seen him, and seeing him tomorrow will not satisfy, and the same illness, like a hunger, will come to you, stronger each time you see him. No, I have not explained it. I was working today, writing. My *head* was busy: my mind was filled with the work. Yet all the while I was conscious of a physical pain—a gnawing—as if a piece of me had been cut off. And the mind could do nothing about it. It was physical: it was in the veins, in the blood, in the skin. That is why human relationships are dangerous—because the mind has no power over them.

And then there is the inevitable foolish, feminine question: Am I not beautiful enough? As if those things were a matter of weights and measures. When I know better than anyone that beauty is not a material object but an effect—a miraculous alchemy —a quality of impression, and that, therefore, there is only the question: Do I *seem* beautiful to him? To be answered only by him, not by me. Yesterday I went to his room, and we made up curtains and a couch cover out of my turquoise-green bedspread.

Today I helped a Vice-President with his shopping and met Natasha at the Café du Rond-Point. I wore my turquoise cape and hat and sandal-shoes; everybody looked at me, men followed me, and, like the very child-woman I most despise, I was dreadfully amused by all my little triumphs. Natasha was late. As I sat in the café the chasseur [bellhop] came with a letter. "Will you come and have tea with me at the Ambassadeurs, Madame?" Signed with some man's name. At first I had refused to take the letter, guessing its contents, although it was the first time this technique was tried on me. Then, furious at my own childish haughtiness, I took the letter, read it, and said: "There is no answer." And five minutes afterward another letter—with an address. This time I looked at the man. He was quite remarkably decorative, even interesting. I thought, how easy it is to begin different lives! How easy it is to live foolishly! I was laughing at this man, and he knew it. He kept the letter, to use probably on another woman. I was a woman among women. Somehow this vast head I carry on my shoulders, with its complicated, symbolical, nuanced world, didn't show. I was outwardly like everybody else—a wonderful feeling. A woman men want. An ordinary woman—to certain men.

To a man who has seen the inner woman, I am a woman one cannot toss an address to, with such an acceptance of simple animal laws. One man can only see me physically, another only mentally; Hugh can see me both ways, and I run from Hugh to the visionary and from the visionary to the café men, and I make many notes in my notebook, on the bus, going from one to another. That is my business. It is very interesting. And neither Hugh, nor Eduardo, nor the café men would like what I am writing: "Her blood eventually turned to ink. It was very economical."

With deviltry, I read Hugh what I wrote this afternoon. And he enjoyed it. A marvelous thing—his love of my writing. And he says, furthermore, that the only *right* point of view is the artist's. That is what makes him tolerant, wise, and so clever with me, so flexible. That is why when he says he does not want to limit me I believe it; his attitude does free me. I owe my good work to his great capacity for being impersonal. Of course, within reason. How far can I go, I ask sometimes, and then jealousy awakens in him. There was never a more generous, more intelligent man. I often test him with readings from my Journal. He responds as a poet. It is no wonder I so often feel inferior to him, because creative gifts do not make up for weaknesses of character. In some ways I am too poor to pay him back. One trait should be measured with an equal trait. In us it is unequal. He is generous; I am not generous. I make him a beautiful home, which is irrelevant. He is kind; I am not kind. I write "W.N.M.C.H.," which stirs him, which is beside the point. He is faithful; I am not faithful. I write things in my Journal which make him aware of riches and conscious of wonder. I give *taste* to our life together. Unequal values. I often measure them, back and forth, upside down, inside out, cubistically and logically. I always get the same sum: unequal values, positive qualities against possible achievements. He is satisfied with our accounts, but I am not. I may be if I do something really wonderful. I think I will. . . .

September 6. The desire grows stronger in me "to live in my own world continuously." Everything else now seems to me as if I were bumping myself against a wall or playing the part of a dwarf, twisted and shrunk to proportions painful to my body. Yesterday I spent three sweet hours with Eduardo, sewing while he read to me. In the evening we went to hear *Carmen*, that horror, with two Vice-Presidents. No humor, no artistic attitude, could console me for the evening. Will I become more and more uncompromising? Is it dangerous to live only in your own world? Natasha does, with violence and cruelty and door-banging. No compromise of any kind. If she is working, the King would be thrown out of her studio. Eduardo wants to try this. I will try it in Louveciennes. I am going to choose my friends, not be chosen by them. I want to know Aldous Huxley.

A cheerful spot: Eduardo read me yesterday a marvelous article on "Costume" by a man who had studied the subject deeply and who differentiates between "costume" and clothing, and begs us to keep alive the stage privilege of *costuming* instead of *clothing*. An idea I reached long ago, by my own instincts and which I have consistently developed. Eduardo understands how true I have been to the extension of stage-costume wonder into daily life—to give it meaning, character, evocativeness, and profundity.

September 7. I buy pastels to make a reproduction of our house, I get books on decoration from the library, and I begin to make plans and to have new ideas. Hugh calls me a good sport—so I'm happy.

He is playing golf with the Vice-Presidents, and Eduardo and I are going out together. We had both decided to see *La Chute de la Maison Usher* [The Fall of the House of Usher].

Une fête pour l'imagination [A feast for the imagination]. First we saw *Un Chien Andalou*, a film surréaliste by Luis Buñuel, which upset us; its symbolism awakened our own symbolic world with unbearable sharpness. And then came Poe's story—intensely poetic and beautiful. I, who am not often floored, was floored. It seems to me it will take days to absorb it all.

We talked about observation. Eduardo complained that I did not observe "reality." I said I did at *moments*—at other moments I closed my eyes to reality and used my vision. I let the "unconscious" work. Eduardo said he was beginning to see things that way, that he not only believed in such observation but he thought it was the only kind that *produced*. A purely surface observation, however complete, without an abstract alchemy produces nothing —as, for example, in Horace, who sees everything and sees nothing. I do not see everything always, but at moments I see more than everything.

Eduardo has a basic sincerity and a boundless faith in my basic sincerity. We never lose that, and therefore we can go on long imaginative voyages and never get lost. I do not lie to him as I lie to other people, because we share a big enough imaginative world. Things happen when we are together; there is not a moment of dullness. It is only in dull moments that I lie and invent, when I feel the necessity of stimulating people by a fantastic statement or of stimulating my own life, which is in danger of dying in their presence. And so I lie, for the wonder of it. I sent myself flowers when I was a girl because nobody sent them, and I played with the great pleasure it gave me to receive flowers. I told my Aunt Anaïs that my train to New York had been attacked by strikers and there had been a fight and bloodshed—because I enjoyed seeing her frightened and jolted. At the end of dull days I have invented adventures for myself, or magnified very little ones. I have endowed people with mots d'esprits [witticisms] which did not come from them, for the humor of it, for the colorfulness and fun of it. I have told myself stories, as when I fancied myself about to meet John instead of calling on a Vice-President's wife—again, for the wonder of it. In Eduardo there is wonder, and so I do not need to create it. What we talk about is a constant, though ever-changing symbolical world, layer upon layer, always full of surprises. So it is with Hugh. When I lie to him he knows it, and it amuses him and I know he knows it, and it is only a game.

September 8. It was so true, as [Orbert] Burdett wrote of Blake—that he could preach theories that succeeded well in his life because he had fine impulses. Furthermore, I believe, as Burdett says, that such men as Blake are primarily to be taken as *stimulators*, not as guides. We must be our own guides and find our own truths once we are stimulated by men like Blake and Lawrence. They are not literally guides; we cannot live as they lived or copy them indiscriminately.

I am the wind itself for my own sailboat. I do not say: I would like to be a drama critic. But I am a drama critic. And immediately I must find a way to live up to my own words. To want to be and to be are the same to me. And so, I am the wind itself for my own sailboat.

"Nettles—for Women."
She could not bear the smell of honeysuckle
Nor the caress of men's willful hands
Was cursed for dreaming foolishly
That they should always come together
While men's caresses would come at hours
And for reasons
She could not understand
The hour, place and scent having no meaning
For them, the woman yes
And pretty soon it was the men
Who could not bear her
Because of that honeysuckle feeling.

Two Americans have said, "Oh, John Erskine? John Erskine has 'Dropped out'." Poor John. Is that due to the fickleness of "fads" in America, or to his own fault? He has not been serious enough. Sinclair Lewis has not dropped out. John has time to find himself. How I wish I could tell him the truth, for I know the truth.

September 9. Eduardo and I went to see St. Anne at the Louvre. He had written a poem about her and me. Afterward I begged to be shown the poem. It was very beautiful. I judged it apart from its personal significance, which we did not discuss. But it is strange to hear him speak of his own *deadness* with lyrical intensity—strange how he makes poetry out of it.

Sitting before him I felt again that deadness enfolding me, and myself becoming a St. Anne, not in the foreground, fleshy, the mother of a child, but in the background, dispensing understanding and feeling and wisdom—the woman who *has* lived and now looks down intelligently on the beginning of another life, on the doting, oversweet, over-self-effacing, uninteresting mother. It is St. Anne the detached, the woman, who is more interesting than the mother, who lived in the child. St. Anne herself lives expectant, yet knowing, profound—entire. Eduardo would eliminate the mother and child (because to him they are the symbol of the love which has unmanned him) to reach St. Anne the woman.

Whatever he will reach, I sit enshadowed, knowing everything, aware of everything—savoring the poetry of his resplendent death and the possibility of his resurrection.

To Eduardo, in a note in which I had to excuse myself for a slip in observation of reality (a certain tearoom where we were to meet does not exist any more): "I will instead come to your place to sew. I did observe that you had a tear in your pants, but my divinatory vision tells me you must have holes in your socks."

I have the marvelous power to let myself live.

September 11. Long trips in the Métro (beginning the business of moving and preparing the house), long thoughts, long soliloquies, long dreams. Beginning to fear that the intensity of my imaginative life makes actual experience a perpetual disappointment. It is not the old story of disillusion, because my illusions were pale and uninteresting compared with what I have lived through. No, what I have lived through has roused imaginative reactions, roused an enthusiasm which more and more living does not abate. In fact, I am hungrier every day—that is all. Intellectual tapeworm, as I said before. Interesting malady.

Hugh, having read some old pages of my Journal, would like me to check up on a few things I have written about him, because he says they are no longer true. I must keep his portrait up to date. But I accused him of making no portrait whatever, which is worse. I cannot very well write down the beautiful things he says to me, as when he calls me his "harem" and his "little mistress" and when he acts like a wildly infatuated lover, crying out his enjoyment of me, and when he tells me I make him profoundly, unspeakably happy, that our life together is miraculous and wonderful. There would be too much of me. But I must tell about him completely.

September 12. Today all was definitely settled between Eduardo and me. After the poem, ending on a note of hope, he had recurrences of his old trouble. We met, both brisk, a bit tense, and hotly discussed other things so as not to hear the sound of our feelings— me, recoiling and shivering; he, insufficient—hurting each other a lot, though we would not admit it for the world. The one who cannot *feel* always blames the other, even if he does not want to. Eduardo is truthful enough to blame himself, but at the same time he builds up a false image of me as an overintellectual person, disregarding the impulses he cannot respond to as if they did not exist. I would die in his world if I had to live in it; his feelings, falling short, give me a terrible shivering. The poetry, for a moment, illuminated his world. He wrote some and I wrote some, but it was a false illumination; something real and warm is not there, and at certain moments, as today, we both found it wearisome. There was charm in our relationship, but not when I feel too clearly his conscious straining after feeling. . . . FINIS.

September 16. Not finis! Last night, in front of the fire, the two of us reached a wonderful realm, not through rational thinking but through mysticism, a language we both understand. He had written another poem—received, as he said, another revelation. Our relationship was finally "fixed" with mystic symbols. On a rational plane, I taught him that a woman's nature does not change with the possession of an intellectual world. I told him the end of my sequel to "W.N.M.C.H." He understood.

Hugh is in Biarritz on business. Eduardo came for dinner and we went out to dance. But I was surprised to see that he felt utterly detached from that life, so strongly has he entered his creative world. He is more intense, more self-reliant, more determined than I at first realized. What a delight! We enjoyed the actual dancing together, yes, but not the place or the people. We sat out in the Dôme and talked. Then he brought me home. We had held hands, firmly promising to be good friends—friends with tenderness.

Before that I had my first experience with an Editor. I had gone to see Edward Titus to ask him about the MSS. I had left with him. He said, "I have had so much to read since I came back from my vacation that I cannot say I have read carefully enough—but your work stands out. I was particularly interested in your essay on Lawrence—remarkable for a young woman to write. The long story was original, but too long for my magazine. Your work needs editing. I do not object to the foreign 'tournure de phrase' [turn of phrase] but to some defects of English. I would not have bothered about the manuscripts in another case, would simply have returned them without a word, but I thought it a pity that a little editing should be an obstacle to you, because the work has quite a bit of merit. You are one of those little persons who has a lot to say."

I was very nervous and very shy. When he questioned me about my education, I said, "None—but grammar school and a lot of reading." I finally scuttled off—really, I did not leave with dignity. How I detract from the value of my work by my "sauvagerie." I was so upset to have been so nervous—yet I realized something good had happened—that I had won Titus's attention, that he was really interested, that this was an unusual reception for a young unknown writer.

How right my poor darling had been. How much I owe to his beautiful English. Where would I be without his teaching and hard work? I wrote immediately to tell him so. Then I began to wonder what I could do about it. Study English. I wish I knew what Conrad did. Titus said so understandingly that someone must edit my work without touching what is original and exotic but only what is *defective*.

Every now and then Eduardo would say, "I am contented, I'm happy."

"Why?"

"Because everything is right between you and me. Because everything is so pleasant between you and me. Occasionally," he said, "it makes me feel very bad, the knowledge that you keep a diary. I am one of those persons who think aloud—I do not always mean everything I say—"

"Don't you think I understand you well enough not to write down things which are not permanently you?"

Then my own problem came back to me and I asked him how he would feel if I published whatever I wrote about him (he was suggesting I should publish my Journal). He was undecided. I told him my idea. I didn't mind anything as long as it only concerned me, because I seek truth and ultimately I don't care what is known of my faults, etc. But about others—I have already torn out something that directly concerned John and would have hurt him if it were published. It is the last thing in the world I want—to devour others as I devour myself. Instructions will be left to Hugh or Joaquin to destroy whatever concerns others if I die—unless these others feel about themselves as I feel about myself, which I doubt. Eduardo thought he would not care as long as many years lay between what I published and his present self—in other words, he would not mind if I published now my Journal of ten years ago.

5:30. A dark afternoon. In the studio, sitting on the rug before the fire in a long amethyst chiffon dress and sandals. Awaiting Eduardo, who is coming to dinner.

September 17. Last night Eduardo read me poetry. His voice is rich and varied, and he has the dramatic quality. It was a deep joy to hear him. I asked him to read me "Tishnar" to see how it sounded. It was so moving, to hear it; I was astonished at my own writing. He alone knows how it should be read, and he read it as I heard it in my own head when I wrote it.

Today I awoke to an odd day—to joyful solitude. In the morning the idea came to me for a mystical story about a houseboat we saw at Etretat. Between buses and Métros and much walking, I managed not only to do all my errands but to arrive at a kind of peak of realization. I knew for a day exactly my own true value, the value of my writing; how I could continue to grow, how I could stand at the center of my own world while yet able to perceive other worlds, how I needed my individuality because otherwise I would be unbalanced by sentimentality and pity, how I need this new feeling of not caring about the opinion of people on any matter: my writing or my living. I know now when I am right and when others are right. I must not be self-satisfied, but very sharply, shrewdly, intelligently self-confident. In one of our conversations I understood Eduardo to mean he thought I was an egotist. It hurt me because it came from him. But it did not hurt my *mind.* I knew I was *right*—that if he called whatever I do egotism, well, let it be egotism. I could carry the word on my shoulders—I could live with it. It was a necessary appearance I must accept for the sake of the underlying values I am after.

I did take the time to try to explain, and then we discovered he had *not* meant that. Of course I was relieved, relieved of the emotional pain—but my mind, my world, my strength have not for a moment wavered, and I have not looked back, wished for the pale, weak, sensitive, unintelligent 1830 person-self. I exult in my strength. I can bear criticism, both just and unjust, I can bear to be despised. Nothing matters but the sweet new sureness.

September 20. Cold rain. I crouch before the fire—after having been for hours very busy, very much the little French practical woman, very reasonable, very calculating, very neat.

The map of my world has temporarily tidied my mind, too, and I try to keep it so. But it cannot remain so because it is quite clear now that I am more of a poet than an intellectual, that I feel more than I think. Eduardo tried a psychological test on me, made me lie down and relax, and sat behind me, saying words. I had to say what image or feeling they suggested to me. Oftener it was a feeling—oftener than either a thought or an image. It was because I was relaxed, a bit mesmerized by the silence and Eduardo's concentration. It was because my mind, which usually watches, was still and quick that the feelings came out on top.

That is why I was unreasonably moved at the movies by Eduardo's tender-heartedness—exactly like mine, exactly like a woman's. He laughed at the comedian and was concerned about his troubles. Who ever heard of a man being concerned about a comedian's troubles? I listened to his laughter and exclamations and pitying sighs and was moved to find that woman's tender heart in him. We call it, in full daylight, sentimentalism. But last night it seemed like something else. I could not help admiring and desiring; it seemed more like Lawrence's tenderness—that extraordinary tenderness of the poets.

Vallia Melnikoff says: "While people talk, all is well. We fashion our own meaning out of their words, and using our own understanding and our own knowledge, we attribute to these people intelligence or a sense of beauty. But let them put their words into images, let them *make images*—for example, a house or a costume for themselves—and then you see that they have no intelligence and no sense of beauty."

Yes, that is so. But there are people who simply cannot make images, such as Eugene, for instance, though they lack neither intelligence nor a sense of beauty. But Vallia is right; and is that why I give images such a great importance, is that why I do not consider a philosophy or a feeling or a dream complete without exteriorization? How fervently I believe in images! Words are something we must give a shape to with our hands before they have any meaning. Hands. Earth. Clay. Tools. Carving. Painting. All these and more. And poetry to fix and transmute the images.

But, oh, god, how it hurts to love images, to love work, to love poetry and to love love as I do. Yet if I didn't always feel hurt it would be death. Very often, just like a doctor, I lean over myself and touch my body, which is sore with excitement and pain, and I say, "It hurts there, it hurts here, does it? All is well. You are alive. I shall not have to give you medicine. Everything is functioning properly."

Sameness is a torment. Differences are a torment. To have such "twin feelings," as Eduardo and I have, is almost unbearable. He cannot bear it. He says it is like loving himself. Phrases come out of him which startle me into absolute silence. It is as if I were talking to myself. I get our ideas so mixed up I don't know at times whose idea it was. He leads me up to the end of my thoughts. It makes me think of a phrase in Christopher Morley's marvelous book *Thunder on the Left*: "Our minds are engaged. Let us announce that our minds are engaged."

But I feel my physical being in revolt. We do not even shake hands. Yet at moments he seems to be violently pushed toward me in some awkward collision—and we bump, ungracefully, like two somnambulists, shoulder to shoulder. Or he takes my arm and presses it to neutralize by physical tenderness the effect of a bit of teasing. All the while, of course, the two physical images match, look in harmony. People notice us in the street, eyes linger on our two faces, people feel we are "bound," and the deception is complete. And now that he is accustomed to my fantastic dressing and likes it, he shows me off like a man and takes pleasure in people's thoughts.

I am disarmed. I never could play the callous woman, the indifferent woman, although I should have. My enthusiasm always burns in my face and gestures, with a child's damnable naturalness. In that, I am a rotten actress. My feelings are too true. I am conquered, I am beaten, by Hugh, by John, by Eduardo. Until I learn the other game I shall never be successful. People love to give pain. In such matters it is a duel. I never shoot first, and certainly someone has to shoot first. I wait. Hugh tormented me, John did, Eduardo does. But I shall get so strong that being shot at will only harden me more.

Just now I do not want to hurt Eduardo. I could, and most

probably if I did he would be piqued, worried, and more interested. But what a game for intelligent people to play! What a comedy, when you know the primitive reactions in such comedies. I refuse to play it—to play on the cock-and-hen instincts of contradiction. Matters of unequally shared feelings cause a great deal of bitterness between men and women because of vanity. Eliminate vanity, and what do you find? Truth! Women cannot stand truth in matters of love. They always take it *personally*. "He doesn't love me" —a personal insult. There is no question of insult unless there is vanity.

September 21. Eduardo spent the afternoon with me. We read and talked endlessly. He said I had helped him when he came here first and was in such a torment about his friend. He said I concealed my intellectuality and that is why I attracted; that, anyway, he considered me an exception among intellectual women—he enjoyed it in me. "But," he challenged, "I do not believe you have a better mind than mine, or ever will."

I laughed. "Why better? Why even the same? Must there be a hierarchy?"

"There must be."

He wishes I possessed more science, more knowledge, wonders how I have done without Freud and Jung, though at the same time he admits they do not seem necessary to me. He says in spite of my Journal and love of truth I shall not know myself until I know psychology, because psychology discovers motives we can never imagine in ourselves. However truthful, I must always idealize myself, not necessarily through self-deceit but through *ignorance*. For a moment he troubled me. He was talking of his own clairvoyance. There is no doubt he *has* it. It sparks right out of him. I have already said he knows me infinitely well. I wondered. Why not knowledge? I spend and waste much time finding everything out by myself. I have grown very strong and individualistic because of that. Now I could use knowledge. It is like my decorating the house first, and then reading books about it, to compare, to criticize, find out my errors and also what natural gifts I can lean on.

For example, he has found traces of narcissism in my Journal. I contended narcissism was self-love whereas what I had for myself, at moments, was admiration; but love—I was always in love with others. This he had to admit was true!

And so it goes. From twelve o'clock until nine o'clock at night seems only an hour. When Eduardo talks he is resplendent. I see in him the incarnation of my own enthusiasms. The theatrical gestures of his hands, the lifting of his face, the full, frank, sensuality of his mouth are all appealing. It seems extraordinary that so much brightness should be cold rather than hot. It is like an enchantment, a curse, a spell, the most diabolical of all nature's tricks.

All day alone, loving my house here, parting from it in fits of rapt admiration. The last fire burned yesterday for Eduardo. I sorted out papers, tore up all old manuscripts, first drafts of this year's stories, useless letters; I cleaned my paintbrushes for tomorrow; I wrote letters; I made plans. I thought and thought about my Hugh, whom I miss terribly, as I write to him, his beautiful animal-like disorder. Where I live it is almost ghostly, untouched and tidy. It does not seem as if the bed had been slept in, the room occupied; the bathroom is spotless. And I imagined him here, like a child, scattering all his clothes about, the contents of his pockets, his big shoes, spilling medicines as he takes them, throwing the towels on the floor, forgetting to put out the lights, tossing in the bed until the covers fall to the floor.

I was lonely tonight, and as I undressed quietly I began to think of my Journal and how I would take it to bed with me and how out of its pages would come such a story of struggles and ecstasies that I would be lulled and enchanted by it and finally fall asleep with a head full of images and stirring phrases, and promises of more and more strange happenings. . . . And so I am in bed with the black book propped against the quilt, and the story has filled my time and helped me to forget my sweet yet unbearable solitude —but I am disappointed in the woman. I cannot help wishing that she should love exclusively and fiercely the *best* of the three men— *but it is true that the love I have for Hugh is the deepest, the only enduring and integral love I have ever felt.*

September 27. Eduardo and I painted one small room in the villa. I had said, "I am going down to Louveciennes Monday."

"I want to go down and help," he said. "What can I do?"

So Tuesday we met on the 2:29 train. I was carrying "enduit" [primer] paint, and brushes, etc. It was a small attic room with a small window. I gave Eduardo a blue blouse and put on a pink one. We pulled the paper down and then found it needed plastering and cleaning. Eduardo was not discouraged. We cleaned, we pulled down cobwebs, we scraped off paper, we plastered the holes, we put the enduit on and tomorrow we paint.

He had books in his pockets. His beard is growing fast. The room is, for him, an experiment in discipline. And working side by side, we reached a new realm. I was in plain old clothes, stripped of a great deal of artificiality, more like the Swiss woman. And then I realized that Eduardo was enjoying our rough work for many reasons. In that little room he seemed suddenly to become tyrannical and overbearing, and I to grow more pliable and small. And then in an explosion of frankness, he confessed he did not want to accept me as a sibylline woman, but as one who had to grow all over again with him, from the beginning. He repudiated the ready-made woman who was not his.

Intellectually this amused me, and I knew he was not being wise, for it is the created woman in me who is wise and who is his best friend—the other would be an emotional and demanding person. But deep down, I was happy, for I realized he was trying to find his very own image of me, to exist exclusively for him alone—and his exacting nature pleased me. I explained the danger of my not being an intelligent and wise woman, and he understood and did not tease me any more. How he tried to tumble down, in a way, what was already there, my newborn confidence and sharpness and little vanities and outward sureness—in order to take possession of his own image of me, molded to fit well into his life. How sweetly egotistical and masculine and unfair. I had noticed that he criticized me because he thought others had spoiled me; that he would go out of his way to find a different way of treating me from what he imagined others to have done. In order to take hold of me in his own way he tyrannized—and I enjoyed it keenly. He is jealous. He said, "I want you to be more real with me." He did not mean more real, but a me that is for no one else. We stopped painting, facing each other, brushes in hand, tense and excited; I, explaining that the real me was not as fine as the intellectually projected one whose wisdom, gained without him, he did not enjoy; he, realizing that in rousing the real me he was rousing again a troublesome affection, whereas the wiser me kept finely balanced a most delicate and intricate relationship. He was conscious at last of wanting to possess me mentally, of wanting me to yield, woman-like, to a symbolical assertion of himself, and I was conscious of yielding, of the deep joy of yielding. He, brush in hand, takes up his painting again and sings to cover up his perplexity; for now that he has asserted himself and I have yielded, he does not know what else to do, since it is all a dream, a mystical venture, and there is to be no human transfiguration. And I also take up my brush again, face turned away, to conceal my little tremors of womanly triumph at having been conquered, thinking meanwhile that woman's true nature does not change. And at the bus stop, while I signal my bus man to stop, he generously concedes, "After all, you were sibylline today. . . ."

In the train, reading together from a book on Blake, as I grow thoughtful over some ideas he is giving me, he exclaims, "I tire you with my intensity!" That cry, so often on my own lips, never uttered, a real fear I have had in the presence of such men as John, his saying it now, was so startling I could barely answer him. What irony—I to be told that by a shamefaced cousin. Oh, what a joy to find an equal measure of that odd, rare quality of intensity which makes people see more deeply.

Today as Hugh, Joaquin, and I walked in the Bois, Eduardo was still a little jealous and ready to hurt and strangely aware of many things I tried to guess. He did not like Joaquin talking aside with me or taking my arm. He did not like Hugh bringing me beautiful Chinese pajamas from Biarritz. And when I sat next to the fire on the rug in my Chinese red-and-black silk coat, he watched me fixedly. And I came out with defiant remarks, saying I disliked *Phèdre*, which he likes, and telling him he shouldn't read *Le Figaro* because it is too conservative; but what small challenges. Tomorrow, in the train or while painting, I shall feel "envahie" [invaded] again, a bit vanquished, though outwardly I will show only a mind watchful not to spoil the fine, intricate balance with my excess of feeling.

Meanwhile, my Cat comes home, ardent and passionate, and I must confess to him that I cannot write about our hours of love because it is the one thing for which I have infinite, awesome respect. But he did desire and love me twice within a few hours, and I was almost dazed by his vehemence and startled by the vigor of his love. My wonderful Cat, who does spoil me, I admit.

In the house, plumbers, painters, etc. (Eduardo and I cannot do the painting with the condition the rooms are in; it took us five afternoons to do a small room.) I go every day.

Hugh is now in bed by my side, reading *Sons and Lovers* (Lawrence). I must introduce one of the dogs we bought from the house's tenant. He is called Ruby, but in spite of the cheap name he is a white, fluffy, intelligent and expressive little Pomeranian, whom I am growing to love.

September 29. Eduardo's consciousness of his incapacity to love woman and me when he wants to do so made him absolutely diabolical during our week of painting. Thrust after thrust, he vented his suffering on me. Suddenly our week together took on another light. I realized he wanted to make himself feel strong by making me weaker. The philosophy he tried to build up around and for his nature was distasteful to me, but I was so eager to help him find his philosophy that I did not worry about the pain it caused me. But he cares enough to hate himself for his perpetual destructive analysis. And so after being subdued for several afternoons, soft and all that is expected of woman, and seeing him build up this false strength and enduring his tormenting moods, I suddenly felt the pain too sharply, and my strength came back to me. I found the courage to say to him, "I am going away."

"Going where?"

"Back to my own world."

He was hurt. But he knew I was right. I am not the woman for him. Nor is he a man to my own measure. He is obsessed by me but also obsessed with his incapacity to possess what he admires, to dominate, to hold. And so he cries: Be small, be passive and warm and mindless.

Oh, I am tired of his antediluvian ideas (as Frieda said she was tired of Lawrence's). I am tired of men who are afraid of a woman's strength. I am tired of discussions, of trying to prove anything, of struggling for truth. I have been so gentle, tender, careful, subtle, so keenly watchful of his needs, tuned to his moods, intent on effacing my mind, on concealing and softening my strength. I have been so woman. I am tired of all that. I re-enter my own world with relief, and joy—wide horizons, air, space, soaring again. How sweet the freedom! Somehow I seem to be living pages out of my own story of "W.N.M.C.H."—the woman with the musician.

"Understand, be intelligent, have vision and talent—only to worship me," says Eduardo. And when I said, for the sake of theorizing, "But I love and have faith in your 'world,' " he answered, "How can you when you have a world of your own? You just cannot believe in mine and in my goal as much as you believe in your world and your goal." He also said, "The trouble with woman today is that she lives by men's philosophies."

"But which she interprets with her own nature. It is only stupid women who do not readapt men's philosophies before using them—"

October 8. Chez Mme. Lafont, Louveciennes. Not a single idea in my head, no more theorizing, no more subtleties, just work, formidable work, three times as much as at 47 Suchet, because the house was so old, so decrepit, so primitive in comfort, so dirty, so damp, so full of problems and obstacles. We moved October 3. Inwardly, I wasn't very brave. Outwardly, I let the world occupy me wholly and apparently had no time for regrets. Since then I have not dreamed or thought for a minute. In between organizing and watching the workmen I cleaned the garden, with Mother and Hugh, and the garage, by myself, raked, painted, washed, etc.

Today was the first sweet moment. The blue mosaic fireplace is up in our future library and we make the first fire! Then I began to relax, because the rain made gardening impossible, thought of my Journal and longed for a moment of peace. Ruby lies at my feet on the bed, so brightly fluffy and demonstrative, full of tricks and intelligence. I really love him. So I begin to peep out of the avalanche, and for the first time I do not feel overtired. One gets so hungry here. The air is stingingly fresh, the solitude and peace are soothing, the old houses, old walls, old vegetation are interesting. I am going to love Louveciennes; perhaps I do already. Friends are at such a safe distance.

October 11. Depression due to the reading of literary reviews, which made me feel I am wasting time. I wish I were back to work, to my writing. I pray ardently that this will be the last house I create and waste time on. From now on I only want to write. Nothing else means anything to me. On cold bleak days it is the only thing which still stirs me, warms me. Dancing, decorating, and people particularly pall on me. I suppose that is only the mood which leads to creation. How painful it is to have the mood without the creation to follow it, with paper, typewriter, and books locked up, and a long list yet of things to be done.

Another word about John. I blame myself entirely for my present underrating of him. It is due entirely to my own peculiar trick of overrating people, so that when they fall short, I am doubly severe and rank them as far down as they have gone up. Poor John stands really in between the two extremes, and I miss his real value altogether because of my own exalted nature. So let John remain the value that Lilith may think he is, and let people like myself stay out of such problems altogether in order to be just. In short, let me "shut up." And Lilith can write his biography.

Thus John is saved from falling into my hands by my own clairvoyance. And let us thank the gods for women like Lilith, who use real measuring tapes with the inches all printed out—the kind that even the carpenters and plumbers use and understand.

Wisdom teeth growing painfully. A note from Eduardo, gentle and flattering and thoughtful. Joaquin stayed a week with him while we moved and is convinced he cannot triumph over his nature by a mental decision. I have rid myself of all cumbersome feelings about him, but that is probably because they were not profoundly set in me, but the outgrowth of a warm imagination.

Gray day. Joaquin learning to drive the car with Hugh. Mother feeding the chickens. And I sit in our old-fashioned room, feeling everything standing still while I write—exactly as if the holding of a pen arrested for a few moments the revolving of the whole world. The car is running along; the chickens gather noisily around Mother; Paula and Lola are cooking lunch—and it is I who lie so still, bowed over a little book, concentrated, owl-like, alone, unfriendly, taking stock of things without a real measuring tape, so that things of small importance to others take up two pages of my Journal and the major events are left out altogether.

October 16. A sweet moment yesterday in the dull mess of the house when the first room (Joaquin's studio) emerged in salmon-rose color (red, yellow, and white mixture). I had a fireplace and bookcases built in. He will have some of my turquoise curtains, cut down. The house, being dark and small, will be mostly in that apricot color—maids' rooms rose, my bedroom pale coral, dining room, as usual, deep coral. No more turquoise, because it is a cold color.

Pleasure, too, in visiting the "pépinière" [nursery garden] to buy evergreens. How the house is changing—it is incredible. Joaquin's studio looked dark and half the size on account of a flowered orange paper with black stripes and other colors on it. It will never be as beautiful as 47 Suchet, which I still regret deeply, but it will be charming, in a small, undignified, unspacious, stingy way!

October 29. It was better not to write and not to think. The work and the discomfort have been overwhelming—and I let them overwhelm me, worked myself to death so I could just fall asleep the moment I went to bed. My only joy was the arrival of the *Canadian Forum* with my essay on Lawrence in it. It reads well, compactly and determinately.

Friday morning we move into the villa. The atmosphere of the place was made cheerful by the near-strangling of the Mayor's maid on a dark road ten yards from our own place while we were having dinner. Hugh bought a revolver, and no one can stay alone in the villa. I sound complaining. I cannot cure myself, although I force myself to take an interest in everything and am reading books on gardening. In spite of all I do, I feel out of the show, and the solitude I desired in Switzerland was not like this: it was something thorough, absolute, and with grandeur. This is mediocre and lukewarm, a middling measure, for I have to see people, since I am not in Caux, and to see them is an expedition. I am ashamed of my unhappiness. Anyway, only my Journal knows it.

Have gained a "point" in my character—I remember every morning now to brush Hugh's suit, hat, and coat, to put the buttons on his shirt, to lay out his socks, handkerchief and keys, and to fill his cigarette case and pocketbook, a little task I have always done intermittently and carelessly. Also I study the menus and remember to bring special things home.

What I don't like about my own attitude is that it is a crime against *enthusiasm*, which I have never lacked. My only alibi is health. Two weeks of acute pain, of sleeplessness, of overdoses of aspirin, all due to my wisdom tooth, which finally had to be extracted. But how I peek out, alive and excited, to talk books with Mr. Davies at Brentano's and to devour *transition* [a literary magazine] and Lawrence's last, *The Virgin and the Gipsy*, my true love. And I have a little mystical story in mind. And a dream for the book of dreams. Soon, perhaps in a week, I may be able to get to work again.

I enjoy the mischievous trick I played on John: I sent him, through Hugh, my study of Lawrence! Why? Because I knew he wouldn't like it, neither Lawrence nor me, and that way the disappointment, mine in him and his in me, will be evenly balanced. Women are hateful. I am hateful. No better than a primitive Spaniard knifing a friend for his indifference. What are you going to do about it? Confess and chuckle over it, secretly; I have really been so good for a month now that it is palling on me. Think of it —no Eduardo, no coquetry—oh, yes, just a bit of delicate, delicate ironic sentiment with Mr. Davies, who finds it so wonderful to talk to me and whose wife is just a pretty little thing without brains who doesn't understand him and his nice Welsh-Irish temperament.

It's funny—I am all cheered up. On the whiteness of the paper the finely scrawled misfortunes look short and simple. Besides, in the messy house I have unpacked an empty notebook like this one, the future Journal, and so I can talk freely now, carelessly, complaining if I wish—it will soon be over, this bad period, and certainly for the new Journal I will find strange happenings and my old enthusiasm.

November 4. Two and a half yards by two and a half yards of space—my writing room for the winter—with heat, a little bit of disorder yet, books on the floor. Mother, in her bedroom, cross and domineering in crises. Lola and Paula, in the kitchen preparing lunch. Banquo, the police dog, keeping guard, barking at innocent schoolchildren. My "cave à bois" [wood cellar] is my pet accomplishment. It's funny how I like to pick up wood and make fagots. Probably because it does not require any brains. So I have neatly and Frenchily piled up logs and fagots in the cave à bois, after cleaning them of all the imaginable dirt. The garden, too, is in my care. I have done unbelievable things. I am tired, healthy, coming out on top again. As soon as I produce the red watch light, the Florentine coffer, a few books, my soul comes to life again. Hugh, too, begins to live. For him also "creation" of a home is only complete when it satisfies visually. We sleep soundly. He works hard on weekends, chops wood, attends to the furnace. At the same time we appear at a formal dinner, the first winter dive into social life. And as usual I wish I had no friends—at least no friends who can ask: "What dresses are you having made this winter?" "Don't you find yourself getting careless and frumpy in the country?" "Why do you live so far away?" "Are you writing? Well, why don't you dance?" Or if you say you are dancing they say, "Why don't you write?"

This is an "introduction" to my work. I expect to begin this afternoon, having gardened enough for the morning. It is also, to be frank, an evasion. It is hard to sit down directly and write. Especially when I have been so utterly "abrutie" [stupefied] by work that the flow of thought comes rushing back incoherently and wildly, almost painfully, and certainly awkwardly.

I'm always so glad when I have exercised my own faculties. For example, I asserted in my article on "Stylization in Decoration" that there should be a transitional style. Then I found an article in *Studio* magazine that speaks of the "intermediate" style. Also I said I thought we should not discard the old accents, as I did in my homes. Then I read Emily Post, who says, "Modern style will not be satisfactory until it makes a place for prized possessions." In each case the idea was better exposed by the others, but I must certainly have gained by reaching them through my own mental progression. I now believe a child should be taught to build his own world from the very beginning, to use his eyes, hands, senses, imagination, and inventiveness. It is bad to rely too much on the knowledge of others, to lean on books of reference.

November 7. I met Eduardo unexpectedly. Hugh brought him to have tea with us after some of my shopping. No feeling. A stranger. No power whatever over me. What have I learned in this extraordinary month? To bristle up against sensibility like a porcupine—to bristle with activity, intellectuality, creation so nobody can touch me without hurting himself. I, secure, busy and mocking—and Eduardo, puzzled and annoyed. No man now who wants to play the idiotic man-and-woman game with me—you yield, I tyrannize; you tyrannize and I am subjugated; you run away, I hunt; you hunt and I run away—will ever get any affection from me. There are big men who don't play those games, like Hugh, who has an inviolable pride, and big men will be all I ask for. Funny revolutionary song for such a woman as I am—but the real truth is that in that way, I am not woman. If I excel in concealing my strength, I also do not love the men I must conceal my strength from. Finis —until tomorrow, when I may find new wisdom while gathering twigs in the garden for our winter fires.

Mother's intolerable crossness when she is tired, her veritable illness I call "contraditis," a perpetual, willful, contradiction of everything, has at last worn down Hugh's own patience. What a cross my mother has been to me. And my father. Mother's love of "scenes" has almost made me weak through reacting. Our constant bickering is terrible and so destructive, petty, and ugly.

We have to take care of Banquo's infected wound and struggled to steel ourselves to it. Banquo, too, is terribly lovable and pathetic. Affection for the two dogs is already strongly rooted. I drop my decorative manners and costumes to rough it—bathing Ruby, bandaging Banquo, putting coal in the furnace, climbing a ladder to clip some high geraniums at the entrance. And I feel a growing love of rough work in the open, particularly of gardening —although always there is an equally natural love of artificial, luxurious, dainty living and spared hands—for you should see my hands and nails. How can one be useful and beautiful? The courtesans knew one couldn't be both. But I am going to try it.

"God for him, and God in him for her." Half the women in the world are mental cripples, or clinging vines or a stone around a man's neck because they think God is only in man. But the women who find God in themselves have a world of their own, hang on nobody's neck, and do not take iodine when nobody loves them. They are called egotists.

To have the poetical temperament is to have inside of you a kind of perpetual singing. Whether sad or gay the response is a song, a humming, a rhythm, a sweeping and rolling and rushing force.

November 13. The editor of the *Canadian Forum* sends me a congratulatory letter, and Eduardo says he has found his "match" in me—which means simply that when we returned to our analysis of our poor emotions he found me his equal in strength! He was so surprised to find out that I could say to him, "You can go to hell." I did not say it to him; I said it to my Journal, but the result for me was identical. So I told Eduardo to go to hell. And immediately, as in a fairy tale, I shot upward two yards or so in height and strength. So today he bruised himself against my indifference and was elated, enthusiastic over the new woman who frees him, a woman without emotion. Wonderful, my dear. He has got what he wants, but as usual what he wants is less rich than what I might have wanted in his place. Isn't it always so?

"I would never give you what you asked—never surrender my world," I said to him.

"I could make you a submissive, docile woman only if I married you."

"Oh, no, you couldn't."

And I felt so elated, standing there at the station while the train grumbled past us—elated at a *game*, a rather eternal and stupid game full of intelligent and colorful nuances, elated as one gets at any game, games of the body and of the mind.

"Our relationship," says Eduardo, "will be like Lawrence's

and Katherine Mansfield's. He must have enjoyed her manner of thinking, her whimsicality, and her stories." (Must have. We do not know. Middleton Murry gave us her journal full of blanks about Lawrence.) So Eduardo thinks Katherine probably loved Lawrence, while Lawrence was attracted to Murry—and, I thought to myself, you think I love you. But before our day together was over I had made it plain to him that I did not love him. Since when? Since he showed such sadistic impulses when we painted the little room, since he tried to destroy my mind's world simply for the sake of destruction, because he knew well that even if he destroyed my mind, I could never be the "primitive peasant" woman he requires. At that I balked, and at his vanity, for he was so sure, so content that my unwanted emotion would last forever.

Meanwhile, Hugh is in Biarritz for two days. Eduardo is here as a "protector." The salon is painted. The work goes on. Banquo is almost well. Eduardo cleans up the garden. At eight o'clock I yawn desperately, even though he is reading Lawrence's poems.

November 14. In the train, going to Paris—I, to an engagement; Eduardo, home—he suddenly melts and says, "I have never felt so physically attracted to you as I do at this very moment." I smiled. It did not move me at all. It scarcely interested me. He had given me time to become lucid. The man who gives me time to think is lost. And I am saved.

I despise their game and yet I am playing the game, for all this is outside of reality, my real love for Hugh and my real self. But in the center stands Hugh forever, beautifully fixed, the object around which my madnesses and my dreams and my experiments circle wildly without ever destroying the pivot. Yes, it can all be explained, philosophically, psychologically. Yet it is curious that none of the explanations really satisfy me, and that I wish secretly that I were different and not quite so elastic and supple and in flux. The pain of seeing myself as I am today is far keener and more poisonous than my youthful and stupid despair. At the same time, there is a diabolically clear urging of the intelligence not to fear and evade evil, as if there were ultimate wisdom only in ultimate living, absolute truth only in absolute evil, as if balance can exist only when the two platters are full—as Blake says, with both "heaven and hell." And so I pile high my heaven and hell. And the intricate weighing maddens me. I hate the old, superstitious, infantile fear of losing my heaven through my hell, of being made to pay for my Johns and Eduardos and other phantoms—for such are the things we are taught as a child so as to be kept from absolute livingness and absolute truth; because absolute truth is a product of *pure intelligence*, and it leads to a religion where the body and other personal possessions lose all their value, a place where hell is interesting and heaven neutral and negative.

Often I have taken Hugh into my hell and decided to live there permanently, and he has liked the sharp savor of it. But much oftener I have gone there alone, because Hugh must not be worried, because Mother is fifty-nine and must have peace, because Joaquin has work to do. And coming back I have looked at myself in the mirror and hated my face.

Not always. Today I decided to bear the dissatisfaction, too, the self-criticism and the self-condemnation—not through tolerance, but because I have ceased to care about *myself*. Not worth bothering about. Let it wriggle—and work. The wriggling is good for the work. I don't even try to give myself a harmonious philosophy, or seek to satisfy my desires. Need friends? Need passion? Need brilliance? What of it? Go to work. In that, you are good, and in that alone. In that, you can redeem your sophistry, your fallacious impulses, your emotional inflammability, your little spiteful, sharp, jealous sensibilities.

November 24. I wrote down today the story I had in mind about another mystical adventure, on a boat, and temporarily called "Circles." It ends with the phrase "I have been wasting time," which can serve as a title to this volume. With this story begins my real work again.

It is raining. I am knotted up with neuritis and in pain. The house is nearly comfortable.

Eduardo writes that on his last visit I deprived him of his catlike equanimity—and asks for an appointment.

How Hugh and I enjoyed chucking a reception at the Godoys yesterday and going off to the movies.

Reading the last number of *transition* has been tremendous for me. I read all these things after I have done my work and then find an affinity with modernism which elates me. If now I am more conscious of my modernism, at least my work remains *natural*, because modernism came to me through vision and is not, as Gilbert suspected, an acquired tendency.

November 26. Chucking other invitations, to Verneuil's reading of poems, Marie André's recital, etc., etc. I say to myself as a justification: I am not going to waste time this winter.

Dancing again. It has lost its power over me. Why? Because I realize that the essence of my dancing experience was dissatisfaction. Unless carried to extreme artistic development, it remains a superficial thing, a hollow thing. The pleasures I remember are mostly of contented vanity and physical expansion. Somehow or other I have outgrown these things, just as I have truly outgrown personal jealousies and sensitiveness. Yes, I can truthfully say that I now do not require to be the star of every salon and center of attraction in gatherings. I feel curiously detached and measure the full unimportance of these values, particularly of people's opinion —precisely because these opinions have been flattering and *inexact* and thoroughly beside the point in my case. I am coming back to my youthful feeling, the true instinct I had of not even wanting my writing to be read too much or commented on. Coming back to secrecy. Because I am now so dreadfully sure that people in general lie to you through ignorance and sentimentality.

Hugh says, sitting at last comfortably in our cozy petit salon: "You *have* made me another beautiful house—even lovelier. . . ."

I want to weave all my stories together like a Proustian épopée [epic]. I am always haunted by the same characters, so let them return ever and ever again all through my writing—and all that I write will stand together as my own world. For the two years that I have not seen John I have continually returned to his significance and value, as if each day I wanted to add to my understanding, as if I could never be satisfied with a final description. And also when the truth ends, or, rather, when I have set down all I know of the truth, then the invention begins, the deformation, the seed of John grown into multiple impersonations, all kinds of Johns living out his own ideas as he may never do. A strange and profound distortion of one truth to arrive at other truths.

Evening. Wrote another queer story, also with a bus in it like "Tishnar," temporarily called "Truths." I'm working!

November 28. At last I have fixed my writing room as I like it: desk before the window, low divan, portraits of Lawrence, Joaquin, Hugh, Eduardo, and John. Here I rest, too, when I come in from the garden, rather muddy.

I feel that whatever strength I give the house, the house gives me back at such moments—when the beauty and softness of it lulls me, when I enjoy a fire or sitting on the rug or at my now ample, tidy, comfortable desk or eating in the incredibly exotic dining room or smoking with Hugh in the petit salon before the mosaic fireplace.

Discouraged over nonsalable qualities of my writing. No word from Jones.

My clean horizon, without even a speck of a friend in the distance is admirably suited to my mood—or perhaps I have suited my mood to the horizon without friends. I suspect I often do that. I don't want to know anybody now until my writing is read and people come to me on a basis of true understanding.

December 1. Eduardo says about the boat story, now called "A Waste of Timelessness," "I like your manner of not overdeveloping, of indicating and suggesting, so that you get the reader's imagination creating. You make me think of Gide. I can read him over and over again because so much is left to my own development, whereas Lawrence, in spite of my devotion to him, I cannot read more than once on account of his way of saying everything that can possibly be said or felt to the very limit of the imagination."

He really loved and understood the story. Hugh is apt to overemphasize the development idea—always demands that I should say more, and I can't. The story came out in a first writing almost impossible to alter; each phrase simply could not be written in any other way. I had very few corrections to make.

December 2. Boussie came today and found "Waste of Timelessness" so good, and laughed so much at it that she offered to translate it! What a pleasure for me when I know she takes nothing that she does not like and that she does translating after my own heart with such a keen, nuanced mind.

Then Hugh comes home and says: "You ought to rewrite that last part—it isn't clear enough. What exactly did you mean here, for instance?" Talking and discussing—I, defending my final phrases—we really became quite sharp. Hugh went out for a walk alone, and I came up to my writing room and made a typewritten copy for the *Adelphi.* Then Hugh came back and we went to bed, and naturally in bed we were reconciled by the strength of our physical love.

During the whole evening there was already running through my head the idea for the Great Writer story. Before going to sleep I wanted to tell Hugh about it, but somehow, in the middle of our solemn and dramatic reconciliation, it seemed irrelevant to say: "I have an idea for another story." So I did not say anything, and I wrote it this morning. How terribly, terribly difficult to know when I am wrong and when I am right. Was I annoyed last night because Hugh was wrong or because he criticized? Boussie and Eduardo were perfectly satisfied. Whom should I believe? What do I myself think? But then I may be wrong, I may be too self-satisfied. Veritable torment. I do want to make progress. I know Hugh is sometimes right, but I know of one time, a most important time, when he was utterly mistaken. May I succeed in keeping lucid, may I be a true self-critic, may I not be deceived by the satisfaction of others, may I not ever be a damn fool.

December 4. The Great Writer story—called "Alchemy"—is good; I am satisfied with it. I rewrote it today and mailed it to Mencken (what nerve!), saying: "I would rather be damned by you than praised by anybody else." I also mailed the "Waste of Timelessness" to the *Adelphi*. Titus introduces me to Mr. Cole, the man who will edit my essay. "Here is a young woman whose work has a *unique* quality. I intend to publish it. . . ." I listen to the word "unique" with turmoil. Mr. Cole is a graduate of Woodbury, of Columbia, and knows Erskine.

The wrathful finger of the Academic has at last caught me, and it must be a judgment of offended literary heavens: Thou shalt have a Columbia man in thy work (I had escaped poor Richard and others). Anyway, tomorrow we edit. Then I heard Titus was interested in the stage.

I got up this morning and wrote an entire play, *Multiple Lives*, which had been on my mind—first as a story, then as a play —about a week ago. It now needs padding. My back is broken, and I'm nearly blind. Janet Flanner, of *The New Yorker*, and of the publishing firm Warren and Brewer, returns my whole book of stories *without even wanting to take a look at my face*, because publishers aren't interested in books of short stories. And that did hurt me. I mean about the meeting. If I were to read my own stories as though written by someone else, I would at least have felt: I wonder what kind of a head this guy has. Maybe she didn't read them.

I've been very slangy today. It is very invigorating.

December 10. Mr. Robert Cole says: "Your work has impressed me so much—there is so very little I can do. You are a genuine artist. I can only point out a few weaknesses which you yourself will work out of. But let me tell you first of all that there is no trace of the foreigner in it. You have penetrated English feeling as you have penetrated the meaning of the words. 'The Woman No Man Could Hold' was so close to my own personal experience that I could hardly read it impersonally enough to criticize it. I had to read it twice. 'Tishnar' is simply perfect. I can only point out an overuse of adjectives, an occasional overstatement, and sometimes a lack of flow and continuity, which is hard on slow minds which cannot leap as you do. I think you have done more than Lawrence in your attitude toward sex. I admire him but I find him unbalanced—" And so on. And as we talked he crossed out a few adjectives. In between, or, I should say, most of the time, he talked about his experiences, evidently stimulated by my story—and of how *alive* my work was, and how I was not the usual iconoclast but one wholly taken up with *creation*, pure creation. Even though he deviated from the true meaning of my stories, I could not help but be touched and grateful. He, the man who was meant to "edit" my work, turned into an admirer. He had seen few young writers for whom he felt as much sympathy, etc., etc.

Hugh and I had an excited lunch together. This would do me so much good with Titus.

With the excitement of this unexpected encouragement, I took the book rejected by Janet Flanner to Sylvia Beach, to whom I made an atrocious speech of self-introduction. Then I came home and found the *Adelphi* had rejected "Waste of Timelessness."

December 11. A long talk and work with Mr. Cole. Occasionally he would have me replace one word by another. When I think him right, I agree. When I don't, I argue. He is half amused, half piqued. The essay is done and he has looked over the "Woman." I cannot endure this very long, so I will work like the devil so as not to need it. From there to Boussie, who reads me her translation of "Waste of Timelessness" and who says some parts make her think of Waldo Frank—a big compliment.

What a translation! So perfect it seems like another story to me and for the first time makes me feel sad about my having lost my French. How much more pointed and sharp! ("Pointed" would be sufficient—why two adjectives?)

The more I work *into* my writing the less I care about exteriorization, the less I care about Arabian beds, turquoise ceilings, and dancing. Writing is like digging into a tunnel, into darkness, to find the unearthly phosphorescence of minerals and other abstractions of reality. With the unwarm glow of these I am satisfied. When I come out of my tunnel I am blinded by crude daylight, and also speechless (so that is why I cannot talk to Titus).

Hugh says: what a funny, pixie way of writing you have—so quick and changeful and unexpected.

No, my play is not so good. I create callous women because I myself am too soft—reaction, always reaction. If I were not so soft I would not achieve intellectual callousness. If I were callous I would probably write mincingly. If I were neither I would not write; I would sit in a café and watch others come and go by the hour. Because I am both soft and callous I write. I sit in a café and worry about my callous woman and my own distressing softness. People come and go but I don't notice them because I am writing. I do not need to look at them. I need only to write, for when I have finished writing and lift my head I will see in their faces that I am right about them, simply because I am so right about myself.

I am an island now.

I often imagine meeting John in the street, flushed, contented, epicurean, hearty, big, too big, too funny, too brutal, and of my feeling perky and saying: "I am an island now."

I am an island on which nobody can land. Nobody will ever again be allowed to crunch the soft sand, to leave imprints of big confident feet, to write on the sand other women's names with the tip of a wand, to leave the mold of a body where the body has lain.

December 12. Last night the neuritis grabbed me again. I was writing in bed. What I most hate about the infernal pain is that it prevents me from writing. I cannot bow my head, my neck is paralyzed, and my arm hurts so. I need help to sit up. In desperation I got up and sat at my desk as if nothing were wrong. After a while my head *would* bow, and I did write, but then I couldn't straighten up again. I shall keep the writing pose!

Proust's work was a "journal intime," a journal of memories. Mine is a journal of consciousness. Isn't it strange that my fiction should be intuitive and unconscious?

I am convinced now that more writing is intuitive than we know—even John's intellectual pranks. That is why I found John, in actuality, lacking in imagination and understanding, though both these qualities predominate in his work. Also what he writes in certain moments of lucidity he forgets afterward. A writer forgetting what he has written is not at all unusual. So John comes to his moments of living like an ordinary man, divested of genius. The question is: If a man of genius shows no genius in a moment of living, can he still afterward remember the moment, re-create it and see it with genius? Take the moment in which John might have perceived me wholly and accurately. At that moment he was obtuse and awkward. Could there come another moment when he could understand, perhaps even write what the moment signified? Such a moment, I suppose, I had expected. I had imagined that John and I were going to create an astounding interplay of literary-creative affection. I had expected a live correspondence. No more than that, I swear, for I had foregone all physical claims the very day I might have been led to believe I *could* make such claims. I knew too well at the moment, so wisely well, that his impulse was a whim not particularly concerned with *me*. Of course, if he thought me young, if he thought me immature, as I think Eduardo today, if he confused me with other young women who were attracted to him, if he felt no sympathy with my mind—then his stupid letters are understandable. I cannot let the story rest, because it is John himself who has remained unexplained. I think what I have most suffered from is his indifference to my mind.

December 16. Eduardo came for the weekend, unexpectedly. He was in an intellectual mood. He read us from Jung, talked to me two hours Sunday morning. Hugh got tired and went out to the garden. Eduardo and I spent the afternoon in the little writing room, absorbed in talk. I read him my play. When it was dark he went home. I went to bed almost ill with nervous fatigue. The burden of his confidences—he is running after another woman—was heavy, but I took great delight in his ideas.

By the end of our talk we had reached something like this, crudely speaking: There is mysticism and there are our instincts. Instincts would be fundamentally good if we lived alone on an island. But in society it is like spreading out your elbows suddenly; you always stab a neighbor. "Society" is a word I can't stand, because it implies the crowd I see in the Métro, but society, I suddenly realized, is the person I hit with my elbow—Hugh or Joaquin or Mother or John. So I took the word "society" seriously from then on, and we went on with our talk. Our instincts hurt or destroy society. For society, we crucify our instincts. We enter the realm of religious, or nonreligious, mysticism.

So far so good. It all looked very pat. We sighed with relief. All would have been perfect if we had not remembered the exceptional man, the creator, who would not crucify his instincts and who ended up by giving society far more than ordinary comfort, who gave society divine truths: Lawrence. We were all muddled again. And remained so.

"But why," I asked, "must you get your philosophy all pat?"

"I cannot live or work if I do not have a pat philosophy."

"Well, how is it I live and work without any philosophy?"

"I couldn't do it," said Eduardo.

I thought of how often I had gotten my philosophy all pat and neat and dovetailed and then destroyed it in two minutes of living. (A kiss can destroy a philosophy.)

I am going to work and to love. I am going to keep my elbows in. I am going to create. My philosophy will come out of it all, by and by. It will not be planted from a seed nurtured by Jung or Spengler or Bergsen—but will grow with *me*, out of my defects and my shame and my madnesses, and it will make room for a kiss, now and then.

December 18. Out comes a story—"The Curse of Peacock Feathers." I can never rest. It is so much like carrying a child—no rest until the child is delivered. Hugh says: "What a capacity for work you have!"

This morning three hours of steady writing resulted in the first draft of the sequel to "Woman No Man Could Hold." It is written in the same style and even more compressed, if possible. I am satisfied with its bird's-eye view of things, usually obscure and spread out. I feel it is better than the "Woman." It does not matter if it hovers between Lawrence and Gide, so that neither Lawrencians nor Gideans can feel sympathy for it, so that nobody will understand it. I have satisfied the demands of my own mind.

Evening. Hugh likes the story. There are phrases in it that struck him: "The body has a wisdom of its own, as the mind has a wisdom of its own." And again I feel that I have described the "Artist" well. There is also a description of a kiss which I love.

(Ruby has his nose on what I write. I am sitting on what he considers his pillow, next to the fire, so he has climbed on my knees and is sniffing literature. Ruby, literature has no smell. It's the ink and the blotting paper and the leather.)

December 19. Look, John has come through! He has been generous, and he does love ideas above himself. Hugh sent him the Lawrence essay, so he writes Hugh: "It was good of you to send me Anaïs's article which came in due time, and I read it with the greatest delight. I needn't tell you how beautifully it is written nor how penetrating the criticism is—her acuteness of observation both in books and in life is really quite extraordinary. I reflect how terrible a person she must be to live with! Don't you feel thoroughly analyzed? I think also, what has often occurred to me before, that when she gets to the point of writing a straight novel, she will do something quite extraordinary. I am sure she is storing up quantities of worth-while material."

Then he writes to me: "I have just been telling Hugh how much I liked your essay on D. H. Lawrence and asked him why in the world you don't sign your own name to such fine writing! It really is first rate—unusually penetrating and subtle." Up to here it might have been written out of sheer courtesy. But then he takes a real interest in the matter and gives a fine idea. "I liked particularly what you said of *Lady Chatterley's Lover.* It is one of those books that most people will think quite fleshly, but some of us will think unusually spiritual. I was struck by one thing in it, the immense craving on the part of the two chief characters to get out of the formalism of their life and realize their souls. In the 13th century that attempt would have been made in a reaching towards religion: in this book it is made through the practice of sex. Some psychologists would of course think there is not such a profound difference, but I think there is a difference, and an interesting one. But you notice that only once in the whole book the church and the English landscape was mentioned, and then only architecturally. When you consider what the English life is like, it is extraordinary to me that Lawrence diverted his attention so entirely from that aspect of its society. I am hoping that the diary continues and that it is going to be turned into a novel before long. I am backing you as a real modern novelist. . . .

"P.S. Anna says, give you her love and tell you you owe her a letter. I won't tell her how long her father has owed this letter."

John as a "great man" is saved. As a friend he is deader than ever, for, after all, he wrote me because he had to, according to his cult of formalities and courtesies, whereas he did not write me when he did not have to, which is friendship. And so here goes John back on the library shelves, John the writer.

Worked most of the day on extracting from my Journal "Eduardo's story," which interests me deeply as an act of truth: I do not think women either talk or write about such love as his—it is too inglorious. Why I had to work on this immediately, I don't know. I had to. Besides, I have to let the play and the sequel lie still so that I may see them with fresh eyes.

I'm in a big black mood, probably because I am all tied up with extreme neuritis. How can one be at once so miserable and so happy? The writing is a source of true ecstasy. Thank God for the stock-market crash, which has given me Louveciennes and this incredible silence, in which I can work as if the world did not exist.

John still torments me, because I have come to believe that by constant stretching of my elastic imagination I have magnified the entire story, and that perhaps his casual attitude is more logical and natural than my intensity. I no longer understand anything, from thinking too much about it. It would appear from his attitude that everything is normal—the scarce, formal letters, the blanks in between, the lack of even intellectual connection, the long years without meeting. Is it simple egoism? Is it a cure for the benefit of my youthful exultation? Is it a casualness normal among men and women? He may come in July. What does he expect? A frank, natural, confident, friendly manner—*as if nothing* . . . Did we just bump accidentally for one mad hour—which he wants to forget and which I alone remember? I cannot be different. Something keeps me from sending him my stories, from writing. I did not answer his last letter, and he thinks he owes me one. He has forgotten that he wrote me about Graham.

I imagine him arriving in July. I don't know why I see us in the garden. I imagine him *novelistically* curious about me—my saying nothing. Probably all I did say before, he did not understand, or accepted as the confession of the woman to the priest-novelist. Was I a "case"? How acute and blind one can be at the same time. I have gone blind from looking at John so much. I cannot believe that from beginning to end I have been dreaming—dreaming all that I have woven around that hour. Yes, I think I have. I see it now so clearly. John would be so surprised if he knew. It is not John's fault that he stirred my imagination, that I added, invented, expected, remembered. . . . An incidental little hour—a grain of sand—out of which I built a world. Let me not blame those whose words or acts can start me on an infinite journey—for I am a dream swallower, and I poison myself. Why is it nothing in the world has yet equaled in savor his kiss? Is it merely because I have a palate for rare, erratic impulses? And would not familiarity have destroyed that savor?

December 20. I made up Elvira's face today for her appearance at the Vieux Colombier. All the excitement of dressing, of the dancing itself left me peculiarly cold. I would have liked to dance, yes, but I did not want the closeness to the public, the dependence on it, the courting of it. I am not made for public life. I take a secret joy in my independence, in my solitude, in the true value of my mind's work.

It struck me just now that this is what Hugh said of John this morning: "He is a public figure, and he likes to be a public figure." Now I remember his love of presiding at banquets, of speaking, his love of public appearances. And I remember his ambition, at the time surprising to me, of being an ambassador to France. He enjoys all this outward living, he enjoys his "fame," flattery of the most unsubtle kind—so many false values! How different we are! Then what links us? I have disliked his "Americanism," his gargantuan comic moods, his epicureanism, his *puritan* enjoyment of immorality—and at the same time I remember liking other things so well. . . .

There were three distinct moments: one, when he was reading us one of his fairy tales late at night after dinner, and he looked so very tired, almost old, burned up—and he seemed like a giant temporarily conquered by white-heat living; the second, the same evening when he sat on our balcony and was all *yearning*; the third, the morning he came to say good-bye—and I saw him at the last, standing by the little window of the salon, looking more serious than I had ever seen him look. Yes, of course, another John, not the big, brilliant public figure. But however often I place my image over the image of the public figure, the public figure seems to outlive it, to remain aggressive, permanent, ineffaceable.

For his body's lack of courage—his body just *would* not, *could* not escape the formalism of his life—I have pity. For the man who can enjoy the formalism of public life, I have no sympathy.

For my own clinging to a nonexistent connection, I have

nothing but disgust. As in my story: "The mind awoke and murmured: 'two strangers, two strangers who have reached by a kiss something more than life.' "

December 22. Hugh says: "Send John the rest of your work." So I had to explain that John was not a close enough friend for me to want to owe him for criticism or any help whatever. Hugh understood.

I was, last night, in a mood of realization: Hugh's wonderful way of keeping up in spite of the Bank (he is reading *transition*), his quick understanding of the ideas I have so much time to develop, his constantly elastic tolerance and selflessness. He says he is both husband to me as a woman and as a writer and that he wants to be both completely. For the love of the writer the husband of the woman endures many things. He can be so impersonal, so artistic in his judgment. Whatever I read him he always judges as a creation separate from me. There is no smallness in him, no egoism, no vanity. Sometimes the expression of all these feelings and attitudes is so quiet, so unobtrusive that I hardly notice it. It is always there, like part of the air I breathe, and it is difficult to fully realize it. If I were deprived of his body, of his tenderness, of his mind, I could not live.

Evening: One day when Eduardo was reading me from *Pansies and Nettles* [D. H. Lawrence] I said to him: "Someday I'm going to write an answer to all that." Last night I read *Pansies* all through. This morning when I finished writing in my Journal I began to write casually and carelessly, Nettle for Nettle. Hugh was ill in bed. I had lunch by his side and thought of other nettles. I had to take the train to Paris, and I wrote still other nettles in the train and one in the Métro. When I came home I had, in all, twelve nettles, of which three were bad ones. And I was happy, happy, happy. I cheered Hugh up, I sang, I put coal in the furnace, I cuddled Ruby, I played with Banquo, feeling blissful, although the day was cold, although Sylvia Beach told me for the fifth time she had no time to read my stuff, although I went to see Boussie and she was not home, although I missed the 3:39 train home and had to wait three-quarters of an hour in the damp station, although we haven't a cent for Christmas.

Lawrence is my best-loved friend. I felt it more so today, addressing myself to him in a chiding, teasing manner, so intimate and so much in his own tone. For the first time I felt really cured of John. And when I realized how much I owed Lawrence I wondered why I had not before transferred all my love to him.

December 26. These days have been poisoned and embittered by Mother's tyranny and contrariness and irrationalism. She makes a battlefield out of our home; her attitude toward servants is so petty and so terrible that it brings to the foreground the entire mechanics of the house, which ought to be in the background.

I realized that I cannot live with my mother any better than Father could. I come to my creative work harassed by the petty subjects I most despise. Finally Hugh realized the injustice of it all and interfered.

I, who love peace! To have this emotional, uncontrollable, ill-tempered force always loose in the house—it is like a madness. I have fought it, I have tried all remedies. There is only one solution: separation—as much as possible. . . .

In all this was sunk the pleasure we had from Joaquin's triumphant concert in Madrid. He had worked terribly hard, and made a brilliant beginning, as an artist and as a man.

Holidays—separation of the family, because of Mother, so that we each spent Christmas night in our own way. Gifts very few, exchanged without true feeling. Inside of Mother there may be a soft kernel—but her battle armor is invulnerable. At last, on Xmas Day we all go to the theatre together, a lamentable attempt at unity.

I think of other things. The tremendous, immeasurable importance of *transition* for me. This was the island I had been steadily sailing to—dreaming of—but I was not so very certain of its existence. I thought I would have to build it up alone. No. Here is my group, my ideas, my feelings against banal forms. I am glad I found it after I had made my own dreams, because now I come to it very strong, open to influences but with discrimination. I read three numbers with elation. I am trying to get others. And it may continue to be published—it will go on! Now I read Jung, [Eugene] Jolas,[1] like a famished man; here are the minds I love, here are the ideas I have obscurely, vaguely felt. I know now what my instincts were leading me into, why I grimaced at "novels," at *Harper's* poetry, at John's trite characters, at "realistic" stories, why I loathed the "Slippery Floor" as soon as I

---

[1] *American poet and editor of* transition.

had written it. Here at last is depth as I understand it, vision and intellect working in unity. Lawrence and *transition*. What a year for me!

After a strict abstention for the sake of economy we allowed ourselves a few theatre shows for Christmas. What a surprise to see Josephine Baker—the *aristocrat*, finely carved, supple, de belle race—nervous and soft at once, with a sense of tragedy, too. Surprising, because people talked of her as a low savage. She is a very definite personality, self-contained, natural, giving an impression of beauty and brilliance. I can only reproach her for not *dancing* enough and compromising too much with the "music hall" expectations—wearing feathers, mere hopping and parading. What was most distinctive about Josephine Baker was her walk and the beauty of her legs.

In between, I've worked over the sequel. In great contrast to "Woman," the sequel will only need to be rewritten once and nothing cut out. I mean, it didn't take a book to make a story, as for "Woman," which shows I am progressing in my chosen form— or formlessness.

But Mother and I have not spoken to each other for two days. Hugh says that my vulnerability inspires sadism.

❧ *1 9 3 1* ☙

January 1. We have seriously discussed the matter of my taking a job. Hugh says if I do he will have nothing left to enjoy and live for; he says my writing has made up to him for the banking, has inspired him, and that it is I who keep the connection with the mental world he loves. It is, according to him, our only *real* riches. But meanwhile we are poor in every other way, and I cannot pay the bills for our last installation and I cannot save. I know my own physical limitations too well to plan a double career—writing and something else. I tried writing and dancing and it didn't work. In the *conventional* sense of the word I feel like a parasite because I do not earn money, even though Hugh may think I do hold up my own end. It's a hellish problem, and I have thoroughly sifted it today. I have made no decision. The jobs I like would hardly pay (helping Sylvia Beach or Titus or Jolas); the jobs I half like I cannot do because of the Bank: modeling or posing. Teaching dancing is strenuous. Could I write too? It is now an accepted fact that I write unsalable stuff.

Mother and I made up New Year's Eve; we are trying hard to live at peace.

I now am adept at chopping wood of the slender variety. Trees I respect. Hugh and I work in the garden a lot and enjoy being muddy. At the same time I read murky Freud, for the first time. What a mind! His "cases" fascinate me, and I like his tremendous truthfulness, and feel he is right, most of the time. But I could not read him if I did not know that at the end of Freud I could find Jung. Nothing that Freud said *surprised* me; I mean that the accuracy of his science is too obvious; but the precocity of the problems does astonish me. At four or five years of age our destiny begins to shape itself—an accident, a dream, a scene, the nature of others, all can be the cause of a lifelong deviation. The mind is already a deep subterranean world full of phantoms, obsessions, dreams, desires. I must read more of Freud, but I already feel that he has not studied enough of the transposition, sublimation, transfiguration of our physical and mental elements. Forcibly, being a doctor, he would seek to point out where and how such elements destroy us, and how, through knowledge, we can master them; but *how the artist uses them* is another aspect, which Jung magnifies as it should be magnified. In other words, *consciousness* and *knowledge* of our phantom world, of our neurotic instincts, is perhaps not sufficient for the cure, as it seems to me it has not been sufficient for Eduardo, who is more or less *obsessed* with what he knows about himself rather than urged to an energetic application of consciousness to living.

I believe now in the intensification of our personal experience to the point of overflow into the universal—the impersonal experience. It all amounts to a *degree* of intensity. A rich personal intensity breaks its own shell and its own obsessions—and touches the mystic whole.

Conversation—Hugh, Me—in the dark, when we should already have been asleep.

He: "Freud talks about a kind of mind which is not 'all there.'"

"I think that is the peculiarity of your mind. It has taken me seven years to understand it. You are rarely 'all there.'

Before, I used to think it was sheer vagueness and passivity, but now I know where your mind goes."

"Where?" said Hugh anxiously.

"Mostly to Jolas's world of dreams. In fact, you are there most of the time, in a kind of poetic penumbra. It used to be terrible for me. It was in fact, darling, what really drove me to seek friends. Observe that Gustavo's and John's chief characteristic of mind was their 'all-thereness,' brilliancy, immediate response."

"I think you are putting a nice interpretation on mere vagueness."

"No, now I am sure I have understood your mind. I realize that if it was possible for you to understand Jung and Jolas at one bound, as you did, without consecutive reading or time to familiarize yourself, it was because you had lived in such thoughts yourself all along. It *seemed* like vagueness, and it seemed like passivity, but it was the inarticulateness of excessive poetic abstractions. That is why also you cannot turn from banking to writing. If it were ordinary, realistic, literal writing such as John's you could do that all the time, but it is inspired writing, which requires slow meditation and concentration."

"You really believe that? It makes me terribly happy."

"The vision and perception of Gustavo and John have seemed crude and dense beside yours. I soon realized that 'all-thereness' and immediate response also inevitably produced a blindness in the *visionary* world. Your lucidity in the visionary world pro- duces a semblance of colorlessness and unresponsiveness in actual interchange of thoughts, which I now understand and love. I love you *better* now, darling. It has really taken me a long time to understand you fully."

"You make me terribly happy," said Hugh. "I wish I could believe you. But why are you visionary and at the same time *all there* and very *clear?*"

"Probably because I don't have to work in a bank and I have fewer problems than you have, less exercise of control and restraint in the direction of what I love—more opportunity for development—you poor Cat."

We went to sleep in each other's arms.

Before that, I had let him read "Eduardo's Story." He found it intensely interesting, was struck with the delicacy with which I indicated things, the curious mixture of sensuousness and spirituality. And he did say I had a unique manner of writing, a phrase I made him repeat because it gave me pleasure.

Ten A.M. Spent a half hour chopping wood, and then to my desk. But the mail brings me rejections from the *Adelphi* and the *American Mercury*, and for once I am truly distressed and discouraged, because *I know that my work is good* and I cannot understand why it does not sell.

The perpetual pain of craving is the source of the artist's work. Nothing would have distressed me more than to have really had John as a devoted and understanding friend, because I could not have written "Waste of Timelessness," in which Alain Roussel is the symbol of the unattainable. This insincerity sometimes disgusts me and sometimes appears to me as inevitable *artistic integrity*. Was it more important for me to write "Waste of Timelessness" or to have John as a friend?

January 5. A visit from Mr. Davies, of Brentano's, uncovered a pathetic life—but not an arresting mind. Simplicity, quietness, kindness—I don't know what urged him in my path. Then Eduardo called up as soon as he came from London, and here I breathe freely again. He reads the sequel to the "Woman" and likes it even better. I have not shown him his story, because we had no time to discuss it.

Besides, I am afraid of showing it to him. In my real self the story has remained more delicate and more emotional. In the artistic projection it has crystallized and hardened. Also, in writing it from the point of view of the woman, the logic of analysis brought it to an equation which was never formulated in my own mind. In other words, the story measures the incident, which I did not, and suggests a balance sheet—a conflict of strengths which has not developed between Eduardo and me because I appreciate him intensely as he is and there is no conflict; there is understanding. There is not even a shadow of reproach in either one of us. We do not love each other, but he admires me, and I admire him. He told Hugh I did not need psychoanalysis because I was *right*—I was in harmony with myself, proved by my work, and I was on the right track in everything, both in my work and in my life. On the other hand, I keenly enjoy his ideas, his dissertations, his actor's way of penetrating personages (Lawrence, Gide) and living absolutely in them for a while and then passing on to other passive absorptions.

In fact, Eduardo has done successfully what John might have done—transfer a fancy into appreciation, retaining the artist and rejecting the woman, shifting the devotion from one to the other with such delicacy (or was it by delicate silences?) that I can feel the vision in Eduardo, and only crude blindness in John.

I am making a tremendous effort to be fair to John's work, because I fear to be influenced by our personal estrangement. But even when I felt closest to him, I had begun to criticize *Uncle Sam*, and it was the manner in which he received this criticism that afterward came back to my memory when I was trying to fit all I knew together. I am defending his last book from a complaint, in a small article for the *Canadian Forum*.

January 9. Eduardo has evidently been quite struck with the sequel, the power and maturity of it. He tried yesterday by adroit questioning to find out if it had not been the outcome of my formidable denial of further experience. He discovered that I *had* been in such a mood all during the writing. Therefore I proved his idea that an artist must attain such renunciation to reach vision—that is, by annihilation of himself he enters paradise.

Well and good. (All this questioning was also a questioning of his own soul, his own experience, his own artistry.) But I protested that I could not have written the story he admired without the experience which preceded the renunciation. Eduardo was not put out.

A certain amount of experience with the body is necessary to awaken wisdom. But then experience must be discarded for the sake of concentrating strength on artistic work. In other words, he and I have had enough living with our five senses to possess wisdom, and now we can work. This "enough" puzzled and amused me. He had come to the same conclusion as I had, that a laughably small experience could be deepened and magnified by the poet and that the process had to be accompanied by a retrenchment of living.

Evening: Rewrote "Eduardo's Story" with a searching for the depths and softness I had left out in the second version (the first one was direct from the Journal) and finally found myself being *true* to my feeling about Eduardo—and I am satisfied. But there are two curious facts: having yet a *feeling* about the story, I cannot tell if it is good or bad; and I am convinced that I wrote it too soon—and why? I don't know. The ideas in it appealed to me; I could not keep away from them. And now I feel a malaise—a mixture of personal "pudeur," sentimentality, and self-disgust. Again why? I should have waited. But I can't stop writing. Now I have an idea for a kind of "essay in understanding" (of Hugh) which I think would be interesting. People think of understanding as a state of grace, whereas understanding is an adroitness of the mind reached by effort and self-development.

January 12. A nerve-racking weekend which has scattered all my concentration. Sociability kills me. We had friends in for tea Saturday. Eduardo came, too. Hugh and I had to dress up after that and rush to meet an American ménage [couple] (business duty), whom we were taking to the opera. We went to a cabaret, came home at five o'clock.

Mr. S. looked like John, had a voice and a mouth like John's— had a sense of the comic like his and the same brilliance allied to awkwardness with women.

When I first saw him, his presence was a shock to me. Immediately I knew that a division was taking place in me, a division between my mind and my body. My mind knew that here was an utter stranger, a man whose life, ideas, and every word meant nothing to me; my body was stirred by the resemblance to John, to a point of absolute submission. When I looked at his face I saw both the stranger I did not like and the power which held me. I knew he was nobody at all to me, but his presence elated me.

In the Russian cabaret we danced. I enjoyed throwing my head back, as I did when I danced with John. I was out of his ken, and he did not know how to talk to me. We did not understand each other at all. He was a man unconscious of his own physical expansiveness, as John had been. He did not know his own feelings. He had the potentialities of a big, sensual Jew— that is what I found arresting. I do not think he will ever know them unless a stronger experience should arouse him, and then he might remember that he was held by me in a strange state of attraction and bewilderment.

His slightest touch kept me afloat from reality and from will. Power emanated from him with such miraculous steadiness that I sat there for three hours and did not feel the time, or the boredom of our talk and its foolish disconnection. As long as I could hear his voice, I was quite lost, quite blind, quite outside of my own self.

I spent Sunday with my mind stretched out toward an understanding of Eduardo, who was telling me about his life. I had for a day given up trying to understand my own self, trying to mold myself to a philosophic pattern. It seemed to me that my imagination and feelings had expanded to limits no mind could calculate, as if I had taken drugs. Have I not said that drugs are not necessary for intensity of dreams? Did I not the previous night prolong a sensation I had thought lost to me? And if my body did not follow my imagination, if I did not surrender to Mr. S. physically as well as symbolically, it was only because our physical life is thus arranged, tidied by barriers, compressed within customs. But within myself it all happened, and I look down today on this terrible and portentous voyage and cannot help but be glad that my absence has destroyed nothing, that the place and people I come back to are unaffected by my absence, and that the only change is, as always, in the formation and boundaries of my abstract world, where truth and emotion are constantly shifting as if to maintain me in a constant state of flexibility—so that I may sit for four hours quietly listening to the overflow of Eduardo's strange wayward desires and conflicts; so that I may understand everything, accept, and be capable of turning simply to the problem of what can be done with the feelings that *are*.

The same understanding could be reached with the mind alone, but to understand with the feelings is to penetrate within the life of a person. I am afraid of trying to seem to justify myself, as if I felt the need of some point from which to judge. It would seem that I conclude that the only standard of measure of one's acts is the artistic, or to what creative use experience is applied, what discipline of mind follows an intrinsically selfish impulse. Although instincts may not at the moment be pure they may be transformed into wisdom. It is the transformation which is important. If we could use the standard of the artist we would not be far from the truth. The artist is the only one who transforms. Perhaps his life may be measured thus.

It would be a triumph to overcome futile instincts with the instinct of creation. But how impossible it is to determine values. I myself am a stubborn crucible. I may have too much confidence in my strength, too much faith in the wisdom of my body, too great a facility for turning weakness into strength, like a common juggler. And it may be a trick, a simple trick of the intelligence, so I can always appear to be right.

Evening. How strange I feel when I see Eduardo and Joaquin attracted to each other, and Eduardo tells me about it, and I see his love divided now between Joaquin and me; and when I know that one day he and Joaquin will lunch together and then Eduardo and I will spend an afternoon together and that cross-currents of feelings will pass through the three of us, back and forth. All the suggestions of my imagination seem incapable of assimilating those feelings; and I go off on solitary journeys to find my own divine integrity again.

January 13. In the middle of my mood came this letter from John: "Dear Anaïs: I've just received the lovely card from you and Hugh with the greeting to Lilith and me. Thank you, dear friend! The happiest of New Years to you and Hugh and all yours. I've thought of you much in one of the most troubled years I ever passed through, and thoughts of France and good friends there have been a solace. It is probable that I shall come over to Paris for a fortnight or so—I'm thinking of coming towards the end of March. In fact, I have my eye on the Paris sailing the 13th of March. I shall be in Europe again this summer but I'm rather tired at the moment and this would be a good rest. . . . The real reason of the trip is a letter from Pauline suggesting that I go away *alone* . . . get rested, think things over. . . . While there I want to go to Bordeaux to collect the honorary degree they voted me, and I want to see some of the Chateaux again, connected with the life of Diane de Poitiers. If I can persuade you and Hugh to come with me we'll get Charles and his car and spend a few days in that region. . . ."

I read the letter over again and made a decision: Hugh and I are not going with John to visit Chateaux. Of that I am certain. Of the reason I am yet unaware. Do I refuse ordinary events because I am denied the extraordinary ones? Does Pauline's sending John to Europe without Lilith rouse a chivalry in me? How would I have felt if John had decided to come of his own accord when he did not need a rest or to see Chateaux or to call for an honorary degree? Probably I might have made a fool of myself. The fact is that John is out of my ken because he does not know how to express his feelings, and he is unconscious of mine. So that we are bound to act at cross-purposes and to miss the truth in each other. I have learned to read the reversible language of Anglo-Saxons, who say "like" when they mean love and "pretty" when they mean beautiful, and whose enthusiasm is wooden. But even then I see in John's letter a pleasure, not an emotion; a feeling of escape, not a choice; and I have made up my mind not to be taken in by my imagination again.

So let John come. I'll be a good friend.

January 23. Last Friday I went to see Titus with the MS of "Woman." I happened to say that I had written a book about Lawrence—which was a Latin exaggeration. I meant that I had more than the essay—notes, and many ideas. His ears pricked up.

"Can you bring it tomorrow?"

I was caught.

I said it needed revision. Damn little liar. He had a publisher just starving for a book on Lawrence, and Mrs. Lawrence was not satisfied with what had been done. My essay was so good. . . .

"I'll come in two weeks," I said.

I went home. I was fearfully excited. I looked over the notes; there was nothing good—all to be discarded. Saturday morning between nine and twelve I wrote five thousand words. Sunday Eduardo came and we talked. He gave me many ideas and some fine help. We talked and read *Twilight in Italy* until I was almost ill.

Monday I began to sit at my desk between nine and twelve or one, and between two-thirty and seven—every day—until tonight.

It had to be worthy of Lawrence. I slept with a feeling of carrying a hard diamond inside of my head.

It is more or less *done*—22,500 words—needs revising, a few details, but the big, important things are in. I cannot believe it. Throughout, I have been astonishingly sure and confident. Lawrence, Lawrence. My God, it has meant more to me to explain him than to do my own creation. The more I read him the more I found in him. Any other author read as I have read Lawrence would have sickened me. The diamond hardness is still there. Now I must rest and get my distance.

Eduardo swims in a maze of indecisions. He understands Lawrence but he cannot make determinate statements, stick to them, be trenchant, co-ordinate, *believe.* He cannot slice and select dauntlessly as I do. It's funny—I never before thought there must be dauntlessness in creation and in criticism. At certain moments I feared that I lacked maturity, but then I relied on my instinct. I even wrote the book with my body, as Lawrence would have it—not always intellectually. I believe it is good.

February 2. It is done. Titus has the book. I have worked ten hours a day—steadily, with extraordinary intensity and lucidity—with deep joy and satisfaction. Hugh has been wonderful, correcting with understanding and actually writing a few pages himself. Twenty-two thousand words. Compact, of course.

I think more of Lawrence than I ever did, even after the microscopic critical examination. It has been a tremendous piece of *creative* criticism; I call it a study in understanding.

February 3. I need a rest and yet now I feel quite lost without my work. I wish for those two weeks, when I surpassed my own strength and capacity for work. I sit here and wonder how I did it. Eduardo says I am a "medium," simply. That's one explanation.

Titus said: "I see such a big difference between this and the essay. It looks perfectly idiomatic."

Oh, it was not only Hugh's help, because he helped me on the essay; it was my terrific desire and the work.

Eduardo came the first weekend and helped with his ideas and knowledge and scholarliness. I tried to arouse him into writing the book with me. He was willing to talk, but otherwise he was *inert*. It palled on my own energy after a while, and I did not see him any more until the book was done. He was rather hurt—until I explained I had been too busy even to talk. Then he came this last Sunday, read the book and found nothing to criticize except tiny details. In fact, he said I had revealed parts of Lawrence to him, that he would read my book now as a key to certain obscurities in Lawrence.

Hugh was so moved. He was going through a miserable week at the Bank, but he didn't care. He would sit right down to correct what I had written during the day, and I would sit and make the last clean copy. We worked until ten-thirty or eleven. He misses it now, as I do. Last night, foolishly, I dreamed with Hugh of the book's publication. But it may be rejected, by Titus or the English editors.

I went out to the garden for a half hour to chop wood. I used to do this during those two weeks, to clear up my head. Chopping wood is now forever connected with thoughts of Lawrence.

People came on visits; we had to see them. I'm afraid I hardly realized they were there. I am still inflated. Monday I was glowing, walking about Montparnasse, seeing Titus and Eduardo. I couldn't go to sleep. Now I am trying to *return*.

Those two weeks will in a sense remain a blank in the Journal. The book itself should come in here. It is the real stuff that filled the two weeks. I ought to quote it all: *D. H. Lawrence: A Study in Understanding.*[1]

February 4. Peace, calm, solitude. Most of my friends, the conventional ones, are more or less angry with me. I am beginning to live again—or should I say not to live?—for life to me was clearly those two weeks, though of course the human must come in somewhere too, and I suppose I couldn't do without it altogether!

Chop—chop—chop in the garden. The dog is wondering why I do not play with him. It is cold and gray. The first primroses are out, dewy in the grass. The birds are sure it is spring, or at least they are making vocal preparations.

One can love beauty for its very own sake. I can love Eduardo's beauty—but as I love Ruby's, only at moments. Beauty is lovable but not indispensable. It satisfies one of the senses but not all. I suppose modern art was a reaction against insipid, eternal beauty, and it is *right* (while I say so, however, I quake, for I'm one of the beauty-loving fools, and I get as much delight from seeing Ruby aristocratically and languidly lying on the black carpet as I get from the discovery of a metaphysical truth).

While I was working I was impervious to the rejections, but they continue to pour in, quite regularly—even from the *Canadian Forum*, which doesn't pay!

Speaking of spring, I write to Eduardo: "What a pity we are not on flirting terms!"

February 6. I do an unworthy thing. I send John my MS on Lawrence, because I am still interested in him *intellectually* and I wonder if this might not change the frothy course of his writing. The unworthy part is that I sincerely do not care about his opinions *intellectually*, only *personally*. Now here is an entanglement worthy of Lawrence himself. I can't figure it out myself. I care personally about his opinion: therefore there is still a personal attachment left. Not much seems to have changed since last year, and yet I know it has, in *degrees* of caring.

The birds have made a mistake. Winter is back again. It is

---

[1] *Published in Paris in 1932 as* D. H. Lawrence: An Unprofessional Study.

snowing. Eduardo calls me up and addresses me as I signed myself: "Your faithful mental connection."

I'm bursting with the strangest mood. The sap is rising. The birds were right. I feel it in my blood. Every year I say I will not be able to bear the season's renewal because I participate too intensely in it; I can't endure the joy of it.

February 7. I am looking forward to my next exile, and work. Boussie was satisfied without reserve: "This is not an abstract criticism: you feel the person, the writer you are handling. You let him speak for himself. There is a gradual and very attractively presented penetration." She had never read Lawrence, but now she wants to. She sees where he influenced Sherwood Anderson and Waldo Frank—and what a big man he was.

We spent a delightful afternoon together, she reading the Study, and often digressing from it in her talk with me, I sewing and watching the log fire. We took a walk in the garden to see the primroses, and I made her laugh telling her how stupidly I had talked with Titus.

Both dogs felt a particular attraction for her, because she is so real, so simple, and very much of the earth. I now enjoy her tartness, her sharp frankness. We always talk about John, lamenting his last phase and recalling the first, when he was a poet and a philosopher. I asked her to compare *Sincerity* with *Dodsworth*. Neither one of us wants to accept the present John as final. We laughed about the negligee in *Sincerity*, the naïveté of it, for in our present age women do not wear negligees, but pajamas; and modern men do not make a practice of *carrying* women; first, because some of them can't, and, second, because it is a technique of the Middle Ages. Such things interest him because they give him anticipatory frissons [thrills].

Planning new work—studies of Gide and Huxley. Have really nothing to write in my Journal, and yet I feel a desire to handle it, to read it over, to say something to it. It bothered me that while I worked I wrote little in my Journal, as if I thought it had a value of its own for me and had to be kept alive. I know this is so.

February 9. Yesterday, the minute Eduardo stepped inside the house I caught a demoniac glint in his eyes. I can so easily read his expression.

We went, all three, to see a remarkable and unforgettable movie, *L'Ange Bleu* [The Blue Angel], a film of Henrich Mann. I don't remember ever being so moved; it was almost unbearable —a work of realistic, perfect psychological art.

We wore out our nerves and imaginations. Afterward, Eduardo was still keyed up. He talked at the restaurant of his wild days in Havana with his group. I could see the energy beating and rising in him, and the devil sparkling out of his eyes. For a moment I was in sympathy with him. And then I turned away, scornfully. How stupidly he would use his energy, that marvelous overflow—drink and whores. It seemed to me an awful waste. I felt that he lacked imagination in his living, just as John lacked it. How petty the outcome of their impulses. Mine would be quite different—certainly more imaginative. Nothing so trite could satisfy me. Moulin Rouge for John. Wine and whores for Eduardo. Banal. No. I'd rather go quietly home with Hugh than participate in Bacchic moments of such poor quality. Hugh felt the same way. We had our Bacchic moment by ourselves next to the log fire. We were very happy.

Lawrence was fearfully right when he described the oscillations between love and hate. I hate Eduardo when he is banal. He needs wine to become impulsive. When he is impulsive he is silly. The demoniac glint in his eyes, which was so suggestive when I first saw it, by the end of our evening together was translated into ordinary cockiness.

At the same time, he hates my creativeness, though he tries to pretend he likes it. My steady flow of writing irritates him. I try to be self-effacing, and half of what I write I never show him. But how much better he would like me if I depended entirely for my life on the progression of his "Offero," which consists of twenty-seven not very original but very poetic lines, and which I like—but which is as yet an infant, and may take twenty years to write.

February 10. Met an "infant prodigy"—twenty-seven years old, with a mind like flint—devoted to literature, fair, acute, critical faculties, and a peculiar quality of *utter* individuality. He talks almost to himself; he never listens; he never lets go an idea once he gets hold of it; his concentration is astonishing. In anybody else it would be the most intolerable egotism; in him it is the most absolute stage of self-development, and because of the brilliancy of his mind, a source of enjoyment. He quotes books by the page; he knows almost everything that has been written of informal value. He is a lawyer in Hugh's department. Never for a moment any respect for his employer. None for me, as his employer's wife. Hooray! Knows his value exactly, has the assurance of a man of sixty. He sits on the edge of his chair to expostulate, with sweeping eagerness, and that strong Yankee twang—a Connecticut Yankee, if you please.

I have enjoyed my holiday—a week now. After Joaquin's concert I go to work again. Every moment has been a joy. I feel as if I were *swimming* in life, because I feel so thoroughly the impact of it against my body, undulating deftly, surrounded, compressed, and free at the same time.

Alertness of nerve tips, bristling of the skin, circular flow of warm blood, currents of vibrations running through the hair, over the forehead, like light but galvanized fingers, over eyes, mouth, neck and around the conical breasts, and around the belly and between the legs—all, living, budding, relaxed, with shivers of animal plenitude—no climax but a perpetuity of small ecstasies.

February 12. Yesterday I was thoroughly plucked—not a single feather left—by an almighty schoolmarm [Miss Lemer], if you please, who passed scholarly, academic judgment on my work. She had read only "Woman No Man Could Hold" and the sequel (not the Lawrence book). Did not get anything out of it, not one holy idea or feeling, on account of the style: "awful style—trite words or long Latin ones—no sequence—no development." And there followed a complete lecture on beauty of style, the hard work necessary to achieve it, how Conrad did it, the necessity for ten years of rewriting, etc.

To be absolutely truthful, the attack, made with American roughness, at first hurt me beyond description, then I mastered myself, overcame my sensitiveness, and faced it, admitting much of the *truth of it*, since Hugh had already said all that—truth, insofar as style was concerned—but I was overwhelmed by the superficiality of the judgment. I am cursed to be cursed by the Board of Education and every Bachelor of this and that recognizes in me the uneducated upstart. And immediately sets out to squash me.

At the same time, I have a more profound love of style than any of these people, and I am quite willing to work desperately on the possession of English. But, oh, God, preserve me from ever looking at writing thus, from not seeing further. Preserve me from formality and pedantry.

I get a sincere letter from Berta [Hamilton] in which she says the *Forum* committee liked my stories but returned them because they were *too condensed.* Style and brevity having been mentioned now so often, I feel that there is a weakness. So I go to work. But of course I feel raw, because I suspect my realizations have leaped ahead of my technique. And so again what is art? Puissance or perfection?

February 13. For a month now I have been so nervous over my "little brother's" coming concert. Finally last night it came to be. And what an overwhelming surprise! I sat there quivering and frightened, and he comes out with the utmost grace and assurance and plays to perfection right through, arousing warm enthusiasm in the audience. He was master of himself and yet spontaneous, playing everything with utter musicianship and astonishing maturity for his twenty-one years. He startled everybody, even those who knew him best. It was truly a miracle of effort. What nuances, subtleties, and power. It was, for me, another Joaquin. How proud I was. And he was so much liked personally. All our friends came to hear him.

I sit and muse over it: Mother glowing; Hugh's paternal pride; Godoy with tears in his eyes; Boussie shaking her head joyfully; Emma Eames clapping enthusiastically; Nestor, the Spanish painter, with a round grin; Eduardo surprised; Gilbert overwhelmed; the Cubans and Spaniards demonstrative; Gisèle [Couteau], who has made Joaquin work and who treats him as Hugh treats me—courageous, eager Gisèle, quite resplendent; Marie André gushing; the classmates demonstrating their admiration merrily.

Today, Joaquin comes in to borrow my eraser; he is again my soft, fat little brother. He teases Ruby by blowing into his ears. I am feeling quite bowled over. Hugh says: "What's the use of having children! Taking care of Joaquin is more than enough pleasure."

Overwhelmed with Katherine Mansfield's descriptive power, even in her letters. At the same time it is not entirely satisfactory, not quite enough. It is no wonder to me that she failed to understand Lawrence. She was not modern enough, and she failed to understand or realize sex. Unreservedly, I admire her style, her visualizations, her poetic qualities, her oddness. And how beautifully she preserved in a sick, tortured body a sensitiveness to life. It is this last quality and her love of her writing, her profound artistry, which are most admirable. She is one who weighed her words.

Miss Lemer, in handing me Mansfield's *Letters*, intended, of course, to deal out an example to me. Well, it was a sweet punishment. But how much more effective it would be if she first understood what there *is* in me—transcending style.

"You have that style in your house and in your dress, to such a strong degree," she said reproachfully.

However, I am willing, humbly willing, to work. I've invented a little scheme. It is like drawing the objects nearest you— the bed, the sheets, the quilt, the room, Hugh. I describe them as I would draw them. I'm deadly serious about my work. It has got to be right. Of course, for me description must be stylized, essential, brief, as I have always felt it, like lightning and wind— not Proustian miasma or the Katherine Mansfield insistence on details.

February 16. Reading attentively and intensely Jung's *Psychology*. Studying gardening. My work was to begin today, but Saturday morning I wrote a good story, "The Gypsy Dancer." It was impulsively written, that is, with excitement and impatience to catch my running and skipping ideas, but there was a bit more conscious care of the style at the same time, and effort at directing it. It will have to be rewritten only once.

The tragedy of Katherine Mansfield's life weighs on me, as much as Keats's. When she writes that she so much wanted to live! Her talent would have developed in some perfect, lyrical direction in great plenitude if she had been given a whole life. How much is intimated in her writing, as in Keats's poems; how extraordinary, what she accomplished while so dreadfully ill; what courage and profound love of life.

Saturday we heard a Festival Debussy, the musician I perhaps love best. His music is all immaterialized—the climaxes are inner—it is pure poetic impressionism, imagery, so very deep and subtle—Falla has perhaps more blood in the rhythm.⁻ Debussy's rhythms are unearthly, so distant, so abstract. Perhaps between the two they contain all the music I would care to hear.

I came home and began a Symphony in Prose, into which I will pour all the lyricism I possess and which will contain all the poetry I know and feel.

February 17. Heard Chaliapin in *Boris Godunoff.* Very moving and original. Chaliapin is losing his power but remains an artist. I think he is better than Caruso. To listen to an opera one must close one's eyes a great deal of the time, when there is no movement on the stage. In Russian opera, however, when one opens one's eyes they should be doubly open to realize the Byzantine splendor of the decoration and costuming. Such range and coordination of colors as they achieve is an art unknown outside Russia and the Orient. Spanish colors are limited in comparison. I listened to the orchestra as I never did before, catching every tonality and nuance of the instruments, composing my own symphony.

The theatre was packed, excited. Chaliapin exerted a spell as much with the gestures of his hands as with the emotional modulations of his voice and his grandiose presence. During the entr'acte the women seemed dim after the colors of the stage, but the long, flowing movements of their dresses were very insinuatingly feminine. Breasts are very much outlined, and backs are fully exposed, with a knotted necklace falling in the hollow of the spine. It was pure Renoir, such as Katherine Mansfield objected to with English delicacy. I was among the much stared-at women. My stylized Spanish dress and lace scarf attracted much ferocious attention from the ladies. What with Joaquin and Eduardo at my side, with Hugh paternally looming over us, we were a group to be commented on. At such moments I used to feel keenly aware of myself, aware of precisely how I looked and stood, and of the impression I conveyed. But last night I was living inside myself. My body was a bit of a shell, with a layer of down between its surface and my feelings, as when I was twelve and read to the point of feeling drugged.

At the same time I have never experienced life so sensually. The other day we were going to have lunch with Mother in honor of Hugh's birthday. Mother had been preparing it all morning. The table was carefully set. We were called in. I stood a moment by the window, waiting for Mother. A feeling of pleasure came over me; we were going to sit down just for the pleasure of eating. It had never occurred to me before that it could be a real pleasure.

I felt an anticipation of my whole body for that physical enjoyment! The olives, the tomato soup, the Spanish dish, the salad, the champagne, the dessert—how *good*, how deeply *good* everything was, what a satisfaction in tasting and chewing, nourishing one's body.

Swinging, then, from the shell body—a body beautifully clothed, parading down the red-carpeted hallways of the Théâtre des Champs-Elysées—to a body aware of sensuous pleasure in all manifestations of physical life.

The uses of understanding: revealing to Berta Hamilton that she has lived too much for others and so has not fully achieved her self-creation, which is, ultimately, the most important contribution to social life and civilization. So now she finds that of her 126 friends no one but me has really preoccupied himself with Berta's own individual fulfillment and satisfaction, that they all considered unselfish, *impersonal* Berta as either a "crutch" or a confessor. And now that crutch is kicking off in revolt! I had guessed the dissatisfaction and the cause. Our correspondence is getting livelier and livelier, discussing destiny and personal problems of how and where to kick destiny, how and where to accept it.

February 18. "Waste of Timelessness" acepted in French translation by *Revue Nouvelle*, thanks to Boussie, not to any merit. Even in writing it is a game of personalities. But I'm just as excited and delighted. It made my breakfast coffee taste like nectar, even though it was served by another example of the ridiculousness of humanism: Lola, my very much spoiled and kindly treated maid, who leaves me because she doesn't care for country life.

Dark gray day, with characterless snow falling in big flabby flakes. Primping for an interview with Titus. Hours of studious reading of Jung, and hours of technical exercises, my dear, to curb the independent thinker always secretly rejoicing at being uneducated; this is the stuff I work on, like scales: Hugh's horn resounds under the bridge near the station. Soon it will sound imperative, so that the iron grille will be opened. The gravel will crepitate under the wheels of the car. Banquo will yawl with lazy pleasure, smell the packages taken out of the car. Isn't this awfully unacademic? The word "yawl" is of my own invention: a combination of yawn and howl! The word "crepitate" is Latin.

"My dear, you must try to write like George Moore. You are overfond of superlatives."

I'm having a lot of fun working consciously and getting un-conscious results.

February [?]. Interview—Titus-Nin:

Titus [crossly]: Why don't you number your pages? Are you sure you've read all the books? What about the psychology book?

Nin: It was incorporated into the Fantasia.

Titus: Did you write up "Essay on Death of a Porcupine"?

Nin: It is of no importance. I referred to it in the chapter on Language.

Titus: Well I see I can't stick you. [Mollified by my smile.] You know you puzzle me—I can't make you out at all. How much of you is there in that "Woman" story? If it's you, you certainly are a little devil! And yet you look so *demure*, so modest.

[There is a young man waiting his turn in the room and so Titus adds:] We can't talk any more about that today, but I'll see you soon again, won't I? [I was beginning to think my Lawrence book was a failure.]

Titus: I think it's a very readable book indeed.

Nin: Will you send it to the English editor?

Titus: I'll not only send it to him, but I think I'll do more: I'll probably publish a limited edition of the book myself here in Paris, three hundred copies or so.

Nin [mute—floored—dished].

Titus [a moment later]: Why don't you let me see some of your stories? I don't like the "Woman," but that may be because I'm prejudiced the moment a writer makes a writer the hero of his story—that's a terrible mistake. It is like a young shoemaker writing about the shoemaking industry. What do you at your age know about writing? You are not even sure that you are a writer!"

I felt like saying: I'm quite sure I am, and so are you. But I thought I had been quite cocky enough for the present, and, after all, I knew he was perfectly satisfied: the fact is he asked me to add one phrase to the Lawrence. There was nothing said about editing.

So I walked out inflated like a balloon, laughing at all he had said, marveling at my own self-confidence, for I hadn't let him bully me.

He told me a story about Lawrence. Lawrence mailed him a poem for *This Quarter*. Titus thought the poem not good enough, coming from Lawrence. When Lawrence passed through Paris he came to see him. When Titus told him he couldn't accept the poem, Lawrence said: "Well, you're quite right. It is not one of my good ones!"

Titus also refused Lawrence's study of Hardy "because Hardy was not in it!" What a blunder. Who is interested in Hardy?

The worst about writing is that you cannot wrap your "instrument" (yourself) in a humidity-proof case with velvet lining, that you cannot acquire an instrument of special quality like the purchase of a Stradivarius, that no amount of studying scales, of difficult practicing, will make you write. It is purely an occult force.

Today I could not work, only correct and file, etc. The truth is I have been depressed by the following issue: Am I more of a critic than a creator? Is my "Woman" story less good than my study of Lawrence? I love understanding and interpreting and creating, but I also love creation. To have a more powerful critical tendency would be quite consistent with the French quality of my mind. In Gide one tendency did not exclude the other, but it usually diminishes the power of the other.

What will John, the critical writer, think of the MS.? Will he want to help me now, I wonder? I wrote him a most formal letter, but it will look very natural to him!

Every holiday, Hugh and I make plans for the future, so that he may leave the Bank sooner. We sit and figure how poorly we could live. When Joaquin is on his feet, and Mother has a little income from her mother's inheritance, Hugh and I could become bohemianly poor—and just read and write. I would certainly be able to contribute. I might be a drama critic so we could see the shows, a book reviewer so that we could have books. Hugh could do what he pleased, to make up for his eight years of slavery to our comfort and security. That is how we dream and talk, endlessly.

I feel my energy diffused now throughout my life rather than centered on Johns and Eduardos. Hugh alone really holds me profoundly. For him alone I could make sacrifices and really work and really deny myself experiences. Since I have begun to work I feel that I am strong enough to accomplish the transformation. At the same time I am unbearably unhappy, because I feel that I have been trapped somehow, in an *ideal love*. There is no doubt of that high quality in our marriage and that I am the inferior half of it, fundamentally held by high values in spite of all my convictions that high values are no more important than lower ones, and that such distinctions do not exist. I feel honest, I feel serious, and yet I did not aspire to be either, because my wisdom is not of that kind—it is all-embracing. I feel influenced by Hugh as I would never have been by anyone else. I feel that he has participated greatly in the making of the present me.

February 21. I'm twenty-eight. Well, that's one thing I got without working for it! Anyway, for each year I have written a book. We're all having lunch en famille, including Eduardo. It is raining. Lola and I parted after a magnificent row, during which I discovered I can live eighteen months with a vixen and not know it until the thirty-first day of the last month. What an extraordinary critical faculty!

Miss Lemer praised the Lawrence book to the limit, not only as a study of Lawrence, but of life. Style perfect (darling Scotchman). Verdict: my criticism better than my stories.

Ha! said the doctor. Is that where it hurts?

Yes, right here, in the *critic zone*, I answer, and then I ask him: Can't you cure me of criticismitis?

What for?

Because I want to do some of the writing myself.

Impossible, dear lady, criticismitis is a chronic malady, a fundamental weakness.

Whereupon the old doctor will mail me a bill for informing me of something I didn't dare to know, as is usually the case. I read my old Journals with pleasure. Is that narcissism? But I also read other people's journals with pleasure. What do you call that?

Wouldn't it be a breezy thing to do: to write the "Private Life of John Erskine," with sympathy for the big idealist, bound-up giant, being consistently intelligent in his stories and so consistently helpless and naïve, and pathetic and frightened and idealistic in his own private life? To see him as the last victim of idealistic formulas?

February 22. Tonight I felt moody, ill, and tired. And yet at the thought that I could get into bed and write in my Journal about last night, a feeling of pleasure overwhelmed me as keen as the feelings of the actual experience. I would taste it all again, alone, secretly, intensely, *slowly*.

Mother and Joaquin were invited out to dinner at the Godoys'. Hugh had a Club banquet, so Eduardo took me to dinner at the Maisonette Russe—both of us "dressed up," although I had begged for a bohemian evening, because I felt moody and indifferent. During the afternoon, while Eduardo was here, he and I had more or less quarreled twice—I, having ventured my opinions of his girl.

"But she gives me a nice, peaceful mother feeling," he said.

"Oh, hell," was my comment.

At the Russian restaurant, sitting next to each other against the wall (we were not influenced by the music, to which we hardly listened), we began to talk—or, not to talk, but to *delve* into the deeps in our usual way. I was strangely split, aware in my old dim way of the place, people, music, dinner, but externally and without feeling. I could describe it minutely—the red mahogany paneling, the billiard-table green baize on the walls, the unbecoming ceiling lights, the six or seven Russian singers, the pianist, cellist, and violinist, the waiter who looked like Boris Hoppe, the tomato soup with cream, the chicken and mushrooms, the crêpes, the black shoulder strap of my chemise slipping over my shoulder—all so empty, not connected with me, unreal. The intensity was gathered up in that flow of talk between Eduardo and me, and I was straining all my being to a realization of him.

It was he who talked most of the time—about Havana, about his strange experiences. He was conscious of living in the pages of Dostoevski. He acted out his experiences—desire, anger, pity, hysteria, passion. His face would become distorted—the veins swelled on his forehead, his nose seemed to grow wider, his mouth became deformed, pausing before certain sentences, remaining open for a second, inchoate, tormented, as if he were overwhelmed by emotion to the extent of losing control of his body. Some of what he told me roused an understanding response in me. The expression of a hunger for life unnerves me always. He said that when he went out with his friend to dine together, he could not *eat*, and the "tearing" in his "bowels" was terrible. All this I felt in myself, as he said it, remembering my own experiences—and I would gasp at the power of mere memory. The Russians were singing, and once we were hushed reproachfully—but we went on whispering. I stopped smoking. Leaning over the table on my elbows, I kept my eyes fully on Eduardo, absorbing him; our shoulders touched. Out of the intimacy rose a strange exultation, which was not sexual and which was not intellectual. Eduardo felt impelled to touch me. "Let me kiss your hand," he said: "We have never been so close." I did not understand what he felt. I let him kiss my hand. It gave me no pleasure, conveyed nothing to me physically, and I know it did not to him. Intensity of confidences had for a moment startled him out of himself; some impulse flared in him, blind, lyrical, but not sexual. My hand fell on his arm, which I pressed. He pressed my fingers. It was utterly inhuman. Was it I who did not feel, who was insentient?

"It was a wonderful feeling," he said. Was it his own measure of warmth? Were we simply cursed to this insentience of flesh while other parts of us were aroused? I went on looking at him. He was flushed—he was *light* and bodiless, as I was. An entirely new skepticism flashed in me: We are exulted because we have been talking about our experiences, and we are moved by *them*, not by each other.

We spoke a few trite phrases. The intensity was broken. We listened to the music. I wanted to go. Eduardo looked dazed. Then Joaquin appeared at the door, looking for us. I had lost my power of speech. I was floating. Eduardo, too, was floating. Yes, certainly there was a space between the earth and our feet filled with a spongy, elastic substance. At the car Eduardo said, when Hugh offered to drive him to a Métro station: "No, *tonight*, nothing will do but a taxi." As he emphasized "tonight" he looked at me. Then, saying good-bye: "It was wonderful." I was hoping he had not divined the utterly passionless intensity of our closeness, that he would float on his own feelings, oblivious to mine. Perhaps he knew, or perhaps he was deceiving himself again, or perhaps he was simply glad of the closeness. I looked on my passionlessness and was sad.

Was it the birthday of wisdom?

February 23. That idea of "understanding" which has been haunting me is developing into a story, which may be a part III of the "Woman." I'm attempting something very difficult in direct response to my instinct. I'm writing as I love to write: the relationship between the woman, Norman, and Daniel exists in space, not in reality; they three are suspended in a "universe à trois" such as is created by states of consciousness that exclude for a period all awareness of reality. This is my favorite state of essence. In this state alone I feel free and happy.

February 24. I tell Eduardo blankly that it isn't technique he lacks, but the impulse. All his talk about getting the technique first, first the discipline, etc., is an evasion. Work first—the technique will follow. For the first time, he agreed. Other times he has fought me and said I was trying to impose my way of working on him (lucky fellow, for I know his nature better than he does himself). But can one teach an impulse? Better let him find comfort in his technique.

He hits back at me by saying I have too much self-satisfaction! At the first manly peep of my usually timid voice, I get squashed. But I answer, "Hooray, I hope I can get more. For it is indeed what makes me work." Whereupon he reflected on this and examined his own waverings. Then I realized again how irritating is the fullness of a creator to an artist who is, for the moment, empty. God, how carefully one must tread, hide one's joy, one's work. I cannot make up for my fullness by pouring jars of faith ointment on him—on his drawing, on his "Offero" (the unfinished "Paludes"). So I sit meekly on my chair, looking heroworshippy, wishing myself a woman with merely talent for making up her eyes properly and knowing how to choose her perfume.

But, oh, we were not as sharp as all that. He had his moment of pleasure, for I know what it pleases him to hear; he liked discovering that I had the hero-worship instinct to a formidable degree, truly a feminine virtue. Today he was raving about the Luciferian pride which he thinks he, Joaquin, and I have, the pride of attempting high things, of thinking the universe in us, God in us, art our destination, etc. I agreed, although I felt we all paid dearly for our moments of pride by our moments of humility and self-depreciation, which far outnumber those in normal men and women.

Very often Eduardo talks to me as if he were examining my conscience: "What makes you create? What do you think of while you are creating?" And I answer as well as I can, trying not to let him stick me. Then I realize he is examining his own conscience. And then I realize it takes a fantastic amount of impulse to bear consciousness, and that few people have managed, as I have, to feel *naturally conscious* and impulsively conscious!

February 25. Eduardo went straight home yesterday "feeling wonderful," sat down and made six fantastic and excellent drawings. That made me happy.

I visited him between business calls—one, to Titus, who was perfectly wonderful to me, calling me "honey girl," holding my hand, but in such a friendly, warm way I really took a liking to him. Until today I had only felt gratefulness. Our business talk, in spite of Hugh's coaching, is level on his side, and quixotic and sentimental on mine, but we always end by agreeing very nicely. I'm free to shift for myself in regard to the American copyright. The English [rights] will only come up in three weeks, because the publisher Heineman is in New York.

Now that this situation is clear, and I have done all I can do, I feel freer to go to work. I wish I could just do the work and have the selling end handled by someone else, because I'm not much good at it.

Anyway, with "honey girl" still ringing in my ears, I traveled across Paris and home with great cheerfulness. The lovely bear, I thought, how nice he can be when he wants to. In contrast to his boutades [whims], the soft mood was very effective.

I have decided to accept my own nature and to make the best of it—that is, I cannot ever look hard-boiled, so I must stick to my Hindu softness and abide by it and suffer the consequences. That is one thing I have not been able to change. Too bad. I had dreamed of an assertive-looking, determinative, hard-boiled modern appearance and manner. This 1830 face and demureness are a hellish nuisance. But I will accept it. I will try to amuse myself with the shocks and surprises I give people.

February 26. At the end of this day there will be Hugh. However sweet the day, whoever I may be with, the thought of Hugh is a secret solace and a deeper joy. And so I hug my secret while conversation is going on, and everything is bearable. It would not be bearable if there were no Hugh, if I should know that that is all there is to living, just the day, the friend, the family, the talk.

It is all reduced to this choice between several moments of intensity or a long, constructive life. For there is no doubt that the moments of high intensity are destructive, like all inordinate exaggeration. I would give my life for the intensity. But I wouldn't give Hugh's life. So it is settled for me. But because of the sadness in it all, this is the end of my part III [of the "Woman"]: "If it was the birthday of her wisdom, it did not seem to her that she received it with the appropriate gaiety."

Again doing all kinds of little things while thinking of John's coming. Why he should have such power over my thoughts is a mystery to me—perhaps because I have not understood him, because he is foreign to me. And yet, no, it was settled in my mind. He was simply a man who took events as most people do, without thinking or feeling much about them. I am the woman who, like Lawrence, thinks and feels much—more than is reasonable. And that is all.

So I am at it again, against my own will. How different the John in my mind from the real John! In spite of the real John, the John in my mind is a great man, full of brilliancy and warmth and potency—subtle, with a touching love of life and *thoroughly* awake and deep. Curse such dreams, such living with one's own created images. My created image of John was this big, mature friend I have always craved, *compelling my mind*, something to reach out to, something for the high moments, wiser and bigger than me, capable of filling this unfillable craving in me.

I ought to live with my images, as I live with my ideas. I would be meeting Eduardo tomorrow and instead of the diffuseness of a Gide-Lawrence-Dostoevski shadow, there would be a man of unique quality, profoundly rich and utterly impulsive; instead of a "strainer," there would be the condensed, preserved, integral, whole Eduardo.

I would be meeting John, and in his first glance I would see that he understood more than Paulines and Liliths—that he could be capable of sad moments, that he preferred intimacies or solitude with his own soul to public life, and he would not say the wrong thing to me; he would say what I love to hear, not something banal or American.

I see now that I have loved, not *themselves*, but what I conceived to be themselves, expecting always a supernatural John or Eduardo, aroused by the miracle of my faith. What naïveté! John is a busy man who thinks about things for five minutes and then files them away. Eduardo is a man who feels about things for five minutes and forgets them. Il n'y a pas de fond [There is no depth]. I'm always seeking the fond. In meeting reality I have made no progress. When people tell me their idea of John or Eduardo—that one is superficial, the other weak—I do not believe them. They just don't understand, and I stick fiercely to my conception. The depth in John *was* there; it has been submerged. Eduardo has his kind of strength, which is flexibility. Whenever I looked at John I saw what was and what could be; it held me, promised so much to me. My *mind* is not blind. I could judge John's work and Eduardo's lack of courage. But my feelings are blind. In my feelings there is an ever-ready justification, acceptance, *transformation* of reality. Eduardo thinks I deceive myself about myself, but he does not observe that I deceive myself about himself, against the dictates of my mind. Faith—what intelligent woman ever had as much of that as I have? What passive, uncritical doormat of a wife?

March 6. Une source intarissable de joie, de joie douloureusement profonde [An inexhaustible source of joy, of sorrowfully profound joy]. Because one night the moon blazed over the old garden sheathed in frost; because one morning the sun blazed through the old house, and I sat absolutely idle, given wholly to the slow rhythm of imperishable dreams; because I detect new melodies in the birds' songs; because I hear the most penetrating silence of the place; because I found among the boxes of odds and ends in the attic something which can be made into a black transparent chemise; because Eduardo and I have broken through the barrier and can give each other warmth; because John is coming, and, whatever happens, I will hear his voice again, touch him, stand in the circle of his warmth, be teased by him.

The new sap rises and flows to every tip; it was never so hot, this sap, it never flowed so heavily or deeply. All the world is warm to me now. Even the gray rain feels warm on my face. Source intarissable de joie, de joie douloureusement profonde.

So I sit on the coral rug, with all my stockings spread on the floor, and I pick out with delight two pairs of flesh stockings which have not yet been mended. Shall I wear one today? Not today. I look at the calendar. On *that* day I will wear it. I have set aside a holiday, for the sake of the anticipation.

March 7. I think Eduardo is foolish to talk to me about the sensuous vision of Katherine Mansfield. She had it about small things but not about sex. I have it little about details, and profoundly about sex. It is strange that if you write in blue, people ask you why you don't write in rose. To hell with every quality in writing I do not possess. Opinions are not going to stop me. Nothing is going to stop me. I understood Lawrence's writing for what it *was*. Someday they will understand mine for what it is. I'm sick of hearing what it should be. I am the only one to be satisfied.

Part I of Play, "Warmth"
Eduardo and Me.

Me: There are some things you will never understand or see in me because you don't love me, because you do not apprehend me physically.

E.: Yes, I do see everything.

Me: You cannot see that side of me which I show to the one who apprehends me physically. I close that up before you. You have made me sensitive and conscious where before I was natural and spontaneous.

E.: That is true. I shall never forget those first weeks when you were spontaneous and warm with me! You were wonderful. But why, then, the night of the dinner, did you withdraw your hand?

Me: Lack of confidence. I thought *you* might think I was becoming sentimental again. If I had known you understood that I, too, felt merely warmth . . .

E.: I wish we could express warmth without fear of it becoming something else.

Me: I wish it, too—I'm sick of this cold, strained, mental relationship. I liked the dinner. You can have all the confidence in me you want. I shall never go beyond mere warmth again. You have killed the spontaneity forever.

E.: I want to have confidence. Very often I have wanted to express warmth to you and I didn't know how you would take it.

Me: Now you know. Now you know once and forever that I am *woman* even if you do not feel me as one.

E.: I suppose I am always trying to evade the fact.

Me: But I am willing not to be woman with you. Let's be friends.

E.: Hoorah! Give me your hand.
[Out of capriciousness, I didn't. He was a little angry—but very pleased because I was flushed.]

E.: We ought to see each other oftener—now that we are not self-conscious any more.

We did feel at last natural, and rejoiced. He always made me so bristly and sensitive and self-conscious on account of his own self-consciousness and sensitiveness. Each one calls out in the other what is in him. Eduardo has cooled me through his own emotional and physical incapacity—and now he wants to blame me. But he cannot, when he remembers the first weeks at Boulevard Suchet, when my fervor and lack of self-consciousness overwhelmed him! When he remembers that he has regrets. Whereas I am glad I discovered in time his own coldness. He has confessed he has *never* felt for a woman what he has felt for his friend.

While sitting in the doctor's waiting room I "sketch" it minutely, and fantastically. And I get an idea by which I may produce my Journal in disguise—comments, sardonic and mordant by me, on the "imaginary character" (of Anaïs!) expressed in the Journal. Opposition of two characters, with my signature under the "other" character and "myself" denied! What fun! One of these Gidean acrobatics, which I love. Coming out of my exalted self to make the cynical remarks other people *would* make anyway. Ha! Ha!

I have spent too much time denying myself, and now I accept myself, my shortcomings, my idiosyncrasies, my ways, my peculiar, individualistic mixture. After a visit, I used to say, hot-faced with shame, "I have been too silent." Now I say, "Well, what of it!" If I am silent it is because I want to be, because there are in me quantities of strange reserves and secrecy, which are due to my habit of confiding and opening only to writing, only to my Journal, or to those I love at chosen moments. Reticence in talk, yes.

An American woman fires direct, indiscreet, brutal questions at me. I shrink within myself and say nothing. But all day I talk to myself, and later I will talk to my Journal, or I will write a story. That is my way—let it be my way. Even to Eduardo, who thinks he knows me, I either postpone expressing myself, because I feel that I can say it better later in writing, or I have already said it in writing and I am unwilling to say it less well. So be it. My speech, the expression of all of me is in my writing. Eduardo, on the other hand, can talk and cannot write.

The time for self-creation is never over, but the time for accepting what I am made up of, has come—for out of that, and not out of other people's qualities, will come my ultimate being and my ultimate creation.

Eduardo is so weak, so weak, so weak. He hasn't one conviction, one basis, one soul—nothing, nothing but a caméléonesque charm! And on certain days I hate him for my own weakness, for listening to him, for taking him seriously, for counting on him, for being pleased or displeased by his opinions, for having the need of him. I want to stand on my own feet. I want, in Lawrence's own plea, to possess my own soul.

To Eduardo: "No, my dear, I can't come today." And I stay home and write, and sew, and garden, and smoke, and dream, and brush Ruby. You see the injustice? I accept *myself*—yet not others!

Joaquin-Hugh-Me

Joaquin: You and I, Anaïs, never lose the thread of our lives.

Me: Oh, I don't know. I think I do. What about my wild restlessness, my excursions, my gigolos?

Joaquin: In spite of all that, you don't lose the thread.

Hugh: I always knew I was thin, but I never knew I was a thread before.

Joaquin: Anaïs's gigolos are only her "models" anyway. She is studying still life.

Me: I guess Eduardo *is* a still life.

March 13. What a profound joy yesterday when I read John's letter to Hugh—a big, generous, *real* John—my John:

"The book [on Lawrence] seems to me very fine indeed—more concentrated in its thinking than the average readers likes, but altogether a joy to anyone with a decently trained mind. I learned a great deal from it, and profoundly admire what Anaïs has done. Is it fanciful to think that she comes at literature with the same sort of ability with which her father comes at music? I shouldn't be surprised at creative ability in her, but I am amazed at the scholarly and critical reaches—which theoretically no woman should possess! I'll let you or her know at once what I have been able to do about the book and it will be altogether a delight to introduce it to my friends here."

I didn't expect *this*. It touched me beyond words—overwhelmed me. In fact, it made me ill with pleasure. It gave me a fit of heart trouble, which kept me awake half the night and has left me weak and feverish. Today I can only brood. His coming is postponed until April. That was a keen disappointment.

March 18. Grateful letter to John. Blissful hours in the garden, enjoying the first sweet sunshine. Hours of work. Rewrote a weak part of the "Woman" and its end. At work on the idea by which I may publish many pages of the Journal.

Eduardo fascinated by the idea. Strange talks with Eduardo about health. He has discovered the importance of *deep breathing*. I'm impressed, and imitating him faithfully. He has declared to a big American girl that she is his "blood polarity," and she exclaims: "Really! I'm surprised. I should have thought the girl for you was your strangely beautiful and intellectual cousin." We laugh together about it. He explains Blake and Lawrence to her. She is a lesbian. What a mess! He has no emotional impulse whatever—just a feeling of *peace*. It is a kind of cream soup he offers, with the possibility that he may, someday, really be aroused to passion. I can't stand that mush; I like demitints, but not in feeling. Oh, God, the impotence of it. I see why he reads Dostoevski, why he *talks* so much about feeling, why he harps on lack of feeling in others. Leaving all this aside, he is as charming as ever. I'm beginning to lie to him to make things more interesting. We dramatize our lives—when it isn't naturally dramatic. We flirt, in a kind of way. Now that our geographical boundaries are definite, he is not afraid of giving me compliments.

It seems that, again, I talk little, implicate myself little; Eduardo says that I just sit there looking utterly comprehending and make him feel like talking endlessly. So, he says, he is bound to make more blunders. "Do I ever blunder?" I asked him.

"You never take the chance," he said. "You don't talk enough."

I wondered. Perhaps *listening* makes me understand, but it makes others not understand me, except for Hugh, who never has very much to talk about, so that *I* talk!

Well, I will stick to listening, anyway. I talk in my Journal enough, and certainly explain myself.

The Journal idea: the "Other Woman" is Natasia. Natasia keeps *this* journal. "I" make the commentaries. "I" am French—critical, realistic. This is what you might call a dialogue between my two souls—a dramatization of my own duality. I am talking to myself. This procedure is natural enough to me, and it should be a good talk, for I do talk well with myself!

March 19. My one desire is to be out in the garden all day. Perfect days—sunshine, freshness, eloquent birds, daffodils blossoming. Primroses have long been scattered all over the grass. I work in the garden, breathe deeply, think less than usual. Worked on the "Woman" stories. Came in to sew. I love to sew sheer lingerie or summer dresses while thinking of summer and anticipating events:

John, the possibility of two months in Mallorca, a month in New York, meeting Eduardo's brilliant friend, meeting the Mexican painter Zaraga, the appearance of my Lawrence book, a possible meeting with Mrs. Lawrence—and all kinds of events which I sense and imagine while I sew, quite badly.

Hugh tired, unresponsive to the season, poor darling. To get him out of the Bank has become an obsession with me—so he will *come to life*. Even his physical love, he expresses more rarely. I notice it with sadness. Is his nature fundamentally quiet, or is it tiredness? Our evenings are dull. I talk a little, and then, getting little response, I take up a book.

An old lament. How I hate myself when I indulge in it. Sometimes I can't help it. Il est lourd dans mes bras, il pèse lourdement sur ma vie—parfois [He is heavy in my arms, he weighs heavily on my life—sometimes]. I love him with pity, I love him with understanding. It is his way to be quiet. I must love him for that too. He is only half alive, fitfully so—it is strange: he cannot *smell*, *taste* or *touch* as I do. So I ask him, Tell me about your *dreams*, then. And about them he does not find much to say. Is it the Bank which weighs him down so much, which saps his strength, his mind? How he enjoys his vacations, and he is *different*, then. So I shall think of Mallorca.

March 20. As it happened, Hugh came home last night a little brighter. We take our electric sun bath together, and—well, we had to turn off the sun-bath. We lay together in the dark, and he was impetuous and warm, and I responded deeply. Afterward we laughed about it together, and I confessed what I had written. He asked me to take it all back. So I'm taking it all back. These Scotchmen! They burst forth so unexpectedly!

Eduardo is going through a *cheap experience* and is cheapening himself in my eyes. F. (Hugh and Joaquin say) is not only homely but common and ordinary. Joaquin is disgusted. If only it had been a woman with beauty or talent or charm, or something— but the commonplace type! I wouldn't let myself sink into such an association. I would have too much pride. My God, what infantilism in living he shows, what immaturity, lack of imagination, lack of pride, lack of greatness. My John is at least a great man! Hugh is "de bonne race." Gustavo was brilliant, even if an adventurer, with personality and power. Eduardo himself is somebody— "un animal de belle race," anyway. He is afraid of people of his own size, even more of those bigger than himself. He must preen himself before nothingness; he must breathe a medium atmosphere, not too fine or strong a one. I am hard on him, but it does not please me to be shared with an F.

What I have just written is not true. An ordinary person *can* give Eduardo a wonderful feeling. He is blind to the commonplace girl and seeks his "peaceful feeling." I do understand. I was writing *superficially*. But, just the same, that his feeling should be roused by an ugly or commonplace woman makes *him* less profound, weaker, and more commonplace himself. Such a thing would never happen either to Hugh or to John. There is wisdom in them.

March 24. Café du Rond-Point. Eduardo, Me, and a few other people—waiters, passers-by; much noise of traffic.

Me: Do you remember our pact to interfere with each other's experiences if they were cheap or detrimental?

Eduardo: Yes.

Me: Well, the time has come. You are going through a cheap experience. Worst of all, you are covering old ground, retracing your steps. This has happened to you sixteen times before. . . .

E.: Fifteen.

Me: All right. Fifteen. It is enough.

E.: But it is altogether *different* this time.

Me: You always thought it was different—at the moment. I can see that it isn't. And you needn't mistrust my feelings as the feelings of a jealous woman, since you know that I do not want you for myself.

E.: I know you couldn't be jealous.

Me: Not of a girl like her anyway.

E.: I would marry her against my family's opinion.

Me: You will lose me too.

E.: (momentarily taken aback): Very well. It is best to be at peace with one's inner Holy Ghost than with a thousand Anaïses.

Me: No, because a thousand Anaïses will give you more trouble than one Holy Ghost.

E.: Don't worry. She is going to Greece for a while.

Me: Good.

E.: (not very much worried, and quite pleased with my interference): Now, about this problem of the solar plexus. I have discovered a new book. Lawrence, as you remember, went to India, and there he must have been influenced [etc., etc.]. I would like to write an essay about it.

Me: Do write it. [I say this with great admiration of his research talents and discoveries, knowing well that he will talk to me for two pleasant hours but that I will write the essay, not he.]

Eduardo claims that I am a decidedly unique specimen, that he cannot find a synthesis of me in any book or any description of physiological, biological, psychological, pathological, or anthropological types. Perhaps there is a resemblance to the whale who has an eye on the back of its head and whose mind must coordinate its double vision into a comprehensive unity.

March 30. What happens if you sift, mix, and bake the following ingredients? Exhilaration at spring, gardening, deep breathing, errands, spring shopping, a permanent wave, [H. A.] Keyserling, Max Plowman, much inner singing and lyricism? A cold—a neat, noiseless, well-baked cold. I chuckle to myself: it happened on purpose. I have had rendezvous with the hairdresser, Eduardo, Boussie, and Mother-the-dressmaker. So today I have a rendezvous with my Journal. Bed, a plate of oranges, literary reviews, fermentation of thoughts, amusement. Why am I always amused when I am sick? I take a sort of superior, whimsical, patronizing tone about myself, as if it required a sense of humor to bear my own company in the restricted area of a bedroom.

I was just about to shellshock Eduardo with my idea about self-acceptance when I found he had been doing his own bombing. By other routes, other sequences of thoughts, he had arrived at the acceptance that he has no *creative genius* but an understanding of it, a sympathetic participation in it; that he must work and understand—and also stop squabbling and lamenting. The elements of Eduardo's nature are now finite, in a sense. He will always attract such a various set of people as Mrs. Eames (social, aristocrat, dilettante, superficial), F. (ordinary, undistinguished, banal), Joaquin (artist-friend), me (stimulating creative companion). He will always get entangled, waver, dissolve, extricate himself. (He has extricated himself from F. partly through me.) He will always evolve philosophies and forget them (as when he has proposed love to Joaquin).

Meanwhile, Joaquin is going through Lawrence's experience with Miriam—exactly. We have talked about it. He will read Murry's book on Lawrence the man, and it will reveal him to himself (chapter on *Sons and Lovers*).

Murry's book I cannot write about yet, having only read Chapter 1. I divine that it is good, and that my instinct was right when I feared writing Lawrence's life because of things I sensed and would not reveal to people who do not love Lawrence as I do and who would judge him. Murry has dared.

Reading the psychoanalysis of America by Keyserling [*America Set Free*] has been for me the deciphering of John's Americanism. Insofar as he is American, he is different from me, and does not understand me.

To tag John with American defects is to acknowledge him a man made by his environment, not a homeless, unique, unclassifiable exception, as I viewed him for many years in my own mind.

In the same way, of course, I could tag myself with European defects. For better or for worse, America's influence on me is wearing off. I cling to the language with fervor—and to the Celtic elements in the language and to many Anglo-Saxon qualities—but more and more I uproot myself from everywhere. Every day I am more homeless, more rootless. Why do I think I would have been John's Latin experience? Reading about Americans makes me realize my European soul. But if I were to read about Europe I would realize my non-Europeanness. However, I think I have the basic Latin faults and qualities. Even Slavic. Oriental. But American, certainly not.

My chest is screwed up with pain. I have eaten three oranges. I have stared at the copper beech in blossom. The afternoon is graying. Occasionally Joaquin comes in to show off his more assertive cough. Mother is relieved to see me busy writing, since she has so much to do. I do not weigh on the family. When alone I always mean to talk about the people with whom I fill my particular world. I pass to an admission of Eduardo's particular power, which is charm. Purely charm. A formidable element to deal with. I may rave against him in my Journal, judge him to his own face, criticize and lament. But he has only to come and spend a few hours here to recover his lost ground. His mere greeting, his tender-whimsical smile, his clear green eyes, the way he sits, his eagerness in talk, his mental and physical suppleness, his pockets stuffed with books, his drifting talk, his idiosyncrasies are all-enveloping, caressing, disarming. His weakness makes him less than a man, but more than a woman; his beauty is that of a woman—so beautiful, the smile, the chiseled features, the fullness of the mouth, the glances, the attitudes, the suppleness of the body, and the color of his skin. But his *whole* self, which appears at moments, is man—man with power over the female, such as woman does not rouse, ever. Dangerous power—man to woman; no, half-man to woman; insaissisable always, appealing; calling to the female, and when she answers, then only he reveals the feebleness of the call. And the female sees in him the love of man to man—a world of men, from which she has not yet been positively rejected; so she goes, hoping.

A strange explanation occurs to me of the *necessity* of John in my world. Love is sometimes an urge for what we do not possess. The kind of strength John has which impelled me is that very blind, insensitive, unfeminine strength opposite to Hugh's. Is it possible I should have sought intuitively in someone else the very crudity which would make me suffer extremely in order that I might gain in resistance (for Hugh does not resist me)? Is it possible that without the knowledge of John, I might never have known how delicate Hugh's perceptions are? Is what we call obscure instinct the impulses of an instinctively wise body? Would a kind of blindness to Hugh's unarresting delicacy have befallen a less susceptible and more loyal woman than myself?

Is there a reason for my being handled thus by John, treated as an ordinary woman, a deeper reason than I could at first fathom? At moments I see a reason in all paradoxes of instinct. Then everything holds together with a superhuman unity. Every event takes its proper place and is justified by the ensemble. And at such moments I am so glad to have surrendered to the impulse. But at other moments I simply think I am the most diabolical of sophists.

The moderns have confessed the love of ugliness in their art. Such a love is true. If you live by your feeling rather than by a style, then feelings are roused by either beauty or ugliness. The modern worship of ugly bodies or ugly houses is the acceptance of a human feeling as against an aesthetic formula. I love beauty but I find it easier to reject it now because I love other things more than beauty: genius, charity, passion, nature—all of which are often manifested without beauty of form. I love ugliness because it expresses strength. My dramatic lie to Eduardo was about a Russian violinist, about whom I have imagined a great deal, because I wanted to own a Russian like that. He was poor, he played in a movie to earn his living. I used to go and see him at the movie and we would talk between the acts. He was madly in love with me in an elemental way. He called me his "little Hindu girl" (nobody has ever said that, and I wanted that said to me). And so on.

Once he wrote me that he was ill and I went to see him in his meager hotel room. There he told me he had an engagement in Hollywood, and would I go with him and dance there, as we had planned to do once. It was the test of my devotion. I had to admit I didn't love him. The scene took on the proportions of a Dostoevski chapter. In came a strange, long-eyed, exotic Caucasian woman, who began to tell me how much she hated me: "You are shallow. Why don't you at *least* love him?" And she tried to cure him by exposing my indifference to him. He began to sob. I felt so bad that out of pity I almost said I did love him. Then I pulled myself together and said definitely no.

All this was very much heightened in the telling, for I have so much loved those Russian characters and wanted to be involved, but certainly not in that primitive way. However, at the moment I couldn't think of a better story. I was so interested in conveying my Russian and his elemental, emotional nature, and the Caucasian woman who couldn't understand my not loving him. Eduardo was quite subjugated by the *feeling* in it.

March 31. Throwing off my cold, I went to Paris. Eduardo and I had a studio to look over. We finally drifted into a tearoom. That man's world I was talking about—I was taken into it through Eduardo's confidences. Both he and Joaquin take me into it, as the woman of understanding and pity. I sit *caught*, subdued, and forgiving—and I need to be forgiving—but sometimes I stifle in their strange world.

What an effort to understand Joaquin, all pride, resistance, wholeness, fighting off experience, mother-bound—Eduardo and I urging him, by our talk and our own lives, to escape, so as to loosen the mother bond, the sexual reserve. Joaquin is mistrustful of Eduardo, because behind Eduardo's talk lurks his desire for Joaquin. Not love, desire. Joaquin, immersed in his pride, resists like a puritan, trying to give himself to Gisèle, and discovers his emotional impotence. Eduardo wishes for Joaquin's freedom and maturity, sincerely, for Joaquin's own sake. But Joaquin feels Eduardo is not disinterested. And so they fight, talk, pity each other. Eduardo resents his own openness, which lays his thoughts bare before Joaquin. Joaquin has the advantage of reserve, of half-confidences.

I sit between them—between Eduardo's vulnerable weakness and Joaquin's utter pride. Now Eduardo is angry and hurt; Joaquin has rejected him.

Somehow they are both so enmeshed. Joaquin is a sophist, and

Eduardo is a primitive. I feel so helpless. I know now one cannot direct others' lives. They only ask me to receive. It is all very heavy.

Joaquin knows he is a divided man. Eduardo is a divided man. They cannot put their souls into what their bodies do. If you do not put your soul into everything your body does, then it will all be worthless.

I am a *whole* woman. I have put my soul into everything my body has done, fearlessly, and that is why I am now so strong, that is why I have not been humiliated. I have not had to deceive myself, have had no need of sophistry, no need of pride to sustain me. I have given, often unwisely, and I have lost nothing!

April 1. Last night I came home revolutionized; but at the same moment I had a strange awareness of my closing up against life, of my gathering myself together, of my withdrawing. I said to myself: Now I am going to work.

I had absorbed enough. My shell was tightening. How clearly I felt the tightening. I didn't even know what I was going to work at. I was *sprouting* in the void.

Today I know. I am at work on an answer to Murry's book on Lawrence. I haven't even finished the book, but I know what it contains and I know my answer. Hugh placed the riddles before me and I answered, unhesitatingly.

April 2. I have killed the dragon Murry; now I feel I can breathe—and read the book through! My introduction is written—in my own way—which means "sketched" to others.

At the same time the singing inside has gone. I don't know why. The strain of the delays of publication is unbearable to my impatient nature. So is the postponing of John's visit. A nervous interview with Titus, who is an ordeal for my shyness—such a bully he is and so roughly kind and unexpectedly sentimental. He does not like my stories ("Tishnar," "Waste of Timelessness," "Alchemy").

Come, pull yourself together. Everything is *not* poetry, but you are a poet, and so you must sing. And by singing I mean no jolly rhymes—no—even sad, tragic singing is allowed, but it must be music, not that flat phonograph voice of everyday banality. I've written some sad things in my introduction: "the creator's voracious craving for climaxes—climaxes which life cannot offer the creator." And, "A knowledge of death is necessary to life." I suppose my songless days are to be my knowledge of death. At work on the double-personality journal. Have such a good little page on the experience with Gustavo, the cocotte-adventurer.

I say to Natasia: "What did you make out of *that* cheap experience."

Natasia: "I don't know. I'm just glad to have understood Gustavo."

Me: "But he is nobody, nobody."

Natasia: "Yes, it is true—I've understood nobody."

Me: "And aren't you humiliated?"

Natasia: "No—I'm not humiliated. This nobody aroused in me such a lot of feelings, and knowledge."

Me: "What did you learn?"

Natasia: "I learned to forgive."

Murry's book is great—deep and true, true to the actual Lawrence. I have found another truth, and I also have been true to Lawrence —*true to his dream.*

To be altogether wise I still have too much *faith.* All day I've read Murry and pondered. I have added to my introduction, which contains all of my creed—so far. Deep inside of me I am dissatisfied; I do not go far enough—*in between.* In between, I am superficial. Murry's book is therefore weightier and more convincing. God, I have a lot to learn yet. To *accept* everything is to deny the *dream.* I cannot deny the dream. My dream about a person is as essential to me as the actual person. There is too much wish fulfillment in the writing of stories, but isn't it the most practical way to fulfill a wish? Have I not been inspired myself by other's stories to be what I am?

I am humble today—humble before my faults as a writer and a thinker. I was supremely satisfied with my book until now. Just today I have outgrown it. Already, I could write a better one, a deeper and more thorough one. I made no pretense at thoroughness. I knew my limitations. But there should be no more limitations. I must study, write, know, work like the devil. I must learn *sustained* thinking; mine goes by leaps and bounds always.

I do not justify myself by saying I am only half Murry's age. That gives me no satisfaction. I should have done as well as he has. Such a *beautifully* written book—so full and thoughtful. So persistent and so logical. When I said I had killed the dragon I meant that I had been obliged to find my ground—what ground I could fight from to save my truth about Lawrence. In several ways I have made mistakes. Murry is right about *Women in Love.*

It is strange to think that Eduardo came, made me suffer, became an important personage in my life just so that I might understand Lawrence!

April 4. Making notes for a possible future essay or an answer to some of Murry's ideas.

When I think I have reached a knowledge of the limits of consciousness (Eduardo and myself) and of intelligent sophistry and labyrinths (Gide) then I strike a book—*Journal du Séducteur* by S. Kierkegaard—which I dislike intensely and find *obscene,* because it is intellectual perversity, an experience in *the mind* which cannot blossom into physical culmination—worse than narcissism, or worse than homosexuality. He only enjoys the pursuit and his mental possession of the woman. When she gives herself, he loses interest. There is something rather dead about all this which is as yet beyond me. That is, I don't know exactly why I dislike it. I know it is an intellectual exercise in the style of Gide, and I usually appreciate that sort of thing. Then what do I miss? Humanity? No. There is humanity of the highest kind in the séducteur's *aesthetic development* of the jeune fille's soul through experience.

The Surprise

A business dinner. Two Presidents of Big Companies and their wives. Also, one of the President's daughters, and a young man employed in one of the companies. All from Kansas City. First, they are aristocratic, in a sense, fine-looking, idealistic, good. True, the two magnates, the Telephone King and the Soap King, are quite nonexistent on any plane but that of their achievement, their work. Conversation impossible because our sense of values is so opposite, ranging from a difference of ideas on food to those on American civilization.

At my right sits the Young Man, who looks like a German student, and I observe he cannot talk very well with the Magnate or the Magnate's daughter. He seems to be holding back something all the time. True to my new philosophy of throwing out highbrow baits to the crowd with the hope of capturing an individualist, I throw off the two words casually: music and books.

The Young Man catches fire. Now it has become impossible to stop him from talking, and more difficult for me to pay attention to the conversation of the Magnate. The little German Student, blank-eyed through the diffuseness of his eyeglasses, talks about music, books, the French life, how all his *values* are shifting, how he is here alone and friendless and glad to be alone, how he cannot tell his Kansas City friends that he does not miss them, how much he suffers in their company, how they *will* take him to Deauville in spite of himself, and how he hates it. So after a while I don't throw a bait, I throw a bomb. D. H. Lawrence. He gets red in the face when I tell him about my book: "My God, and I have been talking like a fool!"

He has been reading *all* of Lawrence, with passionate interest. From now on we do not converse, we gush. During the jazz, the dancing, between intermittent remarks of the Magnate, we gush. Small talk with the others becomes more and more difficult. The funny little German Student. His name is Kniffin. There I sit talking with Kniffin, while I could be talking to the magnificent Magnate, who is so big, so very handsome, who *owns* an island to live on, who grips your hand with murderous virility, a real giant, a sap-head. Oh, God, the power of what does not *seem* like power, the power that Magnates have overlooked, absolutely overlooked. And you feel that any day Kniffin could overthrow the Magnate, though now the Magnate says kindly and paternally: "Oswald, how is your distribution going?" (His name wasn't Oswald but I can't remember what it was.) And so Oswald quotes figures. Mrs. Magnate is really lovely—a refined American—so rarely seen. And my Surprise is sitting there so tense and uncompromising and caught in a trap; he didn't want to come to this damn business dinner and meet the damn Guilers.

April 5. I have certainly a nature like a matchbox: when it catches, all the matches burst into flame at once and the box disappears. How to burn my matches one by one and preserve the box is a big problem. A friendship—flash! All the box gone. Dancing—whiff! All the box gone. John—bang! All the box gone. A book—whoof! All the box gone. And so on. Then I have to go to the doctor for heart-trouble. In between big events I have to reconstruct the box —rest, deep breathing, relaxation.

And so Saturday I rested. But Sunday, because Eduardo came for a few hours, I went up in smoke. See the little grease spot? That is all that is left. Fifteen drops of belladonna three times a day. Poor box! Tonight the heart is fluttering and leaping; its knocks reverberate in my head. That means a bad night. It means sitting up a little to dominate the turmoil of heart and head, which makes the night seem ominous and dangerous, for it is terrible to feel the beats of the heart, to be conscious of that little kernel of life, so frantic and noisy and undependable; it makes life appear too frail a thing and the will to live too futile, for it all comes down to that noise, that awful fluttering—not strong enough to bear life.

Talk, talk—so exciting: Murry, Lawrence, Vivekananda, marriage, homosexuality, my work, my defects, physical states of being, Keyserling, Hugh's legal defense of Lawrence, our dreams, the subject of tampering—Eduardo and I tampering with Joaquin's life; Eduardo tampering with my writing; I tampering with Eduardo's girlfriend; Hugh's family tampering with Hugh, trying to make the basis of his life spiritual (moral) when it was naturally physical.

Eduardo proclaims that his basis *is* spiritual. I ask what mine is. Nobody can say. So I fall into the category of nonbasis people, who, according to Eduardo, are eccentrics—artists. All right. Eduardo sits in the Oriental fashion on the carpet; I breathe deeply in my tight old rose bodice. Physically, I am in such a mood of love and surrender—diffuse, clinging—now to Hugh's hairy, firm wrists, now to Eduardo's extraordinarily beautiful profile. His "acceptance" of me has taken the proper form: Despite my deficiencies in living, I am otherwise a superior person. It is what I said of Lawrence: Certain weaknesses make a man subject to having certain revelations.

April 6. Hugh is more severe with Murry than I am because I was more preoccupied with what was *true* in what he said. But I agree with Hugh that the sum total of his work shows the danger of dealing psychoanalytically with imagination and genius.

I have now decided to wait and to write a long, slow book much later, when I can have the last word! My contribution is going to be the psychoanalysis of the creator exclusively, so that once and for all he will no longer be confounded with the ordinary man. Jung has already suggested the way; I will begin from there. I have almost determined to turn away from fiction to psychology, philosophy, and criticism, and I would do it except that I mistrust the capacity of a female mind on those subjects. Yes, sir.

It was a "little life" today. Hugh was not well and stayed in bed, and we so enjoyed each other's mere presence that again we wished ardently for his retirement. I was busy on little things. One of them was the care of my body—a veritable aesthetic ritual: the warm bath, the deliberate and careful soaping and cleansing, then the thorough oiling, the spreading of roseate pearl lacquer on toenails, the massaging of the face with cold cream until it glows, the astringent brushing and oiling of hair, and finally the care of the hands. To be clean all through, and soft—what a delicious sensation! I love to feel so beautifully in order—thus, to begin the week. It is as though I try to smooth down an overexcited body, to gain an ascendency over my nerves, and thus to maintain lucidity and measure. So French! So French, my orderliness, neatness, all to be blown away in a minute by an emotion.

April 7. Keyserling has been a *big* voyage for me—although not an altogether satisfactory one. I have taken many notes. Sometimes I feel that I would like *everything* in my Journal—not only personal things but also the reading I do and my work. The work is so intimately part of my world. And so is the reading. But very often I assimilate it unconsciously. I cannot make very clear or obvious remarks at first. My notes are chaotic. Then one day it all becomes synthesized and the fragment has become part of the whole. Keyserling's thought has penetrated—what I want of it. And the Journal, meanwhile, is left out of the activities. Sometimes the synthesis appears here, in one of those brief, rootless, condensed phrases which nobody understands because they fall, apparently, like a shooting star—from the unknown. If I would carefully give the roots, the map, the progression, it would not be so mystifying. Certainly I live according to Keyserling's dictate: I supply the *creative activity* for all information or suggestions given to me. Therefore I am doing a lot of independent thinking. And I cannot take my Journal everywhere or it would lose its life in the Deluge.

Eduardo has a faint suspicion that I have not changed quite as much as I appear to have changed. He stands watchfully expecting the betrayal of the 1830 type he knew. I have not betrayed myself. I know that *literally* I have not lived or experienced very much— not half of what he has—but *imaginatively*, yes. He often uses his actual experience as a weapon, to defeat my truths. I have felt the need of equal weapons, because *his* mind is in some ways literal. When I saw him trying to assert his superiority, and having no faith in my psychology because I was not the "Woman No Man Could Hold" but the 1830 bundle of femaleness preserved from the world, I struck a new and overwhelming pose, which I have kept ever since. I *was* the "Woman No Man Could Hold." I had gone through those experiences. John, for instance, had been my lover. In fact, everything that my imagination has played with this year has been presented to Eduardo as a reality. Imagine his confusion: two superimposed images—one, a strange, deceitful experienced woman; and the other, cool, creative, imaginative, distant, poetic, naïve. His instinct tells him the 1830 type is not dead. But there are my words, my stories, my confidences. It is to the *woman* he has talked and given his own strange confidences. If he only knew that the experiences of this woman are imaginary —that most of her which fascinates, repels, astonishes, and interests him is *imaginary*! How often I have amused myself with my impersonations. The demoniac has at the same time made him unable to understand me. I *look* so true and so whole and so simple! It is impossible for him to make me out, to completely understand me. He says I am "strange." I should hope so. My imagination has absorbed what my body has not tasted, so that I can give Eduardo the comprehension of the woman who has lived. What fun! And fundamentally, this satisfies me. These delusions and inventions do not weigh on me. Our relationship has been so enriched. What a woman he has known! (Nonexistent.) What a man he has revealed to this woman—how stimulating the enigma of my being. I can talk with *authority*! And the loveliest quality of my disguise is that I thus conceal again, as always, my true self.

April [?]. Joaquin's tormenting restlessness was not sexual but due to an inflated imagination (the same inflation which produces creation). Eduardo and I made the mistake of urging him to *sexual* experience. That was not his need. At the same time, what we felt to be an excess of pride and self-sufficiency was the isolation of a very young soul which had perceived and sensed experience without having lived and was proud of its nonparticipation. The only falsity here was that big, impersonal, cosmic curve of love embracing the void without contact with life itself. For that, there is a remedy: a concentration on personal, *human* relationships (not necessarily sexual), a contact with the earth, a repose of the imagination, as soon as it ceases to be distended beyond recognition, so as to find true values again.

Suddenly, this afternoon, after Joaquin had been talking with Gisèle and later reading to her from his diary, the terrific tension broke. He drew close to Gisèle and to me. Lucidity returned—a lucidity which consists in not being wholly and irrevocably taken in by the creative and destructive imagination, and in finding one's thread again.

I am fortunate in having Hugh, my beloved thread. Joaquin's thread is less steady. Gisèle is not always there, and she may marry. Certainly under the pressure of an inflamed imagination there seems little we are not capable of doing, for the image is momentarily substituted for the reality or the truth (like my image of a fantastic, vivid, brilliant, genius-permeated and errant life), and the mirage leads to sheer destruction (wouldn't I end in a sanatorium but for my truly regular and secure life?). Joaquin has yet to learn the regular descent into normality, the drawing of new and pure energy from the earth (the garden, the house, the animals) and pure love from relationships in which sacrifice and fairness have a share.

Hugh is right in observing that it is the swiftness and thoroughness of Latin love affairs which make them so true. The equivocations and half-measures of puritans are the elements that create a heavy and stifling falsity. Gisèle is natural, and therefore she puts her relationship with Joaquin on a natural basis, as I try to put mine with Eduardo. But John ruined and falsified our impulse with unnatural scruples (he couldn't even write spontaneous letters!). Ours has been an unfinished, awkward relationship because of his unnaturalness. I tried to put him at his ease with my letters, and he couldn't follow me. Now I remember his marveling at my naturalness!

April 13. A wasted day, receiving friends who mean nothing to me, hearing their insincere comments on the house, for they do not like the country or the garden or the dogs, really, and they are so out of place, and yet the comedy of friendship, which is so humiliating, must drag on, for the "form" of it. For a day, at least, I feel utterly depressed and so painfully and hatefully *superior.* I hate to feel superior. I like to live on my own level, or with those superior to me.

Joaquin and I both have a curious idiosyncrasy: before the very people who, we instinctively feel, do not estimate our true value, we will make a statement we *know* they will interpret against us.

I had that impulse with the Guilers. I talked once about how dangerous it was to live with such an unselfish person as Hugh because it was so easy to let one's self become selfish. His mother did not interpret this as my effort to give Hugh as much as he gives me but as an admission of my selfishness, and I knew she would interpret it unfavorably when I said it. The feeling which follows such candor is a strangely religious one, as after confession and penance—the same I had as a child when I served myself the worst piece of meat, or the burned part of the rice or a rotted banana. I do not understand it. These are strange, quixotic moments of truth, which we usually dominate and handle as we wish.

Why does Eduardo have power when he is here, and none when he is away? Away, he dissolves. The contours of personality, no longer insinuating, now seem merely vague and fluid. Whereas John can be felt at a distance.

I try to combat the devastating effect of cold on myself with the rubbing of oil—which occasionally accomplishes a truly Biblical resurrection. Why does one's body never learn assimilation of a climate? I yearn painfully, profoundly, and always for the tropical. In the tropical climate alone do I really blossom physically.

April 14. The songless days are unbearable. Even though I have written a story which has been on my mind for a long time, about a woman, a "partouze" [orgy] in the Bois, and a deer. It ends: "The deer, soft-footed and timid, led her back to the waiting car." Led her symbolically away from the orgy by the fact of his appearance, his pride, and his animal fineness. When human beings imitate the animals, they are not as beautiful as the animals. In other words, I put certain ethical restrictions on Paganism.

April 15. I pursue a continuous, studious reading, all of the kind which demands application and concentration. Occasionally, I feel a bit overwhelmed. What is neo-Platonism? The true definition of mysticism? Besides, I like to wander off with these reveries—in between—and with these books you can't do it, or you get lost.

Do I pretend to make up for my lack of education? I think so. I feel my originality and independence quite strong enough. Witness the anarchistic notes on the books I read. I have no respect for anybody! Knowledge does not appear imposing to me, nor does anybody have the last word for me, whoever he may be. I have to be deeply convinced. Logic, beauty of style, grandeur of construction, sanctification and beatification of name—nothing. My reading is a perpetual transcending, from my own personal evaluations. In a way, I may only build a philosophy from the element of my individuality. Everything else appears baseless to me, because one theory is as good as another, and only assumes a degree of utility in relation to the individuality that can live by it.

April 17. My darling is away for a week. When he is not here I'm only half alive. I've tried to keep busy. Have gone out a great deal with Mother and Joaquin. Met the composer Florent Schmitt at the Lumleys'—a small, sharp gray-haired man with a mischievous mouth who is always flinging out direct questions like an indiscreet child, which amuses everybody. "Who are you? What do you do for a living? You're not married? *Why* aren't you married?" He took quite a fancy to my face and immediately invited us all to his house.

Last night heard [Felix von] Weingartner direct the Pasdeloup orchestra—a serious, lucid, precise, energetic man—really interesting. But I didn't care for Beethoven's *Pastoral* or Berlioz's *Fantastique*. Both too literal and descriptive. Prefer suggestive music like Debussy's and Falla's—something more subtle, more indirect. Gilbert told me modern music will go one way or the other: toward more suggestivity or back to classical impersonality, like Bach. So now I know why I dislike Bach: classical impersonality! Boredom! Colorlessness! Restraint! Hell! Poor Bach, he missed a lot of fun being impersonal. I would give twenty years of my precious life to be able to write as Debussy composed, to be able to give that profound, intangible, wordless sensation. I suppose Lawrence achieved that. It is so penetrating, so infinitely more than Beethoven's cooing birds and Berlioz's timpani storm, although Berlioz sometimes achieved almost unearthly sounds, which seemed to come from outside the instruments.

In all this, realism is left far behind—but what a problem in writing. Music can do without a concrete image—even the names on the programs are not necessary—but writing appeals to the image-making mind, and so to give a sensation you must produce an image, and the image must be drawn with the forms we know, or remain an abstraction. Music has a right to be abstract. It goes directly *through* our senses, whereas only a certain kind of writing will go through our senses, and it is this penetration I seek; for ideas, to me, are not cool emanations floating in the void, but warm revelations which course through my blood. Only, how to inject them into the blood of others, instead of vaporizing fumes around them, at which they can always throw cold water. You can't throw cold water at music. The minute you hear, it is inside your body. Joyce probably meant to achieve this by demanding to be read aloud, hoping to attain the senses directly.

Oh, well, I have set myself a rather distant star to shoot down. And probably at sixty, when I am all through, someone will pipe up: "It all lacks plot." And I will be sent to a bird-stuffer to be padded as a complementary ornament to Don Quixote.

April 18. Jung defines the nondirected thinking of our epoch: "We no longer compel our thoughts along a definite track, but let them float, sink, and mount according to their own gravity." It seems to me that this is how the moderns have approached the dream realm. It is the basis of Proust, Joyce, and Jolas's efforts in *transition.*

To be intelligent and yet sentimental is my great misfortune. To be taken in not only by others, but by myself, is the extraordinary truth about me which I cannot change. Why am I like a person who is susceptible to hypnotism in my susceptibility to the different powers of people? What is this capacity for submitting, melting, losing myself, in spite of my tremendous unity of purpose and my absolute, profound love of Hugh and of my work? Is it a capacity to live almost impersonally? How well I remember the tremendous curiosity about dancers and stage life I had, which took the form of an unusual devotion to my old, homely Valencian teacher—such sympathy, such patience and friendliness I showed —the hours we sat in cafés; I, listening to his stories, entering into his life so thoroughly that I felt and acted like a cheap little ballet dancer who "spoofs" her teacher along so as to get on in life!

Doctor's Waiting Room: Synthesis of one million salons—the legs of the piano on glass holders, a rug of monkey brown, upholstery of tapestry with overgrown leaves, a couple of porcelain lovers under glass, legs of chairs twisted like roots of ancient trees, flowers fadeless, scentless, a fireplace of veined marble, andirons of highly polished copper. A bunch of real poppies looked like nouveau-riche intruders, even at fifty centimes a bunch!

April 20. There was once a woman who had one hundred faces. She showed one face to each person, and so it took one hundred men to write her biography.

When individuality reaches such a fishlike propensity to multiply, it is time to stop and think. Personality is not what lovers of unity would have us believe. It is a succession of reincarnations within the space of one human life. That is, if you take the imagination seriously. But what is the *kernel* of personality? [Ramón] Fernandez [in *De la Personalité*] doesn't know much. I'll have to find that out for myself. The center of my existence is my love for Hugh. How is that proved? He is the only one for whom I would make sacrifices—*any* sacrifice. All this week I have loved him with extraordinary tenderness, extraordinary selflessness. He has unbounded power over a realm in me which lies *between* the soul and the body, grasping both. I would love it if he could encompass both absolutely, but some essence always slips out of his grasp, and it is that fragment which bothers me. I do not resign myself to my one hundred faces, even though they are definitely classed as imaginative, Hugh alone being the imaginative reality.

How clearly I feel the *urge*. I cannot pretend not to notice it. Even today, as I sat copying and working, I felt that I had stayed in one place long enough, that I must move on. Where? Is it in my life I must make a move, or in my work? In five minutes I *outgrow* both. I feel the shell too tight. Move. Move. Where? How? This is the way my voyages begin. My love arrives tomorrow morning, early. And then? And then? I wish for two things violently: the coming of John so that I may get cured and outgrow him; and the beginning of my new book in a purely modern style, which means that I want to shed this one, the worn one. I feel that the Joyceans are right, that Jolas is right. My state of hallucination is continuous—not so my power to transpose it. If I turn passionate I fall into cheap words, as Lawrence did. I cannot return to classicism. Those few days when I studied what is considered beautiful style I realized its deadness. Yet I love clarity, and my hallucinations and imaginings are not entirely chaotic, but intense, and it is this intensity of vision which classicism does not contain. See Bach. Bach suffocates me. I feel like breaking my chair with my feet, like screaming, sobbing, beating the musicians, setting fire to the concert hall, when I hear Bach. What of serenity? Yes, I *know* serenity—occasionally—the serenity between high moments—but that is not Bach's serenity. His is discretion, permanent good taste. I wish I had known and married him. Married to him, my eccentricities would be justified, my madness plausible.

I don't like the silence of a room, the ticking of the clock, the purring of the fire, when I am about to *move*, to go on a voyage. At such a moment such things appear mediocre to me, keep me from having visions. At other moments, they seem peaceful, healing, and precious. Normalcy. Pink underwear thrown over the green-and-black armchair. What a terror I have of happiness, as others have of the unknown.

A long time ago I stood in the middle of Boulevard Montparnasse and wondered what would happen if I wrote *all* I thought. I was desperately trying to break through my reticence. I have now broken through. There only remains to be written the revelation of the deeper dreams, which slip out, always, between over-definite words.

My darling arrives tomorrow, and my human body rejoices deeply. I wait for him by the quiet, low fire, while the creator vagabonds in the night.

April 22. The minute we were home from the station, at eight A.M., we lit a fire in our room and sat before it, but Hugh had taken all my clothes off, and our desire for each other was a true climax. The newness of it was incredible. As if I had never tasted his kisses before, as if I had never felt his body against mine.

In the afternoon I dressed carefully and tremulously for *him* —we were going to a boring concert together. He was amused by me, pleased, teasing. Our new love was very well, but what was the matter with the old—was it worn? I laughed. Perhaps not worn, but certainly too familiar, too peaceful. So now we are eager, eager lovers.

Today I worked—merely copying, which I hate, but then, it is really for my Love, and if my book appears, it brings his retirement nearer by so many days. So I copied, copied, copied. To soothe my nerves, I tried to compose another chemise out of odds and ends. At six o'clock I stopped. I went down to the "cave" and got a basketful of wood, which I arranged in the fireplace in the salon, for evening. I also instructed Emilia to make a newly invented dessert. In a little while I will go and powder and fix my hair. Hugh will just grin, a little perplexedly, but as long as he takes his lover's job seriously . . .

Parallel to my ascension, every moment of my life, there runs an obstinate falling short of *everything*—the concert, people, friends, world happenings, loves, books. That falling short should arrest my personal movements, but it doesn't. Ridiculously unequal, run the two lives. I dress for events that never take place; I live outside the circle of reality; I do not find my level; no intelligence, aside from Hugh's, answers my own. I love for two, three years a man who has never apprehended me. I sit outside his world talking to him in a voice which does not get to him—in my Journal. It is a vast allegory of delusion, fantasies, and escape; yet I survive. I neither die nor turn bitter. I shall be urged to create my own answers, my own questions, my own understanding of myself, my own world, my own characters, my own fulfillments.

Last night at the concert I realized my strangeness. I saw myself in an utterly original rose dress and coat of my own design, oddly painted, special, wearing jewelry as I alone wear it, in barbaric combinations, and I felt what a void my originality created around me, what a distance. Nobody came near me. The women threw uneasy and quick questions at me which I answered badly. The men were kind. I felt myself beautiful in an isolated, unclassifiable way. So I was left out. When I danced it was worse; the women were afraid of me. They wondered how is it literature doesn't tone me down? How does it give me time to appear in that outrageous rose costume? I see in Elvira's eyes that she has been talking about me. Always the insinuations, cattiness coming out. I divine it all. I wonder what it is that unleashes it against me, for each woman has her own kind of prettiness; why should mine offended them?

I could say, like Lawrence, "They all wish to destroy me because of my non-conformity."

April 23. For me it is not so much an issue of classical English or modern English as English English or Latin English. My tendency is to Latinize English.

The secret of what is called my *condensation* is that I am writing in English for French minds. Boussie is not bothered by my condensation; she *gets* it.

April 26. The tremendous voyage of which I had a premonition was into Rimbaud's world. It is as if I had gathered all the strength of my mind and imagination to leap *outside*, once and forever, outside reality, which stifles me.

My last cry was about the falling short, the falling short of everything and everybody—and then the leap, the leap into the unimaginable. Today I am gone and for good. In Rimbaud I have found the spaces, the air, the movement, the fullness I sought. I do not remember being so lightning-struck by any book as this, *Rimbaud* by Jacques Rivière.

I have traveled warily into the modern chaos, conserving my intelligence at first, then realizing, through Lawrence, that truth is apprehended through emotion and temperament; then sensing that the visions which demand annihilation of our intelligence and surrender to perception are those for which I would give up a thousand lives. As far as I can see, if Rivière is right, Rimbaud explodes reality, takes one into mysticism—and that is all.

Is this the level I seek—more than ever in isolation from human contact, with a companionship of abstract substances only? Is Rimbaud's *Illuminations* to be my universe—the insaisissable, the vertiginous?

It is done now. I can never retrogress. The basis of reality has been blown away by the very pressure of my imagination—other regions, other air to breathe, no boundaries. I tried for many years to fit into the actual world; I starved. I am ready to give myself to the other.

April 28. My *friend* now is Boussie. I have at last grown up to a full appreciation of her. It was in this place, in this garden, that she blossomed and was revealed to me. And in the long hours of quiet visits, of gardening together, I realized the riches in her.

Yesterday we read Rimbaud together—or, rather, she read Rimbaud to me. How far her mind goes, how quickly, and how promptly. I, who talk little usually, talk by the hour to her, about everything. And she told me about the man she had loved, who died in the war, about her worship of her mother, her feeling of having fully lived, having had her children through her teaching. She is fifty-one and I thought she was thirty-five. Teaching for her is an art and a creation. Translation is a creation. She has a gift of naturalness that I have never seen in anyone else. She is the same for everybody. Nothing intimidates her. Ease, independence, enthusiasm, an unusual gift for languages, a sane, healthy physique, an utter absence of materialism, a flexibility within a very definable personality.

April 29. Eduardo returns with a greater assurance and affirmation. He is himself convinced that he is a *great actor*—but that the day will come when he may outgrow all his incarnations.

He thinks he recognizes me in one of Grimm's fairy tales, where the lovely girl who is hated by her stepmother is sent to pick strawberries in the middle of the winter, comes upon three gnomes in a house and does not see them as ugly or despicable at all.

In a sudden mood of confidence I read him many pages of my Journal (description of our dinner at the Maisonette Russe— evening with the man who resembled John) and at last he is entirely converted to my way of writing, which bothered him before because he thinks I have not carried my evocative power into my stories, with the exception of part II of the "Woman" and the Boat Story. In short, I do not convey the moods as successfully outside of my Journal as I do inside it. I happened to be reading to him for personal reasons, but he became objective and judged it as writing, and was *entirely satisfied.* Which pleased me deeply. What is the answer? That I shall be creative merely in the Journal—and outside of it, critical and philosophical but not artistic? Eduardo almost agreed.

I explained to him the blessed innocence which I live in because of my lack of knowledge, which forces me to do my own seeking, always—even to find out afterward that an idea is stale. Often when I give him an idea he says: There is a book by So-and-so, and another book by So-and-so on that subject. News to me. But he now approves my efforts, which really lead somewhere new very often. We talked about evocative writing and music until we were quite dry. His writing will be primitive, all based on images, allegories, myths, fairy tales. Mine the very opposite.

Now we part ways and begin resisting each other, which will be interesting and beneficial to both. He realized the Frenchness of my mind by my feeling for Rimbaud. He will defend Blake, and I know Blake did more, was a richer mystic, a more complete poet, a man of great personal value, but it comes down to a matter of temperament. Rimbaud, and not Blake, carries me.

Yet I gave myself to the Anglo-Saxon language *because* of its poets and mystics. What has happened? There is a poetic quality in the Anglo-Saxons which is absent in the French. Why do I suddenly react to a French poet? Am I less poetical or less mystical? Have I become French?

April 30. Yesterday when Eduardo left me I fell into a strange state of pure, undirected thinking and fantasy-making. I wrote fifteen little pieces like bits of prose-poems, continuing the mood of the morning.[1] They would fit in *transition*. And immediately I made a note on the psychoanalysis of the creator: "creation by undirected imagining—a state of being like a trance—produces subconscious poetry."

It puzzled and amused Hugh and Joaquin, who felt that the pieces seemed deeper than they really were, probably because they were stirred indirectly.

It's funny—days ago I was longing to achieve Debussyism.

Visit to Florent Schmitt a failure. Nobody else there who could distract Mother's attention, and so she and Florent could dislike each other freely. At such moments I get so painfully sensitive, I can only plead with my eyes, now to Mrs. Schmitt, now to Florent. He is a strong character, droll, mordent, and Mother takes him seriously. And when Mother dislikes somebody she talks twice as much, dominates the conversation aggressively, and you feel her so overwhelmingly that even Schmitt was silent —poor man—and annoyed. Joaquin and I could not float; we sank. She delivered a lecture on Godoy (whose poetry of course they don't like), she insisted on being called Mrs. Culmell and *not* Mrs. Nin, she would not let Mrs. Schmitt and me talk peaceably about books. Even my passport (my face), though it smoothed Mr. Schmitt's nerves, could not neutralize Mother. When he came with unusual affability to survey my diet at the tea table, he was confronted with Mother the dragon, who accepted the cakes he intended for me. And all the hopeless subjects: what is the best route from the station, the Spanish revolution, the awful spring weather.

Mrs. Schmitt, who is ill, painfully wasted, had forgotten her kettle on the fire. M. Schmitt reminded her: "It is always the same." She justified herself: "Because sometimes I am thinking of something else." When he left the room she justified him: "He is in the middle of some work—he is tired. And when he is working, he is like the water, he boils over."

"Why don't you put the lid on him?" asked Joaquin.

Fortunately for him, we left early.

---

[1] *The beginning of* House of Incest.

Wrote ten more bits for the set of I don't-know-what I began yesterday. I'm entering a new phase in my writing.

Disrupt the brown crust of the earth and all the sea will rise— the sea anemones will float over your bed, and the dead ships will end their voyages in your garden.

The house had a roof of gold dust and windows the shape of stars—the door was arched in a half-moon, and a rainbow circled around it. The sun lived then and nobody else could live in the house but a blind cat—and I, when nobody is looking.

The house had the shape of an egg, and it was carpeted with cotton and windowless—one slept in the down and heard through the shell the street organ and the apple vendor—who could not find the bell. Exorcise the demons who ring the hours over your head—at night—when all counting should be suspended—they ring because they know that in your dreams you are cheating them of centuries—it must be counted like an hour against you.

Play the lutes which were brought from Arabia and I will feel inside my breast the currents of liquid fire which run through the channels of the Alhambra—from room to room—to refresh me from the too clear water.

May 1. Something has *finished* today, and I don't know what it is. John is not coming, and I no longer have the strength to live on imaginings. It was too much of a promise, too abrupt a denial. I cannot bear it. It found me weak, vulnerable. What has died is my hope. Now at last I feel the physical pain, the horrible emptiness of having desired violently in the void. The body rebels. Bitterness at last burns me. And this, when I was full of poetry, and therefore more than ever stretched out toward a climax.

May 2. As if it were in quest of a new life, I went to buy a new journal, and it amused me to barter to bring its price down, to deny myself the luxurious bindings, the prosperity and impor- tance, "because, you know, I have to buy so many—I must get something reasonable." And I bought two, one for now, for the work, one for Mallorca, and I give myself the length of those two books (equivalent to this one fat one) to be cured, to change the current of my feelings.

Last night we went to the movies, to see a sentimental *Charlot*. I was dressed in my Asiatic-Russian old rose costume, as for a Byzantine opera. Coming back in the car, again gasping in the void of an insufficient reality, I surrendered to visions—I sang, "the dead ships will end their voyages in your garden." I felt that seeping of liquid fire through me, the response of my body to a self-created ecstasy, like the rupture of sweet-acid which comes with the spasm of sexual union. The images make my blood rush back and forth, my nerves leap from tip to tip; until now I did not know what it was to *taste* poetry, to apprehend sensuously, to be connected to life by the channels of the senses. The beacon-mind, watching against dangerous ecstasies, is now useless; resistance to exultation has broken. Where life failed to flow, now the fantasies rise like the sea and fill me, fill the void. My world rises, an immense edifice of visions, stronger each hour.

May 3. The bursting of strength, and with it the bursting of anger, bitterness, hatred, all the dark and acid moods I never knew. Je me sens forte et méchante [I feel strong and wicked]. It is in such moods that Lawrence and Rimbaud lived. It is my descent into hell.

I curse what I love with a voluptuous pleasure. I myself am cursed now to love only the special or violent flavors of life.

Evening. Something moved me, and my mood altered. It was the laughter of the children at the movie. I laughed with them. My strength, which I carry inside a ball of lead, still hurts—but I am even stronger than my strength, and I *will* it to become poetry, not destruction.

May 5. Flabbergasting conversation with Eduardo and Boussie. We seem to be digging in the same direction; we all offer our experiences, our knowledge, to extend the same voyages. At a café or in the garden—Blake, Lawrence, Rimbaud. They are the Signs.

We dig into people, into books, into ourselves. Eduardo is flushed with nervous intensity. I am wrecked. Boussie is elated but poised. She instills naturalness and trueness and a kind of simplicity. We do not talk together; one day, Eduardo and I; another, Boussie and I. But it all flows together. Today the balm of Boussie's humanness was sweet and yet devastating. She has the intelligence which tempers. Involved as I was in a painful knot about John—desiring him, criticizing him, loving and hating him, blind with my obsessions—I let her analyze him, telling her more than I had ever done before.

It comes down to Eduardo's idea of planes: the necessity for completing a stay on every plane—the Circle to be completed. Reactions leading us from one phase into another.

John, according to this theory, would be reacting against his overserious youth, the discipline of professorship, his overserious beginnings in literature, discovering his own youth. Success, adulation and popularity content him. Everything else is for him connected with early disappointment (the failure of marriage, the futility of loyalty, the deadness of idealistic formulas). His present plane occupies him.

This is all very true. The difficulty is that the woman he loves must be on the same plane. Lilith is. John and I have been cursed never to really *meet*, to know true contact, for our evolutions are not in harmony. In fact, we are always at opposite poles. His poetic transition came too soon for me. I missed his poetic plane. We never speak the same language.

I meant this to be the end of my speculations on the nature of John. It would be good to end on a note of sympathy, to still my dreams and expectations, to be French, sadly tolerant, understanding, above everything else. In such a mood I want to meet him.

Eduardo and I, because our ideas are constantly getting married, can never entirely relinquish a certain overflow of warmth.

The other day Eduardo said: "I feel that if you were suddenly left alone, I would marry you and I would love you perfectly and entirely."

"That's only a dream!" I said.

"The Eameses think I am in love with you."

"Did you tell them the truth?"

"But it *is true*; I am in love with you."

In a sense, yes: standing on a traffic island together, waiting to cross the street, we seem to have elected, for the moment at least, a perfect feeling of union. I have learned to give myself up to the mood—it is very sweet. I meet his impulses toward me— when they come. And then I leave him, upset, and never say another word, never *cling*, slowly shedding the warmth, which is a little too fervent to bear in comradeship, shedding it as best as I can—to leave him perpetually free, unoppressed. And he is grateful for the freedom.

May 11. If I had not created my whole world, I would certainly have died in other people's.

May 12. I just cannot write a natural letter to John. I've made three drafts to get it *really natural* and it doesn't go. My imagination has completely confused things. I refuse to write him like an old woman, as he writes me—pater familias, etc., and I cannot find any familiar ground. The last one left, the literary, he has cut off by saying literary opinions are cold things and to please write him a nice gossipy letter! This simply means that I cannot adjust myself to the reality, I cannot conceive of a diminished John.

May 18. Back to regular hours of work, after much misery. Entertaining Hugh's aunts. Aunt Lisa Parker, who is Swedish and married into the family, is cultured and intelligent. But his aunt Annie, whom I had idealized through his eyes, is absolutely and astonishingly narrow-minded, insular, and British, and garrulous and impossible. We sacrificed three days and we're ill over it.

But we saw Ruth Draper—to me, the finest actress of our epoch, the most profoundly imaginative and creative of all actresses. Her impersonation of "Three Women and M. Clifford" flabbergasted me. To be noted: the absence of cruelty in her caricatures. Note, too, her economy of means—no make-up, the smallest quantity of costume: merely a hat, a scarf, an umbrella.

The beauty of her voice when expressing love and the simplicity of her bearing after the show reveal her own self as superior to all the women she portrays. Her power to transform herself and fill the stage with imaginative characters is unique.

"She has a nice smile," said Aunt Annie. And in front of the temple at the Exposition she said: "It's time for tea. Isn't there a tearoom about? We *must* have tea."

As soon as we were home, my poor darling blew up and said: "You are really all I have left in the world. But how do you think I can come from such a family?" An unanswerable question.

I was cross to have wasted so much time—besides entertaining the aunts I've had to go out with the new manager and his wife. Thank God, at last, a delightfully pretty woman who won't hate me.

Oh, I forgot a lovely moment. When Hugh was reading one of my stories to his aunt in the garden, she didn't get it at all. Suddenly I observed he was reading it aloud with pleasure and a *new* understanding of all its points. Afterward he said: "I was all wrong about that story ["Waste of Timelessness"]. It didn't need to be developed. I got *it all* today. It is very subtle and very suggestive." That was the one we had a tiff about and I wouldn't change! I was blissful.

May 20. A stupid day: Titus in bad humor, winter weather, my darling away in Biarritz, Mother cross, no good work done, fatigue after Segovia's boring concert (too much classical music)— so I come to you.

It's funny that I sense a *presence* in my Journal—and I did so even as a child. As if by excessive imagination I had created a companionate character, a responsive pal. It is incredible, but I did feel, when I undressed and got ready for bed, that I was preparing not for solitude but for a talk, a visit, a give-and-take. I bring you a fretful, discouraged, restless being—at war against the invasion of Mother's friends, at war with her own horrible timidity, which makes her say silly things to Titus, and obsessed with her own defects.

The Journal is waiting. Oasis. However terrible the day, however futile—the reality of my self-made world. Escape. Cowardice. In dark moments I will admit that I lack courage. I cannot bear anything: the bad smell of a workman sitting next to me in the train; the cold snap of wind; the awkward silences of Titus, who cannot talk to me quite as well as he talks to other people; futile trips in the Métro and in the bus; *waiting* for anybody; the admiration of old men. I know I will come home and, like Ruth Draper, hold conversations on an empty stage, create characters, give all the answers, think desperately of a story, as of an avenue, a quiet, free avenue leading out.

My moods carry me down into the realms of deeper knowledge. The Journal, which I feel is the presence of something, will go down with me, as far down as one can go. There, I am fearless.

May 23. In bed, at nine, alone—*bursting*—with the joy of consciousness of living, that deep consciousness I achieve alone, at such moments as this. Mother and Joaquin entertaining friends. Distant music and laughter. The silence of my room. Huxley's *Brief Candles*, as a prop to the Journal; his astonishing story "After the Fireworks" upset me. But then everything upsets me, because I am *in* everything. So I was in the story. John was in the story. And then I am angry and pleased and disgusted with Huxley for his lucidity, because now he adds emotion to it—

damn him—and so I am moved as well. Or am I just movable, susceptible? No, it is only when I relive my life in literature and find a terrible closeness with it.

The story of Pamela, who was a "spiritual adventuress—didn't want large pearls and a large motor-car—but a large soul—a large soul and a large intellect, and a huge philosophy and enormous culture, and outsizes in great thoughts"—but being young and not in the same sphere with her fifty-year-old novelist, gets a voracious physical love instead—ha! ha! I laughed at the story. For she didn't like it—she didn't really love him—she didn't want to be an eternal mistress; while I . . . Our story in a way was more interesting. But I didn't get the voracious lover, and I would have liked that. I am franker than Pamela: I say I do not love John, but occasionally I desire him; and I would like to be merely a firework for him.

I'm getting to the end of this Journal. After that I have sworn to be quiet—until I can do something and *finish* John. How I dream of six days on board ship when my "firework" will probably fail, both as a firework and as the extra-large friend I craved. I've got to go forward, and for some reason I can't. It is just as if I cannot write another story because I cannot find the end to this one.

Anyway, I was able to enjoy Huxley's story to the utmost, to understand it perfectly, to read it breathlessly with an ingenuous thrill. Literature spoils nothing. If you have enough flesh and blood, it becomes real again in your hands.

Mother's friends are gone. Banquo barks in his midnight-watch voice. I feel slightly uncomfortable because of the many lies I have been telling—fixing up things, I call it, with embroidery, lace, frills and dramatics—to Eduardo and the aunts. To the aunts, in order to hide my real self; to Eduardo, to efface his unimaginative friends. Truth only to my darling.

How to go about debunking myself? Delightful pastime. Where to begin? Whenever I see an objectionable female lampooned by clever men, I wonder if I fit the part. Somehow or other, I always slip out again into my own uniqueness. Why? Because I'm a little more taken in by my own dreams; perhaps because, as I have said before, I act spontaneously and calculate afterward, therefore being objectionable only on second thought.

I mean, I first jump at John's neck, and then, only then, do I begin to gab. Therefore the spontaneous acts are, for better or for worse, absolutely innocent.

John really missed something good: an absolutely intelligent female, really subjugated. And honest-to-goodness élan in a creature whose critical capacity could, at moments, match his. It would have been a rare firework.

God, Mr. Huxley, my story is better than yours. Except that it is so one-sided, and I've got to get John's side down, in all fairness to him. And wouldn't it be comical, wouldn't it, if John said: "Oh, about that little kiss—why yes, I'd quite forgotten it. Why? Was there anything particular about it?"

I suppose the only particular thing about it was that it was given to a woman who likes particular kisses and not the usual currency. Or maybe it was an accident, a slip—of the tongue.

May 25. What is Paradise? A summer day in an old garden, under a laburnum tree in flower—golden rain; staring up at the pink hawthorns; at the elm, Chinese-looking; smoking, with Hugh at my side.

How the cares fall off. The body heals, the nerves are untied. Two days ago I was near a breakdown. For a moment I thought I was losing my reason, my control, my power over life. I felt frustrated, tricked by my body. I had begun to fear that creation could not satisfy me, that I would wither through denial, that my blood was whitening. Hallucinations. I owe the trees my health— the beauty of blossoms, the beauty of things growing. Above all, the softness of the air breaks down my intensity.

And Hugh the lover begs: "Come into the house with me, come to our room—I want you."

A moment of bliss—and then peace again. I can meet tomorrow with strength. I would be so happy if tomorrow I wrote something. The Journal is too much a lament, while my work is a realization. The Journal is only half of me, the troublesome half. What a fine tomb inscription for the volume: The Journal is only the troublesome half of me! It is so fitting I won't write anything else—will sacrifice a perfectly good blank page and a half to that idea.

June 5. A pair of lace gloves, a red picture hat, a little red jacket, a Robertson clan plaid skirt, the turquoise cape dyed black, several evening dresses lengthened, new petticoats made out of artificial silk, much hunting after practical clothes and buying the unusual, a tremendous struggle to get myself into a tailored suit . . . The worship of clothes. Pretext: preparations for the trip. Hugh says: "Get me a couple of ties and a sweater."

I had not wanted to write here until we were in the train, but I was bursting with a love of costuming and the realization that it would all be for the last time, because I must sober down, in harmony with our new life. After all, clothes are the trip. You begin to travel when you try on that red picture hat whose wings will flap so becomingly in the sea breeze. John won't be on board, so I will manage to keep him out of the Journal, as I had promised. I got an immediate answer to my natural (?) letter, a nice, friendly, exclamatory one.

Had a terrible fright reading a eulogy of Dorothy Richardson, thinking someone had usurped my place or, rather, preceded me in literature. But it was a false alarm. Not me, not me, but it is very good. Cannot say more, since I have read only one volume. The love between women now appears possible to me, a mixture of fraternity and curiosity and perversity. I have only felt the curiosity so far. It is something new to explore—my feelings if I were a man novelist and powerfully desirous of stripping and devouring a woman. I should love a woman because I have never penetrated any woman but myself. It seems miserly of me. Colette must have understood more. But I cannot *imagine* the woman I could love—what pride! I have seen beautiful and desirable women, but I have never known a match for my mind. Colette is too French; Rebecca West, too intellectual, too English; Ruth Draper, too strong. Some women, especially American women, seem too strong to me, with a strength like a man's, and then, I am all feminine.

I wrote (perhaps with a premonition) in my "Woman" story that it was bad for a woman to feel masculine, and that a stronger man should make her woman again by assertion—so she submits and is saved. There is a masculinity in me only as an artist; as a writer I have the desire to pry into women, to escape from my own womanhood. Another voyage. Voilà tout [That's all]. It is begun. It began one day in the garden when I was seeking peace from the obsession and defeat of my other voyage. It seemed to me at the moment that woman had been deluded by the dream that she would know better than man *how* to love a woman.

June 9. To Eduardo: "I've just been shopping. Don't I look stupid?"

"No, you look particularly glowing."

A trivial life beautifies. Ecstasy over a pair of shoes to which there is nothing but a sole, a heel, a strap around the ankle, and two little straps over the toes. Ephemeral. Somebody will surely say: "My dear, how unpractical for rainy weather."

And I will answer: "But the feet can dry more quickly."

Brusque return to profundities. Thinking of my future work on the Journal and the psychology of the creator. I have a presentiment I am not going to rest in Mallorca.

June 10. Ten minutes later I began my life's real work, the transposition of my Journal into a printable form: use of "she," of continuous inward consciousness, a kind of Proustian tapestry. At each step I encounter a difficulty: the truth about myself doesn't matter or bother me, but the truth about others . . . We'll see. I have so often begun this work and found it impossible. But now my technique is firmer, and also the condition of misery I am in is when I do my best work. When I feel life is really devouring me, with its teeth in me, then I feel most like chanting lyrically about its power. Perfectly logical. It is also because *I don't want to die.* If it is cold (it was cold yesterday) and I have neuralgic pains all over, and the shopping is over, and I get a conventional letter from John, and answer him humorously, and Joaquin plays a Liszt sonata which upsets me, and Eduardo floats unwarm in my memory, and Hugh is so busy, and I feel small and weak, castaway, shipwrecked, then I am driven out of the sweetness of living into the powerful exuberance of the vision, a state of misery which is only slavery to life; and the more life buffets me, the more conscious I am of my worship of it; for the wonder of what I can feel and the depths of my misery are extraordinarily beautiful. I love it all, deeply, as when I first discovered violence and pain in passion, and that one can love to exasperation, to cruelty, that a kiss is secretly a bite, a caress a crushing . . . la douce violence [sweet violence]. Everything that is strong hurts. I like to feel the strength of life, its dark violences, its instincts, its climaxes.

I write this while looking up at the acacia tree in bloom, black Japanese branches and full white flowers. The peace of the garden and I meet. I surrender. All my strength is in being penetrated. Only at the moment of writing do I come out aggressively, to project what I have received.

My Journal is packed. My soul is packed. Lovely hours with Eduardo in the garden. He is painting. He let me hold the palette, the paint. What joy! He had given up the little sketch and allowed me to play with it. I painted in my own face and put an imaginative pose and costume in place of the realistic one, and so he went to work again and finished it. Collaboration. Sweetness. His fluid beauty, his green eyes and gold-cream skin . . . But I'm packed. I don't want to give anyting, I don't want to be so fond of Eduardo. I try to sever this connection, wondering how it is he can persistently give me a certain kind of life; I owe him a great deal, as a critic and collaborator, as the one it is possible to talk to because he is never too busy and never unreceptive, and he has such extraordinary ideas, such a talent for slow development, patient unfolding. Here is a friend. Why am I wary, cautious, parsimonious? Fear of my need, of my dependence. So I withdraw. I know my tenderness, so I reject it before it has time to unfold. Lovely hours in the garden, insidious, persistent, like the smell of honeysuckle at night. Oh, Eduardo, what a good friend I make you; you are the leader, as you wished to be. I wait and watch over my own overflowing self, to obey your needs. As it happens, you do not need tenderness from me. So I will keep myself permanently packed, ready to leave at the necessary hour.

The craving for friends and the rejection of friends. To be strong is not to wear one's self out against the strength of others, in love or hate; to discover one's own self-sufficiency. That, I will never know. I have loved these hours in the garden, even though my love of them has fallen quietly into a journal. He has gone home so light with the light burden of his self-sufficiency, and I have stayed and felt so heavy with my story—my story of measures. I have been strong at the moment of leaving, and in the Journal I sigh. And then in the story I will be strong again.

I read this to Eduardo. He was amused at my femininity. "You are not used to not being loved." And so I take mean little digs at his lack of masculinity (talk about his white love, his unwarm nature, etc.). And we laugh at our little war. And the comradeship is re-established. We sat and talked about his friend. I understand. I guess everything. I know that he has a certain kind of love for me, but in spite of my understanding, I feel a physical aversion. That, I cannot tell him.

July 1. St.-Jean-de-Luz. During my traveling I have a feeling that I want to keep my new eyes open, a fear that I may be looking at everything with yesterday's eyes. What an effort I make not to retrogress, not to fall back into memories, recollections, into past moods, but to remain independent of the past and thus to leap forward. The Basque region reminds me of drab days, tragic days: the first visit to Mother when Joaquin was ill. So I shake this off. It is all forward: I am better dressed, I am in better health, I love Hugh more solidly, I love my mother but I am not enslaved by her, she is strong and well, Joaquin is strong and well. But none of this helps. I am too fluid. I come to new countries without stability, receptive, open, dissolved. I do not imprint myself on the place; I let the place imprint itself on me. It makes me furious. This time I want to carry myself along, through the whole voyage, protect myself, open wide the new eyes of a definite being.

July 14. Mallorca.

To Eduardo:

A big mountainous island, with tropical vegetation, olive trees, orange trees, lemon trees, bamboo, almost trees, cactus, rocks, sienna-colored earth; think of a country where even the earth is not a dull brown (it was the color of this earth which made me feel I had found my physical home). A cool white house with a brook running alongside of it . . . cooking over two braseros . . . Emila washing clothes, kneeling beside the brook . . . Grecian earthen jugs to fetch water from the fountain across the road . . . dazzling white dusty roads, as in Cuba. The sea between the mountains . . . buzzing flies . . . grasshoppers buzzing heat . . . at night the sound of the brook . . . cats fighting . . . a bird different from those at home . . . in the morning a donkey sobbing . . . a sheep calling for its mother . . . books on psychology lying dead on the Spanish coffer, gathering dust. Long walks down the mountain to a small bay for sea bathing. We come out covered with sea weeds. Laura Riding, who writes for *transition*, lives around the corner, also several fake painters. We only talk to the natives, when we buy fish. . . . Inexorable diamond sunlight; heavy, nerveless, fat, gathering days.

As a vacation it began sadly. Hugh was quite ill, and I thought I had brought my poor Scotchman to a tropical island on which his Scotch nature couldn't thrive. I got tired out playing nurse. That is why I didn't feel like writing you. . . .

To say our vacation began sadly was to put it mildly. To surprise Hugh I arrived at Barcelona earlier than we had planned so that I might meet him at the boat. His boat arrived three hours before scheduled time and we missed each other. He went on a tour of the city, and I stayed around the hotel in case he should be calling there. I was bewildered by the gallant attentions of Spanish men, all out in the street because it was Sunday. The hospitality and warmth of the people penetrated through the crust of my tiredness, distress, anxiety. Before that, I knew I had found my physical home when I saw, from the train, the sienna-colored earth.

When I meet Hugh at the station Sunday evening at the appointed time, I faint in his arms. In our hotel room we talk until two A.M. His enthusiasm for Spain is very vivid. He, who as a boy would save flies from the flypaper, was subjugated, fascinated by the corrida.

The next day he went to the Bank, and I went to Tibidabo, to see Barcelona from a mountaintop—a big, flat-roofed city at the foot of a mountain flanked by the sea, which meant nothing to me when reduced to personal terms but a Spanish balcony where my conscious life began. This balcony, on an ordinary-looking apartment house, Hugh and I went to see together. On the sea, stimulated by the pain of leaving Spain and my grandmother, I began my Journal in a school notebook. I did not know then that the pain was because I was leaving my sienna-brown earth, my diamond glittering sunlight. Coming back from gray lands and brown earth, I blink and quaver before the light: I am bewildered, stunned. We ride in a car from Palma, with all our baggage, and our maid Emilia, to seek a house. We find one by the road, on the outskirts of Deya.

Hugh's illness predominated for five days. Mechanically I change the cold wet rags on his forehead, I administer medicine, read the thermometer, and watch over him, and sink into a depression. My own tiredness stifles me like a thick crust. Neuralgia tightens my body. Mallorca is a strange island, dispensing nothing but a heat that weakens my poor Scotchman, perhaps a pernicious tropical fever. In my imagination I have already killed him. I curse the inexorable sunlight and the red parched earth.

This morning we awoke healthy. The cheerful letters we wrote home were at last to come true for ourselves. Mallorca was wonderful. I wrote the truth to Eduardo!

I wear cretonne pajamas and alpargatas [rope sandals]. Our hair is black with olive oil. Hugh has a young, lobster-colored skin. I am already gold-nut brown, since I am not a Nordic. We write on the kitchen table while Emilia sweeps upstairs. The sun is milk and diamond white on the flagstones of the little terrace. "Pescado, señores," shouts the fisherwoman at the door. She is dressed in black and wears a straw hat as big as a modern lady's umbrella.

July 18. In the garden, in Louveciennes, I told Eduardo one afternoon that I wanted to become a psychoanalyst. I am absolutely determined. I am studying here, stubbornly. A strange thing happened which ought to augur well for my future work. I discovered my own illness and am taking care of myself.

Analysis One. Symptoms: excessive irritability; excessive sensitiveness to noises; fears of all kinds, which I never felt before: of lightning, of being alone in the house, of walking alone in the city; excessive and inordinate anxiety and imaginings concerning those I love: when Hugh was ill I could see him dying of a tropical fever; when he received a business cable I thought something had happened to Mother; fainting—several times in one month; many morbid broodings and long-lasting black moods; heart trouble. All this is duly described by Freud and is called anxiety neurosis. Cause? Sexual.

Now two or three times I had observed my increasing nervousness and morbidity in Louveciennes, but immediately I boasted: It will all dissolve in creation. And I created a home, a book, friendships, gardening, poetry. I would not admit myself defeated. I would not be so helpless as others. Creation would save me from the desires of my dual nature, from the necessity I felt to be in love with Hugh and infatuated with someone else. And so I worked. But today I admit myself defeated. My control is broken. My nerves are shattered by the constant leaping into space, which is creation. I see it all very calmly today, with painful lucidity.

First I assumed it was fatigue, worry over Hugh's health, our finances, the strain of moving to Louveciennes, the strain of writing my book; then I was more truthful with myself and I realized I had tried the substitution of many things in place of the one thing I wanted and was deprived of: John. This did not come to me as a simple Freudian logic, which is sometimes too logical. I struggled for my own truth. I began my analysis of myself and my condition in my usual strange way: by putting all my clothes, papers, house, and accounts in order. I always do that first. At home I clean up my desk and closets. Here I did all my accounts, tidied my clothes, wrote all the letters I had to write, sent Emilia and Hugh to the beach, and then I felt I could set myself in order. The outward order is a preliminary entertainment.

I cleaned up my conscience: the obsessions with John, which are apparent in my Journal; my tremendous dream of creation and creative living to cover that lack; the struggle to reason myself out of my attachment by finding out carefully how incompatible we are; the occasional emotional retrogressions; the struggle to supplant John by Eduardo, who is spiritually closer to me, and the lack of physical feeling in our relationship constantly recalling to me the sweetness of the other purely physical current; the full richness of my creative life the past year—how I made use of my poor dreams and emotions to write poetry; the struggle to achieve physical balance by the love of the garden and the dogs . . . simplicity; seeking purity in Boussie's companionship, self-sufficiency, and the absence of physical tremor. A terrible moment when all these things failed me, and my anger that they should fail. Unconsciously I had been hostile to Freud's theories even when I did not know of them! Today I capitulate.

I have possible before me a beautiful year of creative work: work on hand, in my head, plenty of studies, new intellectual fields for my energies. I have occupations which will richly fill my life: Hugh, psychoanalysis, Eduardo and Boussie, decoration of the house, development of the garden. Is one little physical whim going to destroy me?

Fortunately it will all be over soon. I must, as I said before, intuitively, get cured of my obsession with John. This can only happen by our meeting again. If possible I should have him and so be convinced of what I already know: that my memory of our physical current has been intensified by my imagination and that reality would fall short a hundred times. In some way or other it must be finished. I hope that it may happen instantaneously, that when I see him again I do not desire him.

What an awful thing to think my physical mechanism is truly outside my control, to think that I can be involved in such a slavery precisely because I try to overcome myself. Will it be a relief to admit my weakness to you, when everyone else thinks me superior? This, too, had to happen to me: I had to know my defeat in order to understand the illnesses of others. I should make a good analyst, for I have not been afraid of truth about myself.

Oh, I must rest from the beautiful perfection of myself, the magnified image of a woman who could not be humiliated or become ill, who could substitute grandiose intellectual dreams and achievements for a physical desire. I rest with the diminished woman lying on the terrace, relaxed and beaten by such a small, small object—a love which began with intellectual worship and then, because I am so entire, became also physical.

Analysis Two. The possibility that, according to Adler, I may have set myself too high an ideal, and finding I cannot reach it gives me an inferiority complex and illness. It is true I have failed to achieve perfection of character, although I have achieved a high mark in understanding and intellectual and artistic development. It is true I have elaborated a complex measuring by which I often assure myself that I have artistically and intellectually enriched Hugh's life and that therefore my failure in character is justified. Such a measuring attests to my doubts of the fullness of my gift to him. I also liked telling Eduardo this. Is it possible I doubted the truth of it? I have never known the conventional remorses, but regrets at my own nature, yes— perpetual hankering for perfection, strength, semitoleration of my true nature, which is vagabond, undependable, intractable, baseless. Two failures this year have humiliated me: the failure of my "ideal" character and of health, which does not allow me to carry out all my ideas.

If this were the only true cause of my illness now, there are remedies. Health: recognize the limit of my physical strength and give myself more time than other people to *arrive* (I tried to become a stage dancer in two years and broke down); defeat of idealism: realize that my poverty in character is equally balanced by other riches of the mind, that the ideal of character as mere perfection of conduct is incompatible with the development of intelligent being, that all fullness of being includes an equal portion of the demoniac.

It is possible, too, that I have an inferiority complex due to having been a sickly child and a girl; due to our poverty—in school I felt very embarrassed at being badly dressed; due to my fear of resembling my parents, whose character I did not admire:

in Father I only admired intelligence and feared his cynicism, sophistry, and love of luxury and glory; in Mother I only admired her courage and hard work and kindness but feared her temper, unreasonableness, aggressiveness, and tyranny. However, I don't like Adler's theories and I think he is not very intelligent, so this theory is the least convincing to me.

Evening: All contrasts give me a painfully acute pleasure: Hugh playing the guitar downstairs and my feet beating time with the music while I study the *History of Psychology*. This afternoon while the grasshoppers sang of sweet fragrant heat I studied Freud. This evening while we walked a bit in the twilight I made the Second Analysis. I lie in bed now. Antonio, the stone breaker, who is also a guitarist, is singing. His voice is Spanish— that is, serious and liquid and penetrating. Downstairs it seemed to me I was dancing. Up here I can see the future psychoanalyst taking shape. My mind takes so easily to this young science. I always craved a science, and this one satisfies me. As I write, my eyes fall accidentally on my small, very firm, upward-pointed breasts, showing between the lace, and inside of myself I am dancing to the rhythm of the two guitars and that voice. Again, I feel definitely and eternally, symbolically split.

July 21. Adler, to my mind, has a pea-sized brain. Apart from the general outline of his theory, which is interesting, his development and his book on the *Science of Living* are infantile. His chapter on marriage is laughable, and he bores one like a goody, goody idealist old maid. After the keenness, subtlety, and intelligence of Freud, he is a terrible contrast.

My admiration of Freud is confirmed by reading *Beyond the Pleasure Principle*, which struck me as profound and intensely philosophic. I got at one bound the idea of our "circuitous route to death" and to pleasure. The rest was arduous, and I must read it all twice, but it has a strong hold on me, and I am more willing to make studious efforts than ever before.

But this is not a notebook on psychology. I see I must start one, for notes are raining down. It is curious to observe, however, that all the pain of personal life dwindles in the warmth of purely intellectual research, that thought in itself diminishes the value of personal emotions and re-creates harmony. I love the cool warmth of thought, which frees the body of its restlessness, of its concentrated desires upon a near object. Perhaps I have begun my own cure. Or perhaps the fact that values are finding their true measures again means that I am cured.

I do discover now that I have not told my Journal the whole truth. Whatever I have left out, however, has been justified in two manners: the things that happened to me which I did not realize or face, which frightened or bewildered me; and the things that made no sense in my life, which I could not describe or explain properly. Now the first are the kind Freud would term "unbearable to the ego." Being, at the time, an extreme idealist, I tucked the strange happenings away quickly, convinced myself they did not belong to me or my *real* life, and succeeded in keeping them misty. Of these I now remember a few because now I realize their meaning.

I have always been in a state of amorousness, unconsciously, since a child, and without sexual consciousness at all until I was nineteen or so. My family still laughs at the story, which I remember well, of when I was five years old, in Berlin, and arranged to run away with a little boy because I had been scolded. They watched me pack my clothes and rolls, and go down the stairs. The little boy, six or seven, was waiting around the corner.

At eight years of age, in Uccle, Belgium, I also remember going to church with Henri, a little freckled scapegoat, and we kneeled in front of the altar and were married, to our firm belief. I knew no sexual stirrings at all and remember no games of that nature; except that once four or five of us, about the same age, were found contemplating each other's hindquarters, which we evidently found very interesting.

After that, at eleven, I fell in love with the Captain of the *Montserrat*, which took us to New York. Of this I recollect there is a trace in my Journal in the form of an innocent obsession. Later that passed in favor of Miguel Antonio, a handsome Cuban and the first man to tell me I was pretty. I erased my wild, lyrical outbursts about him from my Journal a year after having written them. I was ashamed of them. I had ardently wished to be married to him. I used to delight in going to bed early, and to sip sweet condensed milk while thinking of him. The taste and thoughts together seemed bliss. After him I became obsessed with Enrique Madriguera, romantically, and without the slightest physical consciousness apart from heart leaps at his approach and jealousy. Then I felt quite stirred by Eduardo, with a faint physical disturbance, awakened by our dancing together, but I had no sexual knowledge whatever (I didn't even know how children came into the world, and I thought a kiss could conceive a child) and no feelings except romantic exultation.

Before I met Hugh I went out a great deal with a big sensual Russian, whose excitement when dancing with me did not cause me the displeasure it should have caused me, and whose struggles occasionally to steal a kiss I did not punish very severely. I remembered wondering a little at this. When I met Hugh I was aroused by true sensual love. I remember I was stirred in the train by the sight of his legs in golf stockings. Our embraces and kisses at the beach gave me a profound, spontaneous joy. I experienced the first love moisture and the beating and excitement of the nerves. At that moment I asked Mother for explanations of sex and the sexual act, and what she told me rather surprised me. She said it was the same as when the man urinates. And I did say: "It doesn't seem very beautiful to me." But I was sure I loved Hugh and Hugh's caresses and I felt the desire for completion in our love. In Havana, Ramiro Collazo stirred me a little for a month or more, but nothing equaled the feeling of physical affinity between Hugh and me.

I did forget that once, when I was thirteen years old, just arrived from Spain, while taking a shower the water happened to trickle directly between my legs and that I discovered it was a pleasurable sensation, which surprised me, but which I did not think about again.

In St.-Jean-de-Luz, I had my one and only strong crisis of narcissism, which bewildered me, and I would not write about it because I could not realize it. It came with full force, a real physical debacle, a sensual desire aroused by the sight of my own body, and which swept over me with tremendous force. But after the satisfaction of it, I felt dull and miserable, and I think nothing remains of it now except pleasure at the sight of my own body.

Since my sensual awakening, however, two years after our marriage, I have been more generally susceptible to sensual emotions of many kinds, more subject to erotic daydreams, to a search for violence and extremes. I made a final and tremendous effort to save our marriage from destruction by speaking openly to Hugh, revealing my mistress sensibilities, and asking him to treat me at our moments of love not like a tender husband but like a lover, begging him to lay aside respect, pudeur [modesty], the feeling of my being his wife, and to my great surprise he responded with a tremendous joy and relief. Together we threw away tenderness, conventional restraint, and plunged into pure pleasure for its own sake. Our joys were very much increased; I had destroyed the last timidity, the false idealism. He answered and often surpassed my own ardor. This is a new phase, which began only in 1931 and which may save our marriage. We take all our experiences together, the demoniac as well; we are truthful about our erotic dreams and wishes; we have a secret under-standing, as between lovers, entirely apart from our marriage, our real life together. We have a tie of pure pleasure binding us. Hugh blesses me for my courage. I often ask him to make himself attractive, to wear this or that which I like. I am creating the infinitely attractive lover, probably for some other woman, but then one must be courageous sometimes, and I accept the gamble.

In some way we have succeeded in making our marriage serve a dual purpose. And, furthermore, I think we have reached a profound truth. If a wife cannot include the prostitute, who is the woman who knows how to play, she is only a half-wife.

Continuation of analysis: I am convinced that my sexual emotions remained imaginative exultations when I was young because of my extreme anemia. At that time I reacted weakly to everything, lacking full physical vigor. When I gained in strength (at Richmond Hill), I began to experience physical tremors. When I was in my best period of health and vigor (in Havana, before my marriage), I experienced full awakening.

I believe that my nervousness now is due to my having been too much ideally loved: by Eduardo, the homosexual; by Hugh, the restrained, ill, and frightened man (as you will see from his confession); by Gustavo, also a homosexual; by Enrique, who was burned up at twenty, old, tired of physical experiences. John's physical feelings for me almost saved me, but he quickly and morally repudiated the feeling after arousing me.

For all this I am myself responsible. I inspire that kind of love. My physical and sensual self has not expressed itself through my body, or at least not yet. My body bears the imprint and mold of my first essence: unduly pure and imaginative and poetic. It is not a true expression of my emotions. Witness my efforts at trying to reveal my true nature through literature and the aston-ishment it caused. Witness a strange thing: the stories I have told Eduardo, the lies I have invented, were all concerned with the elemental and purely physical love So-and-so felt for me (the

Russian, for example). I told all these stories because I wished them to be so. I was conveying to Eduardo that I wished to be loved in that manner. It was my misfortune to arouse extreme admiration, praise, to inspire awe, flattery, everything but purely sensual love. I aroused in men that painful division they make between love and sensual pleasure, since most men have a false modesty with the women they love and reveal their erotic desires only to the women they have no feeling about (the prostitute). Once this became clear to Hugh (as it became clear to me that if it was to continue to be so, I would keep the loves offered me and seek sensual satisfaction also from men I despised), balance returned, a balance which may be permanent.

Analysis of Hugh. During all this struggle, which I did not discuss with Hugh, I was learning much. Slowly, in my talk, he began to sense a new understanding. He had not read the books I had read. I began gently to question him, to seek the cause of his nervousness, to tell him a little about myself. This morning the questions and talk suddenly affected him. We were lying in bed after breakfast. He began to talk about his childhood in Puerto Rico; at four years of age he and Johnnie were bathing together and they began to show each other their penises—perhaps to play together; he does not remember. A Negro servant's head suddenly appeared at the transom window of the bathroom, and then the servant went to tell their parents what she had seen. The children, who had been terribly shaken, were thrashed. Hugh saw his mother feeding his little sister from the breast, and found her breasts so attractive he asked to be fed, too. His father got very angry and thrashed him.

At about six or seven, in Scotland, where he was being brought up by his aunt Annie, Hugh and Johnnie were urinating together over some pigs by way of amusement. A little girl came to watch them. Hugh showed his penis to her. A servant saw him and told his aunt. His aunt called him in and began leathering him for a long time all around the room, until he crawled under the bed. His act was considered a crime.

At this point in his recollections Hugh stopped talking and showed the most terrible nervousness and emotion, and perspiration appeared on his face. He left me for a moment, as if this were all he had to tell me, and then came back. I was so painfully impressed by the story of the beating that I did not talk. Then he went on explaining how his family's attitude in all these matters was of the utmost and darkest severity, in such a way that he began to feel like an abnormally bad child, and began to be secretive, reticent, and to dissimulate. Once, his mother, putting him to bed said: "I am sure that Johnnie is a good boy, but I am not sure about you."

Hugh accepted his humiliation with suffering and with defiance, too. In Scotland, Johnnie, who had had homosexual tendencies, asked Hugh to play with him. Hugh was never attracted to this, but he thought about girls a lot. When he returned to America at the age of fourteen, he met his two sisters again, from whom he had been separated for ten years. He did pursue Edith, but did not know how to proceed; it was more like a game of exhibitionism.

Now poor Hugh, when he came to this part of the story, broke down completely and told it to me with sobs: "It was terrible. I never wanted you to know it. . . . You used to say you were so glad I had come pure to our marriage, but I assure you it was not very serious; it couldn't be . . . I was too inexperienced." He was still filled with scruples and afraid I would be disgusted. I reassured him completely and soothed him. I told him all this showed simply a rich, sensuous nature, which was nothing to be ashamed of, and that it was all very natural, that even loving his sisters as women was terribly natural, that it was society (for the sake of the race) and his puritanical family who had exaggerated the evil of it. He was not very reassured. He was relieved by his confession, I could see, but still afraid. He thought I was reasoning intellectually and scientifically but that my feelings could not possibly be the same.

"Very well, then, if I were merely reasoning intellectually, my body would recoil from you in disgust, whereas I can prove to you that I feel no such recoil."

His face was joyous. He went to lock the door and came back saying: "Give me that proof." He approached me and found me loving. He came with the utmost joy and relief, as if he were being relieved at once of all his pent-up fears and desires.

We talked much more afterward. He realized his first kisses and embraces had been spoiled by his unnaturalness, his fear of being caught, revealed to society (as he was revealed to his parents by the servants). He thought my own courage in admitting my sensual desires had saved him, liberated him. We were really very happy, very relieved after the tension and his suffering and concealments. We ended by laughingly terming him my "first case."

We talked a little about the harms of so-called ideal love. We had been so revolutionized that I was not surprised when a moment later he asked me easily: "You were attracted by John, weren't you?" I said I had been attracted, yes, but no more. For I am strong enough to live with my secrets, and someday Hugh will be able to understand much better than he does now my love for John. I will wait for that day as he waited for the day I could understand his childhood. I felt so sorry for my poor darling, sorry, pitying, upset, and yet scientific too, and impersonal. I said to him that absolute purity was due either to anemia or to coldness of temperament and that I laid no value on it now. My phrase "I love the purity you brought to our marriage" was a relic of the old conventional idealism. Reality of nature, of being, the spontaneous expression of the instincts which are life, are infinitely more valuable.

July 24. It is astonishing to notice the terrific influence of complexes. My treatment of servants, which is abnormally weak, is due to my deep innate fear of the scenes made by both my father and my mother during my childhood (they were both very violent). When I do bring myself to scold a servant I have a feeling that I am being like my mother. To evade a "scene," I am capable of cowardice or lying. I have always concealed the defects of my servants as much as possible, dreading Mother's outbursts. I still get unduly nervous when I hear Mother scolding in a high voice and, usually, entirely out of proportion to the cause. The dislike of quarrels and the association they have for me is deeper-lying, too, than the treatment of servants. Mother and Father's quarreling together when I was a child made a powerful impression on me. I remember once that the quarrel was so violent that I fell into a fit of hysteria, which actually frightened my parents. I was eight years old.

A great deal has changed since I became economically independent from Mother and mistress of my household, and now I have often dominated her in preference to being dominated, and I can say I am emotionally emancipated to a certain extent, having gone so far as to show Mother an equal or worse state of temper in order to override her own. Hugh has reproached me for my weak handling of servants, and I am trying to improve, being at last convinced that my firmness bears no resemblance to the emotional exaggerations of my mother. I take confidence in my natural fairness and sense of logic, in the fact that I always handle people comparatively gently, even when I am angry, because I constantly overestimate their sensibilities.

How amusing it is to find no resemblance between yourself and others around you and then to find yourself portrayed in a book as a type in a philosophic movement (Irving Babbitt on *Rousseau and Romanticism*). My restlessness, pity, flamboyant dressing, individuality, reactions, are thoroughly tabulated. I personally fulfill the description of the romantic ironist. When I get too worried by my problems, I shall look for the usual solution in Babbitt. I can choose madness, suicide, or humanism. But how is it one does not resemble anyone alive and yet one can resemble at once all the romantic fools and diviners in the encyclopedia?

Analysis Three. Hugh and I arrived together at the conclusion I was afraid to formulate. I had obscurely begun to blame Hugh for my neurosis, starting from the point that when I married him I was not at all nervous, and in the best of health, while he was ill of acute indigestion and intense nervousness—so much so that when we married he did not approach me for two weeks, and when he did, two or three times he was impotent with nervousness and fear. At the time, I was profoundly shocked, because I believed he did not love me, and that our marriage was a mistake. However, in Richmond Hill we began to play without complete union. He used to fondle me and lose his strength between my legs, and thought this was coitus. I told him it was not, because I knew I first had to experience pain and lose blood. My virgin's natural recoil from the final surrender and his timidity and gentleness lasted for a year, during which we played at coming together, while Hugh gained confidence slowly, until one day he was strong enough and violent enough to break through. But I had to incite him even then. I did not experience any pleasure until one night in Paris, but I was always loving and receptive and willing for caresses.

Then began my nursing of Hugh, anxiety over his food, his numerous bad nights, the continuous sense of his weakness and exhaustion, the secret fear that too much love would weaken him more. This morning, when we discovered we were both thinking about this, Hugh even went so far as to say that my concern about his weakness probably prevented me from getting total sexual satisfaction, and it is true I often, very often, desisted, surrendered my pleasure, only half realizing that Hugh's energy had been very quickly spent and was very slow to return.

The fact that I am acutely sensitive to his state of being, his moods, would be almost enough to cause my own depression.

Then Hugh himself said: "If I had not failed you in this particular way, you could never have been moved by John. . . ." And I knew he was right. John, in my feelings and in my body, was vitality, power, warmth, sanity. I never deceived myself about his sensual power over me. This explanation I would never have accepted, because it was a shifting of causes to Hugh, but he came upon it himself, and I shall never forget the terrible morning when I awoke and thought to myself: I wish I could get away from Hugh; I am tired to death of his unhealthiness. I made my last great effort the morning of his confession. Now I am worn out. But he has been rid of all poison. He can now heal himself. His great fear of losing my love—because of his childhood actions, because of my desire for John—is eradicated from his mind. He must have been somewhat conscious of danger from John, because he desired me physically all the time. It was his way of holding on to me.

Of course, it is true that I strained myself, nursing not only his physical troubles but also Eduardo's psychological ones. But to this I owe the knowledge of what was poisoning us. However, to have gone to Eduardo with a need and to have again been asked to do nursing was what caused the final debacle of my nerves. I really think that this is the one time in my life when besides feeling sorry for Hugh I have felt sorry for myself.

Hugh and I said jokingly that this was a modern triangle, not a case of he, I, and another man, but he, I, and his complex. However, it would have been easier for him to shoot the other man than his complex, whose address he never knew exactly!

July 30. Hugh and I talked about discipline. I was telling him that the one good thing I had kept from the Catholic religion was the habit taught me by the nuns at an early age, during the retreat periods of meditation and conscious struggle for saintliness. At such times we were asked to meditate on religion, to practice silence and charity, to make sacrifices. I still have little notebooks where I inscribed the progress of my character and religious fervor. Long after I had lost the fervor, I kept up the little practices of denial.

I was not conscious of any morality, but of the desire for discipline, so that I might know I was in control, able to do without what I most loved. I still continue to give away what I am fond of, to say I don't care for the last piece of dessert if someone else wants it, to give away all my feminine secrets for embellishment (which makes Hugh furious). Then he said he thought he had sought discipline in his banking, for certainly his work was a constant discipline: no laziness allowed, no carelessness, no procrastination; continuous attention and effort.

August 1. I often tried to explain, even before I knew psychology, that I believed the writing of a diary would take the place of a confession and give the habit of self-analysis so perfectly that one ought to be liberated by it. Now I see from my own experience that one can start from a false premise (as I did when I said that not having John's love was what harmed me) and fail to achieve absolute knowledge of one's self and also absolute truthfulness. But it now seems to me that if one knows psychology, then the journal can be extremely useful in helping to clarify, realize, and organize the knowledge of one's self.

The value of psychology is enormous. It should be part of our normal education. I certainly want to possess a knowledge of it, a complete and thorough knowledge.

Our cure: Hugh and I have purposely become extremely sunburned, as if we were symbolically changing our bodies. We both look infinitely healthier and different. Hugh brings more vigor into our sexual relations. He helps me when I get tired swimming, and I let him assert his vigor. He loves me more because of my understanding, and I love him more because of his courage in coming out entirely and finding the real cause of the trouble. However, his jealousy has increased. He dislikes my one-piece bathing suit, and he doesn't let me stand about, because I am too much exposed to staring. One young German sculptor with a beautiful, strong body makes him furious because he is always parading before me.

What one learns from Freud is to think scientifically. He is the greatest thinker among psychologists, and his writing is remarkably incisive. Interpreted intelligently and broadly his theories are not as narrow as popular belief would have them be. He is merely a victim of puritanical defenses and fears.

Typical brilliant morning. I, in my colorful cretonne pajamas, read and sew and write. Hugh studies Freud and his Spanish grammar. We eat at eleven, sleep, and go down to the beach. We refuse to meet people, the eight or ten tourists who live around Deya. However, for the future, we have promised to be less "sauvage," as we think our sauvagerie is partly due to lack of courage and strength. Effort of meeting new people has always been a torture. Result: invasion by other people's friends, like Mother's, who in turn make us disgusted with all social life.

This is my only way of judging an action: "Toute sensation absolue est religieuse" [All absolute feeling is religious]. Religion of the artist—which, by the way, is one of the very few intelligent writings of Novalis, who is precisely the kind of ungenuine and weak romanticist Mr. Babbitt is right in lampooning.

Our way back from the beach is through a gorge and up a mountain, all rocky paths, gates to leap over, dried rivers to cross, lasting far longer than is good for my endurance. In fact, the first day I could hardly get to the top, had to stop and rest often, and would swear at the length and difficulty of the walk, so that Hugh called these stops the stations of the cross puss. The women here wear ten-piece bathing suits—stockings, skirts, etc. The German who parades before me is called Folies-Bergère and Narcisse. We speak of Mother's contraditis. And of Hugh's pendentif.

August 2. The quarrels between my parents must have had a profound effect on my childhood.

Now Hugh is precisely the opposite: gentle, tender, thoughtful, with unbounded confidence and faith and understanding. But my terror of his suddenly becoming like my father is such that I frequently dream that he has, and never until now could understand why I had such dreams. I identified myself with Mother's suffering. It took all Hugh's extraordinary gentleness to give me real happiness, real security, but then the last had to be ruined by my anxiety over his health.

Yesterday Hugh taunted me for the third time about the difficulties of the study of psychology, and how thorough I would have to be. When I expressed anger and surprise, because I was so used to having his utter confidence in whatever I chose to do, he admitted he had acted like everybody else, due to a feeling of envy of my genius. Furthermore, he thought it was such envy that prompted most educated and thorough "knowers" to taunt me about my careless studying and lack of plodding. A person like me who does not earn his progress must certainly be irritating, and I feel sorry for my dear Scotchman, reading Freud so carefully and yet unable to trip me up. Once, when he asked me a question, I did not remember Freud's answer to it. I invented one that I thought to be logical. When I looked it up, I found it was Freud's. That's what you call real knowledge. I assimilated Freud so well that I can solve a problem in his way without seeming to remember what I have learned. In other words, I have not studied Freud; I have understood Freud.

August 3. Seeing that there has been so much misunderstanding between us (Hugh, thinking I would be puritanically repulsed by his young sexual instincts; I, thinking he would be repulsed by my erotic desires, shocked by my naturalness), we tried the other day to arrange our future. I long ago asked Hugh whether it would destroy our marriage if either one of us had a little whim. Until the other day I had not succeeded in making him understand that our life together has a kind of perfection over and above us, that it could be possible for us both to have desires outside it, that in such a case we should be tolerant, give each other time to test the desire, because it would be very strange if either one of us did find another person we wanted to live with. It then came out that Hugh had had thoughts of this kind and had deeply feared an emotional and destructive reaction on my part. This fear poisoned him, be- cause he also revered our life together and desired the security of knowing it would not be destroyed by an incident. (He also seemed positive that the incident would be ephemeral.) We both recognize in ourselves a capacity for intellectual tolerance and reasonableness, but also a great fund of emotionalism, and wild jealousy. Even during our talk Hugh showed tremendous jealousy and said that I was not to interpret the desire for security as a sign of greater tolerance on his part, but merely as a greater effort to preserve our love. I confessed having often been nervous thinking of what Hugh might do if I erred in the smallest way. Of course, the display of his jealousy and my realization that his tolerance was but an intellectual pact kept me from telling him about John, a revelation that seemed to me absolutely futile and unnecessarily cruel.

But I do wonder why he should be more loving and more jealous than ever. Is it the discovery of his powerlessness to satisfy me? No, because our sexual relations are very rich and complete, and I have convinced him of my renewed love for him.

He admits all kinds of things which I have tried to keep him from realizing, and I admire his courage and truthfulness. Last night he was talking about my independence and daring in thought, and the fact that my lack of education has not hampered me. He began to prove to me how his thinking had never been original. In college he was influenced by John Erskine and by Eugene Graves. Eugene discovered and led: Hugh followed, although with great fervor and great understanding. After that he fell under my influence. I led, I suggested, I invented. This situation hurt me, because I am by nature Latin, and in my love I like to be led, and I had instinctively craved a great leader due to my fatherlessness. Those were years of deep disappointment for me. I had to realize that Hugh did not have originality. It was then, too, that I turned to John, the teacher. Now I have an appreciation of Hugh's understanding, and of its rarity; and after John failed to lead me, I go ahead.

The Latin desire is satisfied by the fact that I manage to lead without seeming to lead, without noise, without ever hurting Hugh's feelings, and while bringing out all his talents: by urging him to perfect his guitar playing; by the dancing, which gave him so much confidence and success; by my dependence on his learning and education (by which he can always feel superior to me); by encouraging his social poise, which he has got through the Bank and which I do not have; by carefully uncovering and making him conscious of all his qualities and charms—his smile, his humor, his vision in banking, his management of men and women, his seductive way of selling trusts, his superiority in sports. (I have so much feared to crush him by my more numerous gifts in art.) How much I think about these things and what happiness when I see him blossom out: he smiles, he plays tennis glowingly, he is satisfied with his work, of which I show an intellectual appreciation; he proudly shows me his body, of which his family has made him ashamed because Johnnie was fatter and better-looking; he dresses up to please me. I make fearful scenes of jealousy, half in fun, which he enjoys. All this, up to now, unconsciously, but now I see the result of my effort, and how I have tried to make Hugh find his own way of counterbalancing my originality.

The greater part of creative work comes from the unconscious. I have had innumerable proofs of that. Principally in the fact that my "Woman" story contains the whole Anaïs-Hugh story and was written long before I was at all conscious of the situation. A psychoanalyst could have read our life and problems out of it, although I could not myself; for me it was a "story." That is also why different readers get different meanings out of the same piece of writing—that is, according to the degree of one's awareness and to the widening of one's consciousness. The more psychic a being, the more an artist, because the unconscious is more expressive.

August 4. Last night I dreamed of John. We met and he kissed me, and I forgot all my doubts and questions, and it all seemed natural to begin again. I awakened bathed in contentment, and have been singing all morning because I remember the kisses. Oh, God, I am headed clear for destruction because it will not happen as I had dreamed. I cannot think of anything reasonable, cannot see him, or criticize him. I can only feel that I want him physically with all the strength of my being, that I want him, want him, want him.

What almost destroys me at such moments is that having felt him in my dreams I begin to expect him, as though he were in Paris now. All day I have expected him to arrive here, to hear his voice, to feel him at last; my heart has jumped with false sounds or sights. I could not sleep as usual after lunch. This afternoon I am reading philosophy and yearning for reason again. I am dressed as if he were coming. I must, when I get to New York, make sure that he will never come to me.

August 5. At the same time I feel a tremendous bound of affectionate pity for Eduardo and am thinking a great deal about finding a way to solve his psychological entanglements. I write him a loving and playful letter. I am glad to know him happy with his friend. There are many things I wish I had money for: to give Eduardo presents; to send books to Miss Lemer, who is paralyzed; to send art magazines to Mrs. Hernandez, who is out of touch and lonely; to make Joaquin enjoy traveling; to give Hugh a rest from the Bank; to buy more books for myself; to give Mother a new chickencoop and clothes and a little care for her own visits; to send a present to Kay's little boy Paul, who loves the violin; to carry on a magazine for good young writers. Ouch, this sounds like my childhood plans to be a nun and take care of everybody.

August 7. We half jokingly imagined what would happen if Hugh came to me and said: "I am infatuated; give me six months' leave."

My natural answer was: "All right, but I also want six months' leave!"

He said in that case he would give up his "leave," because his jealousy would be stronger than his fancy for anyone. He would rather give up anything than give me up to someone else.

I laughed and said: "At that moment your jealousy would disappear."

He insisted that it wouldn't, because he knew in the back of his head that nobody would be worth as much as me.

"Well, well," I said, "then I must find a way to help you calm your jealousy so that you can enjoy yourself—by secrecy. If we say nothing to each other it will not arouse your jealousy and we will both enjoy ourselves." (I had reasons to know the efficacy of this method.)

We agreed that it would be much better. We also talked jokingly about the inconveniences of such affairs. Hugh likes our home life. He would still have to seem to be living at home for the sake of the Bank, my mother and his mother. "But you wouldn't sleep in my bed," I said. There was my jealousy talking. What a nuisance! (And how could I find pretexts to get away?)

"Suppose," said Hugh, "you had a child?"

"I would bring him home and he would call you 'Uncle Hugh.'"

"But suppose he were black?"

"My fancies don't run in that direction."

"Oh," said Hugh, "this is an abominable talk."

"How angry your . . . woman will be," I said, "when you take me out with a Vice-President and I knock him out."

"Shut up!"

"I'll have to teach your woman to give you enemas!"

"Hell," said Hugh.

"Don't take a Frenchwoman; she'll steal all your money."

"That's true."

"I would feel so much better if you took a Spanish woman, who would adore you and take care of you."

"Let me tell you," said Hugh, "I'm perfectly satisfied with you as an animal woman, as a femme-maitresse. I am going to satisfy you. No more of this nonsense talk."

"But I do think it ought to be a secret."

"I agree," said Hugh.

Now I know perfectly well that I can keep a secret and that Hugh can't, especially if he is miserable, so I see where I get the best of all the bargains we have made in this world.

Hugh remembers very well how natural it was and how much I enjoyed his first caresses, and how it never occurred to me to ask him if he was going to marry me. The puritanism which made me react violently against France was its appearance of calculation and nonspontaneity, its intellectual libidinousness (with lack of virility), which I still feel today.

Why is Hugh more jealous and I less? According to Adler, all my efforts to give him utter confidence will not succeed, nor will my making myself purposely small.

Anyway, I began to call attention to my weaknesses, and together we came to the conclusion that I have an inferiority concerning my physical endurance. At two years of age I had typhoid fever, which deprived me of the plumpness and cheerfulness I was born with, and made my father call me an ugly child, which made me very sad. I never got rid of this belief until I was about fifteen, when I went to a dance and became the hit of the evening. Anyway, I grew up frail and small. At nine I was struck down with appendicitis (a grave, last-minute case with complications which kept me in the hospital three months). I came out a skeleton, and they shaved my hair. From then on I was considered frail and I was made to feel so. People said so. The Spanish golden pallor was overpale. My aunts commented on my thinness. I was anemic. I caught colds often, and they developed into bronchitis. After coming to America, where the supreme idol was health and hardiness, I suffered from my inferiority at the gymnasium in school.

Then with will power I began to want to surpass everyone. I won races, I held myself well, I danced well. I abhorred basketball, but I played it and took some terrible blows. At the same time someone always appeared to protect and serve me. A lovely, big, red-cheeked German girl insisted on carrying all my books home. Poor Eleanor [Flynn] gave up her love of walking so as not to tire me out. Yet I was striving always to show I was not weak. At the time when we moved to Richmond Hill, my desire for health took a definite form. I tortured myself with ice-cold showers, ate apples, and took long walks in the park. And I did get well. But only because all I had to do was the housekeeping. Then I took up posing for artists, which I did with my usual enthusiasm, never wanting to rest if the rest period came at an important moment in the work, being always on time, and never failing to arrive (I was so glad to get work on Sunday). All this, with a sense of elation, driving myself, doing more to deny what others could read in my face, denying my lack of strength. When I took up modeling dresses in the daytime and modeling in the evenings to make more money, I was utterly silly. And it was at that time I didn't eat any lunch so as to have time to write in my Journal. Then, of course, the crash in health came. I was taken to Havana by Tía Antolina. In five months of idleness and pleasurable living, I became well, plump enough, and with a little color.

Then I married Hugh. The feeling of inferiority was very strong; Hugh's sisters, whom I took as an example, could play tennis, dance, and swim in the same day, and I couldn't. I didn't notice that Hugh was not well enough to do these things. I thought he was giving them up for me. I had just enough strength for the housework. I remember that my marketing exhausted me. I wouldn't confess to anyone that my strength was so ridiculously low. Poor Hugh. I always imagined him someday attracted to a big, tall, square-shouldered American girl, playing tennis with her, enjoying her endurance.

When I told Hugh about this during our analysis, he laughed: "Don't you see that she would have killed me in a week, and furthermore despised me for my weakness, for I, too, was forbidden to enter games at college because I was below normal in health."

"Well, well."

"And what's more," said Hugh, "we have exactly the same measure of energy, and we are always tired at the same moment, and tennis tournaments were very bad for me; they exhausted me."

And meanwhile I had been so humble about not being husky and sportive. How many times, I confessed now, I climbed a mountain with him only to conceal my weakness (and then was ill) or swam, or danced, keeping inside of me this bitter feeling: Never mind. Your damn old body is going to do its job properly. But this was unwise, since I always paid with a breakdown. How sensitive I was about being frail. How beautifully the dancing brought me the revelation of the perfection of body. I had, like D. H. Lawrence, a body with a strength of its own. But I had too much will, a power which broke my body ten times at least and which was defeated.

"Now it is clear between you and me," I said. And at that moment Hugh was overwhelmed with love.

I sit here alone, defeated, without strength to go to the beach. This place has not given me as much strength as Switzerland. And so I am going to sail to New York no huskier or fatter than when

I left Paris. But now I am resigned. Hugh has promised me a trip to Switzerland. And besides, I have had enough strength in my life to write much, and to make two homes, and finally to acquire a science which has cured my husband.

Little inferiority insect, you must always be summing up what you have done because you know that there are women in the world who do much more than you do, who have infinitely more physical power.

August 17. I have done something here that I have never done before. On every vacation we evaded people. Here I sought out two girls: one for her extreme beauty, the other because I had heard she was a writer. I invited them to dinner. Hugh was tremendously surprised at me. He immediately tried to find a cause. Is it psychology which gives you a stronger interest in people? Certainly I had no surplus energy to spur me on. What was it? I do think psychology has given me detachment; for instance, I enjoy the older girl's beauty for my own sake. I am not jealous, and I found the writer very interesting and original for a girl of twenty-four. Is this impulse going to last? I find taking care of others a great relief from my painful and continuous obsession with John.

This is what I imagine: that he has settled down again with Lilith and will be as immovable as he was before. That he could never (even if he were not entirely devoted to Lilith) give me the truly unscrupulous kind of desire, a lover who is finished with idealism and moralities and seeks only fulfillment, or a variety of fulfillments. I am going to be glad when the uncertainty is over and I can seek another fulfillment.

August 21. Hotel Tibidabo, Barcelona. Top of a mountain. The necessary wind, clarity, purity, peace, for my regression . . . to those uncounted days before the end of our stay in Deya. I had not been strong enough to go to the beach. I walked to the post office. Several persons were waiting in that whitewashed room. Robert Graves, a German writer, a Swedish painter, and a girl who sat reading with her head bent down. It was one of the two girls I had been told about, it was the writer. I wondered if this was the one who seemed, by her dress, to be a very tall girl I had met coming from the beach some days ago and whose intensity of gaze and beauty had deeply impressed me. I had also seen her one day when I was so acutely sick after the sea bathing that Hugh was carrying me up the mountain. She stood by, suggesting we call the donkey to get me home, and I was so ashamed of being ill before her. So I spoke to the girl at the post office, and it was not the one I had first seen, but she bore a family resemblance and was really nicer than the other. She was the writer, and we immediately found a great deal to talk about. She had written a few short things and wanted to know where to send them, etc. I gave her a lot of advice and when she passed by my house I gave her my list of magazines and offered to read her work and tell her what I thought of it. I liked the girl: she was young and very positive. Her work was good, with many promising qualities—the poetic, the ironic, and the fantastic. Hugh was already grumbling that I was doing too much, "giving myself away" without caution. I myself did not remember having spoken first to anybody.

I went to their house (Vera and the aunt, Mrs. E., whose husband had died three years after their marriage). As I talked to Vera I felt compelled by Mrs. E. and completely subjugated by her beauty. I watched her face, admired her tall, quiet, controlled body, her smile; everything about her seemed extraordinary. She was reserved and cautious indeed, until they both read the manuscript of my book on D. H. Lawrence. They were enthusiastic. They asked me questions about life, as if I ought to know (Mrs. E. was about thirty-five). I talked a great deal, against my usual custom. We had a lot of literary arguments. Hugh and I sought them out. We invited them to dinner. Mrs. E. came in a yellow dress, which set off her gold-brown tan and jade necklace. She had put on rouge and looked brilliantly beautiful. She was becoming more expressive.

Then came the strange moment when, in spite of her magnificent health and poise, Hugh and I said: She is on her guard about something; there is something the matter with her. We almost felt we had been reading too much psychology. Appearances denied this so vividly. Another strange thing happened. In my eagerness to see her I had forgotten to be slightly jealous, as I am usually; I could understand *anybody* feeling as I did toward her. I don't know what she felt. She seemed to argue against psychology and overvehemently about the morbid temperament. She did not like Lawrence but she would read him because she thought so highly of my study. I did not discover until later that Vera clearly recognized that her aunt, "the chief," had met her match and someone who could upset her very firm ideas. How much I upset her, I realized later.

We had gone to say good-bye to them at five o'clock. We were talking, she and I, about psychology. Hugh and Vera were talking about books. A lady, the landlady, came in for a moment when we were both feeling very excited and interrupted us. Mrs. E. suffered from the interruption. I more than her. I could hardly talk. Then when I prepared to leave, she dragged me away into another room. I had been telling her about the fear of the destruction of the ideal effigy of self. That had struck home. While we talked the sirocco, which had been blowing all afternoon, became violent. Twice Mrs. E. had to get up and close the door. I swore. I felt her troubled and I told her how I sensed that she needed psychotherapy, that I wished I knew more, to answer some of her questions, which were difficult. I knew now I had a powerful intelligence before me, who found it hard to find someone superior in learning who might help her. I confessed myself inexperienced. She leaned over the table and said to me: "For ten years my nerves have been driving me to travel from country to country. Now they are absolutely *shattered*." And I had to sit and think clearly. "I must find you a great man, I will do everything possible to find you a really great man." That was part of my own, new, scientific impulse to heal. But the impulse to heal *her* was like that of a tremendous, protective love. We might have talked more, but the others came in. The two women wanted to walk back home with us. The hot, hurricane-paced wind was like a furious whirlpool. Mrs. E. and I, walking, beaten, exultant—now she had lost her reserve, her beautiful calm. How pitiable! She had said: "I reason too much. I wish I could let go, as you do." My very weakness she admired.

I am afraid of the excitement with which I write. Two days have not calmed me. That day when we had said good-bye, they both had moist hands. Hugh and I had to return to get his pipe. They were quietly at dinner. They had been talking together. I looked at Mrs. E. continually. The intensity was gone. I defended James Joyce. Hugh made puns. Vera was comical, too. Mrs. E. had again regained her goddess bearing. Hugh observed my emotions. He said very simply: "I think you love Mrs. E." And I did not protest.

And she was physically that American overstrong, inflexible, too pure type, which until now I had disliked. And I cannot explain it very well, but standing before her and bearing her strength, glorying in it, changed me. At the same time I melted with pity for her, something happened to me. I had loved the utterly unknown, the utterly strange, the unknown strength symbolized in her. J'ai aimée une autre toute differente de moi, d'une autre force [I have loved another, entirely different from me, with another power]. Two "chiefs" with different powers. But, of course, I gave myself away; she has kept herself. I have loved my enemy, my antithesis.

I had prophesied that I would love a woman, too, with Lawrence's center-of-the-body love.

To see someone beautiful, sane, lucid, physically resplendent, and to discover *illness*—that impressed and upset me.

One of the questions she asked me: "I feel that I *know* the cause of my trouble. Should not that be sufficient?" (To cure her?)

I could only tell her that I thought I knew everything about myself on account of my Diary, and how profoundly mistaken I had been.

August 22. On the terrace of the hotel. What makes a dog want to go and play with children? What makes the sea water salty? These are the questions I used to ask my father. He would never answer He would say: "Look it up in the encyclopedia."

Did I pity Mrs. E. so much because she, too, had such a yearning for an older mind? I would like to explain to a psychoanalyst this horrible and endless intellectual and physical starvation, and how much my not having had a father has had to do with it.

Perhaps what happened with John was that I sought a leader and intellectual stimulation such as I have never known, and that I found also a man full of physical warmth, which uncovered my physical hunger as well, so that for three years and three months I could not kill that vision despite all the impassioned analysis.

August 27. Hotel du Pavillon, Paris. Oh, my Journal, give me strength. Today, like Lawrence, I have died. It is not the first time I have died, but this time I died more profoundly, and the agony was the bitterest I have ever known. I cannot bear life. Up to this point I could bear it. Tonight I cannot. I think of death, of my death. Death would be sweet. Especially because my mind is no longer lucid. I cannot bear the pain. Je descend. Je doit écrire doucement, car autrement le dérèglement de mes sens sera visible à tous [I sink. I should write gently, for otherwise the disorder of my senses will be visible to all]. To think I could cling to life with such worship—this life, which can make a person like me desire disintegration and death.

September 2. On board S. S. *Lafayette.* Five days buried. Sleeping, eating, resting. Insentient. Surfeited with pain. Could read, think, only chaotically. John, John, John. The fear of madness. Music broke me up. At last, out of the absolute stillness, the body stirred (but I couldn't bear Hugh's desire of me; I merely submitted). Tonight I asked for my Journal. First sign of life. I only meant to touch it, to hold it. I do not want to go *deeply* into anything. I need all the new-born strength to face New York. I believe I am going to be courageous. And it will be soon over. How I dream of its being finished so that I may progress in my life. I cannot bear this standing still, this chaos, this slavery, this death.

New York. Hotel Barbizon-Plaza. I heard his voice when Hugh talked to him over the telephone. I didn't dare to talk. My heart was knocking and I was trembling. He was not at the pier to meet us. He has forgotten everything, I know now.

September 7. I will see him today. For two days I have been trembling. I got some courage today because last night I forgot my pain for a few hours, as usual with someone I can give myself to: Ethel. Give, give—ideas, feelings, affections, understanding— which alone saves me from the most terrible moods I have ever known. Ethel—her lovely little face, her mature sculpturing and her child's laughter, her small fine hands and firm round body. Her eyes keen, new. She does not realize me, but I don't care.

September 10. Oh, I was not courageous. Seeing him upset me so deeply that I wished for death again. My John, *like my dream John,* incredibly changed physically and mentally. He came to our hotel with Lilith. We sat in the lounge. On the way upstairs he took my arm and pressed it, which made me reel, and I did not respond. I was trembling so much that I could not light my cigarette with his briquet [lighter]. Did he notice it? After all I have gone through, this meeting seemed the most terrible to bear because of Lilith and Hugh being there. Aside from the emotional turmoil, I was intellectually startled by what he had been thinking and discovering, all that I desired, all that I wanted to hear.

Second evening: in Lilith's home, for dinner. Talk flowing more easily. John talks to me as he used to do. But he is more serious than the first day. I cannot analyze, cannot describe anything. My awareness of John's presence is too strong. How hard it is to talk to Lilith.

Hugh effaces himself. I have no strength left to meet anything, nothing but that inner agony, and I let my eyes absorb him. What I most wanted in the world was for him to come and see me. He does not ask to. Why? I think my happiness at seeing him could be almost enough. Just to hear him talk, to feel his eyes on me. Does he know? Does he know his power?

Thursday evening: Solitude in the hotel room. At last strength. At last the body ceased to tremble, and I give myself to the enjoyment of his mind and work, all to myself. His book is on my knees. He is with Lilith. But tonight it seems to me that *I* am blessed. I owe him the greatest joy and the greatest suffering I have ever known. Destruction is over. I have found my serenity through the intellect again. I belong only to myself and to my work.

September 11. John said: "What happened that morning was that when I went to see you I wanted you—I was mad about you—but at the moment of taking you I thought. I thought first of all about Hugh—and then about Lilith but not in connection with loyalty at all. I realized at the moment that although I thought what Lilith had done in giving herself to me was courageous, you were so much more, so passionate and whole. . . . It is fatal to think at such moments, Anaïs. I'm a mess, you know . . . a bluff." And also: "Women who have anything to do with me will have a terrible time, because I am constantly changing."

To hear that about our hour in Paris was for me the end of all pain and of that experience. Because now I enter a new one: a matching of strength. John seeks his match (Lilith has failed), and I am emotionally unequal to face him. Intellectually, yes, at any time, but emotionally I have been weak. Today when he came to see me, in the empty lounge of the hotel, he grasped and kissed me. I showed my turmoil.

September 15. When you have given to the very limit, then only can you measure the foolishness of the giving, the *miserliness* of the other, and then only can you take yourself back entirely. The experience is over. Tout est consumé [All is consumed].

Yesterday I hated him. Of course, one could say that this is but one of the aspects of love. I began to love him less the very afternoon he showed physical power over me by his kiss, and my response to it.

It is very strange. He was talking precisely about my courage. We passed from that into theory. Talk of duality. I made a statement about the possibility of dual living with so much assurance that John asked: "Have you tried it?" (Having a lover.) I was silent, and his face lit up with interest and curiosity. "You little devil," he said, "why didn't you tell me about it?" When I made it clear I had no lover, he was disappointed. He was more interested in life indirectly (story of me and my lover) than directly (story of my love for him). Anything that touches him directly frightens him. He would choose to live obliquely, in most cases, preserve himself whenever possible, because otherwise he would have to give a little, too. The inhumanity of this suddenly chilled me. The passion slowly dissolved. His power was over. The conflict, lying in watch between us, flared. He must have unconsciously felt it.

He attacked mysticism, modernity, Joyce, abnormality, D. H. Lawrence, Gide. Undirected warfare. I watched my intellectual strength returning, but I was not happy. At least not until it was quite, quite over. Last night as he sat reading an article on American civilization, I hated him. A passionate hatred, because of the kinship which had existed, because of the tantalizing closeness, because I knew then the body has no wisdom of its own, because I knew then I had to fight for my life, which had been so nearly swallowed by his.

What brought on the crisis was, as I knew it would, my showing him the "Woman" story, parts two and three. Fundamentally he did not like the story, although he admired it intellectually. I think that through it he sensed my intensity, the mystical leanings. The compactness of style itself he did not mind, but he wished for the human padding. His ideal now is to create characters like those of Shakespeare or Balzac. I am swinging far from realism. He did not like the essence, the extract, the synthesis, the ideation. Yes, he got mostly ideas out of it, but to him ideas are not human. It was amusing. I did not budge an inch. On the contrary, my resistance crystallized. I had written to satisfy my own mind, not his. He was writing to communicate with people. Paradox: I would probably communicate more by satisfying the demands of my own mind, since I know my mind is not the only one of its kind. He would rather be Shakespeare than Baudelaire, Balzac than Rimbaud. He said my attitude toward art was not sane. I might have answered his was socialistic. On my knees, I pray that I may never be liked by the crowd, so that I may never be aware of working for anyone.

"I'll save you from Joyce yet," he said.

"I've scarcely read Joyce," I said.

"But it's in the air."

My modernism, so sincerely arrived at.

In all this I wondered what place my Journal would take—as my best work? Because of the creation of my own character? No, I feel the sophistry somewhere. I can't put my finger on it. When I came out of the apartment, in the middle of Fifth Avenue, I exploded with an astonishing assertion: Tonight I am aware of my own genius. Because of my sureness? Because in the fencing with John I felt my agility.

It is simply this: there are sides of John's mind which belong to me, by right of understanding. To understand John has been one of my life's tasks. It has made me old.

I say that I like the French idea that a young man's life begins with an experience with a married woman, from whom he learns so much—love-making, wisdom, maturity. Lilith said: "But how much sweeter when they can begin together, two young things . . ."

Such sentimentalism. John sits between us. He loves Lilith for her idealism, probably. How fresh she is. I seem like a deep dark personage beside her (she is much older than I am). I found out later that he preferred my idea. He was too cowardly to say so.

September 16. Now I understand it all. In Mallorca I had a premonition that John's kiss would not be as wonderful as his first. In reality, it was where our experience together finished. His kiss upset me but not passionately, although I was still in a condition of exultation. However, I would not admit that to myself, neither on that day, nor in fact until today. Because my passion died at that moment, I know now, I was able to remain lucid and realize there was no spark in him either; there were only memories. I came to my senses. I even decided I would tell him so, to finish it. As events turned out, I was right.

This means that for people like John and me, love and passion have no continuity: we have our self-created impetus, we stand on our own feet, we have our own élan and progressions. Occasionally in the progression we meet others. This is the moment of intensity I used to think about. John has given in to it as I will give in when the time comes. The explosion. However, the tremendous experience with a man of John's physical and mental power came rather soon. I was young. I was emotionally toppled over. But it aroused my own strength at the same time. What an extraordinary thing! I give in, I am wrecked, swallowed, devoured, in all appearance too young and too weak to meet it—yet, no, not in reality. I meet John again; I face him intellectually. All by myself, I realize the meaning of it all and face the physical truth: *I don't want John,* in spite of the fact that the old emotion is still there to deceive me, the memory of the first shock. When I realize all this, the wonder of life comes back to me.

However, if John had not given me time to think, if he had come straight to me the first day, I know I would have surrendered emotionally, and the experience would have ended badly. There is, therefore, no wisdom in the body. Wisdom is in the afterthought. That is why men like John always wait, stand still, think, laugh if possible, and there you are. When they leap they are sure. Of course, he did not wait before Lilith Two. They had their night together. But afterward, and today, he is writing, thinking, before he brings on all the rest of it.

I am afraid I do not wait. So far the time to wait has come to me by accident (a trip with Hugh away from Gustavo, moving to Louveciennes away from Eduardo, the two or three days between John's first visit and his second visit, because we were both busy). But the body does have a wisdom of its own: when I gave myself to John I was wise; when John gave himself to Lilith One and Two. At *moments,* then. And how is one going to know? By the strength of the impulse?

September 17. I have reached a conclusion. I was not toppled over because I am young, but because I am more passionate. John is one degree less passionate. I recognized this in myself with an acute intuition at the moment when he should have been living rather than thinking. I must admit he did some good analysis. Now I know that as I get older I may handle my life better but I shall always lose my balance, and be glad to have done so.

With John it is not a matter of less passion, but less facility in expressing it physically. It is the Scotch restraint and caution, which existed also in Hugh. I could not wait, I could not conceal or calculate. If John and I had met again physically, it would have been a failure because of that difference. In balance there is neutrality. He who weighs does not love, and loses life.

I am astonished at myself, sitting here in the middle of a tumultuous New York, almost glad of an illness which keeps me from engagements, from living as others do, so that I may live in my own way, all by myself, in retrogression. Yet this frightens me, too, for the first time. It is too much like Proust. I always say it is merely because I want time to assimilate what happens to me. I want plenty of time in between things. I never want them to happen at once. Now I am afraid. Life *itself* seems to be too acute, too fantastic, too tragic, and too painful for me. I am happier when I am dissolving it and liberating myself of its tremendous effects on me.

I say this because today I am not strong.

Yesterday, watching an interplay of feelings between Johnnie Guiler, his little English wife, Mother Guiler, and Ethel, I caught myself analyzing the small phrases and ordinary incidents which revealed a pathetic situation, so that when the evening was over I was just as tired as they were, although I might easily have remained outside the conflict. I was reading characters. Well, read the characters and leave them alone; but oh, no, there had to be pity, and there had to be an effort to try to force petty Mother Guiler and Ethel to understand. Pity will always save me from inhumanity.

John remembers that I told him in Paris three years ago that he would be greater when he put in his books the pity he showed for people and their lives. He said that I had influenced him in the writing of *Unfinished Business*.

But is there so much difference between my pity now and the pity I called sentimentalism? Yes, it doesn't interfere with the movements of my intelligence.

I have started Hugh thinking hard. It is as if we were now in two boats, and I were pushing him off so he would follow his own course. For a while I was doing the thinking for us both, and his boat depended on the guidance of mine. It seems fairer this way. I give him the benefit of all I have learned about life without giving him the pain of finding out *how* I have learned it. I will succeed in enriching it without harming him. Doesn't this justify my existence? Someday he will even be led by me into the joys of another love. Everything I will have taken away from him I will return to him.

This I have done by opening his eyes to his own desires, dreams, feelings, to his own nature, and to the beauty of other women, by freeing him from any tie to me, by telling him all I know about "high moments," though how I can do so without telling him the sources of my knowledge is almost incredible. The day Hugh lives such a moment outside of our relationship I will be free. I will wait for that.

I have an enormous amount of concentration; that is what makes me stick to a line of thought until I get to the very end of it. Thus, too, I wrote a book, and will do all my work. A less flattering description would be "obsessional." I feel that my obsession with John will resolve itself into a complete and final analysis, into understanding. If I were not obsessed with ideas and problems, I would never get anywhere. I would be bright, gay, and changeable. This, I said to myself this afternoon, and so I see myself not as a sickly Proust but as a hard worker. (What nobody understands, though, is that Proust, poor Proust, was a hard worker, a courageous builder, not a weakling retired from active life.)

This is the way I invariably obtain confidences from everybody: I meet other people with thoughts of *them* first. I am expectant, silent, watchful. I do not take the first step. I immediately sense the other's *mood*. If I talk, I say enough, just enough, to make sure of the mood. The talk then comes, from the other. I wait. I watch for what will need to be said to show understanding. It is done. Within the talk, once the other person has directed it, I will say as much as I feel they want, and no more. It is a game of feeling. In that game I felt John didn't ask very much. He likes to fill the space with the richness of his own being. He is not really interested in the other person except as a stimulant to his own pursuits.

It is the one who is confided in who is blessed.

I realized one thing today: John is a strong mixture of idealism and deviltry, of sophistry and truth, of moods and ideations—just as I am. When he has exhausted all his Liliths he will come to me for that high degree of passion he first detected in me and also for the deviltry. But I won't want him then.

When he talks poetically I feel a kinship. When he talks plainly and coarsely, I understand that, too. (Sexual love is, after all, only an inner sneeze, he said.) His devil and his passion are as yet unadmitted.

September 18. Just as I wrote those things down about Hugh, how I had passed on to him all my experiences without the knowledge of its source, he himself came to a partial realization of the truth. I knew he would when he was ready to understand it.

Last night, after dinner, as we walked slowly back to the hotel, he began to question me very gently and quietly. He now knew the cause of my breakdown, the unfinished business. Fortunately his questions came when I was absolutely sure I didn't want John any more. So I began by that, to make it all less painful. I told him how John had aroused me, mostly imaginatively, to a love of a man who never existed. I didn't use the word "love." I used "curiosity," "interest," "preoccupation," for I sensed, and rightly, that the physical would be unbearable to him.

I will never be able to tell Hugh. I suddenly entered a new phase, a new condition in our marriage. We felt so strange, talking about all this, that we could not even be sad. Both of us smiled evasively, even laughed with unnatural, unreal nervousness. There were no tears. Hugh was ripe for utter understanding. We talked abstractly. I tested him by confessing to the kiss which proved to me I did not want John. The idea that I had wandered off from absolute devotion was enough to bear. What was stranger still was that both Hugh and I realized that my experience with John had saved our marriage. Hugh said he had unconsciously felt the competition, had felt challenged, and had come to life, where, before, his mind was dull. Also the suffering I have gone through, which has made me old, has made him older, too, and unexpectedly revealed to me as the more mature man of the two, as the man of understanding.

Intellectually it sounds desirable. While our feelings floundered, gnawed us, we tried to keep our heads. Hugh tried to understand. I told him all but the physical facts. There was no more ideal me. But now Hugh says he loves me because I have suffered. He is relieved to be able to love someone who is no longer ideal either, who confesses that this had to happen to him or to me, to put us both on a basis of reality. The fact that it is I who was first is, of course, a painful realization for him. But this morning and last night he seemed more willing to accept the knowledge.

I knew that by going so deeply into life I had gone of my own will into hell. But I never wished for our old, peaceful, falsely ideal and unreal marriage.

Hugh realizes how terrible even the mental experience I have gone through has been for me, for my body. He wishes, as I do, that I had gone through all physically and quickly, so that it might not have lasted so long and broken me. I could not tell him that this was an accident, for he must believe I refused the physical. I haven't the courage to tell him. Is it necessary? I don't know any more. It seems to me that this he could not bear (how badly he took the story of one kiss). I don't want to destroy all our life together. I have done enough so that he will never suffer as I suffered. That is fair. I have made him mature. I am *real*, alas, quite. He can love me as a woman, not as an effigy; he can hurt me without remorse. The young faith is over—for a woman who acts thus once may act thus again.

That gentle, slow, wise talk with Hugh was the most terrible thing of all. I wish he had not been so calm. It was way down in him, held down.

"Tell me . . . did he hold you in his arms? He kissed you . . . on the mouth? It was my fault, because I was not keeping by your side."

"But this last year you were. I was startled by you when you helped me with my book on Lawrence. That was the first time our minds worked together. Then I told you how extraordinary it was when, after spending your whole day in the Bank, you could come home and read *transition* and Gide and understand them both."

"You made me what I am."

"Nobody can make anything out of anybody if it is not in the person already. I only brought you out. I turned you inside out. And look what I have found: a man of genius."

September 23. That evening of our talk we went to sleep without rousing in each other too acute a realization of anything but the barest facts. We were both a bit crushed, a bit afraid, a bit too peaceful. The next morning we took up the talk again. What most deeply affected Hugh was the confession that on board ship one night I considered jumping overboard. I thought at the time it would be best. Hugh would go on living. I would not hurt him. I had gone too near the edge: everything was failing me, health, courage, my creative power. I was alone to solve the whole thing.

I had borne too much secrecy, too many torments. At other times I had been able to return by way of the intellect. This time I could not return from the edge—it was disintegration, without, as it seemed to me at the moment, the possibility of renewal, of rebirth.

Hugh was hurt by my lack of confidence in him, but above all he is now afraid of me and of my impulses. He made me swear again I would never break up our marriage, and *death* would be a breaking of my promise. He begged me for his sake to save myself, physically and mentally. I cried in his arms and promised I would find peace and strength again. Going to the edge of experience was too dangerous for a person like me, and, above all, too dangerous for our love. Our poor love, so worn, so tragic just now, so inhuman. As we talked it was clear to us both that my life was divided: what enriched my creative life endangered our personal life. Hugh, so tired and thin, holding me in his arms with pity for my own strained, thin body, for my few but very bitter tears.

I promised all he asked.

I know he felt I had taken him to the edge with me. He may yet have to live out his own experiences, but I made him know hell by merely living with me. It seemed that we had suffered enough. Yet what Hugh also felt, and did not know he felt, was a doubt of my love for him. We went through the day heavily. The next morning, Sunday, lying in bed, we talked again, going over the whole thing, hurting each other, trying to understand, to explain. Hugh, to lighten my own self-reproaches, was magnifying his own restlessness, and his comparatively trivial experience before our marriage. As he talked and dwelt on the possibility of his wandering off, I felt a sharp pain. I could not bear the thought of it just then. I broke down. Hugh suddenly realized the significance of this: I loved him, then! We lay together, at last close, at last sure. I had exhausted all my capacity for pain. I let him possess me, too weary and broken to respond. I think the rebirth began then. We spent the day by ourselves, in the park. I could feel the tension over. John was quite finally, quite wholly, out of my body.

There only remained the slow re-creative process, after the disintegration. That came to me one morning when I realized John had no power to make me change my writing. I cared deeply for his opinion, and yet when we disagreed one evening I did not give in. He made me feel his wrath. He gave me what he thought to be a healthy little lecture (two of my short stories were refused by *Vogue*). Then his better impulses came back to him, and he said he would take one of the stories for a magazine he is to manage.

We were talking over the "Woman" story. He thought it needed padding. I explained to him my idea of abstract writing. He then said I did not have a healthy, sane attitude toward writing. He said he had gotten ideas out of my story, but no movement, action, or life. I said, "Ideas *are* life." I was thinking of how he had ruined his ideas by mediocre storytelling, how he had been padding in the most inartistic, boring way with realistic details which meant nothing to him and therefore nothing to the reader. He is a genius of ideas: he is a philosopher, not a storyteller. He talked to me about the limitations of subtlety—quoted what had been said of Valéry: "Such pure poetry, after a while, is composed mostly of silences." I might have known that stylization would not appeal to him.

A few days after that *Vogue* rejected "Alchemy" and "Waste of Timelessness." Because the "note of fantasy and charm" was not good for their magazine. John sent me this with the words: "Now you have a proof of how much subtlety the public can stand." A very equivocal phrase, rather reproachful, to my mind. His letter about the MS on Lawrence had been quite different. He sympathized with me, not with the public. Here, it seemed to me, he sympathized with the public. I took in the full significance of this and sent them both to the devil. My work would be done, anyhow, to suit my inner necessity, and in my own way. I would willingly fight the world. I would willingly relinquish all pleasure of publication, communication, renown. This was a sign that I was not to succeed in publishing, but it did not shake me. It saddened me; oh, yes, more than that, it hurt me acutely, but it wouldn't ever change anything in me.

It was at this moment that my emotionalism died, and that I began to transpose everything into creation, to transmute unbearable and tremendous events. The artist was bearing up the woman.

When John took one of the stories for his magazine I knew it was kindness. I was already at work (explaining, reporting, analyzing in the Journal), and all feeling was gone.

Meanwhile, Hugh said to me that he loved my adventurous spirit, my courage, and my suffering. That it was an adventurous life he wanted. We would have the courage to be adventurous together. We would preserve our love and marriage and yet enrich our life with whatever passion or experience came our way.

When we were very close again, he confessed he could not have borne my having a *physical* encounter as well. I already knew that. I was glad I had effaced the physical scene from the story. It was unnecessary. It was not important to the understanding, to his knowledge of me; its only significance was that it had a mortal effect on my body—that it hurt me. I am the only one concerned.

John told me about Lilith Two. Meeting. Immediate ignition. A night together. Then talk. A trip to Paris. A trip from Paris to New York. Then she discovers existence of Lilith One. And so, says John, "on our trip back we behaved ourselves." Why did they behave themselves? How could they behave themselves? What a revealing story. Reserve. Self-restraint. They call it passion. They don't know what passion is.

It was such a relief to me to discover I did not love John anymore and that I could love Hugh forever. It was then I was really resurrected. By which I mean become an artist again, and have no desire to die over any man. In the very middle of it all I began to write, in between engagements, in the evening, anytime. I have just come back from the theatre with Ethel. I'm waiting for Hugh. We are going out to dinner. John lives twenty yards away and it means nothing to me, absolutely nothing, though I feel sorry for him because of the tangles he gets into.

I had lunch with Lilith One, which was really dramatic. I pitied her and was upset by her confidences, but when she said: "I love him so much," I did not feel like chiming in: "And I"; but I felt sorry she should love him so much. Before, I would have perished with jealousy. The first days here I loathed her. Now I feel sorry for her. Why is John the kind of man who loses the love of a woman so wholly as he has lost mine? Why cannot one have a middle-course feeling about him?

Lilith was very upset because she has just decided to leave New York so as to let John discover what he wants. She does not know about Lilith Two. He does not want her to know, so that she does not think it is the discovery of Lilith Two that has finished his love for her, but that it has died a natural death.

Her tears upset me. It struck me that I personally liked her better for her weakness but that it was strength John required and demanded; the strength to bear the truth about John, the truth about love, passion, life, and Lilith Two. Funny there was never a woman Stoic, no Mrs. Marcus Aurelius. You see, women are the sensitive half of the universe, but man would like sensitivity to be more easily turned off than it is, especially when Lilith Two enters his life. Why do women cling?

There are only two remedies: intellectuality or work, and adoption of masculine attitudes in love. Women are still too idealistic to admit duality, which can be achieved only by a comparative atrophy of feelings. You love and you desire. When love and desire go together, very well. If love is lost, woman thinks she has lost life, but that is not so: life is also in desire, also in work. When one fails you the other two can keep you alive. Woman has not realized that desire can be fulfilled independently of love, because desire seemed to be an attribute of man: man could desire, woman could only be desired. Biologically this still stands, and that is the root of woman's misery. Woman cannot go forth and win her desire; she has to wait for it. We are biologically imperfect. We can only move in an indirect way; we can try to arouse the man's desire, that is all. Some of us haven't the means. But a man without means can always find an object.

The only way out is to eliminate feeling. One man is as good as another, biologically speaking. I write this and I absolutely cannot convince myself. One cannot commandeer strength. Poor Lilith lost hers when she most needed it. I could only sympathize. I was melting with pity. I told her I liked her all the better for not being hard. I saw her at her loveliest moment: when a woman takes down her hair. In that action there is something so intimate, so disarming, that it is as if she had bared her most feminine secrets. I looked at her and reflected, this is the way she looked when John was possessing her. And I felt as if I ought to help her keep John, as if I were now bound to help her, just because she had taken her hair down before me, trustingly, knowing I would measure her loveliness against mine, and at that moment she won me. I said: "You look like a girl of sixteen." "That helps," she answered. And as I realized the utter absence of jealousy in me I realized the utter death of John.

I felt old and tired after this encounter. When I got to my room I called up John to help him clarify whether or not Lilith One should be the enduring love of his life, hoping to persuade him she was. He was out. I left a message. He did not call up again. I no longer interfered with events. My own impetus was carrying me at top speed, away from John.

I am on the upward curve. Writing, realizing. I met Frances Schiff. She has been standing very still, for the sake of peace and security, enwrapped in baby, husband, garden. Quite jellified.

My visit to her was an explosion, of ideas, moods, and experiences, brought to climaxes by my own intensity. She was pushed off her base. She was sad. In an uncanny way I saw myself as John talking to Hugh and me when we were so young and unshaken by life. I was to Frances what John was to us at that time: a stirring, stimulating, powerful upsetting influence. My work overwhelmed her as John's overwhelmed us. I know I was making Frances unhappy, even dissatisfied, but I couldn't help myself.

Then I provoked a full talk with Ethel, and discovered that she and Edith had been going through experiences Hugh and I never imagined—that we did not know them, and that they did not know us in the least, because of reticence, false impressions. I thought Edith ethereal, unearthly, inexperienced, passionless (it is only her face I judged her by), whereas she has suffered and known life, and thought me detached, poetic, ethereal, inhuman. I thought Ethel adventurous, but she is wise and cautious. They thought Hugh was old-fashioned, and intolerant. One false opinion after another.

Yesterday we talked ourselves out. We were surprised at our discoveries. What silly things we had been saying, how much we had reserved and concealed. We had been to the theatre together. I, in my usual indirect way, had been throwing bait in the hopes of getting a response from Ethel. It was simply while we sat before a little table sipping our frosted chocolate that I became aware of undertones and overtones, aware that our conversation was running far from the current of our thoughts. I took the initiative and called her up the next day and asked her to come and see me. I don't quite know how, but after a while my phrases, my attentiveness and receptivity unleashed confidences, talk flowed, and I brought home triumphantly to Hugh a new knowledge of his sisters.

While Ethel talked, I was aware of the connection between incidents, of their interrelation, of how one could not have happened without the other. This was something brought out by my talk with Frances, who explained to me that when she wrote her journal each piece was disconnected and after a while appeared utterly futile to her, deserving only to be dropped and forgotten. Thus, with the same sense of futility, she would drop hobbies, interests, or people. Nothing seemed important enough to follow to the end intensely. This was startling to me and the very opposite of my feeling. I never drop anything. I feel every detail important, I have to finish everything. Old pages of my Journal certainly do appear foolish, sentimental, exaggerated, unwise, but as a whole they lead me somewhere—there is no feeling of futility or unimportance. On the contrary. It is all a heavy weight which has to come with me in my very positive moving forward. Blunders are part of all the movement. My mistakes, my defects, all part of it.

In the end, it seems to me, Frances may know all there is to know and have no more surprises, expect nothing, but she cannot have this feeling of ecstasy I have when I am fully alive and moving forward and struggling. Futility has only come to me occasionally, when I am ill or tired: disintegration and the desire for death have come too. But even that appears to me now as a very important, very creative portion of my life, something which has made me more alive. And I would not mind dying over and over again, for to be in *movement*, whether toward death or toward life, is living.

More moving than all the abstractions and theories in the Lilith-John story are the little details: John is moving into a new apartment which Lilith had hoped to live in as his wife. In our presence they had discussed the colors of the walls. She wanted a brighter green than John did. The morning I came to see her she had been painting garden furniture for the terrace of the apartment; yet all around them the feelings and the desires and connections were breaking down.

I do fear myself at certain moments. I do not know what I might be capable of doing when my emotions are aroused. See what I did when John aroused me: flung out two years of my life and might have given up my life because of it. When I listen to music there is nothing I might not do, when I feel the spring there is nothing I might not do. But also, when I am bursting with creation there is nothing I might not write. This is what I feel this morning.

September 29. Hugh, in trying to explain things to Ethel, puts it more perfectly than I ever did: "As an artist you work at your sculpturing in two ways: you study, you learn anatomy, you know geometry and proportions, and all the technical approaches to art, but when the moment comes to create art you just let go— forget all you learn, and work by impulse, instinct, or intuition, or genius, whatever you may choose to call it. Knowing when to give in to life, and when to resist impulses, can only be compared to the artist's work."

That is what I meant by the psychic force which compels us to live, and which is simply composed of knowledge, thought, the everyday additions we make to the outline of character and ideas. However, if you live on a low basis from day to day, you cannot expect the inspirational outburst to be very wonderful. A creation is not a thing of the moment, instantaneously formed, but very slowly and gradually shaped out of infinitesimally small pieces. We think it is instantaneous because the process is more or less hidden and apparently mysterious. Here at last is the link between art and life which I have been seeking. Here is what I meant by saying that the artist's standards are the only ones we should apply to life when we wish to judge it. Here is what I meant by the ultimate importance, not of experience itself, but of its creative application. I have studied in myself the continuity of the artistic perception carried into life. And it is that I wish to explain and tell others.

September 30. The question did come to me: Is John right, or am I right?—his holding back from getting deeper into life, and my going in too deeply. Frances tried to answer that question for me: "What is right for John is not right for you. You must first satisfy yourself." I agree. I do satisfy myself. I answer my own demands about my writing and about living. Then John can and must only satisfy himself (which he does by writing *Unfinished Business* in precisely the way he has written it). Very well, then, I won't try to find out who is right. There is no such thing. Frances is wise. We are different.

And as Frances said: "Right about what and how? Do you mean wiser, or more sincere, or more intelligent, or more moral?"

"I suppose I mean right in depths of living . . . simply that I feel more profound."

"I don't know," said Frances. "John might think you are simply younger and more intense, and he is older and wiser in remaining on the surface."

"But you, what do you think?"

"I think something very trite," said Frances. "I think that there is that difference between all men and all women."

"There are men like Lawrence . . . but now that I think of it he was half woman."

Frances went into her experience as wholly as I did, toppled over. She also measured the emotional inequality. I told her nothing in the world could tempt me now but an emotional equality. But then, when I first knew John I thought he was that very equality I craved.

Yesterday I could not understand John letting Lilith visit his new apartment and help with the choice of curtains when they are parting definitely on Thursday. I could not understand his bringing Lilith on our good-bye visit (I had offered to go and see her alone), where awkward situations would arise: "I'll see you again sometime, Anaïs." "Of course." (Knowing I would never see her again.)

John's cruelty seemed unfathomable. She was so evidently under a terrible strain. The cult of stoicism. Would it be mean of me to say that John had less to be stoical about, and always would have less? That is what the woman must learn above all else—that, after all, we have made a cult of man's love and should not have; that we do not yet realize the importance of work so as to be less vulnerable to transitions in love.

Frances's husband was afraid to meet me after reading the "Woman" story. He expected a strange, very strange person. Said I *was* strange and different, but nice and likable too.

Lilith's wisest and nearest approach to grace is in leaving for Chicago. But before she leaves I know she will say some ungainly things. Yesterday she could not refrain from making general statements—life is very strange, the world is very small, who knows where we will meet again, who knows what may happen, etc. So many trite phrases. I felt enormous pity for her, yet she is forty-two and should know better.

I was quite wrong about Frances. She was casual about her life, her husband, and her writing. She gave them little importance, she dismissed them in conversation. I took her seriously, and since she had little to tell, I found a lot to say about my life, my husband, and my writing. But when I saw her in her home, met Whitney, the baby, and read her stories, I realized they were all important and rich and wonderful in themselves, and all I had said to her the first day in favor of restlessness seemed very foolish in the face of Whitney, who is worth living for all by himself. I told her so today. However, she did insist that her personal life was placid and secure, overplacid, and that it was not as rich as mine, and that she had little to write about. So we had it all out about the writing. Writing springs directly from the personal life. It is a question of how much of your personal life you will sacrifice to its feeding, and as the writing in turn feeds the personal life (my work has meant a lot to Hugh), this is one problem I will never solve.

I shoot down on a bullet elevator, thirty floors, to meet John— my long dress swishes because of the swift descent. Sandaled feet are not heard on the thick hotel rug. The green Fifth Avenue bus. Dust. Black dust on the face and in the eyes. The tune of "Sweet and Lovely" heard from radio stores; also heard in our room while we are dressing up for a formal dinner. Hugh says: "Did you remember to bring my white silk scarf? It used to be kept in the dark closet of the house at Louveciennes." There is peace. Too much peace. "Sweet and Lovely" cuts into my memories. I hear a clamorous fire engine over the sound of all other traffic. The radio makes me bleed. If there were no music in the world I would never bleed. I would be stoical. But when it comes, the mooning, crooning song, it lifts events out of any ordinary tunelessness. The telephone rings. We have reservations on the *Ile-de-France*. It is a good boat and the food is excellent. We sail at ten. A knocking at the door; a man brings Hugh's blue suit, which has been pressed. I have time to redye my black gloves with India ink. They were worn and turning white. "Sweet and Lovely" teases me. I can sit and write a few lines, it will be like dropping a heavy package at the desk. But I must shoot down in the elevator and go down, down through secondhand bookshops to look for Freud's other books. If I take an impersonal interest in others' lives I might save my own personal life. The maid has brought clean towels. Ethel's bus is zigzagging up Fifth Avenue. Then the telephone rings: "Miss Guiler downstairs." And a tune on the radio will be turned off and go on running inside the machine, as tunes would go on running inside me even if there were no music in the world.

To write at the same temperature at which I live I should write nothing but poetry.

To have imagination is to sit in the subway in front of a man with a gray hat, to look at the gray hat and have its colors remind you of the rocks in Mallorca, and the ancient bark of olive trees— the same gray worn by the Spaniards at the bullfight—and thus to be off around the world, because the man sitting in front of you in the subway wears a gray hat.

To have no imagination is to stare for twenty-seven minutes

at the gray hat and observe that it is stained, and that after a long while you will arrive at Tenth Street. There are two ways of living.

Some people are passively affected by life and all is well. Others are terribly excited by it and must respond in an active way, and here the trouble begins; I must always respond extremely.

You cannot live life according to a pattern. You can only prepare yourself for the unexpected by a long and continuous state of wonder.

I gave Ethel a bracelet and necklace I loved. The impulse to give it was stronger than my impulse to enjoy it myself, and at the same time I felt I was punishing myself. For what? I miss the necklace, but this will be my tribute to an obscure ethical sense. Keeping accounts, hurting myself in my deep love for things.

October 2. Sailing postponed. Last night we knew how much we regretted leaving New York. We were having our last soda, after seeing the Ziegfeld *Follies* with a Bank Vice-President. We were elated by the beauty of the show, by the contact with luxury (we have been to the most expensive homes and restaurants; have had caviar, fowl from Scotland, and 1920 champagne; have sat in the Casino restaurant with a five-dollar cover charge, and at the St. Regis; and have driven in Packards, Rolls-Royce, etc.). The sense of adventure is strong in us. Our talks together are even flippant. Coming out of the show, Hugh said the Ziegfeld girls were beautiful, but that they did not move him.

"Well, you're difficult to move," I said. "If I were a man, I would be knocked off my feet."

"You see, I thought it all out, and I knew I wouldn't be satisfied."

"If we were two men," I said, "tonight you would be thinking and I would be gone, off, under, to try to find out by actual experience whether I would be satisfied or not. I might reach the same conclusion, but afterward. You may be wiser, dear, but I would be the one to have all the fun. Now don't think I'm urging you to fall in love with a Ziegfeld beauty. I'm just urging you to find out whether you are quite sure of what you want out of life. You were never sure. I naturally love you wise, but I don't want this wisdom to be merely ignorance. I want to watch over your life. I just want you to be sure."

He was very sure, because at that moment he happened to be in love with me. He saw me as a stage person, wearing feathers and lace, dancing and posing. He imagined me in place of the others. He was satisfied.

I'm a ship that sails easily, with an anchor made of bamboo shoots. Hugh is a ship that sails off slowly, with much foresight, and his anchor is heavy. That is why he went into the Bank instead of into acting or writing. And has regrets. But how I watch all this now—so that twenty years from now he will have no regrets. Last night he was saying he was sorry to have missed seeing the Ziegfeld show when he was a bachelor and so eager to see beauty. And why didn't he? It was not the custom in his family to go to the theatre. He followed the custom and did not even know he wanted it.

I wish in a way that I could cut myself off from John *completely*, because it is necessary to my integrity. The balancing of friendship's loyalties against literary and personal truths has always been a little too much on the side of friendship. Of course, my Journal is full of truths, but I am thinking more of a public appraisal of his work and life. *Then* I would not be as truthful. For a moment I considered writing a study of his work because I know that in himself he is aware of tragedy within comedy, but he has expressed no such feeling or ideas in his books. Here, my personal knowledge of his life misled the critical judgment.

From now on my *imagination* is half of my life. I cannot live without it. These days, because John was too wrapped up in his own life and troubles to give me anything of himself, I have had to invent again. Invent a friend, a future friend who is to fill the gap. This is to ease the strange and now incurable pain of my self-depreciation. I need, I crave, the appreciation of others too deeply. I am not sure of my own value. Deep down I know I am more than Lilith, for instance, mentally and physically, but it is Lilith who gets what I want, and I begin to wonder if I am anything outside of my own imaginative world, which I inhabit so richly with a rich self! I get knotted up with sensitiveness. I imagine myself unlovable. Reality begins to slip away from me. I am in my Journal, and in my Journal only, nowhere else. Nothing shows on the outside. Perhaps I do not exist except as a fantastic character in this story.

On board S.S. *Lafayette*. But I would not give him up without achieving three things: having him understand our life; stirring up his intellectual curiosity and interest; finding out if he regretted his unfinished experience. This I decided could be done devilishly by my telling him I had a lover. He came Wednesday morning, the day we sailed. I said to him: "Wish me luck, I'm started on my dual life."

"Do you mean you have a lover?"

"Yes."

"Anaïs!"

He was fantastically surprised, moved, upset.

"Are you surprised?"

"Yes, I admit I am." He took hold of my hand. "What about Hugh?"

"Hugh would be living through the same experience if it were the moment for him. I have taught him that." Then I explained to him how we were living out the theories we decided to live out when the time came. The fact that we were not, really, did not matter, but the dramatization was necessary for John, who is more literal, and I had decided to make a dramatic impression. Inside myself I was laughing. I had even chosen the man, a man equally brilliant and clever: Aldous Huxley, to put it on a high level. John wished me happiness. He described our theories about living as the rationalization of a physical impulse. I could see he could not swallow the fact easily, especially as I added that I would go on and on, that this was only a beginning. He suggested—American style—that I should leave Hugh and go and live with Huxley. I explained to him that I loved Hugh best of all, and that he was the only man I wanted to live with. He grasped the complexity but said he couldn't live like that. Everything had to be one hundred percent and clear-cut. He admired me for keeping balance in such a mix-up. I demonstrated all my complexity, quoted Lawrence on the "sides of our nature which eluded fulfillment in one kind of love," etc.

He said he wished he were in Aldous's place—that if he had not been quite so decent (about Hugh) he would be. He laid his hand on my knee (he had not done this at our other meetings). I could see he had a few regrets, a great deal of interest, and an understanding of our life. He said: "You won't have a dull life, anyway."

We talked for three hours about many things, even Lilith Two. He said: "I find it hard to say good-bye."

We got up. He came quite near and said: "If you didn't belong to Aldous, I would take a kiss."

"You forget about Hugh."

He found something else to talk about, and we sat down. He took my hand and said: "You know, I am *terribly* fond of you, Anaïs." He also said what he had never said before: that I had a great deal of maturity of mind, but that I was young in experience, and one had to catch up with the other. Before I had a lover he urged me to ideal faithfulness, declining the responsibility of my adopting a life like his own. Now he was introducing me to my own fallacies. I could see he knew that, from Aldous on, I would become infinitely more interesting. Inside myself I was laughing, laughing. . . .

We got up a third time. He had his arm around my waist. We swayed a little together—and I shook his hand. One must be rigid about boundaries of possession!

It occurred to me afterward I should meet Aldous Huxley and tell him all about this, since he would appreciate it.[1]

But how sweet, how amusing this scene was, John so aware of me now that I was lost—so interested he forgot to worry about Hugh. And I, so pleased with my deviltry, realizing that most people love to be lied to, that imagination heightens life, that whenever there is a gap, or a little lukewarm condition I can start the play going again. That even an imaginary lover gave me a color which my idealism did not have, and gave John an interesting three hours. I left New York amused, elated, happy, and blue, too, sorry to leave such a nice John.

That to me was an artistic finish, a glossy one, you might say. It did me a lot of good to have something to flourish. Before that, things had been a bit flat. He never liked me better (next to our hour in Paris) than when I flourished Aldous.

Evening. Hugh and I had our final crisis. We were looking out to sea. He was saying he wished my experience had been physical so that I might have suffered less. I reminded him he had said he could not have borne the physical. I knew then I would have to tell him the whole truth. I began very slowly, painfully and shakily. I told him all the physical facts: John had kissed me and caressed me and stirred me with his hands. I responded fully and when he asked to see my breasts I showed him my body. And I told him how John's sexual impulse had failed him, and how he had been overcome with scruples and thoughts about Hugh. "You will now hate me for this. I responded

[1] *A.N. eventually met Huxley in Los Angeles in 1958.*

fully. I do not know half-measures. I was ready to go through to the very end."

Hugh was terribly shaken, but with pity. He pitied me, he pitied me deeply. He said: "Let's go down to our room and I will tell you how I feel about this." When we were in the cabin, he said: "Do you remember how you felt when I told you about Aunt Annie beating me for showing myself to a little girl? Well, that is how I feel about you. Terribly sorry for you, and I love you for it, I love you for it all. It only shows me your passionate nature, your sensitiveness. I just love you for it, my poor darling. Now I know how much you have suffered."

"I was afraid it would spoil our physical love."

"Spoil it? Look what I really feel." He showed me that he desired me, and came into me with unusual fervor. I was overwhelmed with gratitude. I couldn't believe it. His pity was so soothing to me, so wonderful. That was one of the most beautiful moments in our life together. His pity and admiration and incredible understanding. We could not go much further. I was so relieved, as he had been in Mallorca. I never knew so much love was possible. We were passionately drawn together, three times in one day, wanting so much to belong to each other again. We talked ourselves into a perfect and complete understanding. Hugh read all my Journals. He knows that I love only him.

We even laughed about certain sides of it. Hugh said the whole thing was a play created by me.

"Well, you played the best part," I said.

"You made me," said Hugh. "I learned generosity in Mallorca from you. Everything comes from you."

"Oh, Love," I said, "of what use would it be for me to create such a big play if you weren't in it. I couldn't make you act as you did today. It is in you. I only indicate."

Then we were sad, because we realized this was at the root of our trouble: the fact that in thought and living I have been the leader because Hugh is in the Bank. It is not quite right that everything should come from me just because I have more time to think. Later he was struck by the fact that all this would make an extraordinary story, and he said I should write it all down. I said it was all written down. He laughed: "I don't feel sorry for you any more."

This was his first reaction, and an intellectual one. He thought of me first; he gave me pity and understanding. His love warmed me, penetrated me. We had a terribly strong desire to belong to each other over and over again. Every impulse in my being was now turned toward him; I never knew at any other moment of my life such a yearning and rushing out toward anyone such as I knew now for Hugh. I would have liked to have dropped the past forever and to give myself entirely to this new Hugh, and our new passion. But now, after the first intellectual understanding, pain was awakening in his body; he suffered from a physical realization of the physical part of my experience. It was this pain I dreaded for him, and no amount of love from me could heal it. The image of John kissing me was intolerable to him. That night I fell asleep because I had taken a sleeping pill. He stayed up and wrote in his journal. It was his turn to die, to suffer, to be tormented by jealousies and doubts and regrets, to touch the bottom of suffering.

The next day, every moment we wanted to be locked up in each other's arms—passion rushed through us again several times. We sought desperately, profoundly to be united. Hugh's questions tormented me; the aching in him took the form of questions, doubts, fears, curiosity. One moment he would understand that the experience had enriched our life, the next moment he only wanted to know what had become of our love, whether I had ever hated him, whether I had loved John more than himself. I could hardly answer his questions, because I could not bear to see him suffer. I did tell him many times that I had never loved John, merely desired him once, that all through, my love of Hugh had been strong, immovable, that the two feelings clashed, and hurt me, but that the feeling for him had been a steady undercurrent fully realized. I read him the pages in my Journal that proved this. He was suffering deeply from jealousy and yet with a terrible desire to know, to know. That night I had to tell him the whole scene in every detail. With his head on my breast, I realized fully that what I had thought a peak moment had become for me an hour to loathe.

Then came the moment I could never forget: the explosion, through suffering, of such passion between Hugh and me as I never conceived or experienced before, the blinding realization of his preciousness to me, the realization of the inseparableness of our two bodies. I broke out in bitter sobbing, for *his* pain more than for mine.

More questions. He is brooding. I cannot heal him except

with the gift of my body, and my body's impetuosity convinces him. And we talk, especially at night, in bed. When memories or an image torment him, he comes to me. I am so open to him, so blissfully whole in my desire for him. At last he knows, through the body, he knows what we had intellectually understood from the first: that without all this his whole extraordinary being would not have flared before me as it did, and my love for him would not have flared so acutely either—that we have discovered each other.

Monday. It may not be our last talk on the subject, but it was certainly the most final. We were realizing this morning that John was entirely a figure of our imagination from the time of Hugh's days at college, when John was exalted by him as a teacher and poet, to our mutual admiration of him as a great writer and still-greater man, and my personal subjection to the *sensual* man—all nonexistent. But what we created in our minds was a tremendous goal which we slowly reached and surpassed, an idea called John, with which John had nothing to do.

I had endowed John with the supreme poetical qualities, particularly imagination and fineness of feeling. When I discovered that he did not possess these feelings and qualities, why didn't I cease to be attracted to him? Because what really subjugated me was the big, dark, sensual power of the man. My imagination and my poetic nature suffered but my body was enthralled. I liked to remember extremely physical and coarse expressions and words; they seemed part of his sensuality, and his sensuality answered a need in me, was a response to a craving. If it had been an intellectual or poetic passion, I would long ago have been cured. In that respect it was Lawrence who satisfied me, not John. But if it was physical and sensual, how could I be cured without the physical experience? Because in New York I discovered in several ways that there was no sensuality in John, that it was all on the surface, in the vitality, in the powerful voice and body, in the eyes; there was vitality, intellectual force, vigor of speech—everything but real sensuality. I might have known, from our first moment together, he lacked the pure sensual impulse which does not fear or analyze. But I was blind then. Infinite sensuality seemed to be aroused in me, and the idea of his sensuality was magnified by my imagination. I felt this when I saw him again, and his talk about himself, me, and the other women revealed the rest.

In Hugh there is sensuality, in his passionate physical jealousy and possessiveness, and now that he has discovered the very
bottom of my own sensuality, it is expressed in us with such
abandon and fullness and intensity that we are like two mature,
experienced lovers, adept at extracting violent pleasures, fierce
joys from our conjunction.

We pretend to be newly married, not as mere children, but
as two mature, experienced persons who have known and suffered
life, who are divested of foolish ideas, notions, scruples, and
timidities. Man and woman, conscious of dark sensual desires
as well as companionate and tender love.

What children we were! At what cost and pain to both of us.
How cruel to each other we were. How false the idealizations.

We began with such impetus and trueness. Hugh loved me
instantly, and dreamed the very first night we went out together
of taking off all my clothes and lying with me. I responded fully
to his caresses at the beach. One afternoon we were so stirred
Hugh made as if to push my bathing suit aside, and I gave little
screams of timidity, "Oh, no, not that," which chilled him; but
if he had known better he would have known that all women's
first instinct is flight, and that wise caresses can win them. I
would not have hesitated one moment if he had tried more
delicately. I would have acted exactly as I acted toward John later.

When we married I was open and ready and desirous. And
then Hugh was frightened and paralyzed, probably with a false
notion about me because of my fright at the beach. This was
such a shock to me that I in turn closed up against him, and
thus we lived, unable to meet at the right moment.

When we came to Paris, Hugh was sexually starved. He
looked to France as the haven of sensuality. To his surprise I
reacted violently against its influence. It seemed flippant to me.
As our marriage had not roused me, I hated books and plays
and people that suggested pleasure and physical fulfillment. Hugh,
poor Hugh, was again repulsed by my severity. He closed up and
was full of shame, as in his boyhood, for his erotic impulses.
Then came my awakening, not through him, but through dancing.
I couldn't talk to Hugh—what would he think of my feelings
and susceptibilities? I could talk to Gustavo because he had written
an erotic book and had said I did not look sensually satisfied. I
remember asking him questions. He asked me once if I knew
violence and hatred in passion, if I had ever wanted to bite some-

one in the moment of pleasure. Now all books and people and pictures were fascinating and moving beyond words. And Hugh had conformed to my ideal and become gentle and colorless. Then came John, who made it possible for me to surround my physical impulse with imaginative, poetic, and intellectual trappings. And then, in my own time, I appeal to Hugh to save our love and reawaken his own erotic desires. How we blocked each other through misunderstandings, feelings always at cross-purposes, and how well this explains my continuous realization of my love for Hugh running as an undercurrent.

And now we know one more thing: that this may happen again, and that there is a need of balance.

Hugh feels a terrible need of also having an experience, to relieve the effect of his pain, to free me of self-reproaches, to balance. We may both be again pulled apart physically. But we know that our marriage stands, our love will accept and understand, and that we will not tell each other until the experience is over, because we cannot know, at the moment we are in it, what the meaning of it is, or estimate its importance. In other words, we are glad that I waited. Hugh is glad to have had intuitions of what was happening, but at the same time a sense of fatalism and wise patience, which prevented him from interfering. He knew it had to be.

Through it all I was revealed to him. We did not know each other, and we were seeking each other for eight years.

If I had not loved him above all, I would not have wanted to die on board ship, die in order to preserve him from pain. I would have been selfishly rejoicing at seeing John again.

What a difference between this trip and the other. Before, I couldn't bear Hugh's desire for me. I was profoundly sorrowful, I was ill. I couldn't write or think. I desired death, oblivion. This time I am feeling wonderfully well. Hugh and I desire each other all the time. The days seem too short now. He is healing. We play games together on the top deck. My joyousness is contagious. He feels enveloped in my love. He is sure, he knows. We kiss on deck, like two lovers who are obliged to steal kisses because they do not live together.

We talked last night about the drab side of married life. We have both wished to be unmarried, or married to others, so that we might enjoy in each other only the high moments. "Think of it," I said. "You would only see me three or four times a week.

I would come to you all dressed up, and fresh, and looking my best and with news to tell you."

"But I don't know that I would like the prepared moments," said Hugh. "I don't know that I particularly love you best when you are all dressed up and prepared. I remember one day in the garden at Louveciennes when we were working together, and it was raining, and your face was wet and your hair messy and I remember that I loved you at that moment."

"And if we met like that, only occasionally, there would not be moments like the spring evening when we took the kitchen table out in the garden to have dinner. And think of the times we might meet for love when one of us is just not in the mood, and the other thinks it is indifference."

"Yes, whereas this way we are always together when the mood comes, and we are also there when the other is depressed or worried or tired."

"Let's not get divorced," I said. And we both started to look forward to our old house and life, and to make plans for work, improvements, things we would do on weekends.

"Did you suffer from . . . humiliation?" Hugh asked once.

"Humiliation? No, I don't think so. It would have been, it seems to me, rather petty. I tried to understand him, and his side of it. It doesn't seem to me that there was any question of humiliation. At least I didn't feel it. . . ."

October 19. Bliss, bliss, bliss. From morning until night, singing, singing, singing. The sunlight in our beautiful room, breakfast in the royal Persian bed. Emilia's smiling face. The family, so sweet, so sweet—my Joaquin, whom I worship so; little Mother to love and care for. Talk, talk about everything. Who would guess it . . .

Joaquin has been gravely ill and is barely recovering. He lies on a chaise longue in my room. I spent three days in bed with a nasty grippe, but how happy we are. Eduardo came to see us; I felt so much tenderness for him. We unpack the trunks. We play the new records. I show Mother the curtain material from Woolworth's. I pile up the new books, American silk stockings, boxes of candy received when we left.

How eager I am to get to work. Please, please, Emilia, hurry up, bring my desk back into the little room where it was. Here it is, at last. Hurry, bring my typewriter. I write in my notebook: "Have vacuum cleaner repaired. Give black dress to the cleaner. Paint ladder. Have curtains made. Accounts. Get rose dye for the sheets. Write letters." There is a lot of work to be done in the garden. Some painting in the house. I've lost interest in the postman. I do not look backward. When I hear "Sweet and Lovely," I think only of the story I want to write, and of the gas bill I must pay. In the attic I found some stuff which will make a beautiful evening dress. Everything is new. Our love is new; Hugh is new. Life is so rich. It is a high adventure. Though I double the dose of my sedatives, it is no use. I'm dancing inside myself with a new bliss.

❦ *Index* ❧

Blake, William, 320, 327, 334, 339,
    349, 357, 401, 423, 426
Blanco y Negro (publication), 88
Bohnen, Carl, 166, 168, 171, 172
Bolton, Whitney, 477
Bonifacio (dancer), 73, 135, 137, 154,
    258, 283, 284, 285, 286, 287,
    301
"Book of Dreams and Nightmares"
    (also "Life on the Moon,"
    project by A.N.), 316
Botticelli, Sandro, 120
Boussinescq, Hélène, 19, 22, 25, 26,
    42, 46, 49, 50, 53, 54, 55, 60,
    63, 66, 69, 87, 88, 105, 106,
    127, 198, 233, 245, 303, 304,
    305, 360, 361, 362, 369, 382,
    385, 388, 404, 421, 422, 438
Brandes, Georges, 13
Brief Candles (Huxley), 429
Brocqua, 280, 284, 289
Brownlee, John, 5
Bruckner, Ferdinand, 257
Brull, Mariano, 48, 69
Buhlig, Richard, 4, 11, 12, 13
Buñuel, Luis, 338
Burdett, Orbert, 339
Burns, Robert, 149
Byron, Lord, 19

Cabrera, Lydia, 264
Canadian Forum (publication), 309,
    326, 353, 356, 375, 381, 389
Canard Sauvage (Ibsen), 181
Cantacuzène, Prince, 69, 123
Carco, Francis, 24, 138
Cárdenas, Antolina Culmell de
    (aunt), 74, 85, 101, 102, 103,
    105, 166, 456 ꞏ
Cárdenas, Antolinita de ("Baby")
    (cousin), 101, 102, 103, 177,
    306
Cárdenas, Carlos de (Charles)
    (cousin), 132
Carlyle, Thomas, 284
Carmen (Bizet), 337
Carnaval de Schumann, Le (Godoy),
    28, 32
Caruso, Enrico, 387
Castro, Fabian de, 284
"Casutza" (article by A.N.), 317
Catholicism, 228
Chaliapin, Feodor, 287, 387

Chant de la Montagne, Le (d'Indy),
    46, 64
Charlot (Charles Chaplin), 425
Chase, Edelmira Culmell de (aunt),
    93
Chase, Gilbert (uncle), 93, 306
Chase, Gilbert (cousin), 5, 13, 14, 93,
    104, 105, 132, 147, 148, 150,
    152, 198, 201, 203, 207, 210,
    211, 228, 229, 246, 256, 276,
    303, 307, 316, 317, 358, 385,
    417
Chase, Kathleen, 211, 256
Chateaubriand, François-Auguste-
    René de, 152
Chekhov, Anton, 325, 326
Chien Andalou, Un (film), 338
Child-Munros, Mr. and Mrs., 6, 162
Chute de la Maison Usher, La (film),
    338
"Circles" (unpublished story by
    A.N.), 358
Cities and Souls (Chase), 203
Claudel, Paul, 260
Cole, Robert, 361, 362
Colette, Sidonie Gabrielle Claudine,
    28, 29, 67, 138, 141–42, 316,
    432
Collazo, Ramiro, 105, 442
Colloque de la Joie (Godoy), 47
Columbia University (New York),
    124, 125, 237, 361
Conrad, Joseph, 83, 84, 108, 342, 384
Constant, Benjamin, 151, 309
Couple, Le (Aurel), 171
Cour de Cassation (Paris), 161
Couteau, Gisèle, 280, 385, 407, 415
Criminals (Bruckner), 256–57
Cubans (in Paris), 47–49
Culmell, Enrique (uncle), 101, 103,
    116, 129
Culmell, Julia (aunt), 101, 103, 116
"Curse of Peacock Feathers, The"
    (story by A.N.), 365
Curtis Brown (literary agents,
    London), 317

D., Jeanne, 158–59, 161, 162, 163, 164
"Dancer" (story by A.N.), 243
"Dangerous Perfume, A" (story by
    A.N.), 302
d'Annunzio, Gabriele, 213, 314
Dans la Rue (Rice), 241

Erskine, Pauline, 93, 100, 121, 123,
124, 127, 128, 131, 132, 144,
154, 159, 161, 166, 167, 173,
174, 176, 177, 188, 191, 212,
213, 252, 257, 282, 378, 396
Erskine, Rhoda, 191, 202
Escudero, 65, 70
"España Cañi" (dance), 40, 49, 57
"Essay on the Journal" (article by
A.N.), 243, 246, 256, 273, 277
Etienne (Deval), 305
Europe and Europeans, 2, 12, 43, 44,
52, 242, 264, 265

F., Miss (friend of Eduardo Sanchez),
402, 403, 404
"Faithfulness" (story by A.N.), 225,
243, 245, 302, 322
Falla, Manuel de, 3, 31, 64, 68, 70,
71, 72, 227, 249, 298, 303, 306,
386, 417
Farrère, Claude, 249
"Fear of Nice" (story by A.N.), 231,
243, 297
Ferber, Edna, 230
Fernandez, Ramón, 419
Ferrara (Cuban Ambassador), 129
Ferrero, Guglielmo, 83
"Fêtes" (Debussy), 252
Figaro, Le (publication), 349
Flanner, Janet, 361, 362
Fledermaus, Die (operetta), 171
Flynn, Eleanor, 455
Folies-Bergère (Paris), 100, 121, 122,
160
Ford, Ford Madox, 216
Forest Hills (New York), 32, 58, 87,
91, 97, 177
Fort, Paul, 249, 251
France, Anatole, 213, 314
Frank, Waldo, 22, 66, 106, 228, 242,
261, 264, 268, 271, 362, 382
Freud, Sigmund, 269, 346, 372, 437,
438, 440, 441, 449, 450, 451,
478
Freyre de Andrade, Maria Teresa,
260–61
Fuller, Loie, 115

Garzon, M., 66
Gibson, Charles Dana, 35
Gide, André, 78, 122, 331, 332, 360,

365, 374, 382, 390, 396, 399,
410, 463
Giraudoux, Jean, 22
Godoy, Armand, 18–19, 20, 22, 28,
32, 35, 46, 47, 48, 49, 59, 63,
72, 74, 79, 80, 88, 89, 121, 122,
137, 149, 154, 158, 161, 166,
198, 214, 229, 233, 249, 250,
280, 358, 385, 392, 424
Godoy, Julia, 63, 64, 72, 88, 89, 122,
137, 161
Godunoff, Boris (opera), 387
Granados, Enrique, 15, 35, 36, 49, 55,
57, 65, 67
Grande Chaumire, Académie de la
("Grand Poussière"), 9, 26
Graves, Eugene, 42, 46, 55, 91–92, 93,
94, 205, 254, 306, 344, 452
Graves, Robert, 457
Greco (Barrès), 261
Guicciardi, Count, 57, 63, 64, 158
Guicciardi, Horace, 6, 7, 10, 20, 32,
37, 57, 58, 63, 64, 87, 88, 104,
105, 112, 117, 198, 237, 255,
265, 338
Guiler, Edith (Hugh's sister), 91, 92,
105, 108, 109, 217, 306, 445,
456, 474
Guiler, Ethel (Hugh's sister), 93,
105, 108, 109, 216, 217, 456,
461, 466, 472, 474, 478, 479
Guiler, Hugh (Hugh's father), 74,
90–91, 97, 98, 99, 101, 206, 227
death of, 90–91, 97
Guiler, Hugh Parker, 1, 2, 3, 4, 6, 7,
9, 10, 15, 17, 18, 20, 26, 29, 30,
31, 37, 40, 41, 45, 48, 49, 52,
53, 55, 56, 57, 58, 61, 62, 63,
64, 69, 70, 72, 73, 77, 78, 80,
83, 87, 88, 92, 93, 94, 100, 104,
107, 108, 110, 111, 112, 113,
114, 115, 116, 117, 118, 120,
121, 124, 125, 127, 129, 130,
133, 134, 136, 137, 139, 140,
142, 143, 144, 145, 148, 155,
156, 159, 160, 161, 165, 168,
169, 171, 172, 174, 175, 176,
177, 181, 182, 184, 188, 189,
190, 191, 194, 198, 200, 201,
206, 207, 211, 212, 213, 215,
217, 218, 219, 220, 221, 223,
225, 228, 229, 232, 233, 234,
235, 238, 239, 242, 243, 244,

0 00 02 0404310 3

MIDDLEBURY COLLEGE